A PRACTICAL APPROACH TO

ALTERNATIVE DISPUTE RESOLUTION

A PRACTICAL APPROACH TO

ALTERNATIVE DISPUTE RESOLUTION

Susan Blake

Barrister and Associate Dean of Learning and Teaching,
The City Law School, City University

Julie Browne

Barrister and Deputy Course Director of the BPTC,
The City Law School, City University

Stuart Sime

Barrister and Course Director of the BPTC, The City Law School,
City University

OXFORD
UNIVERSITY PRESS

OXFORD

UNIVERSITY PRESS

Great Clarendon Street, Oxford OX2 6DP

Oxford University Press is a department of the University of Oxford.
It furthers the University's objective of excellence in research, scholarship,
and education by publishing worldwide in

Oxford New York

Auckland Cape Town Dar es Salaam Hong Kong Karachi
Kuala Lumpur Madrid Melbourne Mexico City Nairobi
New Delhi Shanghai Taipei Toronto

With offices in

Argentina Austria Brazil Chile Czech Republic France Greece
Guatemala Hungary Italy Japan Poland Portugal Singapore
South Korea Switzerland Thailand Turkey Ukraine Vietnam

Oxford is a registered trade mark of Oxford University Press
in the UK and in certain other countries

Published in the United States
by Oxford University Press Inc., New York

British Library Cataloguing in Publication Data

Data available

Typeset by Newgen Imaging Systems (P) Ltd., Chennai, India
Printed in Great Britain
on acid-free paper by
CPI Antony Rowe, Chippenham, Wiltshire

ISBN 978–0–19–959186–2

3 5 7 9 10 8 6 4 2

PREFACE

Alternative Dispute Resolution, or 'ADR', has developed apace in recent years. The phrase itself does not have a fixed technical meaning, but encompasses a wide umbrella of dispute resolution processes that may be used as alternatives to litigation in the courts. It is frequently regarded as a modern development, but parties have been negotiating settlements of disputes since time immemorial, and arbitration can be traced back to ancient Greece. Over time various different ADR processes started to develop, but in more recent years the importance of considering ADR when dealing with litigation in court has brought the subject into the centre of civil practice. In particular, the developments in 1994–97 discussed in Chapter 1 (the requirement in commercial court cases to consider ADR; the extension of that practice into the High Court in 1995; the Central London County Court mediation scheme of 1996; and the mediation scheme of 1997 in the Court of Appeal) marked a watershed in cases conducted in England and Wales. This was cemented by the introduction of the Civil Procedure Rules 1998 and their related pre-action protocols. These require parties to consider ADR before issuing proceedings, and give the courts power to impose sanctions if this is not complied with.

In the near future, an even greater emphasis on the use of ADR is contemplated by the Review of Civil Litigation Costs by Sir Rupert Jackson (2009). This Report is aimed at seeking to reduce the overall costs of resolving civil disputes. The Report recommends that there should be a serious campaign to ensure that all litigation lawyers and judges are properly informed about the benefits that ADR can bring, and to alert the public and small businesses about the benefits of ADR. It also recommends that an authoritative handbook should be prepared, explaining clearly and concisely what ADR is and giving details of all reputable providers of mediation. It is hoped that this book will provide the equivalent information for practitioners and students. This is of particular importance for students on professional courses training to be solicitors and for the bar. The professional regulators have increasingly recognised the importance of ADR, and the Bar Standards Board, for example, has included the resolution of disputes out of court as a compulsory component of the course for intending barristers.

Part of what is required by practitioners and intending practitioners is a rounded understanding of the full range of ADR processes that are available, combined with an appreciation of their strengths, weaknesses, and processes. These divide into non-adjudicative and adjudicative processes. Negotiation and mediation are among the most prominent non-adjudicative processes, with arbitration and adjudication among the most well-known adjudicative processes. The basic difference is that non-adjudicative processes seek to facilitate a negotiated settlement of a dispute, whereas in an adjudicative process a tribunal will come to a decision on the dispute.

This book seeks to adopt a practical approach to the consideration of the full range of ADR processes, covering both a knowledge of each process, and insight into the skills required to obtain a good outcome for a client. It will look into the various different forms of ADR and will consider the range of difficulties and issues that have been found commonly to occur in these processes. The intention is that students and practitioners will gain a systematic understanding of the entire subject. Processes covered in this book include:

- negotiation
- mediation
- early neutral evaluation
- expert evaluation
- conciliation
- complaints and grievance procedures
- ombudsman procedures
- expert determination
- construction industry adjudication
- arbitration.

In addition to the various processes, the book will also consider matters such as tactics and styles, preparation and conducting ADR processes, professional ethics issues involved in ADR, costs, the interrelation between ADR and litigation, and the enforcement of compromises and awards. The intention is to provide a practice-focused oversight that is not necessarily available elsewhere.

The authors appreciate all the assistance and experience that has been shared with them by colleagues at The City Law School, who work constantly to enhance the training provided for those going into practice as lawyers. We are particularly grateful to Margot Taylor and Nigel Duncan, who each played a substantial role in the development of our understanding of negotiation practice, tactics, and strategies. We are also grateful to Ros Carne for commenting on portions of the manuscript in draft, and to Paul Banks for his expertise in tracking down difficult sources. We are also grateful to Katy Elton for her assistance in preparing a number of the flow diagrams used in the book.

Finally, we would like to thank Rebecca Gleave, Suzy Armitage, and Olivia Rowland at Oxford University Press for their assistance in bringing this book to publication.

Susan Blake, Julie Browne, Stuart Sime
May 2010

ACKNOWLEDGEMENTS

In chapter 11, the Annual ADR pledge statistics are reproduced by kind permission of the Ministry of Justice.

In chapter 14, the flowcharts showing the procedure for direct referrals and court referrals are reproduced by kind permission of the Ministry of Justice.

In Appendix 2, the National Mediation Helpline Agreement to Mediate is reproduced by kind permission of the Ministry of Justice.

In Appendix 2, the CEDR ENE Agreement and notes, the CEDR Code of Conduct for Third Party Neutrals and the Model Mediation Agreement and Procedure are reproduced by kind permission of the Centre for Effective Dispute Resolution.

In Appendix 3, the CEDR Model Expert Determination Agreement and guidance notes are reproduced by kind permission of the Centre for Effective Dispute Resolution.

The documents are updated regularly; readers should consult www.cedr.com, www. nationalmediationhelpline.com, and www.justice.com to obtain the most up-to-date versions.

CONTENTS SUMMARY

Preface   v
Acknowledgements   vii
Glossary and abbreviations   xxiii
Table of cases   xxvii
Table of statutes   xxxv

PART 1 HISTORY AND RANGE OF ADR METHODS

  1   Introduction   3
  2   Review of ADR options   22
  3   Factors influencing the selection of an ADR option   38
  4   Costs of ADR procedures   58

PART 2 THE INTERPLAY BETWEEN ADR, CPR AND LITIGATION

  5   The approach of the courts to ADR   75
  6   The sanctions for refusing to engage in ADR processes   93
  7   Recovery of ADR costs in litigation   108

PART 3 NEGOTIATION AND MEDIATION

  8   Styles, strategies and tactics in negotiation   117
  9   Preparing for negotiation   132
 10   The negotiation process   149
 11   Mediation   176
 12   Preparation for the mediation   203
 13   The mediation process   218
 14   Court mediation schemes and other schemes   249
 15   International mediation   270
 16   Professional ethics in negotiation and mediation   279

PART 4 EVALUATION, CONCILIATION AND OMBUDSMEN

 17   Early neutral evaluation   297
 18   Conciliation   304
 19   Complaints, grievances and ombudsmen   309

PART 5 RECORDING SETTLEMENT

 20   Recording settlement   319

PART 6 ADJUDICATIVE ADR

21	Expert or neutral determination	341
22	Construction industry adjudication	353
23	Arbitration	370
24	Arbitral tribunals	394
25	The commercial arbitration process	403
26	International arbitration	432
27	Arbitration awards and orders	453
28	High Court jurisdiction in arbitration claims	462
29	Enforcement of settlements and awards	485

APPENDICES

APPENDIX 1 ADR providers	499
APPENDIX 2	503
National Mediation Helpline Agreement to Mediate	503
CEDR Model mediation agreement	507
CEDR Notes to model mediation agreement	512
CEDR Code of Conduct for third party neutrals	513
APPENDIX 3	517
CEDR Model Expert Determination Agreement	517
CEDR Early Neutral Evaluation Agreement	524
APPENDIX 4	531
Key provisions of the Arbitration Act 1996	531
CPR Part 62	569
Bibliography	579
Index	583

TABLE OF CONTENTS

Preface   v

Acknowledgements   vii

Glossary and abbreviations   xxiii

Table of cases   xxvii

Table of statutes   xxxv

PART 1 HISTORY AND RANGE OF ADR METHODS

---

1   **INTRODUCTION**   3

    BACKGROUND   3

    WHAT IS ADR?   5

    WHY IS THERE A NEED FOR ADR?   6

    THE GROWTH OF ADR OPTIONS   7

    RECENT DEVELOPMENTS   9

    ADR AND THE REVIEW OF CIVIL LITIGATION COSTS   11

    THE INTERNATIONAL CONTEXT   11

    SOME ISSUES WITH REGARD TO ADR   12

    POTENTIAL ADVANTAGES OF ADR   13

    POTENTIAL DISADVANTAGES OF ADR   15

    WEIGHING UP ADVANTAGES AND DISADVANTAGES, AND THE INTERFACE WITH LITIGATION 17

    ASSESSING THE SUCCESS OF ADR   17

    OVERVIEW OF REGULATORY FRAMEWORKS   18

    OVERVIEW OF TRAINING AND ACCREDITATION   20

    KEY POINTS SUMMARY   21

---

2   **REVIEW OF ADR OPTIONS**   22

    KEY ELEMENTS OF ADR OPTIONS   23

    THE ROLE OF THE LAWYER WITH REGARD TO ADR OPTIONS   24

    NON-ADJUDICATIVE ADR OPTIONS   25

    ADJUDICATIVE ADR OPTIONS   32

    OTHER OPTIONS   35

    KEY POINTS SUMMARY   36

3   FACTORS INFLUENCING THE SELECTION OF AN ADR OPTION   38

LEGAL ADVICE ON APPROPRIATE DISPUTE RESOLUTION OPTIONS   38

ADVANCE SELECTION OF AN ADR OPTION   41

FACTORS INFLUENCING ADR SELECTION   42

POTENTIAL CONCERNS ABOUT ADR   50

SECURING AGREEMENT TO ADR   53

CONFIDENTIALITY IN RELATION TO ADR PROCESSES   54

KEY POINTS SUMMARY   57

4   COSTS OF ADR PROCEDURES   58

COSTS CONTEXT   58

GENERAL COST CONSIDERATIONS   59

ELEMENTS OF COSTS   61

COSTS OF ADR PROCESSES   62

EFFECTS OF THE FUNDING BASIS   66

COSTS OF THE PARTIES   67

OVERALL FINANCIAL ANALYSIS AND RISK ASSESSMENT   68

BASIC EXAMPLE OF ADR COST CONSIDERATIONS   70

KEY POINTS SUMMARY   71

PART 2 THE INTERPLAY BETWEEN ADR, CPR AND LITIGATION

5   THE APPROACH OF THE COURTS TO ADR   75

THE HISTORICAL BACKGROUND TO THE CPR   75

THE COURT GUIDES   76

PRE-ACTION PROTOCOLS   79

THE OVERRIDING OBJECTIVE AND ADR   82

ACTIVE CASE MANAGEMENT AND ADR   82

CASE MANAGEMENT POWERS AND ADR   83

ALLOCATION STAGE QUESTIONNAIRES AND ADR   83

GRANTING STAYS FOR ADR   85

JUDICIAL ENCOURAGEMENT OF ADR   85

THE APPROACH OF THE COURTS TO CONTRACTUAL ADR CLAUSES   87

COURT MEDIATION AND EARLY NEUTRAL EVALUATION SCHEMES   90

CAN THE COURT COMPEL THE PARTIES TO USE ADR?   90

KEY POINTS SUMMARY   91

6   THE SANCTIONS FOR REFUSING TO ENGAGE IN ADR PROCESSES   93

INTRODUCTION   94

THE COURT'S GENERAL POWERS TO MAKE COSTS ORDERS   94

ADVERSE COSTS ORDERS AGAINST A PARTY WHO UNREASONABLY REFUSES
   TO CONSIDER ADR   95

REQUESTING FURTHER INFORMATION OR CLARIFICATION OF THE ISSUES
   BEFORE ACCEPTING ADR   100

REJECTING ADR BEFORE ISSUE   101

FAILING TO INITIATE ADR PROCESSES   102

REJECTING ADR AFTER JUDGMENT AND BEFORE THE HEARING OF AN APPEAL   103

DELAY IN CONSENTING TO MEDIATION (OR ANOTHER ADR PROCESS)   104

PULLING OUT OF MEDIATION (OR ANOTHER ADR PROCESS)   104

UNREASONABLE CONDUCT IN THE MEDIATION   105

IMPOSING A COSTS CAP ON SOLICITOR–CLIENT COSTS FOR FAILING
   TO PURSUE ADR   105

INDEMNITY COSTS ORDERS FOR FAILING TO CONSIDER ADR   105

BOTH PARTIES AT FAULT IN FAILING TO CONSIDER ADR   106

HOW DOES THE COURT TREAT PRIVILEGED MATERIAL WHEN SEEKING TO
   IMPOSE SANCTIONS?   106

KEY POINTS SUMMARY   107

7   RECOVERY OF ADR COSTS IN LITIGATION   108

INTRODUCTION   108

COSTS OF INTERIM APPLICATIONS RELATING TO ADR   109

RECOVERY OF THE COSTS OF UNSUCCESSFUL ADR PROCESSES   109

KEY POINTS SUMMARY   114

PART 3 NEGOTIATION AND MEDIATION

8   STYLES, STRATEGIES AND TACTICS IN NEGOTIATION   117

THE IMPORTANCE OF STYLE, STRATEGY AND TACTICS   117

STYLES   118

STRATEGIES   119

TACTICS   125

KEY POINTS SUMMARY   131

9   PREPARING FOR NEGOTIATION   132

THE IMPORTANCE OF PREPARATION   132

IDENTIFYING THE OBJECTIVES   133

THE IMPORTANCE OF THE PROCEDURAL STAGE THE CASE HAS REACHED   134

IDENTIFYING THE ISSUES   135

THE RELEVANCE OF THE LEGAL CONTEXT   136

PREPARING TO DEAL WITH FACTS AND EVIDENCE   137

PREPARING TO DEAL WITH FIGURES   139

IDENTIFYING PERSUASIVE ARGUMENTS   140

PLANNING POTENTIAL DEMANDS, OFFERS AND CONCESSIONS   143

LINKING CONCESSIONS   146

IDENTIFYING THE BATNA   146

IDENTIFYING THE WATNA   147

CLARIFYING YOUR INSTRUCTIONS AND AUTHORITY   147

KEY POINTS SUMMARY   148

10   THE NEGOTIATION PROCESS   149

WHEN, HOW AND WHERE   150

WHO   151

COMMUNICATING EFFECTIVELY   152

STRUCTURE AND AGENDA SETTING   155

OPENING   156

SEEKING INFORMATION   160

MAKING YOUR CASE ON THE ISSUES   161

PLANNING AND TIMING CONCESSIONS, OFFERS AND DEMANDS   163

MAKING PROGRESS   169

DEALING WITH DIFFICULTIES   170

REACHING A CLOSE—SETTLEMENT OR BREAKDOWN   173

KEY POINTS SUMMARY   175

11   MEDIATION   176

WHAT IS MEDIATION?   177

THE DIFFERENCE BETWEEN NEGOTIATION AND MEDIATION   177

JUDICIAL ENDORSEMENT OF MEDIATION   179

DISPUTES SUITABLE FOR MEDIATION   179

THE ADVANTAGES OF MEDIATION   181

DOES MEDIATION WORK? 182

WHY DO THE PARTIES USE MEDIATION? 183

WHY IS MEDIATION AN EFFECTIVE ADR PROCESS? 184

THE DISADVANTAGES OF MEDIATION 185

WHAT CAN BE DONE TO MAKE A RELUCTANT PARTY ENGAGE IN MEDIATION? 185

THE TIMING OF MEDIATION 186

THE DURATION OF MEDIATION 189

SELECTING A VENUE 189

THE COSTS OF MEDIATION 190

THE FUNDING OF MEDIATION COSTS, FEES AND EXPENSES 192

SELECTING A MEDIATOR 193

STYLES OF MEDIATION 197

TRANSFORMATIVE MEDIATION 200

THE ROLE OF THE MEDIATOR 200

KEY POINTS SUMMARY 202

12 PREPARATION FOR THE MEDIATION 203

THE MEDIATION AGREEMENT 203

PRE-MEDIATION MEETING/CONTACT 205

THE ATTENDEES 205

EXPERTS AND LAY WITNESSES OF FACT 207

THE POSITION STATEMENTS 208

THE KEY SUPPORTING DOCUMENTS 210

DISCLOSURE OF POSITION STATEMENTS AND DOCUMENTS 212

OTHER DOCUMENTS THAT THE PARTIES MAY WISH TO BRING TO THE MEDIATION 213

OTHER INFORMATION THAT THE MEDIATOR MAY SEEK FROM THE PARTIES
   BEFORE THE MEDIATION 213

OTHER STEPS THAT NEED TO BE TAKEN TO PREPARE FOR THE MEDIATION 213

TACTICS AND STYLES TO BE EMPLOYED IN THE MEDIATION 215

CONCLUSION 215

KEY POINTS SUMMARY 217

13 THE MEDIATION PROCESS 218

THE STAGES IN MEDIATION 219

THE OPENING PHASE 219

THE EXPLORATION/INFORMATION PHASE 226

THE NEGOTIATING/BARGAINING PHASE 229

JOINT OPEN MEETINGS IN THE EXPLORATION OR BARGAINING PHASE   230

THE SETTLEMENT/CLOSING PHASE   230

THE CLOSING JOINT MEETING   232

TERMINATION AND ADJOURNMENT OF THE MEDIATION   232

THE MEDIATOR'S ROLE FOLLOWING THE CONCLUSION OF THE MEDIATION   232

THE MAIN VARIATIONS IN THE PROCESS   233

THE ROLE OF THE ADVOCATE IN MEDIATION   236

THE WITHOUT PREJUDICE RULE AND THE NATURE OF CONFIDENTIALITY IN MEDIATION   240

LEGAL ADVICE PRIVILEGE IN MEDIATION   243

CONFIDENTIALITY   244

THE MEDIATOR AS WITNESS   246

CAN A MEDIATOR BE SUED?   247

KEY POINTS SUMMARY   247

14   COURT MEDIATION SCHEMES AND OTHER SCHEMES   249

INTRODUCTION   249

THE NATIONAL MEDIATION HELPLINE   250

COURT MEDIATION SCHEMES   254

MEDIATION IN SPECIFIC CASES   258

MEDIATING MULTI-PARTY DISPUTES   262

OTHER SCHEMES   264

SECTOR MEDIATION SCHEMES   266

THE PENSIONS MEDIATION SERVICE   267

THE PERFORMING ARTS MEDIATION SERVICE   268

COMMUNITY MEDIATION   268

PRO BONO MEDIATION AND LAWWORKS   269

KEY POINTS SUMMARY   269

15   INTERNATIONAL MEDIATION   270

INTRODUCTION   270

THE ADVANTAGES OF MEDIATION IN INTERNATIONAL DISPUTES   271

PREPARATION FOR MEDIATION IN INTERNATIONAL DISPUTES   272

THE PROCESS IN INTERNATIONAL MEDIATION   273

THE GROWTH OF MEDIATION IN EUROPE   273

A MOVE TOWARDS HARMONISING PRACTICES IN INTERNATIONAL MEDIATION   274

THE EU DIRECTIVE ON MEDIATION IN CIVIL AND COMMERCIAL
CASES (DIRECTIVE 2008/52/EC)   274

THE EUROPEAN CODE OF CONDUCT FOR MEDIATORS   277

ENFORCEABILITY OF INTERNATIONAL MEDIATION SETTLEMENT AGREEMENTS   277

KEY POINTS SUMMARY   278

16   PROFESSIONAL ETHICS IN NEGOTIATION AND MEDIATION   279

INTRODUCTION   279

ADVISING ABOUT ADR OPTIONS   280

LAWYERS PROVIDING AN ADR SERVICE   281

LAWYERS ACTING FOR CLIENTS IN AN ADR PROCESS   281

DUTIES WHEN ADVANCING A CLIENT'S CASE AND DRAFTING DOCUMENTS   285

THE DUTY OF CONFIDENTIALITY   286

DISCLOSURE OF OTHER INFORMATION   288

AUTHORITY TO SETTLE   289

THE RELATIONSHIP BETWEEN BARRISTERS AND THEIR PROFESSIONAL CLIENTS IN ADR   290

ETHICAL CONSIDERATIONS AFFECTING MEDIATORS   290

KEY POINTS SUMMARY   293

PART 4 EVALUATION, CONCILIATION AND OMBUDSMEN

17   EARLY NEUTRAL EVALUATION   297

WHAT IS EARLY NEUTRAL EVALUATION   297

AT WHAT STAGE SHOULD IT BE EMPLOYED?   298

WHEN SHOULD IT BE USED?   298

WHO SHOULD BE APPOINTED TO CARRY OUT THE EVALUATION?   298

THE PROCEDURE   299

NEUTRAL FACT FINDING   299

JUDICIAL EVALUATION   299

EVALUATION IN PERSONAL INJURY CASES   300

SOCIAL SECURITY AND CHILD SUPPORT TRIBUNAL ENE PILOT SCHEME   301

JUDICIAL ENE   303

KEY POINTS SUMMARY   303

18   CONCILIATION   304

WHAT IS CONCILIATION?   304

AN OUTLINE OF THE PROCESS   304

ADVISORY CONCILIATION AND ARBITRATION SERVICE CONCILIATION   305

CONCILIATION IN FAMILY CASES 307

KEY POINTS SUMMARY 308

19   COMPLAINTS, GRIEVANCES AND OMBUDSMEN 309

INTRODUCTION 309

COMPLAINTS AND GRIEVANCE PROCEDURES 309

OMBUDSMEN 314

KEY POINTS SUMMARY 316

PART 5 RECORDING SETTLEMENT

20   RECORDING SETTLEMENT 319

REACHING A CLEAR OUTCOME 319

FORMS OF RECORDED OUTCOME 320

RECORDS MADE DURING THE ADR PROCESS 321

WHO SHOULD PRODUCE A FORMAL RECORD 322

ENFORCEABLE FORMS FOR RECORDING SETTLEMENT 322

DRAFTING TERMS OF SETTLEMENT 323

METHODS OF RECORDING SETTLEMENT AGREEMENTS 324

TERMS AS REGARDS COSTS 336

INFORMING THE COURT OF SETTLEMENT 337

KEY POINTS SUMMARY 338

PART 6 ADJUDICATIVE ADR

21   EXPERT OR NEUTRAL DETERMINATION 341

INTRODUCTION 342

WHEN SHOULD NEUTRAL OR EXPERT DETERMINATION BE USED 342

AGREEMENT TO USE EXPERT (OR NEUTRAL) DETERMINATION 343

APPROACH OF THE COURTS TO EXPERT DETERMINATION 344

ADVANTAGES OF EXPERT DETERMINATION 344

DIFFERENCES BETWEEN EXPERT DETERMINATION AND NEGOTIATION, MEDIATION AND
      NEUTRAL EVALUATION 345

SIMILARITIES WITH OTHER FORMS OF ADR 345

SELECTION OF THE NEUTRAL OR EXPERT DETERMINER 345

THE PROCESS 346

CONFIDENTIAL INFORMATION 347

THE NATURE OF THE DECISION 347

REASONS FOR THE DECISION 348

CHALLENGING A FINAL DECISION BY COURT PROCEEDINGS 348

PROCEDURE FOR MAKING A CHALLENGE 350

ENFORCING A DECISION 350

SUING THE EXPERT 350

HOW NEUTRAL OR EXPERT DETERMINATION DIFFERS FROM ARBITRATION 352

DISPUTES REVIEW PANELS 352

KEY POINTS SUMMARY 352

22   CONSTRUCTION INDUSTRY ADJUDICATION 353

INTRODUCTION 353

NATURE OF ADJUDICATION 354

REQUIREMENTS 355

EXPRESS CONTRACTUAL RIGHT TO ADJUDICATION 357

DEFAULT PROVISIONS IN THE SCHEME FOR CONSTRUCTION CONTRACTS 358

COMMENCEMENT OF THE ADJUDICATION 358

PROCEDURE BEFORE THE HEARING 365

ADJUDICATOR'S DECISION 367

BINDING, BUT INTERIM EFFECT, OF DECISIONS 368

OVERALL COST 368

ADJUDICATION IN RESIDENTIAL BUILDING CONTRACTS 369

COURT ENFORCEMENT OF SUM FOUND DUE ON ADJUDICATION 369

KEY POINTS SUMMARY 369

23   ARBITRATION 370

INTRODUCTION 371

ARBITRATION AND LITIGATION 372

FUNDAMENTAL CONCEPTS IN ARBITRATION 372

HISTORY OF ARBITRATION 372

INTERPRETATION OF THE ARBITRATION ACT 1996 373

CONTRACTUAL FOUNDATION TO ARBITRATION 373

REQUIREMENTS 375

OVERVIEW OF ARBITRATION PROCEDURE 382

GENERAL PRINCIPLES AND DUTIES	382
FAIR RESOLUTION OF DISPUTES	384
PARTY AUTONOMY	385
COURT APPLICATIONS	386
DIFFERENT TYPES OF ARBITRATIONS	387
STATUTORY ARBITRATION	388
CONSUMER ARBITRATION	389
MULTI-TIERED DISPUTE RESOLUTION	389
ONE-STOP ADJUDICATION	390
EUROPEAN CONVENTION ON HUMAN RIGHTS AND ARBITRATION	390
MAIN FEATURES OF ARBITRATION	390
KEY POINTS SUMMARY	392

24 ARBITRAL TRIBUNALS — 394

INTRODUCTION	394
COMMENCEMENT OF ARBITRATION	394
NOTICE OF ARBITRATION	396
APPOINTMENT OF ARBITRAL TRIBUNAL	396
CONTRACTUAL BASIS OF THE ARBITRATORS' MANDATE	399
TERMS OF REFERENCE	400
REMOVAL, RESIGNATION AND VACANCIES	400
IMMUNITIES	402
LIABILITY FOR ARBITRATORS' FEES	402
KEY POINTS SUMMARY	402

25 THE COMMERCIAL ARBITRATION PROCESS — 403

INTRODUCTION	403
DEFINITION OF 'COMMERCIAL'	404
PRIVACY AND CONFIDENTIALITY	404
RANGE OF PROCEDURAL APPROACHES IN ARBITRATION	405
PROCEDURAL RULES GOVERNING THE ARBITRATION	406
ROLE OF LEGAL REPRESENTATIVES IN ARBITRATION	407
COMMENCEMENT	409
'LOOK–SNIFF' ARBITRATIONS	409
SHORT-FORM ARBITRATIONS	410
GENERAL PROCEDURE IN COMMERCIAL ARBITRATION	410

EXAMPLE OF ARBITRAL RULES THAT CLOSELY FOLLOW COURT PROCEDURES   427

KEY POINTS SUMMARY   431

26   **INTERNATIONAL ARBITRATION**   432

INTRODUCTION   432

MEANING OF 'INTERNATIONAL' IN ARBITRATION   433

ADVISING THE CLIENT   434

SEAT   434

PROBLEMS CAUSED BY DIFFERENT SYSTEMS OF LAW   436

APPLICABLE LAW   437

OBJECTIONS TO JURISDICTION   441

PROCEDURAL MATTERS RELEVANT TO INTERNATIONAL ARBITRATION   445

ICC RULES OF ARBITRATION   447

UNCITRAL MODEL LAW ON INTERNATIONAL COMMERCIAL ARBITRATION   449

KEY POINTS SUMMARY   452

27   **ARBITRATION AWARDS AND ORDERS**   453

INTRODUCTION   453

PROCEDURAL ORDERS   454

INTERIM AWARDS AND AWARDS ON DIFFERENT ISSUES   454

SETTLEMENT   455

MAIN AWARDS   455

AWARD OF COSTS   460

KEY POINTS SUMMARY   461

28   **HIGH COURT JURISDICTION IN ARBITRATION CLAIMS**   462

INTRODUCTION   462

ORDERS TO PREVENT PARTIES BREACHING AGREEMENTS TO ARBITRATE   463

APPOINTMENT, REMOVAL AND REPLACEMENT OF ARBITRATORS   465

PROCEDURAL ORDERS TO ASSIST IN THE DETERMINATION
OF ARBITRAL PROCEEDINGS   467

JUDICIAL REVIEW OF ARBITRAL PROCEEDINGS   470

PRELIMINARY POINTS OF LAW   470

SERIOUS IRREGULARITY   471

APPEAL ON A POINT OF LAW   475

PROCEDURE IN ARBITRATION CLAIMS   478

	APPEALS TO THE COURT OF APPEAL	483
	KEY POINTS SUMMARY	484
29	**ENFORCEMENT OF SETTLEMENTS AND AWARDS**	485
	INTRODUCTION	485
	BASIC METHODS OF ENFORCING COMPROMISE AGREEMENTS	486
	MERGER, OR DISCHARGE OF ORIGINAL OBLIGATION, BY COMPROMISE	486
	MAKING A CHOICE ON ENFORCEMENT OPTIONS	487
	ENFORCEMENT OF COMPROMISES RECORDED AS A CONTRACT	488
	CHALLENGING A SETTLEMENT RECORDED AS A CONTRACT	489
	ENFORCEMENT OF COURT ORDERS	490
	COSTS ONLY PROCEEDINGS	491
	ENFORCEMENT OF CONSTRUCTION INDUSTRY ADJUDICATION DECISIONS	491
	ARBITRATION SETTLEMENTS AND AWARDS	492
	KEY POINTS SUMMARY	494

APPENDICES

APPENDIX 1	ADR providers	499
APPENDIX 2		503
	National Mediation Helpline Agreement to Mediate	503
	CEDR Model mediation agreement	507
	CEDR Notes to model mediation agreement	512
	CEDR Code of Conduct for third party neutrals	513
APPENDIX 3		517
	CEDR Model Expert Determination Agreement	517
	CEDR Early Neutral Evaluation Agreement	524
APPENDIX 4		531
	Key provisions of the Arbitration Act 1996	531
	CPR Part 62	569
Bibliography		579
Index		583

GLOSSARY AND ABBREVIATIONS

AAA	American Arbitration Association
ACAS	Advisory, Conciliation and Advisory Service in relation to employment matters
Ad hoc	An arbitration not administered by an arbitral institution
ADR	Alternative dispute resolution
Adjudication	Adjudicative dispute resolution procedure for construction industry disputes, providing a binding, speedy but temporary decision
AICA	Association of Independent Construction Adjudicators
Arbitral institution	An organisation, which may be international, professional, trade or independent, which administers arbitrations within its area of interest. They often also publish their own institutional arbitration rules
Arbitration	Adjudicative dispute resolution procedure under which the parties agree to submit their dispute to an impartial tribunal appointed by a process agreed by the parties
CA	Court of Appeal
CEDR	Centre for Effective Dispute Resolution
CIA	Chartered Institute of Arbitrators
CIETAC	China International Economic and Trade Arbitration Commission
Claimant	Party bringing a claim, particularly in litigation and arbitrations
CMC	Civil Mediation Council
Complainant	Person making a complaint
Confidentiality	The duty not to disclose information or documents about a dispute to outsiders. In relation to dispute resolution procedures this will usually mean that disclosure will be limited to the parties, their lawyers and the dispute resolution provider
CPR	Civil Procedure Rules 1998 (SI 1998/3132), the procedural governing litigation in the High Court and county courts
Court	In litigation this describes the tribunal appointed to decide the issues between the parties (typically a judge or appeal court). In arbitration a court is usually a governing body of an arbitral institution, and usually has no judicial function
Curial law	The procedural law governing arbitral proceedings. Also known as the *lex arbitiri*
DAC	Departmental Advisory Committee on Arbitration, set up by the Department of Trade and Industry, whose reports formed the basis for the Arbitration Act 1996
Defendant	Party responding to a claim (particularly in arbitration and litigation). Often used interchangeably with 'respondent' in arbitrations
Determiner	Expert or other person appointed to decide a matter referred to expert determination or neutral determination

ECHR	European Convention on Human Rights
EU	European Union
FOSFA	Federation of Oils, Seeds and Fats Association
GAFTA	Grain and Feed Trade Association
HKIAC	Hong Kong International Arbitration Centre
HL	House of Lords. Replaced as the highest domestic appeal court by the Supreme Court in October 2009
ICA	International Court of Arbitration, the arbitration body attached to the International Chamber of Commerce
ICC	International Chamber of Commerce
ICE	Institute of Civil Engineers
ICSID	International Centre for Settlement of Investment Disputes, which is affiliated to the World Bank
IMAC	International Mediation and Arbitration Centre
IMI	International Mediation Institute
Institution rules	The rules published by an arbitral institution regulating arbitrations which may be adopted by the parties for their arbitration
JCT	Joint Contracts Tribunal Limited, which publishes standard contracts and also ADR rules for use in the building industry
Judicial review	Describes going to court to challenge an arbitral award for want of jurisdiction or for serious irregularity, or to appeal to the court on a point of law
Jurisdiction Regulation	Council Regulation (EC) No 44/2001, which replaced the Brussels Convention on Jurisdiction and Enforcement of Judgments in Civil and Commercial Matters 1968
Kompetenz-Kompetenz	Power of arbitrators to rule on their own jurisdiction
lex arbitiri	The procedural law governing arbitral proceedings. Also known as the curial law
LCIA	London Court of International Arbitration
LMAA	London Maritime Arbitrators' Association
LME	London Metal Exchange Ltd, a metals industry arbitral institution
MEDAL	International Mediation Services Alliance
Model Law	Model Law for International Arbitration (1985) promulgated by UNCITRAL
New York Convention	International convention (1958) on the recognition and enforcement of arbitration awards
Ombudsman	Traditionally ombudsmen acted as umpires in cases of alleged maladministration, although their current roles include considering whether services accord with reasonable commercial practice
Party	Generic term used to describe a person involved in a dispute either by bringing the claim or by disputing it
PCA	Permanent Court of Arbitration
PD	Practice Direction. Each 'Part' of the CPR has one or more practice directions which add procedural and practice details to the main provisions of the CPR

Redfern schedule	Four-column document giving disclosure of documents in arbitrations
Respondent	Party responding to a claim or application (particularly in arbitration and litigation). Often used interchangeably with 'defendant' in arbitrations
RIBA	Royal Institute of British Architects
RICS	Royal Institution of Chartered Surveyors
Scott schedule	Multi-column document used in construction disputes for setting out defects or disputes on an item by item basis, with columns for the responses of the other parties and the court or adjudicator
Seat	The jurisdiction where an arbitration is proceeding as a matter of law. Actual hearings may take place in another country without affecting the seat of the arbitration
Separability	Concept, particularly in arbitration, that an agreement to arbitrate has a life which is separate from the underlying contract
SIAC	Singapore International Arbitration Centre
TCC	Technology and Construction Court, a specialist court within the High Court
TeCSA	Technology and Construction Solicitors' Association
Tomlin order	Consent order in litigation which stays a claim on terms set out in a schedule
Tribunal	Body appointed to determine a dispute. It is often used interchangeably with 'the arbitrators'. It is also used to describe the court, judge or jury in litigation, and in relation to statutory tribunals
UNCITRAL	United Nations Commission on International Trade Law

TABLE OF CASES

Abrahams v Lenton [2003] EWHC 1104 (QB) 477
Adonis Construction v O'Keefe Soil Remediation [2009] EWHC 2047 (TCC) 356
Aird & Aird v Prime Meridien [2007] BLR 105 . . . . .57, 177, 240, 242, 244
Ali Shipping Corp v Shipyard Trogir [1999] 1 WLR 314 405
Amec Projects Ltd v Whitefriars City Estates Ltd [2004] EWHC 393 (TCC) 368, 492
Andrews v Bradshaw [2000] BLR 6 466
Anon [1468] YB 8 Edw IV, fo1, p1 8
AOOT Kalmneft v Glencore [2001] 1 Lloyd's Rep 128 482
Arenson v Casson Beckman Rutley and Co [1977] AC 405 350
Arthur J S Hall & Co (a firm) v Simmons [2002] 1 AC 615 19
Ascot Commodities v Olam [2002] CLC 277 375
Asghar v Legal Services Commission [2004] EWHC 1803 (Ch) 381
ASM Shipping Ltd of India v TTMI Ltd of England [2006] 1 Lloyd's Rep 375 . . . . 444, 472, 474
Assimina Maritime Ltd v Pakistan National Shipping Corporation [2005] 1 All ER (Comm) 460 . . . 468
Athletic Union of Constantinople v National Basketball Association [2002] 1 WLR 2863 484
Athos, The [1981] 2 Lloyd's Rep 74, [1983] Lloyd's Rep 127 480
Atkinson v Castan, The Times 17 April 1991 490
Aughton Ltd v MF Kent Services Ltd [1991] 57 BLR 1 379
Aveat Heating Ltd v Jerram Falkus Construction Ltd [2007] EWHC 131 (TCC) 357, 358, 367
AWG Construction Services Ltd v Rockingham Speedway Ltd [2004] EWHC 888 (TCC) 368

Ballast plc v The Burrell Company [2001] BLR 529 492
Bank Mellat v Helliniki Techniki SA [1984] 1 QB 291 441
Barder v Caluori [1988] AC 20 334
Barnetson v Framlington Group Ltd [2007] EWCA Civ 502, [2007] 1 WLR 2443 55
Belair LLC v Basel LLC [2009] EWHC 725 (Comm) 468
Berg v IML London Ltd [2002] 1 WLR 3271 57
Bernard Schulte GmbH v Nile Holdings Ltd [2004] 2 Lloyd's Rep 352 347
Berry Trade Ltd v Moussavi (No 3) [2003] EWCA Civ 715 57
Birkett v James [1978] AC 297 416
Booker Belmont Wholesale Ltd v Ashford Developments Ltd (2000) LTL 18/7/2000 337
Boulos Gad Tourism and Hotels Ltd v Uniground Shipping Co Ltd (2001) LTL 21/2/2002 423
Bradford v James [2008] EWCA Civ 837 187
Bradford & Bingley plc v Rashid [2006] UKHL 37, [2006] 1 WLR 2066 56
Braes of Doune Wind Farm (Scotland) Ltd v Alfred McAlpine Business Services Ltd [2008] 2 All ER
    (Comm) 493 . . . . 434, 435
Brandeis Brokers Ltd v Black [2001] 2 Lloyd's Rep 359 472
Brawley v Marczynski (Nos 1 and 2) [2003] 1 WLR 813 113
Brennan v Bolt Burden (a firm), The Times 7 November 2003 489
British Russian Gazette and Trade Outlook Ltd v Associated Newspapers Ltd [1933] 2 KB 616 487
British Shipbuilders v VSEL Consortium plc [1997] 1 Lloyd's Rep 105 349
Brown v Rice [2007] EWHC (Ch) 625, [2007] EWCA Civ 625, [2007] All ER (D) 252 204,
                                                                                                231, 241, 242
Brownlee v Brownlee, decision of the South Gauteng High Court of South Africa, 2008/25274 105
Bruce v Carpenter [2006] EWHC 3301 (Ch) 347
Buckland v Farrar & Moody [1978] 3 All ER 229 19
Burchell v Bullard [2005] EWCA Civ 358, [2005] BLR 330 . . . . 10, 40, 87, 101, 179

C v D [2008] Bus LR 843 435

Cable & Wireless plc v IBM United Kingdom Ltd [2002] EWHC 2059 (Comm), [2002] 2 All ER
(Comm) 1041 . . . . .42, 89, 183, 512
Calderbank v Calderbank [1976] Fam 93 8–9
Campbell v Edwards [1976] 1 WLR 403 349
Cape Durasteel Ltd v Rosser & Russell Building Services Ltd [1995] 46 Con LR 75 89
Carleton (Earl of Malmesbury) v Strutt and Parker [2008] All ER (D) 257 105
Cetelem SA v Roust Holdings Ltd [2005] 1 WLR 3555 . . . . 469, 484
CGU International Insurance plc v Astrazeneca Insurance Co Ltd [2006] CLC 162, [2007]
Bus LR 162 . . . . 437, 484
Chanel v FW Woolworth [1981] 1 All ER 745 322
Channel Tunnel Group Ltd v Balfour Beatty Construction Ltd [1993] AC 334, [1993] 1 All
ER 664 . . . . 36, 89, 344, 352
Chantrey Vellacot v The Convergence Group plc [2007] EWHC 1774 (Ch) 112
Checkpoint Ltd v Strathclyde Pension Fund [2003] 1 EGLR 1 . . . . 375, 426, 457, 474
Choudury v Kingston Hospital NHS Trust [2006] EWHC 90057 373
City of London v Sancheti [2009] Bus LR 996 464
Clarke v Redcar & Cleveland Borough Council [2006] IRLR 324 306
CMA CGM SA v Beteiligungs-KG MS 'Northern Pioneer' Schiffahrtgesellschaft mbH and Co
[2003] 1 WLR 1015 . . . . .477, 478
Compagnie Europeenne de Cereals SA v Tradax Export SA [1986] 2 Lloyd's Rep 301 464
Connex South Eastern Ltd v MJ Building Services Group plc [2004] BLR 333 . . . . 356, 380
Conoco (UK) Ltd v Phillips Petroleum Co UK Ltd (unreported, 19 August 1996) 349
Corby Group Litigation v Corby DC [2009] EWHC 2019 TCC 101
Corenso (UK) Ltd v Burnden Group plc [2003] EWHC 1805 . . . . .97, 180
Cott UK Ltd v F E Barber Ltd [1997] 3 All ER 540 . . . . 89, 344
County Personnel v Alan R Pulber [1987] 1 All ER 289 19
Coventry Scaffolding Co (London) Ltd v Lancsville Construction Ltd [2009] EWHC
2995 (TCC) 492
Cruden Construction Ltd v Commission for the New Towns [1995] 2 Lloyd's Rep 387 376
Cuflet Chartering v Carousel Shipping Ltd [2001] 1 Lloyd's Rep 707 473
Cumbria Waste Management Ltd v Baines Wilson [2008] EWHC 786, [2008] BLR 330 243
Cutts v Head [1984] Ch 290 . . . . 55, 57

D (Minors), Re [1993] 2 All ER 693 57
D & C Builders v Rees [1966] 2 QB 107 489
Daniels v Commissioner of Police for the Metropolis [2005] EWCA Civ 1312 96
de Lasala v de Lasala [1980] AC 546 333–334
Dearling v Foregate Developments (Chester) Ltd [2003] EWCA Civ 913 113
Delta Reclamantion Ltd v Premier Waste Management Ltd [2008] EWHC 2579 (QB) 377
Demco Investments and Commercial SA v SE Banken Forsakring Holding Aktiebolag [2005]
EWHC 1398 (Comm) 475
Detz v Lennig [1969] 1 AC 170 489
Deutsche Schachtbau-und Tiefbohrgesellschaft mbH v Ras Al Khaimah National Oil Co [1987]
2 All ER 769 440
Deweer v Belgium (1980) 2 EHRR 12
DGT Steel & Cladding Ltd v Cubitt Building & Interiors Ltd [2007] EWHC 1584 (TCC), [2007]
BLR 371 . . . . 89, 344
Dickinson v Jones Alexander & Co [1990] Fam Law 137 19
Dolling-Baker v Merrett [1991] 2 All ER 891 422
Donohue v Armco [2001] 1 Lloyd's Rep 425 377
Dorchester Hotel Ltd v Vivid Interiors Ltd [2009] Bus LR 1026 367
Downing v Al Tameer Establishment [2002] 2 All ER (Comm) 545 377
Dunnett v Railtrack plc [2002] EWCA Civ 303, [2002] 1 WLR 2434 . . . . 10, 101, 103, 179,
255, 280
Dyson v Leeds City Council [2000] CP Rep 42 . . . . 85, 100, 105

E F Phillips and Sons Ltd v Clarke [1970] Ch 322 336
Econet Wireless Ltd v Vee Networks Ltd [2006] 2 Lloyd's Rep 428 . . . . 467, 469
Edmund Nuttall Ltd v RG Carter Ltd [2002] BLR 312 376
EDO Corporation v Ultra Electronics Ltd [2009] Bus LR 1306 468
Egan v Motor Services (Bath) Ltd [2007] EWCA Civ 1002, [2008] 1 WLR 1589. . . . . .87, 187
Egon Oldendorff v Liberia Corporation (No 2) [1996] 1 Lloyd's Rep 380 . . . . 435, 439
Emmott v Michael Wilson & Partners Ltd [2009] 1 Lloyd's Rep 233. 415
Essex CC v Premier Recycling Ltd [2007] BLR 233. 475
Estor Ltd v Multifit (UK) Ltd [2009] EWHC 2108 (TCC), (2009) 126 Con LR 40. . . . . 356, 492
Et Plus SA v Welter [2006] 1 Lloyd's Rep 251 381

Farm Assist Ltd (in liquidation) v The Secretary of State for the Environment, Food and Rural
    Affairs (No 2) [2009] BLR 399 . . . . 243, 245, 246
Fastrack v Morrison [2000] BLR 168. 492
Fidelity Management SA v Myriad International Holdings BV [2005] EWHC 1193
    (Comm) 473, 474
Fili Shipping Co Ltd v Premium Nafta Products Ltd [2007] Bus LR 1719 . . . . . . .372, 374, 381, 390, 445
Fiona Trust & Holding Corporation v Privalov *see* Fili Shipping Co Ltd v Premium Nafta Products Ltd
Food Corp of India v Achilles Halcoussis [1988] 2 Lloyd's Rep 56. 381

Gaston, Broughton v Courtenay [2004] EWHC 600 99
Gbangola v Smith & Sherriff Ltd [1998] 3 All ER 730. 384
Geogas Ltd v Trammo Gas Ltd [1991] 1 Lloyd's Rep 349 . . . . 477, 484
Gill v Woodall, Lonsdale and the Royal Society for the Prevention of Cruelty to Animals
    [2009] EWHC 834 (Ch) 106
Glencot Development & Design Co Ltd v Ben Barrett & Son (Contractors) Ltd (unreported,
    13 February 2002) 234, 492
Glidepath Holding BV v Thompson [2005] 1 All ER (Comm) 434. . . . . 468, 469
Green v Rozen [1955] 1 WLR 741 . . . . 329, 331
Groundshire v VHE Construction [2001] 1 Lloyd's Rep 395 474
Guinle v Kirreh [2000] CP Rep 62 84–85

Halifax Financial Services Ltd v Intuitive Systems Ltd [1999] 1 All ER 303. 42
Halifax Life Ltd v Equitable Life Assurance Society [2007] 1 Lloyd's Rep 528, [2007] 2 All ER
    (Comm) 672. . . . . .287, 347, 348
Halki Shipping Corp v Sopex Oils Ltd [1998] 1 WLR 726 376
Halsey v Milton Keynes General NHS Trust [2004] EWCA Civ 576, [2004] 4 All ER 920, [2004] 1 WLR
    3002. . . . . .10, 12, 40, 83, 85, 90, 91, 95, 96, 99, 100, 101, 102, 103, 105,
                                                                  106, 110, 179, 180, 240, 254, 280
Harley v McDonald Harley (a firm), The Times 15 May 2001 19
Harper v Interchange Group Ltd [2007] EWHC 1834 (Comm) 344
Harris v Manahan [1996] 4 All ER 454 334
Harrison v Bloom Camillin, The Times 12 November 1999 19
Hart v Smith [2009] EWHC (TCC) 2223 368
Hawk Shipping Ltd v Cron Navigation [2003 EWHC 1828 (Comm). 426
Herschel Engineering Ltd v Breen Property Ltd [2000] 70 Con LR 1 89
Hickman v Blake Lapthorn [2006] EWHC 12 (QB) 96
High Court Practice Note (Civil Litigation, Case Management) [1995] 1 All ER 385 9
Hinde v Hinde [1953] 1 All ER 171 332
Hiscox v Outhwaite [1992] 1 AC 562 458
Hodgkinson & Corby Ltd v Wards Mobility Services Ltd [1997] FSR 178 56
Homepace Ltd v Sita South East Ltd [2008] EWCA Civ 1. . . . . 349, 350
Huddersfield Banking Co Ltd v Henry Lister & Son Ltd [1895] 2 Ch 273 489
Hurst v Leeming [2002] EWHC 1051, [2003] 1 Lloyd's Rep 379 . . . . 96, 99

Hussmann (Europe) Ltd v Al Ameen Development and Trade Co [2000] 2 Lloyd's
Rep 83. . . . . .439, 443, 457

Industrie Italia Centrale v Alexander Tsaviris and Sons Maritime Co, The Choko Star [1987] 1
Lloyd's Rep 508 464
Instance v Denny Bros Printing Ltd [2000] FSR 869, The Times 28 February 2008 241
International Sea Tankers Inc v Hemisphere Shipping Co Ltd [1982] 1 Lloyd's Rep 128 477

Jackson v Tharker [2007] EWHC 271 (TCC). 324
Jameson v Central Electricity Generating Board [1998] QB 323 487
Jarrom v Sellars [2007] EWHC 1366. 101
John Barker Construction Ltd v London Portman Hotel Ltd [1996] 83 BLR 31. 349
Jones v Sherwood Computer Services plc [1992] 1 WLR 277 . . . . 348, 349
Joseph Finney plc v Vickers [2001] All ER (D) 235 376

Kastner v Jason [2004] 2 Lloyd's Rep 233 459
Kelaniya, The [1989] 1 Lloyd's Rep 30 477
Kinstreet Ltd v Balmargo Corporation Ltd [2000] CP Rep 62 84
Kitcat v Sharp [1882] 48 LT 64 56
Kollerich & Cie SA v The State Trading Corporation of India [1980] 2 Lloyd's Rep 32 349

Lazenby (James) & Co v McNicholas Construction Co Ltd [1999] 3 All ER 820 416
Lead Technical Services Ltd v CMS Medical Ltd [2007] BLR 251. 492
Leicester Circuits Ltd v Coates Brothers plc [2003] EWCA Civ 333 104
Lesotho Highlands Development Authority v Impregilo SpA [2006] 1 AC 221 . .372, 390, 472, 473, 476
Lobster Group Ltd v Heidelberg Graphic Equipment Ltd [2008] 2 All ER 1173. 111
Locabail (UK) Ltd v Bayfield Properties Ltd [2000] QB 451 466
Longstaff International v Evans [2005] EWHC 4 (Ch). 106

Macob Civil Engineering Ltd v Morrison Construction Ltd (1999) 64 Con LR 1 . . . . 354, 367
Marco v Thompson (No 3) [1997] 2 BCLC 36. 349
Margulead Ltd v Exide Technologies [2005] 1 Lloyd's Rep 324 . . . . 384, 472
McAlpine PPS Pipeline Systems Ltd v Transco plc [2004] BLR 352 . . . . 361, 368
McCash v Williams [2003] NZCA 192 247
McCook v Lobo [2002] EWCA Civ 1760. . . . . 44, 99, 180
McE v Prison Service of Northern Ireland [2009] 1 AC 908. 446
McGlinn v Waltham Contractors Ltd [2005] 3 All ER 1126. 112
McMillan Williams v Range [2004] EWCA Civ 294. 104
Memory Corporation v Sidhu [2000] 2 WLR 1443 19
Mercury Communications Ltd v Director General of Telecommunications [1996] 1 WLR 48. 350
Metalfer Corp v Pan Ocean Shipping Co Ltd [1998] 2 Lloyd's Rep 632. 395
Metcalfe v Clipston [2004] EWHC 9005 373
Michael Wilson & Partners Ltd v Emmott [2008] Bus LR 1361 405
Midland Linen Services Ltd, Re [2004] EWHC 3380 (Ch) 99
Muman v Nagasena [2000] 1 WLR 299 85

Nagusina Naviera v Allied Maritime Inc [2003] 2 CLC 1. 482
National Bank of Jamaica Ltd v Olint [2009] 1 WLR 1405. 470
National Navigation Co v Endesa Generación SA [2009] 1 Lloyd's Rep 666 440
National Westminster Bank plc v Feeney and Feeney [2006] EWHC 90066. . . . . .111, 112
Naviera Amazonica Peruana SA v Compania Internactional du Seguros del Peru [1988] 1
Lloyd's Rep 116. 440
Neal v Jones Motors [2002] EWCA Civ 1757 103
Nema, The [1982] AC 724. 477
Newfield Construction Ltd v Tomlinson (2004) 97 Con LR 148 474

Nigel Witham Ltd v Smith [2008] EWHC 12 (TCC)........................... 104, 187

Nikko Hotels (UK) Ltd v MEPC plc [1991] 2 EGLR 103........................... 348

Nisshin Shipping Co Ltd v Cleaves and Co Ltd [2004] 1 Lloyd's Rep 38 379

Nordsee Deutsche Hochseefi scherei GmbH v Reederei Mond Hochseefi scherei Nordstern AG &
Co KG Case 102/81 [1982] ECR 1095........................... 376

Northern Pioneer, The *see* CMA CGM SA v Beteiligungs-KG MS 'Northern Pioneer'
Schiffahrtgesellschaft mbH and Co

Norwich Pharmacal Co v The Commissioners of Customs and Excise [1974] RPC 101 468

Nova (Jersey) Knit Ltd v Kammgarn Spinnerei [1977] 1 WLR 713........................... 439

Oceanbulk Shipping & Trading SA v TMT Asia Ltd [2010] 1 WLR 1803 56

Oceanografia SA de CV v DSND Subsea AS [2007] 1 Lloyd's Rep 37 380

Ofulue v Bossert [2009] UKHL 16, [2009] 1 AC 990........................... 55

Omnibridge Consulting Ltd v Clearsprings (Management) Ltd [2004] EWHC 2276 (Comm)...... 472

Oxford Shipping Co Ltd v Nippon Yusen Kaisha [1984] 3 All ER 835 404

P4 Ltd v Unite Integrated Solutions plc [2006] EWHC 2924, [2007] BLR 1 97

Pacific Maritime (Asia) Ltd v Holystone Overseas Ltd [2008] 1 Lloyd's Rep 371 469

Painting v Oxford University [2005] EWCA Civ 161, [2005] PIQR Q5........................... 102

Palfrey v Wilson [2007] EWCA Civ 94 98

Patel v Patel [2000] QB 551 373

Peacock v Peacock [1991] Fam Law 139 489

Pegram Shopfitters Ltd v Tally Weijl (UK) Lt d [2004] 1 WLR 2082........................... 492

Petroships Pte Ltd v Petec Trading and Investment Corporation [2001] 2 Lloyd's Rep 348 472

Pickersgill v Riley [2004] PNLR 31 19

Pinnel's Case (1602) 5 Co Rep 117a........................... 487

Pitt v PHH Asset Management [1993] 4 All ER 961........................... 42

Porter v Magill [2002] 2 AC 357 .... 400, 466

Practice Direction (Family Proceedings: Ancillary Relief) [2000] 3 All ER 379........................... 82

Practice Note [1927] WN 290 334

Practice Note (Civil Litigation: Case Management) [1995] 1 All ER 385 76

Practice Note (Commercial Court: Alternative Dispute Resolution) [1994] 1 All ER 34 76

President of India v La Pintada Cia Navegacion [1984] 2 All ER 773........................... 323

Project Services v Opek Prime Development Ltd [2000] BLR 402........................... 492

Purcell v F C Trigell Ltd [1971] 1 QB 358........................... 332

R (Bradley) v Secretary of State for Work & Pensions [2009] QB 114 316

R (Channel Group Ltd) v Secretary of State of the Environment, Transport and the Regions
[2001] EWCA Civ 1185........................... 382

R (Cowl) v Plymouth City Council [2001] EWCA 1935, [2002] 1 WLR 803 .... 67, 86, 192, 280

Raja v Van Hoogstraten (No 9) [2009] 1 WLR 1143 424

Ranko Group v Antarctic Maritime SA (1998) LMLN 492 458

Rederij Lalemant v Transportes Generales Navigacion SA [1986] 1 Lloyd's Rep 45............... 375

Reed Executive plc v Reed Business Information Ltd [2004] EWCA Civ 887, [2004] 1 WLR
3026........................... 57, 103, 106

Reliance Industries Ltd v Enron Oil and Gas India Ltd [2002] 1 All ER (Comm) 59 475

Retla Steamship Co v Gryphon Shipping Co SA [1982] 1 Lloyd's Rep 55 471

Ridehalgh v Horsefield [1994] Ch 205 19

RJT Consulting Engineers Ltd v DM Engineering (Northern Ireland) Ltd [2002] 1 WLR 2344 354

Rofa Sport Management AG v DHL International (UK) Ltd [1989] 1 WLR 902 490

Rondel v Worsley [1969] 1 AC 191 19

Roult v North West Strategic Health Authority [2010] 1 WLR 487 332

Roundstone Nurseries Ltd v Stephenson Holdings Ltd [2009] EWHC 1431 (TCC)........104, 106, 111

Rowallan Group Ltd v Edgehill Portfolio No 1 [2007] EWHC 32 (Ch)........................... 106

Royal Bank of Canada v Secretary of State for Defence [2003] EWHC 1841 (Ch) 95

Rupert Morgan Building Services (LLC) Ltd v Jervis [2004] 1 WLR 1867 492
Rush & Tompkins v Greater London Council [1989] AC 1280 . . . . 28, 55
Rustal Trading Ltd v Gill and Duffas SA [2000] 1 Lloyd's Rep 14. 444

SAB Miller Africa v East African Breweries [2010] EWCA Civ 1564. 470
Savings & Investment Bank Ltd v Fincken [2003] EWCA Civ 1630, [2004] 1 WLR 667 57
Sayers v Clarke Walker [2002] EWCA Civ 910 57
Scott v Avery (1856) 5 HL Cas 811, (1856) 25 LJ Ex 308 . . . . 42, 382
Seabridge Shipping AB v AC Orssleff's Eft's A/S [1999] 2 Lloyd's Rep 685 373
Shashoua v Sharma [2009] 2 Lloyd's Rep 376. . . . . 435, 441
Shell Egypt West Manzala Gmbh v Dana Gas Egypt Ltd [2010] 1 Lloyd's Rep 109 475
Shirayama Shokusan Co Ltd v Danovo Ltd (No 1) [2003] EWHC 3306 (Ch). 84
Siebe Gorman and Co Ltd v Pneupac Ltd [1982] 1 WLR 185 333
Smith v Shirley and Bayliss (1875) 32 LT 234 487
Smiths Group Ltd v George Weiss (unreported, 22 March 2002) 241
Société Internationale de Télécommunications Aéronautiques SC (SITA) v The Wyatt Co (UK)
     Ltd [2002] EWHC 2401 . . . . .98, 107, 112, 180
Sonatrach Petroleum Corp v Ferrell International Ltd [2002] 1 All ER (Comm) 627 440
Soulsbury v Soulsbury, The Times 14 November 2007 322
Stax Claimants v Bank of Nova Scotia Channel Islands Ltd [2007] EWHC 1153 (Ch) 55
Stretford v Football Association [2007] Bus LR 1052. 390
Strover v Harrison [1988] Ch 390. 19
Sudbrook Trading Estate Ltd v Eggleton [1983] 1 AC 444 347
Sumukan Ltd v Commonwealth Secretariat [2007] Bus LR 1075. 390
Sun Life Assurance Company of Canada v CX Reinsurance Co Ltd [2004] Lloyd's Rep IR 58 380
Sunrock Aircraft Corporation Ltd v Scandinavian Airlines System Denmark-Norway-Sweden
     [2007] EWCA Civ 882, [2007] 2 Lloyd's Rep 612. . . . . 89, 344
Sutcliffe v Thackrah [1974] AC 727. 350

TAG Wealth Management v West [2008] 2 Lloyd's Rep 699 416
Tapoohi v Lewenberg [2003] VSC 410 247
Thames Valley Power Ltd v Total Gas & Power Ltd [2006] 1 Lloyd's Rep 441 . . . . 344, 348
Thomas and Co Ltd v Portsea SS Co Ltd [1912] AC 1 379
Thomas-Fredric's (Construction) Ltd v Wilson [2004] BLR 23 492
Three Rivers District Council v Bank of England (No 5) [2003] EWCA Civ 474, [2003]
     QB 1556 . . . . 55, 243
Thwaite v Thwaite [1981] FLR 280, [1982] Fam 1. . . . . 333, 490
Thyssen Canada Ltd v Mariana Maritime SA [2005] 1 Lloyd's Rep 640. 444
Tilia Sonera Ab v Hilcourt (Docklands) Ltd [2003] EWHC 3540 (Ch). 458
Toepfer International GmbH v Societe Cargill France [1998] 1 Lloyd's Rep 379. 382
Tomlin v Standard Telephones & Cables Ltd [1969] 1 WLR 1378 56
Tongyuan (USA) International Trading Group v Uni-Clan Ltd (unreported, 19 January 2001). 493
Tropwind, The [1977] 1 Lloyd's Rep 397. 480

UBS AG v HSH Nordbank AG [2009] 2 Lloyd's Rep 272 380
Unilever plc v Procter & Gamble Co [2000] 1 WLR 2436 . . . . 56, 242
Union Discount v Zoller [2001] EWCA Civ 1755, [2002] 1 All ER 693, [2002] 1 WLR 1517 . . . . . 89, 344
Ursa Major Management Ltd v United Utilities Electricity plc [2002] EWHC 3041 (Ch) 347

Vale of Glamorgan Council v Roberts [2008] EWHC 2911 (Ch) 102
Veba Oil Supply and Trading GmbH v Petrotrade Inc [2002] 1 Lloyd's Rep 295 349
Vedatech Corp v Crystal Decisions (UK) Ltd [2003] EWCA Civ 1066. 240
Venture Investment Placement v Hall [2005] EWHC 1227 (Ch) 204, 241, 244
Virani v Manuel Revert Y CIA SA [2003] EWCA Civ 1651, [2004] Lloyd's Rep 4 103

Walford v Miles [1992] 1 All ER 453 42
Walker v Wilsher [1889] 23 QBD 335 . . . . 56, 106
Watkins Jones and Sons Ltd v Lidl UK GmbH (2002) 86 Con LR 155 376
Weissfisch v Julius [2006] 1 Lloyd's Rep 716. . . . . 439, 445
Wentworth v Bullen (1840) 9 B & C 840 332
West Tankers Inc v Riunione Adriatica di Sicurtà SpA (Case C-185/07) [2009] 1 AC 1138 445
Wethered Estates Ltd v Davis [2005] EWHC 1903 (Ch), [2006] BLR 86. . . . . 100, 106
Whitworth Street Estates (Manchester) Ltd v James Miller and Partners Ltd [1970] AC 583 435
Wicketts v Brine Builders [2001] CILL 1805. 415
Widlake v BAA Ltd [2009] EWCA Civ 1256, [2010] PIQR P4 102
Williams v Hull [2009] EWHC 2844 56
World Trade Corporation v Czarnikow Sugar Ltd [2005] 1 Lloyd's Rep 422 457
Worldwide Corporation Ltd v Marconi Communications Ltd, The Times 2 March 2004 19

Youell v La Réunion Aérienne [2009] Bus LR 1504 440

TABLE OF STATUTES

United Kingdom statutes

Administration of Justice Act 1920 574
Arbitration Act 1697 8
   s 11 67
Arbitration Act 1950 . . . . 372, 569
   s 26 . . . . .572, 573
Arbitration Act 1975 569
   s 3(1)(a) 572, 573
   s 4 573
Arbitration Act 1979 372
Arbitration Act 1996 . . . . xxiii, 18, 32,
      352, 371, 372, 373, 375, 376, 377, 378, 380,
      382, 385, 386, 388, 390, 392, 402, 404,
      405, 406, 408, 410, 411, 413, 417, 418, 419,
      421, 423, 431, 433, 434, 438, 440, 452, 456,
      461, 463, 465, 467, 473, 474, 482, 483, 531,
      569, 570, 571, 575, 576, 577, 578
   Part I 379, 567
   ss 1–84 . . . . 440, 444
   s 1 . . . . .372, 382, 399, 462, 534
     (a) 384, 410, 420
     (b) 412, 455, 462
     (c) 415, 443, 462, 484
   s 2 534
     (1) 440
     (2)(a)–(b) 436
     (3) 435
     (4) 571
   s 3 . . . . 387, 433, 435, 440, 535
   s 4 . . . . .387, 535
     (2) 406
     (3) 386, 406
   s 5 . . . . .380, 476, 535
     (1)–(4), (6) 380
   s 6 . . . . .389, 390, 536
     (1) 376, 390
   s 7 . . . . .374, 387, 536
   s 8 . . . . .387, 536
     (1)(b) 380
   ss 9–11 386
   s 9 . . .374, 377, 443, 464, 484, 536, 570, 571, 575
     (1), (3)–(4) 464
   ss 10–11 537
   s 12 . . . . 386, 395, 537, 570
     (1) 465
     (2) 395
     (3)–(4) 465
   s 13 . . . . 386, 538
     (1) 395

s 14 . . . . .387, 396, 538
   (1) 395
   (3) 395, 396
   (4) 395, 396, 397
   (5) 395, 396
ss 15–22 387
s 15 538
   (1)–(3) 396
s 16 539
   (1) 397
   (3)–(6) 398
ss 17–19 399
s 17 539
   (1), (3) 466
s 18 . . . . 442, 539
   (3) 466
s 19 540
s 20 540
   (3) 398, 455
   (4) 398, 457
s 21 540
   (3) 398
   (4) 398, 457
s 22 . . . . .457, 540
s 23 . . . . .387, 541
   (1), (3), (4) 400
s 24 . . . . 386, 399, 400, 401, 466, 482,
                             541, 571
   (1) 466
   (4) 401, 568
s 25 541
   (1) 401
   (3) 401, 467
     (b) 568
   (4) 401, 467
s 26 542
   (1) 386, 401
s 27 542
   (1) 401
   (2)–(3) 401
   (3) 466
   (4) 401
s 28 . . . . .386, 482, 542,
                             568, 571
   (1) 402
   (2) 567
   (5) 402
s 29 . . . . 386, 542
   (1), (3) 402

s 30. . . . . .387, 445, 543	(3)–(4). 471
(1). 443, 445	(6). 567
ss 31–73 444	ss 46–58. 467
s 31. . . . . 386, 442, 543	s 46. . . . . .387, 548
(1). 442, 444	(1). 426, 437
(4)(b). 444	(b). 437
s 32. . . . . .386, 442, 543, 577	(2). 437
(2). 442	(3). 437, 438
(b). 483, 577	ss 47–49 387
(4). 442	s 47. . . . . 454, 548
(6). 567	(2). 454
s 33. . . . . .386, 399, 426, 472, 544	s 48. . . . . .467, 549
(1). 384, 423	(1), (3). 458
(b). 399, 410	(4). 458, 473
s 34. . . . . 386, 544	(5). 390, 458
(1). 412, 416	(a) 459, 467
(2). 412	(b). 458
(b). 446	(c) 459
(d). 416, 420	s 49. . . . . .459, 549
(e) 384, 385, 423	(3)–(4). 459
(f) 420	s 50. . . . . .549, 568
(g) 367, 385, 423	s 51. 549
(h). 423	(1). 455
(3). 412	(2). 455, 573
s 35. . . . . .387, 544	(3). 455
s 36. . . . . .387, 545	ss 52–58 387
s 37. 387, 467, 545	s 52. 550
(1). 422	(1), (3)–(5). 455
(2). 386	s 53. . . . . .436, 458, 550, 571
ss 38–41 387	s 54. 550
s 38. . . . . .390, 447, 545	(1)–(2). 458
(3). 412	s 55. 550
(4). 413, 467	(2)–(3). 459
(6). 467	s 56. . . . . 386, 459, 482, 550, 568, 571
s 39. . . . . .390, 412, 545	(1). 402, 568
(2)–(3). 412	s 57. . . . . .476, 551
s 40. . . . . 386, 546	(4)–(6). 568
(1)–(2). 384	s 58. 551
s 41. 546	(1). 459
(1). 415	s 59. 551
(3). 415, 416	s 60. . . . . 386, 551
(5)–(7). 415	(1)–(2). 459
ss 42–44. 382, 568	s 61. 552
s 42. . . . . .415, 546	(1)–(2). 459
s 43. . . . . 386, 425, 467, 468, 547, 577	s 62. 552
s 44. . . . . . .382, 387, 468, 469, 470, 547, 571, 577	s 63. 552
(2). 468	(4). 569
(b). 468	s 64. 552
(c) 413	s 65. 552
(e) 469, 470	s 66 . . .386, 389, 442, 495, 553, 569, 572, 573, 574
(3). 469, 570	(1). 493
s 45. . . . . 387, 483, 548, 572, 577	(2). 442
(1). .455, 470, 471	(3)–(4). 493
(2). 471	ss 67–69 484
(b). 471, 483, 572, 577	s 67. .386, 443, 553, 572
	(2). 443

s 68 . . . . .374, 386, 444, 458, 471, 472, 473,
　　　　　　　474, 484, 553, 572
　(1) 471
　(2) 472, 473, 474
　　(a) 472
　　(b) 472, 473
　　(d), (g) 473
　(3) 474
　　(b)–(c) 474
　(4) 483
s 69 . . . . .387, 390, 455, 473, 475, 476,
　　　　　　　478, 480, 483, 484, 554, 572
　(1) 475, 476
　(2) 476
　　(b) 476, 572
　(3) 477, 577, 578
　　(a) 478
　　(b) 476, 478
　　(c) 478
　　(c)(ii) 477, 478
　(5) 483
　(7) 478
　(8) 567
s 70 . . . . 386, 555
　(2) 443, 459, 476, 478
　(3) 443, 458, 459, 476, 478, 483,
　　　　　　　484, 572, 577
　(4) 473, 474
s 71 . . . . 386, 555
s 72 . . . . .374, 386, 442, 444, 556
　(1) 442, 444
s 73 . . . . .386, 442, 443, 474, 484, 556
　(1) 444, 474
s 74 . . . . 386, 556
　(1)–(2) 402
s 75 . . . . .386, 557, 569
ss 76–79 387
s 76 557
s 77 557
　(2) 569
s 78 557
s 79 . . . . .478, 558, 569
s 80 558
　(5) 482
s 81 559
s 82 . . . . .356, 376, 443, 559
　(1) 475
s 83 559
ss 84–86 560
ss 85–88 432
s 87 561
s 88 561
ss 89–91 . . . . 389, 404
s 89 561
s 90 . . . . 404, 561

s 91 562
s 92 562
s 93 . . . . 562, 567
　(1), (6) 399
ss 94–98 388
s 94 562
ss 95–98 563
s 99 . . . . 494, 564
s 100 564
　(2) 493
　　(b) 458
s 101 . . . . .493, 564, 572, 573
　(3) 493
s 102 . . . . 564, 573
　(1) 493
　(2) 494
s 103 . . . . 494, 564
　(2) 442
　　(a) 381
s 104 . . . . 493, 565
s 105 565
　(1) 483
ss 106–109 566
s 110 566
Sch 1 . . . . 385, 567
Sch 2 . . . . .399, 567
Arbitration (International Investment
　　Disputes) Act 1966 . . . . .574, 578
　s 1 574

Companies Act 1985 417
Companies Act 2006
　s 31 381
Consumer Credit Act 1974
　s 60 324
　s 61 324
　s 65 324
Contracts (Applicable Law) Act
　　1990 . . . . 438, 439
Contracts (Rights of Third Parties) Act 1999
　s 1 379
　　(1)–(2) 379
　s 8
　　(1) 378, 379
　　(2) 379
Courts and Legal Services Act 1990 66

Disability Discrimination Act 1995 308

Employment Act 2002 310
Employment Act 2005
　s 5 306
Employment Rights Act 2003
　s 203 261
　　(3) 261

Employment Tribunals Act 1996
s 18
(2)–(3)............................ 306
(7)............................... 305

Family Law Act 1996................... 258
Foreign Judgments (Reciprocal Enforcement)
Act 1933
Part I 574

Housing Grants, Construction and
Regeneration Act 1996 ....360, 362,
368, 369, 492
Part II.....................354, 356, 369
s 104............................. 355
(1), (2)–(3)..................... 355
(6)(b)........................... 355
s 105............................. 355
(1)............................. 355
(2)............................. 355
(d)............................. 355
s 106......................... 355, 369
s 107......................... 355, 356
(1)–(4), (6)..................... 356
s 108.....................354, 358, 491
(1)............................. 356
(2).....................355, 357, 358
(c) 357, 367
(d) 357, 367
(e) 366
(f) 367
(3)....................357, 358, 368
(5)............................. 358
s 109............................. 354
s 112............................. 354
s 113............................. 354

Insolvency Act 1986................... 489

Law of Property Act 1925
s 136............................. 324
Law of Property (Miscellaneous Provisions)
Act 1989
s 2............................... 324
Legal Services Act 2007................39, 310
Limitation Act 1980 ....277, 279, 395, 396
s 14A............................. 395
s 14B............................. 395
ss 2, 5 395

Mental Capacity Act 2005 381

National Insurance Act 1911 8

Parliamentary Commissioner Act 1967....... 8

Proceeds of Crime Act 2002.......... 246, 292

Senior Courts Act 1981
s 31............................. 463
s 33(2) 468
s 34(3) 468
s 37........................... 443, 470
s 51.....................94, 110, 112
s 51(6)............................ 69
Statute of Frauds 1677
s 4.............................. 324

Tribunals, Courts and Enforcement Act
2007 8

Unfair Contract Terms Act 1977....... 247, 352

European legislation

Brussels Convention on Jurisdiction and
Enforcement of Judgments in Civil and
Commercial Matters 1968, OJ L 299,
27.09.1972..................xxiv, 440

Council Directive 93/13/EEC of 5 April 1993 on
unfair terms in consumer contracts, OJ L
95, 21.04.1993 389
Council Regulation (EC) No 2201/2003 on
the jurisdiction and recognition and
enforcement of judgments in
matrimonial matters and matters
of parental responsibility, OJ L 338,
23.12.2003......................278
Council Regulation (EC) No 44/2001 on
jurisdiction and the recognition and
enforcement of judgments in civil and
commercial matters (Brussels I Regulation,
Jurisdiction Regulation), OJ L 12,
16.01.2001 ....xxiv, 440
Art 1(2)(d) 440

European Convention on Human
Rights 377
Art 6.......................382, 390, 393
(1)............................. 391
European Parliament and Council Directive
on Mediation in Civil and Commercial
Cases 2008/52/EC, OJ L 136,
24.05.2008.................. 274, 279
Recital 11....................... 275
Recital 23....................... 276
Recital 25....................... 277
Art 1...........................274
Art 2........................... 275
(a) 275
Art 3(a)........................274

Art 4
(1) 275
Art 5 91
(1)–(2) 275
Art 6 ....91, 276
(1)–(2) 276
Art 7 246
(1) 276
(2) 277
Art 8 277
Art 9 277
Art 13 274

European Parliament and Council Regulation
    (EC) No 864/2007 on the law applicable to
    non-contractual obligations (Rome II), OJ
    L 199, 31.7.2007 438
European Parliament and Council Regulation
    (EC) No 593/2008 on the law applicable to
    contractual obligations (Rome I), OJ L 177,
    04.07.2008 .... 438, 452
Art 1(2)(e) 440
Art 3
(1) 438, 439
(2) 438
Arts 4–8 438
Art 4
(1)(a)–(b) 439
(b) 439
(3) 439
Art 5(1), (3) 439

Rome Convention on the law applicable to
    contractual obligations 1980, OJ C 027,
    26.01.1998 438

International instruments
Convention on the settlement of investment
    disputes between States and nationals of
    other States 1965 (ICSID Convention)...574

ICC Rules of Arbitration 2008 (ICC
    Rules) 433, 452
Art 2(1) 447
Art 3(1) 447
Art 4
(1) 447
(5) 448
Art 5
(1), (4)–(6) 448
Art 7(2) 448
Art 8(1), (4) 448
Art 14
(1) 448
(2) 449
Art 16 .... 446, 447

Art 18 .... 400, 448
(2) 448
Art 20
(1) 449
(2) 449
(3) 449
(4) 449
(6) 449
Art 21(3)–(4) 449
Art 22 449
Art 24
(1)–(2) 449
Art 25(2) 449
Art 27 449
Art 28(6) 447, 476
Art 30(1) 447
Art 31(3) 449

International Convention on the Recognition
    and Enforcement of Arbitration Awards
    1958 (New York Convention)....... xxiv,
        277, 381, 389, 404, 433, 442, 455,
                458, 461, 493, 494
Art 1 493
Art 5 436

Model Law for International Arbitration 1985
    (UNCITRAL Model Law) .... xxiv, 18,
                274, 387, 432, 449–452
Art 1
(1) 404
(3) 433
(4)
(a) 433, 436
(b) 433
Art 2A(1) 449
Art 10
(1)–(2) 450
Art 11
(3)(a) 450
(4) 450
Art 12 400
(1) 466
Art 16 450
Arts 17–17J 450, 467
Art 17
(1)–(2) 450
Art 17A 450
Art 17B(1)–(2) 450
Art 17C(4) 450
Art 17E 451
Art 17F 451
Art 17G 451
Art 17H 451
Art 17I 451
Art 18 452

Art 19
  (1) 451
  (2) 451, 452
Art 21 450
Art 22
  (1)–(2) 446
Art 23 451
  (1) 451
Art 24
  (1) 451, 452
  (2)–(3) 451
Art 26(1)(a)–(b) 451

Art 28 452
  (4) 438
Art 29 . . . . .451, 452
Art 31(2) 452
Art 32 452

United Nations Convention on Contracts
  for the International Sale of Goods
  1980 437

United States legislation
Uniform Mediation Act 2001 18

PART 1

HISTORY AND RANGE OF ADR METHODS

1

INTRODUCTION

BACKGROUND 1.01

WHAT IS ADR? 1.11

WHY IS THERE A NEED FOR ADR? 1.16

THE GROWTH OF ADR OPTIONS 1.20

RECENT DEVELOPMENTS 1.22

ADR AND THE REVIEW OF CIVIL LITIGATION COSTS 1.25

THE INTERNATIONAL CONTEXT 1.27

SOME ISSUES WITH REGARD TO ADR 1.28

POTENTIAL ADVANTAGES OF ADR 1.29

POTENTIAL DISADVANTAGES OF ADR 1.42

WEIGHING UP ADVANTAGES AND DISADVANTAGES,
AND THE INTERFACE WITH LITIGATION 1.52

ASSESSING THE SUCCESS OF ADR 1.55

OVERVIEW OF REGULATORY FRAMEWORKS 1.57

OVERVIEW OF TRAINING AND ACCREDITATION 1.65

KEY POINTS SUMMARY 1.71

BACKGROUND

In many jurisdictions a court system has come to be seen as a superior way of settling civil **1.01** disputes, especially where that system is seen as independent, inspires the respect of society, and has rules for procedure and evidence that have been refined over a long period of time to seek to ensure fairness.

1.02   The strength of the court system in England and Wales is such that over several centuries it has evolved as the main method for resolving legal disputes within the jurisdiction. The respect in which this system is held can be seen in the extent to which other jurisdictions have copied aspects of it, and this respect can still be seen in the extent to which parties making commercial contracts will often select English law and jurisdiction for the resolution of any disputes that may arise. London is seen as one of the main litigation capitals of the world, with reasonably clear and comprehensive rules for procedure, and with confidence in judicial decision making.

1.03   The pre-eminence of the court system is such that other forms of dispute resolution are commonly called 'alternative' dispute resolution (or ADR), carrying the implication that litigation is the normal first choice. However over the years doubts have been expressed as to whether litigation is always the most efficient and effective way of dealing with a dispute. The potential for delay, complexity and cost was illustrated by the fictional case of *Jarndyce v Jarndyce*, in *Bleak House* by Charles Dickens. It has always been the case that many cases settle rather than go to trial, and over the last few decades there has been a steady growth in the use and variety of forms of ADR.

1.04   The growth of ADR has now reached the stage where it is formally acknowledged by the Civil Procedure Rules (the CPR) as being potentially relevant to all civil actions, to the extent that it is positively encouraged both at a pre-action stage and after litigation has commenced, with potential sanctions in appropriate cases where an ADR process is not followed, for which see Chapters 5, 6 and 7. In the 'Review of Civil Litigation Costs' carried out by Lord Justice Jackson, the Final Report issued in December 2009 included as recommendation 6.3 the view that ADR has a vital role to play, and that there should be a serious campaign to ensure that all litigation lawyers are properly informed of how ADR works and the benefits that it can bring.

1.05   These points mean that it is now crucial that all lawyers should be aware of:

- the ADR options that may be available for a client;
- how each ADR process operates;
- the potential strengths and weaknesses of each option, as regards other ADR options and litigation;
- the potential impact of ADR options with regard to matters such as costs, disclosure and enforcement;
- what the role of the lawyer is with regard to each ADR process.

1.06   The reasons why litigation lawyers in particular need such knowledge are:

- the provision of a good service to a client requires the recommendation of an ADR option where that offers potential benefits eg as regards costs and time;
- lawyers who do not advise sufficiently on appropriate ADR options may leave their clients open to significant penalties in costs, even if a case is won;
- in areas such as commercial law and family law clients are showing an interest in and use of ADR solutions, and if a lawyer cannot provide a service that includes ADR the client may go elsewhere;
- it is foreseeable that lawyers will be subject to complaints, and possibly even wasted costs orders or actions for negligence, if they proceed with litigation in a case where ADR could have achieved a quicker, cheaper or otherwise better outcome.

It is the purpose of this book to provide an overview of the ADR options that a lawyer in **1.07** practice in England and Wales should be aware of. We outline the processes involved, the options that should be put to a client, and the sorts of decision that may need to be taken. In doing this we take a practical approach that should be of value to a lawyer in a case, with step-by-step guides and bullet point summaries where appropriate. Due to the relative informality of some ADR processes it is not always possible to provide a systematic guide, but the summaries and checklists should provide a sound foundation.

We seek to cover the full range of ADR options, with a focus on negotiation, mediation and **1.08** arbitration as those are most commonly encountered in practice. Some ADR options are quite specialist, or not commonly used, in which case we provide an overview with references to other books and resources. Some ADR options, such as mediation and arbitration, are quite well supported by not-for-profit or commercial providers, and reference is made to publications and websites that provide useful further information.

It is important to appreciate that ADR does not provide a single 'menu' of alternatives to **1.09** litigation from which a lawyer and client select a single option when a dispute arises. Many cases will move from one option to another—a case that is eventually decided by a judge may have gone through some negotiation, or a case that has been substantially prepared for litigation may be resolved by mediation. The effective lawyer needs not only to advise on an appropriate dispute resolution option, but to keep options under review, to be prepared to move from one option to another, and to consider how one dispute resolution process might impact on another if there were to be a change in how a particular case is being handled.

It is also relevant to be aware that ADR processes are not used only by lawyers. Techniques **1.10** such as negotiation and mediation are often used in business, and dispute resolution processes are common in relation to employment and sale of goods and services. Many clients will therefore have some experience of such processes.

WHAT IS ADR?

The term 'alternative dispute resolution' or 'ADR' does not have an agreed definition. Some **1.11** might argue that arbitration is not a form of ADR because it is a regulated adjudicative system, and others might say that negotiation is not technically a form of ADR as it involves lawyers and their clients but no third party. Terminology and methodologies with regard to ADR are still evolving. For the purpose of this book we are taking the phrase to cover the full range of alternatives to litigation that might be available to a lawyer and client to resolve a civil dispute.

There are also debates as to whether the term 'alternative dispute resolution' should be **1.12** used at all. Options are only really 'alternative' if the use of litigation is seen as the norm, but statistics show that most cases settle rather than going to court for decision, so that settlement rather than litigation is actually the norm. Also many cases use a mixture of court procedure and ADR rather than relying solely on one 'alternative'. For such reasons it has been argued that it may be more accurate to talk of 'appropriate dispute resolution', or to use other terminology. Rather than be drawn into such debates, we take the pragmatic view that 'ADR' is a term generally accepted as covering alternatives to litigation, defined as follows.

1.13   'ADR' is taken to cover alternatives to going to court where:

- there is a dispute between two (or more) parties;
- that dispute relates to civil legal rights and/or duties;
- the dispute could potentially go to court for resolution;
- the dispute is resolved through some other process, usually with a more flexible structure;
- the process is essentially confidential;
- the process involves individuals other than the parties in dispute who add some degree of objectivity, be it lawyers, or an independent and normally neutral third party.

1.14   Alternatives to litigation potentially include the following factors:

- a process that is formal (like arbitration), or informal (like negotiation);
- the involvement of lawyers and clients only (like negotiation) or third parties (like mediation);
- the involvement of specialists or experts;
- a process provided or facilitated by a commercial or not-for-profit organisation;
- processes that operate within this jurisdiction, or are available in this jurisdiction but can operate internationally (with national and international systems for arbitration, and few jurisdictional limits for processes such as mediation);
- a process that is based on meetings, or documents, or that is wholly or partly remote (with some growth of IT-based systems).

1.15   There is no single appropriate terminology for those participating in an ADR process. For example, if a dispute is settled before the issue of proceedings there will never be a claimant or a defendant. The general approach in this book is to refer to those involved in a dispute as the 'parties' to the dispute, whether or not they are formally parties to an action. Much of the text is directed to lawyers advising 'parties'.

WHY IS THERE A NEED FOR ADR?

1.16   A sound and just court system is undoubtedly a primary choice for dispute resolution. Clear and fair procedural rules should ensure that both parties are able to put their case properly. Balanced and transparent rules for evidence should ensure that relevant information is admissible, and that irrelevant or prejudicial information is excluded. A respected judicial system and a process for appeals should ensure that no injustice is done. A state-supported system should ensure reasonable access for potential litigants, and support for the enforcement of judgments.

1.17   That said, no system can be perfect, and there are various ways in which a good court system may nonetheless fail to meet the needs of all individual litigants. Any of the following factors might cause a potential litigant to look for alternatives to going to court.

- The very strengths of a court system can include potential weaknesses. Rules for civil procedure may need to be quite complex to be fair, but this complexity may of itself extend the time needed to resolve the dispute, and the costs of the action.
- Evidence rules for disclosure and inspection may assist justice, but they may be burdensome where a wide range of documents are potentially relevant, or where a client is concerned about issues such as confidentiality.

- It is a central objective of the court system to provide justice for individual litigants—in terms now enshrined in the overriding objective in the CPR: see Chapter 5. However the court system also has other objectives, such as the development of law through the precedent system. It may be necessary to go to the Court of Appeal or even the Supreme Court to resolve a point of law, and this may be something an individual litigant would prefer to avoid.
- The court process in England and Wales is essentially adversarial. This ensures that the case for each side is fully presented and effectively challenged. However an adversarial process may not always be very appropriate, for example where the parties are likely to have an ongoing relationship (maybe as regards business dealings or the care of a child) that may be threatened rather than assisted by an adversarial approach.
- The full range of the litigation process may not be appropriate—if a case turns largely on a specialist matter requiring expert evidence it may be more appropriate to focus on determination by an expert rather than follow a full trial procedure.
- The court system is based on the role and power of the judge, a point reinforced by the Woolf reforms and the growth of judicial case management. While this offers clear benefits for justice and the conduct of cases, it may not suit clients who would prefer more personal control over a dispute resolution process and outcome.
- Normally the focus in court is on a past factual scenario, such as how an accident happened. Sometimes a party might prefer a dispute resolution process to cover a wider range of matters, to take into account points that are not necessarily technically relevant, or to look more clearly to the future.
- In court a judge can only make such decisions or orders as he or she has the power to make, though there is some flexibility, for example as regards what might be put into a schedule to a consent order. A party might prefer a process that could look at decisions and outcomes beyond the technical powers of a judge.

None of these points means that an ADR process is necessarily better than a court process. Indeed each of these points is open to argument—for example civil litigation procedure rules include significant flexibility for controlling time and cost, and options such as the fast track. The point is rather that all of these factors may be relevant in considering options for resolving a dispute. **1.18**

Also these points are not necessarily reasons for rejecting litigation. Many clients will continue to see bringing a legal action as the natural choice when a dispute arises, and if a negotiation or mediation is not successful then litigation will often remain the fallback. Most ADR processes will take place within the context of what a judge might decide if the case went to court, and an outcome to a mediation or negotiation is only likely to be agreed if it compares adequately to the likely outcome of litigation. The point is rather that a good lawyer should not focus exclusively on litigation without considering the possible benefits of alternatives, and should not allow a case to move automatically from one step in litigation to the next without reviewing options. **1.19**

THE GROWTH OF ADR OPTIONS

With current attention and publicity there might be a perception that ADR options are a relatively recent development. However it has always been possible to settle a case rather **1.20** than go to court, and the range of alternatives to litigation has developed over a prolonged period. The following outline of major developments provides a context for the current position, and some insight into what motivates the use of ADR.

- The first English statute relating to arbitration was the Arbitration Act 1697 (9 & 10 Will III c15), which stopped parties from withdrawing from arbitration right up to the last moment if the case seemed to be going against them. It is clear that arbitration was being used well before that date, with the earliest reported case being *Anon* [1468] YB 8 Edw IV, fo1, p1. The Victorians developed the use of arbitration, with further regulation by statute.
- Tribunals to adjudicate disputes with administrative agencies grew throughout the last century. It is generally thought that the first tribunal was that set up under the National Insurance Act 1911, and there was substantial growth and review throughout the century, leading to the creation of a new unified structure for tribunals under the Tribunals, Courts and Enforcement Act 2007.
- A different option for dealing with disputes relating to administration is the use of an ombudsman. The term 'ombudsman' is derived from old Swedish, and while there may be some debate about its original meaning, from about 1800 the term has been used to mean an independent official who could review the actions of executive government to address the concerns of individual citizens. In the United Kingdom the term is used for the Parliamentary Commissioner for Administration, whose office was set up under the Parliamentary Commissioner Act 1967. This initiative has been followed by the creation of a range of other 'ombudsmen' whose role is to address complaints by investigation and who attempt to resolve matters without litigation: see Chapter 19.
- The area of employment saw substantial growth of the use of ADR processes during the last century. In 1975 the Advisory, Conciliation and Arbitration Service (commonly known as ACAS) was set up. Although funded by the government, this body is independent, and focuses on supporting employment relationships, where it is often more important to seek to resolve a dispute and move forward rather than to take an adversarial approach. For more information see www.acas.org.uk.
- In 1990 the Centre for Effective Dispute Resolution (commonly known as CEDR) was launched with the support of the Confederation of British Industry and some leading law firms. This body is based in London but has a national and international presence with regard to promoting and facilitating ADR, and in particular mediation, especially with regard to commercial cases. For more information see www.cedr.co.uk.
- There has for many years been a concern about the high level of costs incurred in personal injury and medical negligence cases when compared to the amount of damages received by claimants. In 1995 the National Health Service started a pilot scheme to use mediation for medical negligence claims. While there was a relatively low take up of the scheme, it proved quite successful in dealing with the cases where it was used.
- Over the last 20 years there has been steady growth in the numbers of commercial and not-for-profit bodies, and the number of solicitors' firms and barristers' chambers, offering mediation and other ADR services.

1.21 There has also been a steady growth in recognition of, and support for, ADR options within the litigation system:

- Steps to support settlement have been taken within the litigation framework. For example the use of offers to settle was encouraged in *Calderbank v Calderbank* [1976] Fam 93, which made it clear that a written offer to settle could be brought to the attention of the judge when costs were considered. More recently this has been formalised into the system for Part 36 offers, with clear potential costs penalties where a party presses on with litigation but fails to improve upon an offer for settlement.

- Initial interest in the use of ADR in relation to court actions arose in the context of commercial cases. In 1994 the Commercial Court issued the 'Practice Note: Commercial Court; Alternative Dispute Resolution' [1994] 1 All ER 34, which requires lawyers to 'consider with their clients and the other parties concerned the possibility of attempting to resolve the particular dispute or particular issues by mediation, conciliation or otherwise', and to 'ensure that parties are fully informed as to the most cost-effective means of resolving the particular dispute'. Although this approach was a little slow to take off, it moved on to quite successful take up rates and improved client satisfaction.
- This was followed in 1995 by the High Court Practice Note (Civil Litigation: Case Management) [1995] 1 All ER 385. While essentially providing for greater judicial control of cases, this included questions on whether legal advisers had discussed the possibility of using ADR with their client and the other side, and whether they had considered that some form of ADR might assist in resolving or narrowing issues. This showed recognition of ADR, while not at that stage taking significant steps to support its use.
- In 1996 a pilot scheme in Central London County Court offered time-limited voluntary mediation in any defended case where the claim was for over £3,000. This became a model, and led to pilot schemes in other county courts, including Exeter, Manchester and Reading. Evaluation of these schemes provided the foundation for the current approach to county court mediation.
- A mediation scheme attached to the Court of Appeal was established on a voluntary basis in 1997. As leave to appeal is given on the basis there is a real prospect of success it is logical that the parties should review their positions prior to the appeal hearing, and the scheme has a reasonably good success rate.

RECENT DEVELOPMENTS

Over the past decade there have been a variety of moves to embed acknowledgement of **1.22** the potential benefits of ADR more clearly and strongly within the civil litigation system. The current position is considered fully in Chapters 5–7, but key elements are summarised here as they provide an important context for the general development of ADR within this jurisdiction.

- Encouragement of the use of ADR was built into the Woolf reforms, and expressly and by implication in the Civil Procedure Rules 1998 that followed. The overriding objective expressly includes saving expense and dealing with case in a proportionate way, CPR r 1.1. Judges are also expected to encourage the parties to co-operate, for example 'encouraging the parties to use and alternative dispute resolution procedure if the court considers that to be appropriate and facilitating the use of such procedure' and 'helping the parties to settle the whole or part of a case', CPR r 1.4.2 (e). See 5.33.
- ADR is expressly encouraged prior to litigation see 5.18–5.28. The reasonableness of pre-action conduct can be relevant to a costs order, including whether proceedings were issued prematurely: CPR r 44.5, see 6.38–6.39. Pre-action protocol requirements were amended

from 2003 (30th update) to say that the letter of claim should state if a party wishes to enter into mediation or another form of ADR. In 2006 (41st update) the approach to ADR in the protocols was standardised to say that the parties should consider whether some form of alternative dispute resolution would be more suitable than litigation and, if so, endeavour to agree which form to adopt. Parties may be required by the court to provide evidence that ADR was considered, and that conduct in this regard can be relevant to costs: see 5.18–5.28.

- ADR is also expressly encouraged during litigation. It is provided that 'A party may when filing the completed allocation questionnaire make a written request for the proceedings to be stayed while the parties try to settle the case by alternative dispute resolution or other means': CPR r 26.4, see 5.40–5.48. If all the parties request a stay or the court of its own initiative considers such a stay appropriate the court will direct that the proceedings be stayed for a period of one month, which can be extended. From 2005 (41st update) where a court gives directions on its own initiative without holding a case management conference: 'In such cases as the court thinks appropriate, the court may give directions requiring the parties to consider ADR'.

- From 2007 the use of ADR has been standardised in county courts, and from 2008 there is a full-time mediation officer in each area. This provides a common and subsidised mediation procedure supported by the National Mediation Helpline: see 14.02–14.09, and www.nationalmediationhelpline.com.

1.23 This development of procedural regulation has been accompanied by a development of judicial attitude. This is important because the rules have expressly opened up options for judges, but have quite specifically stopped short of making any requirement that a party enters ADR. It is therefore essential to consider how the judges use their discretion. The following key cases are fully discussed in later chapters.

- In *Dunnett v Railtrack* [2002] 1 WLR 2434 the courts showed that they were prepared to impose a costs penalty on a party who failed to take part in an ADR process. Although the defendants won their case on appeal they were denied their costs because the court had stated that the parties should attempt mediation but the defendant had refused to consider it. See 6.47.

- In *Halsey v Milton Keynes NHS Trust* [2004] 1 WLR 3002 the court reviewed practice relating to ADR, and accepted the potential benefits of ADR, especially a voluntary process such as mediation. It concluded that a party could not be compelled to use ADR, but that a costs penalty could be imposed on a party who unreasonably refused to consider ADR. See 5.60–5.62 and 6.09–6.13.

- In *Burchell v Bullard* [2005] BLR 330 a dispute over building work involved a claim for £18,000 and a counterclaim eventually judged to be worth about £14,000, so that less than £5,000 changed hands following judgment. The costs of the case were over £160,000. The claimant had suggested mediation at an early stage but the defendants refused. Although the judge was not prepared to impose a penalty as the original case was some years old he made it very clear that ADR should have been attempted. See 5.49.

1.24 These changes have all led to a significant growth in the use of ADR. Useful information on the growth of use of ADR and research into its success can be found on the website of the independent organisation ADR Now, and especially in the ADR Research section: see www.adrnow.org.uk. There has also been a downward trend in the number of court actions

started due to the use of ADR: see for example Ministry of Justice statistics on www.justice.
gov.uk/publications/courtstatisticsquarterly.htm.

ADR AND THE REVIEW OF CIVIL LITIGATION COSTS

The question of costs is one of the main reasons for choosing ADR, and the recent develop-   **1.25**
ments outlined in 1.22–1.24 largely relate to costs issues. ADR options may be attractive in
terms of lower potential costs, more predictable costs, and potentially more control over
costs. The Review of Civil Litigation Costs (December 2009) carried out by Lord Justice
Jackson included in its final Report a number of recommendations designed to bring the
costs of litigation under closer control. These include fixed costs for fast track cases with
a value up to £25,000 where the trial can be concluded within a day, and a more robust
approach to costs management, including the provision of costs budgets and a standard
costs management procedure.

The Final Report also concludes that 'ADR (particularly mediation) has a vital role to   **1.26**
play in reducing the costs of civil disputes, by fomenting the early settlement of cases':
Recommendation 6.3. Lord Justice Jackson feels that ADR is under-used, and he also recommends 'a serious campaign to ensure that all litigation lawyers and judges are properly
informed of how ADR works, and the benefits that it can bring'. He concludes that ADR
should not be mandatory for all proceedings, as the circumstances for which form of ADR
should be used and when will vary from case to case, and this should be left to the judgment
of experienced practitioners and the court: Recommendation 6.3. These recommendations
are considered further in Chapter 4.

THE INTERNATIONAL CONTEXT

There has also been a significant growth in the use of ADR in many other jurisdictions   **1.27**
round the world. While many of these developments are beyond the scope of this book,
they cannot be ignored.

- There is a separate system for international arbitration based on international arbitration
  institutional rules: see Chapter 26. This must be distinguished from the system for arbitration within the jurisdiction which is based on statute and has a very different character:
  see Chapter 23.
- Mediation is an informal process based on agreement, and it is therefore not necessarily
  jurisdiction specific, though its use is regulated in different ways in some jurisdictions.
  For some further discussion on this, and the position within the European Union, see
  Chapter 15.
- Options developed in different parts of the world in relation to different types of cases can
  provide useful models for effective dispute management and resolution processes. There
  is for example the development of the use of collaborative law in North America. Some
  states in the USA have experimented with the use of more compulsion as regards the use
  ADR, with for example case settlement conferences, and court-directed arbitration or
  mediation.

SOME ISSUES WITH REGARD TO ADR

1.28 The speed and level of development might make it appear that ADR is now fully formed and accepted, but there is still significant ongoing evolution. Various issues are still being debated, and there will undoubtedly be change as ADR is more widely used. The flexibility of some ADR options means that change can come about quite quickly.

- A key issue is whether a party can ever be forced to use ADR. In particular it is possible that there might be a breach of Art 6 of the European Convention on Human Rights which provides that 'In the determination of his civil rights and obligations . . . everyone is entitled to a fair and public hearing within a reasonable time by an independent and impartial tribunal established by law'. It seems clear that an order or agreement to use ADR which prevented access to a court would potentially breach this right, though the European Court has accepted that a party can waive article 6 rights in for example agreeing to a binding adjudicative process, so long as there is not undue pressure and the right to trial is retained: *Deweer v Belgium* (1980) 2 EHRR.
- Within this jurisdiction judges considered the issue of compulsion to use ADR in *Halsey v Milton Keynes NHS Trust* [2004] 1 WLR 3002, though possible breach of Art 6 was not fully argued and comments by Dyson LJ were obiter. The position is that no party can be forced to enter into any form of ADR, or to agree an outcome to a non-adjudicative ADR process. The position is rather that a party should consider ADR, and risks a costs penalty where ADR is unreasonably refused. Obligations on parties to litigation have become much more intrusive, and there are now many things that a litigant should do before a court hearing, including compliance with pre-action protocols. Such requirements are not seen as breaching Art 6, and the distinction seems to be that sanctions can be used to support compliance with procedural requirements, so long as enforcement is not by penal sanctions such as imprisonment or a fine for contempt, and the party is not deprived of a right to trial.
- In some jurisdictions mediation is regulated through statute or court regulations. This is not currently the case in England and Wales, where various not-for-profit, commercial organisations and individuals offer mediation services on a self-regulated basis. It is likely that over time some form of regulation will emerge. One possible model is the European Union Code of Conduct for Mediators: see Chapter 15.
- There are a number of jurisprudential issues to be developed with regard to the inter-relation of litigation and ADR. Might there be circumstances where a judge might properly make a wider use of his or her powers to encourage a party to continue with ADR, or to try harder to reach an agreed solution? Might more detailed terms be evolved for the basis upon which a claim might be stayed? Are there problems with regard to the inter-relation of litigation and ADR when a case moves from one to the other?
- There are issues with regard to the traditional concepts of privilege and confidentiality and ADR processes. Client confidentiality is protected by the doctrine of legal professional privilege, which protects communications between a lawyer and client when preparing a case from disclosure when litigation is contemplated. There are significant queries about how this applies in relation to ADR and problems can arise where information is disclosed in an ADR process, and with regard to issues such as whether a mediator can be called as a witness: see 3.71–3.83 and 13.94–13.122.

POTENTIAL ADVANTAGES OF ADR

There are many potential advantages that ADR can offer, though the actual advantages that **1.29** may be available in a specific case will need careful professional consideration by the lawyer. The potential advantages are summarised here, and are developed in Chapter 3 with regard to selecting a specific ADR process. Whether potential advantages are actually achieved will depend on the type of ADR selected, and how the case is pursued.

Lower cost

Using ADR may be significantly cheaper than going to court, especially if the case is settled **1.30** at a relatively early stage before costs build up, and if a relatively inexpensive method such as negotiation is used. This potential advantage will decrease if ADR is not attempted until a relatively late stage (as costs will already have accumulated), and/or if a relatively expensive form of ADR such as arbitration is selected. See Chapter 4 for more guidance on costs.

Speed of settlement

A case can take months or even years to reach resolution in court, and that time frame **1.31** may be extended if there is an appeal. Some forms of ADR, such as negotiation or mediation, can be conducted quite quickly and quite soon after the dispute arises. This potential advantage may be less fully enjoyed if ADR is not used until a relatively late stage in the case, or if the ADR process used is itself protracted, as an arbitration might be. Speed of settlement can substantially reduce the stress and distraction that may be caused to the parties in the case.

Control of process

Once proceedings have been issued, a court case is essentially under the control of the judge. **1.32** A lawyer should always act within client instructions, but in practice many clients may feel that litigation is substantially guided by the lawyer because the client is unfamiliar with procedural rules. Many clients, especially those accustomed to running their own businesses, may prefer the greater control that can come with an ADR process such as mediation.

Choice of forum

In litigation there are some choices, for example as regards the court in which a claim is com- **1.33** menced. However there are many rules about case management, tracks for different types of cases etc, and the parties will have no choice as to the judge in the case. In a process such as arbitration or mediation the parties are able to agree who should hear the case or provide the mediation process, taking expertise and experience into account as they wish.

A wider range of issues may be considered

Sometimes a client will present a lawyer with issues that are not easy to categorise in legal **1.34** terms, or where the law is complex or unclear. Such issues may be difficult or expensive to litigate and ADR may provide a more practical alternative. That said, ADR should never be followed simply in an attempt to sidestep a problem—the need for case analysis and legal research are just as high in an ADR process because of the need to convince an opponent or a third party.

Wider range of potential outcomes

1.35   Essentially a judge in court can only order something that is within the powers of the court, such as damages or an injunction, and the order can only relate to the issues before the judge. If a judge makes a consent order it may be possible to put wider terms into a schedule to an order, but such a schedule may not be an appropriate form, for example to govern an ongoing commercial relationship. Negotiation or mediation can result in any terms that suit the parties, and can be particularly useful where a case includes a future relationship.

Flexibility of process

1.36   A case that goes to court must follow a set process that generally includes a pre-action protocol, rules for commencing the claim, rules for possible interim applications, rules for trial etc. Some of the rules are quite detailed and technical. In contrast an ADR process such as negotiation can be relatively informal. The range of ADR options provides a range of relative formality—mediation will follow an agreed process, and arbitration has procedural rules of its own.

Flexibility with regard to evidence

1.37   The rules for evidence in civil cases have been relaxed in various ways over recent years, but litigation still involves detailed rules for disclosure and inspection and the admissibility of evidence. An ADR process will normally be much more flexible as regards information and evidence—indeed in negotiation and mediation it is essentially for each party to decide what to reveal. This does not mean that the rules of evidence can be ignored—the lawyer will still need to consider what information might be obtained through litigation, and must take some care over what is revealed in ADR in case the process fails and the case goes to trial. In some cases disclosure might be very burdensome and expensive, and this might be avoided through ADR.

Confidentiality

1.38   Most litigation processes are open, so that justice can be seen to be done. There may be various reasons why a client would prefer a more private settlement, for example to keep personal or business information or the outcome of the case confidential. This can be achieved through ADR, which is a private process, and confidentiality clauses are a normal part of an agreement for or reached as a result of ADR.

Use of a problem solving approach

1.39   The emphasis of litigation tends to be on past events, focussing on what happened in the past and on allocating blame. This can be a negative process for both sides, and the adversarial process can lead to parties becoming entrenched. ADR options can be more forward looking and constructive—for example mediation can help to move parties away from intransigence.

Possible reduction of risk

In aiming to find a winner and a loser, litigation can sometimes be a relatively blunt instru- **1.40**
ment. Liability is decided on the balance of probabilities, which could potentially be as
close as winning if the judge is 51% convinced of a case, or losing on 49%. The level of risk
is heightened by the rule that costs will normally follow the event, so that the loser will
potentially bear the costs of both sides. If the chances of winning in litigation are not very
clear cut, proceeding to trial can carry significant risks that will need to be carefully evaluated. An ADR process may be less focussed on finding a winner, and can thus be a better way
of managing risk where there is not a strong chance of success, or where it may be difficult
to assess risk.

Client satisfaction

Even parties who win tend to express some dissatisfaction with the litigation process. This **1.41**
is perhaps inevitable—a client can all too easily have unrealistic expectations, or underesti-
mate the strength of the case for the other side. Nonetheless this cannot be ignored by any
lawyer concerned to provide a good service for a client. Clients tend to express higher levels
of satisfaction with a successful negotiation or mediation process, perhaps because they
have been involved in agreeing the outcome, and have felt more in control of the process
and the outcomes. See 1.55–1.56 and 11.15–11.19 for research on this issue.

POTENTIAL DISADVANTAGES OF ADR

The potential disadvantages will not apply to every case, and they may be largely avoided with **1.42**
careful choice of an appropriate ADR option, and careful pursuit of the case. The potential
disadvantages are also developed in more detail in relation to ADR options in Chapter 3.

Increased expense

An ADR process needs to be carefully selected and efficiently handled to be successful. If **1.43**
ADR is used in an inappropriate way or at an inappropriate time, or if the clients and lawyers
do not put reasonable preparation and efforts into success, the process may fail. Failed ADR
may add expense to resolving the case if the case still has to go to trial. The different costs
implications of different types of dispute resolution must also be kept in mind. A party who
wins in court is likely to get an order that his or her reasonable costs will be paid by the
loser, whereas a settlement will normally leave the party liable to pay his or her own costs
unless some payment of costs is agreed as part of the settlement. This is considered further
in Chapter 4.

Additional delay

An ADR process that fails may cause delay if the case then has to go to court for resolu- **1.44**
tion. It is important to assess carefully when ADR has a reasonable chance of success. This
can lead to complex considerations where one party is keen to use ADR but the other is
obstructive.

Possible reduction in outcome compared to a court judgment

1.45   A client who feels that he or she has a strong case as regards liability and remedy may prefer to go to court to achieve the full potential of the case, including a costs order. ADR may involve some concession or compromise. That said, a non-adjudicative ADR process can never force a client to accept anything less than the client thinks is fair, and some reduction may be justified where time and costs have been saved.

1.46   This can be a strategic issue—a party with a relatively weak case may seek ADR in the hope of getting an offer of something where going to trial might mean losing and having to pay the winner's costs. Litigants with a strong case may understandably be reluctant to enter ADR in such circumstances, and may need persuasion to do so.

Lack of a clear and public finding

1.47   Some clients value a public finding by a judge, and a finding that they have 'won'. It may vindicate a stand the client has taken, or may create a precedent that the client can rely on in relation to other potential claims. However it should be remembered that a finding or agreement reached through ADR can always be made public by agreement.

1.48   There is also a public interest in having a sufficiently comprehensive range of court judgments for the law in an area to be reasonably clear. An ADR process will usually take place within the context of what would happen if the case went to court, so ADR is to some extent reliant on continuing litigation producing precedents. As ADR reports are not normally published it can be very difficult for anyone other than a practitioner regularly involved in ADR in an area to see how practice in settlements is developing.

Loss of potential strategic use of procedural steps

1.49   The range of pre-action and interim applications that can be made in relation to court proceedings can be strategically very useful. For example it may be very relevant to a particular case to seek an interim injunction, or security for costs. Summary judgment can resolve a case quickly. Some such outcomes may be achieved in an ADR process, but arbitrators have much more limited powers, and mediators rarely have any power in such areas. It is important to consider what procedural applications might be useful for a client before selecting an ADR process. This may also be a reason for starting an action and making constructive use of procedural possibilities before moving to an ADR option.

Loss of potential advantages of evidential rules

1.50   If court action is contemplated, evidential rules provide for disclosure and inspection of relevant documents held by the other side, with a variety of possible applications to court if information and material is not made available. Pre-action protocols provide for early availability of such material in many cases. The importance of litigating with 'cards on the table' has been emphasised following the Woolf reforms. Adjudicative ADR options may also have some requirements as to the material to be made available, though this is usually subject to the agreement of the parties. Mediation and adjudication do not normally have mandatory requirements for the disclosure of evidence, and a party may choose to keep relevant material secret. It is important to consider what information and evidence you may need from the other side, as well as what information and evidence you might disclose voluntarily, before selecting an ADR option. This may again be a reason for at least going through the pre-action stages of litigation before moving to ADR.

Confusion of process

In some cases there is a clear choice—for example to use arbitration instead of litigation. However the fact that ADR is not always a full alternative to a court process can lead to real difficulties in analysing a case and pursuing it in a comprehensively strategic way. Negotiation and mediation can arise at various stages before and during a court action in a way that can hamper coherent progress of the case and cause confusion for lawyers and clients. For example a phone call from one solicitor to another or a discussion by barristers prior to an interim application may give rise to some suggestions relevant to settlement while a litigation process is in progress. It is important to try to define ADR and settlement possibilities separately from the steps for ongoing litigation.   **1.51**

WEIGHING UP ADVANTAGES AND DISADVANTAGES, AND THE INTERFACE WITH LITIGATION

The discussion at 1.21–1.51 shows that there can be quite strong reasons for using, or not using, ADR. They also show that the situation can be quite complex, with some factors favouring ADR and others not in the same case. All the factors are considered more fully in Chapter 3 in relation to advising a client in relation to the selection of an ADR option in a particular case.   **1.52**

It is important to emphasise that a decision about ADR is rarely a decision to be taken once only in a case. The factors in a case may change over time, so a decision about ADR may need to be reviewed. This is also considered more fully in Chapter 3.   **1.53**

It is important to appreciate that a case may move between litigation and ADR options, for example starting under a pre-action protocol, then attempting mediation, but if that fails moving to the issue of proceedings and perhaps some interim applications. A Part 36 offer may then lead to negotiation, but then perhaps go to court for a consent order. It may not be so much a question of alternative dispute resolution, or even appropriate dispute resolution, but more a question of blended dispute resolution.   **1.54**

ASSESSING THE SUCCESS OF ADR

Both lawyers and clients may be interested in information as to how successful an ADR process may be. Substantial research has been carried out in a range of jurisdictions, and there is for example quite a body of research into negotiation and mediation in the USA. In particular the Harvard Negotiation Project has a strong international reputation: see www.pon.harvard.edu/research-home/.   **1.55**

In England and Wales there has been important research in particular into the usefulness of mediation. Much of this research can be accessed through the ADR Research section of the ADR Now website: see www.adrnow.org.uk. The Ministry of Justice also provides access   **1.56** to relevant research through its website: see www.justice.gov.uk/publications/research. htm. Probably the most important studies are those that have assessed the relative success of court-related mediation, for which see 11.15. Some of the key studies of ADR are:

- *Twisting Arms: court referred and court linked mediation under judicial pressure. A review of the Central London County Court Scheme* by Professor Hazel Genn and Professor Paul Fenn (Ministry of Justice, 2007);
- *Small Claims Mediation. A collection of 4 research reports on pilot schemes in County Courts* (Department for Constitutional Affairs, 2006);
- *Picking up the Pieces: Marriage and Divorce two years after Information Provision. A study of the pilot scheme for the use of mediation as a part of the divorce process* by Professor Janet Walker (Department for Constitutional Affairs, 2004);
- *Court of Appeal Mediation Scheme. Court—based initiatives for non-family civil disputes* by Professor Hazel Genn (2002);
- *NHS pilot scheme. Mediating medical negligence claims: an option for the future?* by Professor Linda Mulcahy (Stationery Office, 2000).

OVERVIEW OF REGULATORY FRAMEWORKS

1.57   The regulatory framework for arbitration in England and Wales is provided by statute. This framework has been updated on various occasions, and the current regulation is provided by the codification in the Arbitration Act 1996: see Chapter 23. There is ultimate oversight by the courts: see Chapter 28.

1.58   The regulatory framework for international arbitration is provided by international treaty. There are also various agreements that provide a framework for international arbitration including the International Chamber of Commerce Arbitration Rules 1998, and the UNCITRAL Model Law on International Arbitration. Detail is provided in Chapter 26.

1.59   There is as yet no statutory or regulatory framework for mediation in England and Wales, though there is in some other jurisdictions, such as the Uniform Mediation Act in the USA. There are references to ADR and to mediation in the CPR (see Chapters 5–6), but these do not regulate the process itself. There are a number of mediation schemes linked to courts (see Chapter 14), but these provide access to a process rather than further regulation by the courts. Other mediation processes are provided by organisations that provide mediation training and services (see 1.65–1.70 and Chapter 14), but there is no general oversight. The European Union has drawn up a Code of Conduct for Mediators, but it is not yet clear how far this will be adopted in England and Wales (see Chapter 15).

1.60   Some other ADR processes take place within a statutory or regulatory framework, and where this is the case it is covered in the relevant chapter of this book.

1.61   There is no regulatory framework for lawyers taking part in a negotiation or mediation, save the need to abide by appropriate rules of professional conduct and ethics (see Chapter 16). If a client is dissatisfied with the standard of work done by a lawyer then a similar range of options will be available as where a client is dissatisfied with other legal work, though how these rules apply with regard to ADR processes is still being developed.

- Each firm of solicitors and each set of barristers' chambers is required to have a procedure for dealing with complaints under the requirements of the relevant codes of conduct. A dissatisfied client should normally use this as a first step.
- A complaint may be made to the appropriate professional body.
- A complaint can be raised with the Office for the Legal Services Complaints Commissioner: see www.olscc.gov.uk, and 19.06.
- The concerns may be addressed as part of decisions about costs, so that costs are not granted or are disallowed: see Chapter 6.
- There may be a wasted costs order due to an improper, unreasonable, or negligent act or omission on the part of the lawyer, provided there is a causal link between the poor conduct and the costs wasted: *Ridehalgh v Horsefield* [1994] Ch 205. This could include a failure to secure a reasonable outcome to an ADR process.
- In an extreme and appropriate case, a claim may be brought for professional negligence. The standard to be expected is that of such care and skill as would be exercised by a reasonably competent practitioner in conducting an ADR process, and it remains to be clarified what standards will be seen as the norm. In making an assessment the court can take into account that the case may settle or proceed to court: *Harrison v Bloom Camillin* (1999) Times, 12 November. It will also be relevant of a client could still litigate even if ADR has failed. The immunity from an action for negligence based on anything done in court defined in *Rondel v Worsley* [1969] 1 AC 191, was limited in *Arthur JS Hall & Co (a firm) v Simmons* [2002] 1 AC 615, where the House of Lords held that there should no longer be a general immunity in respect of the conduct of a case in court.

Examples of claims for professional negligence that have succeeded include: **1.62**

- The failure of a lawyer to investigate the facts of a case properly so that the client recovered less than they should: *Dickinson v Jones Alexander & Co* [1990] Fam Law 137.
- The failure by lawyers to pass on important information to their clients: *Strover v Harrington* [1988] Ch 390.
- The failure by lawyers who had negotiated a business lease to notify the client of an unusual clause with regard to rent that was used to raise the rent dramatically: *County Personnel v Alan R Pulber* [1987] 1 All ER 289.

Examples of where a claim for negligence has not succeeded include: **1.63**

- The mere fact that advice given by a lawyer is not ultimately successful cannot found an action, or no lawyer would risk giving advice where the law was not clear: see *Buckland v Farrar & Moody* [1978] 3 All ER 229.
- A lawyer only has to act within the scope of their instructions. If for example the client is an experienced businessman the lawyer has no obligation to investigate matters outside their instructions, or to provide warnings about the commercial risks of a transaction: *Pickersgill v Riley* [2004] PNLR 31.
- A lawyer is not necessarily in breach of duties of competence and care by pursuing a very weak case, though this will depend on the circumstances: *Harley v McDonald Harley (a firm)* (2001) Times, 15 May.

Note that a client is bound by a lawyer's assurances to a court even if the lawyer may   **1.64**
be subject to a negligence claim: *Worldwide Corporation Ltd v Marconi Communications Ltd* (1999) Times, 7 July. If there is a conflict of duties, the court will look at the background: see *Memory Corporation v Sidhu* [2000] 2 WLR 1443, where on an interim application there

were problems with what the lawyers told the court as regards the terms of an order, and as regards the evidence supplied by the client.

OVERVIEW OF TRAINING AND ACCREDITATION

1.65   There are separate training and accreditation systems for arbitrators and for mediators. Many barristers and solicitors have trained as arbitrators or mediators in addition to their legal qualification, usually with a view to working in such a role in the area in which they practice. Some firms and chambers offer mediation and/or arbitration services, usually putting summary information on their website.

1.66   While the majority of arbitrators and mediators have a legal background many have other professional backgrounds, eg as accountants. It has also become increasingly common for senior managers in business to have negotiation or mediation training, so it is important to remember that a client may have relevant expertise.

1.67   The professional training and accreditation of barristers is overseen by the Bar Standards Board. From September 2010 training in ADR has become a compulsory part of the Bar Professional Training Course. The professional training and accreditation of solicitors is overseen by the Solicitors' Regulation Authority. Training in ADR is not compulsory for solicitors. Relevant sections of the relevant professional Codes of Conduct are addressed in Chapter 16. Some Bar and Law Society associations support the use of ADR, for example in commercial and family law areas.

1.68   The training and accreditation for arbitrators is overseen by the Chartered Institute of Arbitrators: see www.ciarb.org. They provide three levels of membership, associate, member and fellow, based on specific training courses that include arbitration, international arbitration and adjudication. They also provide accreditation for training meeting their standards that is provided by other bodies.

1.69   The training and accreditation for mediators is provided by a range of bodies. Courses can focus on different specialisations such as commercial law or family law, and have different coverage and length. As there is at present no body that provides formal accreditation or oversight, it is important to check the content of training you might undertake, and to get some information about those who have undergone the training to evaluate a course. When looking for a mediator, qualifications and experience should be checked with a body providing mediation services, and/or with the individual mediator. Information about training provided and services offered is normally available on the relevant website. The following are examples of mediation training providers:

- The Centre for Effective Dispute Resolution: www.cedr.com/training/;
- Mediator Training: www.mediatortraining.org.uk;
- The ADR Group: www.adrgroup.co.uk;
- The TMC Group: www.thetmcgroup.com;
- National Family Mediation: www.nfm.org.uk.

1.70   No formal training is needed to negotiate, save that negotiation has been a compulsory part of the training of barristers for over 20 years. However, many training courses are available, for example from CEDR, and many practical and accessible books provide insight, for example *Getting to Yes: Negotiating Agreement without giving in* by Roger Fisher and William Ury (Random House Business Books, 2003). Such sources can be important because of the extent to which success can depend on the skill and experience of the negotiator.

KEY POINTS SUMMARY

- The use of ADR has grown substantially over the last 20 years, with support now being seen in the Civil Procedure Rules, in other court processes, and in judicial comment. Costs penalties can follow a failure to participate in ADR.   **1.71**
- It is now crucial that a lawyer has sufficient knowledge of ADR options to provide a full range of advice for a client. This is supported by Lord Justice Jackson in a recommendation in the Final Report of the Review of Civil Litigation Costs.
- There is no agreed definition of ADR, and this book takes a wide approach, looking at all the alternatives to litigation. ADR processes are still evolving.
- ADR options offer many potential advantages in terms of saving time and costs, providing confidentiality and increasing client control.
- ADR has some potential disadvantages, especially if it is not used appropriately, and some of the strategic opportunities available in litigation may be lost.
- Arbitration is founded on statute law, but most ADR options have a less formal basis.
- Training is available for arbitrators and mediators, the latter being currently unregulated.

2

REVIEW OF ADR OPTIONS

KEY ELEMENTS OF ADR OPTIONS 2.06

THE ROLE OF THE LAWYER WITH REGARD TO ADR OPTIONS. 2.09

NON-ADJUDICATIVE ADR OPTIONS. 2.12

ADJUDICATIVE ADR OPTIONS 2.42

OTHER OPTIONS 2.60

KEY POINTS SUMMARY. 2.68

2.01   The range of ADR options is quite wide. At one end of the scale are adjudicative processes such as arbitration that have similarities to litigation in that they involve a set procedure and result in the giving of a decision. At the other end of the scale are processes that are relatively informal, such as a negotiation between lawyers representing the parties. This chapter outlines the range of ADR options that are available to parties to a dispute in England and Wales. A lawyer should have a working knowledge of all ADR options that may be relevant to the fields in which they practice, so as to be able to advise a client on which option(s) might best meet the client's needs and objectives. It is important to make a carefully considered choice that as far as possible secures the potential advantages of ADR while avoiding the potential disadvantages, as outlined in Chapter 1.

2.02   There is no overall system for managing or providing ADR. For example mediation services may be provided by courts, commercial providers, not-for-profit providers, solicitors' firms or barristers' chambers. The range of types of ADR is perhaps inevitable given the need for flexibility and the range of types of case, but one would echo the recommendation of Lord Justice Jackson in his Review of Civil Litigation Costs that the provision of a handbook with up-to-date information on reputable providers would be helpful. This book seeks to include references to all the main current sources of information, including websites, though the range is now such that comprehensive up-to-date information is not easy to provide.

2.03   An ADR option may be selected in advance and built into a contract, which may happen in a large commercial agreement. In some areas, such as construction disputes, a norm exists for a particular form of ADR to be used within the industry: see Chapter 22. In some areas a particular type of ADR is seen as normally appropriate for a particular type of dispute, as is for example the case with mediation and conciliation for employment disputes, or ombudsman-type processes for complaints against public bodies. It has also become the norm for certain types of ADR to be used in certain areas of practice—for example mediation is more commonly used in commercial and family disputes than in some other areas of practice.

If no ADR option has been selected in advance, or if there is no norm for a particular type of dispute, a range of ADR options may need to be considered. Those most commonly used are arbitration, mediation and negotiation, which are developed further in later chapters. While only one type of ADR should be used at a time, options are not necessarily exclusive. For example if negotiation between lawyers has led to deadlock, perhaps because of the strict instructions given by clients, a good mediator may still be able to take matters forward. **2.04**

There is no definitively agreed terminology with regard to many ADR options. ADR processes have developed in different ways, in different jurisdictions, and in different areas of law, words can have slightly different meanings. There is no need for this to lead to confusion or difficulty—it is rather a question of avoiding assumptions and checking with relevant people if the meaning of a term is important. **2.05**

KEY ELEMENTS OF ADR OPTIONS

The main purposes of ADR options are as follows, though each occurs to a different extent in different forms of ADR: **2.06**

- The focus is on settlement rather than conflict (though the need for those involved to be able to put their case is seen as important).
- Some level of objectivity is introduced to try to assist the achievement of a settlement through facilitating communication.
- Those involved have some level of control over the process and the decision taken.
- There is a level of flexibility in the process.

This does not of course provide a complete contrast between ADR and litigation in that the purpose of a trial is to provide objective determination by an independent judge. The difference is really one of emphasis in that in litigation the main focus is on the adversarial process right up to the time that the judgment is given. In ADR processes there is more focus on agreement. **2.07**

The main factors that differentiate ADR options are: **2.08**

- whether the process involves an independent third party (as most ADR options do), or only the parties and their representatives (as is the case for negotiation);
- whether a binding decision at the end of the process is made by a third party (adjudicative) or by the parties themselves by agreement (non-adjudicative);
- whether the process may result in a non-binding finding or proposal being made by a third party and, if so, what the role of that finding or proposal is. For example early neutral evaluation normally produces a report for the parties to consider;
- the extent to which there is a set procedure—which is more likely in an adjudicative process so the parties have a fair opportunity to put their case to the third party. There is no set procedure for a negotiation;
- the extent to which a third party controls or facilitates the process. In adjudication the adjudicator normally has a high level of control, whereas the role of a mediator is largely facilitative;

- the extent to which the parties control the process. There is always some control, in that for example the parties will agree on the appointment of an arbitrator, even if the arbitrator then takes over control of the process. In a negotiation the parties keep substantial control through the instructions given to the lawyers;
- the role of lawyers varies in different ADR processes. This is dealt with in 2.11;
- the potential costs of ADR processes vary substantially, depending on the process and the individual case. An arbitration might cost as much as a trial, whereas a negotiation may only cost the fees paid to the lawyers for the time spent negotiating: see Chapter 4. The costs of an ADR process can normally be reasonably predicted and agreed in advance, whereas it can be more difficult to provide a budget for likely litigation costs, albeit that the Jackson Review is proposing a move to fuller budgeting for litigation.

THE ROLE OF THE LAWYER WITH REGARD TO ADR OPTIONS

2.09   A lawyer might conduct an ADR process. A number of lawyers have trained as arbitrators and mediators, and this is covered in 1.65–1.70. More commonly a lawyer may represent a client with regard to a dispute. In any ADR process the lawyer must of course act within the instructions given by the client, and where the lawyer plays a role in agreeing the final settlement, as in negotiation, the lawyer must act within the authority to settle provided by the client.

2.10   There are various points where the lawyer may be involved in an ADR process:

- The lawyer should be prepared to advise orally or in writing on what ADR options might be appropriate as an alternative to litigation.
- That advice should include sufficient information on the relative strengths and weaknesses of each option to assist the client in taking an informed decision. Either the lawyer or the client can consult a potential ADR provider if more detail would be useful.
- The lawyer will need to consider how and when ADR might best fit with a litigation process, and advise the client on that.
- The lawyer will need to help to prepare the case for the ADR process in an appropriate way. This will need to include defining client objectives, preparing information for use, and preparing relevant arguments. Consideration should also be given to how the case should proceed if the ADR fails. For preparing for a negotiation see Chapter 9, and for mediation see Chapter 12.
- If the ADR process produces a potential settlement, or an objective evaluation, the lawyer will need to advise the client on how that relates to what is realistically obtainable if the case is pursued in any other way, eg litigation. In non-adjudicative ADR this might include advising the client on whether to accept a proposed settlement.
- If the ADR process results in agreement, the lawyer is likely to be involved in reviewing the proposed terms and helping to convert them into a final agreement. See Chapter 20 for the options for recording a settlement.
- The lawyer might be asked to advise on enforcing a settlement: see Chapter 29.

2.11   When an ADR process is undertaken, the role the lawyer varies with the process:

- In an adjudicative process like arbitration the role of the lawyer may be broadly similar to the role of the lawyer in a trial in presenting the case to the arbitrator.
- In early neutral evaluation or expert-assisted determination the process may be largely paper based, and the lawyer may be mainly involved in providing information and

assisting in defining issues. If an evaluation is produced the lawyer might advise with regard to its effect.

- In mediation the lawyer will have a more mixed and less formal role, sometimes playing a part in presenting the case, and sometimes advising the client on options. This is developed in Chapters 11–13.
- In a negotiation the lawyers of one party will often deal directly with the lawyers for the other party, a process that gives the lawyer a large role in taking the case forward, but which can also be quite challenging due to limited formality. This is developed in Chapters 8–10.

NON-ADJUDICATIVE ADR OPTIONS

A non-adjudicative process does not provide for a third party to take a decision, or for an outcome to be imposed upon the parties. The purpose is rather to investigate options for settlement in less formal ways, which leave control of the process and the possible outcome with the parties. **2.12**

Inter-client discussion

A party to a dispute may settle the dispute personally. Even if a party has consulted a lawyer for initial advice on rights and possibly as regards a letter before claim, the party may then seek to resolve the dispute personally rather than instructing the lawyer to negotiate. For example this may happen with a commercial client who has experience of negotiating and simply wants advice on the legal context. The lawyer might wish to warn the client of any possible admissions etc that might prejudice the position of the client should the case not settle. The lawyer might also usefully advise about how any agreement should be made legally enforceable. **2.13**

Written offers

An offer to settle a dispute can be made in writing, normally in the form of letter. If the offer is accepted then an agreement is reached. While an oral acceptance could be binding, acceptance would normally also be in writing. Enforcement of such an exchange of letters would follow normal contractual principles: see Chapter 20. **2.14**

Many written offers are now made under the CPR Part 36. The main advantage of this procedure is that it potentially shifts the burden of costs if the offer made is not exceeded in a later court judgment. This potential advantage is such that a Part 36 offer should normally be made if litigation is likely to be pursued, once the case has been sufficiently explored and evaluated for the appropriate level for a Part 36 offer to be calculated. Such an offer needs to be carefully calculated to do its job in protecting the client, normally tempting the other side to consider accepting, but not so generous that any unnecessary concession is made. The Part 36 process is discussed in Sime, *A Practical Approach to Civil Procedure*, 13th edn, OUP, 2010, ch. 42 and is not dealt with in detail in this book. **2.15**

A written offer is one of the simplest ways to seek to settle a dispute. However significant analysis and skill may be required to calculate what should be offered, and to make the offer in a clear form. This approach is probably most suited to a case with a relatively limited **2.16** number of issues to avoid complexity and misunderstanding with regard to the terms of the written offer. A written offer normally relates to a figure for damages, but a more complex offer can be made with careful drafting.

2.17   There are potential problems in making a written offer in a letter. In keeping the terms of an offer clear it is best to leave out much by way of justification or persuasion, which may limit the chance that the other side will accept the offer. Exploration of terms may lead to a further exchange of letters, and confusion as to what is being offered may arise if this is not carefully controlled. Quite often a written offer will lead to a negotiation, and this is further explored in 2.18–2.24.

Negotiation

2.18   A negotiation is a relatively informal process involving the discussion of some or all of the issues in a case with a view to resolving them on agreed terms. The process may be quite simple, or may involve substantial use of strategy and tactics. A negotiation may be carried out in writing (by letter or e-mail) if the issues are relatively few or simple. Alternatively a negotiation may be carried out by telephone or conference call. If the negotiation is carried out face to face, this often happens at the office of one of the lawyers, or at some other location that the parties agree as being appropriate and neutral. Negotiation between lawyers can happen at the door of the court when the parties to litigation go to court for an interim hearing or for trial. For the purpose of this book it will be assumed that lawyers are involved in helping to settle a legal claim.

2.19   There is no set procedure for a negotiation, and the process is very much within the control of those taking part. This can be challenging for a lawyer more comfortable with a set process, but it also offers many opportunities for a lawyer who prepares well to present a case in its best light, and to use strategy and tactics to best effect (see Chapter 10). The key elements of a negotiation are as follows:

- The lawyer analyses the factual background, and ascertains the client's objectives. The lawyer advises when the case is in a state where it can appropriately be negotiated. A lawyer should act within the instructions provided by the client, and any terms agreed are normally subject to client approval before becoming fully effective. Detailed preparation is the key to success in a negotiation (see Chapter 9).
- The lawyers agree when and where the negotiation will take place and who will attend.
- The negotiation process normally starts with the agreement of an agenda to decide what issues will be covered in what order (see Chapter 10).
- The negotiation normally goes through a discussion stage where the parties seek and provide information relating to facts, objectives etc.
- Either as part of the discussion stage or immediately afterwards the parties use argument, persuasion, strategy and tactics to seek to secure the agreement of the other side (see Chapter 8).
- The parties then seek and offer concessions with a view to reaching a settlement
- The parties make offers for settlement of each issue, or of the case overall, and explore those offers.
- To the extent agreement is reached, the terms need to be clarified and put into an enforceable form (see Chapter 20). It is very important to agree the essence of the terms in writing before the end of the meeting to avoid any later misunderstanding. Outline terms are normally subject to client approval.

Attendance at a negotiation is a matter of agreement based on what is appropriate to the case. The following are all possible, though coverage in later chapters is based on the norm that each client instructs a lawyer to negotiate on their behalf.   **2.20**

- It is possible for the parties to negotiate themselves on the basis of advice given, if for example the issue in the case is one of interpretation, rather than a personal dispute where there is significant acrimony.
- The solicitors in a case might negotiate, if instructed by their clients to do so. Solicitors might negotiate by exchange of letters or telephone.
- The solicitors and clients in a case might negotiate together, especially in a case where litigation is unlikely.
- The barristers in a case might negotiate. This is quite common in a case where litigation has been commenced or is a serious likelihood. While barristers might negotiate by telephone they normally negotiate face to face, in chambers, or at the door of the court if there is a court hearing.
- The barristers, solicitors and clients in a case might all meet to negotiate. This is a more expensive and complex option, but it might be justified by what is at stake in the case if there is a realistic hope of settlement.
- In complex or commercial negotiation, it may be necessary to take careful decisions as to who should attend. It is important to involve either directly or through availability on the telephone those with relevant information, and those with the ability to take and implement decisions.
- Because the process is informal it is possible, though unusual, to agree that someone else be present at a negotiation, eg an expert.

A negotiation may take place at any stage in a case and may relate to any issues. There may   **2.21**
well be more than one negotiation in a case. The timing of a negotiation is very important.
The case must be properly evaluated and researched before any negotiation takes place so as
to enable proper preparations to be made for the negotiation, and to enable the negotiator
to act effectively. The main stages at which lawyers may be instructed to negotiate a settlement are:

- early in the case, shortly after initial instruction and evaluation, and before proceedings are issued. Negotiation at this stage is supported by pre-action protocols;
- following a written offer to settle the case, where the offer is sufficiently tempting to be explored, but not good enough for immediate acceptance;
- in relation to interim applications. For example an application for an interim injunction may lead to negotiation outside court that may relate to the application itself, and also to the whole case;
- outside court before a judge hears the case. The attractions of negotiating at this stage are that both sides have fully prepared their case, and a resolution may be reached while the parties still have control of the case saving the expense of the trial. The drawback of leaving negotiation till this stage is that the majority of the costs are likely to have been incurred.

The main potential advantages of negotiation are: **2.22**

- It is very flexible and comparatively low cost, making it one of the commonest forms of ADR.
- Clients retain control of the outcome through giving instructions and approval of any agreement reached.

- Many lawyers favour negotiation because of the control over process and outcome that it offers to them.
- The negotiation process is private, confidential and 'without prejudice'; *Rush & Tompkins v GLC* [1989] AC 1280. This means that no reference can be made to what happened in the negotiation, save if relevant as regards to a later costs order, or as regards the terms of any agreement reached. For further discussion of this see 3.78–3.83.

2.23   The main potential drawbacks of negotiation are:

- Success depends to quite a significant extent on how well the case has been researched and analysed, so that the case on each issue can be put strongly.
- Success can depend on the skill of the negotiator, and the strategy and tactics employed.
- Negotiation can lead to a relatively weak outcome for a client if the strengths of a case are not properly exploited.
- Some clients may be dissatisfied if they not involved in the negotiation and are left feeling that the lawyers have taken over the case.
- The relative informality of negotiation can lead to confusion if a negotiation drags on in a vague way through prolonged correspondence.

2.24   A negotiation is most likely to succeed if the lawyers are properly prepared, and if the clients on both sides are prepared to make sufficient concessions. There are four main reasons why a negotiation might fail:

- Over optimistic client expectations and instructions can bind a lawyer too tightly. If there is little flexibility then offers and possible concessions may be difficult to address. This is best avoided by the lawyer discussing reasonable expectations sufficiently with the client before the negotiation, and seeking to ensure that instructions include adequate flexibility. It may also mean that mediation might be a better option than negotiation.
- Insufficient preparation may make it difficult to make headway against a well-prepared opponent. The flexibility and speed of a negotiation mean that agility in dealing with aspects of the case is a great advantage.
- The negotiation process can get bogged down. If issues are quite complex and neither side is open to making concessions it may prove difficult to reach agreement. Some ways of dealing with such problems are set out at 10.109–10.121.
- If the lawyers continue to see litigation as the primary process and are not fully committed to achieving settlement negotiation may fail. This is to some extent understandable—a lawyer might feel they have more expertise in litigation. While the lawyer may get higher fees if the case continues, it is clearly the lawyer's duty to settle if that is the best option.

Mediation

2.25   Mediation involves a neutral third party who seeks to facilitate the resolution of a dispute. The process is quite flexible, and will normally be agreed in advance in a written agreement. The third party will meet the parties together, and/or separately, helping them to find possible terms of settlement. It can be agreed who will attend a mediation session, but later chapters are largely based on both the parties and their lawyers attending.

2.26   Various types of mediation services are available, provided by the courts, or by commercial or not-for-profit organisations or by individuals. Some services provide for specific types of case such as commercial disputes, family disputes, or landlord and tenant disputes. It is not compulsory for a mediator to be trained, but normally parties will want to use someone with appropriate training and experience: see 1.65–1.70.

There is no set procedure for a mediation. A mediation service provider may offer a standard **2.27** process, but details are usually a matter of a written mediation agreement, which will be an enforceable contract between the parties: see 12.01–12.06. The time frame can also be agreed—many mediations take 1–2 days, though a court-based programme may be much simpler, offering a limited time frame of 1–3 hours. The normal key elements of a mediation process are as follows (more detail can be found in Chapters 11–13):

- The possibility of using a mediation process is raised at an appropriate point in a case by one of the parties or, if litigation has been commenced, by the court.
- If both parties are prepared to consider mediation, the parties will discuss and agree which mediation process or mediator should be used. The choice of a mediation service and/or individual mediator can be key to the success of the process. The requirements for a good mediator are dealt with further at 11.59–11.76.
- A mediation agreement will be signed. Some mediation services offer a set service (as tends to be the case with court mediation models), or offer a standard form agreement (as tends to be the case with major mediation service providers). The agreement will usually cover details such as when and where the mediation will take place, the format to be followed, and the fee to be paid: see 12.01–12.06.
- Lawyers may prepare a mediation file, with an opening position, options on figures, potential offers, and maybe a draft agreement. This file will be private to the lawyer and client, but will provide a basis for the mediation process.
- The mediator may be briefed prior to the mediation. This would typically be done with written summaries from the parties and an agreed set of documents.
- A mediation will normally start with a joint meeting of the mediator and the lawyers and clients for both sides. This may be the first time the clients have met face to face so as to put their cases directly to each other. Opening statements may be made by lawyers and/or clients (see 13.08–13.20), followed by questions and discussion. The intention is to clarify objectives, and the strengths and weaknesses of each side's case.
- There may then be separate meetings between the mediator and the lawyers and/or clients for each side to explore their cases. There can also by agreement be meetings with an expert etc. There may be further joint meetings if that might be useful.
- Depending on what has been agreed in the mediation agreement, the mediator may seek to facilitate agreement in a very general way, exploring options with each side, and/or may make non-binding suggestions for settlement.
- If an agreement is reached the mediator will confirm the details of the agreement and ask the parties to sign a written memorandum of agreement.

It is a matter of agreement who should attend a mediation: see 12.11–12.18. The main **2.28** options are:

- The mediator meets the parties without their lawyers, but the parties act on advice provided in advance by their lawyers. This may be effective if the problem is mainly a personal one, or if the parties do not necessarily need lawyers with them (for example a family case).
- The mediator meets the parties and their lawyers. This is probably the most common format, though the mediator may meet the parties and the lawyers separately if this might

help to take the case forward. The relevant lawyers may include in-house lawyers, solicitors and barristers. It may be necessary to ensure that there are not too many lawyers so that the focus remains sufficiently on the parties.

- Exceptionally and by agreement a mediation may be attended by another relevant person such as an expert, or an insurer, or a key witness: see 12.11–12.22.
- An unrepresented party can present problems in a mediation if the other side is represented, and make the role of the mediator rather complex.

2.29   The timing of a mediation is important, or the mediation may fail and the fees be wasted. Mediation should not happen before the case is sufficiently evaluated, but it may be most effective before the parties become too focused on trial. Mediation may not be necessary if the case can be settled by negotiation—the timing of the involvement of an independent third party is important, see 11.24–11.36.

2.30   The lack of a clear process in mediation can be challenging for a lawyer used to litigation, especially as mediation tends to focus on clients, and the mediator takes some control from the lawyer. The role of the lawyer may be very different depending on the type of dispute, the client, and the composition of the legal team. The main role of the lawyer is as follows (this is developed at 13.75–13.93):

- advising on when to mediate, and who to use as a mediator;
- advising on the terms of the mediation agreement;
- drafting of written summary to brief the mediator, and/or making an opening statement. An opening statement can be strong, but needs slightly different presentation skills from trial advocacy to include the client and address the opponent;
- it may be advisable to have a meeting to prepare the client for the mediation, to discuss the strengths and weaknesses of the case and the possible outcomes, and the role of the client in the process. A client has a much more direct involvement in a mediation that in a negotiation;
- advising the client on any offers or options that may emerge;
- looking carefully at the position as regards evidence. While the process is confidential, if there is a risk the process may fail it will be important to keep an eye on what may happen if the process reverts to litigation;
- ensuring any agreement reached is properly recorded and enforceable: see Chapter 20. It may be a term of the mediation agreement that the parties enter a written agreement or contract at the end of the process, and some standard forms are available for recording agreements. If the parties find it difficult to reach agreement the mediator may make proposals, and/ or continue to work with the parties by agreement. If the parties agree in advance the mediator may make a non-binding or a binding recommendation, or an independent evaluation of the case.

2.31   The key potential advantages of mediation are as follows (and see 11.14):

- A neutral third party may be able to help a party to see the strengths and weaknesses of a case more clearly, and/or may help them to see the dispute in a different light.
- A mediator can help parties step outside an adversarial framework and entrenched positions, which can help mediation to work where negotiation has failed.
- A mediator can strip away false optimism and make possible concessions look more acceptable.
- Mediation offers a potentially much larger role for clients than negotiation, and this can assist clients in feeling that they have had their say, and in seeing the case for the other side.

- Because the process is flexible, a client can be allowed to make a statement to give the client the feeling of 'having their day in court'. A mini trial or an examination of a key witness can be included by agreement if this might deal with a key block in the case.

The potential disadvantages of mediation are: **2.32**

- The involvement of a third party removes some control from the parties themselves.
- Success depends party on the abilities of the mediator.
- Lawyers may feel less comfortable with mediation as they have less control than in a negotiation.
- Mediation may make a party feel they are expected to make concessions and therefore get a worse result than might come from some other form of dispute resolution, though there is no reason why this should be the case.
- Mediation is unlikely to work if the parties are deeply antagonistic.

A mediation is most likely to succeed if both parties take a realistic view of the strengths and weaknesses of their case, if care is taken to agree a process that is likely to work, and if the mediator is reasonably skilled. **2.33**

A mediation is most likely to fail if the parties are unrealistic in their objectives, are falsely optimistic about the strengths of their cases, or are very antagonistic. A mediation can be defeated by one party being unreasonable. **2.34**

Conciliation

Conciliation is in many ways similar to mediation. Both involve an independent third party who seeks to help parties in dispute to reach a settlement There is no agreed distinction between the two, but mediation is more likely to involve some level of helping the parties to evaluate their cases, while conciliation is more likely to be purely facilitative in helping parties to reach agreement on disputed issues. There are also differences in the types and content of meetings held. A number of bodies offer conciliation services, and probably the best known is the Advisory, Conciliation and Arbitration Service (ACAS). There is more detailed consideration of conciliation in Chapter 18. **2.35**

Early neutral and/or expert evaluation

An early neutral evaluation is an assessment of some or all of the issues in a case by an independent third party. This may be appropriate where the case wholly or largely turns on limited issues that may require particular expertise or interpretation, and an appropriate agreed expert can provide a view that both parties will respect, which should help them in evaluating their own case and reaching a resolution. The third party may be an expert or an independent person with legal knowledge, and will normally be asked to produce a written report on specified issues. The report can include findings or provisional recommendations as requested by the parties. **2.36**

There is no set procedure. The key elements of the process are likely to be: **2.37**

- A contract specifies that early neutral evaluation should be used in the event of a dispute, or the parties agree that it would be useful once a dispute has arisen.
- The parties agree who to approach for an evaluation, what issues to seek evaluation of, what information should be provided to the evaluator, and what fee should be paid. An

evaluator can be asked to make findings of fact, findings on likely outcome, proposals for appropriate remedies etc.

- Information will be provided to the evaluator as agreed. This is normally done in writing, but there can be a meeting for discussion with any agreed relevant people present if this might be useful.
- The evaluator produces a report as requested.
- The parties decide how to take the case forward in the light of the report. The report may be so clear that terms may be agreed by letter, or a negotiation or mediation might take place.

2.38 To be most effective it is clearly important that the early neutral evaluation be held as early as is reasonably possible, once the parties have sufficient information to identify the issues to be addressed, and to brief the evaluator.

2.39 The potential advantages are that an independent report may well facilitate the early settlement of the whole case, or at least some of the issues, especially where the third party has a good professional reputation and is respected. This can avoid or limit litigation and save costs, not least as there is little point in using a full litigation process for limited or technical issues. An agreed evaluation can be less intrusive and expensive than a full mediation.

2.40 Possible drawbacks are that work will be required to agree what materials and issues to put to the evaluator, and success will depend on the quality of the report produced. It is of course possible that an independent report will fail to support a party's case, and therefore make settlement more difficult, though it is probably better to see potential weaknesses at an early stage.

2.41 There are some special forms of early neutral evaluation, for example in the Commercial Court and Technology and Construction Court, where a senior judge or lawyer can evaluate the likely outcome of case on the basis of a summary brief. For more detail on early neutral or expert evaluation see Chapter 17.

ADJUDICATIVE ADR OPTIONS

2.42 An adjudicative ADR option involves a decision on the case being made by an impartial third party. The main difference from litigation is that the parties have much more control over the process, and the choice of the arbitrator.

Arbitration

2.43 An arbitration is a consideration of a case by a specially appointed impartial third party that leads to a decision about the case being taken by that arbitral tribunal. The tribunal and the process to be followed are agreed in advance by the parties. There is a great deal of variation and flexibility, and an arbitration can be anything from a consideration of written submissions to a process which is broadly similar to that of a trial.

2.44 Arbitration has developed as an alternative to litigation over many years. Because it is an adjudicative option that can lead to a decision binding the parties, arbitration is formally regulated in many jurisdictions. In England and Wales this is done by the Arbitration Act 1996. Because it can operate outside the courts of individual jurisdictions, arbitration is very popular in commercial cases, and in other cases with an international dimension. In a case with international elements it is vitally important to distinguish between a case where the parties have agreed to an arbitration in England under the Arbitration Acts (see Chapter 23), and a case where the parties have agreed to an international arbitration under a relevant treaty or agreement (see Chapter 26).

The key elements of an arbitration are: **2.45**

- An agreement to go to arbitration is triggered by a clause in a contract, or by an agreement between the parties once a dispute has arisen: see Chapter 23.
- The parties agree which arbitration service/arbitrator to use. This may be decided by the arbitration clause, or by agreement at the time. For more detail on arbitral tribunals see Chapter 24.
- The parties enter a written agreement setting out how the arbitration will be conducted. This will normally include timescale, how evidence and other submissions will be made, what form the arbitration decision will take, and how costs and fees will be paid. Many arbitration providers or regulators provide model terms for agreement.
- The parties take such pre-hearing steps as have been agreed. This may include providing information etc to the arbitrator.
- The arbitration takes place. In a simple case this may just involve the consideration of written submissions and other material by the arbitrator. In a more complex case the procedure can be very similar to a court hearing with lawyers on both sides making oral submissions, calling witnesses etc.
- The arbitration decision is given. This is normally a written decision delivered after the arbitration. Depending on what was agreed it may or may not include detailed reasons. For details see Chapter 27.
- In certain circumstances there may be an appeal to a court from an arbitration decision: see Chapter 28.
- As regards the enforcement of arbitration awards, see Chapter 29.

An arbitration can be held in any suitable, and usually neutral, place agreed by the par-   **2.46**
ties. It is for the parties to agree who should attend where there is to be a hearing. It would be normal for lawyers to attend and to conduct the case at an arbitration hearing. As it is a decision-making process, an arbitration should not be held until both sides have adequately prepared their case, the timing being a matter of agreement between the parties.

The main attractions of arbitration are that: **2.47**

- the process can be closely tailored to the needs of a specific dispute, for example providing for specific evidence to be submitted by both sides, rather than the need to follow generic procedural rules for disclosure etc;
- the parties can select an arbitrator with appropriate expertise and experience, rather than being allocated any judge from the court where proceedings are issued;
- the process is private, unlike a trial in open court, so privacy can be maintained, save to the extent that the parties agree to make any statement about the case and its outcome;
- the fact that the process can be relatively like a trial may make it relatively attractive to lawyers.

The potential drawbacks of arbitration are that: **2.48**

- the fact that some arbitrations can be relatively like a court trial can mean that arbitration is not necessarily a cost-saving option;

- the process results in a decision by the arbitrator, so the parties do not have the control over the outcome that they would have in a non-adjudicatory process such as mediation;
- an arbitration process cannot deal easily with a party who fails to cooperate, such that interim orders and sanctions might be needed in a court action;
- an arbitrator may have relevant knowledge without necessarily having the robustness of a judge with substantial experience of litigation.

2.49   Arbitration is most likely to succeed where the parties put sufficient effort into agreeing the arbitration process, are adequately committed to the process, and select the arbitrator with care.

2.50   It is more likely to fail where the arbitrator is not appropriate for the case, or fails to understand the case for a party properly so that the party is dissatisfied with the outcome.

Adjudication

2.51   There is a variety of other processes in which a neutral third party acting under an agreed process can reach a decision on the whole case, or on specified issues. Some operate under litigation or regulation, and some by agreement between the parties. An adjudication process is most likely to be appropriate in a specialist commercial field where the parties prefer a system adapted to the needs of their industry or business. The adjudicator used is most likely to be someone with appropriate specialist knowledge. One of the best known adjudication processes is that used for construction disputes: see Chapter 22.

2.52   An adjudication process should be fully agreed between the parties. The process to be used is normally laid down in advance in terms agreed by the industry, and/or by the body or person who provides the adjudication. The parties normally agree in a commercial contract to be bound by the relevant adjudication process should there be a dispute.

2.53   The key elements of an adjudication process tend to be broadly similar to those for an arbitration, but they are adapted to industry needs, and may provide for processes to deal with particular types of dispute quickly. By agreement, the adjudication may lead to a binding decision, or to a decision that will only be binding if the parties agree to it, or if neither party appeals within a set period.

2.54   The potential benefits of adjudication are that:

- the process can be carefully adjusted to the needs of a particular industry or business;
- the process may be governed entirely by agreement between the parties, and can therefore be more flexible than arbitration or litigation;
- an adjudication can be one of the most cost-effective ways of getting an independent decision in a case.

2.55   The possible drawbacks are that:

- tailored adjudication processes are not available for all types of dispute where they might be useful;
- adjudication may be quite expensive if the adjudicator has to do a lot of work to understand the case;
- if the adjudication agreement does not provide that the adjudicator's decision will be final and binding on both parties, costs may be wasted and litigation still necessary.

Expert determination

The possibility of an expert opinion assisting non-adjudicative dispute resolution was considered at 2.36–2.41. The view of an expert may be equally useful in an adjudicative process. There are various possibilities depending on the needs of the case. **2.56**

One option is that the expert may be appointed to decide the case. This may be appropriate where the only or main issues in the case require expert knowledge and a full adjudication procedure is not needed. For more information on expert determination see Chapter 21. **2.57**

Another option is that an adjudication may take place, but the adjudicator may not necessarily have appropriate specialist knowledge, so it may be appropriate for an expert to assist in the determination of a case. This might for example be on the basis that a neutral expert would report on specified issues to the adjudicator. **2.58**

Using an agreed independent expert in an appropriate way may well save both time and costs, especially if the alternative would be that the parties would both get reports from separate experts and present them to an arbitrator or adjudicator. However it is important that the expert be carefully chosen so that the parties will accept the expert's report. **2.59**

OTHER OPTIONS

The options most commonly used for ADR are those set out above. However this is not a definitive list. People with a dispute can agree to any approach that they think can assist them in reaching a resolution, and any government or private body can offer dispute resolution processes. There is constant development, and also some further options that do not fit under the headings of adjudicative and non-adjudicative. **2.60**

Hybrids

It is possible to choose an option that combines the advantages and disadvantages of different ADR options. For example a 'med-arb' can be set up with an agreement to mediate, but to allow the mediator to impose an outcome if the parties fail to reach agreement. This means that the dispute will be resolved by agreement if possible, but by a decision from an agreed informed person in default of that: see 13.63–13.69. An alternative is an 'arb-med', where the parties may set up an arbitration, but then the arbitrator may try to mediate an agreed outcome before giving a decision. **2.61**

Such hybrids can present problems, but if the goal is to settle the dispute they may provide the best way forward. All ADR processes in any event have such flexibility that they can be adjusted to needs eg an arbitration may be delayed while the parties negotiate, or a mini trial may take place within a mediation. **2.62**

Processes for dealing with grievances

There are various processes that provide for a person or body to look at a dispute or complaint. The process may provide for various forms of investigation, suggestions for outcome, or decision making. One example is the use of ombudsman-type processes, for which see **2.63**

Chapter 19. Such processes generally apply to concerns in a particular area. An ombudsman may have a facilitative role, or may be empowered to take a decision.

Specialist systems

2.64   Some industries have developed special procedures to meet specific needs. One example is the construction industry, where a dispute may be serious and potentially very expensive, and may involve a range of parties, but need to be dealt with quickly. Construction industry adjudications provide for quick interim decisions with the possibility for later arbitration or litigation. For detail see Chapter 22.

IT-based options

2.65   Over the last few years there has been an increase in the provision of ADR options via the internet. Essentially these services are provided by businesses or individuals who offer versions of mediation, arbitration, adjudication or expert determination based wholly or largely on electronic communication. Submissions and evidence are provided electronically and a decision may be made on the basis of that material. If there is any kind of discussion or hearing it may well be based on video conferencing. As regards mediation, see 13.74.

2.66   Clearly such an option could only be used by agreement, and on the basis of an agreed process. A potential advantage of such a service is that it can cut costs, and it may well be useful for a relatively low value dispute where the parties are some distance apart. However one would have to consider very carefully whether a dispute could be dealt with in an appropriate and satisfactory way with such a process.

Dispute management systems

2.67   Some disputes can be very large or complex, and may involve a large number of potential parties. It can be very difficult to find a single appropriate process to manage and resolve such a dispute, but equally the flexibility of ADR methods can be used very imaginatively to address needs. It may prove possible to adapt and mix ADR approaches to put together a system for moving forward. One example of this is the way in which complex disputes relating to the building of the channel tunnel were addressed: see *Channel Tunnel Group Ltd v Balfour Beatty Ltd* [1993] AC 334. Another example in the way in which concerns relating to the retention of organs from dead children by hospitals was dealt with. Group mediations were used to raise and vocalise the sometimes emotional concerns of parents, and this helped to settle many issues so that only limited parties and issues eventually went to trial.

KEY POINTS SUMMARY

2.68   • A lawyer should be familiar with the range of ADR options and be able to advise a client on them as appropriate. This includes familiarity with each process, when it should be used, who might attend, and key strengths and weaknesses.
      • All ADR options focus on settlement and offer process control to the parties. A process may be set in advance or agreed after a dispute arises.

- Mediation and arbitration processes are often based on a written agreement between the parties
- ADR options can be broadly divided into processes that are adjudicative (where a third party takes a decision) and those which are non-adjudicative (where the parties approve any proposed settlement).
- The main non-adjudicative options are negotiation and mediation. In both cases the outcome is by agreement of the parties. The main difference is that a negotiation is normally conducted by lawyers, where a mediation includes a neutral third party.
- The main adjudicative options are arbitration and expert determination. These provide for a third party to take a decision.

3

FACTORS INFLUENCING THE
SELECTION OF AN ADR OPTION

LEGAL ADVICE ON APPROPRIATE DISPUTE RESOLUTION OPTIONS . . .3.02

ADVANCE SELECTION OF AN ADR OPTION 3.11

FACTORS INFLUENCING ADR SELECTION. 3.16

POTENTIAL CONCERNS ABOUT ADR 3.50

SECURING AGREEMENT TO ADR 3.64

CONFIDENTIALITY IN RELATION TO ADR PROCESSES 3.71

KEY POINTS SUMMARY 3.84

3.01 The range of ADR options and the different advantages and drawbacks of each was considered in Chapter 2. Many factors may influence the selection of an appropriate dispute resolution option for an individual case, and it will be necessary to consider carefully which factors are most important. Sometimes the selection of an option may be relatively straightforward, but in a large or complex case it may be necessary to compare different ADR options carefully with litigation. One of the main potential factors is cost, and this is considered more fully in Chapter 4.

LEGAL ADVICE ON APPROPRIATE DISPUTE RESOLUTION OPTIONS

3.02 If ADR may be appropriate in principle, then the lawyer should consider and advise on the most appropriate form of ADR for the case. As with all advice, at the end of the day the decision lies with the client. The role of the lawyer is to provide sufficient advice for the client to take an informed decision.

Overcoming possible problems in advising on ADR

3.03 Practical knowledge of ADR within the legal profession is perhaps inevitably somewhat uneven, ranging from lawyers who are themselves qualified as arbitrators or mediators, through lawyers who use at least one form of ADR within their practice on a fairly regular basis, to lawyers who rarely if ever use ADR.

There are reasons why a lawyer may not find it easy to advise on ADR: **3.04**

- Litigation lawyers are familiar with the litigation process, and may feel they can do the best job for their client if they work in the area with which they are familiar.
- Lawyers may think it is difficult to advise on ADR before a certain stage in litigation. It may be difficult to assess a case fully until full information is available following disclosure. Indeed in a complex case the lawyer may fear a complaint or even an allegation of negligence if the case is settled for less that it is worth before full information is available.
- The litigation process has a life of its own and naturally moves from one step to the next following a timetable in an automatic way so that ADR might appear to be an intrusion.
- The position of a lawyer is less clearly defined in some ADR processes than it is in litigation, and the lawyer may have concerns about having less control of the process.
- A lawyer will have a natural concern about fee income, and may not find it easy to advise on options that will potentially reduce that fee.
- It can be quite challenging to compare the potential advantages and disadvantages of litigation, and more than one form of ADR, because of the number of possibly relevant factors.

The position is changing rapidly, so that lawyers should feel more confident in giving   **3.05**
advice:

- ADR options are not far outside the experience of most lawyers. The main ADR options are broadly based on negotiation (like mediation) or a trial-type process (like arbitration).
- Most ADR processes take place to some extent in the context of litigation. A settlement should always be based on a careful assessment of the best the client can hope to get in legal terms, and what would be the most likely outcome if the case went to court.
- The importance of disclosure has changed with the growth of pre-action protocols. Much of the key information in a case is now potentially available before the issue of proceedings.
- With the growth of judicial case management under the CPR lawyers have less control over the conduct of litigation than was formerly the case. ADR processes are flexible and subject to agreement, so potentially offer more control.
- In marketing terms clients are likely to be attracted to lawyers who offer a service that includes ADR options for quicker and cheaper settlement given the often high cost of litigation. This can only grow with the opening up of the market with the implementation of the Legal Services Act 2007.
- There has been a massive growth in the availability of information and training with regard to ADR, including internet resources, and ADR providers who offer quite comprehensive packages.

The professional duty to give advice

General legal professional and ethical duties with regard to advising on ADR remain to be   **3.06**
more fully developed by the relevant professional bodies. Currently it is the general professional duties with regard to advising a client that apply. As an example, paragraph 303 of the Code of Conduct for the Bar provides that a barrister must promote and protect fearlessly and by all proper and lawful means the lay client's best interests and do so without regard to his own interests or to any consequences to himself or to any other person. Similarly the Solicitors' Code of Conduct provides in paragraph 2.02 that a solicitor must identify clearly

the client's objectives in relation to the work to be done, and give the client a clear explanation of the issues involved and the options available to the client. For possible penalties where proper advice on ADR options is not provided see 1.57–1.64.

3.07 It is the question of what is in 'the client's best interests' that governs how far it is a duty to offer advice on ADR. It is suggested that it is normally in the client's interests to be made aware of relevant ADR options where they could lead to a more cost-effective or quicker resolution of the client's case, with an outcome that meets the client's objectives to the best reasonable extent. This approach is supported by judicial statements including:

- Dyson LJ in *Halsey v Milton Keynes NHS Trust* [2004] 4 All ER 920: 'All members of the legal profession who conduct litigation should now routinely consider with their clients whether their disputes are suitable for ADR';
- Ward LJ in *Burchell v Bullard* [2005] EWCA 358: 'The court has given its stamp of approval to mediation and it is now the legal profession which must become fully aware of and acknowledge its value'.

3.08 It is clear that a lawyer has a professional duty to discuss ADR with a client to comply with relevant civil litigation rules (and this is considered further in Chapters 5–7):

- in order to comply with a pre-action protocol, or the spirit of a pre-action protocol;
- in order to consider the possibility of a stay for ADR to take place once proceedings have been issued;
- where there is any possibility of a costs sanction if there were any refusal to engage in ADR;
- if the other side proposes an ADR process.

When to give advice on ADR options

3.09 The main opportunities for giving general advice on ADR options are as follows:

- *When giving initial advice.* Relevant ADR options can be broadly outlined, including pros and cons, implications, and potential cost. This could be done generally through a website or brochure.
- *When holding a conference or meeting.* It is natural to review when a Part 36 offer should be made and how much should be offered. It is equally useful to review when and how negotiation or mediation might assist in taking the case forward, helping to achieve the client's objectives.
- *When writing an opinion.* As part of advising on next steps a barrister might well advise on Part 36 offers and/or ADR options.
- *When reviewing a case prior to issuing proceedings.* ADR should be considered not just in relation to a pre-action protocol, but as part of a comparison of litigation and ADR options.
- *When reviewing a case prior to a court hearing.* Preparation of a case for hearing often leads to a consideration of when and how the case might be settled. This may lead to negotiation or mediation.

3.10 The main stages in litigation where the position relating to ADR might most usefully be reviewed are:

- *When the case first comes to the lawyer.* This is the best opportunity to save costs and time if there is an appropriate ADR option, such as expert determination. However ADR should not be used before it is possible to assess the strengths and weaknesses of a case properly.

- *Before proceedings are issued.* Pre-action protocols now require the exchange of information that is normally sufficient to allow an assessment of the strengths and weaknesses of a case, and require the consideration of ADR. This is still a good stage to save significant costs and time, unless there is a good reason to start litigation, for example to make use of procedural and evidential rules.
- *At the track allocation stage or a case management hearing, to comply with civil litigation rules.* There may be a risk of sanctions for failing to consider or engage in ADR: see Chapters 5–6. This can include a failure to comply with the principle of proportionality in the overriding objective if costs are built up unnecessarily through a failure to use ADR when it could have saved costs.
- *After disclosure and inspection of evidence/exchange of witness statements.* It is often suggested that this is a good time to review ADR options because this is the stage at which you are likely to know the full case for the other side. However this is not necessarily true—collecting and dealing with all this material can be very time consuming and expensive so it is only important to wait till this stage when you expect something quite important from it.
- *When a Part 36 offer is made.* The offer is in itself an attempt to settle, but the options are not only to accept or reject it. The making of an offer can be an appropriate time to consider negotiation or mediation if the offer has some possible merit but is not good enough.
- *Just before trial.* A significant amount of negotiation and some mediation takes place just before trial. There is a logic to this as it is the time when lawyers and clients will have made a final assessment of the strengths and weaknesses of the case, and it offers a chance to save some of the cost of trial, and to agree an outcome rather than leaving it to a judge whose view may not be easy to predict. On the other hand, if there is no real reason why the case could not have settled much earlier, it is a waste of time and cost to leave settlement to the door of the court.

ADVANCE SELECTION OF AN ADR OPTION

It is increasingly common for parties entering an agreement, especially a commercial contract, to include a term that in the event of a dispute arising, a form of ADR will be used to settle it. Lawyers advising on the drawing up of an agreement should consider whether such a term should be included, and while a standard term can be used, the clause can be tailored to meet specific requirements. There are many potential advantages in taking decisions about dispute resolution options while a relationship is positive:

3.11

- It can be useful where informal or private resolution is desirable, for example in a partnership agreement, or where specialist knowledge might be needed.
- The parties can agree on the form of ADR to be used, and can even identify an ADR body or an individual to act if needed.
- The parties can agree the process and the timescale for the ADR, and how costs will be met.
- The parties can effectively draw up their own pre-action protocol for what should happen before courts are involved.

- This can help to ensure a constructive approach if there is a dispute, so that parties focus on trying to find resolution rather than escalating the dispute.

3.12   In addition to prescribing ADR in an individual agreement, some large bodies and other organisations have made public commitments to use ADR where appropriate. This includes a public pledge made on 23 March 2001 by the government of the United Kingdom to use ADR whenever it was sought by parties with whom the government was in dispute, in appropriate cases.

3.13   Any clause agreeing to the use of ADR must be drawn up carefully as it will potentially be enforceable as a term of contract. The terms must be sufficiently clear to be enforced: *Cable & Wireless v IBM* [2002] EWHC 2059 (Comm), where there was comment obiter by Colman J that clear procedures such as CEDR's should be enforceable. It would seem that an agreement to use a named expert, or a named ADR provider, or a process like early neutral evaluation would be specific and enforceable. A court can require the fulfilment of certain procedures before the start of arbitration proceedings: *Scott v Avery* (1856) 5 HL Cas 811. However, if the early stages are too vague a court may not be prepared to enforce them, so a stay will not necessarily be ordered to force the use of non-determinative ADR: *Halifax Financial Services Ltd v Intuitive Systems Ltd* [1999] 1 All ER 303. For more detail on the enforcement of agreements to go to arbitration see 23.11.

3.14   However the form of ADR selected may have implications for whether the agreement can be enforced. Negotiation or mediation are consensual processes and a court cannot easily force a party to take part in them, and certainly cannot force a party to agree an outcome. In *Walford v Miles* [1992] 1 All ER 453 it was said that an agreement to negotiate is not enforceable, though that case related to interpreting a collateral provision rather than the use of ADR. This approach was endorsed in *Pitt v PHH Asset Management* [1993] 4 All ER 961, where Bingham LJ emphasised that the problem was that negotiation was a wide and vague obligation, a party could stop negotiating at any time and the court could not really assess if that was for good reason, or force the party to reach an agreement. Even if a term to negotiate were enforceable, it is difficult to see how damages for breach would be assessed, or whether damages could be more than nominal.

3.15   As both the CPR and the approach taken by judges has moved to support to use of ADR over recent years it is to be anticipated that courts will move further to support the enforcement of clearly defined and reasonable ADR agreements. However it is likely that the focus will remain on supporting clearly defined processes—difficulties in enforcing a more open process or a particular outcome will remain. In practice enforceability is rarely a problem. If the parties have voluntarily agreed to ADR they are likely to comply voluntarily. In any event they should normally follow a pre-action protocol, which will require the consideration of ADR, and the pre-agreed form of ADR may be an appropriate way to do this.

FACTORS INFLUENCING ADR SELECTION

3.16   In most cases there will be no pre-agreement as to the form of ADR to be used. This means that the following factors will need to be weighed up. In each case consideration will have to be given to which factors apply, and to their relative importance. This may change at different stages in the case. In taking decisions about dispute resolution options it is vital to consider the advantages and disadvantages of each ADR option as against litigation. The details of the litigation process itself are well dealt with in other sources and are referred to rather than dealt with fully in this book.

Is jurisdiction an issue?

Jurisdiction may be a crucial issue for litigation. In many cases both parties will be based within a single legal jurisdiction. If they are not then the procedural rules of any potentially relevant jurisdiction will need to be used to determine where litigation should take place. Some forms of ADR are only available in a particular jurisdiction, for example because they have been set up by legislation or by court rules. **3.17**

Jurisdiction is not normally an issue for ADR, because it is undertaken by agreement, and indeed ADR can provide a way of overcoming jurisdictional issues. International arbitration may be a solution where for example parties from different jurisdictions do not wish to submit to the courts of a single jurisdiction: see Chapter 26. There is also potential for international mediation: see Chapter 15. By its very nature, negotiation can take place without regard to jurisdiction. Many ADR organisations can provide services both within and outside specific legal jurisdictions. Remember however that jurisdiction may be relevant to an appeal, or to enforcement of an agreement. **3.18**

Is ADR inappropriate?

Any case can potentially be resolved through ADR, but it is sometimes said that some types of case are inherently unsuitable for ADR. It is certainly right that ADR is not the best way forward for some individual cases, but query if any category of cases should never use ADR. Some of the possible problems with ADR generally can be resolved by choosing a specific method of ADR. **3.19**

The main areas where it might be suggested that ADR is not appropriate are where: **3.20**

- *A court judgment is needed as a precedent.* Only a court judgment can provide a precedent to bind other cases. Query however whether the parties to an individual case really need a legal precedent—they can for example agree that the outcome of one ADR process will bind them for other similar cases. See 3.21–3.23.
- *Where the powers of the court to make interim orders are important.* In particular cases the powers of the court may be needed, for example to grant an interim injunction or provide security for costs. Note however that this does not rule out using ADR in a case once appropriate interim orders have been made. See 3.24 and 3.44.
- *If the client has a very strong case.* There may be a fear that agreeing to an ADR process will necessitate the making of concessions, so that ADR should not be used where a case is strong. It may be better to issue proceedings and apply for summary judgment. This is a risk but it is not inevitable—if a case is put strongly in mediation it may force the other side to see that their expectations are unrealistic and save costs on a longer litigation process.
- *The law is very complex.* An area where the law is complex may indeed be best dealt with by a court, especially if clarity of law in that area is important. However it is not necessarily in the interests of an individual client that their case be used to clarify the law, especially

if the area of law is not of general importance. ADR may achieve a practical solution without the need for full legal debate. Alternatively early neutral evaluation may assist in clarifying the legal issues.

- *The facts are very complex.* Complex facts may be appropriately considered in court, especially if there is a fear that witnesses are not telling the full truth and cross-examination may be important. However it can be very difficult for a judge to reach a decision on complex facts, which can leave the parties at risk of losing in court. An arbitration or expert-assisted determination may be just as effective in dealing with complex facts in a specialist area. Negotiation or mediation where key facts are discussed but the parties focus on a satisfactory outcome rather than on detailed analysis of past facts may lead to a satisfactory result.
- *There are many parties to the action.* The rules for civil litigation provide a structured way for a number of parties to be engaged in a dispute. However it is quite possible for an ADR process to be structured to involve a number of parties, with adjudication being quite capable of dealing with a number of parties in a construction case, or mediation being used where there are a number of potential claimants in a negligence action.
- *There is great animosity between the parties.* A process that has to work by agreement may well be doomed to failure if there is great animosity between the parties. However providing a day in court is not necessarily the best way forward if one party will win and the other will remain resentful. A good mediator can be very effective in managing emotion at face-to-face meetings, helping the parties to reach a more mutually acceptable outcome.
- *There are quasi-criminal allegations.* Cases involving allegations such as fraud or libel may not be suitable for non-adjudicative ADR, though this will depend on the facts of the case. Cases involving domestic abuse or similar allegations may be unsuitable for non-adjudicative ADR, unless it is possible to facilitate a real change of attitude to protect the abused party.
- *A matter of public policy is involved.* It is said that public matters such as environmental or government regulation issues are not suitable for ADR because the process is essentially private, however ADR has been used successfully in some such cases where the process is carefully set up.
- *The claimant wants to make a public point of going to court.* Some claimants see having a day in court, with publicity for their case, as being one of their primary objectives, as may happen for example where a well-known figure brings an action for libel. However it is worth remembering that a court hearing will be public whatever the outcome. While ADR processes are private, a public statement can be one of the agreed outcomes, with the client having more control over the words that reach the press.

Is a court decision creating a precedent important?

3.21   It may be important that a judicial precedent is created, eg interpretation of a clause in a standard form contract (see *McCook v Lobo* [2002] EWCA Civ 1760). An important concern about the growth of ADR is the extent to which the doctrine of precedent may be undermined. The development of the common law depends on courts taking decisions which are reported and used as the basis for later decisions. An ADR process is private, with only such public report as the parties may agree, and a consensual agreement or a decision by an arbitrator or expert cannot have the precedent value of a decision by a judge.

3.22   This is an important concern, not least because ADR is partly dependent on court decisions. In presenting a case in an arbitration, or in deciding what to accept in a negotiation, the lawyer will always take as a benchmark what would be likely to be the outcome if the case went to court. ADR processes would be undermined without the development of the law through reported cases, and there is a risk that the law would ossify, or would develop in a way that lawyers could not easily track due to the lack of reported cases. It is vital that a sufficient number of cases continue to go to court for the law to continue to be publicly developed and clarified.

That said, for many years only a small percentage of disputes have gone to trial, with an **3.23** even smaller percentage resulting in reported decisions. Individual parties should not be expected to go to the expense and stress of trial if it is not in their own interests, and the need for precedent should not hold back appropriate development of ADR.

Is a court order necessary?

Sometimes a court order is the only way of achieving a particular outcome. For example a **3.24** declaration of legal rights or an injunction can only be ordered by a court. Some technical orders can only be made by a court, for example an amendment of the register of members of a company. Even if an ADR process is followed, a court order may be required to approve it, for example court approval is required for a settlement made on behalf of a minor or a patient.

What is the relative cost of possible options?

The cost of litigation is one of the main concerns of those who have a legal case, and can **3.25** remain a complaint even of parties who win in court and recover the major part of their costs from the loser. Costs will be an even greater concern for a loser who may have to pay the costs of the winning party as well as his own. The level of concern about incurring and paying costs is such that this is one of the main reasons for choosing an ADR process to settle a case. While ADR is likely to prove cheaper than taking a case to trial, ADR carries its own costs, and savings will depend on the form of ADR chosen and how early in the case it is used. An arbitration might be as expensive as a trial, and negotiation may not save a lot of money if it takes place just before trial. For more detail see Chapter 4.

How important is expert knowledge?

Although expert knowledge is relevant to a wide range of cases, the normal approach **3.26** is to try to have this admitted through an expert report. If an expert can be agreed and jointly briefed this is a cost-effective approach. However some cases require general expert knowledge, for example of how a particular industry functions, or very specific expert knowledge on a core part of the case, such as the maintenance of specialist machinery. It may be quite expensive to litigate such a case because of the amount of evidence that will need to be presented to a judge, and the clients may not have great faith in a judge without specific expertise. An ADR process may be very helpful in such circumstances, and in particular an adjudicative form of ADR would allow the parties to agree on an arbitrator or adjudicator with appropriate expertise, or expert-assisted determination might be appropriate. It is possible for experts to be involved in a negotiation or mediation, but this may be less successful if the issue needing expert input is strongly contested.

Is confidentiality important?

3.27   A desire for confidentiality is another important reason why a client may choose ADR. Most civil trials are held in public, whereas ADR processes are agreed and carried out privately. A desire to avoid publicity may be a key reason for using ADR, for example to protect information about a business, or to keep personal matters private.

3.28   That said, the position on publicity is not entirely straightforward. There can be some privacy in a trial process, for example the detailed outcome of a case can be kept confidential through a schedule in a Tomlin order. Equally there are ways in which an ADR process may become at least partly public. As an ADR process is based on agreement it is quite possible to agree that any kind of public statement be made as part of the outcome if the matter is resolved. There may be an appeal from an arbitration to a court. It is also emerging that there are some problems as regards the application of traditional concepts of privilege and confidentiality to some ADR processes, especially mediation: see 3.78–3.83 and 13.109–13.126.

How much control does the client want?

3.29   On the face of it an adversarial court process provides a large degree of control for the parties as each side prepares and presents their own case. The degree of control can appear particularly strong for a litigation lawyer who is familiar with the process and how to use it. However there are limits to the control that the parties have, especially with the growth of judicial case management, and the use of sanctions for non-compliance. Process control is especially limited when the case reaches trial—a judge is allocated to the parties, that judge can only make such orders as he or she has power to make, and the parties are faced with the decision of the judge, the only option if they do not like it going to appeal.

3.30   ADR options potentially offer much more control. The parties can agree the process that they wish to follow, making their own decisions about time frame, presentation of evidence etc. They can also select and agree an arbitrator, mediator or other third party to suit their needs. The control that they have over the decision made in the case depends on the type of ADR selected. An adjudicative form of ADR, such as arbitration, will normally reach a binding decision, whereas in mediation or negotiation the outcome will remain within the control of the parties and they only need to accept it when they are satisfied.

What are the main objectives of the client?

3.31   Any dispute resolution process should centre on the objectives of the client. It is what the client wishes to achieve that defines both the dispute and when the client will see it as being resolved. The litigation process has many strengths in obtaining objectives for a client—a range of remedies has been developed over many years with great sophistication in areas like the assessment of damages. Court orders are authoritative documents, and they carry with them the enforcement powers of the court. An adjudicative ADR process such as arbitration can lead to a decision, but that will only be binding as regards the parties who have agreed to the arbitration, and the decision will not be directly enforceable by the court.

3.32   A possible drawback of litigation is that a judge only has the power to make such orders that remedy the cause of action argued by the successful party, though this can be mitigated if a judge makes a consent order in terms agreed by the parties. In contrast an arbitrator or adjudicator can make a decision within whatever parameters have been agreed by the parties, which potentially offers the possibility for innovation, and remedies tailored to meet the case. In mediation or negotiation the parties can focus entirely on their objectives, and they can agree any outcome that is acceptable to the parties. Mediators will normally focus on the objectives of the parties, and with the agreement of the parties a mediation can be very forward looking, without the need to reach a decision on factual issues from the past that are not of ongoing interest to the parties.

Is a future relationship important?

Litigation is adversarial—it is based on a contest between the parties. It is also essentially an historic process. It is designed for example to look at the facts of a contract made in the past or an accident that happened in the past, to try to establish truth and apply existing law to issues. A court only looks forward where there is a specific reason for doing so, eg to assess damages for future losses.   **3.33**

An ADR process can take a similar approach, for example if expert-assisted determination is a useful way to decide why a machine malfunctioned and the parties make representations to the expert. However an ADR process can also take a rather different approach, because it does not have to be adversarial, does not have to take decisions about the past, and does not necessarily have to apply existing law. Mediation in particular can be a creative and forward-looking process, which only needs to deal with the past in so far as the parties wish that, and can focus on future relationships. This is why mediation is already used to a significant extent in commercial cases, where businesses may want an ongoing commercial relationship, and in family cases, where parents may need to deal with contact with children for some years.   **3.34**

Are the chances of success relevant?

Some clients are very competitive and focus primarily on 'winning', and being 'proved right' by the endorsement of a decision by a judge. Such clients tend to see any form of compromise or concession as a weakness. This approach is fostered by the adversarial system, and indeed can be seen as the main objective of litigation. This is the approach of many barristers and litigation lawyers. Such an approach is entirely understandable where a client has been injured in an accident, or has a business put at risk by a breach of contract. Doing the best for a client is very important, but the choice of litigation should not be an emotional decision, but should depend on a careful assessment of the strengths and weaknesses of the case, and a careful explanation of the likely chance of success to the client. A case with at least an 80% chance of success may justify going to trial, but the client should understand clearly the risks where there is only a 60% chance of success.   **3.35**

The point is not to suggest that ADR is appropriate for weaker cases—a weak case is unlikely to get any significant outcome from any dispute resolution process. The point is rather that the comparative strength of the case is an important part of risk assessment, managing cost etc. so that ADR may simply be more cost effective where the chances for success are not very high. Equally ADR does not automatically involve compromise—a case can be put as strongly in negotiation or mediation as in litigation.   **3.36**

What are the attitudes of the parties?

3.37   Some clients are very keen to have a 'day in court'. The client may want to be present at the event of a trial, seeing the process as providing an appropriate end to a very serious experience. The client may want to have the attention of a judge, and to see cross-examination of an opponent. However this experience may only prove satisfactory and provide a vindication if the case has a good chance of success. Also the fact that much evidence is now provided in writing in advance as witness statements, skeleton arguments etc can make a day in court a much less cathartic experience. There are ways in which a day in court can actually be quite frustrating for a client, for example because he or she can only sit and watch for most of the time. Some of the aspects of 'a day in court' are available in ADR—for example an arbitrator can reach a decision that endorses a client's position, and clients can find that they can be more involved in putting their case personally in a mediation. Witnesses can be called and questioned as part of many ADR processes.

3.38   Other clients may not really want the stress of a day in court, but may see an apology from the other side as being of crucial importance. Mediation is likely to the best process for a client for whom an explanation and/or apology is an important objective. Mediation may also prove a satisfactory experience for a client who wishes to play a greater role in talking through the experience that is the basis of the action.

3.39   With competition between legal service providers, levels of client satisfaction cannot be ignored. Research tends to show that clients are often dissatisfied with litigation even when they have won a case—the outcome may still not be quite what they wanted and costs may be resented. Clients tend to be more satisfied with an ADR process, probably because they have had a greater role in agreeing the outcome. That said, negotiation can be an unsatisfactory experience for a client if the negotiation is carried out by lawyers in circumstances in which the client feels marginalised rather than fully involved in setting goals and agreeing the outcome.

Would neutral assistance be valuable?

3.40   It is part of the role of a legal representative to provide objectivity in a case, with a dispassionate analysis. In many cases lawyers provide sufficient objectivity to be able to negotiate a settlement to a case, sufficiently meeting client objectives and cutting costs. That said, a lawyer is briefed by a client as a representative, and it is the lawyer's task to act within instructions. If the client is too controlling or too optimistic about a case the instructions provided may not leave a lawyer with scope to negotiate. An experienced mediator may be able to assist as a mediation process can be quite effective in showing a client the weaknesses in a case—the client then has the option of agreeing an outcome rather than going to court with a significant risk of losing.

What stage has the case reached?

3.41   The stages at which a lawyer might be asked to advise on ADR are outlined at 3.10. Some forms of ADR are likely to achieve best results if commenced at an early stage. Adjudicative ADR such as arbitration is effectively a direct alternative to litigation and should therefore normally be selected before steps are taken with regard to litigation. Some non-adjudicative ADR, such as early neutral evaluation, is by its nature effective if it is incorporated into a case reasonably quickly. It is only logical that any form of ADR is most likely to be cost effective if it is carried out sooner rather than later—the later the ADR the more the likelihood that costs have already accumulated. There may still be some potential for cost saving in a negotiation just before the final court hearing, but there is much greater potential cost saving in negotiating before the issue of proceedings.

It would however be far too simplistic to suggest that ADR should only be considered at an early stage. Deciding on the best time to try ADR is an important professional judgment. ADR should not normally be recommended before sufficient information is available to evaluate the case. Presentation of a case in a negotiation or mediation normally requires just as much analysis as for advocacy in court. The lawyer will need to consider very carefully whether, for example, information provided under a pre-action protocol is sufficient to settle the case without seeing a formal particulars of claim of defence. It may or may not be important to wait for disclosure or exchange of witness statements. Specific information can be sought from the other side if needed. However ADR should be considered when there is realistically little likelihood of further significant information emerging.

3.42

On this basis non-adjudicative ADR may be considered at any stage. Indeed it is quite possible that a case that is being litigated will at some point be negotiated, and/or go to mediation. This is most likely to happen when one or both parties feel they are able to evaluate their case sufficiently, it may be triggered by an interim hearing or a Part 36 offer, or the court may order a stay: see Chapters 5–6.

3.43

How important might interim orders be?

Judges have wide powers to make interim orders, including security for costs, interim injunctions, and freezing injunctions. As non-adjudicative ADR is carried out by agreement no such orders are available. The parties can by agreement give an arbitrator or adjudicator some powers in regard to giving directions, but these will never have the potential range and force of court orders. If it is unlikely any such orders will be needed this factor will be irrelevant, save that if interim court powers are not important query whether litigation is to be preferred to ADR. If such orders are needed it does not mean that ADR is not an option. Proceedings may be commenced to provide a basis for seeking relevant interim orders, but once that is done the case could move to an ADR process.

3.44

Might orders relating to evidence be needed?

The litigation process provides for the systematic disclosure of relevant evidence. This is done in stages with key material normally being exchanged pre-action, but then with disclosure of all relevant documents and later of witness statements. There are also court powers with regard to the production of evidence, search orders etc. In non-adjudicative ADR information will only be disclosed by agreement. In adjudicative ADR the arbitrator or adjudicator may have some agreed powers to ask for information, but will not have the powers of a judge to compel the production of material. For clients who are concerned about confidentiality and who do not wish to make full disclosure, for example to protect commercially sensitive information, this may make ADR positively attractive. On the other hand a client whose case depends on getting information

3.45

that the other side will not easily make available voluntarily may need to start an action to get disclosure.

Is there a direction of the court?

3.46   As there is a right to a court hearing, no party can be compelled to settle a case through an ADR process. At most a party can be asked to consider ADR, and the strongest power available to the court is to stay an action, normally for no more than a month, for ADR options to be considered: see Chapters 5–6. Failure to comply may lead to a sanction.

3.47   It is not entirely clear how strong the influence of a court stay is. The wording of an order is quite important, and it will usually require 'best endeavours' or 'good faith' with regard to seeking a solution through ADR. There is little authority, but it appears that some courts will go so far as to propose a particular form of ADR such as mediation, and possibly even a mediation service provider. It appears that the order can provide a strong form of encouragement provided there is not compulsion. If there is a stay the lawyer would need to consider all the factors relevant to ADR with the client, and in particular the likely chance of success of the case in litigation, and the risk and possible implications of a cost penalty. Serious thought should be given to doing at least enough to comply with the order, such as seriously discussing ADR with the other side, making an offer to settle, or proposing a negotiation.

Might enforcement be an issue?

3.48   A potential advantage of ADR is that because the parties agree to the process (in the case of adjudicative ADR), and in many cases also agree to the outcome (in non-adjudicative ADR) there is rarely a difficulty with enforcement. Enforcement is a much greater potential problem in litigation where a party who has lost in court may well be unwilling to meet the judgment.

3.49   In any case where enforcement might be a problem, enforceability options must be considered. A court judgment will carry the advantage of the full enforcement powers of the court. An agreement reached without any court involvement will normally be enforceable as a contract, and a separate action will need to be brought to enforce the agreement, which would be more complex than enforcing an existing judgment: see Chapter 29. Note however that ADR can result in a court order where negotiation or mediation takes place after the issue of proceedings, and the judge is prepared to make a consent order: see Chapter 20.

POTENTIAL CONCERNS ABOUT ADR

3.50   A decision about the use of an ADR process to resolve a dispute should be based on a sufficient understanding of ADR processes, and an objective consideration of the relevant factors set out above. Many lawyers and clients see the potential benefits of ADR in appropriate cases, as is seen in the growth of mediation in commercial law and family law cases. However it is only realistic to accept that a number of lawyers and clients are resistant to the concept of ADR. Some of the most common concerns, and the potential response, are as follows:

ADR can undermine litigation

It is perhaps understandable that litigation lawyers, and barristers in particular, might see their expertise in litigation as being of primary importance in taking a case forward. They focus on statements of case to define issues, the use of interim orders etc. The lawyer may want to keep key points to be used in advocacy at trial. An ADR process may be seen as a threat because it may remove attention from preparation for trial, and may make the other side aware of points so that they can prepare better for trial. **3.51**

Query how far such a view is justified by the modern 'cards on the table' approach to litigation, where substantial information is available at an early stage under pre-action protocols, and where it is virtually impossible to keep any significant point secret until trial. A case should not be allowed to take on a life of its own where the next step in litigation is seen as more important than reviewing whether litigation remains in the client's best interests. The strengths of a case may be argued just as effectively in an ADR process as in court, so there should be a good reason for continuing with litigation if ADR could properly meet a client's objectives. **3.52**

Proposing ADR suggests a lack of faith in your case

In an adversarial system where the lawyer is the representative of a client a competitive approach is inevitable. The client will want to see his or her case in the best light, and it is the lawyer's task to argue the client's case in the best possible way. It might therefore be seen as a sign of weakness to talk of ADR rather than to insist on going to court. **3.53**

In a world where many commercial organisations choose arbitration or mediation such a view is clearly outdated. The less formal process of a negotiation or mediation can provide a very good platform for presenting a strong case. Many litigation lawyers are competitive negotiators. And at the end of the day 'see you in court' is an attitude that should only be sustained when the objectively assessed chances of success are high. **3.54**

ADR can undermine a lawyer's control of a case

It is understandable that litigation lawyers feel they have best control of a case within a litigation process. It is not always easy to see where a quick-fire negotiation might go, and an informal mediation process may be controlled as much by the mediator and the parties as by the lawyer. **3.55**

While this has some truth, it is only *some* truth. In litigation it is the judge rather than the lawyer who is in charge of the trial, and it can be much easier to deal with an arbitrator or a mediator under an agreement than it can with a judge in court. A lawyer has more direct control in negotiation than in any other process. The lawyer's analysis of the case will remain key in any ADR process, and the client can be briefed in advance about how to approach an ADR process. If the lawyer lacks personal knowledge of an ADR process, that can be remedied quite easily through information from an ADR provider. **3.56**

ADR does not really save costs

While saving costs is often an important factor in choosing ADR, it is quite true that ADR will not always save costs. Arbitration can be as expensive as a court hearing, and a settlement **3.57** negotiated at the door of the court may not save much. A non-adjudicative ADR process that does not resolve the case might be seen as wasted expenditure.

3.58   To achieve the best cost savings it is important to select the most appropriate form of ADR at the earliest reasonable opportunity. It is also important to plan for what may be gained from an ADR process even if the case does not settle. Mediation and negotiation can be used to gather information, and to convince the other side of your case in certain areas, even if immediate concessions are not forthcoming. Even if there is not an overall settlement, most ADR processes help to limit the issues, or lead to a settlement at a later date even if not immediately.

ADR is a way of getting something for a weak case

3.59   There is some concern that an ADR process may be abused by a party with a weak case who would lose if the case went to court. This may cause the party on the other side to resist ADR. Such an attitude may be justified in some cases, but it is not justified as a generic response to ADR. A mediation process where lawyers and clients are all in the room can be very effective in making it clear to potential litigant how weak their case is (subject to keeping the cost of the mediation itself low).

ADR involves too much pressure to settle

3.60   In a non-adjudicative ADR process such as negotiation or mediation it is right that a main purpose of the process is to settle the case. An effective negotiator or mediator can certainly exert pressure to try to ensure that a settlement is reached, and indeed this is quite appropriate where the case on an issue is relatively weak.

3.61   However it is equally true that non-adjudicative ADR can only reach any settlement by agreement. It is always possible to say no and walk away, and that provides a strong weapon. A claim can be resisted by making the strengths of your own case and your own bottom line very clear, and this resistance can put pressure on the other side. Testing your case can also help you to prepare it more fully if you do go to trial.

ADR is used as a delaying tactic

3.62   It is sometimes said that an ADR process may be used as a delaying tactic to put off the issue of proceedings or the setting of a trial date. This may have some truth where something relatively inexpensive is done, such as sending a letter that vaguely suggests a possibility for settlement without engaging in realistic negotiation. That said, it is difficult to see that ADR can easily be used to cause any substantial delay. The bluff can be called of a party pretending to negotiate without making any real progress. Any stay for ADR will normally be of no more than a month.

ADR is not a robust process

3.63   Lawyers may have some concern that an ADR process may lack robustness. While arbitrators and mediators are trained they may not have the same length of training and experience as a judge, and they may not have the standing or personality to take a robust approach. While this may have some truth in some cases it is again not a generic concern. Arbitrators and mediators may be like judges in being qualified lawyers with many years of experience in practice, and they may also have substantial experience in ADR processes. While robustness may be a good quality, other factors such as analysis and communication skills may be just as important in securing agreement.

SECURING AGREEMENT TO ADR

Using the factors set out above to decide that an ADR process may be in the best interests of a client will not be an end of the matter. Litigation may be forced on a defendant by the issue of a claim form, but ADR can only be carried out by agreement. It will be necessary to get the other side to agree to the use of ADR. This may just be a matter of asking, but if the lawyers on the other side have some reservations, or have a different view of the interests of their client, then they may need to be persuaded to agree. The following approaches may assist: **3.64**

Suggest specific benefits that ADR might offer

Potential benefits that you identify for your client may also be potential benefits for the other side. There may be other benefits listed in 1.29–1.41 that might apply to the other side. Try to identify positive suggestions, and possibly ways ahead on some issues. **3.65**

Offer information about ADR options

While not being patronising, it may be possible to form some view as to whether the lawyer on the other side has significant knowledge and experience of ADR options. Even with lawyers you do not know it may be possible to get information from the website of the chambers or firm. If the lawyer may not have significant relevant knowledge or experience it may be possible to suggest tactfully that they get information from relevant ADR service providers. Do not rush to suggest a specific mediator as this may make an opponent suspicious, but sending a copy of a typical mediation agreement for consideration might be helpful. **3.66**

Propose a simple ADR option

It may be possible to tempt a party into ADR. A Part 36 offer may encourage a party to enter a negotiation. A suggestion of a negotiation may succeed as many lawyers feel confident with the control they can have. A well-handled negotiation that fails to resolve all issues may encourage the use of mediation to reach a full agreement. If there is a relevant court scheme a lawyer may feel more comfortable with that. You could try an open approach, such as a telephone conversation simply to discuss the possibilities for ADR. **3.67**

Address any concerns that you think they might have

You may form the impression that an opponent has a general concern about ADR, like those raised in 3.50–3.63. If so, try to find out what their concerns are so that you can try to address them. Make it clear that you are open to their arguments about ADR, and perhaps leave it to them to suggest a form of ADR. It may be possible to offer a carrot, such as a willingness to consider a particular concern their client has, so long as ADR is attempted. **3.68**

Offer to pay reasonable ADR fees

3.69   Any such offer should be clear and not open to any misunderstanding as to what will be covered, but one party might for example offer to bear the whole fee of a mediator to encourage the other to enter mediation.

Seek to persuade a judge to order a stay

3.70   Once proceedings have been started it may be possible to ask a judge to order a stay for ADR: see Chapter 5. This should be a last resort rather than a first step as ADR is most likely to be successful if it is used by agreement rather than being forced. It may be most useful to try at least one of the suggestions above first, and this may assist in preparing an application to the judge.

CONFIDENTIALITY IN RELATION TO ADR PROCESSES

3.71   The point was made above that privacy can be one of the main attractions of an ADR process. Whereas litigation normally takes place in open court, ADR processes are private. It is vital to be aware that there is no absolute right of privacy for ADR processes. Privacy depends on three concepts developed in relation to litigation, and it is maintained by:

- any contractual agreement between the parties;
- by legal professional privilege;
- by the privilege from disclosure of oral or written communications made with the intention of seeking a settlement.

3.72   It will immediately be seen that while these concepts, especially the third, are very useful, they are open to interpretation. Problems may arise in particular if:

- the ADR process breaks down and there is any attempt to use something revealed in later litigation. (Note that if a document is disclosable, using it in an ADR process will not give it any privilege.);
- there is any dispute about the terms agreed;
- there is an attempt to call anyone involved in the ADR process as a witness in later proceedings.

3.73   The application of the principles developed in relation to litigation within an ADR process are still being developed. In recent years this has happened particularly in the mediation context, and this is considered at 13.94–13.122. The following sections outline general principles for ADR. It should be emphasised that there is general protection for communications and possible problems are not a reason not to use ADR, but a reason to take appropriate care with sensitive information. If the ADR is successful there will probably not be any issues.

Contractual principles

3.74   It is normal for an arbitration or mediation agreement to include a confidentiality clause, and this may well also be the case in other ADR processes where a person is involved by contract. The confidentiality clause will be binding as between the parties, and can be enforced if necessary through a contractual action. If any third party becomes involved in an ADR process, thought should be given to including a confidentiality clause if any sensitive information. It will not necessarily be binding on a court if some more important principle applies, though if a case does go to court the privilege for without prejudice communications may apply. For a discussion of the use of confidentiality clauses in mediation see 13.94–13.122.

Legal professional privilege

Legal professional privilege applies to communications between a lawyer and client made for the purposes of giving or receiving legal advice: *Three Rivers District Council v Bank of England (No 5)* [2003] EWCA Civ 474. Privilege applies to the giving of advice on what should be done, and should therefore include advice on ADR options, so long as the getting of legal advice is the dominant purpose of the communication. **3.75**

Privilege also applies to communications between a client or solicitor and a third party where the dominant purpose is to help in the conduct of litigation that is reasonably in prospect. It has been held that a meeting between lawyers on opposing sides to discuss 'battle tactics' will not be protected by this privilege (*Stax Claimants v Bank of Nova Scotia Channel Islands Ltd* [2007] EWHC 1153 (Ch)), which has implications for the application of this privilege to ADR. **3.76**

Legal professional privilege does not apply directly to an ADR process, but the separate principles developed to protect without prejudice communications made with a view to settlement are outlined below. Where ADR and litigation are both being used in relation to a case it might be possible to argue that a document is privileged having been developed with a view to litigation. **3.77**

Without prejudice communications

This is the widest potential protection for communications in an ADR process, but it is important to appreciate that the principles have been developed to apply to settlement attempts during litigation. It appears that the principles will apply appropriately in mediation (see 13.94–13.122), but the application of the principle to ADR is still being developed. **3.78**

In litigation, all communications passing between the parties, whether orally or in writing, which are made in an attempt to settle a dispute, are protected from disclosure in both the present and in any subsequent proceedings between the same parties and connected with the same subject matter: *Cutts v Head* [1984] Ch 290. Communications made for the purpose of settlement with a different party within the same litigation are also inadmissible whether or not settlement is reached with that party. Public policy operates to protect those communications from being disclosed to third parties: *Rush and Tompkins Ltd v Greater London Council* [1989] AC 1280, [1988] 3 All ER 737. If the communications were privileged in earlier proceedings, then they will be also inadmissible in any subsequent proceedings between the same parties that involve connected issues: *Ofulue v Bossert* [2009] UKHL 16, [2009] 1 AC 990. The without prejudice rule will prevent disclosure of communications aimed at settling a dispute, even if litigation had not yet begun; the only relevant question was whether both parties contemplated or might reasonably have contemplated litigation if they could not agree: *Barnetson v Framlington Group Ltd* [2007] EWCA Civ 502, [2007] 1 WLR 2443. They **3.79** are protected from disclosure whether or not the word 'without privilege' is used, provided the communications are genuinely aimed at settlement of a dispute.

3.80 The rule is founded on the public policy of encouraging litigants to settle their differences rather than litigate them. They should not be discouraged by the knowledge that anything said in negotiations may be used to their prejudice in the course of proceedings. They should be able to put their cards on the table, without fear that any statements they make in the course of settlement negotiations might be used against them on the question of liability. The rule therefore enables the parties to be able to conduct negotiations freely, in the knowledge that they can make concessions and offers and change their positions in settlement discussions, without these matters being used against them in the litigation if settlement is not reached.

3.81 The court will not dissect negotiations in order to isolate statements that will be admissible from those that are not. That would give rise to practical problems and would undermine the whole purpose of without prejudice communications: *Unilever Plc v Procter & Gamble Co* [2000] 1 WLR 2436 and *Williams v Hull* [2009] EWHC 2844.

3.82 The rule has no application to communications sent on an open basis, such as those sent to discuss payment in relation to an admitted claim, rather than to negotiate a compromise in respect of a disputed liability: *Bradford & Bingley Plc v Rashid* [2006] UKHL 37, [2006] 1 WLR 2066.

Exceptions to the without prejudice communications rule

3.83 The rule is not an absolute one and there are a limited number of situations when without prejudice communications can be disclosed to the court in the interests of justice. The main exceptions are as follows.

- To determine whether a settlement was reached, or to prove the terms of the settlement: *Walker v Wilsher* [1889] 23 QBD 335 and *Tomlin v Standard Telephones and Cables Ltd* [1969] 1 WLR 1378. However the court will not admit without prejudice communications to assist in the proper interpretation or construction of an agreement to ascertain the meaning of the contract or the parties' intentions. To do so, would lead to arguments about the implication of terms into written settlement. Although there is a policy of affording the court the best and most useful evidence as an aid to interpretation and in ascertaining the parties' intention, this policy did not trump the policy of preserving the without prejudice principle: *Oceanbulk Shipping and Trading SA v TMT Asia Ltd* [2010] 1 WLR 1803.
- If rectification of the agreement is required : *Oceanbulk Shipping and Trading SA v TMT Asia Ltd* [2010] 1 WLR 1803.
- To determine whether any settlement agreement apparently reached during the negotiations should be set aside on the grounds of misrepresentation, fraud or undue influence.
- Even if there is no concluded settlement agreement, communications may be admissible to show that a statement was made by one party in negotiations with the intention that the other side should rely on it, and on which they acted, thus giving rise to an estoppel: *Hodgkinson & Corby Ltd v Wards Mobility Services Ltd* [1997] FSR 178 and *Unilever plc v Procter & Gamble Co* [2000] 1 WLR 2436 per Walker LJ at 2443.
- The rule is being abused eg by threats, dishonest, oppressive or disreputable conduct, perjury or blackmail: *Kitcat v Sharp* [1882] 48 LT 64. However the privileged nature of the

communications will not be lightly lost; an inconsistency between a pleaded case and the stance taken in negotiations will not result in the privilege being revoked, nor will putting forward an implausible case; nothing less than unambiguous impropriety will suffice: *Savings and Investment Bank Ltd v Fincken* [2003] EWCA Civ 1630, [2004] 1 WLR 667; *Berry Trade Ltd v Moussavi (No 3)* [2003] EWCA Civ 715; *Aird & Aird v Prime Meridian* (2006) EWHC 2338 (TCC).

- There may also be an exception where there is a risk of serious harm to a child: *Re D (Minors)* [1993] 2 All ER 693.
- There may be an exception in some interim applications to explain delay in commencing or prosecuting litigation, or to obtain relief from sanctions: *Berg v IML London Ltd* [2002] 1 WLR 3271.
- Both sides may consent to the privilege being waived so that the documents can be put before the court, although no inferences should be drawn from a refusal to waive privilege: *Sayers v Clarke Walker* [2002] EWCA Civ 910; *Reed Executive plc v Reed Business Information Ltd* [2004] EWCA Civ 887, [2004] 1 WLR 3026.
- If the parties have made it clear that the communications can be looked at on the question of costs (for example, by marking the documents 'without prejudice save as to costs'), then the court can look at the communications after judgment has been given on liability and before it determines the question of costs: *Cutts v Head* [1984] Ch 290. However the court has no power to look at without prejudice communications on the question of costs unless the parties have negotiated on the basis that they reserve the right to bring the communications to the court on the question of costs, or all parties subsequently agree to waive the privilege: *Reed Executive plc v Reed Business Information Ltd* [2004] EWCA Civ 887, [2004] 1 WLR 3026.

KEY POINTS SUMMARY

- A lawyer has a general professional duty to advise on ADR options, and there are identifi- **3.84** able points in a case and in litigation where this is particularly important.
- There are many factors that may be relevant to the use of ADR, and to which form of ADR is most appropriate, including cost, the nature of the dispute and the objectives of the parties. It is important to select the ones relevant to each case.
- No type of dispute is inherently unsuitable for ADR, though an individual case may be.
- Various concerns may be expressed in relation to ADR, but all can be addressed.
- There are ways to encourage a reluctant opponent to use ADR.
- ADR processes are private, but confidentiality depends on contractual provisions, legal professional privilege, and privilege for without prejudice communications.

4

COSTS OF ADR PROCEDURES

COSTS CONTEXT 4.01

GENERAL COST CONSIDERATIONS 4.06

ELEMENTS OF COSTS....................................4.15

COSTS OF ADR PROCESSES 4.22

EFFECTS OF THE FUNDING BASIS 4.48

COSTS OF THE PARTIES 4.60

OVERALL FINANCIAL ANALYSIS AND RISK ASSESSMENT........4.62

BASIC EXAMPLE OF ADR COST CONSIDERATIONS.............4.71

KEY POINTS SUMMARY..................................4.76

COSTS CONTEXT

4.01 Cost is one of the most important issues with regard to dispute resolution. There is widespread concern about the potential cost of litigation, and a desire to save costs may be one of the most important factors in choosing to use an ADR process. The Woolf reforms in the CPR have led to a decrease in the number of issued cases, but the costs of litigation have continued to increase.

4.02 There are many reasons why litigation costs are high. The work needed to prepare a case for court in terms of collecting evidence, preparing papers etc is time-consuming and often specialist work that is almost inevitably quite expensive. It is now government policy that the civil court system be self-funding, so the level of court fees has risen. It is not surprising that costs can sometimes outstrip the amount in dispute in a case, attracting adverse comment from judges, and that even clients who win a case in court may express concern about the costs involved.

4.03 The details of funding systems, potential costs orders and the assessment of costs with regard to litigation are discussed in Sime, *A Practical Approach to Civil Procedure*, 13th edn, OUP, 2010. However the potential cost of litigation provides a background against which a lawyer and client must consider the potential cost of an ADR process, so this chapter makes reference to such matters in so far as they are directly relevant to the consideration of costs in relation to ADR. Chapter 7 provides detail on the possibility of recovering ADR costs in litigation, and Chapter 6 provides detail on possible costs sanctions where a party refuses to engage in ADR.

Concern about the cost of litigation is at such a level that it has been the subject of a major **4.04** investigation in the Review of Civil Litigation Costs carried out by Lord Justice Jackson. The Final Report from the Review was issued in December 2009 and it includes a number of recommendations for reducing and controlling costs, including the following general endorsement of the use of ADR:

> 'Alternative dispute resolution ("ADR") (particularly mediation) has a vital role to play in reducing the costs of civil disputes, by fomenting the early settlement of cases. ADR is however under-used. Its potential benefits are not as widely known as they should be. I therefore recommend that:
>
> - There should be a serious campaign to ensure that all litigation lawyers and judges are properly informed of how ADR works, and the benefits that it can bring.
> - The public and small businesses who become embroiled in disputes are also made aware of the benefits of ADR. An authoritative handbook for ADR should be prepared, explaining what ADR is and how it works, and listing reputable providers of ADR services. This handbook should be used as the standard work for the training of judges and lawyers.
>
> Nevertheless ADR should not be mandatory for all proceedings. The circumstances in which it should be used (and when it should be used) will vary from case to case, and much will come down to the judgment of experienced practitioners and the court.' (Recommendation 6.3)

The Review of Civil Litigation Costs also includes recommendations for greater attention to **4.05** be paid to costs management (Recommendations 6.10 and 6.11), including greater training in this area for lawyers, and a greater use of costs budgets. Ideally it should be possible for a lawyer to offer a client a budget estimate for pursuing a case through litigation, and an alternative budget estimate for an appropriate form of ADR. This may be possible at the start of a relatively straightforward case, and especially where a relatively low amount is in dispute so that there may be fixed costs for litigation. However in many cases, especially where significant costs have already been incurred, the position on costs may need quite complex analysis, as outlined in 4.62–4.75.

GENERAL COST CONSIDERATIONS

The likely costs of an individual ADR process can be estimated as set out in 4.15–4.47. **4.06** However the cost of that process can only be considered in isolation where it is decided to use ADR at the very start of a case. In most cases some costs will already have been incurred before ADR is considered, and in some cases the proceedings may move from one process to another, for example from litigation to negotiation to litigation to mediation, in which case an ADR process will need to be put into a wider context to ensure that the client is kept in the best overall position in relation to costs.

The main factors to be considered in assessing the likely costs in a case, and who may be **4.07** liable to pay those costs at the end of the day, are as follows:

What are the main elements of costs in the case?

4.08   The costs that a party may incur can vary massively from case to case, depending on factors like the complexity of the factual issues, the clarity of the law etc. The lawyer should try to identify as early as possible in each case what the main cost elements are likely to be. Strategic decisions may need to be made as to how much of this potential cost is essential, especially as regards the costs of gathering evidence. The potential cost benefit of an ADR process can be undermined where substantial costs have already been incurred.

How is the litigation being funded?

4.09   In general this chapter relates to privately funded cases. There may be different considerations as to costs and ADR options where the case is being funded in some other way, such as a conditional fee agreement, or by public funding. See 4.48–4.59 for more detail.

How much is at stake in the case?

4.10   There may be many things the lawyer could do to collect evidence, research law etc, but the potential cost of these steps may be disproportionate to what is at stake in terms of the amount of damages being sought, and the importance of any other remedies. Proportionality is part of the overriding objective under the CPR, which means an ADR process may be attractive as being potentially cost effective.

The extent to which costs have already been incurred

4.11   A lawyer will need to carry out some evaluation of a case before advice on how to pursue the case can be given. In many cases this will extend to starting to take steps potentially relevant to fulfilling a pre-action protocol, and perhaps even extending to issuing proceedings. The extent to which costs have already been incurred, and whether those costs might be potentially at least partly recoverable, must be part of considering the overall possible financial attractiveness of an ADR process.

The chances of success

4.12   Potential cost saving is rarely a simple matter of comparing the likely costs of litigation with the potential costs of an ADR process. The chances of success must also be factored in. Asking a client to pay £10,000 for litigation you have advised is 90% likely to succeed carries limited risk, but if litigation costs are likely to be £10,000 with only a 60% chance of winning the risk is much greater, making the costs of an ADR process rather more attractive as a way of lessening risk. See 4.62–4.70 for more detail.

The possibility that liability for costs may shift

4.13   The situation on costs is made potentially fairer, but also significantly more complicated, by the fact that liability for the costs of litigation may shift from one party to another. The main way in which this might happen is that the loser is normally ordered to reimburse the winner for costs reasonably incurred. A second possibility is that a Part 36 offer may lead to costs being shifted from the last date on which an offer could have been accepted where the offeror does not go on to beat the terms of the offer.

This may significantly complicate a decision as to whether an ADR process may be cost **4.14** effective. Even if the costs of litigation are relatively high, the party incurring those costs may be less concerned if the costs may be substantially recovered if the case is won. This makes it particularly important to assess the chances of success of a case as accurately and realistically as possible. False optimism may lead a client to reject ADR but then go on to lose a case and be badly out of pocket when ADR could have provided a much better outcome. The relevant arithmetic and the choices that may be available are explored further in 4.62–4.75 below.

ELEMENTS OF COSTS

There are basic elements of cost in any process for dispute resolution. These elements are **4.15** listed here because they can all form part of the costs of an ADR process as well as part of litigation costs.

In a privately funded case each party will incur their own costs for having a case investigated **4.16** and getting advice on it. Each party will be liable to pay these costs, which will normally be incurred on the basis of a retainer agreement between a client and solicitor. Liability to pay these costs will remain with the party who incurs them unless there is a court order as to costs (which can only be made as part of a litigation or arbitration process: see Chapter 7), or by agreement (which may be done as part of an ADR process). Someone other than the party may be liable to pay the costs depending on how the case is being funded: see 4.48–4.59.

Solicitor fees

A solicitor will normally charge an hourly rate, the details of which will be set out in a **4.17** client care letter soon after the solicitor is first retained. This rate will be charged when the solicitor is working on the case in any capacity, including advice and research as well as engaging in correspondence, drafting and attending meetings. Different rates may be charged where solicitors with different levels of experience work on a case under the supervision of the solicitor with primary responsibility. The solicitor should provide updates on accumulated fees, and is likely to ask for payments on account to cover fees.

Barrister fees

A barrister will normally be paid a separate fee for each task for which the barrister is **4.18** instructed. There will be separate fees for providing an opinion, for appearing in court to deal with an application etc. Each fee will cover ancillary work such as research.

Evidence and information

Normally the solicitor will be responsible for collecting information and evidence. Much of **4.19** the cost will therefore be paying for the solicitor's time to do this. There will be additional costs where a third party charges for information or for copies of documents—for example an expert will charge a fee for a report, and copies of documents on disclosure must be paid for.

Disbursements

4.20 All cases will have incidental costs such as travel costs, photocopying etc. The solicitor will normally add such disbursements to the bill that is payable by the client.

Process fees

4.21 Fees will be charged for any formal process, eg court fees for issuing proceedings.

COSTS OF ADR PROCESSES

4.22 Many of the costs for an ADR process will fall under the heads outlined in 4.15–4.21. If lawyers are instructed to negotiate or assist in a mediation they will need to be paid to prepare and attend etc. There will often be process fees, though they will cover the ADR process rather than court fees. This means that ADR is not necessarily cheaper if lawyers are involved and a case is fully prepared for hearing, as in an arbitration. What will often make an ADR process less expensive is that it will reach a solution more quickly, will take significantly less legal time, and that potentially time-consuming and expensive processes such as disclosure can be avoided.

4.23 Most ADR processes can be carried out at various levels with a range of costs. Just as litigation costs can vary substantially between a small case in the county court and a large case in the High Court, so mediation may cost very little if the parties attend a free service without lawyers, but it can be very expensive if a big case is mediated over several days with lawyers retained by both sides. An indication of possible fees is given in the following sections, but actual fees should be checked at the time—many ADR providers include information on fees on their website.

ADR provider's fee

4.24 Some ADR provision is free. An ombudsman or complaints process may make no charge. Some mediation processes are offered without charge by a court or by a charitable or not-for-profit organisation. As an example, the Law Works organisation offers up to three hours of mediation free to a party who is on benefits or has a very low income: see www.lawworks.org.uk.

4.25 Most ADR service providers will charge a fee. The fee may be charged by an ADR organisation that provides a service package, for example for arbitration or mediation. Some of the bigger providers, such as The Centre for Dispute Resolution, offer a range of services related to ADR, and these are outlined on their website: www.cedr.org.uk. This fee may cover the cost of a location for the ADR process, support services, refreshments etc as agreed. If it does not this cost may need to be added. There may be a set fee, or a fee that is negotiable depending on what is included. Most fee structures relate to the time that will be taken and/or the value of the claim. Many other websites offer advice on fees: see for example the Dispute Mediation Services site, www.disputemediationservices.co.uk.

4.26 Most individuals who provide ADR services will also charge a fee. A mediator or arbitrator may be engaged personally, and may charge a set fee or an hourly rate. If the mediator is paid hourly, they will want to be paid for preparation as well as the mediation itself. An arbitrator or mediator might also expect to have travel expenses paid. Some mediators charge a higher fee if they do facilitate a settlement of the case. Many firms and chambers offer ADR services, and details are often available on their websites.

The fee for an arbitration may be several thousand pounds for a hearing that may take more than a week. If the case is more straightforward and can be completed in less than a week the fee might be similar to that for a mediation. A paper-based or IT-based arbitration might be based on an hourly fee for the arbitrator and cost only a few hundred pounds. **4.27**

The fee for a mediation might typically be in the region of £300 for a case worth less than £10,000 that can be settled within a day. Many mediations are concluded in less than a day. For a case that might take 2–3 days and be worth over £100,000 the fee would typically be at least £1,000. For more detail on mediator fees see 11.45–11.52. **4.28**

The National Mediation Helpline

There is government interest in providing subsidised ADR services to save judicial time. From 2007 there has been a scheme for county court mediation through the National Mediation Helpline. Their website includes quite detailed guidance on process and fees: see www.nationalmediationhelpline.com. For a small claim (that is a claim worth less than £5,000, or £1,000 in the case of personal injury) the service is offered at no charge once the claim form has been submitted to the court. Each court area has a full-time mediation officer based in a county court who can offer advice and information, and who can provide mediation in a meeting or by telephone. **4.29**

For a fast track or multi track case the fee is subsidised. At the time of writing mediation for a fast track claim (with a claim between £5,000 and £25,000) would cost £300 + VAT per party for three hours. For a multi track case with a claim over £25,000 the cost would be £425 + VAT per party for four hours. The parties are put in touch with a local mediation provider who will make arrangements. **4.30**

Negotiation

The format for a negotiation will be entirely a matter of agreement between the parties. This leads to a very wide variation in potential methods for negotiating, from a brief telephone discussion to a formal meeting, and equally wide variation in potential cost. **4.31**

The main cost of a negotiation will be the fees charged by the lawyers. A negotiation may be carried out by solicitors alone, or barristers may be briefed, in which case they will normally be accompanied by instructing solicitors. Overall cost will depend on the hours of work for the solicitors, and any brief fee for a barrister. The charge for the lawyers may increase if additional time is needed to draw up a settlement after the negotiation. A telephone conversation might take relatively little time, but preparing for and attending a negotiation meeting would be likely to cost a minimum of several hundred pounds. **4.32**

A further significant cost might be the cost of a location for the negotiation, though many negotiations take place at the office of one of the solicitors or at no extra cost. Clients may or may not attend a negotiation, as agreed. If they do attend the clients may themselves incur costs in taking time off work, travelling etc. **4.33**

4.34   A negotiation in a major case may thus be quite expensive. If for example barristers, solicitors and clients agree to meet on neutral ground for at least a day the costs could easily be several thousand pounds. There are however many circumstances in which a negotiation would be much cheaper. Lawyers attending court in relation to an application may, if so instructed, take the opportunity to try to negotiate a settlement and this may be at no greater cost than that incurred to attend the hearing. In a relatively straightforward case a negotiation may be conducted by telephone or by letter, with the lawyer time involved being much shorter and therefore less expensive.

4.35   Each party will pay their own costs in a negotiation, unless it is a term of the negotiation that all or part of the costs of one party are paid by the other party. This may be used as a tactic, with one party offering to pay the reasonable costs of the other for the negotiation in order to secure a concession, or an overall agreement. It would be possible for a judge to make an order as to costs if court proceedings had been initiated, though this would normally only be by agreement if there had been a successful negotiation.

4.36   If a negotiation is otherwise successful, it may be relevant to agree what should happen as regards other costs previously incurred in the case. It is important to have a reasonably accurate estimate of costs to date available at the negotiation for this purpose. Unless any other agreement is reached, each party will pay their own costs. However if, for example, one party has been largely successful that party might ask for reasonable costs spent in pursuing the claim, as might have been ordered had the case gone to court. The parties might agree a global payment to include damages and costs, or a separate additional payment in respect of costs. Other options may be appropriate; for example, if a case is settled after proceedings are issued it may be agreed one party will pay the other party's costs on the standard basis, subject to detailed assessment if not agreed.

Mediation

4.37   There are many possible formats for a mediation, depending on the needs of a case. In a complex commercial case a mediation might last 2–3 days or more and involve a number of people in appropriate neutral accommodation. In a smaller case a mediation would typically take only a couple of hours, possibly without significant cost.

4.38   Major potential costs are the fee for the mediation service provider, and/or the mediator. It is common for a mediation to take place on neutral ground, so there will often also be an accommodation fee. This may be an office provided by the mediation service, or possibly a conference facility in a hotel. It is important to have sufficient space for joint and separate meetings.

4.39   It is a matter for agreement whether lawyers attend a mediation, and if so which lawyers. In a commercial case both parties may bring in-house lawyers, a solicitor and a barrister to provide ongoing input as to the legal options. In family cases the parties may attend without lawyers, though often on the basis of having consulted a lawyer about their potential rights in advance, and possibly seeking advice about a potential agreement after the mediation. If lawyers attend they will normally charge for preparation, which may well involve the preparation of a written and/or oral summary of the case. The extent of lawyer involvement will of course have a major impact on the overall cost of the mediation.

4.40   While clients will not always attend a negotiation, they will always be part of a mediation. This may not be very expensive where they attend a local service, but it can be expensive for a big case. In a case involving a business it is important that sufficiently senior people with decision-taking powers attend, and it may also be important to have others with direct knowledge of the matters in dispute. If these people do not attend the mediation itself, it may be desirable to have them available for telephone or conference calls. While it is not common for experts or other witnesses to attend, this can be done by agreement.

The way in which the costs of a mediation will be met will normally be covered by the writ- **4.41** ten mediation agreement. Many mediation providers will offer standard form agreements, though these may be varied with consent. A mediation agreement is a contract, enforceable as such, and a court will not have power to vary it: *National Westminster Bank v Feeney* [2006] EWHC 900. Normally each side will bear their own costs, and the fees for the mediation will be shared equally whatever the outcome of the mediation. Alternatively it may be agreed that the fees will count as costs in the case if the dispute is not settled and goes to trial. If one party has much greater resources than the other party, or is keen to use mediation, that party might agree to pay the whole fee.

If a mediation is otherwise successful, it may be relevant to agree what should happen as **4.42** regards other costs previously incurred in the case, on a similar basis to the comments in 4.36 in relation to negotiation.

Arbitration

An arbitration procedure is broadly similar to a trial procedure in that both sides present **4.43** their case to an arbitrator with a view to the arbitrator reaching a decision. There may be less formality than in a litigation process as regards procedure before the hearing. At the hearing witnesses and experts may be called as agreed. This all has implications for costs.

One major potential cost is the fee for the arbitration service provider, or the arbitrator. **4.44** Sometimes it may be agreed that an arbitration is to be conducted by a three-member tribunal. It is common for an arbitration to take place on neutral ground, and a relatively large room may be required, depending on the number of people attending. The hearing may only take a day, but in a complex case an arbitration may last for several weeks, with consequently high tribunal and accommodation costs.

It is normal for each party to have legal representation at an arbitration, with possibly a bar- **4.45** rister, a solicitor and an in-house lawyer. The cost of legal representation may be similar to the cost at a trial. The clients may choose to attend an arbitration as they may attend a trial, with consequent costs to them as regards loss of earnings and travel.

The payment of the arbitration fee will normally be covered by the arbitration agreement. **4.46** The costs incurred by each party before the arbitration and at the arbitration will be borne by the party incurring the cost, although often the arbitrator is given discretion to make orders about the tribunal's fees and the parties' costs.

Other forms of ADR

It is not feasible to run through the potential costs of every possible form of ADR. Each will **4.47** be based on the same elements as the main types of ADR illustrated above. A complaint procedure or an ombudsman system may be relatively inexpensive, but an adjudicator or an expert carrying out an early neutral evaluation will require an appropriate fee.

EFFECTS OF THE FUNDING BASIS

4.48 The actual effect of costs on a party will depend on the way in which the party is being funded. The basis for funding may also be relevant to the relative attractiveness of an ADR process. This area is potentially quite complex and the following points are simply indicative of what may need to be considered in relation to ADR as regards the main alternatives to private funding.

Conditional fee agreement funding

4.49 If a client enters a conditional fee agreement (CFA) then there is a shift in some of the dynamics relevant to ADR options. The client may be less concerned about costs as the lawyer's fee will only be payable if the case is won, though the client will still be liable to pay disbursements (which will include the costs of expert fees, and also the barrister's fee if the barrister does not also act under a CFA). The lawyer may be more concerned to keep costs down, especially if there is a significant risk that the case may not succeed, as the lawyer might be left out of pocket (though a weak case would not normally be taken on a CFA basis).

4.50 A CFA must comply with the Courts and Legal Services Act 1990. A CFA provides that the client will not pay legal fees if the claim is lost, but if the claim is won the client will pay the lawyer's normal fee plus a success fee, which may be up to a 100% increase on the normal fee. A party using a CFA will normally also take out after the event (ATE) insurance, to cover the potential liability to pay the costs of the other side if the case is lost. It may be a term of such insurance that a reasonable offer to settle should be accepted.

4.51 A CFA will usually include terms for what happens as regards fees if the case is settled. The settlement of the case will normally mean that the fee and success fee are payable, depending on the outcome reached. The overall figure that the client will be left with needs to be considered—a negotiation or mediation will often try to provide that the costs and success fee of a winning party are paid by the other side, but this can be a very contentious issue. A lawyer may sometime reduce a success fee to help to ensure agreement. Note that the success fee does not have to be revealed in advance as part of discussions as this would disclose the lawyer's view of the chance of success, but otherwise there are clear rules relating to notifying the other side where a party has CFA funding.

4.52 A CFA can therefore provide a problem for settlement for the claimant, though the claimant is still likely to want to settle to keep disbursements down. A CFA can also put pressure on a defendant to settle because if the defendant is unsuccessful the success fee and the ATE insurance premium are potentially recoverable by the claimant as part of the costs.

Insurance or other third party funding

4.53 A party may have insurance for legal costs, or an insurance company may take over the conduct of the case where for example the party has relevant insurance as a driver or a professional. The insurer may then have a view on whether ADR is appropriate, and on what form of ADR should be used. The insurance may provide a maximum amount for legal costs (and note that the maximum may need to cover all costs if for example the party has to pay any costs for the other side).

Legal Services Commission funding

A party who meets the conditions for LSC funding and makes a successful application for funding is in a relatively strong position. As the other side will face paying their own costs even if they win (as a result of the Administration of Justice Act 1920, s 11), they are more likely to make an offer for settlement. LSC funding will normally cover reasonable costs of negotiation or mediation provided that is the most cost effective way of proceeding, but this should be checked before undertaking the process in a specific case. The costs of other ADR processes such as early neutral evaluation or expert determination may also be covered as a disbursement. **4.54**

Public funding may not cover a trial unless reasonable attempts to settle have been made, and it may be withdrawn if a party unreasonably refused to settle a claim in mediation. **4.55**

The Court of Appeal has said that publicly funded claims should be mediated, if appropriate, in order to save costs: *R (Cowl and other) v Plymouth City Council* [2002] 1 WLR 803. The Funding Code recognises that mediation costs can be publicly funded in family work and family mediation procedures are funded directly by the Legal Services Commission. **4.56**

The LSC must be told of a Part 36 offer, as the chance of success of the case is relevant to funding. If an assisted party fails to beat a Part 36 offer they will have to pay the defendant's costs since the offer could have been accepted, which will eat into the sum recovered. The case may need to be compromised to avoid such an effect. **4.57**

However the client with LSC funding is in a weaker position in that the LSC's statutory charge may reduce the sum the client actually receives. The change can bite where costs incurred by the LSC in relation to a party are not fully recovered in an order made against the other side. The LSC has a statutory charge over money or assets recovered or preserved to recover such costs. **4.58**

This needs to be taken into account in the arithmetic in a negotiation or mediation, and steps should be taken to avoid or decrease the effect of the charge. One approach is to keep the issues in the case to a minimum as the charge will only bite on property and money at issue in the case. Another possibility is to keep costs low so that the charge is relatively small. A third possibility is to agree that the other side will pay the costs so that no charge arises. If the case proceeds to litigation and the party with LSC funding wins, that party would normally get a costs order against the other side, and this point should be pursued in an ADR process. The charge may be avoided in a settlement made in a family mediation. **4.59**

COSTS OF THE PARTIES

Putting together the above elements: **4.60**

- Each party to a negotiation will bear their own costs, unless there is any agreement or order as to the payment of costs.

- The costs of each party will be made up of the elements set out in 4.15–4.21.
- The actual liability to pay the costs may vary depending on how the party is being funded.
- The costs of an ADR process will be made up as indicated in 4.22–4.37.
- When considering costs in relation to ADR, it is important to bear in mind costs that have already been incurred. These costs will still be payable by the party, unless any agreement is made as to the payment of those costs in the ADR process.
- In taking a decision it is important to bear in mind the likelihood that the ADR process will succeed (or the costs of the ADR process may be at least partly wasted).
- It is also relevant to bear in mind any other option there may be with regard to costs, for example through making a Part 36 offer.

4.61   Costs payable may be affected in other ways:

- If there has been some litigation, the costs on some applications may have been decided by summary assessment.
- There may be an existing Part 36 offer that is affecting current liability for costs.
- There may be a costs sanction relating to a failure to engage in ADR (see Chapter 6).
- If the case goes to litigation and is won the loser is likely to be ordered to pay the reasonable costs of the winner.
- It is possible that ADR costs may be recoverable depending on the basis on which a settlement is reached if a claim has been commenced. For example, if a claim is formally withdrawn or discontinued, the claimant would normally be expected to pay the defendant's costs because the defendant would technically have won.
- It is also possible that ADR costs may be recoverable in litigation (see Chapter 7).

OVERALL FINANCIAL ANALYSIS AND RISK ASSESSMENT

4.62   The above elements and factors outline how complex financial decisions relating to a case can be. The lawyer will need to take a relatively systematic approach to the analysis of figures and to risk assessment before putting options to a client and advising on whether it is best to pursue a case though litigation or an ADR option. For more detail on the importance of managing risk see *A Practical Approach to Effective Litigation*, 7th edn, OUP, 2009, ch. 6.

4.63   As regards figures, the following is a basic checklist of figures that may be relevant:

- the maximum and minimum sum of damages that is realistically at stake in the case
- your own costs to date
- your likely further costs up to and including trial if the case is litigated
- the extent to which all your costs are likely to be recoverable on assessment if you win at trial
- the likely costs to date of the other side
- the likely further costs the other side will incur up to and including trial if the case is litigated
- the costs of the other side you are likely to have pay on assessment if you lose at trial
- the potential costs of each potentially appropriate ADR process.

4.64   As a solicitor has a duty to keep a client updated as to costs, and the CPR provides for estimates of costs to be made available as a case progresses through litigation, relevant figures for some of these heads should be to hand, but others may require investigation.

Complexity arises because a decision cannot be taken on arithmetic alone. It is important to **4.65** factor in risk assessment and tactics to be able to take a realistic decision.

Risk assessment relates to the likelihood that the case will be won if it proceeds to trial. **4.66** In an extreme case it is possible to win at trial, but to lose overall because of the impact of costs.

- If the likely costs are £10,000 and there is a 90% chance of success then the likely outcome is that the claim will be won, and therefore reasonable costs will be paid on a standard basis. While the standard basis is unlikely to cover all costs, it will normally cover about 90% of them, so £9,000 in costs will be reimbursed leaving the party only £1,000 out of pocket on costs. If the damages recovered are £25,000 this will simply mean that the sum left overall is £24,000.
- If the likely costs are £10,000 and there is only a 60% chance of success there is a 40% chance the claim will be lost. If that happened the party would have to bear those costs, and would be likely to be ordered to pay the costs for the other side. If the other side has costs at a similar level, and with a similar assumption as regards the assessment of costs, the party will pay £10,000 and £9,000 in costs and be £19,000 out of pocket. If damages of £25,000 are also payable the total cost is £44,000.

The first scenario is reasonably attractive, to the level where a client may be attracted to **4.67** incurring extra costs to try to ensure that the case is won. This has an element of gambling, but it may seem sensible to spend more even if the chance of winning is only increased marginally to get the best chance of a positive outcome. The second scenario is very unattractive, but the contrast shows how crucial it is that the chances of success in a case are carefully assessed. The chances of success will of course include matters like how clear the law is, how strong the evidence is, whether cross-examination will succeed and so on.

It is this sort of calculation that can illustrate the potential value of ADR. Rather than go **4.68** to court and risk the difference between the two scenarios above it may be worthwhile spending a few thousand pounds on an ADR process. This may require some compromise as regards the first scenario, but it can help to avoid the second scenario. Of course thought must also be given to how likely it is that an ADR process might work. Alternatives might include making a Part 36 offer to encourage negotiation. If the other side has not done a realistic risk assessment, this may be something that a mediator may be able to help with as part of encouraging a settlement.

The calculation may be made more complicated because developing case law gives rise to **4.69** some uncertainty about likely costs orders. Rather than a simple order for costs based on a winner and loser, an order may be made on the extent to which a case has been won—if there were several issues in the case and some were won and others lost an appropriate proportion of costs may be ordered, or there may be an issues based assessment under CPR 44.3.4.

Despite these complexities, the lawyer should deal with arithmetic and risk assessment **4.70** objectively and put the options to the client. The lawyer's motivation may be complex if they might be paid more if the case went to trial in some months rather than settling soon. Nonetheless the client's best interest must come first. As clients become more aware of ADR there may be a possibility of a complaint if options are not fully considered, or possibly a wasted costs order against the lawyer if litigation is prolonged improperly when a case could be settled: Senior Courts Act 1981 s 51(6) and CPR Part 48.7.

BASIC EXAMPLE OF ADR COST CONSIDERATIONS

4.71   The claimant's lawyer in a negligence claim assesses potential damages at £50,000 minimum to £70,000 maximum if the case is won. The chance of winning on the balance of probabilities is assessed at about 70% (because there are some weaknesses in the evidence). The defendant has indicated that he will claim contributory negligence of 25%. Appropriate pre-action steps have been taken, but a claim form has not yet been issued.

4.72   The costs to date of the claimant are £10,000, and it is thought that the defendant's costs are about £8,000. If the case goes to trial the costs might be up to £10,000 more each, largely because of disputes in the evidence about what caused the accident.

4.73   The claimant's calculations might be:

- It is clearly more likely than not that the case will be won. The best case scenario is that the claimant would get damages of £70,000 with no finding of contributory negligence. His costs after trial will be £20,000, and he would be likely to get about £18,000 reimbursed after assessment. Thus the most attractive outcome is getting a payment of £88,000, which will leave the claimant with £68,000 due to partly unrecovered costs. This may make litigation look attractive, but it is the most favourable rather than the most likely outcome.
- At the other end of the scale, the worst case scenario is that there is a 30% chance that the case will be lost at trial. With weaknesses in the evidence this risk must be taken seriously. If the claimant lost there would be no recovery of damages, and the claimant would bear costs that would by then be £20,000. In addition the claimant would have to pay the defendant's costs, which would by then be £18,000, of which the claimant might have to pay £16,000 after assessment. This would leave the claimant £36,000 out of pocket.
- Depending on the details of the case, a reasonable mid range outcome might be that the claimant would win, but might get only £60,000 in damages, with a finding of 20% contributory negligence. This would provide a payment of £48,000, plus costs.

4.74   The defendant's calculations might be:

- There is a 30% chance the claimant will not win. If the claimant does lose at trial the defendant will not have to pay damages. The claimant will have to pay his reasonable costs, so he will only be out of pocket to the extent his costs are not reimbursed. This is the defendant's best case scenario.
- Even if the claimant wins at trial he may only get damages £50,000, less 25% for contributory negligence, which is £37,250, though the defendant would have to pay the claimant's costs (say £18,000 on assessment) as well as his own (£18,000), a total of £36,000.
- The worst case scenario is that the defendant loses at trial and has to pay the claimant £70,000 in damages. With costs this would be a total payment of £106,000 in all.

4.75   Possible options as regards dispute resolution and costs are:

- Proceedings are issued and the case goes to trial. This holds some attraction for each side because it might achieve their own best case outcome. However there is significant risk that their best case outcome will not be achieved. This option will incur £20,000 extra in costs, and total costs will then be £38,000 against a maximum claim of £70,000.
- Either side might make a Part 36 offer. This will potentially protect their position as regards costs not yet incurred. The offer should be pitched to give away as little as possible, but

should be sufficient for the other side to consider it. The defendant might offer £37,250 on this basis. The claimant might not be prepared to accept less than £60,000 on a Part 36 basis.

- The parties might instruct their lawyers to negotiate, exploring the ground between their potential Part 36 positions. This might work, but if one or both parties are still primarily focussed on their best case scenario the lawyers may not be given sufficient scope within their instructions to reach a settlement.
- The parties might use mediation. Mediation could probably be completed within a day with a total cost of perhaps £6,000. The mediator would objectively help the parties to look at the strength and weaknesses of their cases, and the sort of financial risk assessment outlined above. This might lead to settlement, or it might help the parties to refine their Part 36 offer, or to limit the issues to be pursued in litigation, thus reducing the future costs of litigation.

KEY POINTS SUMMARY

- Costs are a major motivation for undertaking ADR, but the costs position can be quite **4.76** complex. The separate elements of costs must all be considered.
- The Review of Civil Litigation Costs carried out by Lord Justice Jackson and reporting in December 2009 has recommended that ADR has a vital role to play in reducing the costs of civil disputes.
- Although a process like arbitration can be expensive, most ADR processes are relatively inexpensive, and information on costs is quite easily available from ADR providers.
- The basis on which a party is funded is relevant, and the implications of CFA, LSC and third party funding must all be taken into account where appropriate in an ADR process.
- While it is possible to estimate the likely cost of litigation or of ADR in a case it is not easy to make comparisons because a case may move between litigation and ADR, and because the burden of costs may shift.
- It is important for the lawyer to make an overall analysis of the financial position and risks to assist the client in taking an informed decision about litigation and ADR options.
- Costs must always be considered as part of any ADR process, and should be built into a mediation or arbitration agreement, and be part of a negotiated or mediated settlement.

PART 2

THE INTERPLAY BETWEEN ADR, CPR AND LITIGATION

5

THE APPROACH OF THE COURTS TO ADR

THE HISTORICAL BACKGROUND TO THE CPR................5.01

THE COURT GUIDES......................................5.07

PRE-ACTION PROTOCOLS 5.18

THE OVERRIDING OBJECTIVE AND ADR.....................5.33

ACTIVE CASE MANAGEMENT AND ADR 5.34

CASE MANAGEMENT POWERS AND ADR 5.38

ALLOCATION STAGE QUESTIONNAIRES AND ADR.............5.40

GRANTING STAYS FOR ADR.............................5.44

JUDICIAL ENCOURAGEMENT OF ADR 5.49

THE APPROACH OF THE COURTS TO CONTRACTUAL ADR CLAUSES..5.51

COURT MEDIATION AND EARLY NEUTRAL EVALUATION SCHEMES ..5.58

CAN THE COURT COMPEL THE PARTIES TO USE ADR?..........5.59

KEY POINTS SUMMARY.................................5.66

THE HISTORICAL BACKGROUND TO THE CPR

ADR has grown at a rapid rate in the last 20 years, initially mainly in America and Australia, **5.01** but then also in the UK and throughout Europe as a direct response to the cost and delay that was a main criticism of litigation systems. Several comprehensive empirical studies carried out in the USA showed that those who used ADR processes enjoyed substantial savings in costs in comparison to those incurred in litigation, a speedier resolution of the dispute and a more satisfactory outcome for the parties. The historical background to ADR is set out in more detail in Chapter 1.

5.02 In the UK, although the Supreme Court Rules and the County Court Rules (the predecessors to the Civil Procedure Rules) did not promote ADR, the courts started to do so from about the mid 1990s onwards. The Commercial Court and the High Court required lawyers to consider with their clients the possibility of resolving the dispute by mediation, conciliation or otherwise and to ensure that parties were fully informed as to the most cost-effective means of resolving their dispute (*Practice Note: Commercial Court: Alternative Dispute Resolution* [1994] 1 All ER 34; *Practice Note (Civil Litigation: Case Management* [1995] 1 All ER 385).

5.03 However the main growth in ADR in recent years has occurred as a direct result of the Woolf Reforms and the introduction of the Civil Procedure Rules 1998 on 26 April 1999.

5.04 In the final Access to Justice Report of 1996, Lord Woolf regarded delay and expense as the twin scourges of the civil justice system. One of his aims was to encourage a less adversarial approach to litigation by encouraging co-operation between the parties and the ethos that litigation should be seen as the last and not the first resort in the attempt to settle a dispute. Parties should settle their dispute before resorting to the courts wherever possible. Where litigation could not be avoided, then the parties should attempt to settle their dispute at the earliest possible stage in the litigation.

5.05 The Woolf reforms placed ADR at the centre of the civil justice system and the spirit of the CPR is that ADR should be the primary method for resolving a dispute, with litigation the last resort. It is therefore not surprising that since the CPR came into force there has been a marked increase in the use of ADR processes, particularly mediation, both before and after issue of proceedings. There has been a corresponding increase in the number of ADR service providers and the number of lawyers being trained as mediators.

5.06 The encouragement to parties to use ADR to resolve their dispute comes from a variety of means:

- court guides;
- pre-action protocols;
- the court's inquiry at track allocation stage whether ADR could be employed;
- case management ADR orders;
- the court's willingness to grant a stay for ADR to be considered and used;
- judicial encouragement for ADR as developed in case law;
- the willingness of the courts to uphold and enforce ADR clauses in a contract;
- the Government's pledge to use ADR to resolve disputes where it is appropriate to do so;
- the court's willingness to make adverse costs orders or other sanctions against a party who unreasonably refuses to consider ADR (considered in Chapter 6);
- the promotion of court mediation schemes (considered in Chapter 14).

THE COURT GUIDES

5.07 There are a number of specialist court guides, each of which contains guidance relating to the use of ADR. The main guides are as follows:

- *The Admiralty and Commercial Courts Guide* (8th edn, 2009);

- *The Chancery Guide* (October 2009, amended April 2010);
- *The Queen's Bench Division Guide* (2007);
- *The Technology and Construction Court Guide* (2nd edn, revised October 2010).

The Admiralty and Commercial Courts Guide

Section G of the *Guide* encourages the parties to consider the use of ADR to resolve their dispute or issues within it. It requires legal representatives to consider with their clients and the other parties involved whether their dispute, or particular issues in it, could be resolved through ADR (para G1.4). Parties who want to consider ADR can apply to the court for directions at any stage, including before service of the defence and before the case management conference (para G1.5). At any case management conference, the judge can invite the parties to use ADR, and he may adjourn the case for a specified period of time to encourage and enable the parties to use ADR and, in doing so, he may extend the time for the parties to comply with any requirement under the Civil Procedure Rules, the *Guide*, or any order of the court. If the court makes an order providing for ADR, it will also consider at which point in the timetable there should be compliance with it. For that purpose it will take into account the likely costs of litigation and ADR and whether the ADR process is likely to be more successful if there has been completion of statements of case, disclosure of documents and exchange of witness statements and expert evidence (paras G1.6 and G1.7). The court will usually make an order in the form set out in Appendix 7 of the *Guide* (see Figure 5.1 below). This order has also been followed in other courts. **5.08**

At a case management conference the court may consider that an order directed to encouraging bilateral negotiations between the parties' respective legal representatives is likely to be a more cost-effective and productive route to settlement than that afforded by a formal ADR or early neutral evaluation (ENE) order (see Chapter 17 for ENE). If so, the court will set a date by which there is to be a meeting between the respective solicitors and their respective clients' officials responsible for decision making in relation to the case (see para G1.12). **5.09**

An example of an ADR order in the Commercial Court is set out in Figure 5.1 below. **5.10**

The Chancery Guide

The Chancery Division of the High Court similarly encourages the parties to use ADR to resolve their dispute (see *The Chancery Guide*, Chapter 17). The judge or master at any case management conference will usually inquire about steps that can usefully be taken to resolve the dispute by settlement negotiations, ADR or other means. The parties should be in a position to tell the court what steps have been taken or are proposed to be taken (para 17.3). Like the Commercial Court, the Chancery Court will extend the time for compliance with the CPR, or court orders to enable ADR to be attempted. **5.11**

Figure 5.2 shows a typical ADR order that may be made in the Chancery Division. **5.12**

The Queen's Bench Guide

This is in much the same terms as *The Chancery Guide* (see para 6.6 of the *Guide*). Paragraph 6.6.3 informs the parties that information concerning ADR can be obtained from the National Mediation Helpline (see Chapter 14). The National Mediation Helpline is a scheme **5.13**

Figure 5.1 An example of an ADR order in the Commercial Court

IN THE HIGH COURT OF JUSTICE   2010 Folio 276
COMMERCIAL COURT

BETWEEN

BEELER ENGINEERING PAGE PLC

<u>Claimant</u>

and

GREEN AND MORROW LIMITED

<u>Defendant</u>

IT IS ORDERED THAT:

1. On or before 4th October 2010, the parties shall exchange lists of 3 neutrals or individuals who are available to conduct ADR procedures before 14th November 2010.
2. On or before 11th October 2010 the parties shall in good faith endeavour to agree a neutral individual or panel from the lists so exchanged and provided.
3. Failing such agreement by 4pm on 18th October 2010 the Case Management Conference will be restored to enable the Court to facilitate agreement on a neutral individual or panel.
4. The parties shall take such serious steps as they may be advised to resolve their disputes by ADR procedures before the neutral individual or panel so chosen by no later than 4 pm on 14th November 2010.
5. If the case is not settled by 19th November 2010, the parties shall inform the court by letter by 27th November 2010 what steps towards ADR have been taken and (without prejudice to matters of privilege) why such steps have failed. If the parties have failed to initiate ADR procedures the Case Management Conference is to be restored for further consideration of the case.

Dated 22nd September 2010.

that was set up by the Ministry of Justice in conjunction with the Civil Mediation Council (CMC) to give court users ease of access to an ADR provider for the resolution of disputes by mediation.

The Technology and Construction Court Guide

5.14   *The Technology and Construction Court Guide* also encourages the parties to use ADR. The court will, wherever appropriate, facilitate the use of ADR. Legal representatives must ensure that clients are fully aware of the benefits of ADR and that the use of ADR has been carefully considered with them prior to the first case management conference (para 7.1.3). ADR may be appropriate before proceedings are issued or at any subsequent stage (para 7.2.1).

5.15   At the first case management conference, the court will want to be addressed on the likely efficacy of ADR, the timing of it, and whether a short stay of proceedings should take place. Having considered the representations of the parties, the court may order a short stay to facilitate ADR at that stage. Alternatively, the court may simply encourage the parties to use ADR without imposing a stay of proceedings (para 7.2.3). At any stage after the first case

Figure 5.2 A typical ADR order that may be made in the Chancery Division

IN THE HIGH COURT OF JUSTICE   2010 HC 1276
CHANCERY DIVISION

BETWEEN

TIMOTHY SMALL

Claimant

and

PRICE WATCH PROPERTIES LIMITED

Defendant

IT IS ORDERED THAT:

(1) This claim be stayed for a period of one month until 6th December 2010 for the parties to try to settle the dispute by alternative dispute resolution or other means.
(2) The parties shall notify the Court in writing at the end of that period whether settlement has been reached. The parties shall at the same time lodge either:
    (a) (if settlement has been reached) a draft Consent Order signed by all the parties; or
    (b) (if no settlement has been reached) a statement of agreed directions signed by all the parties or (in the absence of agreed directions) statements of the parties' respective proposed directions.

Dated 1st November 2010

management conference and prior to the commencement of the trial, the court will, either on its own initiative, or if requested to do so by one or both of the parties, consider afresh the likely efficacy of ADR and whether or not a short stay of the proceedings should be granted to facilitate ADR (para 7.2.4). The court may make an ADR order at any stage of the proceedings in the terms of Appendix E. If such an order is made at the first case management conference the court may go on to give directions for the conduct of the claim up to trial (in the event that ADR fails). Such directions may include provision for a further case management conference to take place (para 7.3.2).

The usual ADR order will provide for the parties to agree on the identity of the mediator or other neutral person. If they do not, the court will usually select such a person from the lists provided by the parties. To facilitate this process, the court would also need to be provided with the CVs of each of the individuals on the lists.   **5.16**

If an ADR order has been made, the court will expect each party to co-operate fully with each other in making arrangements for the process, otherwise cost orders or other sanctions may be ordered against the party in default (para 7.4.2).   **5.17**

PRE-ACTION PROTOCOLS

Under the CPR, protocols were introduced to set out the steps that the parties should follow before issuing proceedings, as part of reasonable pre-action conduct. These marked a very significant change in the culture that had prevailed in litigation prior to the CPR.   **5.18**

5.19 There are currently 11 specific protocols relating to personal injury claims, road traffic accidents, disease and illness claim, clinical negligence, housing disrepair, defamation, judicial review, professional negligence, construction and engineering disputes, possession claims based on rent arrears, and possession claims in respect of mortgage arrears in residential properties. There is also an over-arching *Practice Direction Pre-Action Conduct* that applies in all cases, including those that have no specific protocol.

Practice Direction Pre-Action Conduct

5.20 The aims of the Practice Direction Pre-Action Conduct are to enable parties to settle disputes without the need to start proceedings, and to enable proceedings to be efficiently managed by the court and the parties if litigation cannot be avoided. These aims are achieved by encouraging the parties to exchange information and consider using ADR (see para 1.1).

In cases not subject to a particular protocol

5.21 Proceedings should only be started as a matter of last resort, and they should not be commenced if a settlement is still being actively explored. Although ADR is not compulsory, the parties should consider whether some form of ADR process should be used before starting proceedings, and the court may require evidence that the parties considered ADR (PD Pre-Action Conduct, para 8.1). ADR procedures can include negotiation and discussion, mediation, early neutral evaluation or arbitration. The parties should also explore settlement at all times, even after proceedings have been issued, and up to and during any trial or final hearing (para 8.4).

5.22 Unless the circumstances make it inappropriate (eg because the limitation period is about to expire), the parties should exchange sufficient information about the matters in dispute to enable them to understand each other's position and make informed decisions about settlement and how to proceed. They should also make appropriate attempts to resolve the matter without commencing proceedings, and in particular consider the use of an appropriate ADR process in order to do so (para 6.1).

5.23 Before starting proceedings, the claimant should send the defendant a detailed letter before claim and the defendant should send the claimant a detailed response (paras 7.1 and 7.2). The letter before claim and the defendant's response should contain the information set out in Annex A in respect of the substantive issues in the claim, and should set out the form of ADR that the claimant considers suitable and invite the defendant to agree to this (Annex A, para 2.2(2)). As well as dealing with the substantive claim, the defendant's response should indicate whether the defendant agrees to the claimant's proposals for ADR and, if not, it should state why not, and suggest an alternative form of ADR or give reasons why ADR is not appropriate (Annex A, para 4.3(4)).

5.24 The court will expect the parties to comply with the Practice Direction and any applicable protocol, and may ask them to explain what steps have been taken prior to the start of the claim. Where a party has failed to comply, the court may ask that party for an explanation (para 4.2).

In all cases

5.25 The claimant is required to state in the claim form or the particulars of claim whether he has complied with the requirements of the Practice Direction Pre-Action Conduct and any relevant protocol (para 9.7). The defendant will have to admit or deny this statement in the defence (he cannot require the claimant to prove it because it will be within the defendant's knowledge whether there was compliance or not). This therefore makes the reasonableness of the pre-action conduct one of the issues in the case that the court will consider in making case management directions, orders about costs and other sanctions for non-compliance (see Chapter 6).

The pre-action protocols

The general position

All of the protocols have the same common purpose, which is to: **5.26**

- encourage pre-action conduct between the parties;
- encourage the early exchange of information about the issues in dispute;
- encourage the parties to use ADR processes to settle the dispute before proceedings are issued; and
- enable proceedings to run to timetable and efficiently if litigation cannot be avoided.

Although the precise detail varies a little from protocol to protocol, all of them have the **5.27** same general requirements in relation to the substantive dispute. The relevant protocol should be consulted for details of precise requirements in each case. In general terms:

- The claimant should give early notification of the claim to the defendant.
- The claimant should send the defendant a detailed letter before claim before issuing proceedings, which gives sufficient information to the defendant to enable him to assess liability and quantum.
- The defendant should be given a reasonable time to investigate the claim and respond (this can range from 7 days to three months or perhaps more in complex claims).
- The defendant should send a detailed letter of response, indicating whether liability is in dispute.
- The parties should give early disclosure of relevant documents.
- They should co-operate by jointly selecting (or jointly instructing) experts.

All of the protocols encourage the use of ADR. All of them require the parties to consider **5.28** whether some form of ADR would be more suitable than litigation and, if so, endeavour to agree which form to adopt. The parties may be required to provide evidence that ADR was considered, and that if the terms of the relevant protocol are not followed, the court will have regard to this conduct when determining costs. However all of the protocols recognise that no party can be forced to mediate or enter into any form of ADR.

The Pre-action Protocol for Construction and Engineering Disputes

Although this Protocol has the same general aims of all of the others, it is unique in requiring **5.29** the parties to have a pre-action meeting within 28 days of receipt of the defendant's letter of response (or, where there is a counterclaim, within 28 days of the claimant's response to the counterclaim) (para 5.1). The aim of the meeting is for the parties to agree the main issues in the case, to identify the cause of disagreement in respect of each issue, to consider how the issues might be resolved without litigation and, if litigation is unavoidable, how it can be conducted in accordance with the overriding objective (see 5.33 below for the meaning of the overriding objective). In such cases there may be a need for more than one meeting.

5.30 The court will normally expect the meeting to be attended by the parties, representatives who have authority to settle the dispute, legal representatives, a representative of insurers and a representative of any relevant third parties (such as sub-contractors) (para 5.3). Any party who attended a pre-action meeting is at liberty to disclose to the court:

- the fact that the meeting took place;
- when and who attended the meeting;
- the identity of anyone who refused to attend and the grounds for the refusal;
- reasons why the meeting did not take place (if that was the case);
- any agreement reached between the parties; and
- whether any form of ADR was considered or agreed.

5.31 Otherwise the pre-action meeting is to be regarded as 'without prejudice' (paras 5.6 and 5.7).

Family proceedings

5.32 In ancillary relief proceedings in family cases, solicitors are required to consider and keep under review whether it would be appropriate to suggest mediation in the proceedings (Practice Direction (Family Proceedings: ancillary relief) [2000] 3 All ER 379).

THE OVERRIDING OBJECTIVE AND ADR

5.33 The fundamental overriding objective of the CPR is set out in CPR 1.1, which provides that the CPR are a new procedural code with the overriding objective of dealing with cases justly. CPR 1.1(2) provides:

'Dealing with a case justly includes, so far as practicable:

(a) ensuring that the parties are on an equal footing;

(b) saving expense;

(c) dealing with cases in ways which are proportionate to the amount of money involved, the importance of the case, the complexity of the issues and to the parties' financial position;

(d) ensuring that it is dealt with expeditiously and fairly;

(e) allotting to it an appropriate share of the court's resources.'

ACTIVE CASE MANAGEMENT AND ADR

5.34 The CPR are a new procedural code with the overriding objective of enabling a court to deal with a case justly. Dealing with a case justly includes, so far as is practicable (CPR 1.1):

(a) ensuring that the parties are on an equal footing;

(b) saving expense;

(c) dealing with the case in ways that are proportionate to the amount of money involved, the importance of the case, the complexity of the issues and the financial position of each party;

(d) ensuring it is dealt with expeditiously and fairly; and

(e) allotting to it an appropriate share of the court's resources, while taking into account the need to allot resources to other cases.

The court is required to further the overriding objective by actively managing cases (CPR 1.4(1)). This, in effect, moved control of the pace and form of litigation from the parties to the court. In furthering the overriding objective, the court can and will encourage the parties to use ADR methods to resolve the dispute. **5.35**

Active case management includes (CPR 1.4(2)): **5.36**

(a) encouraging the parties to co-operate with each other in the conduct of the proceedings;
(b) identifying the issues at an early stage;
(c) deciding promptly which issues need full investigation and trial and accordingly disposing summarily of others;
(d) deciding the order in which issues are resolved;
(e) encouraging parties to use an ADR procedure if the court considers that appropriate and facilitating the use of such procedure;
(f) helping the parties to settle the whole or part of a case;
(g) fixing timetables or otherwise controlling the progress of the case;
(h) considering whether the likely benefits of taking a particular step will justify the cost of taking it;
(i) dealing with as many aspects of the case as it can on the same occasion;
(j) dealing with the case without the parties needing to attend court;
(k) making appropriate use of technology; and
(l) giving directions to ensure that the trial of a case proceeds quickly and efficiently.

The parties and their lawyers are also under a duty to assist the court further the overriding objective (CPR 1.3). **5.37**

CASE MANAGEMENT POWERS AND ADR

The court can also direct the parties to consider ADR at a case management conference or pre-trial review. Such an order can also be made at any case management conference attended by the parties. The Court of Appeal approved the use of such an order in *Halsey v Milton Keynes General NHS Trust* [2004] 1 WLR 3002 at para 32, describing the Commercial Court order (see Figure 5.1 above) as the strongest form of encouragement, but falling short of compulsion. **5.38**

An order (referred to as the Ungley Order, after Master Ungley) may also be made in the form set out in Figure 5.3 (see PD 29 para 4.10(9)): **5.39**

ALLOCATION STAGE QUESTIONNAIRES AND ADR

Cases proceeding in the courts will be allocated to one of three tracks: the small claims track, the fast track, or the multi-track, depending on the value of the claim or any counterclaim or additional claim, the nature of the remedy sought, the complexity of the issues in dispute, the number of parties, the importance of the case and the circumstances of the parties (see CPR 28.6). **5.40**

Figure 5.3 The Ungley Order

IN THE HIGH COURT OF JUSTICE　　　　　　　　　　　　　　　2010 HC 1276
CHANCERY DIVISION

BETWEEN

JOHN SMITH

Claimant

and

LEAKE CONSTRUCTION LIMITED

Defendant

IT IS ORDERED THAT:

1. The parties shall by 20th December 2010, consider whether the case is capable of resolution by ADR.
2. If any party considers that the case is unsuitable for ADR, that party shall be prepared to justify that decision at the conclusion of the trial, should the trial judge consider that such means of resolution were appropriate, when he is considering the appropriate costs order to make.
3. The party considering the case unsuitable for ADR shall, not less than 28 days before the commencement of trial, file with the court a witness statement, without prejudice save as to costs, giving the reasons upon which they rely for saying that the case was unsuitable.

Dated 1st December 2010

5.41　　When the defendant files a defence, the court will serve an allocation questionnaire on the parties, which each party must complete and return to the court within 14 days of the date on which it was deemed to be served on them (CPR 26.3). The allocation questionnaire will ask the parties, among other things, whether they are willing to settle the dispute by other means and whether they wish to request a stay of proceedings for ADR to be attempted. If they do not, they are asked to explain the reasons why ADR or a stay is not appropriate. The court can also order a stay on its own initiative (see 5.44–5.48 below for more detail on stays).

5.42　　The court does not have to accept the reasons put forward by any of the parties for refusing to consider ADR at this stage. If the court considers those reasons to be weak or inadequate, it will direct the parties to attend an allocation hearing, to consider whether ADR should be attempted. In *Kinstreet Ltd v Balmargo Corporation Ltd* [2000] CP Rep 62, the court directed the parties to attempt ADR even though one party objected to this, because the costs of going to trial would exceed the amount claimed. In *Shirayama Shokusan Co Ltd v Danovo Ltd (No 1)* [2003] EWHC 3306 (Ch) the defendant sought an order for mediation in the terms of the Commercial Court ADR order (see Figure 5.1 above). The claimant resisted the application on the grounds that the court did not have jurisdiction to order mediation where one party was unwilling to mediate and, in any event, since the defendant had made allegations that the claimant was dishonest, mediation stood little chance of success. Blackburne J held, granting the application, that the court did have jurisdiction to order mediation irrespective of one party being unwilling to mediate and that a mediation order was in accordance with the overriding objective. He relied on the fact that the court had ordered that the parties attempt mediation, even in face of objections from one party, in *Guinle v Kirreh* [2000] CP Rep 62, and *Muman v Nagasena* [2000] 1 WLR 299. *Shirayama* was cited in the skeleton arguments in *Halsey v Milton Keynes General NHS Trust* [2004] 1 WLR 3002 and, although it was not considered in the judgments of the court in *Halsey*, it is still good law, as the order was made in the form set out in Figure 5.1 and this form of order was approved in *Halsey*.

The court can therefore critically review the reasons put forward by the party for their contention that ADR was not appropriate or a stay should not be granted to attempt it. If those reasons are plainly inadequate or ill-founded, the court may direct the parties to consider ADR, and grant a stay of its own motion, at the track allocation stage or at any other time, for ADR to be considered but it will stop short of actually compelling them to undertake ADR (see 5.59–5.65). **5.43**

GRANTING STAYS FOR ADR

The court's general powers of management include the power to make orders staying the whole or part of any proceedings until a specified date or event (CPR 3.1(f)). Any such stay will usually be for a period of one month although the court has power to extend this period. If the court has stayed proceedings at track allocation stage, then the case will not be allocated to the appropriate track until the end of that period (CPR 26.4 and 26.5). A stay operates to suspend the directions that the court has made or the steps that the parties would be required to take in relation to the proceedings. **5.44**

A stay will be sensible so that the parties are spared the expense of complying with the procedural timetable and case management orders (such as disclosure of documents and exchange of witness statements). A stay therefore enables an ADR process to be explored litigation while, is suspended avoiding a party having to prepare for the ADR process and the various stages of the litigation process at the same time. **5.45**

A stay can be ordered at track allocation stage (see 5.40 above) or at any stage of the proceedings, and on the application by one or both parties, or by the court of its own motion. The courts have also been willing to grant a stay to enforce an ADR clause in the underlying contract between the parties (see 5.51–5.57). **5.46**

If a stay is granted for ADR to be attempted, the parties must keep the court informed about the outcome of the ADR process. If it results in settlement, the parties will probably wish to lodge a settlement order with the court (see Chapter 20). If no settlement is reached during the ADR process, then the claimant will need to apply to the court to get the stay lifted (if it has not expired) and for any further relevant directions so that the litigation can proceed. **5.47**

An example of an order granting a stay is set out in Figure 5.4 below. **5.48**

JUDICIAL ENCOURAGEMENT OF ADR

The courts have repeatedly encouraged the parties to use ADR. **5.49**

- In *Dyson v Leeds City Council* [2000] CP Rep 42, in a claim brought by executors against an employer for causing death from mesothelioma due to exposure to asbestos, Lord Woolf stated [at 16]: '...this is pre-eminently the category of case in which, consistent with the overriding objective of the Civil Procedure Rules and the court's duty to manage cases as

Figure 5.4 An example of an order granting a stay

IN THE HIGH COURT OF JUSTICE   2010 HC 2745
QUEEN'S BENCH DIVISION

BETWEEN

JOHN BULL LIMITED

<u>Claimant</u>

and

PALM OIL PRODUCTS LIMITED

<u>Defendant</u>

IT IS ORDERED THAT:

1. These proceedings be stayed until Friday 22nd October 2010 to enable the parties to continue to complete the requirements of the pre-action protocol, and thereafter to consider and adopt any appropriate course of alternative dispute resolution to include but not necessarily limited to mediation.
2. Either party shall have permission to apply for the stay to be lifted and request the court to fix the case management conference on the first available date with a time estimate of 30 minutes.
3. The parties to notify the court by 22nd October whether the action has settled.
4. If the action has not settled by 22nd October 2010, then the Case Management Conference be restored for hearing at 2 pm on 29th October 2010.
5. Costs in the case.

Dated 10th September 2010

set out in r.1.4 (2) (e), we should encourage the parties to use an alternative dispute resolution procedure to bring this unhappy matter to the conclusion it now deserves sooner than later'.

- In *Cowl v Plymouth City Council* [2002] 1 WLR 803, an appeal was brought by the claimant against the refusal of his application for judicial review of the council's decision to close the residential home in which he was a resident. The council was willing to deal with the matter by a statutory complaints procedure. The claimant contended that this was an inadequate alternative to judicial review. In dismissing the appeal, the court held that it was of paramount importance that litigation should be avoided in disputes between public authorities and members of the public wherever possible. The courts should use their powers under the CPR to ensure that such disputes were resolved with the minimum of judicial intervention. To this end, an inter-partes hearing might be required to establish whether a complaints procedure or other form of ADR could be used. Judges could question the parties as to the steps taken to avoid litigation, including requiring them to justify their decision not to embark on ADR. The court should not permit, except for good reason, proceedings for judicial review to continue if a significant number of the issues between the parties could be resolved outside the litigation process. Lord Woolf gave strong encouragement to parties to use ADR to resolve disputes between public authorities and members of the public (at [1] and [25]):

'The importance of this appeal is that it illustrates that, even in disputes between public authorities and the members of the public for whom they are responsible, insufficient attention is paid to the paramount importance of avoiding litigation whenever this is possible. Particularly in the case of these disputes both sides must by now be acutely conscious of the contribution alternative dispute resolution can make to resolving disputes in a manner which both meets the needs of the parties and the public and saves time, expense and stress.'

'Today, sufficient should be known about alternative dispute resolution to make the failure to adopt it, in particular when public money is involved, indefensible'.

- In *Burchell v Bullard* [2005] BLR 330 at para 43, Ward LJ commented on '...not only the high rate of a successful outcome being achieved by mediation but also its importance as a track to a just result running parallel with that of the court system. Both have a proper part to play in the administration of justice. The court has given its stamp of approval to mediation and it is now the legal profession which must become fully aware of and acknowledge its value.'
- The court has recognised the success of mediation at an early stage of the dispute. In *Egan v Motor Services (Bath) Ltd* [2008] 1 WLR 1589, per Ward LJ stated:

'Mediation can do more for the parties than negotiation. In this case the sheer commercial folly could have been amply demonstrated to both parties sitting at the same table but hearing it from somebody who is independent. The cost of such mediation would be paltry compared with the costs that would mount from the moment of the issue of the claim. In so many cases, and this is just another example of one, the best time to mediate is before the litigation begins. It is not a sign of weakness to suggest it. It is the hallmark of commonsense. Mediation is a perfectly proper adjunct to litigation. The skills are now well developed. The results are astonishingly good.

The typical stages of a claim at which ADR may be attempted are shown in Figure 5.5. **5.50**

THE APPROACH OF THE COURTS TO CONTRACTUAL ADR CLAUSES

The court will give effect to ADR by upholding and enforcing ADR clauses. An ADR clause is **5.51** a clause in a contract by which the parties agree to resolve their dispute primarily by ADR. The clause may define a particular ADR method which should be used, such as mediation, or it may specify a number of methods that need to be exhausted in turn before litigation can be commenced or continued. If an adjudicative form of ADR procedure is specified by the clause (such as expert determination, adjudication, or arbitration), the clause may also specify that the parties are to be bound by the decision. Such clauses are becoming increasingly common, particularly in contracts for services, insurance contracts and construction contracts. Some examples of ADR clauses are set out below:

'Any dispute, question or difference of any nature arising under or contained in or arising out of or in connection with this contract, or as to the rights, duties or liabilities under it of the parties shall, in the first instance, be submitted to adjudication in accordance with the Association of Independent Construction Adjudicators (AICA) adjudication rules and thereafter to the exclusive jurisdiction of the English Courts. If the parties fail to agree on the identity of the adjudicator within five days of the dispute, question or difference arising, the adjudicator shall be appointed by the AICA.'

'The parties shall attempt in good faith to resolve any dispute or claim arising out of or in connection with this Agreement through negotiations between the Managing Directors of each Party. If any dispute is not settled through negotiation, then the Parties shall attempt in good faith to resolve the dispute or claim by an Alternative Dispute Resolution procedure agreed

Figure 5.5 The typical stages of a claim at which ADR may be attempted

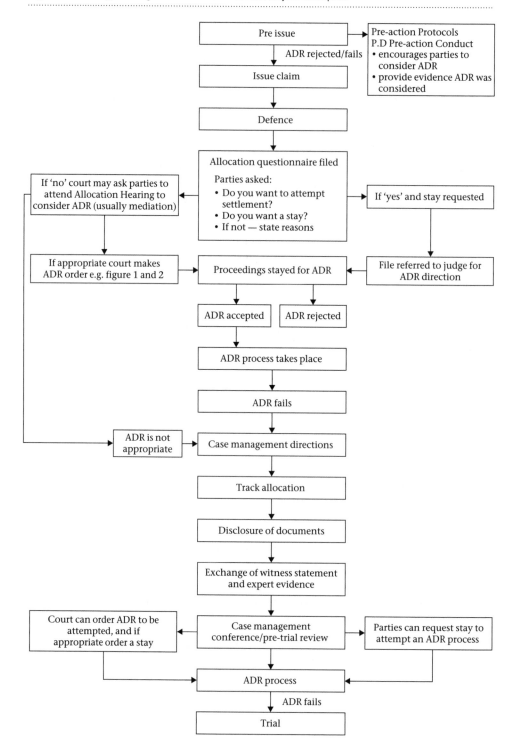

by both parties, and in default of agreement as recommended to the parties by the Centre for Effective Dispute Resolution, before court proceedings are issued to resolve the dispute.'

If the parties have agreed on a particular method by which their disputes are to be resolved, then the court has an inherent discretionary power to stay proceedings brought in breach of that agreement and require the parties to pursue the dispute resolution process that they agreed to use. The court will give effect to ADR clauses regardless of the type of ADR process that the parties have agreed to use.

In exercising its discretion to enforce such clauses by staying proceedings commenced in breach of the clause, the court may consider the following factors (*DGT Steel & Cladding Ltd v Cubitt Building & Interiors Ltd* [2007] BLR 371):   **5.52**

- the extent to which the parties had complied with the requirements in any pre-action protocol;
- whether the dispute is suitable for determination by the agreed ADR process;
- the costs of that ADR process compared to the costs of litigation;
- whether a stay would accord with the overriding objective.

The courts have enforced ADR clauses and stayed litigation commenced before the agreed ADR process had been utilised in *Channel Tunnel Group Ltd v Balfour Beatty Construction Ltd* [1993] AC 334 (where the ADR process agreed upon was expert determination); *Cape Durasteel Ltd v Rosser & Russell Building Services Ltd* [1995] 46 Con LR 75; *Herschel Engineering Ltd v Breen Property Ltd* [2000] 70 Con LR 1; and *DGT Steel & Cladding Ltd v Cubitt Building & Interiors Ltd* [2007] BLR 371 (adjudication).   **5.53**

ADR clauses need to be drafted carefully. The procedure set out in the contract must be clear and unambiguous in order to be enforceable. If it is not, the court will decline to enforce the clause (*Cott UK Ltd v FE Barber Ltd* [1997] 3 All ER 540).   **5.54**

The court has upheld an ADR clause that provided for no particular agreed method to resolve the dispute. In *Cable and Wireless plc v IBM United Kingdom Ltd* [2002] 2 All ER (Comm) 1041, the clause in the contract provided that: **5.55**

> 'The parties shall attempt in good faith to resolve any dispute or claim arising out of or relating to this Agreement . . . promptly through negotiations between the respective senior executives of the parties . . . . . . If the matter is not resolved through negotiation, the parties shall attempt in good faith to resolve the dispute or claim through an Alternative Dispute Resolution (ADR) procedure as recommended to the parties by the Centre for Dispute Resolution.'

The court held that the procedure envisaged by the contract was sufficiently certain to be enforceable, and granted a stay of proceedings commenced in breach of the clause. It also held that for the courts to decline to enforce contractual references to ADR on the grounds of intrinsic uncertainty would be to fly in the face of public policy as expressed in the CPR.   **5.56**

The courts may also be willing to award damages for breach of an ADR clause (*Union Discount v Zoller* [2002] 1 WLR 1517), and to assess damages on the basis of the amount that would have been awarded by the expert had the contractually agreed dispute resolution procedure been followed (*Sunrock Aircraft Corp Ltd v Scandinavian Airlines System Denmark-Norway-Sweden* [2007] 2 Lloyd's Rep 612).   **5.57**

COURT MEDIATION AND EARLY NEUTRAL EVALUATION SCHEMES

5.58   The courts also encourage the use of ADR by a number of court-based mediation schemes, such as the Small Claims Mediation Scheme and the Court of Appeal Mediation Scheme and the National Mediation Helpline and by early neutral evaluation schemes (see Chapters 14 and 17).

CAN THE COURT COMPEL THE PARTIES TO USE ADR?

5.59   Most ADR processes are entered into by the parties on a voluntary basis in order to reach a faster, more cost-effective or creative settlement of the matters in dispute. The court can encourage the parties to attempt ADR by the various means described in this chapter.

5.60   Although the court can direct that the parties should attempt to resolve the dispute by ADR, it cannot make them use ADR and, if they do so, it cannot make them reach a settlement in the selected ADR process. This was recognised in *Halsey v Milton Keynes General NHS Trust* [2004] 1 WLR 3002. In *Halsey,* the court accepted that to require unwilling parties to mediate would infringe Article 6 of the European Convention on Human Rights by which everyone is entitled to a fair and public hearing within a reasonable time by an independent and impartial tribunal established by law. The Court of Appeal also accepted that mediation is a process that is most effective if it undertaken on a voluntary basis. A court can encourage the parties to engage with ADR, rather than compel them to do so. The Commercial Court order was seen as strongest form of encouragement. If such an ADR order is ignored, then the court could penalise the defaulting party by making an adverse costs order against them. Dyson LJ stated at paras [9], [10]:

> 'We have heard argument on the question whether the court has power to order parties to submit their disputes to mediation against their will. It is one thing to encourage the parties to agree to mediation, even to encourage them in the strongest terms. It is another to order them to do so. It seems to us that to oblige truly unwilling parties to refer their disputes to mediation would be to impose an unacceptable obstruction on their right of access to the court. . . . it seems to us that compulsion of ADR would be regarded as an unacceptable constraint on the right of access to the court and, therefore, a violation of article 6. Even if (contrary to our view) the court does have jurisdiction to order unwilling parties to refer their disputes to mediation, we find it difficult to conceive of circumstances in which it would be appropriate to exercise it.
>
> If the court were to compel parties to enter into a mediation to which they objected, that would achieve nothing except to add to the costs to be borne by the parties, possibly postpone the time when the court determines the dispute and damage the perceived effectiveness of the ADR process. If a judge takes the view that the case is suitable for ADR, then he or she is not, of course, obliged to take at face value the expressed opposition of the parties, In such a case, the judge should explore the reasons for any resistance to ADR. But if the parties (or at least one of them) remain intransigently opposed to ADR, then it would be wrong for the court to compel them to embrace it.'

5.61   Dyson LJ went on to add that the form of encouragement can be robust, and an order set out in the terms of the ADR order made in the Commercial Court in the form set out in Appendix 7 of the *Guide* (see Figure 5.1 above) is the strongest form of encouragement. He noted that this form of order stops short of actually compelling the parties to undertake

ADR. He also added that: 'Nevertheless, a party who, despite such an order, simply refuses to embark on the ADR process at all would run the risk that for that reason alone his refusal to agree to ADR would be held to be unreasonable, and that he should therefore be penalised in costs.'

There are many commentators who consider that *Halsey* is wrongly decided in holding **5.62** that the court could not compel the parties to engage with an ADR process on the basis that it would infringe their Article 6 rights. For example Lightman J in a speech entitled 'Mediation: Approximation to Justice' (28 June 2007) has criticised the decision on the ground that the court failed to differentiate between different ADR processes such as arbitration (which does impose a permanent stay on proceedings) and mediation or negotiation (which does not prevent the parties resolving their dispute by trial). Even if a stay is granted, that simply delays the trial process for a short time. He also points out that a number of other nations, who are signatories to the European Convention on Human Rights, such as Belgium, Greece, and Germany, have compulsory mediation processes.

Support for the view that compulsory ADR orders for mediation would not infringe the **5.63** Article 6 rights of the parties can also be derived from the EU Mediation Directive 2008/52/EC. This recommends that courts in member states should encourage parties to mediate. Article 5 provides that:

'(1) A court before which an action is brought may, when appropriate and having regard to all the circumstances of the case, invite the parties to use mediation in order to settle the dispute. The court may also invite the parties to attend an information session on the use of mediation if such sessions are held and are easily available.

(2) This Directive is without prejudice to national legislation making use of mediation compulsory or subject to incentives or sanctions, whether before or after judicial proceedings have started, provided that such legislation does not prevent the parties from exercising their right of access to the judicial system.'

A breach of Article 6 would occur if a party was denied access to the court if they refused **5.64** to consider mediation (by having their proceedings struck out for that reason alone), but it is difficult to see how a party is denied the right to a fair and public hearing within a reasonable time if they are ordered to engage in a mediation process with the right to continue litigation if that process is unsuccessful. A compulsory order to attempt ADR might not even result in a delay in the trial process because the litigation timetable does not need to be stayed or extended in most cases to accommodate ADR; it is simply practical to do so.

However, at present, the courts can only encourage a party to attempt to resolve their dis- **5.65** pute by ADR, and the strongest form of encouragement lies in the form of order made by the Commercial Court (See Figure 5.1). It cannot actually compel them to engage in an ADR process if they are unwilling to do so. It can however penalise a party in costs if they unreasonably refuse to attempt ADR (see Chapter 6).

KEY POINTS SUMMARY

- Parties are required to consider ADR before proceedings are issued by the protocols and PD **5.66** Pre-action Conduct.
- The courts will actively encourage the parties to attempt to resolve their dispute by an ADR process after proceedings have been issued.

- The parties may request or the court may order a stay for ADR to be attempted at the track allocation stage or at any other time.
- If ADR is not undertaken before issue, then it should be considered at the track allocation stage (when all the statements of case have been filed), and again after exchange of documents, and also when witness statements and expert evidence have been exchanged.
- The court will actively consider whether attempts have been made to settle the dispute by ADR at any case management conference, and may direct the parties to attempt ADR.
- If the parties reject ADR, before issue or at any stage of the litigation, they should have reasonable and cogent reasons for doing so and may be required to explain these reasons to the court.
- The courts will uphold and enforce ADR clauses in contracts.

6

THE SANCTIONS FOR REFUSING TO ENGAGE IN ADR PROCESSES

INTRODUCTION. 6.01

THE COURT'S GENERAL POWERS TO MAKE COSTS ORDERS 6.04

ADVERSE COSTS ORDERS AGAINST A PARTY WHO
UNREASONABLY REFUSES TO CONSIDER ADR. 6.09

REQUESTING FURTHER INFORMATION OR CLARIFICATION
OF THE ISSUES BEFORE ACCEPTING ADR. 6.33

REJECTING ADR BEFORE ISSUE 6.38

FAILING TO INITIATE ADR PROCESSES. 6.40

REJECTING ADR AFTER JUDGMENT AND BEFORE THE HEARING
OF AN APPEAL 6.46

DELAY IN CONSENTING TO MEDIATION (OR ANOTHER
ADR PROCESS). 6.51

PULLING OUT OF MEDIATION (OR ANOTHER ADR PROCESS). 6.52

UNREASONABLE CONDUCT IN THE MEDIATION 6.56

IMPOSING A COSTS CAP ON SOLICITOR–CLIENT COSTS FOR
FAILING TO PURSUE ADR. 6.58

INDEMNITY COSTS ORDERS FOR FAILING TO CONSIDER ADR 6.60

BOTH PARTIES AT FAULT IN FAILING TO CONSIDER ADR 6.64

HOW DOES THE COURT TREAT PRIVILEGED MATERIAL WHEN
SEEKING TO IMPOSE SANCTIONS? 6.65

KEY POINTS SUMMARY. 6.70

INTRODUCTION

6.01 The court can penalise a party who unreasonably refuses to:

- comply with an order made by the court directing the parties to attempt to resolve the dispute by ADR;
- accept an offer made by the other side to attempt to settle the dispute using an ADR process before the issue of proceedings; or
- accept an invitation by the other side to use an ADR process during the course of litigation, or even after judgment and prior to the hearing of an appeal.

6.02 The orders that the court can make include:

- depriving the party of costs even if they are successful in the litigation;
- ordering them to pay some or all of the other side's costs even if they are successful in the litigation;
- ordering them to pay costs on an indemnity basis;
- ordering a higher rate of interest to be paid on damages awarded; or
- depriving a party of interest on damages awarded by the court.

6.03 The most common sanction that is imposed for unreasonably failing to consider or use an ADR process to resolve the dispute is to make an adverse order for costs.

THE COURT'S GENERAL POWERS TO MAKE COSTS ORDERS

6.04 Costs payable by one party to another are in the discretion of the court (Senior Courts Act 1981 s 51). The court has a wide discretion in relation to costs, both in relation to costs orders made on interim applications and costs orders following trial. The court has a discretion whether costs are payable by one party to the other, the amount of those costs and when they are to be paid (CPR 44.3(1)). The usual order is that costs will follow the event (ie the overall loser will pay the overall winner's costs), but the court can make a different order (CPR 44.3(2)).

6.05 In deciding what order to make about costs, the court will have regard to all the circumstances, including the specific factors set out in CPR 44.3(4) namely:

- the conduct of the parties;
- whether a party has succeeded in part of his case, even if he has not been wholly successful; and
- any admissible offer to settle made by a party that is drawn to the court's attention (which is not an offer to which the costs consequences in Part 36 apply).

6.06 In looking at the conduct of the parties, the court will look at the circumstances, including the matters set out in CPR 44.3(5):

- conduct before, as well as during, the proceedings, and in particular the extent to which the parties followed Practice Direction Pre-action Conduct and any relevant pre-action protocol;
- whether it was reasonable for a party to raise, pursue or contest a particular allegation or issue;

- the manner in which a party has pursued or defended his case or a particular allegation or issue; and
- whether a claimant who has succeeded in his claim, in whole or in part, exaggerated his claim.

Costs must also be reasonably incurred and proportionate to the subject-matter of the claim and the amount in dispute (see CPR 44.5). **6.07**

The orders that a court may make include an order that a party must pay (CPR 44.3(6)): **6.08**

- a proportion of another party's costs;
- a stated amount in respect of another party's costs;
- costs from or until a certain date;
- costs incurred before proceedings have begun;
- costs relating to a particular step in the proceedings;
- costs relating to a distinct part of the proceedings; and
- interest on costs from or until a certain date, including a date before judgment.

ADVERSE COSTS ORDERS AGAINST A PARTY WHO UNREASONABLY REFUSES TO CONSIDER ADR

The leading case is *Halsey v Milton Keyne General NHS Trust* [2004] 1 WLR 3002. Although there were many cases that dealt with this issue before *Halsey*, this case is a convenient starting point from which to analyse the cases on this subject. **6.09**

In *Halsey* (which concerned two conjoined appeals), the defendants succeeded at first instance and were awarded the costs of the proceedings. The claimant in each case appealed against the costs order on the basis that the defendant should be deprived of costs for unreasonably refusing mediation. The Court of Appeal dismissed the appeals and held that the general rule that costs follow the event should not be departed from unless it is shown that the successful party acted unreasonably in refusing to agree to ADR. The unsuccessful party bears the burden of proving this. The court also found that the Lord Chancellor's pledge in March 2001 (see 3.12) was simply an undertaking to use ADR in all suitable cases. The court should not discriminate against successful public bodies when deciding whether a refusal to agree to ADR should result in a costs penalty. The court found that the judge in *Royal Bank of Canada v Secretary of State for Defence* [2003] EWHC 1841 (Ch) was wrong to attach great weight to the ADR pledge in making no order for costs in favour of the successful defendant. **6.10**

In the first appeal, the defendant refused to mediate on the grounds that it had a strong defence, the claimant's offers to mediate were tactical and the costs of mediation would be disproportionately high compared to the value of the claim. There had been no ADR order and, in the circumstances, the court accepted that the defendant had not acted unreasonably in refusing to mediate for these reasons. It also found that the claimant had not discharged the burden of proving that the mediation would have had a reasonable prospect of success. **6.11**

In the second appeal, the defendant refused mediation because the issue concerned a point of law that required a decision of the court. Again, in the absence of any court **6.12** encouragement for ADR to be used, the court held that the defendant was not unreasonable in refusing to mediate for this reason.

6.13 In deciding whether the refusal to consider ADR was unreasonable, the court should consider all the circumstances of the case, including the following matters:

The nature of the dispute

6.14 Most cases are not, by their very nature, unsuitable for ADR. However there may be some cases in which ADR may not be suitable because the court is required to determine issues of law or construction, a legal precedent is required from the court, issues involving allegations of fraud or other commercially disreputable conduct may be raised that require resolution at trial, injunctive relief, a search order or a freezing order may be required, a point of law may need to be resolved or the case may be a test case. In such cases, a party will not be acting unreasonably in refusing to use an ADR process.

The merits of the case

6.15 The fact that a party reasonably believes he has a strong case is relevant to the question of whether a refusal of ADR is reasonable, otherwise a claimant could use the threat of a costs sanction to force a settlement in respect of a case lacking merit. The courts will be astute to prevent a party using an offer of mediation as a tactical ploy to obtain a nuisance-value offer from a defendant. If a party reasonably believes he has a very strong case, that may well be a sufficient reason for refusing to mediate (or negotiate), particularly if this is borne out at trial. Dyson LJ in *Halsey v Milton Keynes General NHS Trust* [2004] 1 WLR 3002 rejected the view to the contrary expressed by Lightman J in *Hurst v Leeming* [2003] 1 Lloyd's Rep 379. However if the case is a borderline one, then it is likely to be suitable for ADR, and thus a party is likely to be held to be unreasonable in refusing ADR, unless there are factors that tip the scales the other way.

6.16 In *Daniels v Commissioner of Police for the Metropolis* [2005] EWCA Civ 1312, the Court of Appeal held that if defendants, who routinely face what they consider to be unfounded claims, wish to take a stand and contest them rather than make payments (even nuisance-value payments) to buy them off, the court should be slow to characterise such conduct as unreasonable so as to deprive defendants of their costs, if they are ultimately successful.

6.17 In *Hickman v Blake Lapthorn* [2006] EWHC 12 (QB), it was held that the second defendant (a barrister) was not unreasonable for refusing to mediate on the grounds that he believed that he had a strong case. He also refused to participate in any settlement that provided for the claimant to receive the sum of £150,000 against both defendants plus costs. This was an offer the claimant put forward, and amounted to a significant reduction in the total value of the claim. At trial, the claimant recovered £130,000 (which was split 33:66% against the first and second defendant respectively). Despite finding that (i) the settlement could have been achieved at or close to the £130,000 that the claimant was eventually awarded, (ii) settlement had not occurred due to the second defendant's failure to negotiate or mediate, and (iii) the total costs spent by the parties since the refusal of the claimant's offer was £205,000, the court decided that the second defendant had not acted unreasonably in failing to mediate or negotiate. The second defendant's estimation of the strength of the claimant's case was optimistic but not unreasonable, and it was not unreasonable in light of that estimation to refuse mediation. On the facts, this seems a very surprising decision, and one that it is difficult to justify given the outcome at trial (which was very close to the sum that the claimant indicated he would accept), and the costs that had been expended (£435,000 in total).

The extent to which other settlement methods have been attempted

The court will take into account the fact that settlement offers have already been made, but rejected. However this is unlikely to be a decisive factor in deciding whether a party should be penalised for refusing ADR. Much will depend on the facts of the case. If reasonable offers have been made and rejected, then this may show that one party has an unreasonable view of the merits of their case and that ADR may serve no purpose. However the court will also bear in mind that ADR processes such as mediation may succeed where direct settlement discussions between the parties have failed.   **6.18**

In *Corenso (UK) Ltd v Burnden Group plc* [2003] EWHC 1805 (QB), a defendant made two Part 36 offers, the last of which was made (and accepted by the claimant) less than 21 days before trial. In the usual course of events, the claimant would have been entitled to costs up to the date of acceptance, but the defendant argued that the claimant should pay some or all of the defendant's costs because of its failure to respond to its offers to mediate the dispute. The court rejected this submission holding that a party could properly discharge its obligations to consider ADR and to attempt to engage in it, without necessarily being prepared to enter into mediation, if it took the view that there were other forms of ADR that were more appropriate or more likely to produce a result. Provided the parties showed a genuine and constructive willingness to resolve the issues between them, a party could not be automatically penalised because they did not agree to a form of ADR proposed by the other side. The court could only speculate on whether or not a mediator would have achieved any better or quicker result or could have persuaded the defendant to make the eventual offer at an earlier stage.   **6.19**

However a very robust order was made in *P4 Ltd v Unite Integrated Solutions plc* [2007] BLR 1. The claimant's claim was for £70,000. A number of Part 36 offers were made by the defendant, the last one being for £6,000. The claimant recovered £387 at trial. The defendant sought indemnity costs for the whole period; the claimant submitted there should be no order for costs because the defendant had refused an offer to mediate the dispute before proceedings were issued. The defendant rejected the offers of mediation on the following grounds: **6.20**

• It believed the claim was fundamentally flawed on an issue of law.
• It had made other settlement attempts that had been rejected, including a Part 36 offer of £10,000 within a few days of proceedings being issued. Instead the claimant offered to accept £42,000, then increased its proposal to £50,000, showing that the parties were moving further apart.
• It also considered that mediation would be an expensive exercise bearing in mind the sums at stake.
• Mediation did not have a reasonable prospect of success because neither party was willing to concede ground on the issue of law.

The judge (Ramsey J) did not find these to be cogent reasons for failing to engage in mediation. He did not consider that offers of settlement '…can be a proper substitute for the process of ADR which involves clients engaging with each other and a third party, such as   **6.21** a mediator, to resolve a dispute. In such circumstances, the aspirations of each party are soon brought within realistic bounds and a situation in which one party makes increasingly unrealistic offers is avoided. There was no central engagement in the correspondence on the central issues and concerns which are usually the focus of ADR, through such things as position papers in mediation.' He took the view that mediation would have had a good prospect of success, particularly if, at an early stage, the defendant had provided the claimant with information about a particular payment to a sub-contractor. He held that ordinarily, in light of the small amount recovered by the claimant and its failure on the main issues and the early offers made by the defendant, it would have been a case where the defendant would have been awarded the costs of the claim. However up to the date of its Part 36 offer, the defendant's conduct in failing to mediate and provide information, deprived the parties of being able to resolve the case at minimal cost. The defendant was therefore ordered to pay the claimant's costs up to the latest date for acceptance of the Part 36 offer and the claimant was to pay the defendant's costs after that point.

Whether the costs of ADR would be disproportionately high

6.22   This is a factor that will also be taken into account and may be of particular importance if the sums at stake are relatively small. This is because ADR processes, such as mediation, in such cases may cost as much as a day in court. However this is unlikely to be a significant factor in the vast majority of cases, and certainly not in low value cases in the small claims track, where the court operates a free mediation scheme, nor may it be a relevant factor in many fast track cases where fixed-fee mediations can be arranged through the National Mediation Helpline.

Whether any delay in setting up and attending ADR would be prejudicial

6.23   If an ADR process is proposed at a late stage of the litigation and is likely to result in the trial being delayed, this may be a reason to refuse to agree to it. An example is *Palfrey v Wilson* [2007] EWCA Civ 94, where no adverse costs order was made for refusing mediation that was proposed only two months before trial.

6.24   In *Société Internationale de Télécommunications Aéronautiques SC (SITA) v The Wyatt Co (UK) Ltd* [2002] EWHC 2401 (Ch), the defendant settled the claimant's claim at mediation and failed to recover anything against the third party at trial. The claimant contended the third party should be deprived of its costs as it had refused the defendant's offer, made on three separate occasions, to take part in mediation. The court accepted that the third party was not unreasonable in refusing the defendant's first two offers to take part in mediation for the following reasons:

- The mediation concerned the claim between the claimant and the defendant.
- The third party had insufficient time to prepare for the first mediation round as it had only recently been brought into the claim as a third party.
- The defendant's reasons for suggesting mediation was not to settle the third party claim, but rather to persuade the third party to contribute something to the settlement of the claimant's case.
- The offers to mediate were disagreeable in tone and designed to bully and browbeat the third party into mediation.
- The third party was not likely to be liable (an event which was borne out by the trial).

The third offer to mediate related only to the third party claim, and the court also found   **6.25**
that the third party acted reasonably in refusing this offer because it was made too close
to the trial (which was due to take place three weeks later). The court therefore declined to
make any reduction in the third party's costs.

Whether ADR had a reasonable prospect of success

In *Halsey v Milton Keynes General NHS Trust* [2004] 1 WLR 3002, Dyson LJ stated that if media-   **6.26**
tion (or another ADR process) has been refused on the basis that it would have no reasonable
prospect of success, then the burden is on the unsuccessful party seeking to avoid paying
costs to show that the successful party unreasonably refused mediation and that it would
have had a reasonable prospect of success. Dyson LJ remarked that this should not be an
unduly onerous burden to discharge, because the unsuccessful party does not have to show
that mediation would have succeeded. Mediators and commentators have questioned what
is meant by 'success' in mediation. They argue that mediation may be successful even if it
does not result in a settlement because it assists with narrowing and clarifying issues, which
can save time at trial and even lead to a settlement at a later date. That may be so; however
it is clear that the court in *Halsey* was equating success with settlement. See also *Re Midland
Linen Services Ltd* [2004] EWHC 3380 (Ch), where the Court of Appeal refused to penalise a
party in costs for refusing to agree to mediation on the basis that the relationship between
the parties was so bad that mediation did not have a realistic prospect of success.

In *McCook v Lobo* [2002] EWCA Civ 1760, the claimant's appeal against the dismissal of   **6.27**
his claim against the first defendant was unsuccessful. The claimant sought to recover his
costs of the appeal on the grounds that the first defendant had unreasonably refused the
claimant's offer to mediate the dispute. The Court of Appeal found that the defendant had
'a resounding success' before the trial judge and before the Court of Appeal, and that there
was "insufficient room for manoeuvre to make mediation a venture which might have real
prospects of success in achieving compromise".

In *Hurst v Leeming* [2003] 1 Lloyd's Rep 379, a claim was brought against a barrister for   **6.28**
professional negligence. At a hearing for summary judgment, the claimant conceded that
his claim was without merit. However he sought to recover his costs because the defendant had refused his offer to mediate the dispute both before and after the commencement
of proceedings. The court dismissed the claimant's application for costs because in the
exceptional circumstances of the case, it was inappropriate to penalise the defendant for
refusing mediation in view of the claimant's attitude, character and the fact that he was
incapable of a balanced evaluation of the facts and therefore mediation had no real prospect of success. Lightman J however pointed out that to refuse mediation on the grounds
that it has no reasonable prospect of success, although justified on the exceptional facts of
this case, was a 'high risk course to take' because it relies on the court agreeing that there
is no real prospect of ADR being successful.

The court considered this specific point in *Gaston, Broughton v Courtney* [2004] EWHC 600   **6.29**
(Ch). The court ordered the defendant to pay costs for refusing to participate in mediation, despite the fact that the court had ordered, on two separate occasions, a 28-day stay
to enable the parties to consider in good faith whether they could settle the dispute by
ADR and despite a number of offers being made by the claimant to engage in mediation.
The defendant refused to do so on the grounds that there was no foreseeable or realistic
prospect of success. The court found that there was no objective reason to conclude that

mediation had no reasonable prospect of success and that the repeated attempts of the claimant to persuade the defendant to participate in it and to explain its basis and rationale gave positive grounds to encourage hope of success.

Whether an ADR order was made by the court

6.30   Where a successful party refuses to agree to ADR despite court encouragement, the court will take this into account in deciding whether the refusal was unreasonable. In *Hasley* Dyson LJ pointed out at [29]: 'The court's encouragement may take different forms. The stronger the encouragement, the easier it will be for the unsuccessful party to discharge the burden of showing that the successful party's refusal was unreasonable.' If a party refused to engage in ADR, despite the fact that an order was made in the form in Appendix 7 of the *Admiralty and Commercial Court Guide* (see Figure 5.1 above), then '. . . he runs the risk that for that reason alone his refusal to agree to ADR would be held to have been unreasonable, and that he should therefore be penalised in costs'.

6.31   In *Dyson v Leeds City Council* [2000] CP Rep 42, Lord Woolf [at 18] stated:

> 'I would also add the reminder that the court has powers to take a strong view about the rejection of encouraging noises we are making [about ADR] if necessary by imposing eventual orders for indemnity costs or indeed ordering that a higher rate of interest be paid on any damages that might at the end of the day be recoverable.'

6.32   The successful party was also penalised in costs for ignoring two ADR orders made by the court in *Gaston, Broughton v Courtney* [2004] EWHC 600 (Ch) (see 6.29 above).

REQUESTING FURTHER INFORMATION OR CLARIFICATION OF THE ISSUES BEFORE ACCEPTING ADR

6.33   The court in *Halsey v Milton Keynes General NHS Trust* [2004] 1 WLR 3002 made it clear that the factors listed above were not exhaustive. In deciding whether a party was unreasonable in refusing ADR all the facts and circumstances of the case must be considered.

6.34   These include whether a party was unreasonable for refusing ADR where it considered further information or clarification had to be provided before it was willing to do so.

6.35   In *Wethered Estates Ltd v Davis* [2006] BLR 86, the defendant had made a number of requests for mediation, both before and after issue. The claimant expressed willingness to engage with mediation but felt that it was important that each party's case was set out in court statements of case before doing so. After issue of court proceedings, the defendant again asked the claimant to agree to mediation on several occasions. The claimant indicated that it was willing to do so, but it first needed to understand the defendant's case (although it had by then, the defendant's defence and witness statements) and that mediation would be best undertaken when the evidence was final. The claimant only agreed to participate in mediation 15 months after it was first proposed by the defendant. The court held that the claimant had not acted unreasonably by refusing to mediate until the issues in the case were clarified, as the nature of the dispute was difficult to fathom.

In *Jarrom v Sellars* [2007] EWHC 1366 (Ch), the court deprived the claimants of costs in a **6.36** probate claim for refusing the defendant's offer of a settlement meeting before the proceedings were issued. The claimants refused to attend such a meeting until the defendant had provided an agenda, witness statements and detailed proposals. The court found that these reasons were not sufficient to justify the claimants refusing a meeting, as such a meeting would have given them the chance to find out what the defendant wanted, what she proposed and may have enabled the parties to explore how to take the matter forward without the necessity for litigation. The court therefore made no order for costs.

In *Corby Group Litigation v Corby DC* [2009] EWHC 2019 (TCC), the court found that the **6.37** unsuccessful defendant had not acted unreasonably in refusing to mediate in group litigation brought by the claimants until expert evidence had been obtained. Once that evidence had been obtained, the defendant again rejected mediation on the basis that it was unlikely to reach a conclusion of the matter because the defendant's expert evidence supported its stance on each issue and the claimants were adopting a 'scattergun' approach. Although with hindsight the defendant was wrong in their assessment of the litigation, their decision to refuse ADR had to be judged at the time the decision was made, and no adverse costs order was made against them.

REJECTING ADR BEFORE ISSUE

The court will expect the parties to have complied with the Practice Direction Pre-action **6.38** Conduct or any relevant pre-action protocol. It can ask the parties to explain what steps were taken to comply with the requirement to consider ADR. Where there has been non-compliance by a party the court may ask that party to provide an explanation (PD Pre-action Conduct, para 4.2). Where there has been an unreasonable refusal to consider ADR, the court may make an adverse costs order against that party, including an order that costs should be paid on an indemnity basis (PD Pre-action Conduct, paras 4.3 and 4.6).

The nature of any sanctions that should be imposed on a party for rejecting ADR before **6.39** issue of proceedings was reviewed by the court in *Burchell v Bollard* [2005] BLR 330. The Court of Appeal stated that a party should not ignore a reasonable request to negotiate or mediate before proceedings are started. It found that the defendant was unreasonable in refusing an offer to mediate before proceedings were issued, as a small building dispute is, par excellence, the kind of dispute that lends itself to ADR and the merits favoured mediation. The defendant's reason for rejecting mediation because the case was too complex was 'plain nonsense', and any belief that the defendant had in the strength of its own case was unreasonable. The claimant established that mediation would have had a reasonable prospect of success. Despite this, the court declined to make an adverse order for costs because the defendants rejected mediation before the law was clearly developed by cases like *Dunnett v Railtrack* [2002] 2 All ER 850 (see below) and *Halsey v Milton Keynes General NHS Trust* [2004] 1 WLR 3002. However a party was penalised for rejecting ADR before issue of proceedings in *Jarrom v Sellers* [2007] EWHC 1366 (Ch) (see 6.36 above).

FAILING TO INITIATE ADR PROCESSES

6.40   The court makes a distinction between cases where the successful party *rejects* an offer of ADR made by the other side and those cases where there has been a failure by the successful party to *initiate* ADR proceedings.

6.41   In *Vale of Glamorgan Council v Roberts* [2008] EWHC 2911 (Ch), proceedings were commenced by the local authority in relation to a boundary dispute. It succeeded in the litigation. The defendant argued that it should not have to pay all of the council's costs because it failed or refused to accept or engage in serious settlement negotiations or mediation. The court found that none of the defendant's offers positively suggested mediation, so the local authority did not positively refuse to mediate. The court distinguished *Halsey* on the basis that those guidelines did not apply to a case where the successful party did not initiate ADR, and held that it would be going too far to disallow costs incurred by a successful party simply because that party did not initiate suggestions for mediation (or, by analogy, any ADR process).

6.42   However the court in *Vale of Glamorgan Council v Roberts* did not consider the case of *Painting v Oxford University* [2005] PIQR Q5. This was a personal injury case in which the claimant was claiming £400,000. Initially the defendant paid £184,442 into court. Surveillance evidence showed the claimant's injuries were less severe than she alleged, so the defendant withdrew the payment in and substituted a Part 36 payment of £10,000. At trial, the claimant recovered the sum of £23,331. The defendant argued that it should not have to pay the claimant's costs on the grounds that she had exaggerated her claim and, had it not been for the exaggeration, the matter would have been settled early with minimal costs. They also criticised the claimant for failing to take any steps to negotiate, make counter-offers or accept the offers that had been made. The Court of Appeal held that the judge had failed to give proper weight to the fact that the claimant had exaggerated her claim, and had also failed to take into account the fact that, but for the exaggerated claim, the matter would probably have been settled at an early stage. The court also noted that the claimant had not made an offer or a counter-offer and that the court could take a failure to negotiate into account when determining costs. The Court of Appeal therefore ordered that the defendant should pay the claimant's costs up to the date of the payment into court and the claimant should pay the defendant's costs from that date.

6.43   In *Widlake v BAA Ltd* [2010] PIQR P4, the court applied *Painting v Oxford University* and the successful party was deprived of costs because of exaggeration of the claim and the fact that he failed to negotiate, and the court ordered that there should be no order for costs.

6.44   However in either of these cases, it is not possible to determine how seriously the court viewed the claimant's mere failure to take part in negotiations. In both cases there was a combination of exaggeration and a failure to negotiate. In the absence of any exaggeration, *Vale of Glamorgan v Roberts* establishes that an adverse costs order should not be made against the successful party for failing to initiate ADR or mediation in situations where there is no offer to engage in ADR processes by the unsuccessful defendant.

6.45   However it remains to be seen how long *Vale of Glamorgan Council v Roberts* will stand. As stated above, PD Pre-action Conduct and also Part 44 of the CPR gives the court power to take into account conduct, including the extent to which a pre-action protocol is complied with. The obligation is on *both* parties to the dispute to consider ADR. It may be logical to find that a party who ignores the requirements of the protocol, shuts his eyes to ADR and embarks on litigation should find his failure to do so penalised in costs. On the other hand, it may be difficult to justify giving a costs advantage to the losing party if they too have ignored the need to consider ADR.

REJECTING ADR AFTER JUDGMENT AND BEFORE THE HEARING OF AN APPEAL

The court has on several occasions penalised a successful party for refusing ADR after trial and pending an appeal. **6.46**

In *Dunnett v Railtrack plc* [2002] 1 WLR 2434, the single judge, Schiemann LJ, granting leave to appeal, recommended that the parties should try to mediate the dispute using the Court of Appeal Mediation Scheme (which was free to the users at that time). The defendant refused to engage in mediation on the grounds that it was confident it would succeed at trial. Despite the fact that the defendant won the appeal, and the claimant failed to beat a modest Part 36 offer of £2,500 that the defendant had made after leave to appeal had been granted, the Court of Appeal refused to award the defendant the costs of the appeal. The Court held that if a party rejected ADR out of hand when it had been suggested by the court, they would suffer the consequences when costs came to be decided. As the defendant had refused to contemplate ADR at a stage prior to the costs of the appeal beginning to flow, it was not appropriate to take into account the fact that offers had been made to compromise the appeal. Brooke LJ stated (at [15]): **6.47**

> 'It is to be hoped that any publicity given to this part of the judgment of the court will draw the attention of lawyers to their duties to further the overriding objective in the way that is set out in CPR Part 1 and to the possibility that, if they turn down out of hand the chance of alternative dispute resolution when suggested by the court, as happened on this occasion, they may have to face uncomfortable costs consequences.'

In *Neal v Jones Motors* [2002] EWCA Civ 1757, the winning party to an appeal had its costs reduced by £5,000 because it failed to heed advice given by the court to attempt mediation. **6.48**

In *Virani v Manuel Revert Y CIA SA* [2004] Lloyd's Rep 4, on granting leave to appeal, the single judge suggested to the appellant that they could use the Court of Appeal mediation service. They declined to do so and lost the appeal. The respondent was awarded costs to be assessed on the indemnity basis because of the appellant's refusal to mediate. **6.49**

However a different view was taken by the court in *Reed Executive plc v Reed Business Information Ltd* [2004] 1 WLR 3026. Here, the Court of Appeal refused to penalise the successful appellants/defendants for refusing an offer by the claimant to mediate that was made late in the day after the claimant had obtained judgment in its favour, when the defendants would have been negotiating from a position of weakness and on the grounds that it had a reasonable and justifiable belief in its prospects of success in the appeal. This decision is more likely to be in line with the factors that the court considered in *Halsey v Milton Keynes General NHS Trust* [2004] 1 WLR 3002. **6.50**

DELAY IN CONSENTING TO MEDIATION (OR ANOTHER ADR PROCESS)

6.51   In *Nigel Witham Ltd v Smith* [2008] EWHC 12 (TCC), the court considered whether a party could be penalised for agreeing to mediation late in the day when the majority of costs had been incurred, although they did in fact mediate the dispute. The court held that where the successful party has unreasonably delayed in consenting to mediation, this may lead to an adverse costs order, but no order should be made on the facts. The court found that it was not unreasonable for the defendant to refuse to mediate before the proceedings were issued as it was entitled to see how the claimant set out its claim and the claimant's uncompromising attitude meant that an earlier mediation would have had no reasonable prospect of success. The defendant had not unreasonably delayed in consenting to a judicial settlement conference.

PULLING OUT OF MEDIATION (OR ANOTHER ADR PROCESS)

6.52   The court has considered whether a successful party should be penalised for agreeing to explore settlement in an ADR process, and then backing out of it at the last moment.

6.53   In *Leicester Circuits Ltd v Coates Brothers plc* [2003] EWCA Civ 333, the parties agreed to mediate and even got as far as appointing a mediator and arranging the date of the mediation meeting. However the defendants withdrew from the mediation the day before it was due to take place on instructions from their insurers. They lost at first instance but won on appeal. Although the defendants were granted the costs of the appeal, the Court of Appeal was not prepared to allow them to recover costs that were incurred from a date nine days before the date they withdrew from the mediation on the basis that there was at least a prospect that the mediation process would have succeeded if it had been allowed to proceed. Per Longmore LJ:

> 'The whole point of having mediation, and once you have agreed to it, proceeding with it, is that the most difficult of problems can sometimes, indeed often are, resolved.........Having agreed to mediation, it hardly lies in the mouths of those who agreed to it to assert that there was no realistic prospect of success.'

6.54   In *McMillan Williams v Range* [2004] EWCA Civ 294, the parties agreed, after encouragement from the court, to attempt to resolve their dispute by mediation. Two days before the date fixed for the mediation, the appellant decided not to proceed with it, on the grounds that it was not likely to be successful as neither side was willing to change their positions. Despite winning the appeal, the Court of Appeal refused to award the appellant the costs of the appeal. As Ward LJ put it: 'this is a case where we should condemn the posturing and jockeying for position taken by each side in this dispute and thus direct that each side pay its own costs of their frolic in the Court of Appeal'.

6.55   In *Roundstone Nurseries Ltd v Stephenson Holdings Ltd* [2009] EWHC 1431 (TCC), the defendant withdrew from a mediation meeting days before it was due to take place. The court ordered the defendant to pay the claimant's costs thrown away by the late cancellation of the mediation process.

UNREASONABLE CONDUCT IN THE MEDIATION

The principles in *Halsey v Milton Keynes General NHS Trust* [2004] 1 WLR 3002 were extended **6.56** in *Carleton (Earl of Malmsebury) v Strutt and Parker* [2008] EWHC 424 (QB), to unreasonable conduct in the mediation. The court held a party who agreed to mediation and then took an unreasonable stance in that mediation was in the same position as a party who refused to mediate and that *Halsey* applied to this situation. The parties agreed that privilege should be waived in all 'without prejudice' matters. The court found that the failure to mediate before the trial was due to the attitude taken by both parties, and it was not therefore open to one party to claim that the failure of the other should be taken into account on the question of costs. In relation to the mediation that took place following judgment on liability, the judge found that the claimant's position at the mediation was plainly unreasonable and unrealistic and that if they had made an offer that reflected their true position the mediation might have succeeded. He found that the defendants could have protected themselves by making a Part 36 offer, but that justice would be done by awarding the claimant only a portion of their costs to reflect the unreasonable stance they took in the mediation.

It is likely that the court can only enquire into conduct that took place in the mediation if all **6.57** parties to the mediation consent to waive privilege and confidentiality (see 13.94–13.122). As this is not likely to happen often, an order of this type is likely to be very rare.

IMPOSING A COSTS CAP ON SOLICITOR–CLIENT COSTS FOR FAILING TO PURSUE ADR

In *Brownlee v Brownlee*, a decision of the South Gauteng High Court of South Africa, **6.58** 2008/25274, the parties unreasonably failed to mediate in a family dispute. The judge made an order imposing a cap on the solicitor–client costs that could be recovered because he was '... persuaded that the failure of the attorneys to send this matter to mediation at an early stage should be visited by the court's displeasure'.

It is quite possible that the courts in England and Wales could be persuaded to make a **6.59** similar order if the circumstances of the case merited it. The court could also exercise its powers to make a wasted costs order against a legal adviser who failed to give his client proper practical and commercial advice about the benefits of ADR.

INDEMNITY COSTS ORDERS FOR FAILING TO CONSIDER ADR

Although the courts have warned that they have powers to take a strong view about the **6.60** rejection of ADR, if necessary by imposing indemnity costs orders, or ordering that a higher rate of interest should be paid on any damages that might be recoverable (see the comments of Ward LJ in *Dyson v Leeds City Council* [2000] CP Rep 42 at [18]), there are few cases in which orders of this kind have been made.

6.61 An indemnity costs order was made in *Rowallan Group Ltd v Edgehill Portfolio No 1* [2007] EWHC 32 (Ch) where the claimant issued proceedings during the course of a mediation hearing, with no prior letter before claim.

6.62 The court refused to award costs on an indemnity basis against a party who unreasonably withdrew from mediation in *Roundstone Nurseries Ltd v Stephenson Holdings Ltd* [2009] EWHC 1431 (TCC). The court accepted that the defendant's conduct justified them paying the claimant's costs thrown away, but it did not merit assessment of those costs on an indemnity basis.

6.63 However in *Gill v Woodall, Lonsdale and the Royal Society for the Prevention of Cruelty to Animals* [2009] EWHC 834 (Ch) the court was prepared to make an indemnity costs order against the defendant in relation to one issue for refusing to mediate the dispute.

BOTH PARTIES AT FAULT IN FAILING TO CONSIDER ADR

6.64 Where both parties are at fault in failing to consider ADR, the court may penalise both of them by refusing to make any costs order at all, whatever the outcome of the case (*Longstaff International Ltd v Evans* [2005] EWHC 4 (Ch)).

HOW DOES THE COURT TREAT PRIVILEGED MATERIAL WHEN SEEKING TO IMPOSE SANCTIONS?

6.65 Any communications passing between the parties that are aimed at settlement are privileged from disclosure by operation of the without prejudice rule (see Chapter 13). In *Halsey v Milton Keynes General NHS Trust* [2004] 1 WLR 3002, the court accepted that if the integrity and confidentiality of the mediation process is to be preserved, the court should not know, and therefore should not investigate, why the process failed to result in an agreement.

6.66 In *Reed Executive plc v Reed Business Information Ltd* [2004] 1 WLR 3026, the Court of Appeal applied *Walker v Wilsher* [1889] 23 QBD 335 and held that the court has no jurisdiction to order disclosure of oral or written communications that were expressed to be 'without prejudice' (whether in party-to-party negotiations or third-party assisted negotiations) for the purpose of deciding the question of costs and whether a party acted unreasonably in refusing ADR. It found that the decision in *Halsey* did not change that general rule. Even if there were such a jurisdiction, disclosure should be refused as a matter of discretion. It is open to a party to avoid the rule by providing that the communications are taking place expressly on the basis that they are 'without prejudice save as to costs'. The court can then look at those communications after issues of liability and remedies have been determined, in order to decide the question of costs. The court recognised that the fact that it cannot look at 'without prejudice' material means that in many situations it may not be able to determine whether the winning party has acted unreasonably in refusing an offer to attempt to resolve the matter by an ADR method.

6.67 In *The Wethered Estate Ltd v Davis* [2005] EWHC 1903 (Ch), the defendant submitted that the mediation failed because no agreement could be reached about costs and that this was due to the claimant not agreeing to mediation at an earlier stage of the dispute when the costs were significantly lower. The court was not prepared to enquire into the reasons why the mediation failed as it was important that the without prejudice nature of the mediation process was maintained unless the parties themselves waived it by clear and unequivocal consent.

There clearly have been cases where the court has been referred to without prejudice mate-   **6.68** rial in order to decide the question of costs, and in particular whether an adverse costs order should be made against a party for refusing to participate in ADR. This was the case, for example, in *Société Internationale de Télécommunications Aéronautiques SC (SITA) v The Wyatt Company (UK) Limited* [2002] EWHC 2401 (Ch). Here it was apparent that without prejudice material was shown to the judge after judgment on liability had been delivered and before argument took place about costs. The material provided to the judge included letters written in an attempt to persuade the third party to take part in mediation, including attendance notes of without prejudice meetings of the lawyers, which also recorded events that took place at the mediation meeting and remarks alleged to have been made by the mediator. It is not clear whether all of the communications that were referred to the judge were marked 'without prejudice save as to costs'. To the extent that they were not, the parties waived privilege. Such cases are likely to be rare.

It is clear from these cases that if a party makes an offer to explore settlement using some   **6.69** form of ADR process, they should make sure that correspondence is marked 'without preju- dice except as to costs' if they want to refer it to the court on the question of costs if the other side unreasonably refuses to consider the ADR process. Otherwise a party will not be able to refer to the without prejudice material in making submissions about costs, unless all parties to the dispute waive privilege.

KEY POINTS SUMMARY

- The court will look at whether a party complied with the requirements of PD Pre-action   **6.70** Conduct and the Pre-Action protocols in making decisions about costs.
- If a party unreasonably refuses to consider ADR, before issue, after issue, or after judgment and pending appeal, they can be penalised in costs.
- In considering whether a party has unreasonably refused to consider ADR, the court will look at all the circumstances in the case, including the factors identified in *Halsey v Milton Keynes General NHS Trust* [2004] 1 WLR 3002 .
- If a successful party unreasonably refuses ADR, they may be deprived of some or all of their costs or ordered to pay some or all of the losing party's costs, including costs on an indemnity basis.
- Pulling out of an ADR process at the eleventh hour is likely to be judged unreasonable conduct and may result in an adverse costs order.
- The court will not consider 'without prejudice' material in considering costs, unless privi- lege is waived by all the parties to the dispute, or the correspondence is explicitly written on the basis that it is 'without prejudice except as to costs'.

7

RECOVERY OF ADR COSTS IN LITIGATION

INTRODUCTION. 7.01

COSTS OF INTERIM APPLICATIONS RELATING TO ADR 7.05

RECOVERY OF THE COSTS OF UNSUCCESSFUL ADR PROCESSES. . . .7.09

KEY POINTS SUMMARY. 7.28

INTRODUCTION

7.01   The costs of using an ADR process can be significant. If the ADR process results in settlement of the dispute, that may represent a significant saving over the costs of proceeding to trial in litigation. The settlement agreement is also likely to make provision for the costs of both the litigation (if any) and the ADR process.

7.02   The ADR costs will include the costs of lawyers preparing documents for and attending the ADR process, as well as any fees paid to a neutral party such as the mediator's fees or an evaluator's or determiner's fees and other costs such as venue fees (see Chapter 4 for more detail on this). If the ADR process is unsuccessful, the costs of that process will have increased the overall costs of the parties in resolving the dispute.

7.03   This chapter considers the extent to which the court can make orders about costs if:

- an interim application takes place in relation to ADR;
- ADR is attempted, but fails to result in any resolution of the dispute due to no fault of either party (unreasonable conduct by a party could result in an adverse costs order as explained in Chapter 6 above); and
- the main issues are resolved by an ADR process, leaving costs to be determined by the court.

7.04   As mentioned above, if the ADR process is successful the settlement should deal with costs, which is why costs in cases that are settled are not discussed in this chapter, unless there is no agreement between the parties about costs.

COSTS OF INTERIM APPLICATIONS RELATING TO ADR

As stated at 6.04–6.08, the court has a wide discretion in making orders about costs in legal **7.05**
proceedings. The usual order is that the unsuccessful party will pay the costs of the successful party (see CPR 44.3(2)(a)).

Occasionally an application or a hearing will take place in relation to an ADR process. This **7.06**
can happen if:

- the court orders that an allocation hearing or a case management conference should take
  place to determine whether an ADR order should be made directing the parties to attempt
  to resolve their dispute by a particular ADR process;
- the court has made an ADR order, perhaps in a form similar to that set out in Figure 5.1,
  but the parties have not been able to agree on the selection of a suitable neutral person for
  the ADR process, and a further case management conference is required for the court to
  facilitate the selection of the neutral person;
- an application is made by one or all parties for a stay to enable ADR to be attempted;
- an application is made to deal with an issue arising during an ADR process.

The costs of interim applications made in connection with an ADR process will usually be **7.07**
'costs in the case'. This means that the costs of the interim application or hearing forms part
of the costs of the court proceedings, so the party who is awarded costs at the end of the
trial process will recover the costs of the interim application (see PD 43–48, para. 8.5). Such
an order is made because generally there is no overall winner in case management conferences or hearings at which the court gives directions, because such directions (for example
ordering a stay) tend to be for the benefit of all the parties.

However if a hearing has taken place due to one party's unreasonable refusal to engage **7.08**
with or act reasonably in an ADR process (for example an unreasonable refusal to consider
ADR or to co-operate in the selection of a mediator), and the court decides their conduct
was unreasonable or unmeritorious, then there is no reason why that conduct should not
be penalised in costs. The court could order the party acting unreasonably to pay the other
side's costs of and occasioned by the application or hearing.

RECOVERY OF THE COSTS OF UNSUCCESSFUL ADR PROCESSES

ADR processes that deal with costs

Applications in court proceedings for the costs of unsuccessful ADR processes are only likely **7.09**
to arise where the process selected does not include a power to award costs in the event
that the process is unsuccessful. ADR processes therefore fall into two groups, as set out in
Table 7.1.

Table 7.1 ADR processes: power to award costs if the process is unsuccessful

ADR process with no power to award costs if the process is unsuccessful	ADR process with power to award costs if the process is unsuccessful
negotiation	adjudication
mediation	arbitration
conciliation	expert determination with power to award costs
evaluation	
expert determination with no power to award costs	

Costs of failed ADR as part of the costs of litigation

7.10   Whether the costs of a failed attempt at ADR are recoverable in court proceedings depends in part on whether the costs are 'incidental' to the proceedings for the purposes of the Senior Courts Act 1981 s 51, and in part on the agreement of the parties. In general terms, the costs of negotiations are regarded as part of the overall costs of the proceedings (see PD 43–48, para 4.8(6), which provides that the bill of costs can include work done in connection with negotiations with a view to settlement). Otherwise, the costs of work done in relation to other ADR processes are not specifically mentioned in CPR, Parts 44 to 48 or PD 43–48, which are the provisions dealing with costs.

7.11   Despite this omission in the CPR, there is no reason in principle why the costs of the unsuccessful ADR process should not be regarded as part of the costs of the litigation. The court guides published for the specialist courts recognise this. An example is the *Admiralty and Commercial Court Guide* (8th edn, 2009), which states at para. G1.10:

> 'At a case management conference or at any other hearing in the course of which the judge makes an order providing for ADR he may make such order as to the costs that the parties may incur by reason of their using or attempting to use ADR as may in all the circumstances be appropriate. The orders for costs are normally costs in the case, meaning that if the claim is not settled, the costs of the ADR procedures will follow the ultimate event [so the unsuccessful party will be ordered to pay the successful party's costs incurred in connection with the ADR process], or that each side will bear their own costs of those procedures if the case is not settled.'

7.12   In *Halsey v Milton Keynes General NHS Trust* [2004] 1 WLR 3002, the court accepted that the costs of an unsuccessful mediation can be the subject of a costs order by the court after the trial.

7.13   However, whether or not the court can treat the costs of an unsuccessful ADR process as part of the costs of litigation, and order the unsuccessful party to pay the costs that the successful party has incurred in connection with the ADR process, will depend on whether the parties have made any contrary agreement in relation to the costs of the ADR process.

The agreement between the parties determines liability in respect of ADR costs

7.14   If the parties have agreed, for example in a mediation agreement, that they will each bear their own costs of the ADR process, then the court will not look behind this agreement and make a different costs order in the event that the ADR process is unsuccessful.

Typically, the parties will enter into an agreement in respect of an ADR process, for exam- **7.15**
ple a neutral evaluation agreement, or a mediation agreement, which provides that the
expenses of that process will be borne equally by the parties and that each party will be
responsible for their own costs, whether or not settlement is reached during the process.
Such an agreement will bind the parties, and the court will not be able to go behind it to
apportion responsibility for costs in any other way. This is so even if the settlement agreement that is reached in the mediation provides for one party's costs to be assessed on the
standard basis if not agreed and this is reflected in a Tomlin Order (see 20.48–20.54) signed
by the parties, but the settlement agreement does not explicitly deal with the costs of the
ADR process (which are covered by the ADR agreement). In such a case the Tomlin Order
covers the costs of the parties other than the costs of the ADR process, with the costs of the
ADR process being borne equally by the parties in accordance with the ADR agreement.

This was the case in *National Westminster Bank plc v Feeney and Feeney* [2006] EWHC 90066 **7.16**
(costs). The mediation agreement provided that the mediator's fee would be borne equally
by the parties and that each party would bear their own costs. Guidance notes to the
agreement indicated that if the parties wished the costs of the mediation to be taken into
account in any court orders if settlement was not reached, then the standard terms should
be amended accordingly. No such amendment was made. The Tomlin Order that was made
at the mediation provided for the claimant to pay the defendant's costs of the counterclaim,
to be assessed, but did not mention the costs of the mediation process. The defendant then
sought to obtain the costs of the mediation in the assessment of costs undertaken by the
court. It was held that, as a matter of general principle, the costs incurred in a mediation
could form part of the costs of the claim just as the reasonable costs of negotiation could be
recovered as costs of the proceedings (see PD 43–48, para 4.8(6)). However the mediation
agreement showed that the parties' intention was that those costs should not be recovered
as part of the costs of the litigation, and it could not be said that the Tomlin Order varied
or discharged or took precedence over the terms of the ADR agreement. The Tomlin Order
also did not include the costs of mediation by necessary implication. The defendant was
therefore not entitled to recover its costs of and in connection with the mediation from the
claimant. The decision was upheld on appeal (unrep. 14th May 2007).

In *Lobster Group Limited v Heidelberg Graphic Equipment Limited* [2008] 2 All ER 1173 it was **7.17**
held that if the parties agree to bear their own costs of a pre-action mediation, regardless of
the outcome, they cannot subsequently seek to recover these costs from the other party to
the proceedings.

It is likely that if the parties had explicitly stated in the settlement agreement that one **7.18**
party should indemnity the other party in respect of their mediation costs and expenses,
or if they had agreed to vary the mediation agreement to provide that one party should bear
the costs and expenses of mediation, the decisions in these cases would have been different. Parties should therefore give careful thought to the costs position in drawing up the
terms of any settlement agreement.

The parties make no agreement about the costs of the ADR process

In *Roundstone Nurseries Ltd v Stephenson Holdings Ltd* [2009] EWHC 1431 (TCC) the claimant **7.19**
applied for an order that the defendant should pay the costs thrown away as a result of the
defendant's withdrawal from the mediation process. Unlike the cases in the previous section of this chapter, the parties had made no agreement about the costs of the mediation.

The court held that the costs of separate stand-alone ADR processes, particularly where they took place before proceedings were commenced, did not usually form part of the costs of or incidental to the proceedings. However, applying *McGlinn v Waltham Contractors Ltd* [2005] 3 All ER 1126, it was clear that costs incurred during the pre-action protocol process could be recovered as costs incidental to the litigation. The court found that the mediation had been arranged so that the parties could comply with the Construction and Engineering Disputes Pre-action Protocol, which required the parties to have a without prejudice meeting. It was common for this to take place under the umbrella of mediation. In the absence of any agreement between the parties about the costs of that process, the parties could ask the court to determine who should bear the costs of the mediation proceedings. The court held that the defendant was wrong to cancel the mediation hearing days before it was due to take place and, that being so, the defendant should pay the claimant's costs thrown away by late cancellation of the mediation as costs 'incidental to the litigation'.

7.20 Even if the mediation had taken place after litigation commenced rather than pursuant to a pre-action protocol, in the absence of any specific agreement between the parties as to who should bear the costs of the process it is likely that the court has jurisdiction to determine the costs of the process, particularly bearing in mind the court's encouragement of ADR (see Chapter 5).

Agreement between the parties for the costs of the ADR process to be costs in the case

7.21 The court will have power to determine the costs of an ADR process if the parties, agree that the costs of the ADR process are to be regarded as costs in the case in the event that settlement is not reached in the ADR process. The same result will apply if settlement is reached on the substantive issues, but not on costs. In these cases the court can regard the costs of the ADR process as part of the overall costs of the litigation.

7.22 In *Chantrey Vellacott v The Convergence Group plc* [2007] EWHC 1774 (Ch) and *Société Internationale de Télécommunications Aéronautiques SC (SITA) v The Wyatt Company (UK) Limited* [2002] EWHC 2401 (Ch), the courts were prepared to treat mediation costs as costs of and incidental to the proceedings, which meant the court had a discretion to determine who should pay those costs pursuant to the Senior Courts Act 1981 s 51. However neither the parties nor the court considered the effect that the mediation agreement had on recovery of these costs.

7.23 To get round the decision in *National Westminster Bank v Feeney* [2006] EWHC 90066, many ADR providers provide in the ADR agreement that the fees and the party's legal costs and expenses incurred in preparing for and attending the ADR process may be treated as costs in the case in any litigation where the court has power to order or assess costs, even where the agreement also provides that the expenses of the process (such as the mediator's or evaluator's fees) are to be borne equally by the parties. For example:

- Clause 5 of the National Mediation Helpline Agreement provides that: 'Unless the parties agree otherwise, the fees and expenses of the mediator are to be borne by the parties in equal shares. Each party will also pay its own expenses of individual representation in the mediation. The fees of the mediator are payable in advance. In the event that the mediation does not result in settlement, this clause does not prevent a court or other tribunal with appropriate power from treating the mediator's fee and each party's costs as costs of, or incidental to, the proceedings' (see Appendix 2).

- Clause 11 of CEDR Model Mediation Agreement (11th edn) provides: 'Unless otherwise agreed by the Parties and CEDR Solve in writing, each party agrees to share the Mediation Fees equally and also to bear its own legal and other costs and expenses of preparing for and attending the Mediation ('each Party's Legal Costs') prior to the Mediation. However, each party further agrees that any court or tribunal may treat both the Mediation Fees and each Party's Legal Costs as costs in the case in relation to any litigation or arbitration where that court or tribunal has power to assess or make orders as to costs, whether or not the Mediation results in settlement of the dispute' (see Appendix 2).

Settlement or determination on all issues apart from costs

A separate issue in respect of costs can arise where the parties resolve the main dispute between them by an ADR process (such as mediation or expert determination), but they cannot reach an agreement on the costs of the process or the proceedings, or where an expert determiner has no power under the contract appointing him to award costs between the parties. In that situation, in the absence of agreement about costs, the parties are likely to refer the question of liability for costs to the court.　**7.24**

This happened in *Dearling v Foregate Developments (Chester) Limited* [2003] EWCA Civ 913. The parties settled the claim and counterclaim at the trial (after pressure from the judge) but referred the issue of costs to the court. Dyson LJ noted that the principles that were to be applied when a claim is settled without the parties reaching agreement on costs derived from *Brawley v Marczynski (Nos 1 and 2)* [2003] 1 WLR 813. These principles are:　**7.25**

- the court has power to make a costs order when the substantive proceedings have been resolved without a trial but the parties have not agreed costs;
- it will ordinarily be irrelevant that the claimant is legally aided;
- the overriding objective is to do justice between the parties without incurring unnecessary court time and consequently additional cost;
- at each end of the spectrum there will be cases where it is obvious which side would have won had the substantive issues been fought to a conclusion. In between, the position will, in differing degrees, be less clear. How far the court will be prepared to look into the previously unresolved substantive issues will depend on the circumstances of the particular case, not least the amount of costs at stake and the conduct of the parties; and
- in the absence of a good reason to make any other order, the fall back is to make no order for costs.

As mentioned by Dyson LJ, it is difficult, if not impossible to reach a conclusion on the merits without hearing evidence and submissions. The trial judge also accepted that he could form no view on whether the claimant would have recovered more than the settlement figure had the case been fought. In those circumstances, in the absence of a good reason to make any other order, the fall back order of no order for costs was inevitable.　**7.26**

If the court is able to work out, without conducting a detailed investigation into the issues, which party is clearly the overall successful party, then a different costs order may be made.　**7.27**

KEY POINTS SUMMARY

7.28
- The court does have power to make an order that the costs of interim applications in connection with ADR should be borne by one party if that party has acted unreasonably, otherwise the usual order will be 'costs in the case'.
- If the parties embark on an ADR process and make a clear agreement as to their respective liabilities for the costs of that process, the court will not look behind it.
- If the parties make no agreement about the costs of an ADR process, the court can determine liability for the costs of the ADR process.
- If the parties agree that the court can treat the costs of the ADR process as costs in the case, irrespective of who pays the costs, and irrespective of whether settlement is reached in that process, then the court can determine liability for the costs of the process.
- If the parties reach agreement on the main issues by an ADR process and agree that ADR costs should be determined by the court, the court is likely to make no order for costs (meaning each party will bear their own costs) unless it can determine, without trying the case, who would have won at trial.

PART 3

NEGOTIATION AND MEDIATION

8

STYLES, STRATEGIES AND TACTICS IN NEGOTIATION

THE IMPORTANCE OF STYLE, STRATEGY AND TACTICS 8.01

STYLES 8.06

STRATEGIES. 8.12

TACTICS 8.36

KEY POINTS SUMMARY 8.73

THE IMPORTANCE OF STYLE, STRATEGY AND TACTICS

In a courtroom, rules of evidence and procedure, and the oversight of the judge, provide **8.01** structure and relative certainty. In a negotiation there is no set structure (save for whatever is agreed by the parties), and no rules (save for those that come from the context of possible litigation and as matters of professional conduct). This leaves substantial scope for the use of strategy and tactics, to the extent that these can have a significant effect on the outcome of the process and how much a lawyer can achieve for a client.

It is therefore vital to have a practical understanding of what strategy and tactics may be **8.02** used, and what they may achieve. Even if you do not use them yourself they may be used by an opponent, and you will need sufficient insight to identify what is happening, and to address it effectively. A confrontational opponent may appear intimidating, but you need to be able to ensure that this does not undermine what you can achieve for your client.

It may be tempting to think that decisions on strategy can be left until one meets an oppo- **8.03** nent, and that good tactics will occur to you on the spur of the moment, but this would risk losing many of the benefits that strategy and tactics can achieve. The negotiation process offers substantial control to a lawyer, and the opportunities are best exploited with planning. Strategy and tactics may need to be adapted as a negotiation develops, but options should be planned in advance so they can be properly set up, and quickly deployed.

This chapter provides an overview of the general styles, strategies and tactics that may be **8.04** employed in negotiating. There is no clear agreement on the meaning of these terms, but broadly:

• a *style* is the manner of delivery, a negotiator's attitude and demeanour;

- a *strategy* is the overall approach taken to achieve a good settlement;
- a *tactic* is a specific action used to try to achieve a particular end.

8.05 For those who wish to develop their skills, psychological and sociological insights can be helpful. For example some research studies show that those who aim high tend to do better. Research and books on communication skills, emotional intelligence, and working with difficult people can all assist.

STYLES

8.06 Everyone has a personal style. This may be a natural part of their personality, or a matter of how they wish to be seen professionally. A person's style includes a range of factors such as use of language, tone and volume of voice and physical presence (eg the way someone sits or stands). It includes such things as being relatively friendly and talkative, or relatively reserved, and can include matters such as use of humour. Two main styles can be identified.

Cooperative

8.07 A cooperative style is normally seen as being friendly, courteous, and conciliatory, seeking to gain trust. This style is often characterised as being relatively open, providing information, and seeking to cooperate with an opponent in trying to reach an agreement. Some lawyers will go so far as to try to charm an opponent as they might seek to charm a judge.

8.08 Such a style can be very productive if the opponent also seeks to be cooperative, but it is important not to be naive and assume that an opponent will be cooperative simply because a settlement is in the interests of both parties. A cooperative style can easily be exploited by a competitive opponent. Also be careful of someone who apparently has a cooperative style but who is using it to mask a competitive strategy.

Competitive/confrontational

8.09 A competitive style usually consists of making demands, and it is often argumentative. Emphatic language and a strong tone of voice may be used to make the opponent feel uncomfortable and intimidated. It tends to put pressure on an opponent to agree, or may seek to wear an opponent down. In an extreme form this style could be seen as bullying.

8.10 Such a style can be quite effective, especially if an opponent is weak, dislikes confrontation, or is poorly prepared. However this style can be risky, especially if it is sustained throughout a negotiation, as it can easily alienate an opponent, who may well refuse to make concessions so that no progress is made. It is not uncommon for a lawyer to start a negotiation with a competitive style, but to do so with an underlying collaborative strategy that may emerge later in the negotiation once the case has been put in strong terms.

Choice of style

8.11 It is sometimes suggested that one style is inherently more likely to be successful than another, but this is not the case. You should consider what style is most effective for you.

Some individuals are naturally more inclined to be co-operative or competitive, but choice of style should also depend on the type of case, and what you know of the negotiator for the other side. If you have a strong case a competitive style may well be justified even if your natural style is cooperative. It is also important to distinguish style from strategy—the use of a competitive style does not necessarily mean that the underlying strategy is competitive.

STRATEGIES

Your strategy is your overall plan for getting the best possible outcome in a negotiation. Style **8.12** is essentially a matter of presentation and may be relatively superficial, but strategy is key to success. Strategy and style may coincide so that one reinforces the other, or style may be used to mask strategy. A strategy may be selected for a whole case, or for part of a case.

Cooperative

A cooperative strategy focusses on reaching an agreement that is adequately fair and accept- **8.13** able to both sides. Concessions are expected on both sides, and information is shared. The negotiator tries to be reasonable and open, and to engender trust.

Characteristic approach: **8.14**

- Open by stressing the importance of settlement, and trying to build openness and trust with the opponent.
- Offer information to try to promote understanding.
- Move relatively quickly to make and seek concessions at a reasonable level.
- Explain the basis for offers to show that they are fair.
- Use a conciliatory approach to try to secure agreement.
- Tactics are used constructively to foster agreement.

The main strengths of a cooperative strategy are: **8.15**

- Provided an opponent responds by being cooperative, this strategy has a good likelihood of reaching agreement.
- Appropriate concessions are seen as principled and not a weakness.
- It can support a continuing relationship between the parties.
- There are fewer risks that the negotiation will break down. It may also result in agreement being reached relatively quickly.

The main weaknesses of cooperative strategy are: **8.16**

- This strategy can be undermined by a competitive opponent, who may treat cooperation as a weakness.
- It can be too easy to see settlement as the main goal, rather than ensuring that the client's objectives are met as fully as possible.
- Without detailed planning, this strategy can lead to unnecessary concessions and a weaker outcome for the client.
- A cooperative negotiator may be tempted to make unilateral concessions or early concessions to encourage an opponent to be cooperative. This may leave limited room for manoeuvre later.

- A cooperative negotiator may volunteer information while getting little or nothing in return.
- A cooperative negotiator may try to avoid confrontation, ignoring rather than seeking to challenge competitive techniques.
- A cooperative negotiator may fail to press the strengths of a case fully.

Competitive or positional

8.17 A competitive strategy seeks to win, getting the best possible outcome for the client, especially as regards financial issues. The negotiator takes a strong stance on each issue, focussing on demands rather than concessions, and is generally slow to yield. The negotiator will show little if any interest in the concerns and objectives of the opponent. Settlement is not seen as a key goal in itself, and the negotiator will walk away rather than accept terms seen as unsatisfactory. A positional strategy is very similar, with the focus being on the position of the client. This strategy is basically adversarial and may therefore come most easily to a litigation lawyer. It is also commonly perceived as an appropriate strategy for success in business. A competitive strategy is not necessarily presented with a confrontational style— the strategy relates to structure and content.

8.18 Characteristic approach:

- Open by making strong statements about the client's position, with little or no attempt to engage constructively with the opponent.
- Make high opening demands (often unrealistically high), and maintain high demands for as long as possible.
- Demand large concessions from the opponent.
- Make few and small concessions, save on things that do not matter to the client.
- Provide limited argument to support demands, but demand full justification for the opponent's position.
- Give limited information, but often seek detailed information from the opponent.
- Seek success on every issue, including interest and costs.
- Tactics such as threats or bluffs are commonly used.

8.19 The main strengths are:

- This strategy can be very successful in achieving a good outcome, especially against a weak or poorly prepared opponent.
- Research has shown that a high starting position does tend to lead to a better settlement.
- It is likely to be most successful where there are few issues, and where the issues are money based.
- It can also be successful for the stronger party where there is an imbalance of power, for example because one side has a much stronger case.
- There is little chance of exploitation by the opponent because few concessions are made.
- The strategy is relatively easy to understand and use because it involves simple statements and blocking rather than engaging with the complexity of issues.

8.20 The main weaknesses are:

- Many lawyers are not susceptible to the aggressive and manipulative behaviour of a competitive negotiator, so this strategy can make it difficult to reach an agreement.

- This strategy can be damaging in a case where there will be an ongoing relationship between the parties as it can lead to bad feelings.
- The tendency to focus on 'winning' or 'losing' may ignore some of the potential advantages of collaborative negotiation (see below).
- The use of pressure increases tension and stress levels, which may make settlement less likely.
- This strategy can be undermined by a well-prepared opponent who is confident in making good arguments and pointing out weaknesses so that the 'bluster' that is partly inherent in a competitive strategy is exposed
- A competitive strategy is not the most effective to deal with complex issues. The hard stance limits the possibility of exchanging information or discussion, and it is difficult to explore options.
- A competitive strategy is unlikely to work well if you hope to get a significant amount of information from your opponent, who will be unlikely to be disposed to answer questions.
- A competitive strategy tends to emphasise differences, and can increase misunderstanding.
- The negotiation can too easily become a battle between the lawyers who jockey for position over issues, losing sight of the client's interests.

Collaborative—principled or problem solving

A collaborative strategy assumes that the parties can work together to reach an agreement that meets the needs of both and is objectively fair. The process includes the parties exploring their underlying interests, sharing information, and being creative in the options considered. The agreement will not necessarily focus solely on the original issues between the parties but will try to identify options for mutual gain. This strategy involves more than co-operation—it is based on mutual effort and requires advance analysis and planning. Collaborative strategies may be used to reach settlement in difficult political situations, and may be particularly useful where the parties will have an ongoing relationship.   **8.21**

Within the term 'collaborative' different strands may be identified: **8.22**

- A 'principled' strategy tries to achieve an outcome that is objectively fair against some external authoritative norm, for example based on the view of an agreed expert. The principled approach was developed by Roger Fisher and William Ury of the Harvard Negotiation Project. It is clearly and well explained in *Getting to Yes: Negotiating agreement without giving in* by Roger Fisher and William Ury (Penguin Puttnum, 2008). This is developed further below.
- A problem-solving strategy focuses on both parties' real needs and interests, and tries to get a practical solution without building costs. The 'problem-solving' approach was set out by Carrie Menkel-Meadow of UCLA in her paper 'Toward another View of Legal Negotiation: The Structure of Problem Solving' (1984) 31(4) *UCLA Law Review* 754–842.

Characteristic approach: **8.23**

- Working together is stressed at the start of the negotiation, and this approach is sustained throughout.
- Each point is approached constructively, focussing on the best possible outcome for both parties.

- Issues are likely to be approached from the point of view of needs, interests and options rather than fault and blame.
- Both sides work to maintain an open and reasonable atmosphere.
- The negotiators are likely to emphasise objectivity and a potential settlement is often judged against agreed criteria to test fairness.

8.24   The main strengths are:

- A collaborative strategy is capable of achieving very good outcomes because it opens the process to anything of potential benefit to the clients, such as creating new shared marketing opportunities.
- This strategy has a good chance of success because it focuses on the interests of the parties going forward, rather than the issues of the past (though those issues must be resolved as part of the agreement).
- Even if there is no agreement, the areas of conflict are usually decreased.
- Techniques to expand resources rather than simply divide them can be beneficial, especially in a case relating to business interests.
- The rational and reasoned approach is reasonably easy to manage, provided both sides follow this strategy.
- A well-prepared collaborative strategy can be successful against a competitive opponent, so long as you are able to demonstrate the potential advantage for their client.

8.25   The main weaknesses are:

- A collaborative strategy can only really succeed where both parties are prepared to collaborate (though an initial stage of the strategy may be to persuade an opponent to collaborate).
- Effective collaboration may require substantial preparation of options.
- Attempts to collaborate may be defeated, or even exploited, by a competitive opponent, if attempts to collaborate lead to unnecessary concessions.
- This strategy may be difficult to use in court door negotiations because of time pressure, and limited opportunities to look at options fully.
- A collaborative approach may be exploited by a competitive negotiator, who pretends to be collaborative, but who actually seeks to get concessions while offering little.
- A collaborative strategy may have little to offer in a case where options cannot be developed.

8.26   The concept of 'principled' negotiation as developed in books such as *Getting to Yes* includes elements that may be useful whether or not used as part of a collaborative strategy.

- *Separate the people from the problem*. This involves defining the difficulty to be addressed objectively, rather than seeking to attach blame to people. It is sometimes expressed as being hard on the problem but soft on the people. This helps to avoid emotion, and can help people to save face. It can help the parties to understand different perceptions of the problem, and thus make agreement more likely.
- *Focus on interests rather than positions*. A negotiation can too easily focus demands or on who is right or wrong. Issues, positions, interests and needs should be carefully distinguished. To get progress it is more constructive to look at what underlies an issue or a position and see whether a need can be met in a different way (for example through a structured settlement rather than a single financial award). If one person wants a window opened and one wants it closed, it may be more productive to focus on other ways to

provide fresh air or to avoid a draught than to argue only about whether to open or close the window.

- *Look for options that may benefit both sides.* This is sometimes called win–win, or increasing the pie, contrasted to any view that one party will 'win' and the other 'lose' as regards an issue. For example if a business contract has been breached, an advantageous deal for future trading may more than wipe out the losses incurred as a result of the breach. An illustration sometimes used is of two sisters arguing over an orange. Just before they cut it in half their mother asks why they want it—and finds out that one sister wants to eat the inside but the other wants the peel to go into a cake she is making. Both can have what they want—a better result than half each.
- *Use objective standards to justify offers and concessions.* Because a negotiation does not involve a judge, this is an effective way to show that a proposal is principled and justified. This can be done by use of an independent expert, an independent standard, setting objective criteria, or following a precedent.
- *Develop a best alternative to a negotiated agreement (BATNA).* This provides a practical framework against which to judge any possible settlement. For guidance on developing a BATNA see 9.58–9.63.

Pragmatic

A pragmatic strategy involves adapting strategy to meet the needs of the particular negotiation. There is a sharp distinction to be made here. Planned pragmatism, especially in the hands of an experienced negotiator, can be very effective. It involves careful forethought about potentially effective strategy for each separate issue, with provisional decisions about an appropriate strategy for each, but leaving options open for a final decision to be made during the negotiation. Such a strategy may be most effective where you have limited information and need to get more facts in the negotiation before finally deciding how to proceed, and it may be appropriate where you do not know your opponent and cannot predict what strategy he or she might adopt. **8.27**

In contrast, unplanned pragmatism that amounts to little more than 'making it up as you go along' carries a high risk of failure, especially in the hands of an inexperienced negotiator, or against an opponent who has a well-prepared strategy. A negotiation can move very quickly, and while you need to take complex decisions about facts, figures and options, it is very difficult to take and implement the best decisions about strategy too. **8.28**

Choice of strategy

Many lawyers have a personal preference for the type of strategy they find it most natural to pursue. However the strengths and weaknesses of different strategies should be taken into account in making the best choice for each case. Also while consistent use of a single strategy can help to build expertise it can also leave you more vulnerable to an opponent—if someone knows you will use a particular strategy they can plan to undermine you. **8.29**

As part of planning for each case, the planning of strategy should include: **8.30**

- a preferred overall strategy for the case, especially where the strategy needs to be followed clearly and consistently, as is the case with a collaborative strategy;
- how you will open the negotiation to provide a firm foundation for your strategy. This needs care—your opponent may be cooperative and let you follow your strategy, but a

competitive opponent may ignore your strategy, and a very competitive opponent may try to force you to change strategy to undermine your confidence;

- a fallback option for overall strategy should it prove difficult to implement your first choice, for example because of the strategy used by your opponent, or because unexpected information emerges;
- any appropriate change of strategy. You might for example choose to be competitive in going through issues to test your opponent, but then be cooperative in reaching an agreement;
- if appropriate, separate strategies for separate key issues—for example you might chose to be competitive on financial issues, but then collaborative in for example negotiating the terms of an injunction.

8.31   There is much discussion and disagreement about whether one strategy is inherently more effective than another. Perhaps the best overall conclusion is that no strategy is inherently better, but that different options are better for different types of case, depending on the strengths and weaknesses of each strategy as outlined above. There is some research into the effect of strategy, and also gender and culture on negotiations (in particular by the Harvard Negotiation Project). The outcomes of research cannot easily be summarised, but it may be a useful area of study if you would like to become a really effective negotiator.

Interaction of strategies

8.32   It is not just the strategy you choose that matters, but rather the choice of strategy of each negotiator. Some strategies work very well together but others do not. It is important to be aware of the potential interaction of strategies—one does not necessarily trump another like a game of stone–paper–scissors.

8.33   Clearly two collaborative negotiators should be able to make effective progress. Two co-operative negotiators are also likely to be able to agree, but they may not get the best agreement for their clients if there is too much focus simply on agreeing rather than on analysing the case fully and securing the best possible outcome for each client.

8.34   Two confrontational, positional or competitive negotiators may well reach deadlock. This has been confirmed by an American study *Legal Negotiation and Settlement* by G Williams (West Publishing, 1983). However it is possible that two competitive negotiators can cover issues in a way that makes compromise appear unlikely, but then trade offers quite quickly at the end of the negotiation when all issues have been tested.

8.35   Where two negotiators are using different strategies, knowledge of the strengths and weaknesses of each strategy as outlined above is important in dealing with the opponent effectively. It is not essential to change your own strategy to meet an opponent using a different strategy—you can use the strengths of your own choice, and use the weaknesses in their own strategy against them. To give just one example, a collaborative negotiator can succeed against a competitive negotiator by pointing out potential mutual benefits. You should not go too far in exploiting the weaknesses in an opponent's strategy—if a competitive negotiator secures too good an outcome against a co-operative negotiator then the latter's client may simply refuse to accept the provisional agreement. You should of course take care not to let the potential weaknesses of your own strategy be used against you.

Table 8.1 Basic comparison of the main negotiation strategies

	Cooperative	Competitive	Collaborative
Objective	To get a settlement acceptable to both parties	To win best outcome on every issue	To achieve the best outcome for both parties
Manner	Reasonable and seeks to build trust	Tends to ignore needs or interests of others	Open and constructive Focus on working together
Opening	Stress the desire to be cooperative	Strong statement on client's position and demands	Set out the benefits of collaboration
Information	Tries to build openness by sharing information	Demands information be given Slow to provide information	Shares information and tries to open out options
Argument	Explains basis for proposals	Strong stance on every issue Does not justify position, but demands other side justifies position	Justifies proposals in terms of both clients' best interests Looks at needs and interests rather than fault
Tactics	Used constructively to support settlement	Used wherever an advantage may be secured eg threats and bluffs	Used constructively to open discussion and promote settlement
Concessions	Relatively quick to make and expect concessions	Focusses on demands. Slow to make concessions and few concessions	Focus on best outcome and objective criteria
Key strengths	Good chance of success Supports ongoing relationship	Can secure a good outcome for client Limited chance of exploitation Tends to get good outcome on financial issues	Can secure a good outcome for both clients Good chance of success Good for continuing relationships
Key weaknesses	Can be exploited by opponent Tends to focus on settlement rather than getting best for client Tends to concede too easily May fail to press strengths of case	Significant risk negotiation will fail Not good for ongoing relationship Can be challenged by well-prepared opponent Not good for exploring complex issues Fosters stress	Can be difficult to implement unless both negotiators are prepared to collaborate Requires significant preparation Can be difficult to use in limited time May be exploited

TACTICS

A 'tactic' is a type of behaviour or a specific action used in a negotiation to try to achieve a **8.36** particular end. The term 'tactic' is sometimes seen as negative—associated with manipulating or even tricking an opponent to get an unfair advantage. This is not the case—a tactic can be just as useful for a principled negotiator dealing with a confrontational opponent, and a proper use of tactics is part of getting the best possible outcome for a client. Understanding the different tactics that can be used in a negotiation enables you to decide whether and how to use them. Tactics should not be used by a lawyer in an unethical or unprofessional way, and you should neither do this nor accept such behaviour from an opponent. Having a good knowledge of tactics will also help you to recognise when an opponent is using a tactic, and to know how to deal with it so that it does not undermine your case.

8.37   Some tactics are associated with a particular style or strategy. For example a positional or confrontational approach is most likely to involve bluffs or threats. However versions of many tactics can be used in relation to most strategies and styles. Tactics need to be planned in advance because they may need to be set up as part of agreeing an agenda for negotiation, or as part of dealing with a specific issue. It is not necessary to plan tactics for every part of a negotiation—focus on tactics for key issues, and the issues that might be most difficult to address.

Tactics relating to information

8.38   Information may be central to a negotiation, and it is a resource to be dealt with tactically. Use of information is particularly important for a collaborative strategy. You need to gather information to assess the case for each side, to use information as part of persuading your opponent, and to decide what you will and will not reveal.

Questioning

8.39   Questioning is very important in any negotiation. Questions might relate to the facts, evidence or objectives as seen by your opponent, and can be used to probe the strengths and weaknesses of their case. Put questions in a way appropriate for the strategy you are using–questioning can have a negative effect. Questions can be used tactically to put pressure on an opponent: for example 'What is your bottom line on this?', or 'What are your instructions on this'? Even if the process fails you can use questions to find out more about your opponent's case.

Statements

8.40   It is important to make tactical statements about your case. A positional negotiator will make substantial use of statements, for example as regards what their client expects to achieve. A collaborative negotiator might make a statement about what collaboration might achieve. To be most effective a statement should be relatively short and clear, with words carefully chosen. Think carefully about the effect you want the statement to have on your opponent as that is the most important aspect of the statement.

Revealing information

8.41   Treat information as a resource and reveal it for a purpose. It can of course be very helpful to reveal information that shows the strength of your case. However it is important to take tactical decisions about how far to reveal matters such as your client's objectives. To do so may strengthen your case in terms of showing high expectations, but it can be a hostage to fortune if an opponent takes a realistic objective to be merely a starting point to be argued down. Even a cooperative strategy should be conducted tactically—consider not giving information unless you get information in return

Concealing information

8.42   There is no obligation to provide information, so it is quite proper to keep information confidential, or to refuse to answer a question, especially if the information may weaken your case. However remember that concealing information can have negative effects, for example building up costs if settlement of the dispute is delayed.

Reframing

This can be a useful tactic to redress how a difficult opponent is presenting their case. A   **8.43**
competitive negotiator might summarise the facts of an accident in an exaggerated, antagonistic or emotive way. Rather than getting irritated you can politely use more objective
words to say the same thing, and this can show that you are in control and not prepared to
be manipulated. A collaborative negotiator may try to develop a proposal you are not happy
with—trying to reframe it at an early stage is better that letting something you are likely to
reject develop too far.

Tactics relating to offers and demands

Achieving an outcome in a negotiation is done through making and accepting offers, and in   **8.44**
some strategies through demands. Within any strategy offers need to be dealt with tactically
to ensure the best possible outcome—timing and phrasing can be very important.

Pre-conditions and setting parameters

It is possible to have some control over potential offers by setting a precondition, for exam-   **8.45**
ple 'I could not make any offer on this issue unless your client agrees to apologise to mine',
or a parameter, for example ' I have instructions to settle for no more than £ 2,000 on this
point'. This sort of approach is most often associated with a competitive strategy, but it can
be used appropriately in connection with any strategy.

Objective standards

A principled or collaborative negotiator may make frequent reference to objective stand-   **8.46**
ards, but any negotiator may refer to an objective standard as a tactic. An objective standard
can be any sort of business practice, trade standard etc. The standard may be referred to in
order to justify the fairness of an offer or point you make, or to point out the unfairness of
an offer or other point made by the other side.

Authority to settle

The importance of settling within the authority provided by the client is dealt with in   **8.47**
9.67–9.70. A negotiator should make clear any limit on their authority, but a comment
about a possible limit on authority may also be made tactically: for example 'I'm not sure
I have authority to deal with that issue'. If an opponent suggests that they do not have
authority, you may wish to investigate what is being said; for example 'Are you saying your
client has specifically told you she will not accept less than £ 2,000?' Alternatively you can
sidestep the problem, as in 'Your client will not have been able to give you instructions on
the full offer I have made, and I would like you to put it to your client'.

Ultimatums

An ultimatum may be used to try to force a settlement; for example 'Unless you accept   **8.48**
£5,000 to settle this issue I will have to withdraw that offer, and I will make no other offer'.
An ultimatum might relate to withdrawing from the process, or a step the party will take
if agreement is not reached. An ultimatum is most associated with a competitive strategy,
but may be used as a tactic within any strategy to try to move to a settlement when a negotiation risks getting bogged down after an item has been fully discussed and concessions
are proposed but not accepted. An ultimatum should be distinguished from a threat—an
ultimatum should be justifiable.

Proposing additional outcomes

8.49 If it is important to you that a particular offer be accepted, you might choose to tie in some further outcome to make it sufficiently attractive; for example 'If you accept the £ 10,000, I will propose to my client that he should pay the costs to date'.

Tactics relating to structure

8.50 A normal structure for a negotiation is outlined in Chapter 10, but variations on structure can be used tactically.

Imposing structure

8.51 Structure is normally agreed through negotiating an agenda at the start of a negotiation. One negotiator may seek to impose their agenda, seeing an advantage in choosing the order in which topics are addressed. It may be tactically useful for example to start with an area where one has strength.

Ignoring structure

8.52 One negotiator may choose for tactical reasons to depart from an agreed agenda. This might for example be part of a competitive strategy, to try to control the process. It may also be used to try to confuse or surprise an opponent.

Parking issues

8.53 Once you have dealt with information, strengths and weaknesses as regards an issue it is normal to move to possible concessions. If this does not lead to agreement you should park the issue. There is little to be gained from repeating what you have said. If an issue needs to be parked it is tactically important to take charge of the parking by briefly summarising in your words what you want, and why your case merits it. It is useful to note the basis on which an issue is parked.

Moving on

8.54 Part of the purpose of parking an issue is to be able to move on. There may be other tactical reasons for proposing moving on, for example to take charge of the agenda, to avoid discussing a weakness in your case, or to give yourself time to think if you are suddenly confronted with new information.

Reopening issues

8.55 An issue that has been parked should be reopened at a strategic point. It is often best to reopen a parked issue at a time when it may be tied to a concession on another issue so as to reach an agreement on both. It is not good practice to reopen an issue that has already been agreed as this can undermine trust and lead the negotiation to fail. Nonetheless a confrontational or competitive negotiator may seek to reopen a provisionally decided issue as a way to try to make progress on another issue.

'Just one more thing'

8.56 Normally the issues to be discussed are agreed at the start of a negotiation. This is tactically quite important because you are likely to try to balance a concession on one issue against a concession by the other side on another issue, and this can be undermined if you find at a late stage there are more issues than you were aware of. Tactically a negotiator may choose to introduce a new demand near the end of the negotiation, hoping that it will be accepted rather than lose what has been agreed. This is a risky tactic to use as it is likely to irritate an opponent. If it is used against you it is probably best to make it clear that this is an unfair addition and to refuse to accept it.

Avoiding deadlock

Tactics for avoiding deadlock area dealt with in 10.109–10.121.   **8.57**

Tactics relating to presentation

Presentation is as important in negotiation as it is in advocacy. It is normal to present each   **8.58** point clearly, pointing out the strengths of your case and the outcome that you hope to achieve and why. Different approaches to presentation may be used tactically.

Abruptness

A competitive negotiator may address an issue very briefly, perhaps doing little more than   **8.59** making a demand and/or stating a key strength. This can be frustrating for an opponent, who may have little choice but try to pull out more detail, or to state that detail will be needed for progress.

Evasion

Evasion is another tactic most often used by a competitive negotiator. An incomplete or   **8.60** evasive response may be given to avoid providing facts, evidence or arguments in relation to an issue. Again an opponent will need to press for detail, making it clear why it is important. Evasion can be a risky tactic—it may lead an opponent to conclude that a case is weak on a point even if it is not.

Silence

Silence can be used to put pressure on an opponent, or to try to ensure that your opponent   **8.61** goes on to provide more information, or to make a concession. It is important to make it clear that you expect your opponent to say something, for example by looking at them.

Time to think

Most negotiations proceed at a fast pace with relatively few pauses. It may be tactically   **8.62** important to have time to review information and/or options. If you need time, ask for a minute to review the figures, or for a five-minute break to talk to the client. Make it clear that this is a positive decision—just flicking through your papers can appear weak.

Prepare a draft

A tactical way to ensure a focus on your view of the issues is to prepare a draft for use in the   **8.63** negotiation. This might relate to a particular aspect of the negotiation, for example presenting the arithmetic on the damages from your point of view. An alternative is to bring a draft agreement and suggest going through the draft, for example if the negotiation relates to an interim injunction. This can help you control the agenda, and can put an opponent on the back foot in terms of trying to introduce and justify their own points. If your opponent uses this tactic, decide carefully whether you are prepared to use their draft—you might look at it quickly to see what it reveals about their case and then say 'That was very helpful, but perhaps we could discuss the matter first and maybe go back to your draft later'.

Bluffing

8.64 It may be tempting to bluff with regard to the strength of a case, especially if using a competitive style. This can work against a relatively weak opponent, but a well-prepared opponent is likely to challenge such a bluff, seeking detail on the strengths of the claim. A claim that is shown to be a bluff tends to undermine belief in other claims made, so a bluff can be a risky tactic. A bluff should not amount to actively misleading an opponent with regard to facts or evidence, which is likely to amount to unprofessional conduct, see Chapter 16.

Aggression

8.65 Lawyers normally behave in a controlled and objective way. However in negotiation a competitive negotiator might use aggressive tactics to try to put pressure on an opponent and undermine their confidence. There may not be overt aggression, but sarcasm, ridicule, expressions of exasperation etc. If such approaches are used against you, do not react. Ignore it or respond in a rational way, or label the behaviour to defuse it, for example 'Sarcasm is not going to persuade me!'

Threats

8.66 A competitive negotiator may be tempted to make threats, and even a collaborative negotiator might consider some form of threat to try to reach an agreement they think is fair. A client may propose the making of threats in a difficult case where much is at stake. There are grey areas with regards to threats, and careful distinctions may need to be drawn.

8.67 A pure and unjustifiable threat would normally be unethical and might well amount to unprofessional conduct: see Chapter 16. However a statement of fact in relation to something your client has told you, pointing out potential consequences of a course of action, or setting out a step you feel may be justified if an agreement is not reached, could be seen as a statement, even though it might be perceived as a form of threat by the opponent. Saying 'If we cannot agree on this issue I will have to pursue an application for an interim injunction' is a statement, so long as it is reasonably justified. Saying 'My client has told me that he is thinking of reporting your client for tax evasion on the profit from this deal if we don't reach an agreement today' is on the face of it a statement, but is close to being an unjustified threat in a case that relates to contract law and has nothing directly to do with tax. Much may depend on exactly what is said and how it is said. For the sake of professional probity it is best to err on the side of caution.

8.68 There are a variety of ways of responding to a threat. You could ignore it, you could state openly that you refuse to deal on the basis of threats, or you could push it aside with words such as 'If making a threat is your best line of argument...'. In appropriate circumstances you could challenge whether the threat would really be carried out. Making a counter-threat is rarely helpful as it escalates hostility.

Tactics relating to law

8.69 Although legal analysis is vital in preparation, use of detailed law has a limited role in the negotiation itself. As lawyer–negotiators have legal knowledge there is no need for law to be explained in detail. A collaborative negotiator may not see it as productive to carry out a detailed legal analysis of past events. That said, law provides a vital context for the negotiation, and law can and should be used tactically.

Using legal terminology and tests

A point about the legal strength of a case can be made in a shorthand way; for example 'My client properly mitigated his loss and I am not going any lower', or 'If we go to court I will succeed on the balance of convenience test'. **8.70**

Equally, a weakness in an opponent's case can be pointed out briefly, as in 'You may say that, but you would not be able to prove it on the balance of probabilities', or 'Your client may want £500 on that, but there is no causation'. This can be successful against a poorly prepared opponent, who may make a concession rather than get into debate about a point of law they have not prepared. **8.71**

Using research

Mentioning a recent or obscure case as an authority can be an effective tactic in getting a concession from an opponent. It is important to do sufficient legal research in relation to key issues to be able to do this. If this tactic is used against you, take care not to reveal that you have not heard of the case and are a bit shaken. Say something like 'Interesting point, but have you got a copy of the case with you so I can deal with the detail'? **8.72**

KEY POINTS SUMMARY

- A proper understanding and use of style, strategy and tactics is a very important part of securing the best possible outcome for a client. **8.73**
- Style should be distinguished from strategy as an apparent style can mask a different strategy.
- Specific strategy and tactics should be planned in advance for each case so that they can be implemented to best effect.
- The main strategies are: cooperative, competitive, collaborative and pragmatic. Each has strengths and weaknesses.
- A wide range of tactics can be used, relating to information, offers, demands, structure and presentation. Tactics can and should be used to support any strategy.
- In addition to using strategy and tactics effectively yourself, you should use your understanding to identify and address the strategy and tactics used by your opponent.

9

PREPARING FOR NEGOTIATION

THE IMPORTANCE OF PREPARATION 9.01

IDENTIFYING THE OBJECTIVES 9.04

THE IMPORTANCE OF THE PROCEDURAL STAGE
THE CASE HAS REACHED. 9.07

IDENTIFYING THE ISSUES 9.15

THE RELEVANCE OF THE LEGAL CONTEXT. 9.18

PREPARING TO DEAL WITH FACTS AND EVIDENCE 9.21

PREPARING TO DEAL WITH FIGURES 9.31

IDENTIFYING PERSUASIVE ARGUMENTS 9.33

PLANNING POTENTIAL DEMANDS, OFFERS AND CONCESSIONS . . .9.48

LINKING CONCESSIONS. 9.57

IDENTIFYING THE BATNA 9.58

IDENTIFYING THE WATNA. 9.64

CLARIFYING YOUR INSTRUCTIONS AND AUTHORITY 9.67

KEY POINTS SUMMARY. 9.71

THE IMPORTANCE OF PREPARATION

9.01 A negotiation offers great potential to a lawyer. The lack of regulation offers a level of control that is not available in a relatively formal trial process. The flexibility of the process provides possibilities for the use of strategies and tactics, and the availability of outcomes, that may not be possible in a court. However, comprehensive preparation is essential to make the best use of the available opportunities so as to secure the best possible outcome for the client.

9.02 To mould a negotiation to suit your purpose you need a clear list of what you want, and clear plans for how you might get it. While a negotiation normally follows a staged process (see

Chapter 10), it often moves very quickly, and is likely to bring surprises and challenges, especially if your opponent is experienced and/or determined. With preparation you can move forward confidently, make the most of every possible advantage and take the unexpected in your stride.

Because negotiation is a relatively informal process, it might be tempting to take the view   **9.03**
that one could just turn up and see how it goes. For a lawyer such a view is unprofessional and potentially disastrous. Without full familiarity with the strengths and weaknesses on each issue it can be very difficult to put the case coherently and effectively to an opponent, and without a sufficiently detailed analysis of possible concessions it can be very difficult to take justifiable decisions on what to offer or accept. Strategy and tactics also require planning for best effect (see Chapter 8).

IDENTIFYING THE OBJECTIVES

The starting point is to be clear as regards exactly what the client hopes to achieve. Ask the   **9.04**
client to provide clear objectives, and check that the list you have is complete. You will need to check this list as you analyse the case to advise the client what is realistically achievable, but get a full list first. Ask the client to identify priorities—do not make assumptions.

- *Money claims*
  - You need a full list of every potential head of loss, for example in a road accident claim the client may be seeking damages to cover loss of wages, other benefits lost from being laid off at work as a result of the accident, medical expenses, the cost of repairing the car, etc.
  - Consider future loss as well as past loss, such as ongoing loss of wages. Consider whether there are any problems with regard to recoverability of each head, such as foreseeability, mitigation etc.
  - Reach a figure or a range of figures for each head of loss. If it is difficult to calculate a loss eg loss of profit, you will have to propose a method for assessment, as you would have to do if the case went to court.
  - Consider associated matters: When should the sum be paid? Should it be paid as a lump sum or in instalments? Is there a claim for interest? If so, what is the rate of interest and over what period has it been calculated? Are there any VAT or other tax implications for the sum?
- *Other legal rights*. If there is a possible claim for a non-financial remedy such as a declaration or an injunction relating to legal rights, consider whether this can be addressed without going to court, eg through a written agreement. Consider the wording that will best meet the client's objectives.
- *Future relationship*. If there will be a future relationship, for example because the dispute relates to residence and contact in relation to a child, because there is a commercial relationship, or because the parties are neighbours, establish what your client's objectives for the future are. Are there existing terms for the relationship, such as a contract or a contact order? If so, will those terms be varied or will there be a new agreement? What terms does the client want for the future?
- *Personal objectives*. The client may wish to achieve something in addition to enforcing legal rights, for example an apology

- *Costs of the litigation.* Check the costs of the case to date, and the costs of the negotiation itself. Get a breakdown rather than just global figures, and identify any arguments as to which party should pay each element of the costs.

9.05   It is also important to try to anticipate your opponent's objectives as far as you can—what they are likely to want from any settlement, and their probable priorities. Consider what might motivate them to settle. If you are not clear about their objectives you might wish to ask in the negotiation. This will be important to your whole approach if you are likely to use a collaborative strategy. It will in any event be relevant to planning possible concessions.

9.06   Once you have identified and attempted to prioritise the objectives of both sides, you should consider whether there are any that are shared (ie that both parties want), compatible (ie where the parties value things differently), or where there is conflict. This will help you to formulate possible offers.

THE IMPORTANCE OF THE PROCEDURAL STAGE THE CASE HAS REACHED

9.07   The stage that the case has reached provides a crucial context for the preparation that needs to be done. It also gives rise to different procedural possibilities and points that may be made during the negotiation. The main options are as follows.

The case is at a very early stage

9.08   Considering a negotiation shortly after the client has approached a lawyer may be good in terms of keeping costs to a minimum. If you have a relatively strong case there may be benefits in trying to settle before the other side has time to marshal arguments. A solicitor may send a letter proposing a negotiation, on the basis that if agreement can be reached the case will proceed no further.

9.09   However a very early settlement carries risk, unless the case has only one or two issues, such as a claim for money owed. At this stage the lawyer will often have little more than the client's informal statement and any documents the client may have to hand on which to assess the case and the appropriate remedies. Equally the other side may well only have an informal statement from their client. Any negotiation may well need a lot of information exchange and discussion to gain a clearer picture before trying to settle. You are likely to be taken by surprise by some of the points raised by the other side, as each client is likely to have described events from a very different point of view.

The case is at a pre-action protocol stage

9.10   Solicitors will often attempt to negotiate a settlement before a claim form is issued in an attempt to avoid going to court. Consideration of settlement is required under pre-action protocols. This is still a good time to settle in terms of saving costs. As the pre-action protocols require the exchange of quite a lot of relevant information, and a correspondence file is likely to have built up, it should be easier to assess the strengths and weaknesses of the case.

9.11   As neither side is yet committed to a statement of case there will be no formal definition of issues. This can be an advantage in terms of flexibility in the negotiation, though this may be a disadvantage in terms of there being less information about your opponent's case. The possibility of issuing proceedings can be used as a tactic in a negotiation.

After the issue of proceedings

Once all statements of case have been served, both sides will have a much clearer picture **9.12** of the issues and the allegations of fact made. It will also be clear what will go to court if the case is not settled. Further information becomes available step by step as directions are given with regard to disclosure and inspection of evidence, and then the exchange of witness statements. This gives you the advantage of a clearer picture of your opponent's case, the disadvantage being that your opponent will also know more about your case. Appropriate procedural steps, for example with regard to getting further evidence can be taken before a negotiation, or raised tactically during a negotiation.

At this stage you may be negotiating at the court door or prior to an interim application, **9.13** for example an application to obtain summary judgment, or an interim injunction. This can be a particularly challenging type of negotiation because there may be very limited time outside court, and there are several factors to consider.

- Be clear whether you have authority to negotiate the outcome of the whole case as well as the interim application. Ensure you have a full list of issues if you can deal with both, eg costs of the case and of the application.
- If you have authority on both, remember that you will still need to go into court to address the judge as regards the interim application, so you need to decide whether that goes ahead, is abandoned etc.
- Be aware of the possible effect of the application on the case, especially if for example the application is for summary judgment.
- As regards negotiating the outcome of the interim application, bear in mind the test that the court will apply, for example in a claim for an interim injunction, whether there is a serious issue to be tried, whether damages would be an adequate remedy and where the balance of convenience lies. The chances of winning in court are the basis for negotiating.

The case is being prepared for trial

A negotiation at the door of the court just before trial has particular characteristics. This is **9.14** the last stage at which the parties will have control of the outcome rather than leaving it to the judge. The imminence of trial may also focus the minds of the parties on trying to avoid the risk, stress and costs of a full trial. At the door of the court there will also be particular considerations, such as trying to avoid keeping the judge waiting for too long and recording any agreement reached in a consent order. Although the costs may be greater, there may be merit in having a separate meeting before the trial date.

IDENTIFYING THE ISSUES

You need to identify clearly what parts of the case and what issues you are instructed to **9.15** negotiate.

- You may be instructed to negotiate the whole case, or the outcome of a specific application: see 9.12–9.13.

- You may be instructed to deal with certain issues. Some issues may have been settled already, for example through correspondence. It may be agreed to negotiate a specific part of the case, leaving other matters for a later date. For example there may be a negotiation about liability for an accident, leaving damages till later. You might be instructed to negotiate a claim but not the counterclaim.

9.16　　As regards the range of issues in the case, if litigation has been commenced the issues should be largely defined in the statements of case. If litigation has not been commenced the issues will need to be identified from client statements and correspondence with the other side, using a process similar to that used for case analysis in relation to opinion writing or advocacy.

- Identify the alleged or potential causes of action.
- For each cause of action, identify the elements that would need to be proved if each went to court, for example the making of a contract, relevant express or implied terms and breaches.
- Identify which elements are actually in dispute. For example there may be no dispute about the making of the contract or its express terms, but there may be a dispute about implied terms, or there may be an argument that a term was in fact varied.
- Identify on whom the burden of proof lies with regard to each element of each issue.
- Identify alleged or potential defences, eg limitation, or contributory negligence.
- Identify the remedies that are or might be sought.
- Identify any legal issues with regard to each remedy; for example if damages are claimed there may be issues of causation, remoteness, foreseeability, or mitigation.
- Is there a counterclaim?

9.17　　The flexibility of the negotiation process allows you to deal with additional or non-legal issues, especially if your strategy will be collaborative. Check the list of potential issues with the client if you can. The above list will need to be adapted as appropriate if you are acting for the defendant rather than the claimant. In any event you should go through the list from the point of view of your opponent to get insight into the lines they are likely to pursue in negotiation.

THE RELEVANCE OF THE LEGAL CONTEXT

9.18　　Legal principles are central to a trial. The issues in the case are defined by law, the lawyers on each side focus their arguments on how the law supports their case, and the judge makes a decision based on and often setting out the application of the law to the case. For a negotiation the legal context is different, but potentially equally important.

- The potential outcome if the case were to go to court is a key standard against which the parties should measure proposals for settlement.
- Where your case has legal strength you should use this in argument in the negotiation, albeit with reference to relevant legal principles rather than a long argument based on law.
- Where your case has legal strength you should not make significant concessions.
- You can use points of law, such as a recent case, tactically.

Many negotiations turn on arguments on fact and evidence rather than on law, though **9.19** there are still likely to be legal issues such as the wording of an implied term, or whether a particular head of loss was foreseeable. Ensure you identify and are familiar with relevant legal principles as your opponent may take a more legalistic view of the case than you. Also ensure that your knowledge of the law is up to date so that you cannot be taken by surprise.

If there is a more complex issue of law in the case you need to research it as thoroughly as **9.20** you might in preparing the case for court. Consider taking copies of key cases or relevant practitioner texts with you to the negotiation to show your opponent. If case law is relevant, decide which cases support your position, and consider the level of the court involved, and whether the case has been subsequently considered by the courts, including whether it was approved, distinguished or overruled. Consider how you will argue the case supports your client. Also consider how your opponent is likely to argue the point, and which cases they might use. Summarise research that you have done in a way that can be referred to easily in your preparation and in the negotiation itself.

PREPARING TO DEAL WITH FACTS AND EVIDENCE

Most legal negotiations turn wholly or partly on disputes of fact. Indeed it may be problems **9.21** or potential cost with regard to clarifying facts and collecting evidence that lead to a decision that negotiation should be attempted. It is a vital part of preparation to decide how you will deal practically and persuasively with each issue of fact and evidence, especially where there are gaps in information.

Dealing with fact and evidence can be one of the most difficult parts of a negotiation. Unless **9.22** you are negotiating after the action has been started and after disclosure and inspection and exchange of witness statements have taken place, you will have less information than would be available at trial. This makes it particularly important to be methodical and strategic in dealing with the information you have, and with the information you do not have.

The client's view of the facts and evidence

You need a full version of your client's view of the facts. Later in the case this will take the **9.23** form of a sworn statement, but at a relatively early stage in the case there will be an informal summary of what the client says. While you must accept what your client tells you, be wary of assuming that your client has told you the whole truth, or has given an objective summary. The two parties are likely to view the events leading to potential litigation very differently, and are likely to have developed a mental picture to support what they wish to see as an outcome. If you have only an unsworn statement that is likely to be incomplete and over optimistic, you may well wish to test what the client says in a meeting or conference to avoid being taken by surprise by your opponent in the negotiation.

Consider next what information and evidence currently available supports your client's **9.24** view of the case as regards each issue likely to be in dispute. While it is not formally necessary to prove an allegation of fact to an opponent in a negotiation, proof or potential proof will be important tactically in convincing an opponent of your case. Where you do not have evidence, identify what is likely to be easily available, so that you can say at the negotiation that you will seek to get that evidence to support you if the case goes to trial. The relevance, admissibility and weight of existing and potential evidence is important as part of the strength of your case. You can show an opponent evidence that is not technically admissible, but they are likely to be quick to point out that inadmissibility in court is a weakness.

The opponent's view of the facts and evidence

9.25 To determine what an opponent might accept you need to look at the facts from their point of view. Close to trial you will have a sworn statement from the other side to support their case, but at an earlier stage in a case you may have very limited information about how the other side's version of the facts differs from your own. To avoid being taken by surprise at the negotiation, draw everything you can from what your client says and from what documentation is available to try to predict how the other side sees the case. If there is a key issue on which you would like to know their view prior to negotiation it may be possible to ask with a letter or a phone call.

9.26 Early in a case you will know little or nothing about the evidence the other side may have. Make best use of the pre-action protocols to request relevant evidence in the possession of the other side. If you would like to see evidence that is not strictly available under a pre-action protocol you can ask—they can only say no. Bear in mind that when a negotiation precedes to formal exchange of evidence, an opponent may produce evidence in support of their case at a negotiation tactically to try to surprise you.

Dealing with gaps and ambiguities

9.27 Having followed all the above steps, there will be gaps and ambiguities in the information you have, especially early in a case. A successful negotiator is often someone who is able to deal effectively with such gaps. You do not need to know everything about a case to be able to negotiate effectively. Even if a case goes to trial you will not find out exactly what happened—the judge will decide on the balance of probabilities. Do not get distracted by or feel insecure about the various things you do not know—focus on what you really need to know to deal effectively with those issues that are in dispute. Focus on information that is most relevant to winning on the main issues, and to getting the results the client hopes for. This will help you to see that some gaps in information are not very important.

9.28 When a gap in information is important it may be dealt with as suggested above—by asking the client, or by a request to the other side prior to the negotiation. You may collect extra evidence before the negotiation, but only seek evidence that is really important and can be found at reasonable cost.

9.29 Where gaps remain you will need to present arguments to convince your opponent. It is vital to develop arguments on key gaps in the case in advance—good arguments will not necessarily occur to you on the spur of the moment, and arguments need to be integrated with your strategy and tactics. The following might provide a line of argument:

- Given the disparity between the two versions of events, which seems more plausible? Why?
- How can the facts that are known be most convincingly put together?
- What further evidence might each party gain if they needed to?

- Which side would be most likely to persuade a judge if the case went to trial?
- Which side would have the burden of proof on the disputed issue? Will that party be able to meet the standard of proof of the balance of probabilities? Is what they say more probable than not?
- Will their evidence be admissible and their witnesses credible?

Preparing to deal with facts and information in negotiation

Going through the above stages should prepare you to deal efficiently and confidently **9.30** with the facts in a case. There are just a few more things to do to ensure that you can deal with factual information quickly and fluently. Having to check facts in your papers during a negotiation wastes time and provides your opponent with an opportunity to take control of the process. If you make a mistake about facts it may impact on how the negotiation proceeds, and misleading your opponent about facts can be an issue of professional conduct.

- Ensure that you are fully familiar with the facts so that you can deal with them accurately—any errors can undermine the impact you have. You also need to be able to absorb new information quickly to adjust your view of the case during the negotiation.
- Be ready to put the facts on each key issue in dispute clearly and confidently from your client's point of view
- Be ready to use evidence that you have or could easily obtain to best effect to support your client's view of the case.
- Think about which facts are known to both sides and which are not. Early in a case you may be able to make tactical use of information known only to you.
- Prepare a list of questions to put to your opponent to get information to support you client's version of the case and to undermine your opponent's version.
- Have arguments ready to deal with gaps in your case that cannot be addressed in any other way.
- Consider where there may be gaps in the information your opponent has.
- Decide whether there is any information about your case that you might wish to keep secret in case the negotiation fails.

PREPARING TO DEAL WITH FIGURES

Virtually every negotiation includes at least some issues relating to figures. Some negotia- **9.31** tions may turn almost entirely on figures, for example where a commercial contract has been breached, or where liability has been admitted, so that only a figure for damages remains to be negotiated. It is vitally important to be prepared to deal with figures in detail to ensure you get the best outcome for your client, and do not get confused.

- You cannot afford to get confused or make errors about figures in the heat of a negotiation. If you do you will undermine your confidence, waste time and lose the initiative.
- Presenting figures to an opponent who is almost certainly going to argue is more difficult than presenting figures to an objective judge.
- If you are not prepared to deal with detailed figures you may easily make concessions unnecessarily and end up with a deal that is very unfavourable to your client.

- The process of dealing with offers and concessions will mean that you need to be able to amend your figures quickly and correctly.
- Many negotiators will choose a competitive strategy with regard to money, whatever strategy they might use on other issues.

9.32   Steps to take with regard to preparing figures are:

- Identify all issues to which figures are relevant, including each head of loss.
- Collect the figures you need to address each issue, or decide how you will deal with a figure that is not to hand. You might for example propose accepting a figure for damage assessed by an agreed independent expert.
- Ensure that you can justify the case for the figure you say is payable—that the loss is foreseeable, is caused by the breach etc as relevant.
- Check whether there is any basis on which the figure should be reduced—mitigation, contributory negligence etc as relevant.
- Consider any issues relating to calculation, eg how loss of profit should be calculated.
- Consider whether any figure should be adjusted, for example to take VAT into account.
- Consider which figures should have interest added and, if so, the rate and period.
- Consider any issues about when and how money should be paid.
- Ensure you have figures for costs to date, and for the costs of the negotiation.
- Consider how your opponent will see each of the above issues.
- Prepare a summary of your figures to include all the above elements as any of them might be argued in the negotiation. Prepare the summary in a flexible way so that you can quickly adjust figures and recalculate in the negotiation if necessary.

IDENTIFYING PERSUASIVE ARGUMENTS

9.33   The real challenge in any negotiation is getting your opponent to concede what you want for your client. A good negotiator is properly prepared, as outlined in this chapter, and makes effective use of strategy and tactics as outlined in Chapter 8. A good negotiator is also able to persuade their opponent to make concessions. Persuasive arguments need to be prepared in advance for negotiation just as much as they do for advocacy. It could be said that preparation of argument is even more important in negotiation because it is more difficult to persuade an opponent than an objective judge.

9.34   The first step is to identify where you will need persuasive arguments. This should emerge from putting together your analysis of your client's objectives (see 9.04–9.06), of the issues in the case that are in dispute (see 9.15–9.17) and of how far facts and evidence support your case (see 9.21–9.30). You will need the most persuasive arguments where issues are most in dispute, and where those issues are most important to your client's objectives. The importance of developing arguments where there are gaps in the facts was dealt with in 9.27–9.29. Here we look at the wider need to develop arguments to support the case overall.

9.35   Use of argument in negotiation is in some ways similar to use of argument in advocacy. In both you seek to persuade another to meet the claims of a client through promoting the strengths of a case and minimising the weaknesses. Both may depend to some extent on developing a coherent theory of the case, or at least a coherent approach to key issues.

A major difference from advocacy is the way in which you put your case. A case needs to **9.36** be put comprehensively in court, with a set role of an opening and/or closing speech. In negotiation the process is more fragmented, and tends to focus on what is really is dispute. Use of argument in negotiation can be more challenging because the process moves much more quickly than a trial, your opponent may well interrupt, you are more likely to have to deal with new information and points, and the opponent is not an independent arbitrator but a person with a different viewpoint. These differences can make it difficult to present a full and detailed case. If time is limited it is recommended that you focus on identifying about three of the best arguments on each issue and that you work on how to present those arguments in the most persuasive way. By all means note other arguments, but they can be kept in reserve.

You should also be aware of the arguments that are most likely to be used to test you or to **9.37** justify your opponent's proposals so you can be ready to respond to them. This will help you to be proactive rather than merely reactive; for example you may be able to reduce the impact of any argument that may be raised by your opponent before they use it.

Arguments based on the application of the law

If there is a significant argument on what the relevant law is, it is more likely that the case **9.38** will go to court, especially if either party wishes to create a precedent. An argument may arise with regard to an issue because a legal principle is not well established, or if it is argued that it should be reinterpreted or applied in a different way. Reference to the law may be needed where there is dispute about the interpretation of the law as regards a statute, regulation or case law as regards an issue, and the law may need to be argued at sufficient length. The lawyers cannot establish what the law is in the way a judge can, but the lawyers can try to reach agreement on what the law will be seen as being for the purposes of settling the case if the parties wish to avoid the cost of going to court.

Argument is more commonly about how the law applies to facts, for example what the **9.39** standard of care is in a case where negligence is alleged, or whether representations induced a contract. In a negotiation is between lawyers there is no need for law to be stated at length— more commonly there is a brief reference to principle and then a statement as to how it is seen to apply. For example 'We will of course need to satisfy the balance of convenience test and we do that because...' When arguing about law, lawyers typically use shorthand references to principles; for example 'We will not pay £1,000 because you have a forseeability problem in employing a chef for a day'.

Arguments based on facts

Commonly at least some of the arguments in a negotiation relate to what the facts are. In a **9.40** contract case there may be a dispute about whether there was an oral variation of contract, which essentially sets one person's word against another's. In a negligence case there may well be a dispute about exactly how an accident happened. How to deal with argument where there is a gap in the information available is dealt with in 9.27–9.30.

Merit based or moral argument

9.41 A merit-based argument is one that seeks to show an objective reason why a specific approach should be adopted, for example by relating an issue to a set standard. An argument on law will be merit based where you are seeking to argue that a specific outcome is justified by legal principle. An argument on evidence will be merit based where you have clear admissible evidence on a point. A merit-based argument should have a sound base, not relying on an assumption or partisan view, to be successful.

9.42 A moral argument might relate to the beliefs or circumstances of the parties to a case. A specific outcome might be seen as 'right' for those involved, perhaps for cultural or personal reasons. In negotiating a separation between a couple it might be right to take such factors into account.

9.43 More frequently an argument about what is 'fair' might be used. A negotiator might say 'it would be fairer to ...', but this is a very vague term. You need to be able to justify on what basis a particular approach is 'fairer'. Is it more equal? Is it more justified because of the way someone has behaved?

Practical or personal arguments

9.44 Practical arguments might relate to a party's circumstances, or to the practicalities of achieving a possible compromise. Practical arguments might be very relevant in a case relating to a sale between two businesses, or as regards the terms of a proposed interim injunction. A practical argument might also relate to the terms of a settlement, for example relating to terms for payment.

9.45 An argument in a negotiation might relate to the particular people involved, especially where a collaborative strategy is employed. In a neighbour dispute an elderly person might primarily want to secure a peaceful and quiet life. In a business dispute a hairdresser might want to get the right ambience for a new salon. Personal arguments can be powerful if used carefully and at the right time, but they can show weakness if used wrongly, especially if used against a competitive opponent.

Mixed arguments

9.46 An issue might be addressed using several types of argument, either separately or cumulatively. A single issue might be addressed with an argument about the application of the law, and an argument about personal needs. Alternatively an issue might involve an argument about facts, then an argument about the application of the law, then a moral argument about what is fair. The force of some key arguments can be lost if too many arguments are put together.

9.47 First identify the main different types of argument that might be used on an issue. Then think carefully about which arguments are strongest, and whether you might use only key arguments, keeping others in reserve. If you might need to use more than one form of argument, for example about facts and about application of the law, then plan the use of each argument as regards the order in which they are best presented, and how they are best linked.

PLANNING POTENTIAL DEMANDS, OFFERS AND CONCESSIONS

A negotiation is a process for moving towards agreement. It may start from positions that **9.48** are quite far apart, especially where two competitive negotiators are involved. From there a process of demands and proposals will potentially lead to offers and concessions, and hopefully to a point where the parties can agree. In order to ensure you get the best possible outcome for your client it is important to plan in advance when you would envisage these steps taking place. Without planning it can be very difficult to know what to offer when, and it is all too easy to ask for too little or concede too much.

Overall you need to work within a clear understanding of the client's priorities, the most **9.49** the client might possibly achieve, and the least that the client might accept: see 9.04–9.06 and 9.69–9.70. There should rarely if ever be a concession on something that is important to your client and where the case is strong. Any concession should be justifiable by a proper evaluation of the case, as outlined in this section. It is your professional duty to seek the best available outcome for your client, and your plan should be reasonably optimistic. It is not your role just to aim vaguely for a position some way between yourself and your opponent, or to try to impose something you see as roughly 'fair', and such an approach could be exploited by a competitive opponent.

Plan what you will seek from the other side

Planning involves systematic consideration of the client's objectives, the client's priorities, **9.50** and the strengths and weaknesses of the case. It is psychologically helpful to start by identifying where you will seek concessions from the other side.

- What are your client's main objectives? Work from a detailed and prioritised list. Concessions may come from the lower part of the list, but should be limited in the upper part.
- Which issues relate to your client's main objectives? Plan primarily with regard to those issues.
- How exactly is your case strong in relation to key issues? Is it a matter of law, fact, and/or evidence? What sort of legal or evidential issue is it? How good are the arguments you can develop?
- Is your strength on the issue clear (for example because of evidence you hold), or might you need to investigate the issue with them before seeking a concession (for example to see what evidence they have)?
- What exactly are the weaknesses of the case for the other side in relation to the key issues? Are the weaknesses legal, factual or evidential? How can you point out those weaknesses most clearly?
- What are the relative strengths or weaknesses? Can you argue the other side should acknowledge you should win (for example because you have a letter proving a variation of contract, or you will argue a head of loss was unforeseeable)? Can you argue the other side should make a significant concession (for example because you think you can prove 30% contributory negligence)? Can you only argue they should make a small concession (for example because of a limited failure to mitigate loss)?

- Based on the previous point, identify as accurately as possible the largest concession on the issue you can expect the other side to make.
- Identify fall-back positions as accurately as possible. For example if they will not concede 30% contributory negligence, might you argue for 20%? Why?

Plan how and when you will ask

9.51 Gaining a significant concession from an opponent in a negotiation will not be easy. If you just ask an opponent to concede 30% contributory negligence you are likely to be met with a refusal. You need to plan carefully when and how you will seek a concession to maximise your chances of success.

- Decide whether you will make a demand or ask for a concession, or use other terminology, depending on how this fits with your strategy.
- It is usually best to seek a concession specifically, clearly and once. This is most likely to stick in your opponent's mind and to have some effect.
- Support this with a clear summary of reasons. For example 'I think you need to drop your claim for £2,000 for the loss of the wife's earnings. That head of loss was not foreseeable to my client and he had no notice of it. I any event I would argue it did not flow from the breach.'
- Relate concession planning to structure planning and time your approach for best effect. A competitive negotiator might well demand early in a negotiation that an opponent makes a number of concessions. This can be effective as it will often lead to the other side making concessions on at least some of those points. However early demands that are unrealistic and unjustified are likely to fail as they can be challenged relatively easily by the opponent. More commonly a concession would be requested after the relevant issue has been discussed and the case made, so you might want to cover areas where your case is strong early so that you can get justified requests for concessions on the table.

9.52 You may obtain a concession quite quickly if your case is strong (though if you obtain a concession too easily it might mean that you have asked for too little). However you will rarely get a full concession immediately. Once you have made your opponent aware of what you are seeking you may need to move to another issue. You might well be able to get the concession in return for something else later. Repetition is more likely to weaken your position rather than help because your opponent may well repeat a refusal. Do not rush to reduce the concession you are seeking unless there is a good reason—this can look weak.

Plan what you will offer

9.53 You also need to plan carefully what concessions you might make to the other side. You will rarely if ever be able to reach a settlement without making some concessions. Your client will want to achieve their objectives as far as possible, so success depends on making as few concessions as are necessary, with each concession being as small as possible. A co-operative strategy should not lead to unnecessary concessions any more than a competitive strategy.

The process for identifying possible concessions is similar to that for identifying demands: **9.54**

- How exactly is your case weak or their case strong? Is it a matter of law, fact, and/or evidence? What sort of legal or evidential issue is it?
- Should you investigate the issue with them before offering any concession (for example to see what evidence they have)?
- What is the relative weakness in your case? Are you clearly going to lose on the issue (for example because your client admits to you that a key term was not part of an oral contract)? Might you have to make a significant concession (for example because the burden of proof on an issue is on you and you think it unlikely you will be able to get enough evidence)? Are you thinking of a small concession (for example that you will not force the other side to get formal evidence on a particular point)?
- Based on the type and size of the weakness, should you really make any concession at all? Is the weakness something you might address by getting further evidence if the case went to trial? What is the smallest concession on the issue you can expect the other side to consider?
- Is there any more you might concede in any circumstances? If you make any concession an opponent might press for more—your concession should not be more than the relative weakness of your case justifies. Be slow to concede more on an issue of real importance to the client.
- Ensure you are clear what concession you might make—for what reason, how much and in what circumstances.
- Prioritise potential concessions in order of importance to the client, and try only to make ones that are of least importance to the client. The fact that you could make a concession does not mean that you should!

Plan how and when you will make offers

You should plan carefully when and how to offer a concession to ensure that you make as   **9.55**
few concessions as are really necessary. This might well be a part of planning the whole structure of a negotiation. You might well want to make any concession that you offer 'provisional', that is that the concession would only become operative as part of an overall deal with concessions from both sides, and is not a concession that would stand alone.

There may be a tactical reason for making a provisional concession at an early stage; for   **9.56**
example 'I am prepared to say immediately that we will not be pressing ahead with our application for an interim injunction so long as all the issues relating to the agreement between the parties can be settled today.' This can help to lay a foundation for a collaborative strategy.

- You might start with an area where you can make a few unimportant concessions so that you can appear generous. If these are provisional concessions you can use that to put pressure on your opponent to make concessions later.
- You might start with an area where you do not feel you need to make any concessions, to lay a foundation for a competitive strategy.
- It is risky to start with an area where you think you may need to make significant concessions as this can make you look weak, unless perhaps you are sure that both negotiators are committed to a collaborative approach.

- If you need more information to be sure whether a concession is justified, make sure that you ask relevant questions before raising any possible concession.
- Plan to stage concessions. Make small fall-back steps between your opening offer and the least you can accept. Avoid big or rapid increases in concessions or your opponent will realise that more may be gained by pushing you.

LINKING CONCESSIONS

9.57 In seeking to do the best for the client, a concession should rarely be made without getting something in return. In addition to having a good reason for making a concession on a particular point, you should try to make sure that the concession takes the case forward. This is most likely to happen if your concession is linked to a concession by your opponent on another point. Make this clear by saying when you offer a concession that it is provisional on getting something in return. Make sure that you try to link getting a concession on something important to your client to making a concession on something of limited importance. Make sure you do not vaguely trade one concession for another if you are giving away much more than you get.

IDENTIFYING THE BATNA

9.58 In addition to planning potential demands and concessions on individual issues, you need to put a potential settlement into an overall context so that you will be able to judge whether a particular set of terms should or should not be accepted. You will need to be able to compare whatever potential overall deal you are able to achieve in a negotiation with what alternative there would be if no settlement were reached so as to decide whether to accept the deal or walk away. This involves identifying the BATNA (the best alternative to a negotiated agreement). The BATNA is sometimes seen as the 'bottom line', that is the least that should realistically be accepted.

9.59 It may not be easy to identify a BATNA, especially if the client's objectives and priorities are not all financial and there is a variety of issues. In such a case it will be especially important to have a discussion with the client in advance to develop a BATNA, so as to know what settlement terms are acceptable. This can be done by looking at the list of the client's objectives and listing what the possibilities are if no agreement is reached. The client can then help to identify what could best be achieved. This process can also help to provide confidence in a negotiation as it is to some extent a 'plan B'.

9.60 Normally for a legal negotiation the alternative to settlement will be going to court, so that calculation is made in relation to what the client would be likely to get if the case went to court. A client who has been advised that if they go to court they are likely to win and to get £40,000 and costs could see that as a BATNA. However this might be an idealistic rather than a realistic BATNA. It is necessary to take into account the realistic risks that that outcome will not be achieved because the case will not be won. There may be doubts as to whether a legal argument will succeed, as to whether a key witness will come up to proof, or as to whether a judge will be sufficiently convinced by the evidence overall. If the lawyer assesses that these points together mean that the chance of success at trial is 75% at most then a client who might get £40,000 at trial should perhaps consider £30,000 as the BATNA due to the risk.

Another factor is that going to court will incur further costs. If the client might have to incur another £5,000 in costs to go to court, not all of which would be recoverable even if the case was won, then the BATNA might go down to £28,500. This calculation is complicated by the fact that the party who wins at trial will normally get their costs, but at least a broadly realistic BATNA is identified. **9.61**

The better your BATNA the stronger your negotiating position is, because the more likely it is that you will walk away if you do not get a good enough offer. For that reason you might consider revealing your BATNA to the other side for tactical reasons, as in 'I'm afraid you are going to have to make a bigger concession on this. We are confident we have a good chance of getting £40,000 if we go to court'. A competitive negotiator might suggest a high BATNA as a tactic. Do not forget that your BATNA is your bottom line—you should aim to get much more. It is the point where you walk away because you are likely to do just as well going to court. **9.62**

It is also helpful to consider the BATNA for the other party as far as you can from the information available to assess what proposals they may or may not accept. You should try to get a deal that pushes the other side as close as possible to their bottom line. **9.63**

IDENTIFYING THE WATNA

Identification of a WATNA (worse alternative to a negotiated agreement) is also relevant to assessing whether a deal offered in negotiation should be accepted. Here you are seeking to ensure that you do not sink into a worse situation than could happen if there were no agreement. **9.64**

It may not be easy to assess the worst that can happen, partly because a doomsday scenario may not be very likely, and also because it may be difficult to engage a client in considering this when you are trying to convince a client that you are acting in their best interests. **9.65**

In the scenario in 9.60 the worst that could happen is the 25% risk that the client would lose at trial, therefore getting nothing, and probably having to pay the other side's costs in addition to their own. This is not a likely outcome and should not of itself lead to unnecessary concessions, or to settling below the BATNA. The point is rather to stress the importance of assessing the likelihood of success at trial accurately, and thus the risk that the WATNA might happen. If there is only a 60% chance of success at trial a WATNA might need to be taken more seriously. **9.66**

CLARIFYING YOUR INSTRUCTIONS AND AUTHORITY

In professional terms it is vital to be absolutely clear what you are instructed by the client to do, and what authority you have from the client to settle. If you have any doubts about either you should check, and if the client is indecisive or vague it may be best to record the **9.67** instructions and authority in writing. If any doubts arise you may also wish to check during a negotiation that your opponent is acting with instructions and within the authority given.

9.68   Your instructions relate to whether you can negotiate at all and what you can negotiate on. Do you have a clear instruction to negotiate? Does it apply to all issues? If not, which issues are you instructed to deal with? Any doubts must be resolved with the client as it is a matter of professional conduct to act within your instructions. Check whether any proposals for settlement have been made by the other side and, if so, what your instructions are with regard to those proposals.

9.69   Your authority to settle is a different matter. 'Authority' relates to what you are authorised to accept on your client's behalf. Although a lawyer normally has apparent authority to settle on behalf of a client, if you do not act within actual authority you may put yourself in the very difficult position of having made an agreement with the other side that your client is not prepared to honour. A client will often give general authority to negotiate, but on the basis that any agreement you reach with the other side will only be provisional and subject to client approval. This is a helpful basis for you as it gives you flexibility but enables you to make it clear to your opponent that only a provisional agreement can be reached and it will be subject to client approval. You need to raise any limit on authority in the negotiation: see 10.49–10.52.

9.70   A client may give guidelines as to what sort of figures are acceptable on specific issues, often based on the advice the lawyer has given to the client on what can realistically be gained. Sometimes a client will insist on being unrealistically optimistic so that the lawyer only has authority to settle for a high figure. This may make it unlikely the negotiation will be successful.

KEY POINTS SUMMARY

9.71
- The negotiation process is very flexible, which offers a lot of opportunities to a lawyer who is properly prepared to get the most out of the process.
- The purpose of a negotiation is to get the best possible outcome for the client, so planning should be based on a careful identification and prioritisation of the client's objectives.
- Context is very important—consider carefully the implications of the stage the case has reached.
- Identify the issues that need to be negotiated, and analyse the facts, evidence and law to put together persuasive arguments on each issue.
- Be ready to deal with figures fully and in detail so that you can deal with them fluently in the negotiation.
- Evaluate your case carefully to plan potential concessions, demands and offers, so that you are clear what you want to get on each issue, and what the possible fall-back positions are.
- Have planned positions so that you can avoid 'splitting the difference'—this may appear to be fair but is often not justified by relative strengths and weaknesses.
- Plan a BATNA and WATNA to provide a context for assessing offers and the possible overall outcome of the negotiation.

10

THE NEGOTIATION PROCESS

WHEN, HOW AND WHERE 10.04

WHO 10.08

COMMUNICATING EFFECTIVELY 10.11

STRUCTURE AND AGENDA SETTING 10.26

OPENING. 10.32

SEEKING INFORMATION 10.57

MAKING YOUR CASE ON THE ISSUES 10.63

PLANNING AND TIMING CONCESSIONS,
OFFERS AND DEMANDS. 10.77

MAKING PROGRESS. 10.107

DEALING WITH DIFFICULTIES 10.109

REACHING A CLOSE—SETTLEMENT OR BREAKDOWN. 10.122

KEY POINTS SUMMARY 10.130

There is no defined negotiation process, but almost all negotiations include similar identifi- **10.01**
able stages. Understanding those stages will help you to control the process and work with
confidence, so that you can get the best achievable outcome. Many negotiators prefer the
relative security of a conventional structure based on an agenda, though it is inevitable that
discussion will sometimes move away from what was planned, and some negotiators will
fail to follow a set structure as a matter of tactics.

The main stages that can be identified are as follows. They normally come broadly in the **10.02**
order listed, though stages 2–4 are often followed through separately in relation to each
issue. The stages are as follows, and they are illustrated in Figure 10.1.

1. Agenda setting/opening (10.26 and 10.56).
2. Seeking information (10.57–10.62).
3. Discussion of the merits on the issues (10.63–10.76).

Figure 10.1 Overview of the negotiation process

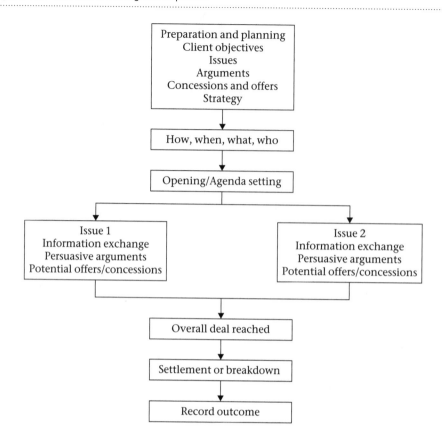

4. Concessions and offers (10.77–10.98).
5. Conclusion (10.122 and 10.129).

10.03   That said, each negotiation is unique. Each case will have different issues and clients with different objectives. There will be different legal and evidential strengths and weaknesses, and the negotiation may take place at a different stage in the case. The negotiators will use different strategies and tactics that affect how the process unfolds. Analysis and preparation, as outlined in Chapter 9, will help to ensure that you can predict and control these differences rather than be confused or tripped up by them.

WHEN, HOW AND WHERE

10.04   The first decision to make is that negotiation is an appropriate process for settlement, and that a good point in the case has been reached to try negotiation. The parties need adequate information to be able to analyse the case sufficiently as outlined in Chapter 9.

10.05   The next question is what form of negotiation to use. A negotiation may be conducted wholly or partly face-to-face, by telephone or in writing. Exchange of letters or e-mails may be appropriate if there are limited issues in the case and proposals can be put quite briefly without the need for much explanation or discussion: this book does not deal further with making written offers. Negotiating by telephone might be appropriate where the barristers or solicitors on each side are instructed to investigate settlement and it is thought that the process will not take too long. A number of the points made in this chapter could apply, but this chapter deals primarily with face-to-face negotiation involving lawyers.

An appropriate location for the negotiation must be agreed, depending on who will attend: **10.06** see 10.08–10.10. Solicitors will often negotiate in the office of one of the solicitors, and barristers may negotiate in the chambers of one of the barristers. A sufficiently large space will be needed for the number of people involved, and a space appropriate for the length of time the negotiation might last. There may be advantages in holding the negotiation in a space you have control of so that you can arrange seats, offer refreshments and so on. Alternatively you may prefer to visit a space where you have no responsibilities, and where you can threaten to leave if you are not happy with progress. A negotiation can be facilitated or frustrated by simple things like comfortable chairs and adequate table space for papers. Space can support your strategy and tactics. Do you want to show a competitive start by taking all the space available for your papers, or do you want to make a facilitative start by arranging chairs comfortably round the table? Making a point about the arrangements at the start of a negotiation may be done as a tactic.

You may have little choice over location if the negotiation takes place outside court. This **10.07** will happen quite often for a barrister early in practice, when appearing on an interim application may provide an opportunity to negotiate. It may also happen when lawyers meet outside court before a case management conference or trial. Many courts have small interview rooms that may be available, but there is often no choice but to use the corridor outside court, which may be noisy or busy. There may be no tables, and possibly no seats, so that it may be difficult to manage or refer to papers. There can also be stress if a case will be called into court at a particular time. You should still do what you can to control the space. Court door negotiations are often carried out between counsel, and it may be important to find space where the solicitor and client can wait away from counsel.

WHO

Decide who needs to attend the negotiation with care. Relevant people need to be included, **10.08** but additional people will increase cost, may slow the process down, and may make it more difficult to control. The negotiation may be just between solicitors, just between barristers, or between teams of lawyers on both sides, possibly including in-house lawyers. The number of lawyers should be justified by the complexity of the case and/or the amount at stake. If there is more than one lawyer on each side the role of each should be decided in advance—will one take the main role and the others provide information? Will each deal with different issues?

The clients may wish to be present. This can make it easier for the lawyers to take instruc- **10.09** tions and review the acceptability of options. However, it may be undesirable because clients may undermine the strategy or tactics being used with oral interjections or body language. If the client is present, the role of the client in the negotiation should be clearly agreed beforehand. It may be better for clients to be available in separate rooms nearby or available for consultation by telephone so that they can be asked for instructions or be briefed on what is happening as and when appropriate.

10.10 Others might usefully attend, or be available for consultation, especially if there are complex issues. An accountant might be present for at least part of the negotiation to assist with figures, or an expert might be asked to attend to help to deal with a specific issue.

COMMUNICATING EFFECTIVELY

10.11 Effective communication is central to effective negotiation. The main purpose of the process is for sufficient communication about the case for each side to take place so that agreement can be reached. Unfortunately the lack of a clear process, different strategies and tactics, and factors such as stress can make communication difficult. This might prevent agreement being reached if you do not avoid or address problems.

10.12 Psychological factors and non-verbal communication should not be ignored. Sitting back, smiling and making open and relaxed body movements can suggest confidence and might encourage negotiation. Nodding normally indicates support. Crossed arms and looking away can show hostility. Failing to meet someone's eyes might indicate that what is being said is misleading. Hunching over a desk or sitting uncomfortably can indicate lack of confidence.

10.13 Make sure that you control your own body language—sitting and moving in a confident way can help to convey your message. Sitting forward with interest when your opponent outlines a point of importance to them can help progress a collaborative approach. Take time to watch videos of yourself performing to see what effect body language has. Body language can provide clues that you can follow up, for example saying 'You do not look comfortable—you don't seem to think your case on this point is strong.'

Reciprocal or 'mirroring' behaviour

10.14 When two people are involved in a discussion, they often unconsciously 'mirror' each other's behaviour. If one starts to express annoyance, the other may take a similar course. You can sometimes take advantage of this to help you to progress a negotiation. If you want to take a collaborative or cooperative approach it can be very helpful to model it by smiling, listening carefully, and expressing what you say supportively. Unless your opponent has a clear plan for another strategy, he or she is likely to be prepared to follow your lead. Do not go too far—do not make too large a concession just to try to encourage an opponent to do likewise.

10.15 Two competitive negotiators can make effective progress, but mirroring can be a problem if one negotiator is confrontational or aggressive and the other is pulled in to behaving in a similar way. This serves little purpose, even if each negotiator feels that their behaviour is justified, and deadlock is likely to result. If your opponent's conduct is unhelpful try to remain calm and constructive. Do not feel compelled to make concessions to appease them—this may be what the tactic is trying to achieve.

Effective presentation

10.16 The way you present your case is likely to have a major impact on the outcome. A mediocre case will often get a better outcome if it is presented confidently and coherently. Being well prepared is half the battle—if you know how you want to argue each issue and what concessions you will seek you can concentrate on what you say and how you say it. A strong case can be completely undermined by mediocre presentation.

- The way you speak can be important—choose your language and tone of voice carefully.
- Keep up a good pace, but do not rush so that points get lost.
- Focus on your opponent as your audience—the point is to ensure that your opponent understands your case and is persuaded by it.
- Make each point as clearly and concisely as you can. Say what you want and why. Focus on your strongest points on each issue.
- Construct arguments carefully, making all your points on an issue together so they build on each other.
- Use appropriate legal terminology, not setting out law at length, but using the right legal words: for example 'Your client is clearly in breach of an implied term' or 'I can't see that there is any problem with foreseeability here.'
- Objective language is often most persuasive, 'My client has good evidence on this issue' is stronger than 'I think my client has a good point here.'
- Reference to the client is generally better than making things personal; for example 'My client would not accept that', rather than 'I won't accept that.'

Presentation can be undermined in various ways. **10.17**

- Speaking at too great a length—if you ramble, or recite information your opponent is already aware of at any length, your opponent will cease to listen and is likely to interrupt you.
- Presenting too many arguments together in a way that is difficult to follow, or where good arguments get lost among weaker ones.
- Repeating points at length—this is more likely to bore your opponent than lead to concessions.
- Failing to notice how your opponent is taking your presentation. If your opponent misunderstands or is bored you need to deal with that.
- Hesitation, or pausing to flick through papers without clear purpose, can allow your opponent to take control.

Presentation should of course be varied to fit with strategies or tactics. A competitive or **10.18** confrontational negotiator is likely to present with extreme self-confidence, whether or not this is justified, and may make sarcastic or condescending remarks about an opponent. Such a negotiator may be argumentative to try to wear an opponent down.

Responding effectively

Responding is almost as important as presenting, but can be rather more difficult, as you **10.19** may have to take into account new information that alters your assessment of the case. It is easy to focus so much on presenting your own case that you fail to respond properly—do not lose a chance to get a point across.

- You need to understand facts presented by an opponent. Follow up detail if you need to. Check key allegations and figures. Do not be content with what is offered if you need more.
- You may need to understand the arguments made by your opponent, but take care how you do this. Do not help an opponent to develop an argument, or allow a weak argument to appear important.

- Test and challenge what your opponent says—if a statement is not properly justified ask for reasons, or for evidence.
- Try to respond as clearly an accurately as you can to what your opponent says. Your response should try to move your case forward, keeping a focus on your client's objectives and your view of the strengths and weaknesses of the case. If you disagree with what the other side has said about law/fact/evidence then make that clear and say why.
- Avoid responding with surprise, or an indication that anything said undermines the strength of your case. If you are aware of a weakness you may have a prepared response; for example 'I accept we do not have evidence on that, but we could seek it if the case were to go to trial'. If you need time to think before you respond, make time by talking about details, or move on to another point and then come back.
- It is normally best not to interrupt an opponent—you may miss something important. If their presentation is long try to make the point by saying something like 'Sorry to interrupt but I think your key point here is that you are denying contributory negligence—can you give me your two main reasons for this.'

10.20　Responding should also fit with strategy and tactics. A competitive negotiator may fail to respond at all to a point made to imply that the point is irrelevant.

Questioning effectively

10.21　Lawyers are used to the need for questioning skills in conferences with clients and in dealing with witnesses in court. Similar skills may be needed to get information from an opponent in a negotiation, be it factual information or reasons for their view of the case. While only a very competitive negotiator would cross-examine an opponent, questions are crucial for testing your opponent in an appropriate way, asking about evidence etc.

10.22　Questions can also be used constructively—a collaborative negotiator will ask questions about what the opponent's client most wants to get from the negotiation. Most questions can be asked in a positive or confrontational way. Saying 'Please could you tell me why your client feels his claim on this issue is strong' is much less confrontational than 'I really can't see why you think you have a leg to stand on. On what possible basis do you make that claim?'

Listening effectively

10.23　A lawyer in a negotiation is often so focussed on putting the client's case and on responding robustly that too little attention is given to listening. Indeed there may be a fear that listening is not a good use of time when you could be presenting. Unless you stay quiet for a long time this is not the case—pick up every clue you can from what an opponent says, what they do not say, and any subtext. A throw-away remark may reveal information you need to follow up, or you may be able to spot a gap in their case from the way an argument is being made. An opponent who appears boring may be someone from whom you can get a concession.

10.24　Concentration is important, and negotiation can be tiring, especially if you are trying to negotiate in a crowded corridor. Make sure you do not miss anything important because you are thinking about something else. Listening can be part of your strategy—listening with interest supports a cooperative strategy, but appearing bored may support a competitive strategy.

What is not said can be very important. Something an opponent is trying not to talk about **10.25** could be an area of weakness. Ask about gaps, and do not feel you need to tiptoe round an issue. Remember that your opponent has a professional duty not to mislead you—if careful but vague wording is being used it may well be because care is being taken not to mislead. Remember there may be a gap between what your opponent has told the client and what they are telling you. The client may have been told the case on a point is not strong, while their lawyer tries to present it to you in a good light—you maybe able to pick up your opponent's underlying view if you listen carefully.

STRUCTURE AND AGENDA SETTING

The lack of a set format for a negotiation process means that structure and agenda setting **10.26** are important. An experienced negotiator will want to use a structure that supports plans for strategy and tactics. An inexperienced negotiator is likely to feel more secure working within an agreed structure. In a big case the coverage and order for a negotiation may well be agreed in advance. In a smaller negotiation the agenda is usually set in the first few minutes of the negotiation.

The potential benefits of a clear structure and agenda are that they should help to ensure **10.27** that:

- time is used efficiently, especially if limited time is available;
- you are able to cover all the things you need to;
- you can work coherently to achieve your client's objectives;
- you can implement your chosen strategy and tactics;
- you can deal with topics in a sensible order;
- you have a plan to fall back on, rather than feeling lost, if something unexpected comes up.

Choices for structure will normally be based on: **10.28**

- what you judge to be the best opening: see 10.32–10.56;
- what you judge to be the most productive order for dealing with topics;
- the need to resolve some issues before others, eg liability before damages;
- the need to gather information and clarify issues before any discussion of concessions;
- whether a few items will dominate the discussion, or whether there are a lot of items.

Despite the importance of structure, various problems may arise in implementing a chosen **10.29** structure:

- An opponent may make a very different choice about structure, such that it is impossible to implement both.
- Your opponent may interrupt you, either with questions and proposals, or as a tactic to undermine your plans.
- Unexpected information or views from your opponent may make it difficult to pursue your structure as planned.
- It may prove more difficult than you expect to deal with a particular issue, so that some parts of the structure overlap or get repeated.
- The negotiation may take an unpredictable turn because of an offer made to you.

10.30 If a difficulty arises try to modify rather than abandon your structure. Abandoning a planned structure can be risky as it might undermine your strategy, or mean that you forget to deal with some important issues. Prepare flexibly, to try to foresee which problems might arise, and be prepared to adapt your structure if necessary

10.31 Sometimes structure is vital to a whole strategy. A problem-solving approach might require the investigation of interests and needs, followed by option-creation, rather than moving straight to issues. A principled strategy might include the consideration of objective criteria for what is fair or just. If you want to follow this kind of strategy there is merit in trying to agree this in advance with your opponent, as it may be difficult to impose without warning.

OPENING

10.32 The way in which you open can set the tone for a whole negotiation. One negotiator may be able to take control of the process, to impose decisions as to structure or strategy in a way that may put the other at a disadvantage. How you deal with opening can give messages about what your client wants, what your strategy will be, how good you are at presenting your case, how well prepared you are, and whether you will make efficient progress in dealing with issues. Choose the messages you want to give and make them clear. You will have most energy and focus at the start of a negotiation and should use this to best effect.

10.33 Possible choices for opening are as follows. Some of them can be combined by starting with one and then moving quickly to another. Some openings are only appropriate in some circumstances—for example a long statement proposing a collaborative approach is unlikely to prove effective if there is limited time to reach an agreement outside court.

Open by agreeing an agenda

10.34 This is the normal way to open when no agenda has been agreed in advance. It has advantages in allowing both negotiators to influence structure, and it provides a relatively objective start in which each negotiator can form an impression of the views and strategy of the opponent.

10.35 An agenda is often proposed by one negotiator. You could start by listing the matters that you consider need to be discussed, and the order in which you would like to consider them. If there is limited time, take this into account to ensure you cover key matters. Your opponent may draw conclusions as to your interests and strategy from what you propose.

10.36 An agenda may be evolved collaboratively. You could open by saying: 'I thought it would be a good idea to agree an order in which to discuss the matters. The order I think would be best is…What do you think?' You can still keep relative control if you set up and manage this approach.

10.37 Alternatively one party may try to take control of the process by imposing an agenda—the other negotiator might chose to go along with this but then start to impose their own agenda at a later stage. Alternatively an objection can be raised—challenge if you are prepared to be competitive, or point out the benefits of a different agenda.

Open with a statement or a proposal

You can start by outlining your view of the case, and of the negotiation. A general outline **10.38** of the merits of the case may be useful if you have a strong case overall that is weak on some minor issues. If for example there is a single breach of contract where your case is relatively clear, but then several heads of loss of mixed strength, it could be helpful to present your overall view of the contract at an early stage. It can also be helpful if you want to stress some particular aspects of the case, or state views about the potential outcome, especially if this includes some things your opponent may not be aware of. A statement can also be useful if you want to set up a particular strategy, for example to explain how a collaborative approach might help.

It might be tempting to make a speech about your case at the start, but there is limited point **10.39** in providing an overview where there are several issues of equal importance but you have a good case on some but not others. You will simply make it clear from the start that your case has a mixed chance of success, and give your opponent advance notice so your opponent will be better prepared to respond. If you over-emphasise a readiness to settle, a competitive opponent see this as a weakness. Keep any statement you make relatively short and clear or there is a risk your opponent will start to argue with you before you can finish it.

It can be very tempting to start a negotiation by setting out the strengths of your client's case **10.40** and, possibly, the weaknesses of your opponent's case. You might include what your client is expecting to achieve, and you might include strong confidence in achieving much if not all of what your client seeks. This sort of opening will appeal particularly to a competitive negotiator, who might use an extreme form of it, such as 'Well, I am here to get the £15,000 my client demands, and I expect interest on it and costs. I can't see that your client has a leg to stand on, so I hope this won't take long.'

It is not very common to start with a proposal related to settlement, but it can be helpful to **10.41** set up a cooperative strategy, or as a tactic to take forward a specific element of your case. For example if a negotiation takes place just before an application for an interim injunction you might propose at the start that you will not pursue the application provided concessions are made on specific issues.

Start by asking some key questions

It is not common to open a negotiation by asking questions, but there are some circum- **10.42** stances in which it may be useful, or even tactical. If there is a key piece of information that you need to be able to assess your case or to frame an offer then you could start by saying 'It would be really helpful if you could let me know the dates when you are saying there was too much noise.'

Alternatively you might ask a question about your opponent's objectives, such as 'Could you **10.43** just tell me how much you are claiming for the damage to the car?' Asking questions constructively can lay a foundation for a collaborative approach, though intrusive questions may alienate the opponent.

Invite your opponent to open

It can be a useful tactic to invite your opponent to open, especially if you have limited infor- **10.44** mation about a case, or you are not sure what view of the case your opponent might take. It may help you to evaluate your opponent's likely negotiating strategy, and what they hope to achieve. It may assist you to gauge whether your strategy will work effectively or should be adjusted. With any luck your opponent might reveal information you are not aware of, or possibly even a weakness in their case. In any event you can ask questions or probe issues when your opponent finishes.

10.45   This way of starting clearly has potential advantages, but you cannot guarantee that they will be achieved, unless your opponent is relatively weak. Your opponent might refuse to start, or do more than make a general comment. This type of opening is also risky, as you are effectively leaving the start to your opponent, who may not cover what you invite them to cover. A competitive negotiator might well see this as an invitation to take control.

Start with items that can be agreed easily

10.46   There may be some issues that can be easily agreed, perhaps because both parties want the same thing, or because the issue is important to one party but of limited interest to the other. This can be especially useful in setting the tone for a cooperative or collaborative strategy. Such an opening must be used with care—if you go so far as to start offering concessions your position may be exploited by your opponent.

Start with items where your case is strong

10.47   You may well wish to start with items where your case is strong, either setting an agenda briefly and then moving straight to this, or by jumping straight in with words like 'I would like to get the issue of whether there was actually a breach of contract sorted out first.' The potential advantages are clearly that you can put your case best while you are freshest, that this can help give a general impression that your case is strong, and that you may get some quick concessions. The possible drawbacks are that your opponent may not be prepared to discuss your strongest issue first, and that if you fail to get a concession on your strongest issue it might undermine your case later on.

10.48   There are certainly advantages in pitching your case at its best and in 'opening' high in terms of what you expect to achieve. Research has shown that higher opening demands tend to lead to higher outcomes. However it is important to pitch an opening demand carefully. If the demand is unrealistically high only a weak or poorly prepared opponent will take it seriously. If the demand has no real justification, the opponent may form the view that the negotiator making the demand is not credible or is not well prepared. The only way to move from a high demand to compromise is to make concessions, and if the demand is very high the concessions may have to be big. The general risk of starting by focussing on the strengths of your case is that you may set a competitive tone for the whole negotiation, or at least antagonise your opponent.

Make limits on authority clear

10.49   Any limit on your authority to settle should be made clear to your opponent, and this is often done with a statement at the start of a negotiation. This is important as an error could lead to the negotiation breaking down, to a breach of professional conduct, and or to a complaint or legal action by your client.

In the negotiation you are acting as the agent of the client, and with apparent authority to bind the client to what you agree with your opponent. Any terms you agree will therefore bind the client, unless you have already made a limit on your authority clear. If you bind your client to anything beyond your instructions from your client, you will be in breach of your duty to your client. If you do that, or mislead your opponent about your level of authority, there may be a breach of professional conduct. If you appear to agree something in a negotiation but later try to say it was not agreed due to a limit on your authority your credibility will be undermined and your opponent will probably refuse to negotiate further. **10.50**

A common limitation on authority is that an agreement reached will only be provisional and will be subject to your client's approval. This is good for the client as they will have final approval, and it provides protection for the lawyer if the negotiation moves outside areas where instructions are clear. **10.51**

If your authority to settle is subject to final approval by the client then say so early in the negotiation. Another possible limit on authority is if you negotiate outside court prior to an interim application. If you only have authority to negotiate as regards the interim application but not the main action you should make this clear. **10.52**

Refer to privilege for discussion

Discussions with a view to settlement are generally 'without prejudice'. This means that what is said is privileged and cannot be revealed in court, so that offers or possible concessions will remain private and cannot be referred to if agreement is not reached. It also means that any information provided cannot be used as evidence, though it may be that admissible evidence can be found in another form. There is an exception in that if agreement is reached there is an enforceable contract, and evidence can be given about that if necessary. It is normal briefly to confirm at the start of a negotiation that the discussion will be 'without prejudice'. See 3.71–3.83. **10.53**

Note that the privilege applies to not referring to the matters discussed in court. It is not a general provision that nothing said in the negotiation can be passed on. If for example one lawyer reveals to the other a detail that benefits the case of the latter's client, the lawyer can tell the client what was revealed. Bar Council guidance makes this clear as regards barristers in its guidance on counsel-to-counsel confidentiality. **10.54**

Dealing with problems in opening

However you plan to open, it may not go as you hope. You should always be ready to modify what you planned, or move to an alternative because you need to start as well as possible to lay a sound foundation for the negotiation. Many negotiators will be prepared to discuss an agenda, but you will need to take on board quite quickly the style and strategy of your opponent, and what opening they have planned. **10.55**

In some cases there will be a real problem and you may need to negotiate how to start. You may plan to be collaborative but be met by an opponent making a very competitive statement to which you may feel you need respond, or you might plan a competitive start to be met by an equally competitive opponent so that deadlock is reached within minutes. You may need to modify strategy so as to make some progress, hoping to return to the original **10.56** strategy later. Alternatively you can name the problem and propose a next step; for example: 'Our clients have asked us to try to settle and we have both set out strong positions. Let's see if we can try to agree an agenda as a way forward.'

SEEKING INFORMATION

10.57　Knowledge can provide power. The negotiator who knows most about a case is likely to be in a strong position. The need to analyse the information you have thoroughly in preparing for a negotiation is outlined in Chapter 9. This is likely to leave gaps in your knowledge of facts, and you may well want to know more about matters like you opponent's objectives. Limited information gathering may be needed in a negotiation just before trial, but if a negotiation takes place early in a case, a substantial part of the negotiation may relate to gathering information. Logically you need to gather information before discussing the merits of the case in detail, either through dealing with information generally early in a negotiation, or though dealing with information at the start of dealing with each separate issue.

10.58　Information gathering will be affected by the strategy and tactics being used by each negotiator. If both are taking a collaborative or co-operative approach then the exchange of information is likely to be relatively free and straightforward. A negotiator following a competitive strategy will use information much more tactically, possibly asking quite intrusive questions, but generally refusing to provide many answers.

10.59　Bear in mind what information is shared. If the case is close to trial then statements of case, formal witness statements and evidence that have been subject to disclosure and inspection will all be shared. There may be relatively few further questions, and no need to discuss this information save as regards how it shows strengths and weaknesses in the case. Early in a case there may be little information that is shared.

10.60　The types of information you might wish to seek include the following. Word questions with care because the other side does not have to provide answers. Try to show how the information will help to progress the negotiation.

- basic factual information relating the an issue, for example 'Your client says there was a lot of noise and disturbance on the Sunday—it would be useful if I could have more detail';
- a general explanation of how they see an element of the case; for example 'Can you explain how you think my client's children caused the death of the fish?';
- basic factual information relating to a remedy claimed; for example 'Could you outline how that loss of profit is calculated?';
- information about what evidence the other side has to support their allegations; such as 'Do you have evidence from anyone who overheard what your client said?';
- information about the other side's objectives, which might help you in framing offers; as in 'How important is it to your client to keep running the machine until 6.00 pm?';
- checking if the other side has information you have (but only if this has a purpose—do not check if you want to use the information strategically later). For example 'There is a letter relating to the cost of repairing the rook—do you have that?';
- information that may be useful to you in progressing the case if the negotiation fails (though your opponent may not be prepared to answer such questions).

10.61　You may need to judge carefully how to respond to a request for information. Even if you are trying to be collaborative it is probably not in your client's best interests to give away information without getting enough information in return, especially if it is information that shows any weakness. If your strategy is competitive you may refuse to answer questions, but take care not to force the negotiation to break down. Possible responses include the following.

- You can refuse to reply, especially if the reply might undermine your case. (However be aware that your opponent might interpret a refusal to reply as an acceptance that your case is weak.)
- You might say that you will deal with the matter later. This might be necessary because of strategic plans. It can also be a tactic to deflect a question that you would prefer not to answer (though your opponent might call your bluff and ask the question again later).
- Give a partial answer, or avoid answering the question directly, to avoid revealing a weakness (though an opponent might press you for a fuller answer).
- Give an answer that reinforces a strength in your client's case (especially if you can add detail or evidence that the other side might not yet be aware of).
- Your duty to protect client confidentiality means that you should not reveal anything your client would not wish the other side to know.

Quite often you will get information that comes as something of a surprise. Your client **10.62** may not have been entirely truthful in revealing possible weaknesses in the case, and your opponent may well have collected extra information for the negotiation and may wish to surprise you as a tactic, especially if there is information that weakens you claim. It is very important not to react with surprise or your opponent will realise you have seen a possible weakness in your case. Try to give yourself time to absorb the information and to think of a constructive way to respond. If you are not sure how to respond it is probably best to move on to another issue.

MAKING YOUR CASE ON THE ISSUES

Making your case on the issues is a major element of any negotiation. You may chose to **10.63** make a general statement about how you see the strengths of the case, but normally the negotiators will go through each issue separately reviewing the strengths and weaknesses of the case on each side. The order in which you choose to go through the issues should be dictated by your strategy and planning, and will normally be agreed as part of setting the agenda at the start of the negotiation.

Normally the negotiators go through the issues one at a time. On each issue they will deal **10.64** with information, then discuss of strengths and weaknesses, and normally deal with possible concessions before moving to the next issue. This stage of a negotiation can get a little confused if problems are encountered or discussion jumps from one issue to another. Such problems are dealt with below, but it is usually constructive to deal with each issue systematically.

Keep a tight focus on the outcome you want to achieve on each issue, and why you should **10.65** get it. Do not digress into general discussion, unless you do this for tactical reasons to distract your opponent. It is very important to deal with strengths and weaknesses effectively and persuasively. If you do not you are likely to find it very difficult to get concessions from your opponent.

Remember that the point is to air the merits of the case and get concessions. You do not need **10.66** to agree on an interpretation of the law, to agree exactly what the evidence proves, or to agree exactly what happened, so do not get distracted. You are trying to see what is reasonably justified as a basis for settlement. As you discuss the merits you will need to monitor how well your arguments are succeeding. Where does your opponent accept a point you make, and where are you impressed by a point your opponent makes? Who would be most likely to win on a balance of probabilities if the case went to court? What remedies would a judge be most likely to award? This will inform what concessions should be demanded or made.

Presenting the merits of your case

10.67 The importance of preparing persuasive arguments was covered at 9.33–9.47, and of clear presentation at 10.16–10.18. If you are properly prepared it should not be too difficult to present the merits of your case on each issue reasonably briefly and clearly. Avoid reciting facts at length—focus on the key strengths of your case to persuade your opponent. Put your main arguments clearly and concisely. If you get distracted or side-tracked make sure you go back to cover or summarise the merits of your case.

Addressing weaknesses in your case

10.68 You should choose strategically and tactically how to deal with weaknesses in your case, especially if they are significant weaknesses, related to a key client objective.

10.69 One possibility is to bring up the weakness yourself, together with an argument to limit the effect of the weakness, as in: 'It could be said that my client might have mitigated his loss by cancelling the holiday, but I would say that would not be reasonable as this was a special holiday for his son's 18th birthday that could never be replaced.' The benefit of this approach is that it can take the wind out of your opponent's sails by undermining an argument they might have made later. The possible problem is that you might bring up a weakness that your opponent had not even thought of.

10.70 A second possibility is to have a response to each possible weakness ready for use should your opponent raise the weakness. This can be effective as you will see what case your opponent makes and fit your response to that, but the drawback is that it lets your opponent have the first word on the issue, and if they make a point of the weakness it may be difficult to recover.

10.71 A third option is to simply ignore or downplay the weakness. A competitive negotiator might well take this approach. This can be effective against a weak opponent, but is likely to be ineffective against a strong opponent. If you refuse to make a case about a possible weakness your opponent will probably insist on taking the weakness fully into account in making offers.

Bringing out weaknesses in your opponent's case

10.72 It is important to point out the weaknesses in your opponent's case, whether they are in law, fact or evidence. Any defence to a potential cause of action should be aired, as should any argument against the availability of a head of loss, or the amount of damages. If you are not sure whether there is a weakness you should probe your opponent's case to find out. This is all part of doing your job for the client, and getting the concessions you should get.

10.73 A competitive negotiator is likely to be keen to voice and over-emphasise every weakness. A collaborative negotiator might well voice a point more constructively, as in: 'The facts do show 30% contributory negligence, and it is only fair to my client that that be reflected in what you pay.' If you feel that your opponent is being too optimistic about chances of success you should point this out.

Proposing an outcome

You will normally wish to explore an issue fully before proposing an outcome. Indeed you **10.74** may choose not to propose an outcome until you get on to the offer and concession stage covered in 10.77–10.106. However it is important that in discussing each issue you raise the arguments that are relevant to how much or little should be offered, and what concessions should be made. This lays a clear foundation so that when you move on to dealing with offers and concessions you have reasons for what you offer or seek. A competitive negotiator might deal with each issue in less detail, but would still be likely to stress the strengths of their case and the weakness of the opponent's case.

Alternatively, you can state the outcome you seek as part of dealing with an issue, and then **10.75** deal with strengths and weaknesses as part of justifying that outcome. This can help you to persuade your opponent as regards what you want and why, but there can be some risk in revealing the outcome you seek before your opponent sets out their case.

Additions to oral argument

The argument in a negotiation is primarily orally. However there is nothing to stop you **10.76** using other things to support your argument. Tactically it can be very helpful to support you case with other resources, as this can help you to 'anchor' the discussion on your viewpoint. To give some examples:

- *Evidence*. If you have a letter, report etc that supports your case you might choose to provide a photocopy to your opponent, especially if you think they may not be aware of it. You might want to show this quickly without providing a copy if part of the document does not support your case.
- *Figures*. It can be difficult to discuss figures, and it can be helpful to prepare a schedule from your point of view for discussion and show it to your approval. This can help you to control discussion, and to get concessions from a poorly prepared opponent. But make sure your arithmetic does not have basic errors!
- *Law*. If there is a legal issue it can help to bring a copy of statute, regulation or case. A lawyer cannot easily refuse to argue a legal point, but may not be able to reply quickly to a point you have prepared.
- *Photos*. Where damages, injuries etc are in issue a photograph can make an impression on an opponent as it can on a judge or jury.
- *Plans*. If any kind of plan can help to understand an accident etc it is a good idea to produce one as it can help you to get control of the discussion.

PLANNING AND TIMING CONCESSIONS, OFFERS AND DEMANDS

Dealing with concessions, offers and demands is central to a negotiation. The point of a **10.77** negotiation is not to determine whether the claimant or the defendant should win, what would be the outcome in court, or whose version of the facts is 'true'. The purpose is for each negotiator to secure the best possible outcome for their client, which is achieved through getting concessions, but not making too many concessions.

10.78   Dealing with concessions is inevitably challenging. A competitive negotiator may find it relatively easy to make high demands, but it can be difficult to move from that to realistic settlement proposals. Co-operative negotiators can find it difficult to secure a deal that really protects the client's interests. The following are important to feeling confident about this stage of a negotiation:

- Have a clear and full list of the issues in the case, and the client's objectives and priorities: see 9.04–9.06.
- Prepare plans for what concessions you should ask the other side to make, and what concessions you should be prepared to make of necessary, including potential staging of concessions: see 9.48–9.57.
- Have standards against which to compare overall offers, with a calculation of what you might get if you went to court, and a consideration of the BATNA and WATNA: see 9.58–9.66.
- Have sufficient familiarity with the figures to be able to add VAT, take away a month of wages etc without a major delay: see 9.31–9.32.
- Get sufficient further information in the negotiation to refine possible formulate offers and concessions: see 10.57–10.62.
- Explore the strengths and weaknesses of the case sufficiently to have reasonable confidence in demands or offers.

Implementing concession plan

10.79   Implementing your plans will rarely be easy, but the earlier stages of the negotiation process should help you to get a feel for the strategy your opponent is following, and where they might be most open to settlement.

10.80   As regards timing, it is best to try to deal with offers and concessions in a reasonably structured way. There are the following options:

- Start with issues where you have a strong case so that you can seek concessions supported by good reasons relatively early on.
- A competitive negotiator might make early demands, though there is normally some discussion of the case before concessions are considered.
- Try to avoid making early concessions unless they are small, part of your strategy, or provisional on you getting something in return.
- Discuss possible offers and concessions at the end of dealing with each issue, once you are able to assess what is reasonable. Either open the discussion yourself with a clear statement of what you want and why, so that you get control of the process, or get you opponent to say what they want and why.
- If nothing can be agreed move on, but take the lead in suggesting an overall deal once other issues have been aired.

10.81   As regards the size of concessions, it should always be your rule to get as much as you can for your client and give away as little as possible. Your planning and further questions during the negotiation should tell you what the range of possible figures is. Start reasonably high, and move down in small, planned and justifiable stages.

As regards terminology, you can talk of offers, demands or concessions. The same potential **10.82** deal can be phrased in many ways, so you should consider what fits with your strategy and is most likely to get what you want from your opponent. A competitive negotiator might say: 'My client will not accept a penny less than £10,000!', where a collaborative negotiator might say: 'It would be fair for my client to get £10,000 on this issue, but perhaps that would be acceptable if your client got the £3,000 he sought on the item we just discussed.' The term 'concession' relates to the outcome as regards a claim on an issue—agreeing on relevant law of on facts may be helpful, but as the negotiation is confidential it has no real effect on the outcome.

Gaining concessions

Gaining a significant concession from an opponent in a negotiation will require skill. Your **10.83** opponent will not want to give anything away, and is likely to challenge your points and may even interrupt or distract you. Keep a tight focus on what is most important to your client and the main concessions you need to get.

- Identify clearly the largest concession on each issue you can realistically get. Aim steadily for that, moving to a fall-back position only for good reason and if there is no option.
- Identify the legal, evidential, factual and other arguments that support your claim on each issue. Identify the three strongest arguments in support of the concession you seek and ensure you make those points in the negotiation as clearly and well as you can. Adding weaker arguments can confuse or undermine your case.
- State clearly what concession you are seeking and why.
- Do not be put off. You will rarely get the full concession you want immediately—if you do it may mean that you have asked for too little. Once you have made your case on each issue restate what you want and move on.
- Take time to respond if a concession is made. Accept it if the offer is good, but pause to consider whether you could get a little more. If an offer seems very generous, consider if your opponent is aware of a weakness in their case that you do not know about.
- If there is any ambiguity in a concession then clarify it. If you would like a modification then say so. If it is not good enough ask your opponent to justify it.
- Do not get distracted by small concessions, or by suggestions one concession be traded for another. Check your client is getting a good deal.

Making demands

While no absolute distinction can be made, concessions generally arise from a discussion of **10.84** strengths and weaknesses, and tend to come with some justification. A demand tends to be made unilaterally, with little or no discussion, with limited justification, and often on the basis the point is non-negotiable.

A competitive negotiator may talk in terms of demands, setting out what their client wants **10.85** in this form. All negotiators may need to make demands if the client wants something that may be difficult to justify.

If an opponent makes a demand you can ask them to justify it. Alternatively you can make **10.86** it clear that you would only consider it as part of an overall settlement, treating the demand as a potential concession.

Making concessions

10.87 You will rarely be able to negotiate a settlement without making some concessions. Success normally depends on making as few concessions as are necessary for a settlement, with each concession being only as big as is necessary. It is the duty of a lawyer to get the best possible outcome for a client, and even a co-operative approach should not lead to unnecessary concessions.

10.88 Before making any concession, check the following:

- Has the opponent given a clear legal, evidential or factual reason why you should make this concession? Be slow to volunteer a concession if your opponent has not asked for it and justified it.
- What is the lowest concession you can make?
- What might you get in return for the concession? Can you link it to the opponent conceding something that is worth as much or more to you?
- Will the client accept the concession as part of the settlement? If not, what do you need to get so the client will accept it?

10.89 Making a concession can be seen as winning or losing on an issue. Refusing to make concessions might be seen as a sign of strength, and being slow to make concessions of any size may improve the deal you get. However unreasonable refusal to make concessions can lead a negotiation to fail, which may not be in the client's interests. If you do make a concession, make it in a clear and confident way, and make it clear if it is conditional. If you look weak or unsure your opponent may seek a greater concession. State the concession you are making clearly, and the reason for it. Do not leave room for confusion. Do not offer a range or your opponent will press for the best possible figure. Either propose to tie the concession to something you want, or make it clear that the concession will only stand if it is tied in with a concession from your opponent.

10.90 If your offer is not accepted then make is clear if it is your final offer on that issue, and whether it stays on the table to be possibly tied in with a concession from your opponent later. Do not offer a bigger concession unless you have planned to and/or it is justified. Move by as small an amount as you can. If your opponent sees it is possible to get you to increase concessions they are likely to try to exploit that.

Linking concessions

10.91 A concession should rarely be made without getting something in return. Even if there is good reason for making a concession on a particular point, there is likely to be a reason why your opponent should make a concession on another point. This can be done most easily where the parties put different values on different items, which can often emerge as the issues and the objectives of each party are discussed.

10.92 Trying to tie concessions together to make an overall acceptable settlement is best done by making it clear from the start that all proposals should be treated as conditional until an acceptable overall package emerges. This gives you flexibility to look at different options, or to withdraw a possible concession if your opponent proves difficult.

10.93 Be very wary of linking concessions that should not be linked because they are not equal. The fact that two issues have a similar face value does not mean they should be set against each other if one side has a much stronger case. Do not be fooled by a comment about the number of concession each side has made—it is the trading of equal amounts that are equally justified that matters.

Making offers

Quite separately from dealing with concessions, you might want to offer something that could assist in the reaching of a settlement. This is particularly likely where a collaborative negotiator wishes to get the best possible outcome, and might for example offer a new business opportunity so long as an agreement can be reached. An offer would rarely be one sided—you would hope to get something in return, linking your offer to a concession by the other side.

10.94

Reaching a deal

An overall settlement is usually based on a proposal for how all the possible concessions, offers and demands fit together. This may emerge naturally if each issue is provisionally agreed as it is discussed, and/or as possible concessions are traded against each other. If it does not, then it is likely that one of the negotiators will propose an overall settlement for discussion.

10.95

It is useful to propose an overall deal yourself so that you can pitch it as closely as possible to what your client hopes to achieve, and you leave your opponent the burden of arguing why it is wrong. Before proposing an overall deal, make sure that you have a complete list of the issues that are to be covered, or your opponent may try to add extra items. A possible disadvantage is that it shows your opponent what you hope to get, and they might seek further concessions.

10.96

Think carefully about the way in which potential concessions are joined together. Base your proposal on what you have argued for, but building in just enough of the concessions your opponent has sought. At this stage in a negotiation the negotiators tend to be tired and can easily get confused. Make sure you do not make more/larger concessions than your opponent overall, and check the deal against your client's objectives and your BATNA.

10.97

Different strategies tend to move to an overall settlement in different ways:

10.98

- A competitive negotiator will open 'high', setting out the highest sustainable goals. They will demand concessions, and is likely to focus discussion on what concessions the other side should make. They will be slow to concede, and will make only small concessions. The negotiator may attempt to impose a settlement that makes the fewest possible concessions. This approach carries significant risk that no settlement will be reached. If settlement is very important to the client a competitive approach may be used to explore issues with a more cooperative approach to reaching final agreement.
- A cooperative negotiator will tend to see concessions as important, and is likely to encourage and note potential concessions by each side as each issue is discussed. The overall deal is likely to pull together those potential concessions. While this approach is likely to reach a settlement, care must be taken to keep a strong focus on client interests rather than just look for a possibly broadly fair outcome.
- A collaborative negotiator will focus on exploring interests and options, and will tend to think in terms of offers. Concessions have less importance as the focus is on an outcome that is 'fair'. Again this approach has a good chance of reaching settlement, but the

strengths and weaknesses of the cases on each side should not be overlooked, producing a settlement that is not sufficiently justified.

Bargaining tactics

Preconditions

10.99 A negotiator might make a demand expressed as a precondition—stating for example that the other negotiator must accept a particular point before a topic is discussed. This may be used to try to force a concession from the other side, or at least put them at a disadvantage. If the precondition has no justification it is probably best to refuse to be 'bullied'.

Extreme demands

10.100 An inflated opening demand can influence how the parties see the 'bargaining range' and produce a higher outcome. However if the demand is not credible it can be easily attacked as being unrealistic. Other ways to deal with an extreme demand are to discuss the issues, or to ignore the demand. Responding with a high demand can make settlement very difficult.

False issues

10.101 A negotiator may suggest that something is an issue when it is not, making an apparent concession on the issue in an attempt to get a real concession from the other side. If you are surprised by an issue, ask questions to check it is a real issue.

Escalating demands

10.102 A very competitive negotiator may increase the size of their demands. This is done to try to test how much they can get the other negotiator to concede, and to increase pressure and stress. This is a risky strategy that can lead to a breakdown. If it is used against you refuse to consider it or insist on discussing the merits.

'Take it or leave it'

10.103 A negotiator may make a single offer and refuse to discuss it. A competitive negotiator may do this, or a collaborative negotiator may do this on the basis what they propose is 'fair'. It may also be done if the negotiation is dragging on. The other negotiator is apparently deprived of the chance of discussing the offer. Asking for the reasons behind the offer may help to open discussion.

Multiple concessions

10.104 A negotiator may try to deal with several issues together, focusing on the number of concessions they have made to argue a position is fair, whereas in fact the overall amount conceded is lower. Check the arithmetic and do not get confused.

Inducing stress

10.105 A competitive negotiator may purposefully induce stress, especially if the opponent seems at all uncomfortable with conflict or confrontation, trying to force concessions. Try to make steady progress rather than show stress, or make a comment like: 'I prefer to deal with the issues objectively rather than get into pressure and emotion.' Do not make an unnecessary concession.

'Splitting the difference'

An inexperienced negotiator might feel that there is some fairness in 'splitting the difference'—that is just taking a figure halfway between what is sought and what is offered. If there is no other way forward you might split the difference, but on many issues it is not at all fair and is a sign of failing to prepare properly or to negotiate effectively. To 'split the difference' is to say that each side has an equal case on the issue, which is rarely true. If your client has a 70% chance of winning a head of damage in court then you are not doing a good job for your client in accepting 50%. Remember that in a civil case the standard of proof is the balance of probabilities—if you have a better than 50% case then you should win and not split the difference.

10.106

MAKING PROGRESS

Making progress means moving through the issues towards a settlement with reasonable efficiency. This is best achieved in a relatively systematic way, reviewing the strengths and weaknesses of each, and potential concessions on both sides. This should happen at a good pace, with an appropriate time being spent on each issue. If there is limited time outside court it may be particularly important to make key points and move on.

10.107

You should keep progress under review:

10.108

- If discussion is spending too long on an issue of limited importance, point this out and suggest you move on.
- If the structure you are following moves away from an agreed agenda, decide what to do. It is not necessarily a problem if something unexpected has come up, and/or if you are still making reasonable progress. If the departure is not justified, suggest returning to the agenda.
- Jumping around from issue to issue almost always causes problems because the case for both sides is not properly explored so it is difficult to move to settlement. If this happens, try to return to a clearer agenda.
- If a problem arises in dealing with an issue, try to identify and deal with it. Is there a problem with information, or a failure to look at possible concessions? Failing to tackle the problem and moving on will often mean you just have to come back to the point later.
- Sometimes the parties get tired or frustrated and points get repeated. This wastes time and serves no purpose. If you are properly prepared make you points and move on. If your opponent starts repeating a point make it clear that that is what they are doing and ask them to move on.
- If at the end of discussing an issue you manage to reach a provisional agreement, make a note of it. This helps to ensure the matter is not forgotten or reopened, and that there is no misunderstanding as to what was agreed. If you make an offer that is not accepted but that you want to leave on the table then make a note of that.
- If you cannot reach any agreement on an issue, note the point you have reached; for example: 'I propose your client pays 70% of my client's losses, but you are proposing only 40%.' It is easy to assume you will remember this, but you may not. It may be easier to address the point once other issues are sorted out.

- Try to think of creative options. Structured settlements were invented by lawyers looking at how to meet the needs of claimants and defendants in personal injury cases: see PD 40C Structured settlements.

DEALING WITH DIFFICULTIES

10.109　Negotiation is a complex and challenging process. Awareness of the sorts of problems that can arise, and potential solutions, can help you to move forward and avoid a breakdown of the negotiation.

Gaps in information

10.110　It may be difficult to reach an agreement because of a lack of a key piece of information. If there is no easy way to check the point, get as close as you can to an agreement rather than giving up, possibly using a formula rather than an immediate solution. For example if you do not know the value of an item you can agree that a party will pay a fair price as assessed by an independent third party. Agree sufficient detail, such as how the valuer will be selected. Be realistic, and try to avoid the expense of a further meeting.

Getting bogged down, or reaching deadlock

10.111　Even with good preparation, and reasonably effective progress, a negotiation can get bogged down at some point. This can be for various reasons—an item may be particularly difficult, there may be new information the negotiators need to consider, or the negotiators may be tired. Rather than repeating yourself or getting frustrated, try to identify what the problem is, so that you can address it.

- In a long negotiation it may best to have a short break.
- It is usually constructive to summarise progress so far and what remains to be done, agreeing an agenda for those items. You may find that one issue has not been fully discussed, or that a new suggestion comes up.
- If it is important to both parties to settle, it may help to focus on the advantages of settlement for both sides. There may be shared interests or a small area of agreement to build on.
- If the problem relates to concessions, you could propose a conditional or hypothetical concession to get things moving, but do not offer a concession that is not justified.
- If there is no more constructive option, state that progress does not seem to be possible and why you think this is, seeing if either negotiator can propose a solution.
- Propose an alternative way forward if you can. Mediation with the clients can sometimes help.

10.112　In an extreme case the negotiation may appear to reach a deadlock, where agreement appears impossible. This may happen if, for example, one side makes a 'final offer' which is refused, if one negotiator is unreasonable or unrealistic in terms of demands, or if one client is over-optimistic about chances of success and has not given realistic instructions about an acceptable agreement. One of the approaches above may help, but if deadlock is inevitable the best tactic is probably to summarise your best reasonable offer, perhaps backing that up with a Part 36 offer later.

Dealing with a poorly prepared opponent

Most lawyers prepare properly for a negotiation, and make a serious attempt to settle. **10.113**
Sometimes a lawyer is not properly prepared, due to lack of time, underestimating the complexity of the case, or over confidence. On the face of it this should not be a problem—the better prepared lawyer should have little difficulty in getting a good outcome—but the lack of preparation can lead to problems.

Your job is to get the best realistic outcome for your client, not to make up for the weak- **10.114**
nesses of another lawyer. Sometimes an underprepared opponent will fall back into being competitive or positional, and your best course is to proceed to make your prepared case. Sometimes the lack of preparation stops you doing your job, because your opponent is not able to answer questions or deal with possible concessions properly. In such a case you should make progress by taking charge with regard to putting your arguments, proposing concessions etc. However you should not go so far as to propose settlement terms that will not be acceptable to your opponent's client. Get the best deal you can for your client that is likely to be acceptable to the opponent's client. It can be difficult to assess this if your opponent is not very forthcoming, but try to ask your opponent about their client's objectives to check.

Dealing with a very competitive opponent

A competitive opponent can put you under pressure with regard to your case, but at the end **10.115**
of the day a good competitive negotiator knows that an agreement should be reached if possible, and that it needs to be acceptable to both clients. Problems are most likely to arise with a negotiator who chooses a competitive strategy but is not sufficiently skilled, so that the result is inflexibility, failure to discuss, attempts at manipulation and bad feeling.

One reaction to a competitive opponent is to be competitive yourself, running a risk of **10.116**
deadlock. Another approach is to be relentlessly reasonable and proactive. Refuse to be manipulated, remain objective and stay cool. If your opponent's approach interferes with process you may need to point that out and explain why that it is a problem for their client as well as for yours. Continue to make objective and justified proposals, and to ask your opponent for objective justifications.

Frustration and emotion

A negotiation between lawyers should be more objective than a negotiation between the **10.117**
parties. However the negotiation is potentially competitive, and even with appropriate professionalism, there may be clashes of personality, style or strategy, and there may be frustration where agreement proves elusive. Rather than giving way to feelings, pretending there is no problem, or letting the negotiation break down, there are some steps that may help. At the very least, keep calm and persevere.

Some useful ways of dealing with a difficult opponent are proposed in *Getting Past No:* **10.118**
Negotiating Your Way From Confrontation to Cooperation, by William Ury (Bantam, 1999). In summary, this book proposes strategies for breaking through five potential barriers to cooperation.

• Your reactions may be a problem, if for example your opponent has irritated you. Deal with this by not reacting. Pause, do not give an off-the-cuff response, and mentally return to a point where you were in control. Keep focused on your objectives. 'Don't get mad, don't get even get what you want!'

- Your opponent's emotions may have a negative effect, if for example they are nervous or defensive. Deal with this by trying to defuse the emotions. Be conciliatory, encourage them to explain their problem, and try to check you understand. Agree with the problem as far as you can, and put your own point of view objectively, trying to rebuild a working relationship.

- Your opponent may be too embedded in a positional approach. If so, try to reframe the process and alter their perception. Do not get sucked in to win or lose, but try to ask problem-solving questions to get information or reasons. Label their behaviour as argumentative etc and ask how it is helping to try to get them to shift ground.

- Your opponent may have doubts about the agreement and whether it is best for their client. They may wish to focus on their proposals rather than look at something which is your idea. Try to build a bridge by involving your opponent in the proposal, ensuring all interests have been explored, and helping your opponent to save face.

- An opponent may perceive negotiation as a power game. Try to show your opponent that negotiation is not win–lose but win–win. Try to keep a focus on reality, and what will happen if agreement is not reached, and give your opponent space to agree.

Concern about possible inexperience

10.119 In practice, particularly in your early years as a lawyer, you will negotiate with more experienced practitioners. Concerns about a disparity of experience could influence how you negotiate. You might assume that your opponent is more skilled or knowledgeable, and be inclined to accept their suggestions about process. You might also find it difficult to argue about their views of the law, or proposals as regards outcome. You must ensure that this does not undermine the outcome for your client. Focus on your preparation and your decisions about the case, and do not accept anything you would not accept in any other negotiation.

10.120 In any negotiation you may have sudden feelings of weakness or indecision. You may have to deal with new information, complex calculations and difficult decisions very quickly. A proposal from your opponent may surprise you when you are getting tired, or temporarily lose concentration, or it may prove very difficult to achieve something you know is important. Feelings like this are inevitable from time to time, and you should not allow them to prejudice the outcome for a client. If you need a short break in a long negotiation ask for it, even if it is just a couple of minutes to check your papers. Alternatively you could move discussion to a more straightforward topic for a few minutes. If the problem is severe, review your analysis of your client's objectives and the merits of the case to check whether there is any alternative.

10.121 Once in a while an opponent will make a point that completely undermines your view of the case and the chances of your client achieving their objectives. If it is early in the case this may be something you had no chance of finding out, or your client may have significantly mislead you. Do not show any sign of panic or surprise. Review whether there is any chance your opponent is bluffing or exaggerating. Go on to complete as much as you can of the negotiation, but it may be that you will only be able to make provisional agreement on a few issues and will need to consult your client about the new information.

REACHING A CLOSE—SETTLEMENT OR BREAKDOWN

Reaching an agreement in a negotiation is an oral contract, but it is no more than an oral contract. When you agree there may well be a sense of relief, and a desire to get on to the next thing you need to do. It is however absolutely vital to check that you have tied up all the ends before you leave, or the terms you have agreed may fall apart when it comes to implementation, so that all your effort will be wasted. **10.122**

Making an oral contract

When you think you have reached a provisional agreement on all issues you should do the following: **10.123**

- Double check your own list of issues to ensure you have gone through every item.
- Ensure you have included all the details such as interest, costs etc.
- Check each term is practical and realistic, especially if you have been drafting terms for something like an interim injunction.
- Check the arithmetic. Check what your client gets overall. If both sides are making payments to each other try to combine the figures into one payment—but make sure the figure is right!
- Check that the agreement on crucial issues, and overall, is within your instructions and reasonably meets your client's objectives. The test is not whether you think it is roughly fair but whether you have achieved a deal as close to your client's instructions as possible
- Go through the agreement on each issue to ensure you and your opponent agree what was agreed, and that details such as dates for payments are included.
- If there are still actions to be taken to complete the agreement, eg an item to be valued, agree how that will happen.
- Remind your opponent that the agreement is provisional and subject to client approval

This process needs doing efficiently and carefully. Do not relax—it is not uncommon for the deal to fall apart at this stage. The following problems may arise. The best way to avoid them is to work to a clear agenda, to deal with sufficient detail as you reach agreement on each issue, and to note down what has been agreed on each issue as you negotiate, checking the wording with the other negotiator at the time. **10.124**

- *Renegotiation of an issue.* In looking at the overall deal, one negotiator may realise that the deal on one issue is not as good for their client as it might be, and will try to renegotiate. If possible insist that the terms are an oral agreement and cannot now be varied.
- *Adding an issue.* Your opponent may want to add an issue at the last moment. Even if it seems a small point, be careful—this may be a tactic to get more and may change the balance of the whole deal.
- *Filling a gap.* While gaps do need to be filled, take care that something that is raised as filling a gap does not turn out to be a renegotiation or an additional issue.
- *Points of detail.* Detail is important, but can be used as a mask for something that turns out to be substantial. Try to agree sufficient detail on issues as you go along rather than leaving it to the end.
- *Confusion.* All too often it emerges that the negotiators did not in fact agree a point that they thought that they had agreed. This happens if the parties voice proposals clearly, try

to give their own favourable interpretation to a point that is not clear, or do not take the trouble to check and note what is agreed before moving on to another issue. Do not accept something vague as it is likely to return to haunt you and may undermine the whole deal—you need to clarify and note detail as you go along.

Recording the outcome

10.125 An oral agreement is potentially enforceable, and it will be enforceable immediately if it is not subject to some condition. Most negotiated agreements are subject to client approval, so will be binding once approved. Even if you fully trust your opponent and there are others present, it is very risky to leave the outcome as an oral contract. It is all too likely that memories of what was agreed will differ, especially once you have moved on to other cases. It is therefore normal to note the terms in writing and to agree how they will be made enforceable.

10.126 It is normal for one lawyer to make a full note of the terms agreed, and to check the words written down with the opponent. A copy of the note might be made and handed over straight away. You may need an accurate record for various purposes—either as a basis for reporting to a judge in court if you have negotiated outside court, or to provide a basis from which to write a letter or contract. It is normally worth writing the agreement out on a fresh sheet of paper to avoid crossings out etc that might cause confusion. You may need a copy for the judge if your terms need court endorsement.

10.127 The options for recording a settlement are dealt with in full in Chapter 20 and are just noted here.

- *Endorsement on briefs*. If barristers negotiate and reach a relatively simple agreement the terms may be written onto the backsheet of the brief and signed.
- *Exchange of letters*. One solicitor may write out the terms in a letter, with the other side replying to agree.
- *A contract or deed*. A complex or important agreement may be drawn up as a contract to be signed by the parties.
- *An interim order*. If the negotiation relates to the terms of an interim application, the terms may be recorded as an interim order by a judge.
- *A consent order*. The terms may if appropriate be recorded in a court order by a judge.

No agreement is reached

10.128 If no full agreement is reached, there may still be some progress.

- If there is provisional agreement on some issues, note which issues have been agreed and on what basis. Is the agreement final so that the point is no longer in issue? If not, on what basis is it provisional? It may be appropriate to confirm this by an exchange of letters.
- If there has been movement on some issues without agreement make a note of the movement. Note extra information has emerged regarding facts, evidence and objectives, but remember that the negotiation process was confidential.

10.129 Even if no agreement has been reached and there is no clear progress, most negotiations provide some useful information or insights.

- Review your plans for the case, and any insights you may have gained with regard to objectives and concessions.

- Decide whether to formalise your updated views of the case into a Part 36 offer.
- Consider whether some other form of dispute resolution might be tried at some point. For example if a negotiation does not succeed, a mediation with the clients present might make more progress.

KEY POINTS SUMMARY

- Good communication skills are very important for effective negotiation.
- Although negotiation is an informal process, it has identifiable stages.
- Using the stages reasonably systematically will assist the negotiator in making best use of the process.
- Each negotiator should make clear any limits on authority, and whether any settlement will be subject to client approval.
- Agenda setting and opening are important in gaining control of a negotiation.
- It is normal to move through each issue reasonably systematically, making best use of information, analysis and presentation.
- It is important to deal with concessions, offers and demands effectively to get the best outcome for the client.
- The negotiator should be able to identify the problems that can arise in a negotiation process, and the techniques that may be used to overcome them.
- If a negotiation is successful an oral contract is reached. The terms should be clarified and recorded.
- Even if the negotiation is not successful, progress may be made with regard to the case.

10.130

11

MEDIATION

WHAT IS MEDIATION? 11.01

THE DIFFERENCE BETWEEN NEGOTIATION AND MEDIATION 11.04

JUDICIAL ENDORSEMENT OF MEDIATION 11.07

DISPUTES SUITABLE FOR MEDIATION 11.12

THE ADVANTAGES OF MEDIATION. 11.14

DOES MEDIATION WORK? 11.15

WHY DO THE PARTIES USE MEDIATION? 11.20

WHY IS MEDIATION AN EFFECTIVE ADR PROCESS? 11.21

THE DISADVANTAGES OF MEDIATION 11.22

WHAT CAN BE DONE TO MAKE A RELUCTANT
PARTY ENGAGE IN MEDIATION? 11.23

THE TIMING OF MEDIATION 11.24

THE DURATION OF MEDIATION 11.37

SELECTING A VENUE 11.39

THE COSTS OF MEDIATION 11.45

THE FUNDING OF MEDIATION COSTS, FEES AND EXPENSES 11.53

SELECTING A MEDIATOR 11.59

STYLES OF MEDIATION 11.77

TRANSFORMATIVE MEDIATION 11.93

THE ROLE OF THE MEDIATOR 11.95

KEY POINTS SUMMARY 11.102

WHAT IS MEDIATION?

The Centre for Effective Dispute Resolution (CEDR), one of the leading ADR service providers, has defined mediation as '...a flexible process conducted confidentially in which a neutral person actively assists parties in working towards a negotiated agreement of a dispute or difference, with the parties in ultimate control of the decision to settle and the terms of resolution'. The National Mediation Helpline has defined it in a slightly different way as 'an effective way of resolving disputes without the need to go to court. It involves an independent third party, a mediator, who helps both sides come to an agreement.'   **11.01**

Instead of conducting a negotiation face-to-face with the other side, the parties do so through a neutral third party whom they select by mutual agreement. Mediation is therefore a form of neutrally assisted negotiation (see *Aird v Prime Meridian Ltd* [2007] BLR 105 at [5] per May LJ). The negotiations will take place with the help of a neutral third party, within a structured process, in a formal setting, during a defined period of time, all of which will help to create an impetus for settlement. The mediator will work to facilitate a settlement between the parties, but will not himself impose one, or decide the outcome of the dispute. There is no determination of liability in mediation, and any settlement that is reached is not necessarily based on the underlying legal rights or obligations of the parties. Instead, the parties, with the assistance of mediator, can reach a solution which is tailored to their real needs and interests.   **11.02**

Mediation is a voluntary process. The court can offer strong encouragement to the parties to mediate their dispute, but it cannot compel them to do so. Despite the fact that there is some support among commentators and providers of mediation for compulsory mediation to be introduced, it looks as though this is unlikely to happen. Lord Justice Jackson, in his Final Report on the Review of Costs in Civil Cases, reported at ch 36, para 3.4: 'In spite of the considerable benefits which mediation brings in appropriate cases, I do not believe that parties should ever be compelled to mediate.' Even if the parties do mediate their dispute, they have the right to go to court to resolve the dispute if mediation does not result in settlement. Mediation can take place before litigation is commenced or it can be a parallel process to it.   **11.03**

THE DIFFERENCE BETWEEN NEGOTIATION AND MEDIATION

The main benefits of negotiation and mediation are dealt with in chapter 2. There are many similarities in terms of cost effectiveness and keeping control of the outcome. Negotiation plays a central part in mediation. Mediators need to have a good understanding of the various styles, strategies and tactics that can be employed in negotiations, and have the ability to counter them in order to prevent the deadlock that may occur in direct negotiations between the parties (see chapter 8).   **11.04**

The key potential advantages of mediation over negotiation are: **11.05**

• The presence of the mediator can help the parties to present their own case more effectively.

- Mediation can create a balance between the different negotiating styles used by the parties. It minimises the pressure that one party can feel when the other side employs a positional, confrontational negotiating style.
- Mediation encourages a more accurate and honest assessment by each party of the strengths and weaknesses of their own case.
- It avoids the direct confrontation between the parties that occurs in face-to-face negotiation.
- It can avoid over-ready concessions between the parties as the mediator will advise on the timing of offers and concessions.
- In mediation, negotiations take place within a defined time frame and within a structured framework.
- Mediation has a high success rate.

11.06 Although negotiation plays a key part in mediation, there are some fundamental differences between the two processes. The main differences are set out in Table 11.1 below.

Table 11.1 The differences between negotiation and mediation

Characteristic	Negotiation	Mediation
A voluntary process?	Yes.	Yes—although the court may order the parties to attempt mediation, it cannot compel them to do so. The court can impose sanctions, such as an adverse costs order, if the parties unreasonably refuse to engage with the process.
A structured process?	Not usually.	Yes.
It takes place through a neutral third party who assists in formulating proposals and testing claims?	No.	Yes (a mediator)—although he will not usually evaluate claims or advise on the likely outcome unless the parties ask him to perform this role.
The parties themselves will have the chance to be heard and will be active participants in the process?	Not usually, if they have instructed lawyers to act for them.	Yes—even if lawyers are instructed and attend the mediation on behalf of the lay clients, the mediator will ensure that the parties themselves directly participate in the process.
Witnesses of fact or expert witnesses may be directly involved in the process?	Not usually.	Although this is unusual, they can be asked to attend the mediation and give a summary of their evidence and, in some cases, can be questioned on their evidence by the parties or the mediator.
The parties choose: (i) the date; (ii) the venue; (iii) the issues to be negotiated; (iv) who should take part.	Yes—although usually negotiations will be conducted between lawyers for the parties rather than the parties themselves.	Yes—although (i) will be subject to the mediator's availability and the mediator may give guidance on (iii) and (iv) and may provide (ii).
The process is likely to result in settlement if the parties have reached deadlock?	No.	Yes—the mediator can help the parties work through the deadlock.

JUDICIAL ENDORSEMENT OF MEDIATION

In many cases, the courts have stressed the importance of mediation, and the flexibility the process affords for resolving disputes.

11.07

In *Dunnett v Railtrack plc* [2002] 1 WLR 2434 per Brooke LJ at [14]:

11.08

'Skilled mediators are now able to achieve results satisfactory to both parties in many cases which are quite beyond the power of lawyers and courts to achieve. This court has knowledge of cases where intense feelings have arisen, for instance in relation to clinical negligence claims. But when the parties are brought together on neutral soil with a skilled mediator to help them resolve their differences, it may very well be that the mediator is able to achieve a result by which the parties shake hands at the end and feel that they have gone away having settled the dispute on terms with which they are happy to live. A mediator may be able to provide solutions which are beyond the power of the court to provide. Occasions are known to the court in claims against the police, which can give rise to as much passion as a claim of this kind where a claimant's precious horses are killed on a railway line, by which an apology from a very senior officer is all that the claimant is really seeking and the money side of the matter falls away.'

In *Halsey v Milton Keynes General NHS Trust* [2004] 1 WLR 3002, Dyson LJ at [15] said

11.09

'We recognise that mediation has a number of advantages over the court process. It is usually less expensive than litigation which goes all the way to judgment.... Mediation provides litigants with a wider range of solutions than those which are available in litigation: for example, an apology; an explanation; the continuation of an existing professional or business relationship perhaps on new terms; and an agreement by one party to do something without any existing legal obligation to do so.'

In *Burchell v Bullard* [2005] BLR 330 Ward LJ (at para 43) endorsed mediation in these terms:

11.10

'*Halsey* has made plain not only the high rate of a successful outcome being achieved by mediation but also its established importance as a track to a just result running parallel with that of the court system. Both have a proper part to play in the administration of justice. The court has given its stamp of approval to mediation and it is now the legal profession which must become fully aware of and acknowledge its value. The profession can no longer with impunity shrug aside reasonable requests to mediate. The parties cannot ignore a proper request to mediate simply because it was made before the claim was issued. With court fees escalating it may be folly to do so.'

Members of the judiciary have also encouraged the use of mediation in numerous speeches and articles. It has been stated on many occasions, that ADR in general, and mediation in particular, must become an intrinsic part of the litigation process with lawyers giving it the same automatic attention as routine matters such as disclosure or expert evidence. A direction that the parties consider mediation is rapidly becoming part of the standard pre-trial case management directions (see Chapter 5).

11.11

DISPUTES SUITABLE FOR MEDIATION

Mediation is suitable for almost all disputes, whatever the subject-matter of the underlying cause of action. It is carried out in all kinds of contract disputes, consumer disputes,

11.12

neighbourhood disputes, housing disputes, tortious claims, regulatory and public sector disputes and family disputes. The factors to bear in mind in selecting a particular form of ADR are dealt with in Chapter 3, where there is also guidance on the types of case where mediation may be suitable.

11.13   The following cases may *not* be suitable for mediation:

- cases where the parties wish the court to determine issues of law or construction of a contract or document;
- test cases that require a judicial precedent eg interpretation of a clause in a standard form contract (see *McCook v Lobo* [2002] EWCA Civ 1760);
- cases that involve matters of public policy (eg environmental or planning cases or the discharge of local government or regulatory duties), on which require public determination;
- cases requiring publicity such as the restoration of a reputation by libel proceedings (although these types of cases are not necessarily unsuitable for mediation because the terms of settlement can provide for a public apology by a method agreed by the parties);
- cases that require a court order, for example amendment of the register of members of a company, or a claim by judicial trustees for directions in relation to a particular beneficiary;
- cases where declaratory relief is sought in relation to legal rights or obligations;
- cases requiring urgent injunctive relief or final injunctive relief (although in some cases it may be possible for the parties to agree terms in a mediation that would meet the same need as an injunction and that could, if required, be incorporated into a court order by way of an undertaking given to the court);
- cases that require court approval for settlement, eg cases involving a person lacking capacity such as a child or protected person. Cases of this type can be settled by mediation, but any settlement will not be binding unless approved by the court;
- if a party has a strong case, it may be more appropriate to issue proceedings, and apply for summary judgment. A refusal to mediate may be reasonable in such circumstances, otherwise a party with a weak case could use the threat of a costs sanction against the other party to force a settlement in respect of a case that lacks merit. However the party declining mediation on these grounds must be reasonable in their assessment of the merits of the case (*Halsey v Milton Keynes General NHS Trust* [2004] 1 WLR 3002);
- cases involving allegations of fraud or other disreputable conduct (Dyson LJ in *Halsey v Milton Keynes General NHS Trust* [2004] EWCA Civ 576). Whether or not an allegation of fraud rules out mediation will depend on a detailed analysis of the facts of the case and the evidence that is available to support it;
- if other factors, such as an unreasonably bullish stance taken by one party, suggest that it is unlikely to have any reasonable prospect of success (*Halsey v Milton Keynes General NHS Trust* [2004] EWCA Civ 576);
- cases in which mediation is proposed at a very late stage and close to trial and/or which would have the effect of delaying the trial (*Halsey v Milton Keynes General NHS Trust* [2004] EWCA Civ 576).
- if more time is genuinely and reasonably needed to obtain further information such as disclosure or exchange of witness statements or expert evidence (see *Société Internationale de Télécommunications Aéronautiques SC (SITA) v The Wyatt Company (UK) Ltd* [2002] EWHC 2401 (Ch) or to explore other settlement possibilities (*Corenso (UK) Ltd v Burnden Group plc* [2003] EWHC 1805 (QB));

- cases involving intentional wrongdoing, an abuse of power, human rights and vexatious litigants, including cases of domestic violence or other physical or mental abuse.

THE ADVANTAGES OF MEDIATION

Mediation has a number of advantages over litigation (see Chapter 3). The key advantages are as follows: **11.14**

- It is a flexible process and can be tailored to meet the needs of the case.
- It results in a speedier resolution of the dispute than litigation. Although many cases settle during the litigation process, this may be at a later stage than settlement reached by mediation.
- It is cost effective. It tends to be a cheaper method of resolving disputes than the trial process. It can result in a significant saving compared to the costs of litigation. This is particularly important where litigation is being funded by public money, as in the case of publicly funded private parties or public sector disputes involving government departments and agencies and in complex cases.
- It can be arranged relatively quickly. Most mediations (apart from mediations in very complex or multi-party cases) can be arranged within a matter of days or weeks from the date the decision is made to mediate. The mediation will typically last for one day only.
- Negotiations can take place with the assistance of a neutral third party, within a structured process, which promotes better communication between the parties. Direct negotiations between the parties may fail because of hostility, distrust, or because one or more of the parties has become entrenched in their position.
- It is a confidential and private process. This is particularly useful if the publicity generated by a trial could damage the reputation or have an adverse effect on the commercial relationships of one or both parties, or would result in disclosure of a trade secret or confidential information. Generally, all communications passing between the parties during the mediation (oral and written) cannot be disclosed to the court or third parties.
- It avoids an adverse precedent being set by the court.
- It avoids the stress and the trauma that some individuals may feel about giving evidence in court.
- A settlement that is reached by mutual agreement is more likely to preserve relationships than a court-imposed solution. This can be important in public sector disputes involving bodies such as a health or local authority and in continuing employment and commercial relationships.
- Mediation enables the parties to be more creative when reaching a settlement. The terms of settlement may provide for matters that could not be achieved within the constraints of the litigation process. The solutions that are agreed in mediation can include matters such as an apology, an explanation, the continuation of a commercial relationship (perhaps on different terms), replacement of goods or services, an agreement by one party to do something that he has no legal obligation to do so (such as the transfer of land to a neighbour for a sum in excess of its market value as a solution to a nuisance/easement/boundary dispute claim) or a change in policy or procedure to avoid such a complaint/dispute arising in the future.

- Even if settlement is not reached at the mediation, going through the mediation process may help the parties to understand each other's case, narrow the issues and, in some cases, settlement may be more easily achieved after the mediation.

DOES MEDIATION WORK?

11.15 Research carried out into court-mediation schemes has indicated that mediation is an effective ADR process for timely resolution of many different kinds of dispute: see for example, Professor Hazel Genn's reports into mediation schemes at Central London County Court between 1996–1998 'The Central London County Court Pilot Mediation Scheme: Evaluation Report' (DCA Research Paper 5/98), the report by Professor Hazel Genn and others, 'Twisting Arms: court referred and court linked mediation under judicial pressure' (Ministry of Justice Research series 1/07), and also Professor Genn's report 'Court-Based ADR Initiatives for Non-Family Civil Disputes: The Commercial Court and the Court of Appeal' (2002). Reference can also be made to the evaluation of Sue Prince and Sophie Belcher 'An Evaluation of the Effectiveness of Court-based Mediation Processes in Non-Family Civil Proceedings at Exeter and Guildford County Courts'.

11.16 Evidence from ADR providers also show that there is increasing use being made of mediation as an ADR method, and that it is very successful at resolving disputes. By way of example, CEDR, reports on its website (www.cedr.com) that over 70% of cases referred for mediation do settle at mediation. CEDR has also carried out a number of mediation audits. In 2007, CEDR's third mediation audit showed that the market had grown by 33% in two years, and that mediation saved UK businesses around £1 billion annually and that a quarter of all mediation referrals came through mediation schemes such as the Court of Appeal Mediation Scheme and the National Mediation Helpline as well as sector specific schemes (see Chapter 14 for details of these schemes). The average fees of a less experienced mediator for a one-day mediation remained at around £1,200, but those for more experienced mediators had risen by 42% over a two-year period to around £3,100 per day. The audit also showed that mediators reported that around 75% of their cases settled on the day, with another 13% settling shortly thereafter, giving an aggregate settlement figure of 88%. In 2010 CEDR's fourth Mediation Audit (published 11 May 2010) records that there is a continued rise in clients making direct referrals to mediators (nearly 65% in 2009, compared to 60% in 2007, 55% in 2005 and 45% in 2003). Around 6,000 civil and commercial cases are referred to mediation per annum (over a 40% increase in activity since the 2007 Audit), with the vast majority of the growth being attributed to schemes (see chapter 14). Average fees for the less experienced mediator have increased to £1,390 and fees for more experienced mediators have risen to £3,450 for a one day mediation. The aggregate settlement rate resulting from mediation had increased slightly to 89%.

11.17 Some evidence about the success and use of mediation can also be obtained from statistics released by the Ministry of Justice. On 23 March 2001, with the aim of ensuring that the Government led by example, the Government pledged to use ADR to resolve any suitable dispute involving Government departments and agencies if the other side agreed. Since then, the Ministry of Justice (and previously, the Department for Constitutional Affairs) have published an Annual Pledge Report which monitors the effectiveness of this pledge. The annual reports can be viewed on www.justice.gov.uk. They record the number of cases referred to ADR each year, in which the government is involved, and the outcome of those cases. Although no breakdown is given in the annual reports between the various types of ADR processes, the illustrative cases used in the reports involve mediation. The following figures are taken from the annual pledge reports from 2001–02 to 2008–09.

Table 11.2 Success rates of ADR in disputes involving Government departments

Year	Number of cases referred to ADR	% settled by ADR	Estimated saving made by using ADR
2001–02	49	—	£2.5m
2002–03	163	83%	£6.4m
2003–04	229	79%	£14.6m
2004–05	167	75%	£28.8m
2005–06	336	72%	£120.7m
2006–07	331	68%	£73.08m
2007–08	374	72%	£26.3m
2008–09	314	82%	£90.2m

While some ADR organisations and the Government publish figures on the number of cases referred to ADR processes, a substantial number of mediations take place by mediators in private practice, and it is more difficult to obtain statistics in relation to these. **11.18**

Some statistics can also be gleaned from submissions made by interested parties for the Review of Costs in Civil Cases by Lord Justice Jackson (see the Jackson report 2010 at www. justice.gov.uk). The Civil Mediation Council's submission of 21 July 2009 recorded that its members reported around 6,473 mediations so far in 2009, which was an increase of 171% over the 2007 baseline. Its members conducted 8,204 mediations in 2008. See 11.72–11.73 for more information about the Civil Mediation Council. **11.19**

WHY DO THE PARTIES USE MEDIATION?

There are a number of reasons why the parties choose mediation as an ADR option. **11.20**

- The parties may have contractually bound themselves by a dispute resolution clause to attempt to resolve any dispute arising out of or in connection with the contract by mediation before embarking on litigation (or arbitration). See for example *Cable & Wireless plc v IBM United Kingdom Ltd* [2002] EWHC 2059 (Comm).
- The court may have encouraged or directed the parties to attempt to settle the dispute by mediation, and the parties may fear adverse costs orders or other sanctions if they unreasonably refuse to mediate.
- The parties may have voluntarily chosen to mediate their dispute because of its perceived success rate and advantages as an ADR method.
- The parties may be referred to mediation by an applicable disputes resolution scheme.
- Practical considerations may lead the parties to choose mediation, such as a desire to settle a multiplicity of claims between the parties involving a number of different but related issues, with perhaps each claim proceeding in a different court and perhaps even in different jurisdictions. Mediation can also be an effective process for settling claims with a

multitude of parties eg a number of defendants and additional parties. In these types of cases, all of the parties and claims can be brought into the mediation process and a settlement can be reached that resolves them all.

- The parties may have tactical reasons for choosing mediation. For example, they may wish to seek clarification of one or more of the issues, or assess the strength (or weakness) of the other side's case. None of these reasons are improper provided they are coupled with a genuine intention to explore settlement. Sometimes parties will enter the mediation process in bad faith, for an ulterior motive, for example to engage in a fishing expedition, with no intention of trying to settle the dispute. The mediator will detect this within a very short time, and he or she is likely to terminate the mediation if this occurs.

WHY IS MEDIATION AN EFFECTIVE ADR PROCESS?

11.21   Mediation is perceived to be effective for a number of reasons.

- Negotiations take place in a structured process (see Chapter 13).
- The appointment of a mediator introduces an element of detachment into the settlement process. He can calm strong feelings such as anger or pride that may lead the parties to adopt entrenched positions in, or even walk away from, direct negotiation. He can help the parties to communicate constructively and effectively with each other and will manage aggressive negotiating tactics that can prevent settlement. The mediator will usually have a great deal of knowledge of and expertise in the skill of negotiation. He will have a sound understanding of the rules of principled negotiation advocated by Roger Fisher and William Ury in their book *Getting to Yes*. He will help the parties (and their lawyers) to work through deadlock that can be created by purely positional or competitive negotiation, by devising strategies that are more likely to lead to settlement.
- Proposals offered through a mediator can be perceived as being more attractive than an offer made by the party directly, and a concession proposed by the mediator may be seen to be more valuable than if it were made by the other side directly. In simple terms, this is because arguments put forward by one side are automatically psychologically devalued by the other side (a process known as 'reactive devaluation').
- The mediation takes place within a defined period of time (usually between three hours and one full day, depending on the type of dispute).
- The parties are likely to be paying for the mediation, both in relation to their own legal costs and their contribution towards the expenses of the mediation (such as the venue) and the mediator's fee (see Chapter 4 and 11.45–11.52) as well as any indirect costs such as their time, lost wages or holiday entitlement caused by their attendance at the mediation. This generates an impetus to settle, so that the costs and time spent in relation to the mediation should not be in vain.
- The court may direct the parties to attempt mediation, thus imposing a requirement on the parties to engage with the process seriously and with the intention of settling the case.
- It allows the parties 'to have their day in court'; they can explain their position to the mediator (and the other side in joint meetings: see Chapter 13) and this can make them more amenable to settlement.
- The parties can explore options for settlement that could not be ordered by a court and can thus reach more creative settlements that reflect their underlying needs and concerns.

THE DISADVANTAGES OF MEDIATION

There are a number of reasons why a party may be unwilling to try mediation. Points such **11.22** as the strength of the case and costs are dealt with in Chapter 3. Other specific points are as follows:

- Suggesting it displays a lack of confidence in the case and gives an impression of eagerness to settle. However the pre-action protocols, the CPR and the courts encourage ADR and mediation in particular, both before issue and at the allocation and case management stages of the case (see Chapter 5). A party who fails to mediate for this reason is likely to face an adverse costs order (see Chapter 6). Far from demonstrating a lack of confidence in the case, taking the initiative in exploring ADR options shows that the party has confidence in their case, it is in good order, they are complying with the CPR and are acting in their client's best interests in trying to resolve the dispute by the most cost-effective means.
- It will delay trial or the litigation process. If mediation results in settlement, a significant saving in the time taken to resolve the dispute is likely to be achieved. Even if the mediation takes place after the litigation has commenced, it need not lengthen the litigation process. Mediation can be attempted without the litigation being stayed. Even if a stay is granted, it tends to be for a short period, usually 28 days. The matter would be different if a trial date or window had been arranged, and a mediation would result in the trial being vacated.
- A party may fear revealing their case. Some parties may view mediation with suspicion because they do not want to reveal the strength of their own case, or fear that the other side are suggesting it to assess the strength of their case. The CPR favour a 'cards on the table' approach to litigation, so this is not likely to be a valid reason for refusing to mediate. If the case has merit, it will be resolved in that party's favour by settlement and/or judgment, so parties with a strong case have nothing to fear. Anything relevant to the litigation will have to be disclosed in due course in any event during the usual process of disclosure. It may cause more concern to parties with a weaker case, because if the weaknesses in the case are exposed, then offers to settle may not be forthcoming at all. However, the parties themselves control the amount of information that they give to the mediator and which they authorise him to disclose to the other side, so parties should not refuse to agree to mediation on that basis.
- A party may fear that information disclosed in the mediation will be used against them in subsequent litigation. However mediation is a confidential, without prejudice process, and that will only be overridden in exceptional circumstances (see 13.94–13.118).

WHAT CAN BE DONE TO MAKE A RELUCTANT PARTY ENGAGE IN MEDIATION?

If one party wishes to try mediation, and the other side does not, a number of steps can be **11.23** explored to bring the reluctant party to the mediation table. General points to encourage a party to engage in ADR are dealt with in 3.64–3.70. Specific points relating to mediation are as follows:

- A letter can be written to the other side, pointing out that the pre-action protocols, the Practice Direction Pre-action Conduct and the CPR all require the parties to consider using an ADR procedure to resolve the dispute. The letter should also put the reluctant party on notice that if they unreasonably refuse to engage in mediation (or another suitable ADR process), then an order for costs, including indemnity costs, will be sought against them at trial (see Chapter 6).
- A party may seek help from an ADR provider. It may be worthwhile approaching an ADR provider (either alone or, preferably, jointly) so that an independent person can advise whether there is any merit in attempting mediation. If only one party approaches the provider, that party will be solely responsible for any fees charged for acting as broker. The person acting as broker will not be involved in the mediation itself. A list of ADR organisations is set out at Appendix 1. If an individual mediator is approached by one party to act as a broker, he may decline to do so on the grounds that it would compromise the other side's perception of him as a neutral. If he does agree to act as a broker to persuade the other side to mediate, he will be scrupulous about disclosing his dealings and communications with all parties. For that reason, the initiating party should be careful about revealing confidential information to the broker at this stage. If the dispute is suitable for mediation, the broker will liaise with the reluctant party and will seek to persuade that party to engage in the process.
- A party may invite the court to stay proceedings (assuming that proceedings have been issued) to enable the parties to attempt to resolve the dispute by ADR (see CPR 1.4 and 26.4, and PD 29).

THE TIMING OF MEDIATION

11.24 Before the parties embark on mediation they should first attempt to settle the dispute by direct negotiation between themselves (see Chapters 8, 9 and 10) as this will normally be less expensive and may narrow issues. If negotiations are unsuccessful, and the dispute is suitable for mediation, the lawyer will have to consider the timing of the mediation. Mediation can theoretically take place at any stage of a dispute. It can take place before issue, after issue, or at any time up to trial and even pending an appeal as is aptly demonstrated by the Court of Appeal Mediation Scheme (see Chapter 14). It can be an alternative process to litigation or arbitration or it can be used in conjunction with those processes. General points about the timing of ADR are covered in Chapters 2 and 3 and 5. Specific points about mediation are as follows:

11.25 There are two important questions which any lawyer advising a client must ask himself:

- Should mediation take place before proceedings are issued?
- If mediation is to take place after issue, at which point in the litigation process should it be employed?

Before litigation begins

The court has recognised the success of mediation at an early stage of the dispute. See for **11.26**
example, *Egan v Motor Services (Bath) Ltd* [2008] 1 WLR 1589, per Ward LJ:

> 'Mediation can do more for the parties than negotiation. In this case the sheer commercial
> folly could have been amply demonstrated to both parties sitting at the same table but hear-
> ing it from somebody who is independent.... The cost of such a mediation would be paltry in
> comparison with the costs that would mount from the moment of the issue of the claim. In
> so many cases, and this is just another example of one, the best time to mediate is before the
> litigation begins. It is not a sign of weakness to suggest it. It is the hallmark of commonsense.
> Mediation is a perfectly proper adjunct to litigation. The skills are now well developed. The
> results are astonishingly good'.

The judge (HHJ Coulson QC, as he then was), had this to say about the timing of mediation **11.27**
in *Nigel Witham Ltd v Smith* [2008] EWHC 12 (TCC) at [32]:

> 'It is a common difficulty in cases of this sort, trying to work out when the best time might be
> to attempt ADR or mediation. Mediation is often suggested by the claiming party at an early
> stage. But the responding party, who is likely to be the party writing the cheque, will often
> want proper information relating to the claim in order to be able to assess the commercial
> risk that the claim represents before embarking on a sensible mediation. A premature media-
> tion simply wastes time and can sometimes lead to a hardening of the positions on both sides
> which make any subsequent attempt at settlement doomed to fail. Conversely, a delay in any
> mediation until after full particulars and documents have been exchanged can mean that
> the costs which have been incurred to get to that point themselves become the principal
> obstacle to a successful mediation. The trick in many cases is to identify the happy medium:
> the point when the detail of the claim and the response are known to both sides, but before
> the costs that have been incurred in reaching that stage are so great that a settlement is no
> longer possible.'

Some cases may lend themselves more to mediation before issue than others and this should **11.28**
also be borne in mind. In *Bradford v James* [2008] EWCA Civ 837, Mummery LJ remarked:

> 'There are too many calamitous neighbour disputes in the courts. Greater use should be made
> of the services of local mediators, who have specialist legal and surveying skills and are expe-
> rienced in alternative dispute resolution. An attempt at mediation should be made right at
> the beginning of the dispute and certainly well before things turn nasty and become expen-
> sive. By the time neighbours get to court it is often too late for court-based ADR and media-
> tion schemes to have much impact. Litigation hardens attitudes. Costs become an additional
> aggravating issue. Almost by its own momentum the case that cries out for compromise moves
> onwards and upwards towards a conclusion that is disastrous for one of the parties, and pos-
> sibly for both. '

In deciding on the most appropriate time to mediate, a lawyer acting for a party should **11.29**
consider the following matters:

- Are the issues fully defined?
- Is the client's own case in relation to the issues clear?
- Has all the key information been obtained?
- Have the main witnesses been interviewed and statements taken from them?
- Is the other party's case clearly developed?

- Have key documents that are material to the dispute been exchanged?
- In a technical case that is likely to turn on expert evidence, is it necessary to obtain an expert's report before attempting to resolve the dispute? It may be that the parties can agree to jointly select the expert, or even jointly instruct the expert for the purposes of the mediation.
- Is this a case where it would be more advantageous to the client to attempt to secure an early resolution of the matter before issuing proceedings, despite the fact that all available evidence has not yet been obtained or disclosed by the parties?

11.30 The advantages and disadvantages of mediating before issue of proceedings is set out in Table 11.3 below

Table 11.3 The advantages and disadvantages of mediation before issue

Advantages	Disadvantages
It is likely to achieve the largest saving on costs.	The issues between the parties may not be clearly defined.
It is likely to result in the largest saving on time.	The parties may not have reached an accurate assessment of their own case. Counsel's advice, or an expert's opinion may be needed, or their advice may only be provisional on further information being obtained.
The parties are less likely to have adopted entrenched positions.	It is more difficult to distinguish between a genuine sustainable position and pure posturing.
The parties have greater incentive to settle the dispute so to avoid the stress and costs and time occasioned by litigation.	There may not be full disclosure of all relevant documents and information, including witness statements and expert evidence.
Relationships are more likely to be preserved.	It may not be possible to evaluate strengths and weaknesses of each party's case with the same degree of accuracy.
Total confidentiality is more likely to be achieved.	It may be more difficult to evaluate arguments made by the opposing party in the mediation and to counter them effectively.
	It may not be possible fully to quantify the claim or counterclaim.

11.31 If the parties have fully defined the issues, disclosed key information and quantified the claim and any counterclaim, then the most advantageous time to embark on mediation will be before proceedings are issued. However if the issues between the parties are not yet clearly defined, or the information-gathering process is so incomplete that an evaluation of the strengths and weaknesses of each party's position cannot reasonably be ascertained until litigation commences, then early mediation is not likely to result in settlement, and, to save costs, it may be best to postpone the timing of it. If a party decides that it would not be sensible to embark on mediation before issue, then that party must be prepared to explain and justify this to the court. The decision should be objectively reasonable on the facts of the particular case. If it is not, then an adverse costs order may be made against that party (see Chapter 6).

11.32 Sometimes the parties may embark on an early mediation, and it becomes apparent that the issues are not clearly defined or that further information needs to be obtained before settlement can be reached. If this happens, the parties, with the assistance of the mediator, may agree a timetable for further information to be obtained and disclosed, and the mediation can be adjourned to another date for that to be done. This will add to the costs of the mediation process.

After litigation begins

The later the mediation takes place in the litigation process, the more clearly the issues will be defined between the parties, and the outcome of the dispute can be assessed with more accuracy. This is particularly so if mediation is undertaken after disclosure of documents and exchange of witness statements and experts' reports. However the costs savings that can result from a mediated settlement decrease the closer mediation is undertaken to the date set for trial. **11.33**

Parties who wish to attempt mediation after issue should consider applying for a stay of the proceedings and a suspension of the timetable set by the court in order to save costs. **11.34**

The court may take the selection of the timing of the mediation out of the hands of the parties. It can grant a stay to enable ADR methods to be tried at the track allocation stage (CPR 26.4). However this occurs immediately after the statements of case have been filed, so it may be the case that the parties have not sufficiently disclosed all relevant information to enable mediation to be attempted at this early stage in the litigation process. It can also grant a stay at any stage for the parties to attempt ADR. **11.35**

If mediation cannot reasonably be undertaken before issue, the best time to attempt it may be after disclosure of documents, or after exchange of witness statements or (if applicable) expert's reports. By then a clear evaluation of each side's case should be possible on both liability and quantum. **11.36**

THE DURATION OF MEDIATION

A typical mediation will last a day, with negotiations not really commencing until some way into the day. However in a case involving few issues or straightforward issues, it may only take half a day. In time-limited court schemes, the mediation will usually last three hours. In more complex, multi-party, or high value cases, it is not uncommon for mediations to last anything between two and five days. Some mediations can also take place on a number of separate occasions arranged over a number of months. This is particularly the case in complex or multi-party disputes or international disputes. A number of meetings also tend to be held in family disputes, particularly in cases involving children. **11.37**

If in doubt about how long the mediation is likely to last, it may be best to book the mediation for one day, but with all parties prepared to adjourn to another day if further time is needed. **11.38**

SELECTING A VENUE

If the parties are using an ADR provider then they may select and book a suitable venue for the mediation on behalf of the parties and may even have suitable rooms at their own **11.39** premises. A mediator in private practice may also conduct the mediation in his or her own premises. Otherwise the parties themselves will have to choose the date and select an appropriate venue for the mediation. A number of practical factors will govern the choice of venue, and these include the costs of the venue, the size of the premises required and the equipment and facilities needed.

11.40   A neutral venue is likely to be best, such as a hotel, or a designated conference centre because all participants are away from their familiar environment and so are likely to focus more intensely on the issues.

11.41   The mediation can sometimes be held at the offices of the solicitor for one of the parties, or even in the chambers of counsel for one of the parties or at the premises of one of the parties. These options may make the other side feel at a disadvantage, although they may result in a cost saving.

11.42   Normally at least three rooms will be required, one for the joint meeting, and two separate rooms, one for each of the parties. Ideally a fourth room is desirable for the private use of the mediator, or for joint meetings (if convened) of lawyers or even experts of the parties during the negotiating phase of the mediation. If there are more than two parties, sufficient rooms should be made available to ensure that each of the parties have their own room. In large multi-party disputes it may be possible for parties of a certain class or those united by a common issue to share a room. It is worthwhile checking that the rooms are sound-proofed if they are next door to one another; if they are not, the parties will not feel comfortable having a frank discussion in private meetings.

11.43   The mediation meeting will frequently last all day, and often run into the evening, so this should be borne in mind when selecting a venue. It would be very inconvenient if the venue had to be vacated at 4.30 pm, just when a crucial stage was reached in the negotiations. It is important that suitable refreshment facilities are readily available in or close to the venue. The venue also should be equipped with all of the usual facilities such as flipcharts (a necessity in all rooms), telephone, facsimile machine, computer and internet points and photocopying facilities.

11.44   The layout of the main meeting room that will be used for the joint sessions is particularly important. It should not be laid out in an adversarial style resembling that of a courtroom. A room containing a single table which is large enough to accommodate all of the parties will be more conducive to a successful mediation.

THE COSTS OF MEDIATION

11.45   The general aspects of the costs of ADR processes are dealt with in Chapter 4. The costs of mediation will include the party's own costs, the mediator's fees and other expenses.

The party's own costs of preparing for the mediation

11.46   This will include the costs perhaps of lawyers preparing position statements, case summaries and other documents for use in the mediation and solicitor's and perhaps also counsel's fees of preparing for and attending the mediation. If experts are to attend the mediation, it will also include their costs. These costs are referred to in this book as 'mediation party costs'

The mediator's fee

The mediator's fee will usually be calculated on an hourly or daily basis or it may be a combination of them both. The hourly rates will usually include preparation time. Daily rates may be advantageous because that is the rate that will be paid irrespective of how long the mediation lasts, so if it goes on into the late evening no additional fees will have to be paid by the parties. However some fees will be set at a certain level for the day (based on an 8 or 10-hour day) with additional fees being calculated on an hourly rate for every hour after a certain time, for example, 6.00 pm. Hourly rates vary greatly between individual mediators, and will depend on the nature and value of the case being mediated, and the experience of the mediator. The hourly rate can range between £200 and £500 plus VAT, and perhaps even more in very high value cases. Daily rates can vary from around £800 per party (for a multi track case up to £50,000 mediated by a mediator with little experience) to £3,000 per party or more in high value cases with a highly experienced mediator. Mediators' fees may be less if a court mediation scheme is used (see for example, the National Mediation Helpline, the County Court Small Claims Scheme and the Court of Appeal Mediation Scheme in Chapter 14). **11.47**

If the parties use an ADR provider, then it is likely that they will charge a fixed fee that will include all associated expenses as well as the fees of the mediator. The fixed fee will be payable irrespective of the length of time the mediation takes or the amount of preparation that is undertaken by the mediator. It is likely to be higher than the fees that would be payable should a mediator be appointed directly by the parties because the ADR provider has to cover their administrative costs in selecting and referring the case to a mediator on their panel and administering the process. A discount on the usual fee may be offered if the ADR provider operates, and the parties select, an express mediation service by which the parties use the ADR provider to select the mediator, but carry out most of the other administrative work themselves, such as booking the venue and the date. **11.48**

Fees payable to a mediator or an ADR provider are usually payable in advance of the mediation (usually around seven days in advance) and if they are not paid the mediation may be cancelled and the parties are likely to have to pay some or all of the cancellation charges. Any additional charges (caused by the mediation taking longer than expected for example) will be billed after the mediation. **11.49**

Expenses of the mediation

These will include other associated costs of the mediation such as the venue and the provision of refreshments. **11.50**

The mediation agreement will usually provide that the mediation fees and expenses (will be borne equally by the parties, and that each side will bear their own costs (ie the mediation party costs). However there is no reason why the parties cannot agree something different if that would be more appropriate on the facts of the case. For example: **11.51**

- One party could agree to pay all of the fees and expenses associated with mediation.
- One party could agree to pay the other side's mediation party costs.
- The parties may agree that all of costs of and arising out of the mediation are to be regarded as costs in the case, so the overall winner (whether by settlement at the mediation,

acceptance of a Part 36 offer made since the mediation or by trial) will pay the overall loser's mediation party costs and the fees and expenses of the mediation.

11.52 In some circumstances, a party may be able to recover their mediation party costs and their share of the mediation fees and expenses from the other side in the litigation (see Chapter 7). Alternatively a party may be able to recover some or all of their mediation party costs and their share of the fees and expenses of mediation by the settlement agreement that is reached in the mediation (see Chapter 13).

THE FUNDING OF MEDIATION COSTS, FEES AND EXPENSES

11.53 The ways of funding ADR costs, fees and expenses are dealt with in Chapter 4. Specific points in relation to mediation are mentioned below.

Public funding

11.54 The Legal Services Commission (LSC) are prepared to fund a party's mediation costs, fees and expenses in appropriate cases. Counsel and solicitors acting in publicly funded cases should ensure that the LSC will fund the costs of mediation before embarking on this process. The Funding Code recognises that mediation costs can be publicly funded in family work and family mediation procedures are funded directly by the LSC (*The Funding Code: Decision Making Guidance 3C-050*, para 7.2.5; see www.legalservices.gov.uk). In *R (Cowl) v Plymouth City Council* [2002] 1 WLR 803, the Court of Appeal stated that publicly funded claims should be mediated, if appropriate, in order to save costs. Mediation in non-family cases, and other forms of ADR such as early neutral evaluation or expert-assisted determination, may be funded by the LSC as disbursements, usually under the category of Legal Help or Legal Representation (*The Funding Code: Decision Making Guidance 3C-050*, para 7.2.5).

11.55 The LSC can require a party to attempt mediation before other steps are taken in the litigation, unless the dispute is not suitable for mediation or the other side refuses. However public funding will only be available for mediation if it appears to be the most cost-effective way of proceeding and the fees of the mediator are reasonable in all the circumstances (*The Funding Code: Decision Making Guidance 3C-054*, para 7.6.2). When the LSC funds mediation, the funding will include all the reasonable legal costs of and related to the mediation, including payment of the mediator's fees. Public funding may be withdrawn if a party unreasonably refused to settle a claim at mediation. The LSC provides mediation through LSC-contracted providers under fixed fee arrangements, and under the terms of the *LSC Mediation Quality Mark Standard (MQMS)* (2nd edn, 2009).

Funding under a CFA

11.56 CFA agreements can impose a great deal of pressure on a defendant to settle because if they lose the claim, the success fee and the ATE insurance premium is recoverable from the losing party as part of the overall costs of the litigation, subject to questions about the reasonableness of the success fee or ATE premium. The terms of the ATE policy may also provide that a party can have the benefit of the ATE insurance revoked if he refuses a reasonable offer to settle the claim.

11.57 Work that a lawyer carries out in connection with the mediation may be covered by the CFA. The fees payable to a lawyer will be affected by the outcome reached at the mediation. If the case settles at mediation, that may trigger payment of the success fee. Sometimes the level of the success fee can be a barrier to settlement, and the lawyer may be asked to reduce the success fee as part of the overall settlement. That can also be a source of conflict between the lawyer's interests and those of the client.

11.58 Mediators can also be instructed on the grounds that their fee is dependent on the outcome of the mediation. If the case settles they will be paid a success fee, ie an enhancement of the fee that they would otherwise have been paid, but if the mediation is not successful, then the mediator obtains no fees. Many mediators will refuse to accept instructions on this basis as there is a perception that such a fee arrangement compromises the neutrality of a mediator.

SELECTING A MEDIATOR

11.59 The parties can approach a mediator directly; alternatively they can engage the services of one of the ADR providers, who will then recommend one or more accredited mediators on their panel, often leaving the final choice to the parties themselves.

11.60 If the parties decide to use a mediation provider, then the shortlist of mediators who have the relevant expertise to mediate the dispute will be drawn up from its panel. The ADR provider will also administer the mediation process. It is likely to:

- arrange the date of the mediation;
- book the venue;
- provide the parties with the mediation agreement;
- ensure that the mediator has no conflict of interest;
- advise on the documents and statements that each party should provide for the mediation; and
- deal with any concerns or queries that the parties may have about the process.

11.61 Some ADR providers (for example, CEDR) may offer a fast track mediation service for parties who book their own date and venue, and only require a mediator, and a discounted rate will usually operate for this more limited service.

11.62 In large and complex disputes, the parties may need to appoint more than one mediator. If so, then there may be scope for choosing mediators with different styles and areas of expertise, so that a complementary mediation team is selected to mediate the dispute.

The qualities required in an effective mediator

11.63 A good mediator is someone who will have good communication skills, diplomacy, incisiveness, empathy, firmness, the ability to inspire respect, good analytical skills, relevant mediation experience, excellent negotiation skills and techniques, good attention to detail, the ability to think creatively when resolving a dispute, persistence, determination and a commitment to reaching settlement. He will also, of course, be neutral and impartial.

Factors influencing the selection of a mediator

11.64 There are a number of factors that will determine the selection of the mediator. Karl Mackie and others in *The ADR Practice Guide, Commercial Dispute Resolution* (3rd edn, Tottel Publishing) (ch 12) set out a comprehensive list of factors that the parties should consider when selecting a suitable mediator. These include the following matters:

Personal recommendation

11.65 Lawyers for the parties may be able to recommend a particular mediator based on personal experience or based on the recommendation of others in their firm or chambers. ADR organisations will usually also be able to make available feedback from clients on particular mediators that they recommend.

Personality

11.66 It is important that the parties have trust and confidence in the mediator and that they feel that they can have an open and effective working relationship. The mediator's personality should work with those of the parties. For example if one of the participants in the process could be categorised as a 'bully' or 'obstinate' or 'rude and arrogant', it may need a mediator with a strong and authoritative personality to enable the mediation to work effectively.

Expertise in the subject-matter of the dispute

11.67 The parties may want to select a mediator who is familiar with the subject-matter of the dispute. This is also likely to be helpful if expert evidence is to be employed in the mediation. The parties are not likely to want a mediator who has a specialist family law practice to mediate a technical commercial supply contract or a construction dispute. The parties will also need to give some thought to how the mediator acquired his expertise (for example, a solicitor or barrister who practised in the particular subject area, or a qualified professional in the field, such as an accountant or an engineer). A mediator who has no underlying expertise at all in the subject-matter of the dispute, whether as a lawyer or an expert in the relevant field, is less likely to focus on the relative merits of each case and the likely outcome if the matter went to trial, and will be more interested in devising a creative solution to the problem. Such a mediator is also more likely to adopt a facilitative rather than an evaluative approach to mediation (see 11.77–11.92).

Expertise gained as a lawyer

11.68 In some cases, expertise acquired as a lawyer may well be very desirable. Such a mediator will appreciate the procedural background and practicalities of litigation, the commercial realities of the matter and the underlying technical issues or the complexities of the legal or factual position of each party. He will also be trained to look at a matter more widely and creatively when facilitating a settlement. Such expertise is also likely to be essential if evaluative mediation is required (see mediation styles below). In cases involving difficult legal issues a lawyer mediator is to be preferred.

Expertise gained as a professional in other fields

A non-lawyer mediator who has expertise in the underlying nature of the dispute, such **11.69** as an accountant or an engineer may be essential if the underlying issues are so technical that expertise is required to understand them in order to facilitate meaningful negotiations between the parties, or if evaluative mediation is sought (see 11.86–11.92 below). However the mediator's expertise in the subject-matter of the dispute may make it more difficult for him to remain or appear neutral, and to keep the parties (and their experts perhaps) focused on settlement rather than debating the merits of complex technical positions.

Preferred style of mediation

The choice of mediator may also depend on the style of mediation that the parties prefer. **11.70** Some mediators work in a more facilitative style, preferring to avoid expressing an opinion on the merits of the case. Others will adopt a more evaluative approach. If the parties do wish the mediator to express a view on the merits of their respective cases, or the likely outcome or offer a range for settlement, it will be particularly important to select a mediator who has expertise in the subject-matter of the dispute. See 11.77–11.94 below for details on mediation styles.

Practical experience as a mediator

Care also needs to be taken to select a mediator with relevant practical experience. The par- **11.71** ties will want to ensure that the person selected is a trained and accredited mediator, with a proven track record in relation to the mediations they have undertaken. The parties should not be afraid to ask the mediator to provide a detailed curriculum vitae, information about the number and type of mediations he or she has undertaken, the outcome of those mediations and the names and addresses of referees.

Accreditation

Although there is no formal system of accreditation or regulation for mediation, there are **11.72** many ways in which some form of accreditation may take place.

- Many ADR organisations have their own systems in place for training and accrediting member mediators.
- Family mediation providers are formally accredited by the Family Mediation Council.
- The Law Society has prescribed training standards and has a system of accreditation for solicitor mediators on its Family and Civil/Commercial Mediation Panels who comply with those standards.
- The Bar Council has also adopted the Law Society Standards for the purpose of accrediting barristers as mediators.
- The Civil Mediation Council (CMC) was constituted in 2003 to represent the interests of mediation providers and mediators, promote mediation and create a culture of best practice in the field. It also lays down minimum standards for ADR service providers who are members of the Council, and those standards are similar to as those operated by the Law Society. The CMC will accredit providers so long as they pay the relevant fee and satisfy the Board of Accredited Mediation Providers that they have met the standards set by the Board. Around 71 ADR providers are accredited members of the CMC plus around 19 workplace provider members. However individual mediators are not accredited by the CMC. They are accredited by the Accredited Mediation Provider which is a member of the CMC. The Accredited Mediation Providers will apply the same standards

as those required by the Board of the CMC. The accredited providers must therefore police the standards of their mediators rather than the CMC doing so. Community and family mediators are excluded from the operation of the CMC. The CMC has also drawn up an Independent Mediation Complaints Review Scheme (2009) although this is not yet in force. It is intended to be open to CMC-accredited providers and also non-members on payment of a fee.

- LSE-contracted mediation providers must comply with the Mediation Quality Mark Standard 2009.

11.73 In order to become accredited, a mediator must satisfy requirements for training and continuous professional development. Although these vary between providers and organisations, they typically involve attending a training course which can range between 3–8 days in duration (for the purpose of accreditation by the CMC, the Law Society and the Bar Council, the training course must include not less than 24 hours of tuition and role play followed by formal assessment). The course will include training in ethics, mediation theory and practice, negotiation and role play exercises. Law Society accredited panel members must also have some practical experience consisting of at least four mediations. Any mediations that take place through the National Mediation Helpline (see Chapter 14) will be handled by organisations accredited by the Civil Mediation Council. A list of accredited mediation providers can be found on the National Mediation Helpline's website (www.nationalmediationhelpline.com). The Civil Mediation Council also provides a list of accredited ADR providers (see also www.civilmediation.org). Most ADR providers will also monitor performance of their mediators through client feedback and peer review, and they may make this available to the parties to assist in the selection process.

Interview

11.74 Bearing in mind the points set out above, the parties may wish to draw up a shortlist of suitable prospective mediators and interview them before selecting and engaging the mediator of their choice. At the interview, the parties will be able to explore some of the points made above which are of particular importance to them.

Language and cultural considerations

11.75 The parties should consider whether it is necessary to have a mediator who can mediate in the first language of the parties. This is particularly important in a cross-border or international disputes. The mediator should also share or be familiar with the cultural background of the parties, and should be sensitive to cultural diversity. See the guide to choosing the right mediator produced by the International Mediation Institute (www.imimediation.org). In cases with an international or European flavour, the IMI also maintains a directory of accredited mediators, which can be found on its website.

A team of mediators

11.76 Some very complex or multi-party disputes or international disputes may require more than one mediator to be appointed. In such cases, care needs to be taken to ensure the team of mediators contains the right blend of expertise, age, gender, professional experience and background as well as compatible personalities and mediation styles. The co-mediators need to ensure that they work as a team in all respects. For a useful perspective on co-mediation, see David Richbell, *Mediators on Mediation* (Tottel Publishing) ch 17 and Lawrence Boulle and Miryana Nesic *Mediator Skills and Techniques: Triangle of Influence* (Bloomsbury Professional, 2009), ch 9.

STYLES OF MEDIATION

Mediation tends to follow two main forms: facilitative mediation and evaluative mediation (sometimes called directive mediation). **11.77**

Facilitative mediation is the norm. However one party or both parties may invite the mediator to undertake a wider role by asking for an evaluation of an issue, the overall case or the likely outcome of the claim. The mediation will then move from being a purely facilitative mediation to an evaluative one. However this will only happen at the request of both parties. If the mediator does agree to perform an evaluative as well as a facilitative role, this should be recorded in writing in the mediation agreement at the outset, or added to it by way of an addendum if the request is made during the course of the mediation (see Chapter 12). **11.78**

The main differences between facilitative and evaluative mediation are explained below and set out in Table 11.4 below. **11.79**

Facilitative mediation

The mediator, as a neutral or impartial third party, helps the parties to solve their own problems by negotiations that he facilitates. A facilitative mediator will focus primarily on the real interests and concerns of the parties that underpin the dispute rather than the strict legal merits of the dispute. **11.80**

Although the mediator is there as a facilitator, his role is not a passive one. He will ask questions that test the strength and weaknesses of each side's case. He will explore each party's situation and help them to identify what they really need or want to achieve from the dispute. He will encourage the parties to think about the likely outcome of litigation and the costs of obtaining that outcome. He will focus each party's attention on their underlying objectives and needs, rather than on a strict analysis and evaluation of the merits of their case. He will help them to work out a creative solution that is in their best interests. **11.81**

The facilitative mediator will also help the parties to negotiate more effectively, formulate offers in a way that will be attractive to the other side and will give them guidance about the timing and staging of offers and concessions. **11.82**

The one thing however that a facilitative mediator will not do is to give his own opinions on the strengths and merits of each party's case or evaluate the likely outcome of a dispute or put forward proposals for settlement himself. A facilitative mediator is also likely to exert less control over the process than an evaluative mediator and will generally be less interventionist and challenging in the questions asked of the parties about the way in which they have assessed the merits of the case. **11.83**

Facilitative mediation is the primary or true form of mediation. Whether any particular mediator favours a facilitative or an evaluative style is something that the parties should **11.84** take into account when selecting a mediator, or in agreeing the scope of the mediator's role in the mediation.

11.85 Most mediators will use both evaluative and facilitative styles during the mediation, but evaluative mediation in the narrow sense means a mediation in which the mediator will evaluate the dispute and express an opinion on the likely outcome of it, or about the range within which the parties should settle.

Evaluative mediation

11.86 Evaluative mediation concentrates on the strengths and weaknesses of the case. The evaluative mediator will evaluate the dispute, exert more control over the process, challenge the parties to re-evaluate their assessment of the case, and give an opinion on the likely outcome. The evaluation will be carried out in a legalistic way, with emphasis on the legal and factual issues and an evaluation of the evidence in relation to the issues. Lawyers or professionals who have expertise in the subject-matter of the dispute have a natural tendency to be evaluative mediators.

11.87 An evaluative mediator will be more challenging in relation to the questions he or she asks the parties about the way in which they have assessed the merits of the issues and the likely outcome at trial.

11.88 The evaluative mediator will generally facilitate settlement by adopting a facilitative style. However he will encourage settlement by evaluating the issue or claim and the strengths and weaknesses of each party's case. An evaluative mediator may also be asked to recommend a form of settlement, or a range of options for settlement. He will usually communicate his opinion to each party in a private meeting, although the evaluation can also take place in a joint meeting. If he is asked to do so, he will set out his opinion in writing. His evaluation is not binding on the parties.

11.89 It is the parties who will determine whether the mediator's role moves from the normal facilitative role to an evaluative one. Both parties may jointly ask the mediator to evaluate the claim, or one or more discrete issues in the claim, or recommend a suitable range for settlement or one party may do so privately in relation to their own position. The mediator will not usually evaluate a claim or issue unless he is specifically invited to do so because doing so may lead to the appearance that he is not maintaining neutrality (on the basis that his assessment of the merits is likely to be more closely allied to that of one party). It is for this reason that some commentators suggest that if evaluation is to be undertaken, it should be done openly, or at least the same advice should be given to both parties in identical terms. An opinion given jointly to the parties is less likely to give rise to undue pressure or coercion than an opinion given to one party alone.

11.90 Some ADR providers do not permit their mediators to express an opinion on the merits of the dispute or give an indication of the likely outcome or analyse a party's legal position. There is a perception that evaluative mediators can coerce the parties into settlement, and by expressing an opinion on the likely outcome they can compromise their neutrality. The mediator will also seldom be provided with all of the documentation in a case. Any evaluation that he provides may not be based on complete information and may therefore be misleading. Providing an evaluation may also expose the mediator to a potential claim in negligence (see 13.123). For these reasons, evaluative mediation is more likely to be the exception rather than the norm. However, some commentators and clients favour it; it can speed up the settlement negotiations, and provide the reality check that is needed to enable the parties to move towards settlement. The Law Society's Code of Practice (See paras 3, 4 and 5 and commentary) provides that:

> 'While impartiality is fundamental to the role of the mediator, this does not mean that a mediator may never express a comment or view that one party may find more acceptable than another. However the mediator must not allow his or her personal view of the fairness or otherwise of the substance of the negotiations between the parties to damage or impair his or her impartiality. The mediator must appreciate that his or her involvement in the process is inevitably likely to affect the course of the negotiations between the parties.....This would be the case whether the mediator intervenes directly or whether he or she deals with issues indirectly, for example, through questions. Consequently, all mediator intervention needs to be conducted with sensitivity and care in order to maintain impartiality.'

> The mediator and the parties should agree, as far as practicable, at the outset whether the mediator's role will be purely facilitative, or whether the mediator may at his or her discretion, provide an evaluative element based on his or her knowledge of the subject matter or legal issues involved.

> The mediator should not impose his or her preferred outcome on the parties. The mediator may suggest possible solutions and help the parties to explore these......'

If evaluative mediation is sought from a mediator, this should be specified in advance (as **11.91** some mediators may be unwilling to do this) and if it is to be undertaken by the mediator, this will usually be agreed at the outset and recorded in the mediation agreement, or added to it by way of addendum if the evaluation is sought during the course of the mediation (see Chapter 12).

Evaluative mediation is very similar to conciliation (see Chapter 18) and some commenta- **11.92** tors refer to it as conciliation. However, in this book, where the evaluation and/or recommendation as to the form of settlement take place in the context of mediation, it is referred to as evaluative mediation rather than conciliation. It is also a form of early neutral evaluation (see Chapter 17) in that the outcome is similar, although the process may differ. Where the evaluation takes place in the context of mediation, it is referred to in this book as evaluative mediation, rather than early neutral evaluation.

Table 11.4 A comparison of facilitative and evaluative mediation

Characteristic	Facilitative mediation	Evaluative mediation
The mediator will make an assessment of the claims for the parties and may even suggest a range for settlement.	No.	Yes—but usually only if he is specifically asked to do so by the parties and he agrees to do so.
The mediator will be interventionist in challenging the parties to re-assess their claim, and will exert more control over the form of the parties negotiations.	Yes—but to a lesser extent.	Yes—to a greater extent.
The evaluation or determination of the mediator will be binding on the parties.	Not applicable.	No—the parties do not have to accept any evaluation by the mediator.

TRANSFORMATIVE MEDIATION

11.93 Some commentators also make reference to a third style of mediation, namely that of 'transformative mediation'.

11.94 Transformative mediation tends to focus on improving the relationship and communication between the parties rather than having the settlement of the dispute as its primary focus. Transformative mediators aim to help the parties to improve their communication so that they can resolve their own dispute. The parties themselves will control the nature of the discussions, with the mediator primarily providing a reflective role. Whilst some mediators will display some aspects of a transformative mediation style during the course of mediation, most will also use elements of a facilitative or an evaluative approach. For further information on transformative mediation see Robert A Baruch Bush and JP Folger, *The Promise of Mediation, The Transformative Approach to Conflict* (Jossey-Bass, 2005) and www.transformativemediaiton.org.

THE ROLE OF THE MEDIATOR

11.95 The mediator's role can be said to fall into three discrete areas:

- organising the mediation process;
- acting as facilitator during the process;
- acting as intermediary between the parties.

Organising the mediation process

Before the mediation

11.96 When appointed, the mediator will usually contact the parties (or their lawyers) and will explain, in a pre-mediation meeting, or by telephone, the nature of the mediation process, how they should prepare for it, his function and the role that the parties will play in the mediation. He will also advise the parties about the costs of the process. He will discuss with each party who should attend the mediation, and will check that the attendees for each party have authority to settle the case. He will endeavour to find out if there are any limits on their authority and, if so, advise on what needs to be done to ensure that settlement is not thwarted because one party lacks authority at the mediation. He will also set the timetable for events that need to happen prior to the mediation such as the date by which the mediation agreement should be signed and returned and the date by which position statements and documents should be provided and exchanged (see Chapter 12). If the parties have used an ADR service provider to provide a mediator, then it is likely that the service provider rather than the mediator will make the arrangements for the mediation.

At the mediation

11.97 The mediator will also perform an organisational role at the mediation. He may set the agenda for the mediation by suggesting the order in which issues should be negotiated. He will control the form that the mediation follows on the day, and decide when discussions should take place in joint or private meetings. He may also impose or suggest a time limit for delivery of opening statements in the joint meeting. He will decide whether further joint meetings should take place during the negotiation phase in addition to the opening joint meeting. He will not permit interventions by the other side during the opening statement of the opposing party and will ensure parity as far as possible in the amount of time he spends in private sessions with each party. He may also control the form of questions that one party may put to the opposing party in the opening joint session. All of these matters are dealt with in detail in Chapter 13.

He will act as a facilitator

The mediator will assist the parties to negotiate with one another in a more effective manner **11.98** than they would be able to achieve on their own. He will help them to identify the legal and factual issues, and their underlying needs and objectives. He will encourage the parties to treat the mediation as their 'day in court' and to air their feelings and emotions, particularly in private meetings, so that the matter can move forward. He will discourage or defuse confrontational or aggressive communications between the parties that will hinder negotiations, and will reframe them if necessary. The mediator will encourage the parties to analyse the strength and weakness of their own case and the case presented by the other side, and will perform the role of 'reality-checker', perhaps by assuming the role of devil's advocate, if they are unrealistic in their assessment. He will encourage the parties to think about the BATNA (best alternative to a negotiated agreement) and the WATNA (worse alternative to a negotiated agreement), and ensure that they have carried out a full risk assessment, including the costs (and irrecoverable costs) of proceeding to trial. He will review the negotiations that have already taken place between the parties, and will encourage each party to reflect on why they failed, and about how they can change their position to move the matter forward. All of these matters are discussed in detail in Chapter 13.

He will act as intermediatory

The mediator will act as the 'go-between' or 'shuttle-diplomat' during private meetings of **11.99** the parties. He will convey offers, concessions and information, rejections, concessions and counter-offers from one party to another. He will enable the parties to negotiate through him as intermediatory, rather than with each other face to face. This can be very effective in achieving progress to an overall settlement. He will keep a record of any agreement reached on individual issues as the negotiation progresses, as this will help with drawing up any final overall settlement agreement.

In order for the mediator to carry out these functions, it is vital that each party trusts and has **11.100** confidence in him. To build up that trust, the mediator must ensure that he is even-handed in his dealings with the parties and that he does not do or say anything that may lead one party to think that he is biased in any way. That is not to say that a mediator should not be rigorous and testing in the way he encourages each side to analyse their case. He may play the 'devil's advocate'. But he should not do or say anything that gives the impression he is not impartial, and he should not force a solution on the parties.

Post-mediation role

Even if the mediation does not result in settlement, it is not uncommon for the parties to **11.101** engage the mediator to broker settlement negotiations at a future date particularly if both parties trust and respect him.

KEY POINTS SUMMARY

11.102   • Mediation is a flexible, voluntary, confidential process.
   • The parties retain control of the outcome.
   • Almost all disputes are suitable for mediation.
   • The assistance of a neutral (the mediator) can result in mediation succeeding where direct negotiations have failed.
   • Mediation should only be conducted when the issues are clearly defined and the merits and quantum can be evaluated.
   • The earlier mediation can be undertaken the greater the saving in costs.
   • Mediation generally results in a more cost-effective and speedier resolution of the dispute than litigation.
   • A wide range of factors can influence the choice of mediator, including whether a facilitative or evaluative style is required.

12

PREPARATION FOR THE MEDIATION

THE MEDIATION AGREEMENT 12.01

PRE-MEDIATION MEETING/CONTACT 12.07

THE ATTENDEES 12.11

EXPERTS AND LAY WITNESSES OF FACT 12.19

THE POSITION STATEMENTS 12.23

THE KEY SUPPORTING DOCUMENTS 12.35

DISCLOSURE OF POSITION STATEMENTS AND DOCUMENTS 12.46

OTHER DOCUMENTS THAT THE PARTIES MAY WISH TO
BRING TO THE MEDIATION 12.47

OTHER INFORMATION THAT THE MEDIATOR MAY SEEK FROM
THE PARTIES BEFORE THE MEDIATION .12.48

OTHER STEPS THAT NEED TO BE TAKEN TO PREPARE
FOR THE MEDIATION. 12.49

TACTICS AND STYLES TO BE EMPLOYED IN THE MEDIATION 12.59

CONCLUSION. 12.62

KEY POINTS SUMMARY 12.63

THE MEDIATION AGREEMENT

In the United Kingdom, with the exception of mediations arranged in employment cases **12.01** through ACAS, mediation has no form of statutory framework. In most cases, the regulatory framework for mediation derives from the contract between the parties and the mediator, comprised in the mediation agreement.

12.02 The parties to mediation will be required by the mediator to sign a mediation agreement before the mediation meeting takes place. The mediator or the ADR service provider that the parties are using will usually send their standard form agreement to the parties (see, for example, CEDR's Model Mediation Agreement and the agreement used by the National Mediation Helpline in Appendix 2). These standard form agreements are amended from time to time, so check the website for the latest edition at www.cedr.com, and www. nationalmediationhelpline.com.

12.03 The mediation agreement represents the contract between the mediator and the parties appointing him. It sets out the terms on which the mediator is appointed and the scope of the mediation.

12.04 Although the detail of the mediation agreement will differ from mediator to mediator, most agreements contain the following key clauses:

- The scope of the mediation: Reference should be made to the dispute that is being referred to mediation. If only some of the issues are being referred to mediation, the agreement should make this clear.
- Practicalities, such as the names of the parties, the identity of those attending the mediation, the date and time and place of the mediation, and confirmation that the parties attending the mediation have authority to settle the case, and the fees payable for the mediation.
- The process is confidential and that the parties will keep confidential all information arising out of or incidental to the mediation (see Chapter 13). If the parties are particularly concerned about confidentiality, they may want to tailor this clause to suit their own circumstances.
- Communications passing between the parties and/or the mediator during the mediation process will be protected from disclosure by the 'without prejudice' rule and should not be disclosed to any third party or used in litigation unless it is disclosable by law (see 13.94–13.107).
- The mediator has no conflict of interest and will not reveal confidential information entrusted to him without the consent of the person who provided it, unless he is required to make disclosure as a matter of law (see 13.109–13.118).
- The parties will not call the mediator as a witness in later legal proceedings in connection with the dispute or in relation to any matter arising out of the mediation and they will indemnify him for the costs of resisting or responding to any application that he should do so (see 13.119–13.122).
- Any settlement reached at the mediation will not be binding on the parties until it is recorded in writing and signed by the parties.
- The agreement will also set out the costs of the mediation and who is responsible for paying them.

12.05 The parties may wish to vary the standard form agreements so that they are more specifically tailored to the circumstances of the particular case. The final mediation agreement should be signed by the parties and the mediator, and returned to the mediator.

12.06 The courts have recognised that mediation agreements are valid and that they contain enforceable terms (see eg *Brown v Rice* [2007] EWHC (Ch) 625). The courts have also granted an injunction to restrain breach of a confidentiality clause in such an agreement (*Venture Investment Placement v Hall* [2005] EWHC 1227).

PRE-MEDIATION MEETING/CONTACT

Once a mediator is appointed, he will read the papers supplied to him. If the mediator **12.07** decides that the dispute is one that is not suitable for mediation, or the position of the parties is so entrenched that mediation is likely to serve no useful purpose, he will advise the parties of that fact. He may also recommend another ADR process if he believes it would be more appropriate than mediation.

If the case is particularly complicated, or there is a need to establish rapport with the parties, **12.08** the mediator may ask to meet privately with the lawyers for each party or perhaps even the parties before the mediation to get a better understanding of the issues in dispute and their needs and objectives. If a pre-mediation meeting takes place, the mediator is also likely to use it to also explore settlement options with the parties.

Even if the mediator does not meet the parties in person before the mediation, he will usu- **12.09** ally contact them (or, more usually, their lawyers) by telephone before the mediation in order to:

- check that the parties understand the process;
- obtain information on any particular needs and objectives that each party may have;
- discuss practical matters such as the venue, the date and time of the mediation, the duration of the mediation and any special arrangements that need to be made for any of the parties;
- identify the parties who should attend the mediation, the documents to be provided, and the preparation that each of the parties should do for the mediation;
- set the timetable for the mediation and the dates by which steps should be taken by each party in order to prepare for the mediation. This is usually also set out in a letter to the parties;
- explore who is intending to take lead in the negotiations and in the opening plenary session, and the role that the lay clients will have;
- explore with the lawyers, particularly where the lay client is a public body, a company, partnership or backed by an insurer, that the representative attending the mediation has full authority to settle the dispute whatever emerges during the negotiation process. If he has not, the mediator will try to persuade the lawyer to ensure that someone more senior, who has the appropriate authority, attends the mediation;
- form a view of the personalities of the parties involved and the way they interact with the other parties and the strength of feeling they have in respect of the issues;
- discuss how he will approach and structure the mediation.

All of these matters are discussed in detail in the remainder of this chapter. **12.10**

THE ATTENDEES

It is very important to identify all of the relevant individuals who should attend the **12.11** mediation. Factors influencing the selection of the participants are fully discussed by Karl Mackie and others in *The ADR Practice Guide, Commercial Dispute Resolution* (3rd edn, Tottel

Publishing) para 12.4, and include the following:

- Who has direct knowledge of the key issues in the case?
- Who is most closely and personally affected by the dispute or the resolution of it?
- If relevant, who has the relevant technical expertise?
- Does resolution of any particular issue require expert evidence and the attendance of an expert at the mediation?
- Who has authority to settle the dispute?
- What message will the identity and status of the participants send to the other side?

12.12   The key attendees will include the following individuals.

Representatives of the parties

12.13   Each of the parties will have to determine who should attend the mediation. If the parties are individuals, then it is likely that they themselves will almost invariably attend as they will have direct knowledge of the facts and issues in dispute. If the parties are public bodies, companies, or unincorporated associations or a partnership, then the representative will most likely be the person who has the most direct personal knowledge of the issues in the case. The parties will also be permitted to bring any friend or relative with them for support, although these individuals may not be able to enter the mediation rooms due to shortage of space. If they are permitted to enter they may be asked to sign a confidentiality agreement.

Person with authority to settle

12.14   If one of the parties is a firm, company, public body or an unincorporated body, it is important that someone attends who has authority to settle the action up to the maximum value of the claim. A failure to do so may render the mediation ineffective. It will usually be an express term of the mediation agreement that each party will ensure that the mediation will be attended by someone who has authority to settle the dispute (in so far as this is possible). If it is genuinely impossible for the party who has authority to settle the dispute to attend the mediation, then they should be available throughout the day to be contacted by email and/or by telephone. It is not uncommon to find that the person attending the mediation only has authority (eg from their board, or claims manager) to settle the dispute up to a prescribed limit. If the proposed settlement exceeds that limit, authorisation will have to be obtained from another person, and it may not even be possible to obtain it that day. In such cases, the parties may have to conclude the mediation by signing a 'heads of agreement' document that sets out the agreed terms, subject to formal authorisation being obtained by one or both parties. This can be risky because there is no binding settlement until authorisation is obtained and the settlement signed, so the parties can resile from their position. An alternative would be to adjourn the mediation until authority has been obtained, or so that the person who has the relevant authority up to the maximum value of the claim can attend the mediation.

Lawyers

12.15   If the parties have reached the stage of instructing lawyers in relation to the dispute, then the lawyers will usually attend the mediation. Usually solicitors acting for the parties will attend the mediation. Counsel may also be instructed to attend instead of or in addition to the instructing solicitor. It is important to have a lawyer present at the mediation to advise the client on offers, concessions and any overall settlement proposals. If a party is unrepresented, then a pro bono organisation such as the Bar Pro Bono Unit, or Law Works, can be approached to see if free representation can be arranged. The mediator cannot advise any party on the merits of the proposed settlement or about their legal position, so legal representation for each party at the mediation is essential in complex claims, although it can and often will be dispensed with in small claims mediations.

Insurers

Thought needs to be given to the position of insurers. If any party is going to be indemnified under a policy of insurance, then a representative of the insurer, who has the requisite authority to settle the claim, may need to attend the mediation, or at least be available on the day so as to approve any settlement. **12.16**

Interest groups

Some mediations may involve other parties, such as representatives of the community. **12.17**

Once each party has identified the members of the team who will attend the mediation, the other side and the mediator will need to be notified of the names and position of each of the attendees. The identity and position held by the attendees may send a clear message to the other side about the value that a party places on mediation and the commitment they are making in the process. **12.18**

EXPERTS AND LAY WITNESSES OF FACT

Experts

Sometimes an expert may need to be consulted during the course of the mediation. This may be the case if there are technical issues that an expert may be able to resolve. Sometimes a mediator may need to obtain assistance from an expert to gain a better understanding of the issues in the case. The expert may be one who has already been instructed for the purposes of actual or proposed litigation. He may have been jointly instructed or jointly selected by the parties, following the steps in a pre-action protocol. Each party may have obtained their own expert evidence, in which case the mediator may ask both experts to be present at the mediation. The experts may be able to meet in a 'without prejudice' meeting during the mediation to see if they can narrow the issues and identify areas of agreement or dispute between them, which may make it easier to resolve the dispute. **12.19**

It may also be the case that the parties have not yet obtained expert evidence, but they and/or the mediator consider that it would be beneficial for an expert to be instructed for the purposes of the mediation. Any instruction for these purposes will usually be made on a joint basis. **12.20**

An expert attending the mediation may make a statement in a joint session (often the opening joint session), and be questioned by the mediator or by the parties on it. If an expert is required to give oral evidence at a joint meeting then this should be agreed with the **12.21** mediator in advance. The expert may also simply be present and available in private meetings, to assist the mediator and the parties with technical issues that arise. For the difference between joint and private meetings, see 13.05–13.33.

Witnesses of fact

12.22 Occasionally, especially where the dispute revolves around the evidence of conflicting factual witnesses, it may be useful for those witnesses to attend the mediation so that the mediator can clarify their accounts, if necessary, either in private meetings or by a more formal process of cross-examination at the opening joint meeting. Even if the witness does not give evidence in the opening joint session, the parties or their lawyers may wish to have key witnesses attend the mediation so that they can answer any issues that arise, or give assistance to the mediator if required.

THE POSITION STATEMENTS

12.23 The mediator will usually ask each party to provide him with a statement setting out their case. This is sometimes referred to as a position statement (which is the term that is used in this text), a case summary, a statement of case, written submission, party statement or even an issue statement.

12.24 The mediator will usually stipulate the time limit within which the position statements (and supporting documents) should be sent to him. This will usually be around 7 to 14 days in advance of the mediation.

12.25 On occasions, particularly if the mediation is taking place before proceedings have been issued, the mediator may suggest that there be sequential exchange of position statements, with the claimant having the right to reply to the position statement of the defendant. If an ADR order is made by the court, then this may also direct the parties to exchange case summaries and supporting bundles of documents for use in the ADR process (see the example of the Commercial Court's ADR order at Figure 5.1).

12.26 The position statement is not intended to be a formal document like a statement of case used in litigation. The document is primarily intended to ensure that the mediator is fully briefed on each side's case. The statements are also usually disclosed to the other party, so they form an important tactical function of giving the opposing party an insight into the strengths of the other side's case, and what they hope to achieve from the mediation.

The aims in drafting the position statement

12.27 There are no set rules for drafting the opening statement or case summary. However it should not read like a statement of case. It should be written in plain English. The aim in drafting it, as with so many other legal documents, is that it should be concise and precise.

12.28 The party drafting the statement should bear in mind the following matters:

- It should be clearly laid out, easy to navigate, with appropriate use being made of headings and subheadings where necessary.
- It should be logically ordered.

- It must be precise.
- It must be concise. Whilst there is no set page length (unless the mediator imposes one), on average it should be between 5–10 pages long, and may be shorter than five pages if the case is relatively straightforward. In any case, it should seldom exceed 10 pages.
- It needs to be persuasive. It should set out the key issues in a focused, concise way, rather than being a detailed discursive document that will lack impact due to over-lengthy explanation.

The content of the position statement

It is suggested that the position statement should set out the following requirements as **12.29**
essential matters:

- *Heading*: It should be headed up with the names and description of the parties (as in a statement of case) and marked 'Without Prejudice and for use in the Mediation only'. It should clearly identify the party on whose behalf the statement is made (eg 'Position Statement on behalf of the Claimant, Jane Beggs').
- *Formalities*: It should also include the date and time of the mediation, the name of the mediator, the party on whose behalf the statement is made, a list of the individuals attending the mediation on behalf of that party and their connection with the dispute.
- *Facts*: It should briefly outline the key facts of the case and the nature of the matters in complaint.
- *Issues*: It should identify the issues in the case, both legal and factual. The statement should also identify the key issues that are of vital importance to the parties at the date of the mediation. This may be different from the list of all of the factual and legal issues that arise in the case as it involves focusing on the matters that are of primary concern to the party. If these issues are resolved, all else tends to follow or fall away, so the mediation will primarily focus on these issues.
- *Outline of the party's case on the issues*: The statement needs to clearly set out the party's position in relation to each of the issues, and explain why the issues should be resolved in their favour. The statement should make reference to statements of case, key documents or evidence and matters of law that support the party's position. It is important that this document persuades both the mediator and the other side of the merits of the case, and therefore the strength of the party's negotiating position in relation to the disputed issues of fact or law.
- *The party's interests and objectives*: The key objectives that the party wants to achieve at the mediation should be identified. This section can draw attention to the costs of proceeding to trial, the element of irrecoverable costs, the desire to preserve relationships, the time it will take to resolve the depute if mediation is unsuccessful or any other factors that influenced the party to mediate rather than litigate the dispute. It should also make clear the party's intention to resolve the dispute, if possible, at the mediation, but also that they are prepared to proceed to trial if no reasonable offers are made by the other side.
- *Further information required*: The statement may identify any further information that needs to be obtained before the matter can be resolved.
- *Negotiations*: Any offers, including offers made under Part 36 of the CPR, or concessions that have already been made, should be explained. It should explain why offers have been rejected. If any issues in the case have already been resolved by negotiation, this should also be noted.

There should be no objection at all to a statement in this form being provided to the other **12.30**
side. However if the case summary is not disclosed to the other side and it is intended to be

a confidential document for the mediator's eyes only, this should be clearly stated on the face of the document.

12.31   The parties may also wish to set out an opening offer, or a road map for settlement (for example, if agreement can be reached in relation to the boundary wall, the claimant will abandon its claim on the driveway).

12.32   If proceedings have been issued and the parties have already prepared an agreed case summary and a list of issues, for example for a case management conference in a multi-track case, then these matters do not need to be set out again in the position statement. Reference can simply be made to that document, and a copy can be annexed to the position statement. If the mediation is taking place before proceedings have been issued, it would be helpful if the position statements set out each party's case as fully and clearly as possible, to enable the mediator and the other side to understand the issues in the case and each side's position in respect of them.

12.33   The position statement should always be accompanied by two separate documents, unless the nature of the dispute renders these unnecessary. These two documents should be agreed with the other side and then all parties can refer to them at the mediation:

- *Chronology*: This should include the chronological dates relevant to the complaint, as well as the chronological negotiation history, and a chronological history of the proceedings (if proceedings have been issued).
- *Dramatis personae*: This document is really for the benefit of the mediator. It should identify the parties, their legal advisors, the experts, the witnesses for each side, the insurers (if relevant), and the name of the person or persons for each party who has authority to settle the dispute.

Joint position statement

12.34   The parties can also agree to prepare a joint statement that they can both use at the mediation, although such a statement is likely to be limited to the facts, the issues and an explanation of each party's case in relation to the issues.

THE KEY SUPPORTING DOCUMENTS

12.35   Each of the parties will have to select and prepare a bundle of key documents for the mediator. These documents will usually support or even prove the assertions and arguments made in the position statement.

12.36   Some parties will wish to send almost all of the documents that they have to the mediator. In a complex commercial dispute, this can run to many boxes of material. If the mediator is charging an hourly rate for preparation and he is required to read several boxes of documents, then the preparation fee alone is going to be substantial. It is usually not helpful to prepare voluminous bundles of documents for use in the mediation. Each party should endeavour to select the key documents only that will help the mediator to identify the issues in the case, support and strengthen their own position in relation to the liability or quantum issues in dispute, or undermine the case of their opponent.

The parties should exercise restraint and ensure that they supply the mediator with key documents only.

Some mediators may stipulate the maximum length of the bundle of documents that **12.37** should be provided by each party. This should be adhered to unless there are exceptional reasons why a greater volume of documents should be provided.

When compiling the documents, the lawyers should bear in mind that the documents are **12.38** necessary to:

- inform the mediator of the issues in the dispute, the strength of the party's case in relation to those issues or that undermine the position of the other side;
- enable the mediator to adequately test the other side's case;
- support the negotiating stance taken by the party and the objectives it wishes to achieve at the mediation.

The documents sent to the mediator should consist of the following categories: **12.39**

- the statements of case together with any case summary or list of issues that has been prepared in the litigation (if proceedings have already been issued);
- any case management orders that have been made (so that the mediator understands the procedural timetable governing the dispute);
- any relevant witness statements of each party, particularly those that focus on key issues of liability and quantum, together with an indication of whether each witness statement has been disclosed;
- any expert reports that have been obtained, or the key sections of those reports (there is usually no need to include appendices), so that the mediator can fully understand the technical issues in the case. An indication should be given whether the report has been disclosed;
- any key documents that relate to the issues in dispute. It is helpful if these can be grouped together in relation to the issues to which they relate;
- any relevant correspondence or other documents such as attendance notes that show the prior negotiations that have taken place between the parties;
- any case or statute law that supports the lay client's case on the main issues that will be discussed at the mediation.

If expert evidence is required to resolve the dispute (eg in the case of a share or asset valua- **12.40** tion) but it has not yet been obtained, then the parties may need to jointly commission an expert's report prior to the mediation (see 13.19).

Agreed bundle

The parties should co-operate with one another in relation to the documents that are pro- **12.41** vided to the mediator and produce agreed bundles where possible. This will be particularly important if the mediator has imposed a maximum page number in relation to the supporting documents that should be provided to him.

The agreed bundle should consist of: **12.42**

- statements of case if proceedings have been issued and detailed letters of claim if they have not;
- witness statements that have been disclosed by the parties;

- any expert reports disclosed by the parties;
- Part 36 offers or other offers;
- any relevant documents that have been disclosed relating to the liability issues in dispute (eg the contract, documents relevant to breach or causation);
- documents that have been disclosed in relating to quantum, such as medical reports, schedules of loss, loss of earnings documentation, share valuation documents or computation of loss of profit;
- any other relevant correspondence between the parties.

Confidential bundles

12.43 If a joint bundle of core documents has been agreed, then each party can produce for the mediator, if required, a small bundle of additional documents that they do not wish him to reveal to the other side. The confidential documents could consist of documents setting out the party's view of the case, issues that they may be willing to compromise on, a draft expert's report or witness statement that has not yet been disclosed to the other side or perhaps counsel's opinion on liability or quantum. These should be placed in a separate bundle and care should be taken to mark these as 'strictly confidential' and to explicitly state that the mediator should not disclose them to the other side.

12.44 Sometimes parties will not want to disclose documents in the mediation because they feel that it will adversely affect the chances of settlement being reached. This may be so if proceedings have not yet been issued or disclosure has not yet taken place. The parties do not have to disclose anything if they do not wish to do so. However in choosing not to disclose documents they should bear in mind the provisions of the CPR and the protocols that encourage a 'cards on the table' approach to litigation. If the document would have to be disclosed in the litigation, it may be best to disclose in the mediation. Failure to disclose crucial documents that have a major effect on the case can give rise to a risk of any settlement being overturned on the grounds of misrepresentation or (less likely, as the parties are not in a fiduciary relationship to one another) material non-disclosure.

12.45 If documents are disclosed to the mediator in confidence he will not reveal the existence or content of these documents to the other side. However, from an ethical point of view, the mediator is likely to refuse to communicate any offer or other information to the other side which is directly contradicted by the existence of a confidential document of which he is aware.

DISCLOSURE OF POSITION STATEMENTS AND DOCUMENTS

12.46 Any documents or position statements that are provided by one party to the mediator will not be disclosed to the other side by the mediator unless the party providing those documents agrees that the mediator has authority to disclose them to the other side. If there is no objection to disclosure, each party may wish to arrange for copies of these documents to be sent directly to the other party or provide additional copies to the mediator or ADR provider with a request that they be sent to the other side.

OTHER DOCUMENTS THAT THE PARTIES MAY WISH TO BRING TO THE MEDIATION

Although the documents to be provided to the mediator are likely to be limited in scope, it **12.47** is often useful to ensure that the complete set of papers relating to the dispute is available at the mediation in case reference needs to be made to them to resolve a matter that arises during the process.

OTHER INFORMATION THAT THE MEDIATOR MAY SEEK FROM THE PARTIES BEFORE THE MEDIATION

The mediator may contact one or more of the parties, by telephone or in writing, before the **12.48** mediation to seek further information. In particular, he may wish to know about the following matters:

- clarification or further information about an issue in the case;
- further information about offers or negotiations that have taken place between the parties and why these have been rejected;
- the key objectives of the party and an indication of concessions or offers that they would be willing to make;
- the method of funding for the case. The mediator will want to know whether the claim is funded by a CFA and ATE insurance, or publicly funded by the LSC as this is likely to have a bearing on any settlement reached (see Chapter 11);
- the nature of any costs orders that may already have been made in the case. These may need to be considered as part of the overall settlement;
- the costs incurred by the parties to date, and the further costs that they are likely to incur if settlement cannot be agreed at the mediation.

OTHER STEPS THAT NEED TO BE TAKEN TO PREPARE FOR THE MEDIATION

The lawyers acting for each party should ensure that a full risk assessment is carried out in **12.49** relation to the client's case before the mediation. The preparation falls into two main areas, each of which is considered in more detail in this section.

- Analysis. This is turn comprises four aspects, each involving analysis of the party's own case and other side's case: legal analysis, factual and evidential analysis, an analysis of costs and finally an analysis of wider considerations. This work will also have to be done as part of the preparation for trial so time spent on this will not be wasted if settlement is not reached at the mediation.
- Preparation of negotiation strategies and tactics to be employed in the mediation.

Analysis

Legal analysis

12.50 Any lawyer retained by the parties to attend the mediation, whether counsel or solicitor or both, must be able to advise the client on any settlement proposal that is put forward by the other side. The lawyer (through the mediator or in a joint meeting of the lawyers) may also wish to persuade the other side of the weakness of their position as a matter of law. He may also be asked to concede a weakness in the lay client's case. It is therefore essential that a clear understanding is required of the legal background underpinning the dispute and an accurate legal assessment must be made about the strength of the case.

12.51 To reach that assessment, the lawyer may need to carry out a great deal of research into the legal issues. The lawyer should concentrate on those elements of the cause of action about which there is a dispute between the parties (for example, whether a duty was owed to the claimant in tort, the defendant's activities were the operative cause of the damage or whether particular statutory regulations apply to the situation). Any authorities that are useful in resolving the issue in favour of the lay client should be copied, brought to the mediation and provided to the mediator and the other side.

12.52 A legal analysis should also be undertaken in respect of the other side's case. In particular any defences that they have put forward should be carefully researched and evaluated. Any case law or other authorities that tend to refute the defences should be copied and produced at the mediation if this is likely to assist the settlement negotiations.

Factual and evidential analysis

12.53 It is important to carry out a factual analysis by checking the evidence that is available to prove each element of the cause of the action. Any gaps in the evidence should be noted and lines of inquiry should be set in motion to attempt to fill these gaps before the mediation if possible. It may be that some important documents that have a bearing on liability have not been located or disclosed to the other side. A relevant witness statement may need to be obtained to strengthen the case on liability. If any of the gaps in the evidence can be plugged with ease and at minimal expense before the mediation then this should be done as it may force the other side to change their position.

12.54 The same factual and evidential analysis should be carried out in respect of the other side's case. Any gaps or weaknesses in the other side's case should be noted on an issue-by-issue basis, so that these can be used and exploited in the mediation.

Cost analysis

12.55 It is important to ensure that a full costs review is carried out before the mediation and the relevant figures are brought to the mediation. A breakdown should be available of the costs and expenses that have been incurred up to the date of the mediation, and the further costs that are likely to be incurred to take the matter to trial, including the likely amount of irre-coverable costs. These figures will be necessary if an overall settlement is reached because the settlement agreement is likely to make provision for costs.

Analysis of other matters that may influence settlement

12.56 Any wider considerations that affect the lay client or the other side should also be borne in mind, such as adverse publicity or the effect that the dispute will have on commercial or personal relationships, financial considerations, or the stressful effects that continuing the dispute or litigation may have on the parties.

Bearing in mind these factors, the lawyer should consider whether there is any scope for 'expanding the pie' by including matters within any proposals for settlement that would be beyond the power of the court to order and that are strictly outside the scope of the dispute. **12.57**

Draw conclusions from the analysis

Having undertaken analysis of the law, facts, evidence and costs, the lawyer should have formed a clear view of the likely outcome of their client's case overall both on liability and quantum and a corresponding assessment of the merits (and quantum if relevant) of the other party's case. Furthermore the strengths and weaknesses of each side's position on each issue should be readily apparent, together with gaps in the evidence that need to be plugged on both sides. It should then be relatively straightforward to reach a clear view on the best alternative to a negotiated agreement (BATNA), that is the best outcome at trial if no settlement is reached and the WATNA (the worse outcome at trial if no settlement is reached). **12.58**

TACTICS AND STYLES TO BE EMPLOYED IN THE MEDIATION

The final stage involved in preparation will be planning a negotiation strategy. Bearing in mind the WATNA and BATNA, the lawyer attending the mediation should give some thought to: **12.59**

- the concessions that could be made by the lay client;
- the value those concessions would have for the other side;
- the timing and order in which concessions could be made;
- what can reasonably be asked of the other side in return;
- the offers that a lay client may be prepared to make;
- the timing of those offers;
- identification of the range within which the lay client could or should settle and the bottom line beyond which he should not settle;
- what information should be sought from the other side.

These matters are also relevant to negotiation and so they are considered in detail in Chapters 8 and 9. **12.60**

The key stages that need to be undertaken in preparation for mediation are shown in Figure 12.1. **12.61**

CONCLUSION

The value of effective preparation for the mediation cannot be underestimated. Effective drafting of position statements and careful compilation of documents will enable a party to influence the mediator so that he is able to be more effective in devising creative solutions and carrying out a 'reality check' with the other side. They will also show the other side the strength of the case. The mediation itself will proceed more effectively and **12.62**

Figure 12.1 The key stages in preparation for mediation

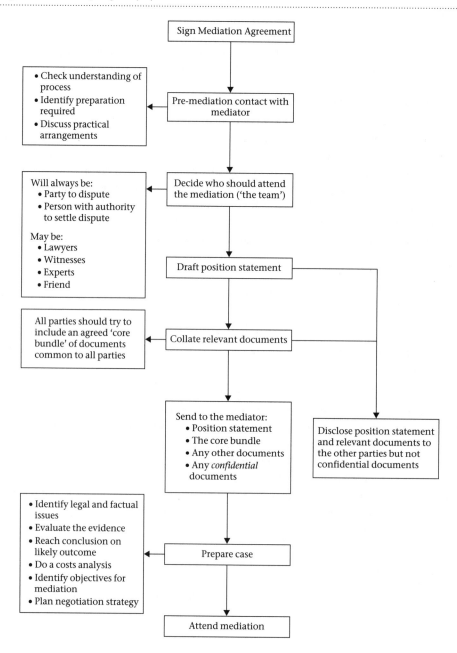

efficiently if each party's position is made clear in advance. In high value cases, the costs of preparation are likely to be very small compared to the sums at stake and the sums that would be spent in litigation or arbitration. However in low value or medium value cases (particularly small claims and fast track cases) the parties will need to take care to ensure that the costs of preparation remain proportionate to the sums sought to be recovered in the claim.

KEY POINTS SUMMARY

- Mediation requires thorough preparation. The lawyer should carry out a legal, factual, evidential and costs analysis of the case before attending the mediation. **12.63**
- The objectives for the mediation and a negotiation strategy should also be prepared in advance.
- A logically structured and persuasive position statement should be prepared to set out the client's position on the issues.
- Effective drafting of position statements, supported by key documents, may strongly influence how the other side and the mediator view the client's case.
- The parties should co-operate to produce an agreed bundle of key documents for use in the mediation.
- Care needs to be taken to identify and secure the attendance of all relevant individuals at the mediation.

13

THE MEDIATION PROCESS

THE STAGES IN MEDIATION. 13.01

THE OPENING PHASE. 13.03

THE EXPLORATION/INFORMATION PHASE. 13.34

THE NEGOTIATING/BARGAINING PHASE. 13.37

JOINT OPEN MEETINGS IN THE EXPLORATION OR
BARGAINING PHASE 13.43

THE SETTLEMENT/CLOSING PHASE 13.46

THE CLOSING JOINT MEETING. 13.51

TERMINATION AND ADJOURNMENT OF THE MEDIATION 13.52

THE MEDIATOR'S ROLE FOLLOWING THE CONCLUSION OF
THE MEDIATION 13.53

THE MAIN VARIATIONS IN THE PROCESS. 13.58

THE ROLE OF THE ADVOCATE IN MEDIATION 13.75

THE WITHOUT PREJUDICE RULE AND THE NATURE OF
CONFIDENTIALITY IN MEDIATION 13.94

LEGAL ADVICE PRIVILEGE IN MEDIATION 13.108

CONFIDENTIALITY. 13.109

THE MEDIATOR AS WITNESS 13.119

CAN A MEDIATOR BE SUED? 13.123

KEY POINTS SUMMARY 13.127

THE STAGES IN MEDIATION

The typical mediation will go through four key stages, which are discussed in detail in this chapter: **13.01**

(1) *The opening phase*. This will consist of introductions and each party setting out their formal position in relation to the issues in the case. It will usually take place in the opening joint session (sometimes called a plenary session, which simply means any session which is attended by representatives of both parties).

(2) *The exploration (or information) phase*. This can take place partly in open joint meetings and partly in closed private meetings, or exclusively in an open joint meeting or alternatively a closed private meeting, depending on the preferences of the parties, the issues in the case and the view of the mediator.

(3) *The negotiation (or bargaining) phase*. This will almost invariably take place in closed private meetings (sometimes referred to as 'caucuses' or 'closed sessions') with the mediator acting as broker between the parties.

(4) *The settlement (or closing) phase*. This will usually take place in joint meetings between all of the parties or between the lawyers of the parties who will have the task of drawing up the agreement.

The key stages in the mediation process are shown in Figure 13.1. **13.02**

THE OPENING PHASE

Introductions

On the day of the mediation, the mediator will usually arrive at the venue early so that he can greet the parties as they arrive and show them to their private rooms. Generally, the parties should arrive at the venue in good time for them to be able to have a final conference before the day begins. The mediator is likely to visit the parties in their private rooms before the start of the mediation in order to meet the members of the team in an informal way and to answer any queries about the process or the timetable for the day. He will also explain the layout of the facilities. He may ask them to clarify who will be making the opening statement at the joint meeting and may even briefly discuss the content of the opening statement. He will check how the parties prefer to be addressed, and whether they are comfortable with first names. **13.03**

If the parties have not yet signed the mediation agreement, then the mediator will ask them to do so before the commencement of the mediation. He will then call the parties together for the opening joint meeting. **13.04**

The opening joint meeting (plenary session)

The mediator's opening statement

The mediator will direct everyone to their seats and then ask everyone present to introduce themselves. The parties, rather than their lawyers, will usually be seated closest to **13.05**

Figure 13.1 The typical mediation process

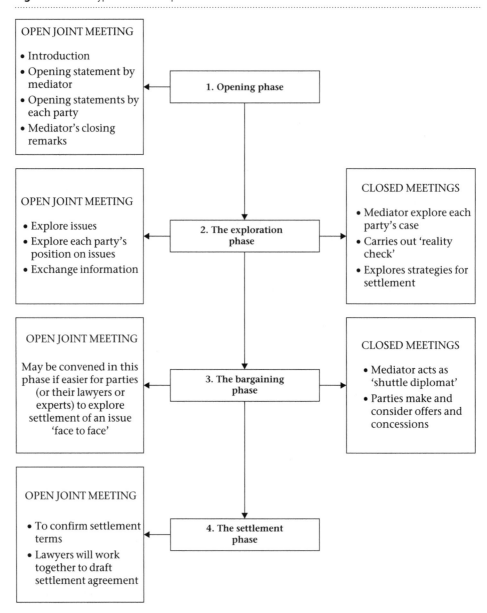

the mediator. The mediator will take a central position at the table (usually at the end of the table), with the parties on either side of him, usually approximately facing each other. The lawyers will sit on the other side of the parties (again usually opposite each other). Any other witnesses, then experts, will be seated on the other side of the lawyers. A diagram showing the typical seating arrangements for joint sessions is set out in Figure 13.2. However the mediator will arrange the parties as he sees fit bearing in mind the relationship between them and the nature of the issues in dispute.

13.06 The mediator will open the mediation by making a formal opening statement. The form of the opening will obviously vary from mediator to mediator and will also need to be tailored

Figure 13.2 A typical seating plan for joint meetings

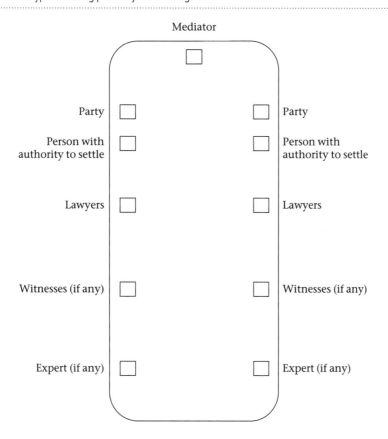

to the subject-matter of the dispute and the issues that have to be resolved at the mediation. The value of the opening statement cannot be underestimated; it sets the tone for the day and can influence the parties' expectations of and attitude towards the day and encourage them to commit to the process.

In his opening statement, the mediator will usually: **13.07**

- introduce himself and give an outline of his qualifications and experience and professional history. This may help the parties to gain confidence in him;
- explain what mediation is about, and perhaps give some general indication of its success rate as a method of dispute resolution. He will explain the course of the mediation, the likely time that each stage of the process will take and the role that each of the parties present will play in it;
- confirm that he is neutral. If he has any interest or connection with the parties or the dispute he will disclose this;.
- explain that he is not there to decide the case, but merely to help the parties reach settlement, that the process is flexible and can be adapted to meet the needs of the parties;
- explain the confidential nature of the mediation process and that anything said during private meetings with him will not be revealed to the other side without the prior express consent of the party making the disclosure. He will also explain that anything that occurs during the process cannot be used in subsequent litigation because the mediation process

is 'without prejudice'. He is likely to highlight the confidentiality provisions in the media-tion agreement that deal with these matters (see 13.94–13.118 below);

- explain the voluntary, non-binding nature of the process and the fact that any or each of the parties can abandon it at any time prior to settlement being reached;
- check that the parties present have authority to authorise settlement or, if not, that the person who has ultimate authority is easily contactable by telephone (or email) and will remain so throughout the day;
- explain the procedure in the event that settlement is reached and the need to have a set-tlement agreement drawn up and signed by the parties before the close of the mediation (unless ratification is required by a board or committee after the mediation).

Opening statements by the parties

13.08 The mediator will usually ask each of the parties to outline their case and what they hope to achieve at the conclusion of the dispute. They may do this by reference to the position state-ment that they prepared, although they may of course depart from this if they wish. The mediator will ask the other side not to interrupt the party delivering the statement.

13.09 It is becoming increasingly common for the opening statement to be made by counsel or the solicitor instructed by the party, but it can be delivered also by the parties themselves. It should be concise. The mediator may impose a time limit on each party. Generally, each party should aim to make their opening statement in less than 30 minutes, and typically around 10 minutes is usual. However the length of the opening will depend on the complex-ity and number of issues in the case.

13.10 The rationale for the opening statement is to:

- let the parties air their views about the matters in dispute;
- enable the parties to persuade the other side of the strength of their case;
- inform the mediator about the nature of each party's case, so that he is in the most informed position from which to facilitate settlement or undertake an evaluative role (if requested) in the mediation;
- point out weaknesses in the other side's case. In effect, the aim is to persuade the other party to take stock of their own case and evaluate it afresh;
- enable the parties to set out the remedy/outcome that they wish to achieve;
- give each party their day in court. Even if the lawyers have delivered the statement, the mediator will almost invariably ask the parties if they wish to add anything and will actively encourage them to do so;
- give the other side (and the mediator) the opportunity to assess the personalities involved in the opposing team and the quality of their arguments and their credibility.

13.11 The mediator will fix the order in which the parties are asked to make these statements. The usual order is that the claimant in the dispute will be asked to begin first.

13.12 Bearing in mind that the purpose of the opening statement is to persuade the other side of the weaknesses of their own case compared to the strengths of the case against them, it should be addressed to the other side, as well as the mediator. In order to persuade the other party and build up a dialogue for negotiation and settlement, good eye contact should be maintained with the other party during the delivery of it. The individuals concerned in the dispute should be referred to courteously by name and title. Some mediators prefer to get the parties at the mediation on first name terms unless they are uncomfortable with this, but sometimes a more formal address such as 'Mr Jones' is to be preferred. However because the opening is delivered directly to the other side, they would not be referred to by description, for example 'the claimant', or 'the claimant's solicitors'.

It should be concise yet persuasive. It should aim to cover all of the issues and the strength of the lay client's case in relation to those issues in a focused way that will make a real impact. It should also address the other side's case in relation to those issues, and deal with any arguments that they have raised in defence of their position. In doing this, the advocate may wish *briefly* to remind all parties present of key statements in the statements of case, documents or witness statements that support the lay client's case and that show that the other side's position in relation to the case or issue is much weaker than perhaps they believed it to be. It may also be necessary to explain why the other side's position is wrong or weak as a matter of law. When doing this, it is important to pitch the statement at the right level so that it persuades the parties. It should not be pitched at the level of a judge. It should explain and justify why the party is not prepared to settle at a figure proposed by the other side in any negotiations that took place before the mediation. **13.13**

The statement should be delivered with confidence and conviction. Thorough preparation and being totally on top of the issues, law, facts and evidence will help in presenting the lay client's case in the strongest terms. The advocate should be sensitive and courteous to the other side when delivering the statement. He should adopt a reasonable tone that seeks to win over rather than alienate the other side. The advocate may be able to empathise with the other side (for example by expressing regret about an injury) or even explain what happened or what went wrong, whilst still maintaining a strong stance on liability or quantum (or both) on behalf of the lay client. **13.14**

If the mediation is to be effective the advocate should ensure that he emphasises the lay client's willingness to settle the dispute. He may even offer suggestions for how a settlement could be achieved. **13.15**

If the lawyer makes the opening statement on behalf of the client, the client should always be invited to speak at the end of it. He may wish to explain the importance of the case to him and state his grievances or concerns. The client should be guided to vent his grievances in a factual measured way, rather than ranting and raving at the injustice caused to him or her by the other side. The aim of the joint meeting is not to escalate or inflame the dispute, but rather to lay the groundwork to enable settlement to be achieved. The lawyers acting for the parties should take great care to explain this to the client. It is often better to ensure that the client vents his emotions in the private meetings rather than in the joint meeting. **13.16**

The team for each party may divide up the delivery of the opening statement between them, with the lawyer (usually counsel if counsel is present, or the solicitor if not) setting the scene and dealing with the legal merits of each side's case, followed by the lay client who may say a few words about any aspect which is of particular concern to him, followed by an expert if the case raises complex technical issues. **13.17**

After each party has delivered their opening statement, the mediator will usually ask any other member of the team if they wish to add anything to the opening statement. At the conclusion of each party's opening statement, the mediator may ask questions to clarify anything which is unclear. He will try to frame such questions in an open and neutral way because a closed question (for example, 'You did not heed the large yellow warning notice positioned in the courtyard did you?') could give the impression that he had formed a **13.18** view of the merits of the case. He may also give the other side the opportunity to ask questions to clarify any matter that they did not understand. However such questions should be framed to elicit further information or clarification of an issue. The mediator will not permit the other side to conduct a cross-examination about the submissions made in the opening statements.

13.19   The second party to deliver the opening statement does not have to respond to the first party's statement. Each side should concentrate on their own position, rather than on answering the position of the other side. However if there are points that can be refuted clearly and succinctly, this can be done. The mediator may occasionally allow the first party to reply to something mentioned in the second party's statement, but this is not usual.

13.20   Further information about the purpose, content and delivery of opening statements can be found in Boulle & Nesic *Mediator Skills and Techniques: Triangle of Influence* (Bloomsbury Professional, 2009), ch 5, Karl Mackie et al *The ADR Practice Guide, Commercial Dispute Resolution* (3rd edn, Tottel Publishing), ch 13 and Goodman and Hammerton *Mediation Advocacy* (XLP Law), ch 4.

Witnesses and experts

Lay witnesses

13.21   Sometimes, it is desirable for live evidence to be given at the mediation. This may be necessary if an issue of fact divides the parties that depends on the evidence of a particular witness and an assessment of their credibility by all of the parties. If a party wishes to call any witnesses at the mediation, then this will usually happen after that party has made their opening statement.

13.22   If a witness is called at the mediation, their evidence will not usually take the form of examination in chief and cross-examination; rather the mediator will ask the witness to give a brief summary of their evidence. The mediator rather than the party calling the witness will usually ask the witness additional questions arising out of his evidence. However the mediator may allow each side to ask additional questions of the witness.

Expert evidence

13.23   The lay witnesses (if any) may be followed by expert evidence (if any). Where there is a dispute between the experts in relation to an important issue in the case, it may be necessary for the parties to reach a view on which expert's opinion is more likely to be accepted by the court before an overall settlement can be reached. The experts can give their evidence at a joint session, or simply be available in private sessions to answer any queries that the parties may have. If the experts do give evidence in a joint session some thought will need to be given as to the form of that evidence. There are two options which may be employed:

- The lawyers for the parties can question the experts within a pre-determined time limit.
- The mediator can question the expert, but in doing so he should not cross-examine or challenge the expert because this may cast doubt on his neutrality. He can ask questions that are designed to get at the truth of the matter and enable all present to assess the underlying factual assumptions and the cogency of the reasoning of the expert on a particular point.

At the conclusion of the opening joint meeting, the mediator will draw together the points **13.24** made by each party, summarise the issues to be resolved and explain the approach he will take to the mediation during the remainder of the day.

Closing the opening joint meeting

When the opening statements have been made, and any relevant witnesses have been **13.25** heard, the mediator will draw the opening session to a close. He will usually summarise the concerns of the parties and any areas of agreement between them, and the areas they need to resolve in the mediation. He will explain that the mediation will now move into the next phase, and that this will take place primarily in private meetings of the parties. He will explain how the private meetings will be conducted and what his role will be. He may explain the confidential nature of the private meetings and that he will not reveal any information that he obtains during these sessions to the other side without consent.

The mediator should be asked to set some sort of timetable for these private sessions, and to **13.26** give some indication about which party he will see first and the initial time he will spend with each party (which will usually be between 30 to 60 minutes per party). The mediator should ensure that the parties are given equal amounts of his time during the initial private meetings. After the first private meeting with each party, it is likely that the pace of negotiations will increase and the mediator will be moving from one party to another with offers and counter-offers on a very frequent basis and in a way which it would be impossible to timetable.

Extension of the plenary session

Some mediators may extend the joint opening session in an attempt to get the parties to **13.27** co-operate with one another or to commence and perhaps even complete the exploratory phase of the mediation in the joint meeting. Such a tactic will not work in all cases, but the process is flexible and can be tailored so that it best meets the needs of the particular case. If the parties are reasonably co-operative and civil towards one another, some mediators have reported that they like to extend the plenary session to:

- get the parties to agree the key issues that need to be discussed, and to agree the order in which they will deal with these issues;
- get the parties to work together to explain a particular issue for the benefit of the mediator;
- enable the parties to plug any relevant gaps in the information;
- brainstorm the figures that comprise the claim and the counterclaim (if any), the costs that each party has incurred to date and the future costs that will be incurred by each party if the dispute is not settled at the mediation. This can be effective in focusing minds on overall figures and settlement, rather than on positional issue-driven bargaining.

The separate private meetings (or closed meetings)

Almost all mediations will involve the parties spending time in closed meetings. These **13.28** meetings are sometimes called 'separate private meetings', 'caucuses' or 'closed meetings' to distinguish them from the open joint meetings of the parties. In these meetings the parties will meet privately, without the other side being present, to explore the issues and discuss settlement. This tends to be the key stage in the mediation process. The mediator will attend the private meetings of each party. The key characteristic of these meetings is that any discussion that takes place within them in the presence of the mediator is confidential. To give weight to this confidentiality process, many mediators will not write down any information that they gain during private meetings with the parties unless they are clearly told that the information can be communicated to the other side.

13.29 The key purpose of private meetings is to:

- give the parties privacy to discuss the issues in the case and their own negotiating strategy and proposals for settlement;
- enable the mediator to meet with the parties privately to discuss the dispute and strategies for settlement and to test the reality of their assessment of the case;
- enable the parties to consider proposals from the other side and make a considered response to those proposals. This may be more advantageous than in face-to-face direct negotiations where an instant response of some kind may be required or spontaneously given in the heat of the moment;
- enable the mediator to frame and communicate offers and counter-offers in a constructive way.

13.30 In the closed private meetings, two phases of the mediation usually take place.

- the exploration/information phase (although in some cases, this can take place in a joint session as described above). Some commentators refer to this as the 'problem-solving' stage;
- the negotiating/bargaining phase.

13.31 Although these phases usually take place in private meetings, there is nothing to stop the parties and the mediator carrying out these stages of the mediation in an open joint meeting if this would be useful in all the circumstances of the case. Mediation is a very flexible process and the mediator will make use of open and closed meetings in a way that best meets the needs of the parties.

13.32 Where both phases take place in closed private meetings, they can happen at the same time, particularly if offers are made early in the process. It may be impossible to draw a clear distinction between the two phases. In other mediations, negotiations will not commence for some time into the process until after the parties have exchanged information and explored positions on the issues in the dispute. However both phases will feature in almost all mediations to some extent (although there are some exceptions, such as mediations in family cases, which usually take place in a joint meeting only).

13.33 It is impossible to state with any accuracy the percentage of time spent in the joint or open meetings because the balance between the two will depend on the type of mediation, the subject-matter of the dispute and the relationship between the parties. To a very large extent, the mediator will go with his instinct on the day having observed the parties and the way they are reacting to one another.

THE EXPLORATION/INFORMATION PHASE

13.34 In the closed private meetings, in the presence of the mediator, the parties can embark on a rigorous assessment of their case without the other side being present, and without losing face if they revise their positions several times on any issue or in relation to the overall settlement that they hope to achieve. The mediator performs a number of important roles during the closed private meetings and these roles are discussed below.

He will carry out a 'reality check'

The neutrality and the 'reality check' that the mediator can provide is an extremely valuable **13.35** part of the mediation process. The mediator will do this in the following ways.

- He will assist the parties to review and accurately evaluate the strengths and weaknesses of their own case and that of the other side.
- He will focus each party's attention on gaps in the evidence, facts which they may have difficulty proving at trial and anything which may affect the court's assessment of the credibility of a particular witness or expert.
- He will also help the parties to work out what their best ,worst and most realistic case outcomes are if the matter proceeds to trial, together with the costs of legal proceedings, including the element of irrecoverable costs which would be payable even if one party succeeds and gets a judgment and costs order in his favour.
- He will make the parties consider the consequences of a settlement not being reached. He will encourage them to let go of the dispute and focus on what they could achieve if they were not expending time, money and energy on the dispute.
- He will also encourage the parties to give vent to their private feelings and concerns, and he will absorb these. This fulfils an important role of allowing the parties to 'have their day in court'. This is also cathartic, and the parties are sometimes only able to move forward to resolve the dispute once they have done so.
- He will ask them to consider any wider factors that impact on settlement, such as adverse publicity, the need to maintain a relationship with the other side, damage to reputation, and the effect that a failure to achieve settlement may have on third parties.
- He will try to get the parties to evaluate the case in the same way, so that the gap between them is narrowed to the extent that they can achieve settlement.

He will devise strategies to help the parties work through deadlock

To move the settlement process forward, some new offer, concession or information will **13.36** have to be placed on the table by the parties, particularly if stalemate has been reached. It is one of the most important parts of the mediator's role to help the parties to explore other remedies and solutions that will enable them to move the settlement discussions forward. The mediator may employ a number of tactics and strategies to move through deadlock:

- The mediator may embark on a rigorous reality check with the parties to get them to reassess their position on the merits.
- He will require the parties to consider their interests (that is commercial and personal needs) rather than the positional approach that they may have taken in the negotiations up to that point.
- He may persuade one party to disclose additional documents to the other side, which might encourage some movement in their position.
- He may suggest that different members of each team should get together to brainstorm settlement options in relation to an issue in the hope that they will introduce new energy into the process.

- The mediator may divide one issue into many, so as to create greater opportunities for settlement. For example if the issue is the amount of damages for a breach of contract, he may divide that into several issues consisting of the amount of damages, the amount of credit that should be given by the claimant, the timing of the payment, how payment will be made and what interest is payable.

- If one party needs time to absorb and reflect on offers that are made, he may adjourn the mediation to another day, rather than allow the settlement opportunity to be lost altogether.

- If the mediator suspects that one or more members of a team are effectively frustrating the attempts of the others to settle (and this may include over-zealous lawyers with an unrealistic assessment of the merits of their client's case), he will see them individually and encourage them to look at the situation objectively and realistically, or else occupy them so that their impact is minimised.

- The mediator may also be able to help the parties to save face in relation to a changing position in a way that cannot be easily achieved in direct negotiations. He may do this, for example, by making a third party the scapegoat (eg the government for changing the tax structure), by encouraging the parties to blame him for a proposal, or by dressing up an offer in such a way as to give the impression that it was engineered by him, or even by giving them a 'cop out' for changing position by trying to pin the change of position on matters that emerged during the mediation even if they were obvious and present throughout the process.

- The mediator will encourage the parties to explore the likely outcome if the litigation proceeds to trial, including the element of irrecoverable costs.

- To bridge the gap in the monetary offers made by the parties, he may suggest, for example, that the claimant accepts less if payment is made immediately, or that the defendant should increase its offer if given a longer period of time in which to pay the agreed sum to the claimant.

- In cases where both teams' lawyers are giving bullish legal advice on an issue, he may create doubt over that advice by telling the parties that their lawyers cannot both be right, to try and force each team to recognise the risks of proceeding to trial.

- The mediator will suggest options for closing the final gap between the parties such as splitting the difference, tossing a coin who see who wins or loses the final sticking point, one party making a charitable donation instead of a payment to the other side, implementing the agreement in relation to all other matters that have been agreed and adjourning the final issue in dispute to be determined by a suitable expert or by discussions with the mediator on another day, perhaps by telephone.

- The mediator will also encourage the parties to be more creative in looking at ways to achieve settlement, particularly in thinking about options that may not readily be available in court proceedings, but which may nevertheless be of real value to the parties. This can involve building into the agreement matters that are outside the scope of the dispute and which a court would have no power to order. For example:
  - in a boundary dispute, agreeing to 'sell' a piece of land to the other side for a sum above its true market value that reflects the importance of that small piece of land to the other side;
  - in a commercial case involving the supply of goods, agreeing to supply goods for a prescribed period of time to the other side for an agreed price that is perhaps lower than the usual market price for goods of that type;
  - in a libel case providing a public apology by an agreed method;

    – agreeing to accept damages by way of periodic payments;

    – devising new systems that will prevent a recurrence of the complaint in the future.

- If quantum remains the sticking point, the mediator may suggest agreement on liability leaving quantum to be determined by another ADR method at a later date.
- The mediator may suggest alternative solutions and settlement proposals for the consideration of the party.
- Finally, the mediator may actually advise the parties, by evaluating the dispute and giving them his professional opinion on the likely outcome of it or in respect of an issue raised in it. A mediator who provides an opinion is said to be an evaluative mediator (see 11.86–11.92). Any opinion or advice given by the mediator is not binding on the parties.

THE NEGOTIATING/BARGAINING PHASE

At some point during the private meetings, the parties will start to think about putting forward proposals for settlement. They may ask the mediator for guidance on how a proposal or offer should be presented to the other side, and about the value and content of the opening offer and the strategy that they should employ in order to move towards settlement. They may commence with less controversial issues on which agreement can be more readily achieved, before moving to the main contentious issues that need to be resolved. In the later stages of the bargaining phase, small issues may divide the parties and prevent them from reaching overall settlement. Mediation can be more effective than direct negotiation at closing the final gap between the parties and the mediator will employ every skill and technique at his disposal to ensure that the parties make the final push towards settlement. **13.37**

Before he leaves a private meeting with a party, the mediator will sum up the discussion that has taken place and any offers or concessions or information that he is authorised to communicate to the other side. **13.38**

The mediator will then 'shuttle' between the parties, putting forward offers, concessions, information and responses to offers for their consideration and generally acting as the intermediary between the parties. This is sometimes referred to as 'shuttle mediation'. He will usually be the judge of when to time offers or concessions and the order in which they should be made during the process, in order to maximise the chances of settlement. **13.39**

There are advantages in the mediator acting as a shuttle diplomat or honest broker in this way: **13.40**

- Offers and concessions made by a mediator will be perceived as having more value than if they had been made by the other side directly.
- It is effective if the parties have a limited range of negotiating skills or the relationship between the parties has broken down.

There are also disadvantages: **13.41**

- The parties are not working together to the same degree.
- Confidential information may be inadvertently leaked by the mediator to the other side.
- The process may take longer.
- It gives the mediator a great deal of control and power.

13.42 For these reasons, sometimes rather than engage in 'shuttle mediation', the mediator will convene a joint meeting, so that the parties can negotiate directly between themselves.

JOINT OPEN MEETINGS IN THE EXPLORATION OR BARGAINING PHASE

Joint meetings of representatives of the parties

13.43 The mediator may call the parties together for one or more joint meetings as the day progresses if he feels it would be would help the parties to reach agreement on one issue or an overall settlement. These joint meetings may be attended by the lawyers acting for each party, or by all of the parties and their representatives. Some mediators favour bringing the representatives of the parties together for offers to be made unless the relationship between the parties would make this counter-productive. The mediator is likely to convene a joint meeting during the negotiation phase if he thinks it would be more effective for the representatives of the parties to make or explore proposals face to face, rather than through him.

Joint meetings between the lay clients

13.44 In some mediations, it may be beneficial for the parties to negotiate some or all of the issues directly with one another. This is only likely to be the case if the parties have a reasonable working relationship with one another. Even if the mediator conducts 'shuttle mediation' for most of the bargaining phase, when the negotiations are almost completed, the mediator may often bring the lay clients together to agree the remaining outstanding issues, particularly if the overall settlement is likely to involve a future relationship between the parties. The mediator may also convene a meeting between the lay clients if no movement at all has been made towards settlement in order to explain the benefit of the process and encourage the parties to commit to it.

Joint meetings of the experts

13.45 If experts are present for each party then joint meetings may be convened between the experts, usually without the representatives of the parties or the parties themselves being present, to see if some agreement can be reached on a technical issues or on issues of quantum.

THE SETTLEMENT/CLOSING PHASE

If settlement is reached

13.46 If a settlement is reached, the mediator will confirm the terms agreed and ask the lawyers of the parties (if they are present) to draw up the settlement agreement. Whatever form the document takes, the mediator will ensure that the parties do not leave the mediation until the agreement is signed by the parties and the mediator as their input is frequently required as the fine points of detail are hammered out between the lawyers. The mediation agreement will usually provide that no settlement is binding on the parties unless it is recorded by the parties and signed by them. Unless this takes place at the mediation, there is always the possibility that the parties may resile from the settlement before the binding agreement has been drawn up.

If the parties are represented by lawyers, they will have the task of drawing up the settlement agreement. This will usually be a joint effort of all the lawyers involved. The mediator will however oversee the process and will mediate any disagreement that takes place between the parties, or their lawyers, in relation to the detailed terms of the settlement. The lawyers should try to ensure that a laptop computer is brought to the mediation for that purpose, together with some sample precedents. **13.47**

If the parties are acting in person, the mediator may draw up a heads of agreement or a memorandum of agreed terms and ask the parties to sign it, with the intention of setting out the terms in writing so that the legal representatives of each party can then draw up the formal settlement agreement (perhaps in the form of a Tomlin order) after the mediation. No binding settlement will be achieved however until this has been done, so there always remains the possibility that one or more of the parties will have second thoughts about the settlement and try to renege from it. However there is little that can be done to prevent this happening. In very simple cases, the mediator may draft a settlement agreement. In order to ensure that a party acting in person fully understands the terms of the settlement and that the settlement is in his best interests, the agreement may provide that it will only be binding if legal advice is obtained within a certain time. The mediator will then maintain contact with the party acting in person after the mediation and oversee the implementation of the agreement. **13.48**

Once the final terms of the settlement agreement have been drafted, the mediator will usually convene a final joint meeting of all the parties and will read through the agreement. Once he is satisfied that the agreement fully reflects all of the parties' objectives, he will ask the parties to sign it. **13.49**

If no settlement is reached

If no settlement is reached, the mediator will record this, and may also set out the reasons why the mediation did not result in settlement. In any event, he is likely to summarise the closing positions of the parties, which may form the baseline for further settlement discussions outside the mediation. In suitable cases, he may invite the parties simply to adjourn the mediation for further information to be obtained, or for the parties to consider their positions. If the parties do not wish to adjourn the mediation, the mediator will remind the parties of the advantages of settlement over litigation and will encourage them to try and close their differences by continuing discussions and negotiations or perhaps by employing some other form of ADR process. He may invite the parties to let their closing offers remain open for acceptance for a limited period of time after the mediation so that the parties can consider them in the meantime. If an offer made in the mediation is accepted outside the mediation meeting it is likely to be regarded as a settlement reached in the mediation, so must be recorded in writing to be binding on the parties (*Brown v Rice* [2007] EWHC 625). In fact many unsuccessful mediations do result in settlement some time after the mediation took place. **13.50**

THE CLOSING JOINT MEETING

13.51   The mediator will convene the closing meeting if:

- a settlement has been reached on all of the issues or on some of the issues, leaving the remainder to be determined by litigation;
- settlement is not likely to be achieved;
- one of the parties wishes to terminate the mediation;
- the mediation needs to be adjourned eg for an expert to carry out a neutral evaluation of particular issues, for further information to be obtained, or if the day has ended without reaching a settlement but the parties feel that settlement could be achieved if the mediation is adjourned to the next available date.

TERMINATION AND ADJOURNMENT OF THE MEDIATION

13.52   The parties may request an adjournment at any time, to consider proposals, to obtain advice or for any other reason they see fit. The mediation can also be terminated at any time by any of the parties or by the mediator.

THE MEDIATOR'S ROLE FOLLOWING THE CONCLUSION OF THE MEDIATION

13.53   In most cases, if mediation does not result in settlement, the mediator will have no further involvement with the case unless, at some future date, the parties refer the dispute back to him for further mediation, or seek his assistance in private negotiations between the parties. The mediator may help to facilitate settlement by conference telephone calls or by correspondence if the parties wish him to do so.

13.54   In cases where the parties are likely to continue to explore settlement themselves after the mediation, the mediator and the parties should agree whether the mediation has merely been adjourned (so that any further settlement discussions between the parties take place under the terms of the mediation agreement) or whether the mediation has ended, so that any further settlement discussions take place outside of it. This can be important in relation to costs, particularly if the mediation agreement sets out the manner in which the parties will bear the costs of the mediation. It can also be important for determining the form of settlement.

13.55   If the mediation does not result in settlement, the parties may ask the mediator to provide a written opinion on the likely outcome of the dispute or a written settlement recommendation (and thus become an evaluative mediator). A separate fee would be payable for this.

13.56   If it is clear that the mediator's involvement with the case has come to an end, he may return the papers he was given to the parties. However some mediators will retain their file of papers in case their assistance is required in relation to any matter arising out of the mediation in the future. Some mediators may destroy confidential information that they were given by the parties during the mediation.

If settlement is reached at the mediation, the terms of the settlement may state that any **13.57** dispute about implementation of the settlement must be referred back to the mediator. This is not uncommon in complex settlement agreements that require a number of things to be done by the parties to implement the settlement.

THE MAIN VARIATIONS IN THE PROCESS

Mediation is designed to be a flexible process. The procedure can be varied to suit the sub- **13.58** ject-matter of the dispute and the needs of the parties. In family proceedings, it is rare for the mediator to convene separate meetings with the parties to avoid any impression that he is not completely neutral. In cases that raise public policy or environmental issues the mediation may take place in public before interested parties rather than in private. If the relationship between the parties has broken down completely the mediation can take place in private closed meetings only.

Full details of the main variations in the process can be found in Laurence Boulle and **13.59** Miryana Nesic *Mediator Skills and Techniques: Triangle of Influence* (Bloomsbury Professional, 2009), ch 9. The key variants in the process are outlined below. Reference should also be made to the various mediation schemes described in Chapter 14.

Evaluative mediation

If the parties have elected to have an evaluative mediation process rather than a purely **13.60** facilitative one, the mediator will give the parties a neutral evaluation of the case. An evaluation should only be given if *all* of the parties agree and request this and the mediator is willing and happy to do so. He is only likely to give an evaluation on the merits of the overall dispute if he has some expertise in the underlying subject-matter of the dispute. He may also be unwilling to do this if each of the parties have lawyers acting for them, as they can properly advise their clients on the likely outcome of the dispute should settlement not be reached. Evaluative mediation is described in more detail in Chapter 11.

The evaluation will usually be undertaken in the exploration or bargaining phase, dur- **13.61** ing private meetings with the parties, although the evaluation provided to each of the parties should be in identical terms. In some cases it may be advantageous for the evaluation to take place early in the mediation so that the parties can bear it in mind when putting forward proposals for settlement. Sometimes the mediator may leave the evaluation until near the end of the bargaining phase and then provide his opinion in a final last-minute effort to persuade the parties to resolve the differences between them. In giving an evaluation of the likely outcome of the case, or when suggesting a settlement proposal for the consideration of the parties, the mediator must take care not to reveal private and confidential information provided to him by the parties that had a bearing on his evaluation.

The mediator can also recommend to the parties that an expert be instructed to carry out a **13.62** neutral evaluation or determination of one or more of the issues in the case. This will normally be discussed and agreed with the parties in advance of the mediation and the expert appointed in good time before the day set for the mediation. Sometimes the need to have a determination or expert evaluation only becomes apparent during the mediation. If this happens, the mediation may be adjourned and then resumed when the evaluation or determination report has been obtained.

MED-ARB

13.63 This is a hybrid process which provides that if no settlement can be agreed at the mediation, the parties may invite the mediator to act as arbitrator to determine the dispute and make an award that will be binding or non-binding as agreed by the parties.

13.64 The main advantage of the process is that the parties have certainty that the dispute will be resolved by one method or the other. The main criticisms of the process revolve around the fact that the same neutral person is both mediator and arbitrator. He will therefore be in possession of confidential information provided by the parties, or the parties will be inhibited in providing confidential information to him for fear that it could prejudice them in any resulting arbitration. Such a challenge was successfully made on this basis in proceedings to enforce an adjudication award where the adjudicator had previously acted as mediator in *Glencot Development and Design Co Ltd v Ben Barrett & Son (Contractors) Limited* (unreported, 13 February 2002). This can be overcome by having a different individual to act as mediator and arbitrator, although this is likely to be more costly.

13.65 The Centre for Effective Dispute Resolution has recently published a report 'The CEDR Commission on Settlement in International Arbitration' (see www.cedr.com/arbitration) recommending that an arbitration tribunal should facilitate a negotiated settlement unless the parties otherwise agree. It has also published 'CEDR Rules for the Facilitation of Settlement in International Arbitration', which provide for a mediation window to be inserted into the arbitral proceedings at the request of the parties, and when awarding costs the tribunal can take into account any unreasonable refusal by a party to make use of a mediation window.

13.66 If settlement is agreed at the mediation, the parties may appoint the mediator as arbitrator and ask him to draw up the settlement agreement as an arbitration consent award, which would then become enforceable at law. If the parties wish to do this, they should commence the process by an arbitration agreement otherwise, if the dispute is settled by mediation, there will be no 'dispute' within which an arbitral award can be made by consent.

ARB-MED

13.67 This reverses the process. A simplified form of arbitration takes place first, followed by mediation. The neutral person will make an arbitration award which is sealed and not revealed to the parties unless they are unable to reach settlement at the mediation that will follow the arbitration. The same neutral person will change his role from arbitrator to mediator. The uncertainty generated by the unknown award often forces the parties to reach a settlement at the mediation. If mediation produces settlement, the arbitral award will not be opened.

13.68 The main criticism of this process is that if mediation results in settlement, the time and money taken to arbitrate the dispute first will have been wasted. There is also the risk that the parties may perceive the mediator as giving some indication of the arbitration award if he makes any evaluative comments in relation to the dispute.

For more detail on MED-ARB and ARB-MED, see the paper by Alan L Limbury 'Hybrid **13.69** Dispute Resolution Processes—Getting the Best while Avoiding the Worse of Both Worlds?' (January 2010) (published on www.cedr.com).

Telephone mediations

In some situations, mediation may need to be conducted by telephone rather than in face- **13.70** to-face meetings. This may happen in:

- the Small Claims Court Mediation Scheme (see Chapter 14);
- if the parties have been restrained by a court order from meeting each other;
- if the parties live a long geographical distance from one another.

Telephone mediations lack the impact of a meeting and some parties find it very difficult to **13.71** communicate via a telephone conference call.

The stages in the telephone mediation process are as follows: **13.72**

- The mediator will hold pre-mediation discussions with the parties as in the main process. This will take place exclusively by telephone.
- The mediation will take place by a telephone conference, with all the parties being telephoned at the same time by the mediator, so that they can hear what is said, and participate, as if they were present at a joint meeting.
- If separate discussions are needed with the parties (to mimic a separate private meeting), then the telephone conference will be terminated and the mediator will then ring each party on their private telephone line and discuss the case with them in much the same way as he would if a private meeting was convened with the parties attending in person.
- The negotiating phase can take place by the mediator acting as shuttle diplomat in separate telephone conversations with the parties, or by the parties making offers and concessions during a joint telephone conference, or a mixture of the two.
- In any event, the mediator should confirm the agreement reached and ensure each party assents by arranging a final joint telephone conference call.
- The mediator may record the terms of the draft agreement in writing and email or fax it to the parties before the end of the joint telephone conference for it to be fully drawn up by their lawyers and signed by the parties.

There are a number of ADR providers who offer a telephone mediation service, for example **13.73** Inter-Resolve.

Internet mediations

Mediation can also take place on the internet (also known as e-mediation or online **13.74** mediation). This can be useful if the parties reside in different countries. A number of internet organisations now offer online ADR services such as Settle Online (www.settleonline. com), Cybersettle (www.cybersettle.com), e-mediator (www.e-mediator.co.uk), the Mediation Room (www.themediationroom.com), and the Online Ombuds Office (www. ombuds.org). Any mediations taking place over the internet will be fully documented by the email and text messaging exchanges that may take place between the various parties, and there may be issues about confidentiality. It may be possible to arrange virtual meetings via webcam conferencing facilities. It is likely that this will further develop in the future.

THE ROLE OF THE ADVOCATE IN MEDIATION

13.75 Lawyers, whether they are a solicitor or a barrister, will carry out a specific role at a mediation that will involve the exercise of the four main skills in their toolbox. These are:

- preparation and case analysis;
- mediation advocacy skills;
- advisory skills;
- drafting skills.

13.76 In many cases, the solicitor acting for the party will attend the mediation without instructing counsel. In some cases, however counsel will be instructed to attend the mediation without a solicitor in attendance. In complex or high value claims, counsel is likely to be instructed to attend the hearing as well as the instructing solicitors. Counsel is also likely to be instructed to attend a mediation on behalf of a child or other person who lacks capacity to conduct legal proceedings on their own behalf. Any settlement reached at the mediation will only become binding when the approval of the court has been obtained, and counsel's opinion on the merits and quantum of the claim and whether the settlement is reasonable is usually required before the court will approve it.

Preparation and case analysis

13.77 Preparing effectively for a mediation is just as important as preparing for trial. An advocate who turns up to the mediation without having undertaken a careful analysis of his client's case is not going to be able to persuade the other side of the strengths of the case in a joint session, nor he is going to be in a position to advise the client on offers made by the other side or the extent to which the client should be making reasonable offers and concessions. He will not be able to properly guide and advise his client through the mediation process.

13.78 The advocate instructed to represent a client at a mediation hearing must undertake a great deal of preparation. He should carry out a thorough analysis of the strengths and weaknesses of the legal and factual and evidential issues in the case and evaluate the prospects of success. He must also undertake a thorough analysis of the position of his client in relation to costs. Finally he should consider the dispute and the position of his client in the broadest possible context, including looking at the practical, commercial and personal considerations that might influence settlement. When he has done that, he should devise a strategy for the mediation. All of these matters are dealt with in Chapter 12.

Mediation advocacy

13.79 The Standing Council of Mediation Advocates (SCMA) has defined mediation advocacy as the technique of presenting and arguing a client's position, needs and interests in a non-adversarial way (see www.mediationadvocates.org.uk). SCMA is a multi-disciplinary cross-professional association established to promote and deliver best practice and professional excellence in mediation advocacy. Its members include sets of barristers' chambers, solicitor's firms, and individual legal, surveyor and construction professionals who represent parties in civil and commercial mediations in the UK. A very useful description of the role of advocates in mediation can be obtained from *Mediation Advocacy* by Andrew Goodman and Alastair Hammerton (XPL Law).

There are a number of key differences between mediation and court proceedings, which **13.80** advocates (and barristers in particular) should bear in mind.

- It is an informal, non-adversarial process.
- There is no opportunity for forensic witness handling skills that are employed in the adversarial process that occurs in the courtroom.
- The aim of the game is not to win, but to ensure that a settlement is reached.
- The focus is on the parties and not the lawyers. The mediator will speak directly to the parties rather than communicating with them through the lawyers. In mediation, the lawyer will have to expect to take a 'back seat' in private meetings with the mediator. The lawyer is a valuable part of the team, but not the leading player in it.
- The mediator will not (usually) be making any determination on the issues on the case, so he does not need to be 'won over' or persuaded of the strength of the lay client's case in the same way as a judge. In saying that it is important that the mediator has a clear appreciation of the merits of the case so that he can effectively counter arguments made by the other side during private meetings with them.
- The mediator is primarily there to facilitate settlement between the parties, not to direct what the outcome should be, and not to give advice on whether any proposed settlement is a reasonable one.

Advisory skills in mediation

The advocate, whether solicitor or barrister, will have an advisory role in mediation. The **13.81** advice that the advocate may need to give to his client at mediation covers a wide range of issues:

- The advocate may need to advise the client about various aspects of the process of mediation and the position of the mediator and the roles that each party will play in the process.
- If the lay client is to deliver part of the opening statement at the opening joint session, the advocate should prepare the lay client to do this.
- The advocate will need to advise the client at mediation about the strengths and weaknesses of their legal position, so that they can evaluate any settlement proposals made by the other side and so that they can make informed offers and concessions themselves as the day progresses.
- The advocate will also be required to give legal advice about issues raised by the other side, the effect of offers and concessions made by the other side and guide the lay client in responding to these.
- The advocate will need to advise the client about offers and concessions that the client may wish to make, or should be advised to make.
- The advocate may need to discuss and agree tactics and a negotiating strategy during the mediation. He may need to 'rein in' a client who wishes to make his best offer first if that would be tactically unwise in the circumstances of the case.

- The advocate will also want to advise the client on any settlement reached during the mediation, and ensure that the agreement is a reasonable one bearing in mind the lay client's underlying interests as well as the merits of his legal position.

Delivery of the opening statement at the opening joint meeting

13.82 It is usual for the advocate to deliver the opening statement in the opening plenary session. As is noted above, the purpose of this statement is to persuade the mediator and the other side of the merits of the lay client's case. The advocate should make the statement to the other side, and maintain good eye contact with the other party and his lawyers during the delivery of it. He should seek to persuade the other side of the strength of the case against them. He should also acknowledge their concerns and position and try to deal with these. Care must be taken not to construct a wall between the parties, or make it higher than it is already. Instead the opening statement should persuade the other side of the need to dismantle the wall, and show them the route that could be taken or explored during the mediation in order to reach that goal.

The advocate's role during private closed meetings

13.83 The lawyer must be sensitive of the need not to 'take over' the private meetings. The mediator will do his best to ensure that he does not do so. The mediator's focus on the private meetings will be on exploring ways to move the settlement process forward with the lay client.

13.84 During the private meetings, the advocate will have to persuade the mediator of the merits of his client's case and the weaknesses in the other side's case. He may also raise questions that he wishes the mediator to convey to the other side in an effort to obtain further information about their stance on a particular issue, or give the mediator information to pass to the other party. He will discuss the case with the mediator and, if necessary, re-assess the merits of the case in light of that discussion or following information disclosed during the mediation.

13.85 The lawyer will also discuss and explore settlement options with the lay client and other relevant members of his team, including the timing of offers and concessions and the negotiation strategy to be adopted.

13.86 The advocate may propose or be asked by the mediator to meet with the lawyer for the other party in a joint meeting to explore settlement of a particular issue rather than communicate second-hand through the mediator. A joint meeting of lawyers may also be held to enable them to explain their case on a difficult issue to each other in the hope that this will cause some movement in their positions.

Settlement

13.87 If a binding agreement is reached during the mediation process, then the mediation agreement will usually provide for the settlement to be drawn up in writing and signed by the parties before it is regarded as a legally binding contract between the parties. The lawyers' role will be to draft this legal settlement agreement before the close of the mediation. There is always a time pressure in drafting the agreement. The deal is usually struck at the end of the day, but no members of the team can be released until the agreement is signed as the drafting of the terms of settlement often throws up points of detail that may need to be further negotiated and agreed between the parties.

Lawyers acting for the parties should always bring a laptop computer to mediation meetings, together with key precedents that they may need to use in drafting the settlement agreement. Many of the settlement provisions can be anticipated and drafted in advance before the mediation and then amended to reflect the actual terms agreed. **13.88**

If it is clear that if an overall settlement cannot be achieved at the mediation, the advocate should ensure that the parties record in writing those issues on which agreement was reached, so as to achieve a narrowing of the issues to be determined at trial. **13.89**

The terms of settlement should include details of some or all of the following matters: **13.90**

- How much is to be paid and by whom and by when.
- If instalment payments have been agreed, there should be absolute certainty as to the time, date and method for each payment.
- Provision should be made for what is to happen if payment is not made by the due date.
- Agreement also needs to be reached on any interest that is to be paid, and when it runs from and at what rate and when interest ceases to be payable.
- If an apology is to be provided, then the wording of this should be agreed and, if the apology is to be made public, the agreement should spell out when and by what means that should happen.
- If one of the settlement terms was that the parties would enter into a new contract, the form and terms of that contract should be agreed.
- Thought should be given to the method of enforcement should there be a breach of the terms of the settlement by any party.
- The settlement agreement should also deal with the costs of any litigation and also the costs of the mediation. It is also always open to the parties to negotiate the costs, fees and expenses of mediation (see Chapter 11) as part of the overall settlement. This is so even if the mediation agreement provides that the fees and expenses of the mediation should be borne jointly by the parties and that each party was responsible for their own legal costs. By the settlement agreement, one party can indemnify the other in relation to costs, fees or expenses paid by them in connection with the mediation.
- If one party is acting under a CFA agreement, then any settlement agreement should make it clear whether the success fee and any ATE insurance premium is included in any terms agreed about costs.
- If litigation has already commenced, the settlement agreement should provide for the means by which the litigation will come to an end. This is usually done by either by lodging a consent order staying the action on the terms of the settlement (a Tomlin order), dismissing the proceedings, or by a consent order made in the proceedings that sets out the terms agreed in the mediation. The Tomlin order is the most effective because it enables the parties, in the event of default, to apply to the court to enforce the terms recorded in the schedule attached to the order without the need to issue fresh proceedings. A second major advantage of a Tomlin order is that the schedule containing the terms is confidential and is not part of the court order itself. If litigation has not yet commenced, then the settlement agreement will usually take effect as a contract between the parties. If the terms are breached, then fresh proceedings would need to be issued for breach of contract.

- Provision may be made for any disputes arising out of the terms of the settlement agreement to be referred to mediation in the first instance.

13.91 If any of the parties lack capacity, such as children, then any settlement reached in the mediation will not be binding unless it is approved by the court. Any settlement will therefore be conditional on court approval being obtained. Sometimes, for example if one of the parties to the mediation is a public body or a company, it may be the case that the settlement needs to be approved by a committee before it becomes binding. In this event, heads of agreement can be drawn up at the mediation although the agreement will not be legally binding until it is approved by the committee and signed by the parties.

Enforcement of settlement agreements

13.92 A detailed discussion about the various ways in which settlement can be recorded is dealt with in Chapter 20. Chapter 29 deals with the methods by which settlement agreements can be enforced.

Setting aside settlement agreements

13.93 A party may be able to issue proceedings to set aside a settlement agreement reached in mediation, or defend enforcement proceedings brought in respect of such an agreement if there are grounds to do so. In *Vedatech Corp v Crystal Decisions (UK) Ltd* [2003] EWCA Civ 1066 one of the parties sought to set aside the agreement on the grounds of fraud, misrepresentation and on the basis that one side had renounced or breached the agreement or that the agreement failed to comply with the formalities essential for a contract as it was not signed by the correct party to the dispute, namely the parent company rather than the subsidiary.

THE WITHOUT PREJUDICE RULE AND THE NATURE OF CONFIDENTIALITY IN MEDIATION

13.94 The nature of the without prejudice rule and the exceptions to it are discussed at 3.78–3.83.

The without prejudice rule in mediation

13.95 The without prejudice rule and exceptions to it apply to communications passing between the parties made in the context of a mediation, so these cannot be relied on or referred to in subsequent court proceedings if the mediation is unsuccessful (*Aird v Prime Meridian Ltd* [2007] BLR 105).

13.96 In *Halsey v Milton Keynes General NHS Trust* [2004] 1 WLR 3002, the court accepted that 'if the integrity and confidentiality of the [mediation] process is to be respected, the court should not know, and should not investigate, why the process did not result in agreement'. The without prejudice rule will clearly apply to communications aimed at settlement that take place between the parties before the mediation agreement is signed, or before the mediation commences, as well as communications that take place during the course of the mediation. For further details about the operation of the rule in mediation see Karl Mackie et al *The ADR Practice Guide: Commercial Dispute* (3rd edn, Tottel Publishing), ch 7.

The without prejudice rule is often specifically stated in the mediation agreement **13.97** between the parties (see, for example, cl 5.2 CEDR Model Mediation Agreement), and is further strengthened by a confidentiality clause. The court will uphold these clauses and grant an injunction to restrain a party from referring to any part of the discussions that took place during the mediation (*Venture Investment Placement Ltd v Hall* [2005] EWHC 1227 (Ch)).

In mediation, the following communications will be protected from disclosure by operation **13.98** of the without prejudice rule:

- any oral or written communications made specifically for the purposes of settlement, such as position statements, correspondence about the mediation, offers or concessions whether made before, during or after the mediation;
- any communications passing between the parties and the mediator before, during or after the mediation with a view to exploring settlement;
- communications created for the purpose of trying to persuade the parties to mediate: *Instance v Denny* Bros Printing Ltd [2000] FSR 869.

The rule will protect communications aimed at settlement which pass between the par- **13.99** ties themselves or between their respective lawyers and it is also likely to protect communications passing between the parties and the mediator (*Brown v Rice* [2007] EWHC 625 (Ch)).

It will also operate to protect investigations carried out as part of the mediation process. In **13.100** *Smiths Group plc v George Weiss* (unreported, 22 March 2002), the agreed mediation procedure provided for each party's expert to meet with employees and former employees with a view to establishing work done by them during a particular year. The mediation was adjourned to enable this to be done. The persons interviewed were told informally before each interview that the interview was without prejudice and that the material would not be used in evidence. The mediation failed to result in settlement and the issue before the court was whether the claimant's expert should be required to expunge accounts of his interviews with the employees from his report. Despite finding that the interviews were part of the fact-finding process and in no sense related to any attempt to settle the proceedings, Mr Roger Kaye QC (sitting as a Deputy High Court Judge) accepted that these interviews were protected by the without prejudice rule, and that the defendant's conduct was not such that they should be estopped from asserting the privilege.

Communications that are not protected by the without prejudice rule in mediation

Although there are few reported decisions in the context of mediation, in view of the fact **13.101** that there is no particular special category of 'mediation privilege', it is likely that the exceptions to the without prejudice rule in general litigation (see 3.83 above) will also apply in the context of mediation.

In mediation, the following communications will not be protected by the without prejudice **13.102** rule:

- open offers;

- offers that can be communicated to the court on the question of costs, after issues of liability and remedies have been determined. If a party wishes to rely on a document in relation to costs, then they should either mark the document 'without prejudice except as to costs' or make a formal offer under Part 36 of the CPR. If the offer is not accepted by the other party, and they fail to beat it at trial, then it can be drawn to the attention of the court in order to persuade the court to make an adverse costs order against that party;
- communications that are not aimed at settlement of a dispute. Not all documents produced at or prepared for a mediation will be protected by the without prejudice rule. The rule will not protect documents that were not created for the purposes of exploring settlement, such as statements of case or contractual documents, documents relating to loss, accident report forms, maintenance records or any other documents of this nature that would have to be disclosed during the course of litigation. It will also not apply to a joint statement made following a meeting of the experts instructed by each party that was created for use in the mediation, as such a statement is one that the experts must produce if the court directs it under CCR 35.12 (*Aird v Prime Meridian Ltd* [2007] BLR 105).

13.103   If the without prejudice rule is abused, eg by a party making a threat about the action they will take if an offer is not accepted during a mediation, then the court will not allow a party to shield behind the rule and will order disclosure (*Unilever plc v Procter & Gamble* [2000] 1 WLR 1436; *Aird & v Prime Meridian Ltd* [2007] BLR 105).

13.104   The court can look at communications that took place in a mediation to decide if the mediation resulted in a concluded settlement. In *Brown v Rice* [2007] EWHC 625 (Ch); an issue arose between the parties as to whether a settlement had been reached at a mediation, even though the terms had not been recorded by an agreement in writing and signed by the parties. The ADR Group was given permission to intervene in the proceedings. They submitted that nothing said or done in preparation for or at a mediation could be disclosed in the absence of impropriety by a party at the mediation. They also submitted that the clause in a mediation agreement providing that there was no agreement unless it was in writing and signed by the parties prevented the court from looking at the events in the mediation to see if there was a concluded settlement because this clause effectively removed that exception to the without prejudice rule. The court rejected these submissions and held that the fact that communications took place in the context of mediation did not provide the communications with a special status. Mediation was simply a form of assisted negotiation and so the usual exceptions to the without prejudice rule applied in the context of mediation. The court could therefore look at the events in the mediation to decide if there was a concluded agreement as an exception to the without prejudice rule. Although the court accepted that an offer had been made, and accepted by the deadline on the day following the mediation, the absence of any provision as to the manner of disposal of the litigation meant that the offer was incomplete. The court also held that the clause in the mediation agreement requiring there to be a written settlement, meant that any agreement reached between the parties could not be completed until reduced to writing, unless that clause was varied or waived or one party was not able to rely on it. The court therefore found that no binding settlement had been reached.

13.105   The mediation agreement itself is not protected by the without prejudice rule and it can be produced to prove its terms (*Brown v Rice* [2007] EWHC 625 (Ch)).

If *all* parties to the mediation waive privilege, the communications can be placed before **13.106** the court. In *Cumbria Waste Management Ltd v Baines Wilson* [2008] BLR 330, a mediation took place between the claimant and DEFRA, which resulted in settlement. The claimant then sued its former solicitors, Baines Wilson, for the difference between its original claim and the settlement amount. The shortfall was alleged to be due to their negligence in drafting the underlying substantive contract. The solicitors (who did not act for the claimant in the mediation) sought disclosure of communications in the mediation and argued that, by bringing the action against them, the claimant had waived privilege and they needed to know what happened during the mediation to assess the reasonableness of the settlement. The court held that the court should support the mediation process by refusing, in normal circumstances, to order disclosure of documents and communications that took place within mediation. Mediators should be able to conduct mediations confident that, in normal circumstances, their papers would not be seen by the parties or others. The privilege belonged not only to the claimant but also DEFRA. In the absence of waiver of the privilege by DEFRA, the court could not order disclosure of the communications within the mediation.

Can the mediator rely on the without prejudice rule?

The without prejudice rule exists for the benefit of the parties and it can be waived by them. **13.107** It is not a privilege of the mediator, so if the parties waive it, the mediator cannot rely on it to prevent non-disclosure of communications arising out of the mediation process or to justify a refusal to give evidence about such communications. This is so even if the mediation agreement contains an express provision as to the without prejudice nature of the mediation process (*Farm Assist Ltd (In liquidation) v The Secretary of State for the Environment, Food and Rural Affairs (No 2)* [2009] BLR 399).

LEGAL ADVICE PRIVILEGE IN MEDIATION

Communications passing between a client and their lawyers made for the purposes of **13.108** giving or receiving legal advice are protected by legal professional privilege (*Three Rivers District Council v Bank of England (No 5)* [2003] QB 1556). Legal advice privilege will also be upheld in mediation. In *Farm Assist Ltd (in liquidation) v Secretary of State for Environment, Food and Rural Affairs* [2008] EWHC 3079, the claimant and the defendant settled the claim at mediation. The claimant then brought separate proceedings against the Secretary of State seeking an order that the settlement reached at mediation should be set aside on the grounds of economic duress. The Secretary of State sought disclosure of documents covered by legal advice privilege both before and during the mediation, consisting of advice about the merits of the claim, the offers to be made during the mediation and the response to offers made by DEFRA. It was argued that privilege had been impliedly waived by impeaching the settlement on the grounds of economic duress. The court held that waiver of legal advice privilege could only occur in proceedings between the client and the solicitor, and that legal advice privilege was not waived by suing a third party (DEFRA) in these circumstances.

CONFIDENTIALITY

The obligation of confidentiality

13.109   The mediation agreement will usually stipulate that neither party can reveal any detail of the mediation process or any information obtained during the mediation without the express consent of the other party. A confidentiality clause in the mediation agreement amounts to a contractual promise on the part of all parties to the contract, including the mediator, not to reveal communications made during the mediation. An injunction can be obtained, in certain circumstances, to restrain breach of this obligation (see *Venture Investment Placement Ltd v Hall* [2005] EWHC 1227 (Ch)). Damages could also be claimed for any breach. Even in the absence of an express confidentially clause, one is likely to be implied, because it would destroy the basis of mediation if either party could publicise the matters that took place within between them and the mediator. The mediator also owes a duty of confidentiality to the parties. A confidentiality clause adds weight to the without prejudice rule and it may be wider than it.

13.110   In *Aird v Prime Meridian* [2007] BLR 105, the court accepted that a confidentiality clause reinforces the without prejudice rule. However May LJ went to state:

> 'This cannot of course be taken literally, since it would obviously not apply to documents produced for other purposes which were needed for and produced at the mediation, for example their building contract or the antecedent pleadings in the proceedings.... but the general intent of the provision is clear, and it accords with the generally understood "without prejudice" nature of mediation'.

13.111   Unless the mediation agreement provides to the contrary, the mere fact that the parties have agreed to try and resolve the dispute by mediation or have had a mediation hearing is not confidential; the confidentiality therefore attaches to the events during the mediation process, rather than the bare fact that the parties are about to or have embarked on mediation.

Example of a confidentiality clause

> Any information, whether written or oral, which is disclosed to a mediator in private will be treated as confidential by the mediator and will not be disclosed to any other party to the dispute or any person whatsoever or to any judge, court or tribunal unless:
>
> (a)   the party making the disclosure agrees that it should be disclosed;
> (b)   the law requires the mediator to disclose the confidential information;
> (c)   the mediator believes there is a serious risk to the life or safety of any person if disclosure is not made.
>
> The parties and the mediator also agree that they will not disclose any information arising out of or in connection with mediation, including the facts and terms of settlement, unless they are compelled by law to do so or except insofar as it is necessary to enforce any settlement agreement.

Information given to the mediator

13.112   Any information given to the mediator during the process and in particular anything revealed to him during the private meetings of the parties is protected by the confidentiality obligation. The mediator cannot reveal this information to the other side or any other party unless the party providing the information expressly consents. The duty of confidentiality will apply even after the mediation process has been completed or terminated.

This is important because it enables the parties to speak frankly to the mediator about their **13.113** concerns or their assessment of the case, without fear that this will be communicated to the other side and exploited by them in the litigation, should the mediation fail to result in settlement. The mediator can also help the parties to decide what disclosures to make to the other side to facilitate settlement.

Can the mediator enforce the confidentiality clause?

The without prejudice rule exists for the benefit of the parties and it can be waived by them. **13.114** It is not a privilege of the mediator, and cannot be relied on by him. However the express or implied term of confidentiality is different. The court in *Farm Assist Ltd (in liquidation) v The Secretary of State for the Environment, Food and Rural Affairs (No 2)* [2009] BLR 399 accepted that the express (or implied) obligation of confidentiality exists not just between the parties themselves, but also between the parties and the mediator, and so it could only be waived by them all.

In *Farm Assist*, the claimant sought to set aside an agreement reached with the defendant **13.115** at the mediation on the basis of economic duress. Both parties waived the without preju- dice privilege and confidentiality in the mediation. A witness summons was issued against the mediator, requiring her to attend court to give evidence about the entire events of the mediation, including private conversations she had with each party. The mediator applied to set the summons aside, relying on the confidentiality provision in the mediation agree- ment. The mediation agreement also provided that the parties would not call the mediator as a witness in any litigation. The court held that confidentiality can be waived but only by the consent of *all* parties. The claimant and the defendant could not waive confidential- ity so as to deprive the mediator of her right to have the confidentiality of the mediation preserved. The court accepted that the mediator has an express enforceable right to keep matters confidential under the terms of the mediation agreement. However, it went on to hold that the obligation of confidentiality is not absolute, and the court has power to permit evidence of confidential communications to be given or produced if it is in the *interests of justice* to do so.

When will the court override the confidentiality provisions in the interests of justice?

It seems likely that the court will override the confidentiality provisions in the absence of **13.116** agreement by all parties only in exceptional cases. In *Farm Assist*, the court did override con- fidentiality because it was necessary for the court to ascertain what was said and done at the mediation in order to determine whether the agreement reached at the mediation should be set aside for economic duress. The interests of justice are also likely to require confidential- ity to be overridden by the court if one party is seeking to vitiate an agreement reached at the mediation on the grounds of duress or undue influence or misrepresentation. The court is also unlikely to allow a mediator to rely on a confidentiality clause so as to prevent the parties from revealing advice given by him during the mediation in respect of any action against him for breach of contract or negligence.

13.117   To permit confidentiality to be overridden in anything other than in very exceptional and limited circumstances will seriously undermine the mediation process. In view of the strong promotion of mediation by the judiciary, this is unlikely to happen.

Other exceptions to confidentiality

13.118   Confidential information may have to be disclosed by the mediator in some circumstances. These exceptions may also be spelt out in the mediation agreement:

- where disclosure is required by law, for example where disclosure is required under the Proceeds of Crime Act 2002, or the HM Revenue and Customs exercise its statutory powers to compel disclosure;
- if the mediator believes there is a risk of significant harm to the health, life or well-being of a person or a threat to their safety if confidential information is not disclosed. This can arise particularly in a family mediation concerning children.
- if disclosure is necessary to prevent criminal activity, or prevent the mediator being charged with colluding in the commission of an offence or if a failure to disclose the confidential information may amount in itself to a criminal offence on the part of the mediator.

THE MEDIATOR AS WITNESS

13.119   The EU Mediation Directive, Art 7, provides that member states should ensure that mediators should not be compelled to give evidence regarding information arising out of mediation. It does however provide for exceptions where all the parties agree or there are public policy considerations that require the mediator to give evidence. The Directive has to be implemented in member states by May 2011.

13.120   The mediation agreement will also usually contain a clause by which the parties agree not to call the mediator or any of his employees or agents as a witness or expert or consultant in any proceedings. Such a clause was considered in *Farm Assist Ltd (in liquidation) v The Secretary of State for the Environment, Food and Rural Affairs (No 2)* [2009] BLR 399. However the clause in that case prevented the parties from calling the mediator as a witness 'in relation to the dispute', meaning the underlying dispute between the parties that gave rise to the mediation. The court (Ramsey J) found that this was different to the dispute that the court was concerned with, namely whether the mediation agreement should be set aside for economic duress. However the court went on to find that even if the clause did apply to the current dispute '... I do not consider that it would in itself lead to the witness summons being set aside. Rather, it would be a factor for the court to take into account in deciding whether, in the interests of justice, a mediator should be called as a witness.' The court found that it was in the interests of justice that the mediator should give evidence as to what was said and done in the mediation and it therefore dismissed the mediator's application to have the witness summons set aside.

13.121   The court was unsympathetic to the mediator's submission that she had little recollection of the mediation as it occurred many years ago and she had conducted up to 50 mediations per year in the intervening period. Ramsey J said this (para 53):

'Whilst the mediator has clearly said that she has no recollection of the mediation, I accept that this does not prevent her from giving evidence. Frequently memories are jogged and recollections come to mind when documents are shown to witnesses and they have the opportunity to focus, in context, on events some years earlier......... ... This is a case where, as an exception, the interests of justice lie strongly in favour of evidence being given of what was said and done.'

The court will therefore override the mediation agreement, and require a mediator to give evidence, if it is in the interests of justice to do so. **13.122**

CAN A MEDIATOR BE SUED?

Legal proceedings

A mediator acts under a contract made with the parties. It is probably an implied term of the contract that he should perform his services with reasonable care and skill. Theoretically, it is possible that a claim could be brought against a mediator for breach of contract, or in negligence if he acted in a way that was not consistent with his duty of care and skill. This may be the case for example if he gave the parties legal advice in the mediation that was incorrect, or negligently evaluated their claim, or brought undue pressure or misrepresented anything to them in order to persuade them to settle the case. If a mediator took it upon himself to draft the settlement agreement (few mediators will do this), a claim could also be brought against him for negligence in this respect. Such claims are likely to be difficult to prove, and will raise difficult issues of causation (particularly where the parties are independently advised by lawyers who are present at the mediation) and loss. **13.123**

If a settlement was reached as a result of undue pressure exerted on that party by a mediator, then this may provide grounds for overturning the settlement agreement. In *Tapoohi v Lewenberg* [2003] VSC 410 an action to overturn a settlement agreement that one party alleged they had entered into as a result of pressure by the mediator was allowed to proceed. The mediator could also be liable if he personally recommends a settlement at a certain level to the parties, if the settlement was unreasonable on the facts of the case (see *McCosh v Williams* [2003] NZCA 192). There have been no cases, as yet, in this jurisdiction in which a mediator has been sued on this basis. **13.124**

Some mediation agreements will contain an exclusion clause that purports to exclude the mediator from liability for negligence or breach of contact (see, for example, cl 4 of the CEDR Model Mediation Agreement in Appendix 2). This may be unenforceable in law or unfair under the Unfair Contract Terms Act 1977. **13.125**

Disciplinary proceedings

It is possible that disciplinary proceedings could be brought against a mediator who acts improperly or not in accordance with the code of conduct adopted by the ADR service provider by whom he was accredited and appointed. **13.126**

KEY POINTS SUMMARY

- The mediation process is flexible and can be tailored to the needs of the parties. **13.127**

- A typical mediation will go through four phases: opening, exploratory, bargaining and settlement.
- The mediation will take place in a mixture of joint open meetings and private separate meetings of the parties.
- The opening statement by the parties should be addressed to the other side.
- The mediator will help the parties to work through deadlock in the bargaining phase.
- Mediation is 'without prejudice', although there are exceptions to the rule.
- Mediation is a confidential process but confidentiality can be overridden by the courts in the interests of justice.
- The mediator may be called to give evidence about the mediation if this is in the interests of justice.

14

COURT MEDIATION SCHEMES AND OTHER SCHEMES

INTRODUCTION. 14.01

THE NATIONAL MEDIATION HELPLINE. 14.02

COURT MEDIATION SCHEMES 14.13

MEDIATION IN SPECIFIC CASES. 14.31

MEDIATING MULTI-PARTY DISPUTES. .14.58

OTHER SCHEMES. 14.65

SECTOR MEDIATION SCHEMES 14.74

THE PENSIONS MEDIATION SERVICE 14.86

THE PERFORMING ARTS MEDIATION SERVICE. 14.87

COMMUNITY MEDIATION 14.88

PRO BONO MEDIATION AND LAWWORKS 14.91

KEY POINTS SUMMARY. 14.92

INTRODUCTION

A number of court and other mediation schemes have developed over recent years. The **14.01** main court schemes are those operated by the National Mediation Helpline and the Court of Appeal Mediation Scheme and the Small Claims Scheme. Other specialist mediation schemes operate for specific types of claims, such as personal injury, family and employment. These are discussed in this chapter.

THE NATIONAL MEDIATION HELPLINE

14.02　The National Mediation Helpline (NMH) provides a low-cost method of mediating a wide range of disputes. This scheme is administered by the Ministry of Justice (MOJ) in conjunction with the Civil Mediation Council (CMC). All mediators used by the scheme are members of accredited mediation providers. A full list of accredited providers who assist in the operation of the scheme can be found on the website www.nationalmediationhelpline. com.

14.03　All county court-annexed mediation schemes now operate through the NMH, with the exception of the Mayor's and City of London County Court Scheme and the Small Claims County Court Scheme (see below). Small claims cases can use the NMH, although the service is not free to the parties, unlike the Small Claims Mediation Scheme, so there is no incentive for them to use it. Any type of case, proceeding in any track or in any court, can be referred to mediation using the NMH. In practice however, it seems to be most used for mediating fast track cases proceeding in the county court.

14.04　A referral to the NMH can be made by the court or by the parties. If the court makes the referral, the judge will usually stay the proceedings for 28 days to enable the parties to resolve their dispute by mediation arranged through the NMH.

14.05　Parties can also refer a case to the NMH directly by completing the online enquiry form available on the website, or they can telephone the Helpline. They will be asked a series of straightforward questions to determine whether the dispute is suitable for mediation. If it is judged suitable, then an adviser will refer it to one of the accredited ADR providers who assist the scheme.

14.06　The Telephone Helplines Association (THA) was commissioned by the Department for Constitutional Affairs to evaluate the operation of the NMH Scheme and Linda Thompson produced a final report in October 2005. This research demonstrated a number of weaknesses with the Scheme, most notably, lack of consistency in information provided to callers and in the processes used by providers, lack of clarity in the referral process where the other party had not agreed to mediation, insufficient monitoring information collected for the process by the NMH, lack of standard procedures for the providers of the scheme and lack of a standard NMH agreement and documentation. The report proposed a number of recommendations that resulted in the scheme being comprehensively revised.

14.07　The ADR providers who assist the Scheme must now comply with a standard procedure, which varies slightly depending on whether the referral is made by the court or by the parties directly. The procedure is summarised below.

- The ADR provider to whom the referral has been made must make contact with the parties, by telephone, within two working days of the referral being received from the NMH. The provider will endeavour to obtain the consent of both parties to mediation. If contact has not been made with all parties within 10 days of referral because one party has not responded or declined mediation then, if the case has been referred by the court, the provider can close the call log and inform the court. If there has been a direct referral, the provider will write a further letter to the parties, giving a seven-day time limit in which to respond. If contact has not been made with all parties by the end of that period, then the call log can be closed and the provider will write to the parties confirming this.

- If all parties agree to mediation, then within 15 days of referral, the provider should have arranged and agreed the date and venue of the mediation with the parties.
- The NMH provider must update the NMH database when mediation is refused and also when the mediation date and venue has been arranged, and also within five days of the mediation taking place.
- If the ADR provider is unable to provide a mediator, then they must return the referral to the NMH within five days and the referring parties must be informed, and the NMH will then contact the next available provider.
- Any complaint must be handled in accordance with the NMH Complaints Procedure.

Flowcharts showing the standard practice procedure for court and direct referrals are repro- **14.08** duced by kind permission of the Ministry of Justice and are set out in Figures 14.1 and 14.2 below. These flowcharts may be amended from time to time (see www.nationalmediation-helpline.com for the most recent versions of these documents).

That ADR provider will require the parties to enter into the NMH standard form mediation **14.09** agreement (which is reproduced in Appendix 2). The provider will also advise parties on the documentation to be provided at or prior to the mediation. Mediations that take place through the NMH tend to be facilitative in nature. The mediator will see the parties individually and shuttle between them with proposals and counter-proposals until a settlement is reached. In order to keep costs down, they are also time-limited mediations.

The fees of the NMH Scheme

There is a fixed scale of fees, depending on the value of the claim, which is calculated by **14.10** adding together the sums claimed in both claim and counterclaim (if any). The fixed fees apply to two-party disputes. If more parties are involved, the next fee tariff may apply as the mediation is likely to take longer. The fee is payable in advance and is also payable in full if the mediation is cancelled five working days or less before the date fixed for the mediation; otherwise any fee paid will be refunded less a cancellation charge of £100 plus VAT. The parties may also have to share the costs of a suitable venue.

- Small claims cases involving sums of £5,000 or less will cost £50 plus VAT per party for a one-hour appointment (which can also take place by telephone), and £100 plus VAT per party for a two-hour appointment, with additional hours costing £50 plus VAT per party.
- Cases with a value between £5,000 and £15,000 cost £300 plus VAT per party for a three-hour mediation appointment, and cases with a value between £15,000 and £50,000 cost £425 plus VAT per party for a four-hour appointment, with additional hours payable at the rate of £95 plus VAT per party per additional hour.
- If the claim is valued in excess of £50,000, the fee will need to be independently negotiated with the ADR provider.

The NMH Scheme is proving to be successful, although it has not grown at the same rate as **14.11** the Small Claims Mediation Scheme. Some commentators have suggested that the reason for this may be that solicitors prefer to deal directly with an ADR provider who is known to them rather than use the Scheme. Around 66% of the cases referred through the NMH result in settlement.

The time-limited mediations taking place under the NMH tend to the follow the same **14.12** process as set out in Chapter 13, although witnesses or experts are unlikely to attend the

Figure 14.1 NMH—Provider standard practice procedure target flowchart for court referrals (April 2008)

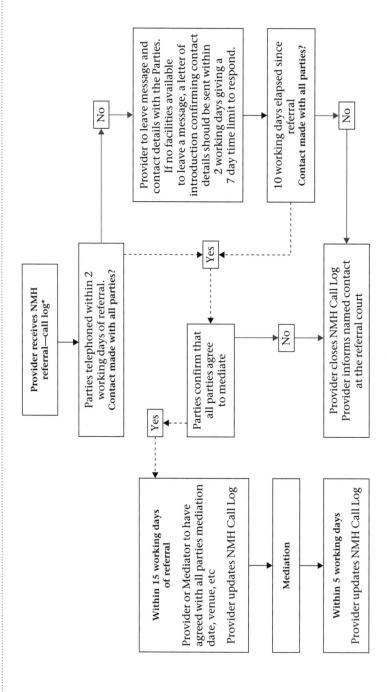

Figure 14.2 NMH—Provider standard practice procedure target flowchart for direct referrals (April 2008)

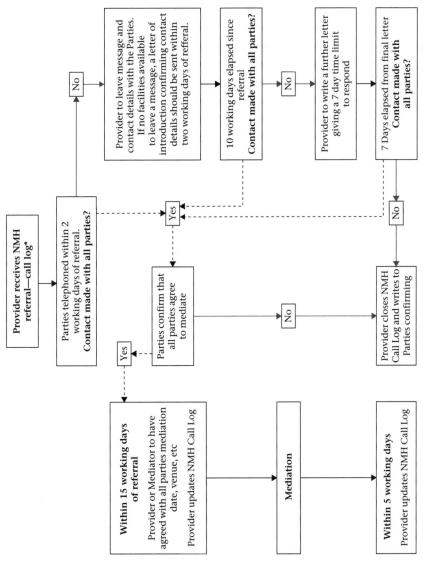

* Initially the call log must be updated within 7 days of referral and at least every 28 days thereafter.

mediation, and position statements may not be required in some cases. The opening plenary session is likely to be significantly shorter or may even be dispensed with altogether and the mediator is more likely to focus on the parties' interests rather than the underlying merits of the dispute.

COURT MEDIATION SCHEMES

14.13   Some county courts have their own mediation scheme, as does the Court of Appeal. These schemes are operated by the court and mediations will be set up directly by the court office. Some schemes are linked to external ADR providers who supply the mediator, but some may have a mediator attached to the court.

The Mayor's and City of London County Court Mediation Scheme

14.14   The Mayor's and City of London County Court Scheme was launched in May 2006. It is a fixed cost time-limited scheme administered by the City Disputes Centre with the assistance of a number of ADR providers. It is a cheaper option for users of that court than mediations taking place through the National Mediation Helpline. Mediations take place at the International Dispute Resolution Centre in Fleet Street, London. The cost to each party is £250 plus VAT for a three-hour mediation for claims up to £15,000 and £375 plus VAT for a four-hour mediation. If the claim is greater than £50,000 or the mediation extends beyond the fixed time limit any additional fees must be agreed with the mediation administrator. The Scheme is reported to have an 88% success rate.

The Central London County Courts pilot schemes

The Central London County Court Voluntary Mediation Scheme

14.15   In 1996, a pilot scheme was set up in the Central London County Court which offered voluntary mediation in any defended case with a claim above £3,000.

14.16   Under the Scheme, parties were offered a voluntary mediation at the court, which was limited to a three-hour slot that took place between 4.30 pm and 7.30 pm. Parties initially paid a fee of £25 each (raised to £100 in 1998) to cover administration costs. Although the Scheme was under-used, it was favourably reviewed by those who did use it. The operation of the pilot was reviewed in 1998 by Professor Hazel Genn (see DCA Research Paper 5/98).

14.17   The Scheme was rolled out at the Central London County Court between 1998 and 2007. Since then, mediations tend to take place through the National Mediation Helpline.

The Central London County Court Compulsory Mediation pilot scheme

14.18   This was set up in 2004 and ran from 1 April 2004 to 31 March 2005. It provided for cases to be automatically and therefore compulsorily referred to mediation unless one or both of the parties gave reasons for objecting to do so. After the decision in *Halsey v Milton Keynes General NHS Trust* [2004] 1 WLR 3002, the judge could not override a party's objections and compel mediation if one party was unwilling to agree to it. If the reference to mediation went ahead, then the proceedings were stayed for an initial period of two months to enable the mediation to proceed (CPR, PD 26B paras 1.1 and 5).

All cases where automatically referred to the scheme except (see CPR, PD 26B para 2): **14.19**

- cases on the small claims track;
- cases where one of the parties was a child or a protected person or a person exempt from paying court fees;
- cases in which the court had granted an interim injunction.

Parties were required to pay for the mediation and the amount of the charge was notified by **14.20** the court to each party, and was payable within 14 days (CPR, PD 26B para 6). The fee was set at £100 per party.

The operation of both the voluntary and the compulsory scheme was reviewed by Professors **14.21** Hazel Genn and Paul Fenn and others in the 2007 report 'Twisting Arms: court referred and court linked mediation under judicial pressure' (Ministry of Justice research series 1/07). This research report showed the following.

- In the compulsory scheme, in 81% of all cases referred in which the court received a reply, one or both parties had objected to the referral. Case management conferences dealing with objections did not generally result in mediation bookings and tended to delay the progress of the case. There was a higher rate of objection in personal injury cases (and this was also the case in the voluntary scheme). Over the year of the pilot, cases in which both parties had initially objected to mediation had a lower settlement rate (48%) than cases where neither party objected (55%). Where mediation had taken place that did not result in settlement, it was felt to have increased overall costs by around £1,000–2,000.
- In the voluntary scheme, there was a significant increase in the number of mediations following *Dunnett v Railtrack Plc* in 2002. However the settlement rate had declined from 62% in 1998 to below 40% in 2003, and the settlement rate had not exceeded 50% since 1998.
- From both schemes, it was apparent that the motivation and willingness of parties to negotiate and compromise was critical to the success of mediation. Facilitation and encouragement, with appropriate pressure, was felt to be more effective than coercing the parties to mediate. Judicial pressure and fear of costs' penalties had resulted in more cases being mediated, but had perhaps brought unwilling parties into the mediation process, which may have accounted for the declining settlement rates since 1999.

The HMCS Small Claims Mediation Scheme

Schemes for mediating small claims track cases were first piloted in the Exeter and **14.22** Manchester County Courts. In the Exeter model, the district judge referred suitable cases to solicitor mediators who gave the parties a 30-minute mediation appointment to explore settlement. The Manchester pilot used an in-house court mediator and operated on the basis of one-hour mediation appointments, which initially involved face-to-face meetings and then latterly telephone mediations. It is this model that is primarily followed in the nationwide Small Claims Mediation Scheme that has been rolled out across the courts. A further pilot operated in Reading, but this was primarily limited to providing parties with information about mediation.

The Small Claims Mediation Scheme was established by Her Majesty's Courts Service **14.23** (HMCS) in 2007–08 following the success of the in-house small claims mediation pilot in Manchester County Court. It is a free service for defended small claims cases and it now operates in all court centres, with the mediators in the employ of HMCS rather than being paid by the parties. The court will refer the parties to the Scheme. If the parties agree to mediate their dispute (and as the service is free, there is little reason for them not to do so), then a court mediator (who is not a member of the judiciary) will contact them usually by telephone. If this is not possible, a meeting can be arranged. The telephone mediations are generally conducted by private discussions with each party rather than in a joint telephone conference call. The mediation, whether conducted by telephone or by a meeting, will typically last about one hour. If the mediation is unsuccessful, then a hearing date is arranged before a district judge.

14.24 The scheme has been very successful. It won the 2008 European Crystal Scales of Justice Award given by the European Commission and the Council of Europe for innovative court practice. It also won CEDR's Sector award and was runner up in the Innovation category of The Guardian Public Service Awards.

14.25 The Government, in its annual pledge reports, has been monitoring the success of the scheme. The Annual Pledge Report for 2007–08 reported that 3,745 cases had been referred to mediation, with 2,527 of those cases settling at mediation (a success rate of 67.5%). The Report for 2008–09 showed that 9,240 cases had been referred to mediation, with 6,675 settling at that stage (a settlement rate of 72%). The Annual Pledge Reports can be found at www.justice.gov.uk.

The Court of Appeal Mediation Scheme

14.26 The Court of Appeal Mediation Scheme was first set up on a voluntary basis in 1997, although it had a low take-up and a less than 50% success rate. A revised scheme was launched in 2003. With the exception of family cases, the revised scheme is currently administered by CEDR Solve. In family cases, the court will select the mediator from the Law Society's Family Mediation Panel, the UK College of Mediators or the Solicitors' Family Law Association.

14.27 The key features of the scheme are as follows:

- If a party has selected or the court has recommended that mediation be tried, the Court will pass details of the case to CEDR Solve, who will then contact the parties.
- If both parties agree to mediation, they will be sent the names of three suitable mediators, and they must select one from this list. In the event of disagreement, CEDR Solve will make the selection.
- The parties will usually find and pay for the venue.
- The preparation for the mediation and the mediation meeting will follow the same steps as those described in Chapter 12, although no witness of fact or expert witnesses are formally called in appeal mediations, although they can attend and give assistance if required.
- The scheme is entirely voluntary and the parties are free to terminate the mediation at any time and without giving a reason.
- The mediator's role is to facilitate a settlement of the matter.
- The parties can ask the mediator to offer his opinion on issues that arise in the case, although he may not be willing to do so.

- As a condition of entering into the scheme, the parties have to agree not to make any claim in relation to the mediation against the mediator, the court or its officials or CEDR Solve, the administrators of the scheme.
- All discussions in and documents created for the mediation are confidential and 'without prejudice' although, as an exception to this, the mediator will make a short report to the court setting out the date and outcome of the mediation; but the court will not have power to enquire into the events that took place during the mediation.
- If settlement is reached, the agreement would normally be placed on the court record, although the parties can keep the terms of settlement confidential if they wish.
- In non-family cases, the fixed fee for each party is currently set at £850 plus VAT, although in exceptionally complex cases or high value cases above £1 million, a higher fee may be proposed by CEDR Solve, subject to the approval of the court. The fixed fee covers four hours preparation time by the mediation and a meditation meeting of five hours duration. Any extension of time for the mediation and any additional fees arising in connection with that have to be agreed between the mediator and the parties.
- In family cases, the parties can opt for a fixed fee of £850, or they can agree to pay the mediator an hourly rate of £170 per hour plus VAT, based on the mediator's actual preparation and mediation time; but the total fee will be capped at £850 plus VAT.
- In all cases, parties of limited means who cannot obtain funding from the Legal Services Commission can apply for the fee to be waived.

Mediation in the Commercial Court

The Commercial Court will usually make an ADR order, which strongly encourages the **14.28** parties to attempt to resolve their dispute by ADR (usually mediation). The order usually requires the parties to co-operate with one another by exchanging lists each containing the names of three mediators who are able to conduct a mediation by the date fixed by the court. If the parties cannot agree, the court will usually select a mediator or provide that the mediator should be selected by an ADR organisation. If the case does not settle, the parties are required to file a statement explaining what steps were taken to resolve the dispute by mediation, and why those steps failed.

An evaluation of the Commercial Court's practice of using ADR orders was undertaken by **14.29** Professor Hazel Genn in 2002 (see DCA research paper 'Court-based ADR initiatives for non-family civil disputes: The Commercial Court and the Court of Appeal'). This showed that ADR was attempted in a little over 50% of the cases in which an ADR order was made and, of those cases, 52% settled through ADR, 5% proceeded to trial, and 20% settled some time after the conclusion of the ADR procedure. In cases in which ADR was not attempted following an ADR order, around 63% eventually settled, but 15% proceeded to trial.

The West Midlands Family Mediation Scheme

This was set up in July 2009 and it aims to offer parties the chance to resolve their dispute **14.30** by mediation rather than by recourse to the courts. Local family mediation providers will operate in local courts, and work with judges to identify cases that are suitable for referral to the scheme.

MEDIATION IN SPECIFIC CASES

Intellectual property cases

14.31   Disputes involving unregistered copyright, registered patents, trademarks and registered designs and all other forms of intellectual property cases have their own specialised mediation scheme. The main tenets of this scheme are similar to the general process that is described in Chapter 13.

14.32   The mediation service in these cases is operated by the Intellectual Property Office, using mediators accredited by mediation providers who are skilled in this type of work.

Complex construction and commercial disputes

14.33   Cases of this type tend to follow the general process set out in Chapters 12 and 13 above but with some differences:

- The mediation hearing will be more formal.
- It will usually involve the presentation of detailed expert or factual evidence.
- The mediator will usually be a lawyer, and may also be assisted in the resolution of the dispute by an expert in the relevant field.
- A formal evaluation of the party's case is likely to form part of the mediation.
- The mediation hearing takes place over several days, with the parties having the ability to make revised proposals and statements as each stage takes place.

Mediation in family cases

14.34   In family cases, the general approach is that the courts should be used as a matter of last resort and mediation has been established as an ADR method since the introduction of the Family Law Act 1996. In publicly funded cases, there is a presumption that mediation should usually be tried before litigation.

14.35   The EU Recommendation on Family Mediation also provides that states should set up mechanisms that would enable legal proceedings to be interrupted for mediation to take place, and ensure that in such a case the judicial or other competent authority retains the power to make urgent decisions in order to protect the parties, their children or their property.

14.36   Family mediation is used in divorce proceedings in ancillary relief claims and in disputes relating to residence and contact arrangements in relation to children. Family mediation is more highly regulated than most other forms of mediation. Family mediators must be qualified and accredited. The Family Mediation Council, which was established in 2007, is responsible for setting and maintaining the professional standards for family mediators and for devising and implementing training standards with which all family mediators must comply.

14.37   Family mediations tend to be undertaken by specialist ADR providers, the main ones being National Family Mediation, which has a large number of affiliated providers in England and Wales, and The Family Mediation Association, Resolution (which is the Solicitor's Family

Law Association), the ADR Group and the College of Mediators (formerly known as the UK College of Family Mediators). These ADR providers are the members of the Family Mediation Council.

In family cases, the mediator will usually meet with the parties in advance to ensure that **14.38** both parties are participating in mediation willingly and that they have not been influenced by threats of violence or other harm (see section 11 of the Law Society Code of Practice for Family Mediation and also the College of Mediators Code of Practice).

During the main mediation meeting, the mediator will seldom conduct private meet- **14.39** ings with the parties, in order to avoid any suggestion of bias. All parties will generally remain in the same room with the mediator throughout the process. If, exceptionally, private meetings are held with the parties, the mediator will usually agree to report back to the other party the substance of the discussions that took place in private meetings. Even if the parties agree that private meetings are confidential, the mediator cannot keep confidential anything that would be open if discussed in a joint meeting. All financial information will therefore be regarded as open information even if revealed to the media- tor in a private meeting and he would be obliged to disclose it to the other party and any financial information disclosed may be used in later court proceedings. The mediator in a family context must not guarantee to keep anything confidential that is discussed in a private meeting (see for example, sections 7.2–7.5 of Law Society Code of Practice for Family Mediation).

The mediation will usually be conducted over several sessions, with revised proposals being **14.40** made by the parties in between each session. Typically the mediation meetings will last for between three and six sessions, each lasting approximately 1.5 hours, although in ancillary relief cases, the meetings may last longer and fewer sessions may be required. There may be a gap of some weeks between each session. Normally lawyers will not be present in family mediations, although the mediator may invite them to participate if he considers this would be useful.

The mediator's role often involves elements of conciliation as well as negotiation He will **14.41** suggest solutions to resolve deadlock rather than leaving it to the parties to devise the pro- posals for themselves. However any proposals that he puts forward are not binding on the parties.

The welfare, wishes and feelings of each child of the family must be considered in appropriate **14.42** cases in relation to any matter affecting them. See also the UK College of Family Mediators Policy on Children, Young People and Family Mediation, which encourages mediators to involve and consult the children in the mediation. Parents should be encouraged to focus on the needs of the children as well as their own needs and to consider the wishes and feel- ings of the children of the family.

Public funding is available for family mediation, subject to satisfying eligibility require- **14.43** ments. Publicly funded mediation work can only be carried out by providers contracted to the Legal Services Commission.

Family mediation is regulated by the Solicitors' Regulation Authority. Parties can obtain **14.44** information about mediation, and be provided with details of mediation providers, and be given information about funding through the Family Mediation Helpline.

Workplace mediation

14.45 This is a growing area of business in the mediation field and it concerns conflict avoidance and management in the workplace. The aim is to resolve internal complaints and disputes and grievances before they result in formal disciplinary or internal complaints investigation procedures and a loss in time and productivity. Workplace mediation can be used to resolve all forms of disputes between employees, or between employer and employee, ranging from relationship breakdown, bullying, harassment, performance and motivation issues, behavioural issues or pay disputes. The 2009 ACAS Statutory Code of Practice on Discipline and Grievance recommends that disciplinary and grievance procedures should be resolved within the workplace if possible, and, if necessary, independent third parties, such as an internal or external mediator, should be used to help resolve the problem. This is an expanding area of business for ADR providers. The Civil Mediation Council maintains a register of mediation providers who are accredited to provide workplace mediations. There are currently around 19 accredited workplace providers who now also accredited as civil and commercial mediation providers.

Mediation in employment disputes

14.46 Mediation can be particularly useful for resolving employment disputes. The DTI have investigated the possibility of making it mandatory in all applications brought before the Employment Tribunal. Although the proposal had a lot of support, some commentators felt that it should not be mandatory for discrimination claims, which merit publicity in the public interest. Other commentators have pointed out that mediation is particularly effective in such cases, as part of the proposed solution can be an undertaking by the employer to change its procedures, provide relevant training, provide a written apology or reference to the employee and, in some cases, enable the relationship between the employer and employer to be preserved. Mediation can also be effective for resolving disputes arising out of a restrictive covenant in an employment contract, where part of the solution can be the redrafting of the covenant so that it meets the real needs of all parties concerned. See the useful chapter 'Mediation in Employment Disputes' by Michel Kallipetis QC in *Mediators on Mediation* (Tottel Publishing, 2005, ch 10) for some observations on the effectiveness of mediation in all types of claims arising out of the employment relationship.

14.47 Mediation and conciliation schemes have been offered by ACAS since 1984. ACAS mediation and conciliation schemes are regulated by statute, unlike most other mediation processes in the UK, which are regulated by the contract made between the parties.

The ACAS Conciliation Scheme

14.48 This is discussed in Chapter 18.

The ACAS Mediation Scheme

14.49 This is an evaluative mediation scheme. It is not free, and the parties have to pay a fee to use the service. It is used in workplace disputes and the key goal is the preservation of the employment relationship. It tends to be used in cases where proceedings have not been commenced in a tribunal and which are not likely to be commenced (if an application has been or is likely to be made to a tribunal, the conciliation scheme tends to be used and it is free to the parties).

A particular feature of compromise agreements that result from the successful mediation **14.50** of employment disputes is the need to ensure that they are drafted in a way that complies with s 203 of the Employment Rights Act 2003. Section 203 renders void any provision in an agreement that purports to preclude a person from bringing a claim under the Act before the Employment Tribunal, unless the agreement complies with the statutory conditions in s 203(3), the most important of which is that the employee receives independent legal advice from a person identified in the agreement who is covered by professional indemnity insurance. Any settlement reached at mediation in relation to a dispute that could be referred to an Employment Tribunal must therefore take the form of a statutory compromise agreement.

Judicial mediation in Employment Tribunals

A judicial mediation pilot was carried out in three regions of England—Newcastle, Central **14.51** London and Birmingham—by the Employment Tribunal Service in respect of all kinds of discrimination cases (age, sex, sexual orientation, disability, race, religion or belief) in the Employment Tribunal between June 2006 and March 2007. Parties were informed at the case management stage of the opportunity to join the judicial mediation pilot, and asked whether they would do so, if their case was selected as suitable for mediation. All of the parties were offered ACAS conciliation before the judicial mediation took place. The pilot was evaluated by Peter Urwin and others in the report 'Evaluating the use of judicial mediation in Employment Tribunals' (Ministry of Justice Research Series 7/10, March 2010). The evaluation showed that judicial mediation had no discernable, statistically significant effect on the rates of cases settled or avoidance of a hearing. Outcomes of judicial mediation were not significantly better than those of unmediated cases. Further, judicial mediation had an estimated cost to the Employment Tribunals Service of £908 per case. The researchers concluded:

> '...judicial mediation was an expensive process to administer and cannot be offset by the estimated benefits (both direct and indirect) of the process. Therefore, it was not recommended that the service be rolled-out to other areas of the ETS [Employment Tribunal Service] in its present form.'

Personal injury mediation schemes

There was a perception by many lawyers and insurers that personal injury claims were not **14.52** suitable for mediation. However in recent years, there has been a growing awareness among personal injury practitioners that mediation is a more effective method for resolving those disputes than litigation, not least because:

- the costs incurred in litigating personal injury claims of modest value are often disproportionate to the amount of the claim;
- mediation will often lessen the stress and trauma an injured claimant will face by attending a trial;
- mediation offers the parties the chance to build bridges by offering an explanation or an apology for the injury, and an acknowledgment of the effect that it has had on the claimant;
- mediation results in a high success rate, with some providers of personal injury mediation reporting settlement figures in excess of 80%.

14.53 A number of ADR providers have set up their own specialist personal injury mediation schemes. Some examples of these schemes are set out below:

CEDR'S Personal Injury Unit (PIU) Telephone Mediation

14.54 CEDR has devised a number of ADR options for resolving smaller value personal injury cases through the creation of its Personal Injury Unit (PIU) which has a team of around 30 specialist mediators. The PIU Telephone Mediation Service enables personal injury claims to be mediated with a minimum of time and cost. There is no need to book a venue as the mediation will be carried out using conference telephone facilities. The mediator will be drawn from a panel of CEDR's mediators who have expertise in personal injury claims, and who have undertaken specific training on carrying out mediations by telephone. The process is very speedy, and may only take a few hours from start to finish. The cost is from £145 per party (this is the current cost quoted on CEDR's website, which is updated frequently, so check www.cedr.com for the most up-to-date information about this scheme). A PIU telephone referral form can also be downloaded from the website.

CEDR'S PIU Mediation

14.55 CEDR also offer a specialist mediation service for personal injury claims up to a value of £100,000. PIU Mediation offers parties either a half-day (four hours) or full-day mediation. The cost of a half-day mediation is £400 per party (which includes two-hour reading and preparation time), while a full-day will cost £700 per party (which includes four hours preparation and reading time). All mediators are experienced in personal injury litigation.

Trust Meridian Ltd's Personal Injury Scheme

14.56 Trust Meridian Ltd provides a fixed cost mediation in personal injury claims, and all of its mediators have professional practice-based experience in personal injury litigation.

The British Coal Miners Mediation Scheme for Respiratory and Vibration White Finger

14.57 This was set up by the Department of Energy and Climate Change to mediate claims for respiratory and vibration white finger in the coal mining industry. The Scheme is administered by the ADR Group.

MEDIATING MULTI-PARTY DISPUTES

14.58 Mediation has proved to be effective in multi-party disputes. Such disputes can take two forms:

- those involving large numbers of claimants or defendants, such as the Alder Hey retained organs claims and multiple holiday claims brought against a tour operator for food poisoning; and
- those cases where there are only a limited number of parties to the main dispute, but a large number of parties have been added to the dispute as additional parties. This is commonly the case in construction claims.

A team of mediators may need to be appointed to mediate multi-party claims. A number of　**14.59**
things make them slightly different from mediation of other claims:

- crowd control;
- information management;
- time management while the mediator is having a private meeting with all of the various
  groups or parties.

In group litigation actions involving a very large number of claimants, it may be necessary　**14.60**
to divide them into a number of sub-groups, each of whose claims raise issues similar to others in terms of liability or quantum, and then appoint parties to represent the interests of
each group. Consideration also needs to be given to the effective management of the large
volume of documents that such cases can generate and the use that will be made of those
documents in the mediation.

During the mediation, the lawyers and the mediator will have to draw up strategies for　**14.61**
management of the idle time that will inevitably occur as the mediator sees the parties or
representatives of each sub-group in private meetings. The amount of idle time in such
mediations can be significant. For example if there are 10 parties or sub-groups and the
mediator spends only 20 minutes with each party, it will be over three hours before the
mediator will get back to the first party, and in fact the time usually spent with parties in
the initial private meeting is likely to be longer than that. It is hard to keep the impetus
and energy for settlement going within each of the teams where there are long periods of
delay.

Mediating very complex claims involving multiple parties will often give rise to issues about　**14.62**
the funding of the mediation, and issues of confidentiality, publicity and about the neutrality of the mediator.

Mediation is a very flexible process, so it can be tailored to meet the needs of a multi-party　**14.63**
dispute. The mediator will discuss with the lawyers the structure and form of the mediation, together with the order in which the issues will be discussed, and the time that the
mediation is likely to take. Such disputes may need to involve a team of mediators. It is also
useful to use the organisational and managerial skills that an ADR provider can provide.
It is usually time-efficient to deal with as many issues as possible in joint sessions in multi-
party disputes, so such mediations tend to have extended joint sessions, with much of the
exploration phase of the mediation taking place in those sessions. Successfully mediating
the dispute may well involve several pre-mediations to resolve issues between different
groups such as disclosure and information requests. They may also involve post-mediation
meetings to divide a global offer between a number of different parties. Mediating multi-
party cases can take several months with various mediation meetings taking place during
that time.

Useful perspectives about mediating multi-party disputes and complex cases can be found　**14.64**
in *Mediators on Mediation* (Tottel Publishing, 2005), ch 13 'Mediating Multi-party Disputes'
by David Richbell and ch 14 'The impossible takes a little longer—Mediating Really Complex
cases' by Eileen Carroll and Dr Karl Mackie.

OTHER SCHEMES

The Family Housing Group Mediation Scheme

14.65   The Family Housing Group are social landlords in London. The mediation scheme is run by CEDR Solve to mediate disputes between neighbouring tenants, in relation to issues such as anti-social behaviour. The scheme is funded by the Family Housing Group and it is free to tenants, and the mediations are time-limited to three hours and will take place at a local Family Housing Group office. Similar schemes are operated by other housing associations, and local community mediation schemes will also mediate disputes between tenants, including anti-social behaviour.

The London SEN Mediation Service

14.66   This is a mediation service, accredited by the Civil Mediation Council, which aims to resolve disputes between local educational authorities (LEA) and parents about the provision of special educational needs (SEN). Such disputes can be brought before the Special Educational Needs and Disability Tribunal Service. Similar schemes operate in other areas. The London service is funded by the LEA members who participate in the scheme. The mediation service is free to parent users. Referrals can be made by phone, letter or email, although a standard form referral form can be found on www.londonsenmediation.org.uk. If parties agree to mediation, this does not prevent them continuing with a claim before the Tribunal. The 2009 research paper 'Dispute Resolution and Avoidance in Education; A study of Special and Additional Support Needs in England and Scotland' by Professors Sheila Riddell and Neville Harris, demonstrated that mediation was under-used in SEN and additional support needs disputes, but where it was used it was valued by the parties.

Project mediation

14.67   This is useful for resolving problems that may arise during the currency of long-term contracts, or contracts involving a lengthy chain of parties such as contractors and subcontactors on a large-scale building project. The aim of project mediation is to prevent problems escalating into entrenched disputes that may hinder or delay the project. The project mediator will usually be selected on the basis of his experience in the relevant industry. He will be available to the appointing parties during the currency of the project and he will have discussions with relevant parties involved in the project in relation to any matters of concern to prevent disputes arising that might impact on the performance of the contract. If needs be, the project mediator will also carry out a formal mediation, although the aim of project mediation is to solve problems before that becomes necessary. For an example of a project mediation scheme, visit www.cedr.com. CEDR have also devised a model mediation agreement, and a model mediation project protocol, which sets out the terms and conditions of its project mediation service, copies of which can be downloaded from the website.

The mini-trial or executive tribunal

14.68   This is a form of evaluative mediation, which can be employed as an alternative to the forms of mediation discussed in Chapters 13. It is particularly useful in corporate disputes. Each party to the dispute will make formal legal submissions to a panel, which is comprised of senior executives from each company and chaired by a neutral advisor. The executives and the neutral adviser will then adjourn to discuss settlement of the issues in the case. The neutral advisor may act as a mediator to facilitate negotiations. If asked, the neutral adviser may also agree to assume an evaluative role by providing his opinion on the merits of the case and the likely outcome if it went to trial.

This process is advantageous because: **14.69**

- it can be arranged relatively speedily;
- it involves key executive officers of both companies at an early stage in the dispute, who have authority to settle the matter;
- it enables the parties themselves to have control over the outcome;
- it is cost-effective and will represent a significant saving in the costs of a trial, particularly if it is carried out at an early stage of the litigation process;
- it enables the parties to create a more flexible settlement outcome than that which could be ordered by the court in litigation or arbitration;
- the procedure is flexible and can be created by the parties, in conjunction with the neutral chairperson, to best suit the needs of the parties and the subject-matter of the dispute.

However the process itself is more formal and structured than a typical mediation. Each **14.70** side will usually make detailed written submissions, supported with relevant documents. The parties control the information placed before the tribunal and can also put confidential documents before the tribunal, although these should be clearly marked as confidential. At the hearing, each party will make formal oral submissions to the Tribunal. The parties may also agree to call evidence from witnesses and experts at the hearing.

The process is useful for resolving disputes of a complex nature. Even if overall settlement is **14.71** not reached at a mini-trial of this nature, often agreement can be reached on some issues, so narrowing the issues that need to be considered at trial.

The parties can select and appoint the neutral person privately, or they may engage the **14.72** services of an ADR provider to nominate a suitable person. If an ADR provider is used, they will probably also provide the venue and manage the process. Some ADR providers have model agreements and a model procedure for executive tribunals, which can be amended to suit the needs of any individual case (see eg CEDR Model Executive Tribunal Procedure at www.cedr.co.uk).

Consensus-building in environmental disputes or disputes that involve public policy issues

A variation in the mediation procedure can take place in cases involving environmental and **14.73** other public policy issues that affect a number of different interest groups. A neutral third party will be appointed to identify and consult all of the interest groups and will promote consultation and negotiations between them with the aim of achieving a consensual outcome that satisfies the parties and all of the various interest groups. This approach is more commonly employed in the USA and Australia.

SECTOR MEDIATION SCHEMES

14.74 There are many specific sector mediation schemes. This book cannot attempt to cover all of them, but a selection is included, in brief terms, to give a flavour of the nature of these schemes.

The Financial Services Authority (FSA) Mediation Service

14.75 The FSA is a regulatory body whose main aim is to maintain confidence in the financial system, reduce financial crime and market abuse and protect consumers. It can be difficult for a regulatory body involved in an enforcement role to participate in mediation because it was initially felt that a regulatory matter was not capable of being 'settled', and the confidentiality of mediation was at odds with the duties owed to the public by a regulator to ensure compliance with the regulatory framework. The commercial considerations that influence most mediations will not arise in a regulatory mediation, which will concern two main issues: (1) whether a breach of regulations has been committed and, if so, (2) what is the right penalty to impose. The mediator will however be sensitive to the fact that the reputation of the respondent will be at stake, and even the future of the business may be under threat. In most cases there will be an on-going relationship between the regulator and the respondent so both parties will be interested to ensure compliance with the regulatory framework in the future.

14.76 The Financial Services Authority has developed a successful mediation model for enforcement cases, namely the FSA Mediation Scheme. The terms of the scheme can be found on www.aci-adr.com. Respondents are entitled to elect mediation at any time during the enforcement process, which usually starts with a warning notice sometimes accompanied by an investigation report, both of which can be very substantial documents. If a respondent selects mediation before a warning notice has been issued or after receipt of a final decision notice, the FSA's consent is required. The scheme is administered by an independent service provider, ACI, who organises and manages the mediation process, including offering the parties a selection of suitable mediators who have relevant expertise and familiarity in the subject-matter of the dispute. Although mediated settlements are usually confidential, the FSA has a statutory duty to publish any penalty imposed for breach of a regulatory matter and, in cases concerning consumers eg wrongful selling of pension or insurance policies, public statements may need to be prepared for release to the public at large and to parliamentary committees.

14.77 A very useful explanation of the practical operation of the scheme can be found in *Mediators on Mediation* (Tottel Publishing, 2005), ch 16, 'Mediation in the Regulatory Context' by Elizabeth Birch.

Mediation schemes in the healthcare sector

14.78 The healthcare sector has now started to embrace mediation and has set up a number of schemes that use mediation.

National Health Service Litigation Authority

The National Health Service Litigation Authority encourages parties to refer disputes to **14.79** mediation. The majority of claims are high value. In most cases, mediation takes place after proceedings have been issued and usually only a matter of months before trial. The liability issues have usually been resolved and mediation in health care claims tends to deal with quantum only.

The Independent Healthcare Forum

The Independent Healthcare Forum is a voluntary organisation for healthcare providers in **14.80** the independent sector, and most independent hospitals are members of it. It has devised a code of practice for dealing with complaints. The code provides for complaints to be dealt with in three stages: (1) local resolution, (2) internal appeal, and finally (3) a further appeal to an independent external adjudicator. The parties can agree to use mediation instead of referring the appeal to an independent external adjudicator. Although the code of conduct provides that mediation can be used at stage 3, there is nothing to prevent the parties from mediating their complaint at local level at stages 1 or 2.

The Independent Doctor's Forum

The Independent Doctor's Forum represents doctors in general practice and consultants **14.81** undertaking private work outside the NHS. It has devised a complaints code that provides for complaints to be referred to mediation if they cannot be resolved at local level.

NHS trusts

Most trusts also encourage parties to refer claims to mediation and some trusts have set up **14.82** specialist mediation schemes that have been designed and are administered by ADR providers using mediators who are skilled in clinical negligence claims.

The CEDR Clinical Negligence Mediation Scheme

The Scheme is available for clinical negligence claims worth £150,000 or less. **14.83**

The parties agree the location and venue and date for the mediation and whether a full-day **14.84** or half-day mediation is required. They then refer the dispute to CEDR Solve, who will then appoint a mediator with expertise in this field.

The Healthcare Commission Mediation Scheme

This is a time-limited mediation scheme (four hours) administered by CEDR Solve, which **14.85** is funded by the Commission and is free to the complainant. The scope of the scheme does not extend to financial compensation.

THE PENSIONS MEDIATION SERVICE

The National Association of Pension Funds has implemented a mediation service to resolve **14.86** complaints between and against trustees and scheme members and between pension schemes and third-party service providers, including funding disputes and changes to schemes (for example from final salary to money purchase schemes).

THE PERFORMING ARTS MEDIATION SERVICE

14.87   The Performing Arts Mediation Service was set up to deal with disputes within the performing arts sector, such as copyright, service contracts, or employment disputes. It is an independent service, administered by CEDR Solve, and any arts organisation can use the service at any stage of a dispute.

COMMUNITY MEDIATION

14.88   There are a large number of community mediation schemes in every area of the United Kingdom. They can be used to mediate a wide range of matters, including disputes about noise, litter, nuisance claims, parking, harassment, pets, some landlord and tenant disputes and small debt claims. Community mediators operate outside the terms of reference of the Civil Mediation Council. There is currently no umbrella group that draws together community mediation services (a company known as Mediation UK did fulfil that role, but it went into liquidation some years ago). It is relatively easy to find a number of community mediation groups local to any particular area by using the internet, and the local council should also be able to help. A fairly comprehensive (but by no means exhaustive) online directory of local community mediation providers can be found by searching the online Directory of UK Mediation on www.intermedial.org.uk. Local community mediation services are usually funded by charities, or have charitable status, and many also receive funding from the local authority.

14.89   The key characteristics of community mediation schemes are as follows:

- They are usually free to the users.
- Lawyers seldom are instructed to attend community mediations.
- Referral is made by contacting the local service directly.
- An initial meeting (usually face-to-face, but contact may be made by telephone) will be made with the initiating party.
- If the dispute is suitable for mediation, the community service provider will usually contact the other party.
- If all parties agree, a mediation meeting is arranged to try to determine the dispute.
- The mediators are volunteers, but they will usually have received mediation training, in many cases by attending training courses organised by the local community mediation provider.
- Co-mediators are often assigned to a dispute.
- The mediation meeting can last from anything between one and three hours, depending on the type of dispute and the number of parties involved and the practice operated by local organisation.
- Each party will outline the nature of the dispute for the mediator and what they wish to achieve by the mediation. The parties will rarely provide position statements or a bundle of documents.
- The venue for the mediation will usually be a local community centre, or the offices of the community service provider.

- The dispute is usually resolved in a joint meeting, although separate meetings can take place if this is appropriate, with the mediator 'shuttling' between the two parties.
- If agreement is reached, it can be recorded in writing, or it may remain as a verbal agreement. In either case, it is unlikely to be legally binding on the parties.

The College of Mediators have recently set standards for community mediators and, to date, over 100 community mediators have met those standards.   **14.90**

PRO BONO MEDIATION AND LAWWORKS

LawWorks is an independent charity that operates throughout England and Wales. It has over 150 mediators who are willing to provide mediation services pro bono to those who cannot afford to pay the usual costs associated with mediation. It is free to both parties if one party qualifies. If a party is entitled to a fee remission in respect of the court fees, then they are also eligible for free mediation through LawWorks. In all other cases, LawWorks will assess whether a party qualifies, by ascertaining if that party's gross annual income is below a prescribed amount or that person is in receipt of a means-tested benefit (see www. lawworks.org.uk).   **14.91**

KEY POINTS SUMMARY

- Time-limited, fixed cost mediations can take place through the National Mediation Helpline.   **14.92**
- Some courts also operate time-limited cost-effective mediations, such as the Court of Appeal and the Mayor's and City of London County Court.
- There are many industry- and sector-specific schemes.
- Mediation can be used effectively in multi-party or complex disputes.
- Mediation can also be used in public sector and regulatory disputes.

15

INTERNATIONAL MEDIATION

INTRODUCTION...15.01

THE ADVANTAGES OF MEDIATION IN INTERNATIONAL
DISPUTES 15.03

PREPARATION FOR MEDIATION IN INTERNATIONAL DISPUTES ...15.04

THE PROCESS IN INTERNATIONAL MEDIATION 15.05

THE GROWTH OF MEDIATION IN EUROPE 15.06

A MOVE TOWARDS HARMONISING PRACTICES IN
INTERNATIONAL MEDIATION 15.09

THE EU DIRECTIVE ON MEDIATION IN CIVIL AND COMMERCIAL
CASES (DIRECTIVE 2008/52/EC) 15.11

THE EUROPEAN CODE OF CONDUCT FOR MEDIATORS.........15.29

ENFORCEABILITY OF INTERNATIONAL MEDIATION
SETTLEMENT AGREEMENTS.............................15.30

KEY POINTS SUMMARY.................................15.33

INTRODUCTION

15.01 The USA was a key player in pioneering the use of mediation in civil disputes as an alterative to litigation. Mediation is now also regarded as an important method of ADR in countries such as Canada, Australia, New Zealand, Hong Kong, Japan, China and India, as well as being commonly used in most countries in the European Union. As in the United Kingdom, there has been a significant increase in the volume of mediations in international disputes in recent years in a wide range of cases such as the sale of goods, supply of services, intellectual property, insurance, international construction and engineering disputes, information technology and pharmaceutical supply contracts.

15.02 In the EU, attempts are being made to standardise mediation procedures and promote mediation throughout member states by the introduction of the EU Directive on mediation in civil and commercial matters (Directive 2008/52/EC), and the development of the

EU Code of Conduct for Mediators. This chapter will concentrate on those developments and will also highlight some areas of practical importance to those wishing to undertake mediation in international disputes. In this chapter, an international dispute means a commercial dispute involving any subject-matter where the parties to the dispute are based in different countries, and which may require the performance of obligations in different countries.

THE ADVANTAGES OF MEDIATION IN INTERNATIONAL DISPUTES

Mediation in international disputes offers all of the advantages that are described in **15.03** Chapters 1 and 11, as well as the following additional advantages:

- The parties can determine where the mediation should take place, which need not necessarily be the place where the litigation would have to be commenced. The parties can select a neutral venue in a neutral country.
- It enables disputes in which there are multiple parties situated in different jurisdictions to avoid problems such as difficult jurisdiction and conflict of law issues that can arise in litigation in international cross-border cases.
- A complementary team of mediators can be appointed to deal with the dispute, to take account of cultural differences and who have between them all the relevant expertise (and linguistic skills) necessary to facilitate a settlement with minimum delay and cost.
- Mediators can assist with communication problems that can arise in international disputes, despite modern communication techniques, because parties are in different geographical areas, many miles apart, in different time zones, with differences in language and culture.
- It enables facilitation of a speedy settlement in cases where there is an on-going valuable commercial relationship between the parties.
- The fact that mediation is a flexible process is particularly important in international disputes because it enables the parties to have a number of mediation meetings perhaps with each party in their own location, before the parties are all brought together at the main mediation meeting. The fact that the parties can decide the number and type of mediation meetings, their frequency, and the issues that each meeting will deal with is particularly useful in complex disputes of this type.
- Mediation also enables the parties to the dispute to rely on local advisers in each relevant country to solve technical, practical, political or legal issues that may arise and that would otherwise block a settlement agreement.
- It is particularly cost-effective compared to litigation and arbitration in such cases. Eileen Carroll and Karl Mackie in *International Mediation—The Art of Business Diplomacy* (2nd edn, Tottel Publishing) at p 69, give an example of clients in one case who made the choice to mediate before arbitration in a dispute involving US $20 million. The mediation took between 2–6 months, involved 100 hours of management time, the mediators cost $17,000, the legal costs were $90,000 and the outcome was an agreed commercial solution. Arbitrating the same case would have taken 24–36 months, involved 700 hours of management time and cost between $400,000–600,000 in legal costs and the costs of the arbitrator panel would have been in the region of

$350,000–750,000 (on the assumption that the same hourly rates could be applied to mediators and arbitrators).

PREPARATION FOR MEDIATION IN INTERNATIONAL DISPUTES

15.04　The preparatory steps for mediation in international disputes will follow the same general processes described in Chapters 11 and 12. However a number of factors deserve special mention:

- The selection of the mediator team will need to be undertaken with care in international disputes. The parties may wish to use an organisation such as the International Mediation Institute (IMI). IMI is a non-profit foundation and registered charity whose aim is to set high competency standards for mediation practice across all fields, worldwide (see www.imimediation.org). It also has set up the Independent Standards Commission which sets uniform standards for certification of mediators. Interested parties can use the search engine on the website to find the right IMI certified mediator for their particular international dispute. It has also published a useful document, *Guidelines for Lawyers Representing Clients in Mediation*, to assist them in the choice and selection of the right mediator with the necessary expertise and mediation style for their particular dispute. This document can be downloaded free of charge from the IMI's website. Another useful source for selecting a mediator is the International Mediation and Arbitration Centre (www.imac-adr.com). Many domestic private mediators and those affiliated to ADR providers will also have expertise in international disputes (see a selection of ADR providers in Appendix 1).
- Many mediators in international disputes will operate under their own rules and codes of practice of their particular organisation. The International Mediation Services Alliance (MEDAL) (www.medal-mediation.com) have developed the MEDAL International Mediation Rules for use by MEDAL member organisations. They set out standards and procedures for initiating the mediation, agreeing the appointment of the mediator, the neutrality of the mediator, confidentiality, the conduct of the mediation and the authority of the mediator. IMI-certified mediators will operate under the IMI Code of Professional Conduct. The IMI Disciplinary Commission will handle formal and informal complaints about IMI certified mediators.
- In international disputes, particular care needs to be given to consideration of how language and cultural differences between parties can be managed.
- The position statement is likely to be longer in international disputes than in most domestic mediations. As a general rule, the mediator will seek to confine each party's position statement to 15–20 pages, with the indexed bundle of other documents consisting of around 3–4 files (see Eileen Carroll and Karl Mackie in *International Mediation—The Art of Business Diplomacy* (2nd edn, Tottel Publishing).
- More preparatory work will need to be undertaken by the mediator in relation to pre-mediation meetings with the parties by telephone or video conference link, or perhaps in person at each party's place of business (and this may mean travelling to several different countries).
- The mediation overall is likely to take longer, perhaps lasting several months.

THE PROCESS IN INTERNATIONAL MEDIATION

The mediation process will follow a similar pattern to that described in Chapter 13, but the **15.05** following factors should be borne in mind:

- In the main mediation meetings, the mediator is more likely to encourage the parties to explore issues in joint meetings and there is likely to be an extended plenary session for that purpose.
- At an appropriate stage, the mediator team will convene private meetings of the parties to explore the issues, and commence the bargaining process by way of 'shuttle diplomacy' as described in Chapter 13.
- Expert evidence is likely to feature to a greater extent in an international mediation. The mediator may hold a meeting of experts or with a single expert on an issue and allow the parties to question them if this is likely to assist in the resolution of a particular issue.
- Time pressures may be more acute in international cases, particularly in the bargaining phase of the mediation due to practical matters such as the fact that the parties may come from different countries and time zones. A binding settlement agreement is not likely to be drawn up at the conclusion of the mediation, even if agreement is reached on all issues, as any final agreement is likely to be the subject of reflection, review and consultation and require very detailed work by the lawyers before it can be signed off by the parties and become binding. If this is so, the mediation may be resumed at a different time, usually some weeks later, with a non-binding framework or heads of agreement being drawn up in the meantime to record areas of agreement. In international mediations it is not uncommon for the settlement phase of the negotiation to last several months.

THE GROWTH OF MEDIATION IN EUROPE

Mediation has grown at a rapid rate across the EU in recent years, although it is has not **15.06** developed at a uniform pace in each of the member states, and there are some differences in the process across member states.

Details of the state of development of mediation in each of the EU countries can be found in **15.07** *The EU Mediation Atlas: Practice and Regulation* by Jayne Singer (LexisNexis). See also chapter 19 'Mediation in Continental Europe: a Meandering Path Toward Efficient Regulation' by Guiseppe De Palo and Sara Carmeli in *Mediators on Mediation, Leading Mediator Perspectives on the Practice of Commercial Mediation* (Tottel Publishing) and chapter 13 of *Mediator Skills and Techniques: Triangle of Influence* (Bloomsbury Professional) by Laurence Boulle and Miryana Nesic.

The growth in mediation across Europe has revealed: **15.08**

- differences in the training and accreditation of mediators between the 27 member states of the EU;
- the lack of a common code of conduct for mediators; and
- differences in the manner and frequency with which ADR in general, and mediation in particular, is promoted and employed in individual states.

A MOVE TOWARDS HARMONISING PRACTICES IN INTERNATIONAL MEDIATION

15.09   As mediation becomes more common in international disputes, there is a need for some elements in the mediation process, including a code of conduct regulating matters such as confidentiality and the impartiality and neutrality of the mediator (see Chapter 16) to be standardised or harmonised.

15.10   To this end the United Nations Commission on International Trade Law (UNCITRAL) has developed a Model Law on International Commercial Conciliation (although it is called conciliation, the process is, in effect, mediation) across international jurisdictions. This Model Law consists of detailed rules governing all aspects of the mediation (see www. uncitral.org). The European Parliament and Council has also attempted to introduce standardisation in EU cases with the *EU Directive on Mediation in Civil and Commercial cases* (Directive 2008/52/EC) and the *EU Code of Conduct for Mediators*. The Council of Europe have also issued a *Recommendation in respect of family mediation* (Recommendation No R(98)1).

THE EU DIRECTIVE ON MEDIATION IN CIVIL AND COMMERCIAL CASES (DIRECTIVE 2008/52/EC)

15.11   The Directive was preceded by a Green Paper presented by the European Commission in April 2002. This sought views from member states and interested parties on measures that could be taken to promote the use of mediation to aid the development of extra-judicial procedures for the settlement of disputes in civil and commercial cases and thus simplify and improve access to justice. The Commission recognised the benefits of mediation, the fact that those benefits were even more pronounced in cross-border cases, and wanted to encourage more use of mediation across the EU. The online consultation can be viewed at http://www.europarl.eu.int/comparl/juri/consultations/default_en.htm.

15.12   The Directive was published in the Official Journal of the European Union on 24 May 2008 and came into force 20 days after that date (Art 13). Member states are required to implement the Directive into national law by 21 May 2011.

The objective of the Directive

15.13   The objective of the Directive is to facilitate access to alternative dispute resolution and to promote the amicable settlement of disputes by encouraging the use of mediation and by ensuring a balanced relationship between mediation and judicial proceedings (Art 1).

15.14   Mediation is comprehensively defined in Art 3(a) as meaning:

> 'A structured process, however named or referred to, whereby two or more parties to a dispute attempt by themselves, on a voluntary basis, to reach an agreement on the settlement of their dispute with the assistance of the mediator. This process may be initiated by the parties or suggested or ordered by a court or prescribed by the law of the member state. It includes mediation conducted by a judge who is not responsible for any judicial proceedings concerning the dispute in question.'

Article 5(1) makes it clear that national courts can invite parties to use mediation, and **15.15** Art 5(2) provides that the Directive '...is without prejudice to national legislation making the use of mediation compulsory or subject to incentives or sanctions, whether before or after judicial proceedings have started, provided that such legislation does not prevent the parties from exercising their right of access to the judicial system'.

The Directive makes it clear that court-ordered compulsory mediation (which exists in some **15.16** member states) is still a voluntary process, despite the fact that parties are ordered to arrange and/or attend mediation, because the parties are not compelled to reach agreement in the process. Member states can promote mediation in whatever form they see fit, whether by a compulsory mediation referral by the court or by inviting the parties to use it. However mediation should not be promoted so as to prevent the parties from litigating their dispute in court.

The Directive does not apply to any attempt made by a judge to settle a dispute acting in the **15.17** course of judicial proceedings and therefore performing a 'judging' role, rather than a pure mediation role.

The application of the Directive

The provisions of the Directive apply only in cross-border disputes, in civil and commercial **15.18** matters (Art 2). However nothing prevents member states from applying any provisions of the Directive to their own internal processes (Recital 8). A cross-border dispute is defined in Art 2(a) as a dispute in which at least one of the parties is domiciled or habitually resident in a member state (meaning any of the 27 states of the EU with the exception of Denmark) other than that of any other party on the date on which:

- the parties agree to use mediation;
- mediation is ordered by the court;
- an obligation to use mediation arises under national law; or
- the court invites the parties to use mediation.

The Directive is not intended to apply to: **15.19**

- pre-contractual negotiations;
- processes of an adjudicatory nature such as judicial conciliation schemes, consumer complaint schemes, arbitration, and expert determination, or to processes by which a formal recommendation is issued, whether or not it is to be legally binding as to the resolution of the dispute. It therefore will not apply to early neutral evaluation (Recital 11);
- revenue, customs or administrative matters or to the liability of the state for acts and omissions in the exercise of state authority (Art 2).

The key obligations of member states

Ensuring the quality of mediation

Member states are required '...to encourage, by any means which they consider appropriate, **15.20** the development of, and adherence to, voluntary codes of conduct for mediators and organisations providing mediation services, as well as other effective quality control mechanisms concerning the provision of mediation services' (Art 4(1)). This is an area on which further work is needed in the United Kingdom, given the piecemeal system of regulation and accreditation that exists for mediators in civil and commercial disputes (see Chapter 11).

15.21 Unfortunately, the Directive falls short of requiring member states to implement a uniform code of conduct for mediators. The Civil Mediation Council (CMC) took steps in this direction by the creation of a Registered Mediation Organisation Scheme in 2009 and a Registered Mediator Scheme, also in 2009, for individual mediators. It also produced the CMC Code of Good Practice for Mediators 2009. These registration schemes and the Code of Good Practice have been developed in conjunction with the Ministry of Justice, the Department for Business Enterprise and Regulatory Reform, the ADR Committee of the Civil Justice Council and the legal professions. However registration on the schemes and adherence to the Code is voluntary. However the public will be encouraged, in due course, to use only a CMC-registered mediator. The CMC schemes are not yet in operation. This is therefore likely to be an area of further development in the United Kingdom.

Training and continuous professional development of mediators

15.22 Member states are required to encourage the initial and further training of mediators in order to ensure that mediation is conducted in an effective, impartial and competent way (Art 4(2)). At present, individual ADR providers tend to have their own training and continuing professional development requirements for their accredited mediators, and there is a lack of consistency in the training requirements between different providers (with the exception of family mediators). The CMC is also taking steps in this direction with the creation of a CMC Registered Training Organisation Scheme, intended to come into operation in 2010, and for individual mediators, a Registered Mediation Scheme 2009, together with a CMC Code of Good Practice. Registration on the Schemes and adherence to the Code is voluntary. This is therefore also likely to be an area of further development in the United Kingdom.

Enforceability of agreements resulting from mediation

15.23 Member states should ensure that the parties are able to request that a written agreement resulting from a mediation is made enforceable by a court, by a judgment or decision or other means in accordance with national law, unless the content of the agreement is contrary to national law (Art 6(1) and (2)). It is likely that many of the current provisions that exist for enforcing settlement agreements (see Chapter 29) comply with this provision. At present, enforcement of settlements reached through mediation which takes place before issue of proceedings is by bringing court proceedings for breach of the settlement contract, which should result in a court judgment that can then be enforced through the courts. There is a doubt whether this is sufficiently direct to comply with Art 6.

Confidentiality

15.24 The Directive recognises that confidentiality in the mediation process is important and that there should be a minimum degree of compatibility of civil procedural rules with regard to how to protect the confidentiality of mediation in any subsequent civil or commercial judicial proceedings or arbitration (Recital 23). Article 7(1) provides that member states must ensure that neither mediators nor those involved in the administration of the mediation process shall be compelled to give evidence in civil or commercial judicial proceedings or arbitration regarding information arising out of or in connection with a mediation process, except in the following circumstances:

- The parties agree otherwise.
- It is necessary for overriding considerations of public policy, in particular to ensure the protection of children or prevent physical or psychological harm to any person.

- Disclosure of the content of the agreement is necessary in order to implement or enforce that agreement.

Article 7(2) provides that nothing shall prevent a member state from enacting stricter **15.25** measures to protect the confidentiality of mediation.

The circumstances in which the confidentiality of mediation can be overridden are nar- **15.26** rower under the Directive than those that exist as a result of recent developments in the courts of England and Wales. As discussed in Chapter 13, confidentiality in mediation can be overridden where the interests of justice require it.

Effect of mediation on limitation and prescription periods

Member states are required to ensure that parties who choose to attempt to settle their dis- **15.27** pute by mediation are not subsequently prevented from initiating judicial proceedings or referring a dispute to arbitration by the expiry of limitation or prescription periods during the mediation process (Art 8). This provision is likely to make it necessary to amend the Limitation Act 1980 to provide for the temporary suspension of a limitation period while mediation is being undertaken. If this is done, more care will need to be taken in defining the start and end date of the mediation. This is particularly important because the media-tion process may continue after the date of the mediation meeting, and at present, in many mediations, it is difficult to pinpoint the end date with any certainty.

Publicity

Member states should encourage the provision of information to the general public on how **15.28** to contact mediators and organisations providing mediation services, in particular on the internet (Art 9). They should also encourage legal practitioners to inform their clients of the possibility of mediation (Recital 25).

THE EUROPEAN CODE OF CONDUCT FOR MEDIATORS

The European Code of Conduct for Mediators has been approved by the Justice Directorate **15.29** of the European Commission. It sets out a number of principles to which individual media-tors can voluntarily decide to commit. It therefore falls very far short of laying down a uni-form set of principles which mediators across member states are obliged to follow. It sets out a range of principles covering matters such as competence, independence and impartiality, the procedure for the mediation, fairness of the process, confidentiality and the termin-ation of the process. The Code of Conduct is discussed in more detail in Chapter 16.

ENFORCEABILITY OF INTERNATIONAL MEDIATION SETTLEMENT AGREEMENTS

An agreement reached in international mediation cannot be enforced in the same way **15.30** as a judgment of a court or an arbitration award. International arbitral awards are readily enforceable in almost every country in the world under the New York Convention 1958 (see Chapter 29). However if the agreement takes the form of a binding commercial contract, it can be enforced in the same way as any other contract. To facilitate that, the parties should consider putting a choice of law clause and an exclusive jurisdiction clause into their settlement agreement so there is certainty in relation to the courts of which country and which system of law governs the contract.

15.31 If arbitration or litigation proceedings have already been commenced, and a mediated settlement is reached during the course of those proceedings, it could be reflected as a consent order in the litigation or an agreed award in the arbitration proceedings. It would then be enforceable as a court order or arbitral award (see Chapters 20, 27 and 29 for details).

15.32 If the consent order is made in the courts of an EU state, reciprocal enforcement arrangements exist by virtue of the Jurisdiction and Judgments Regulation (Regulation (EC) No 44/2001). Consent orders of a court in an EU state which is a party to the Jurisdiction and Judgments Regulation can be registered for enforcement in the courts of England and Wales pursuant to CPR, Part 74. Reciprocal enforcement arrangements also exist in cross-border family cases by Council Regulation (EC) No 2201/2003 on the jurisdiction and recognition and enforcement of judgments in matrimonial matters and matters of parental responsibility.

KEY POINTS SUMMARY

15.33
- Mediation has grown globally at a rapid rate in the last 10 years, particularly in EU countries.
- Mediation is particularly effective as an ADR process for resolving international disputes, because:
  - It enables linguistic and cultural differences to be managed and respected to a greater extent than is possible in court proceedings.
  - It avoids complex arguments about which court has jurisdiction to determine the dispute and which system of law applies to the dispute.
  - It can be speedy and cost-effective compared to the costs involved in arbitrating or litigating such disputes.
  - The flexibility of the process enables the parties to tailor it to their particular needs.
- A team of mediators will usually need to be appointed to mediate international disputes.
- A move to promote and set minimum standards for mediation in EU countries has been created by the EU Directive on mediation in civil and commercial matters (Directive 2008/52/EC).
- EU member states are required to implement the Directive by 21 May 2011.
- Implementation of the Directive will result in some change to domestic law, in particular to the common law developments in confidentiality, and to the Limitation Act 1980.
- A voluntary European Code of Conduct for Mediators has also been implemented.

16

PROFESSIONAL ETHICS IN NEGOTIATION AND MEDIATION

INTRODUCTION....................................16.01

ADVISING ABOUT ADR OPTIONS.........................16.02

LAWYERS PROVIDING AN ADR SERVICE 16.10

LAWYERS ACTING FOR CLIENTS IN AN ADR PROCESS.........16.13

DUTIES WHEN ADVANCING A CLIENT'S CASE AND DRAFTING
DOCUMENTS......................................16.34

THE DUTY OF CONFIDENTIALITY.........................16.38

DISCLOSURE OF OTHER INFORMATION 16.42

AUTHORITY TO SETTLE 16.48

THE RELATIONSHIP BETWEEN BARRISTERS AND THEIR
PROFESSIONAL CLIENTS IN ADR 16.50

ETHICAL CONSIDERATIONS AFFECTING MEDIATORS..........16.55

KEY POINTS SUMMARY...............................16.74

INTRODUCTION

ADR processes, in particular negotiation and mediation, can give rise to a number of ethical **16.01** considerations for lawyers that may differ from those that arise when conducting litigation. Lawyers acting in an ADR process will owe duties to their professional client, the lay client, the neutral third party (such as the mediator, adjudicator, expert or arbitrator) and the court (if settlement occurs that is to be embodied in a court order). Mediators also have to adhere to ethical standards of behaviour in mediation. These matters are discussed in this chapter.

ADVISING ABOUT ADR OPTIONS

16.02 ADR affords clients many advantages over litigation (see Chapter 1). One of the key advantages is the cost savings that can be achieved by settling a case by negotiation or mediation. If a case settles by ADR, particularly before proceedings have been issued, the lawyers in the case will obviously earn less fee income. However lawyers must not let this fact influence them in any way.

16.03 Under the CPR, lawyers have a professional duty to help the court to further the overriding objective (CPR 1.3). They are therefore under a duty to save expense, ensure that the case is dealt with expeditiously and fairly and in a way that is proportionate to the issues, the importance of the case, the amount of money involved and the financial position of each party (CPR 1.1). Helping the court to further the overriding objective will also mean that they must encourage the parties to co-operate with each other and facilitate the use of ADR if that would be appropriate (CPR 1.4).

16.04 Legal representatives, including solicitors and barristers, are under a positive duty to consider routinely with their clients whether the dispute is suitable for ADR. This has been the subject of judicial comment in several cases, such as *Halsey v Milton Keynes General NHS Trust* [2004] 1 WLR 3002, per Dyson LJ at para 11; *Dunnett v Railtrack* [2002] 1 WLR 2434 per Brooke LJ at para 15 and *Cowl v Plymouth City Council* [2002] 1 WLR 803 per Lord Woolf at [27].

16.05 The duty on the parties to consider ADR should be exercised at all stages of the dispute, not just before proceedings are issued. It should be considered, in particular, before issue, at track allocation stage, after disclosure and before the costs of a trial have been incurred.

16.06 Solicitors in particular are under specific duties under their code of conduct to discuss the costs of litigation and whether the potential outcomes of any case will justify the expense or risk involved, including, if relevant, the risk of having to pay the opponent's costs (Solicitors Code of Conduct r 2.03(6)). A solicitor must discuss whether mediation or some other form of ADR procedure would be more appropriate than litigation, arbitration or other formal processes. They must also ensure that the client understands that there may be adverse costs consequences if a party refuses ADR. The Law Society's Practice Advice, issued on 22 April 2005, states that advice about alternative ADR procedures must be given at any appropriate stage of the proceedings, not just at the outset. In assessing whether the matter is suitable for ADR, the solicitor should bear in mind the factors discussed in Chapter 3.

16.07 Both barristers and solicitors are required to act in the best interests of the lay client without regard to their own interests (Solicitors' Code of Conduct r 1.04 and the Code of Conduct of the Bar of England and Wales ('the Bar Code of Conduct') para 303(a)). This will require them to consider, and discuss with the lay client, the most cost-effective and timely way of resolving the dispute by using the most appropriate ADR method. This professional duty is also reinforced by the key court guides (see the *Chancery Guide* para 17.4; the *Admiralty and Commercial Court Guide* para G1.4 and the *Technology and Construction Court Guide* para 7.1.3).

Where an ADR process is to be used in an effort to resolve the dispute, the extent of the solici- **16.08** tor's involvement (and that of counsel) in the process should be clearly agreed with the lay client in advance. Appropriate costs advice should also be given to the client in relation to this, and recorded in writing.

If a lawyer fails to give appropriate advice about ADR or negligently advises the client to **16.09** reject an offer from the opposing party to use ADR, the lawyer may expose their client to a costs penalty (see Chapter 6). The lawyer could be personally liable for a wasted costs order and/or a professional negligence action could be brought against him or her.

LAWYERS PROVIDING AN ADR SERVICE

A solicitor or a solicitor's firm may offer ADR services to third parties, either as media- **16.10** tor, neutral evaluator, adjudicator, or expert determiner. A solicitor undertaking an ADR service of this kind must be truly neutral. They must ensure there is no prior personal knowledge of or relationship with either of the parties to the dispute. They should also ensure that no one within the firm has acted for any of the parties in any matter, even an unrelated matter. This is important to avoid the appearance of bias. If the lawyer, or any member of the firm, has acted or had any connection with any of the parties to the dispute, this must be disclosed to all parties, and the lawyer should not proceed unless all parties consent in writing to the provision of the agreed ADR service (Solicitors' Code of Conduct r 3.06).

Barristers are also permitted to offer ADR services, and many barristers' chambers now offer **16.11** a mediation service. Although barristers generally are not permitted to make any payment to any person for the purposes of procuring professional instructions, they are permitted to pay a reasonable fee required by an ADR provider that appoints or recommends them to conduct mediation, arbitration or adjudication services. They are also permitted to enter into a reasonable fee-sharing arrangement with such an organisation on comparable terms to other mediators (Bar Code of Conduct para r 307(e)).

Barristers are required to act with independence and be impartial. A barrister must not **16.12** compromise professional standards in order to please a client, the court or a third party, including any mediator (Bar Code of Conduct para 307(c)) and must not permit absolute independence, integrity and freedom from external pressures to be compromised (Bar Code of Conduct para 307(a)).

LAWYERS ACTING FOR CLIENTS IN AN ADR PROCESS

Lawyers acting for a client in an ADR process will be under a duty to act in compliance with **16.13** their core professional duties, which apply in all cases. It should be noted that the precise wording of the core obligations differ in the codes of conduct applicable to each side of the profession, although the fundamental core obligations are very similar. These are as follows.

To act within the client's instructions

16.14   It is vital that a lawyer acts at all times within the client's instructions. The objectives in the case, and the priorities, must come from the client and be confirmed with the client, and should not be assumed. In the relative informality of some ADR processes it may be tempting for a lawyer to aim for an outcome that is broadly 'fair', but it must be remembered that the lawyer is in no way a judge who may impose an outcome. The lawyer should advise the client on the strengths and weaknesses of a case, and what is a realistic outcome, but must leave decisions to the client. This is particularly important as regards authority to settle in a non-adjudicative process, which is dealt with at 16.48.

To act at all times in the client's best interests

16.15   Paragraph 1.03 of the Solicitors' Code of Conduct provides that solicitors should treat the interests of the clients as paramount, provided they do not conflict with other professional conduct obligations, or the public interest in the administration of justice.

16.16   The duty owed by barristers is in similar terms. Paragraph 303 of the Bar Code of Conduct provides that a barrister

> 'must promote and protect fearlessly and by all proper and lawful means the lay client's best interests and do so without regard to his own interests or to any consequences to himself or to any other person (including any professional client or other intermediary or another barrister)'.

Advising on ADR options

16.17   A lawyer advising a client about ADR options or representing a client in an ADR process must always act in the lay client's best interests. A lawyer would not be acting in the client's best interests if they advised the client not to pursue a particular ADR option, or enter into a reasonable settlement, because the lawyer wanted to preserve fee income that would result from the litigation continuing between the parties.

Advising on settlement

16.18   A lawyer should also have this duty clearly in mind when advising on any settlement proposal put forward by the opposing side. It is important to ensure that the lay client is properly informed about the merits of the case, the prospects of success, any evidential weakness in the case, the likely outcome at trial, and the costs of proceeding to trial so that the client can make an informed decision. The lawyer should also remember that the decision whether to accept an offer (or make an offer) must be that of the lay client. The lawyer must ensure the lay client is fully informed about his or her position. The lawyer can and should give the lay client the benefit of an opinion, but the ultimate decision is that of the client. Care must be taken not to put improper pressure on a lay client to enter into a settlement if the client is unwilling to do so. If the lay client is publicly funded, the lawyers will have an obligation to report if a reasonable offer to settle is refused (Funding Code Procedures, Section 12 Reporting Obligations C43.2 and c44 i). The Legal Services Commission may withdraw public funding in that event, and the lay client should be advised about this possibility.

16.19   A lawyer acting in the lay client's best interests should also ensure that any settlement reached using an ADR process is a reasonable one. It will rarely be reasonable to advise a client to settle a claim for a sum significantly below that which is likely to be received at trial. A lawyer should also ensure that any settlement agreement is drawn up in a way that best protects the client's interests. This may determine the form the settlement takes. For example, it may be more advantageous to record a settlement in a Tomlin order rather than invite the court to make an order by consent for a specified amount (see Chapter 20).

Conditional fee agreements ('CFA')

The lawyer also needs to consider the best interests of the client when acting under a CFA **16.20** (see Chapter 4). If the lawyer is acting for the client under a CFA, then this can potentially give rise to a conflict of interest between the lawyer and the lay client when considering ADR options or when advising on settlement. This is because the level of the lawyer's fee is likely to be dependent on the fact and terms of settlement. In such cases, the opposing party may make an offer that provides for payment of a lower success fee than that set out in the CFA. In order to act in the client's best interests, the lawyer may have to advise the client to accept a reasonable offer by the other side even if it provides for payment of a lower success fee than that set out in the CFA. This may also require the lawyer to agree with the client to reduce the success fee in accordance with the terms of that offer.

A barrister acting under a CFA must comply with the Conditional Fee Guidance drawn **16.21** up by the Bar Council's CFA Panel. When advising on settlement (or a Part 36 offer), the barrister must bear in mind only the interests of the lay client and not personal interests, such as the fact that a success fee may become payable on settlement under the CFA. A barrister must also bear in mind obligations under para 303(a) of the Code of Conduct.

To be independent

Rule 1.03 of the Solicitors' Code of Conduct provides that a solicitor must not allow his **16.22** independence to be compromised in the face of pressure from the clients, the courts or any other source.

A barrister owes an overriding duty to the court to act with independence in the interests of **16.23** justice' and not to 'deceive or knowingly or recklessly mislead the court and must not permit his absolute independence integrity or freedom from external pressures to be compromised' (Bar Code of Conduct paras 302 and 303(a)).

To act with integrity

A solicitor must act with integrity towards clients, the courts, the lawyers and others and **16.24** must not behave in a way which is likely to diminish the trust the public places in the legal profession (Solicitors' Code of Conduct rr 1.02 and 1.06).

A barrister must not (Bar Code of Conduct paras 301 and 302) engage in conduct that is: **16.25**

- dishonest or discreditable to a barrister;
- prejudicial to the administration of justice;
- likely to diminish public confidence in the legal profession or the administration of justice; or

- otherwise bring the legal profession into disrepute or knowingly or recklessly mislead the court.

Mediation

16.26 A barrister instructed in a mediation must not knowingly or recklessly mislead the mediator or any party or their representative (Bar Code of Conduct para 708.1). ADR processes cannot be conducted in a dishonest way. A lawyer cannot say anything to the mediator, expert or evaluator that he or she knows or suspects is not true (see Bar Code of Conduct para 708.1) even if the client wishes this to be done in order to have a stronger bargaining position over the opposing party. It is also likely that a lawyer cannot withhold information simply on the grounds that it is confidential if the failure to disclose it renders false and misleading related information that has been communicated to the mediator and the opposing party and on which they have been asked to rely. An example of such information may be putting forward a proposal to supply hand-made specific goods from a specified manufacturer in 14 days, but withholding the fact that the manufacturer had just had his leg amputated and would not be able to make the goods within that period.

16.27 If the mediator or evaluator or other neutral in an ADR process suspects or has grounds to believe that a position is being misrepresented or that information given is not accurate, those concerns should be expressed to that party. The mediator is also likely to warn the party and the lawyers of the dangers of misrepresenting the position either positively or by concealing information that renders untrue or misleading a position they adopted in the mediation. If appropriate, a halt will be called to the whole process. Any lawyer supplying false information is likely to be reported to the appropriate professional body and is likely to face disciplinary proceedings.

16.28 A lawyer will also not be acting with integrity if he or she knows that the lay client is engaging in a non-adjudicative ADR process with an improper motive (such as to gain information about the other side's case or delay the eventual resolution of the matter by litigation) rather than with the intention of genuinely attempting to reach a settlement.

Negotiation

16.29 A lawyer must also take care not to mislead the opponent in direct negotiations. A barrister must not engage in conduct that is discreditable, or which would diminish public confidence in the profession (Bar Code of Conduct para 301).

16.30 The different strategies and tactics that may be used in negotiation are dealt with in Chapter 8. The point is made there that a competitive strategy may involve bluff, or sometimes what amounts to threats. There are grey areas about how far it is acceptable to go, but in broad terms in negotiating with the opposing party, a lawyer should not:

- pretend to have evidence if this is not the case;
- misrepresent the evidence;
- indicate that it is the client's final offer if it is not;
- indicate that they have instructions on a matter if this is not the case;
- indicate that they have no instructions on a matter if this is not the case;
- conceal information that should properly be disclosed;

- provide information that the lawyer knows or believes to be false or misleading;
- threaten the other side with improper adverse consequences if they do not accept the client's position/offer;
- change positions and then deny that this has been done;
- make a clear threat that is nothing to do with the issues in the case, eg to report the client or the other side to the tax authorities on the basis of accounts produced in a case.

If an opponent in a negotiation appears to be behaving in an unethical way, the behaviour **16.31** should be challenged. This does not need to be done in a confrontational way, but should be done in a way that defuses any possible benefit from the behaviour. For example: 'It would be helpful to hear your argument on the law on this issue. That did sound a bit like a threat and I don't think that will help us to move forward.'

Fairness

Lawyers must always act with fairness and must not discriminate directly or indirectly **16.32** because of race, colour, ethnic or national origin, nationality, citizenship, sex, sexual orientation, marital status, disability, age, religion or belief (Bar Code of Conduct para 305.1; Solicitors' Code of Conduct r 6.07).

Competence

A solicitor must only act if he is able to provide a good standard of service (Solicitors' Code of **16.33** Conduct r 1.05). A barrister owes similar duties of competence and these are set out in detail in Bar Code of Conduct para 701. This provides that:

'A barrister:

(a) Must in all his professional activities be courteous and act promptly conscientiously diligently and with reasonable competence and take all reasonable and practicable steps to avoid unnecessary expense or waste of the court's time and to ensure that professional engagements are fulfilled;

(b) Must not undertake any task which:

　(i) he knows or ought to know he is not competent to handle;

　(ii) he does not have adequate time and opportunity to prepare for or perform; or

　(iii) he cannot discharge within the time requested or otherwise within a reasonable time having regard to the pressure of other work.

(c) Must read all instructions delivered to him expeditiously.'

DUTIES WHEN ADVANCING A CLIENT'S CASE AND DRAFTING DOCUMENTS

Paragraph 704 of the Bar Code of Conduct provides that: **16.34**

'A barrister must not devise facts which will assist in advancing the lay client's case and must not draft any . . . document containing

(a) any statement of fact or contention which is not supported by the lay client or his instructions;

(b) any contention which he does not consider to be properly arguable;

(c)   any allegation of fraud unless he has clear instructions to make such an allegation and has before him reasonably credible material which as it stands establishes a prima facie case of fraud;

(d)   in the case of a witness statement or affidavit any statement of fact other than the evidence which in substance according to his instructions the barrister reasonably believes the witness would give if the evidence contained in the witness statement or affidavit were being given in oral examination.'

16.35   When drafting a position statement, case summary or any other document for use in an ADR process, a barrister should ensure that all allegations and assertions are properly arguable and supported by instructions. This also applies to drafting a confidential document for submission to a mediator. This is reinforced by para 708.1 of the Code, which provides that in mediation a barrister must not knowingly or recklessly mislead the mediator or any other party or representative.

16.36   When drafting any document for use in an ADR process, the barrister should also ensure compliance with the Written Standards for the Conduct of Professional Work.

16.37   Any allegation or contention that a barrister puts forward in face-to-face negotiations must also be properly arguable. They should not advance a claim that is hopeless and so lacking in merit that it is not properly arguable. They should only assert an allegation of fraud or dishonest conduct if there are clear instructions to do so and reasonably credible evidence that establishes a prima facie case of fraud.

THE DUTY OF CONFIDENTIALITY

16.38   The Solicitors' Code of Conduct provides that all information about clients must be kept confidential (r 4.04). A similar duty of confidentiality is contained in para 702 of the Bar Code of Conduct, which provides that:

> 'Whether or not the relation of counsel and client continues a barrister must preserve the confidentiality of the lay client's affairs and must not without the prior consent of the lay client or as permitted by law lend or reveal the contents of the papers in any instructions to or communicate to any third person (other than another barrister, a pupil....or any other person who needs to know it for the performance of their duties) information which has been entrusted to him in confidence or use such information to the lay client's detriment or to his own or another client's advantage.'

16.39   A separate duty of confidentiality also stems from the following:

- ADR processes are confidential. In non-adjudicative ADR processes, communications that take place between the parties themselves, and between each party and the mediator, evaluator, expert should not be revealed to the court (if agreement is not reached) or a third party, whether or not settlement is reached in that process (see Chapters 13, 17, 21 and 25). Arbitration and adjudication are also confidential processes, although in these processes it is not generally possible for one party to place information before the tribunal that has not been disclosed to the other side.

- Any information that is revealed, whether orally or in writing, for the purposes of settlement will be protected by the 'without prejudice' rule (see Chapters 3 and 13 for a detailed explanation of the without prejudice rule, and the exceptions to it in mediation).

The without prejudice rule will not however apply to open offers, or clear admissions made in the course of negotiations (for example 'my client admits he owes your client £100,000').

- Negotiations taking place between lawyers with a view to reaching settlement are impliedly covered by the 'without prejudice' rule.
- A separate duty of confidentiality exists in mediation where private communications take place between a party and the mediator in private meetings. These communications are confidential unless the disclosing party agrees otherwise. The mediator will also owe a separate and enforceable duty of confidentiality to the parties. See Chapter 13 for specific considerations that relate to confidentiality in mediation.
- Confidential information can also be provided to an expert in expert determination or to an evaluator in early neutral evaluation unless the parties or the court orders otherwise (see Chapters 17 and 21). However it is generally unwise for confidential information to be provided by one party to the expert or evaluator where a decision or evaluation has to be issued with reasons. In such cases, the expert (or evaluator by analogy) should summarise the information provided in private so that all parties can ascertain the information relied upon in reaching the decision or evaluation (*Halifax Life Ltd v Equitable Life Assurance Society* [2007] 1 Lloyd's Rep 528) (see Chapter 21).

In practical terms, this means a lawyer should take the utmost care not to: **16.40**

- inadvertently or deliberately reveal private and confidential information relating to their client. In particular, a lawyer should take care when negotiating face-to-face with the other side in the absence of the lay client. These counsel-to-counsel or solicitor-to solicitor discussions can be fast paced and informal. Lawyers must always guard against revealing something that would be damaging to the client's case during these discussions that ought not to be revealed. If information is revealed by the other side during these negotiations which would assist the lay client's case then this information should be brought to the lay client's attention.
- disclose any information that he gained during the ADR process or reveal details of what took place during that process to any third party, or to the court (if settlement is not reached);
- reveal information that the client wishes to be kept confidential to the lawyers acting for the opposing parties in any joint meetings that take place during mediation or in direct negotiations;
- repeat information gained during settlement negotiations with the other side or the content of those negotiations to the court or any third party.

Before acting for a client in negotiations and mediation and at all times during those processes, the lawyer must take care to obtain clear instructions from the client about: **16.41**

- the information that the client wishes to withhold from the other side (and, if applicable, from the mediator);
- the information that can be disclosed to the mediator on the basis that the mediator treats the information as confidential;
- any open offers that the client wishes to make to settle the dispute (these will not be protected by the 'without prejudice' rule and will not be treated as confidential information);
- any admission that the lay client is willing to make. An admission is not protected by the 'without prejudice' rule and thus can be disclosed by the other side. It is also important

to make sure that the client appreciates the difference between a clear admission and a concession. An admission is an unqualified acceptance of a fact (eg I accept my client must pay for the radios in the sum of £600 as there is no defence to that aspect of the claim). A concession on the other hand is an offer to concede a fact or position in order to reach an overall settlement and without any admission of liability (eg I will agree to pay for the radios if you will waive your claim for the ipods). A concession is therefore protected by the 'without prejudice' rule, and cannot be used against the client or disclosed by the other side in the event that settlement is not reached.

DISCLOSURE OF OTHER INFORMATION

Non-adjudicatory ADR and expert determination

16.42 In most non-adjudicatory ADR processes and also expert determination, the parties usually retain control of how much information to put before the mediator, facilitator, neutral evaluator or expert. The strict rules of evidence and procedure do not apply to these forms of ADR. As a general rule, the parties will disclose information and evidence that is relevant to the dispute, helpful to the case of the disclosing party and that would have to be disclosed in litigation.

16.43 The difficulty lies in deciding whether information should be disclosed that is adverse to the client's case. In litigation, the parties are required to give standard disclosure, namely disclosure of the documents on which they rely, as well as those that adversely affect their own case, adversely affect another side's case or support another party's case (CPR 31.6). However there is no obligation to disclose such documents in advance of the disclosure stage in litigation (unless the documents are required to be disclosed by a pre-action protocol). The party may therefore have a choice whether to make such disclosure in the ADR process.

16.44 The lawyer acting in such cases may be asked to give advice on whether disclosure should be made. The guiding principles are as follows:

- Adverse information may need to be disclosed if failure to do so renders false or misleading some fact or information that has already been disclosed by that party unless the misleading fact or information can be withdrawn or corrected in some other way.
- Otherwise, however unhelpful the information is to the party's case (and therefore helpful to the opposing party), it will not usually have to be disclosed. The lawyer would not have to disclose, for example, the fact that the lay client has a phobia about court, is terrified about giving evidence in court and is likely to be a very nervous and unimpressive witness (but equally, you could not positively mislead the other side by saying the client is looking forward to the trial and will be a very confident witness).

16.45 In order to ensure that a lawyer acts with integrity, and does not knowingly or recklessly mislead anyone, great care will need to be taken in mediation and negotiation in relation to information that is communicated to the mediator and the other side. In particular the lawyer should not:

- make any assertion that he or she knows or believes is untrue (perhaps because it is contradicted or qualified by information that the client does not wish to disclose);

- make threats or bluff (eg stating an offer is a final one, when it is not).

An ADR process will only have value if the other side can rely on information and represen- **16.46** tations made to them during the course of the process. Lawyers and parties should be aware of the fact that although any settlement agreement reached during a non-adjudicative ADR process cannot be the subject of appeal, it can be set aside if one or both parties entered into it under a mistake or misrepresentation or because of duress or undue influence.

Adjudication and arbitration

These processes are more akin to litigation. The parties will usually agree the ambit of dis- **16.47** closure and, in the absence of agreement, the court will determine the scope of disclosure. See Chapters 22–27 for those processes. In practice, the ambit of disclosure tends to be more akin to litigation.

AUTHORITY TO SETTLE

Lawyers acting in non-adjudicatory ADR processes must ensure that they: **16.48**

- understand any limitations imposed on the authority to effect a binding settlement agreement on the client's behalf. If in doubt, always make it clear to the opposing party that any negotiations are on the basis that no binding agreement can be reached until the lay client's express approval or authorisation has been obtained;
- do not exceed the authority given by the client. By virtue of the ostensible authority that a lawyer has as the client's agent, the lawyer can bind the client to an agreement without actual authority to do so. This is likely to result in the lawyer being sued for negligence and breach of contract;
- do not mislead the opposing party or a mediator as to the authority given, for example by representing that he or she has authority to settle the dispute up the maximum value of the claim (say £1,000,000), when in fact the authority is limited to £500,000.
- understand the 'bottom line' figure below which the client is not prepared to settle the dispute, and the range within which the lay client would be prepared to settle the claim. This information will be necessary in preparing the negotiation strategy.
- make and keep an accurate note of offers, counter-offers and concessions made during the course of negotiations. Some barristers will ask the lay client to sign or initial a note of an offer before it is made or rejected. This can be a good idea to ensure that there can be no possible misunderstanding between lawyer and client. The client should also be asked to sign any written settlement agreement recording the settlement (see Chapter 20 for more detail on recording settlement).

When conducting direct negotiations or acting in mediation, it is preferable to have the **16.49** client available so that instructions can be obtained in relation to the settlement proposal. It is particularly important to ensure that the lay client or person who has authority to settle the dispute (for example a representative of an insurer) is present at a mediation. The mediation agreement will typically provide that the person signing the agreement on behalf of a party warrants that they have authority to bind that party to the terms of any settlement.

THE RELATIONSHIP BETWEEN BARRISTERS AND THEIR PROFESSIONAL CLIENTS IN ADR

16.50 A barrister may be instructed to attend an ADR process such as mediation instead of the instructing solicitor. If this is the case, the barrister must ensure that a full and accurate record of what occurs during the process is made and kept. The barrister may be asked to make a copy of this attendance note for his instructing solicitors. At the very least, he or she will have to inform the instructing solicitors of the important events that occurred during the process.

16.51 If a barrister is instructed to attend an ADR process as well as the lawyer, it will need to be made clear where the division of roles lies between them is. This is particularly so in mediation. The barrister may be briefed to attend a mediation to advise on the merits of offers, carry out a re-assessment of the case in the light of information revealed during the process and to draft the settlement agreement. The solicitor may wish to take the lead in the negotiations. It may be that the solicitor will wish the barrister to assume a lead role in the mediation (which is more usual where counsel is instructed). It is important that all parties are clear about this.

16.52 In any event, a barrister should always treat the instructing solicitor with courtesy, and listen to their views and opinion with respect. A solicitor should act likewise.

16.53 A barrister must bear in mind that the primary duty is owed to the lay client rather than the professional client (the instructing solicitor) and must not permit the instructing solicitor to limit the barrister's discretion as to how the interests of the lay client can best be served (Bar Code of Conduct para 303(b)).

16.54 If a barrister forms the view that there is a conflict of interest between the lay client and the instructing solicitor (for example because the barrister considers the instructing solicitor has been negligent), then he or she must consider whether it would be in the lay client's best interests to instruct another professional adviser. If the barrister considers that it would be, then the lay client must be advised about this and take steps to ensure that this advice is brought to the attention of the lay client, if necessary by sending a copy directly to the client as well as to the instructing solicitor (Bar Code of Conduct para 703).

ETHICAL CONSIDERATIONS AFFECTING MEDIATORS

16.55 The number of ADR professionals is growing year on year and they come from a wide range of professional backgrounds. While some are lawyers, many are not. Mediators may be drawn from other areas of professional practice, such as accountants, engineers and other construction professionals, and from the field of psychology. The ADR profession needs regulation. The market is not served by the fact that:

- there is a great deal of variation in the nature of the training courses offered by different ADR providers;
- mediators in private practice do not have to undergo any form of training or accreditation at all;

- there is a multiplicity of codes of conduct among providers.

There is an urgent need for: **16.56**

- uniformity in the professional training and accreditation requirements leading to a formal qualification;
- a common code of conduct which sets uniform standards, which *all* mediators must adhere to;
- an independent regulatory body to oversee the work of *all* ADR professionals, including setting minimum professional standards in the way mediators carry out their business, monitoring those standards, and implementing and operating a standard complaints procedure.

Although the Civil Mediation Council is taking steps in this direction by creating the **16.57** Registered Mediation Organisation Scheme, the Registered Mediation Scheme and the Code of Good Practice, these measures fall short of what is required. There is a European Code of Conduct for Mediators, but it is also entirely voluntary and mediators or ADR organisations do not have to adopt it or operate under it.

The Third Mediation Audit report by CEDR (November 2007) suggests that this would **16.58** find favour with the profession, with 52.3% of mediators welcoming the idea of a single standard of basic professional training of commercial mediators and 58.5% agreed that there should be a single regulatory body for setting and monitoring professional standards of practice by commercial mediators and dealing with public complaints against mediators. These figures were broadly unchanged in the fourth Mediation Audit (2010), being 52.8% and 54.9% respectively.

Most mediators do operate under a code of conduct. Although there will be differences in **16.59** the wording of the ethical and other considerations governing the conduct of mediators, most codes do or should cover the professional standards to be expected of mediators, which are discussed in the remainder of this chapter.

Competence

Mediators must be competent and knowledgeable in the process of mediation. This should **16.60** include proper training in mediation skills and in the process of mediation, and a system for Continuing Professional Development (CPD) to refresh and update their skills. The mediator should be competent to conduct the mediation bearing in mind the nature and complexity of the dispute and the needs and objectives of the parties. Mediators should also provide information to interested parties relating to their background and experience so that they can make an informed choice (European Code of Conduct for Mediators paras 1.1 and 1.2).

Independence and neutrality

A mediator must ensure there is no conflict of interest with any of the parties directly **16.61** or indirectly affected by the dispute. If circumstances exist which do or may give rise to a conflict of interest or affect his neutrality, these should be disclosed immediately to the parties. The mediator should only consent to act in such circumstances if the parties expressly authorise this (in writing) (see European Code of Conduct for Mediators para 2).

Impartiality

16.62 The mediator should at all times act, and endeavour to be seen to act, with impartiality towards the parties (European Code of Conduct for Mediators para 2.2).

The mediation procedure

16.63 The mediator should ensure the parties understand the nature and purpose of the mediation process, the terms of the mediation agreement, the fees payable, and the obligations of confidentiality imposed on the parties and the mediator. The mediator should also explain the procedure to be followed in the mediation, which can be modified or agreed following discussions between the mediator and the parties (European Code of Conduct for Mediators paras 3.1 and 3.4).

Fairness

16.64 The mediator should act fairly between the parties, ensuring that all parties have adequate opportunities to be involved in the process.

16.65 The mediator should also be careful not to put undue pressure on a party to settle the dispute. If this happened, the agreement could be set aside for undue influence or duress. The mediator must not press a party into settlement in order to maintain a high personal settlement rate.

Confidentiality

16.66 Paragraph 4 of the European Code of Conduct for Mediators provides that:

> 'The mediator shall keep confidential all information arising out of or in connection with the mediation, including the fact that the mediation is to take place or has taken place, unless compelled by law or public policy grounds. Any information disclosed in confidence to mediators by one of the parties shall not be disclosed to the other parties without permission or unless compelled by law.'

16.67 The duty of confidentiality in mediation is discussed in Chapter 13. The mediation agreement will usually spell out the circumstances in which the mediator can reveal confidential information. The usual exceptions to the general rule are where disclosure is required:

- to prevent risk of harm to the public at large (eg one party concedes in private discussions in mediation that during a manufacturing process, a brand of breakfast cereal became contaminated by rat poison);
- to protect the life or health of a person or persons;
- by law (eg to comply with reporting obligations under the Proceeds of Crime Act 2002).

Termination of the mediation

16.68 The mediator should terminate the mediation, and inform the parties (if appropriate) if they believe a settlement to be unenforceable or illegal, or that continuing the mediation is unlikely to result in settlement (European Code of Conduct for Mediators para 3.2).

The mediator should also explain that the parties have the right to withdraw from the medi-   **16.69**
ation at any time, and without giving any reason for doing so (European Code of Conduct
for Mediators para 3.3).

If agreement is reached at the mediation, the mediator should ensure that all parties under-   **16.70**
stand the terms of the agreement, and that they consent to it. The mediator may, if requested
by the parties and competent to do so, give advice on how the agreement can be formalised
and made enforceable (European Code of Conduct for Mediators para 3.3).

The mediator should also ensure that any files or documents, including personal notes that   **16.71**
are retained following the mediation should be securely and confidentially stored.

Repeat instructions

In the Third Mediation Report carried out by CEDR (November 2007), concern was expressed   **16.72**
by both mediators and lawyers that a mediator's over-dependence on repeat referrals from
a particular firm could also prejudice their neutrality. However this would not be an issue if
disclosure was made of all prior contacts with referring parties, as well as the parties directly
involved in the dispute.

Practice administration

The Civil Mediation Council Code of Good Practice for Mediators also requires mediators to: **16.73**

- have an efficient system of personal practice administration (para 11);
- have access to a complaints resolution system (para 12);
- make effective arrangements for obtaining peer review and feedback and an effective
  system for obtaining and reviewing feedback (para 13);
- be insured to cover errors, omissions and negligence: the CMC recommends a minimum
  of £1 million of such insurance or a higher level if appropriate (para 14);
- be sensitive to diversity, equality and anti-discrimination issues (para 15).

KEY POINTS SUMMARY

- Lawyers must advise their clients about ADR options, at all stages of the dispute.   **16.74**
- Lawyers can provide an ADR service for clients, provided there is no conflict of interest.
- In ADR processes, lawyers must observe the rules of the Bar Code of Conduct or the
  Solicitors' Code of Conduct.
- If the lawyer is acting under a CFA, care must be taken to ensure that the settlement is in
  the client's best interests, irrespective of whether the success fee becomes payable on settlement or the amount of the success fee.
- When acting in mediation or negotiation, a lawyer must take care not to:
  - mislead the other side;
  - disclose confidential information to the other side (or the mediator) unless the client
    consents;
  - reveal the details of the negotiation or what took place in mediation to third parties or
    to the court;
  - exceed the limits of his authority.

- Mediators are required to act in accordance with ethical standards.
- Although there is no standard code of practice that applies to all mediators, most mediators or ADR providers will devise their own code of conduct or code of good practice, and this will be incorporated into the terms of the mediation agreement made between the mediator and the parties.
- The European Code of Conduct for Mediators and the CMC Code of Good Practice provide a useful benchmark for determining the minimum rules of professional conduct that should be expected from a mediator.

PART 4

EVALUATION, CONCILIATION AND OMBUDSMEN

17

EARLY NEUTRAL EVALUATION

WHAT IS EARLY NEUTRAL EVALUATION 17.01

AT WHAT STAGE SHOULD IT BE EMPLOYED? 17.05

WHEN SHOULD IT BE USED? 17.06

WHO SHOULD BE APPOINTED TO CARRY OUT
THE EVALUATION? 17.08

THE PROCEDURE 17.10

NEUTRAL FACT FINDING 17.14

JUDICIAL EVALUATION 17.15

EVALUATION IN PERSONAL INJURY CASES 17.20

SOCIAL SECURITY AND CHILD SUPPORT TRIBUNAL ENE
PILOT SCHEME...................................... 17.24

JUDICIAL ENE 17.28

KEY POINTS SUMMARY................................ 17.29

WHAT IS EARLY NEUTRAL EVALUATION

Early neutral evaluation (ENE) is an assessment and evaluation of the facts, evidence and/or **17.01** the legal merits of an issue in the case or of the case as a whole. It is usually undertaken by the parties jointly, although in some cases it can be undertaken at the request of one party only in relation to their own case. The parties will usually appoint a neutral third party to evaluate the facts, evidence and law in relation to the issue or case and provide an opinion on the merits. This differs from mediation which is essentially a *facilitative* process. ENE is an *advisory* and *evaluative* process.

As discussed in Chapter 11, there is a close similarity between this and evaluative media- **17.02** tion. However, in this book, the term early neutral evaluation is used when a neutral third party is asked to evaluate a dispute, without themselves becoming involved in any way in the negotiations between the parties. It is this disengagement from the negotiation process that distinguishes early neutral evaluation from evaluative mediation.

17.03 ENE can take place within the court system, in which case the evaluation is usually carried out by a judge. ENE can also take place outside the litigation process, but parallel with it, and even before litigation has been commenced at all.

17.04 Like mediation, it is a private and confidential process, and the evaluator must be impartial. If the evaluator is appointed using an ADR provider, he will operate under a code of conduct that may be the same or similar to the code of conduct that governs the conduct of mediators.

AT WHAT STAGE SHOULD IT BE EMPLOYED?

17.05 ENE is usually employed in the early stages of a dispute (hence its name), but in fact it could be utilised at any stage. Neutral evaluation employed at the early stages of a case can assist settlement by mediation, and can be carried out before or even during the mediation, and before or at any time during the process of litigation.

WHEN SHOULD IT BE USED?

17.06 The rationale for ENE is that an unbiased evaluation of the case and the likely outcome by a neutral party, such as a judge or expert, will help the parties subsequently to settle the dispute by negotiation or even mediation. It can be particularly useful where the parties have taken an unrealistic and entrenched view of the claim and need a reality check and assessment of the case by an independent person.

17.07 The process can be useful in that it enables each party to appreciate the strengths and weaknesses of their case and this in turn can encourage and lead to settlement, even if the parties do not agree to settle on the basis of the evaluation.

WHO SHOULD BE APPOINTED TO CARRY OUT THE EVALUATION?

17.08 The choice of evaluator will depend on the issues presented by the case. It may be that an expert is required, in which case the process will be an expert evaluation. Whether an expert is appointed to carry out the evaluation will depend on the underlying subject-matter of the dispute and whether issues of a technical nature are raised that require expertise to evaluate.

17.09 The parties may privately appoint a neutral. This could be a solicitor or a barrister or an independent third party such as an expert. Alternatively they may enlist the assistance of an ADR provider (see Appendix 1 for a selection of providers) in order to help them select and appoint a suitable evaluator. For example CEDR offer an ENE service and their model ENE Agreement and Guidance Notes are reproduced at Appendix 3.

THE PROCEDURE

The manner in which the evaluation is conducted will be primarily decided by the evalu- **17.10**
ator, although they will usually fix the procedure after consultation with the parties. The
process is flexible and the parties can tailor it to meet the needs of their case. The parties
can control the amount and form of the information that is placed before the evaluator, and
they can identify the issues of fact or issues of law or both that they want the evaluator to
evaluate. The evaluator will be instructed by both parties, and they will agree the terms on
which he is instructed and the ambit of the instructions. The parties can also agree that the
evaluator should carry out his own investigations independently of the parties, and make a
recommendation based on those investigations.

Each party will usually make written submissions to the evaluator, together with such evi- **17.11**
dence and supporting documents as they see fit. It is also possible to agree that each party
should present some or all of their case at an oral hearing. The evaluator may also wish to
interview the parties at a private meeting, or they may conduct an informal meeting at
which both parties are present and are given the opportunity to make submissions to the
evaluator.

The neutral will evaluate the evidence (oral and written) and the law and the submissions **17.12**
of each party and then produce a recommendation setting out his view on the merits of the
dispute and the likely outcome of it. The recommendation may or may not contain detailed
reasons for the decision depending on the agreement reached between the parties and the
evaluator.

The recommendation is usually non-binding, and the parties do not have to accept it, **17.13**
although they can agree to make this binding on them.

NEUTRAL FACT FINDING

A variation in the process is to require the evaluator simply to evaluate the facts in dispute **17.14**
between the parties (but not the underlying issues of law or quantum) and reach a decision
on those facts.

JUDICIAL EVALUATION

The court may provide evaluation of a dispute, in which case the ENE is carried out by a **17.15**
judge.

The Commercial Court may, with the agreement of the parties, in an appropriate case, **17.16**
provide ENE of a dispute or of some of the issues in the case. The approval of the judge
in charge of the Commercial List must be obtained before an ENE is undertaken. If, after
discussion with counsel, it appears to the judge that ENE will aid the resolution of the dispute, they will, with the agreement of the parties, refer the matter to the judge in charge
of the list. The judge in charge of the list will, if the state of business in the list permits,

nominate a judge to conduct the ENE. The judge conducting the ENE will then take no further part in the case, either for hearing applications or as trial judge, unless the parties agree otherwise.

17.17 Judicial evaluation can also take place in the Technology and Construction Court and in the Mercantile Court.

17.18 The judge will usually evaluate the case based on a summary of information provided to him. He may also require the parties to jointly instruct an expert to help him reach a determination of the technical issues in the case. Any judicial evaluation is not intended to be binding on the parties, but rather to help them to facilitate settlement by negotiation or mediation.

17.19 An example of an order providing for judicial neutral evaluation is Figure 17.1.

EVALUATION IN PERSONAL INJURY CASES

17.20 Some ADR providers operate evaluation schemes for personal injury cases. For example, CEDR, has created a range of ADR options for lower value personal injury cases through their dedicated Personal Injury Unit (PIU). PIU eValuate is described as:

> '…A paper evaluation service which gives the parties early judicial insight into a Court outcome. Experienced evaluators with District Judge expertise provide a written evaluation steering the parties to a solution'. A key strength of the scheme is that the evaluator '…will have the some mindset, training and experience as the ultimate arbiter of the dispute.'

17.21 This will enable the parties to have an indication of the likely outcome should the case proceed to trial.

17.22 The scheme is designed for cases up to £50,000 in value (so personal injury cases that would be proceeding in the county court) and the fees start from £195 (this is taken from information on CEDR's website, which is updated regularly: so check www.cedr.com for the latest information about this scheme).

17.23 The key features of this evaluation scheme are as follows:

- An independent evaluator, who will have expertise as a district judge will be selected to evaluate the dispute (this could be the whole claim or an issue in it). The evaluations will usually be carried out by retired district judges who will have a great deal of experience in deciding similar cases.
- The parties will agree on the issues to be evaluated.
- The evaluation is not binding on the parties, unless they elect to be bound by it.
- Each of the parties will send written submissions to the evaluator together with any relevant documents. The submission should identify the issues that the evaluator is asked to assess and set out the party's case in relation to those issues.
- Within 10 days, the evaluator will consider the written submissions and assess the most likely outcomes at trial and report back to the parties.
- The evaluation fee will usually be jointly split between the parties, although the costs of the process can be treated as 'costs in the case', meaning that the overall loser will pay the overall winner's costs of the evaluation.
- The whole process is confidential and without prejudice, so the parties cannot use the evaluation in any later court proceedings.

Figure 17.1 An example of an order providing for judicial neutral evaluation

IN THE HIGH COURT OF JUSTICE   2010 Folio 2976
COMMERCIAL COURT

BETWEEN

MORROW TECHNOLOGY PLC

Claimant

and

BROWNSTONE HOLDINGS LIMITED

Defendant

ORDER

IT IS ORDERED BY CONSENT THAT:

1. The hearing of the early neutral evaluation shall take place at Room E300 on 20th October 2010 at 2pm before Mr Justice James.
2. The claimant shall by 6th October 2010 lodge an agreed statement of issues, a chronology, a bundle containing statements of case, any relevant witness statements/summaries, any experts' reports and essential documents and correspondence.
3. Each party shall lodge at court and serve by no later than 4pm on 13th October 2010 a skeleton argument containing a brief outline of its case.
4. Each party shall have one hour to present its case.
5. Each party shall have 15 minutes to reply to the other party's case.
6. Each party shall have 15 minutes in which they may direct questions to the other party via the judge.
7. The judge will deliver an assessment orally or in writing.
8. Nothing said at the hearing will be used in court for any purpose.
9. The judge shall be disqualified from any further involvement in the case, unless the parties agree otherwise.
10. Representatives of the parties duly authorised to make decisions to resolve disputes between the parties shall be present at the hearing.
11. Each party shall bear its own costs of the evaluation.

Dated 23 September 2010

- The process is relatively cheap, being around £195 to evaluate a single issue, with approximately £65 for each additional issue. These fees are likely to change from time to time and for the up-to-date fee information see www.cedr.com.

SOCIAL SECURITY AND CHILD SUPPORT TRIBUNAL ENE PILOT SCHEME

From September 2007 until the end of January 2009 a pilot ENE scheme was operated **17.24** in the Social Security and Child Support (SSCS) Tribunal in Sutton, Bristol, Cardiff and Bexleyheath. The focus of the pilot was the use of ENE by a tribunal judge of the facts, evidence or legal merits of appeal cases in the SSCS against decisions relating to the entitlement to or level of disability living allowance and attendance allowance.

17.25   The aim of the pilot was to assess:

- the use of ENE as a cost-effective method of resolving administrative appeals without the need for a hearing;
- whether ENE provided a less formal and more convenient method of resolving the dispute;
- whether ENE produced a faster resolution of the dispute;
- whether ENE increased the operational efficiency of tribunals by reducing the number of hearings and speeding up case resolution; and
- to determine what factors contribute to the success of ENE and therefore to understand where else in the Tribunals Service they could be applied.

17.26   The parties were given the option to have the dispute determined by ENE. If they elected to do so, stage 1 of the ADR process involved an ENE by a district tribunal judge (DTJ) within four weeks of receiving the appeal. If the DTJ assessed that one of the parties was likely to lose the appeal, then stage 2 involved a telephone call to that party. If the losing party was likely to be the Pension Disability and Carers Service, then they were invited to reconsider their decision and, if they did not do so, the matter proceeded to a hearing. If the appellant was likely to lose, they were contacted by the DTJ and this was explained to them, and they were invited to withdraw their appeal or alternatively submit further evidence in support of it and proceed to a hearing. If the DTJ was unable to make an initial assessment without a hearing, directions were given for a hearing. Where a hearing did take place, the DTJ undertaking the ENE did not chair the tribunal panel and the panel hearing the appeal were unaware that an ENE had taken place.

17.27   The pilot has been evaluated by Carolyn Hay, Katherine McKenna, and Trevor Buck in January 2010 (Ministry of Justice Research Series 2/10, January 2010, www.justice.gov.uk/publications/research.htm). Key findings from their research are as follows:

- 78% of appellants opted for ENE.
- 42% of opt-in cases had directions (typically for further evidence) issued at the ENE stage and before the hearing compared to less than 1% of non-opt-in cases. ENE therefore resulted in cases being better prepared for the final hearing.
- The telephone calls that took place with the likely losing party at stage 2 of the process were largely positively received by the parties.
- 23% of opt-in cases were resolved without the need for a hearing, compared to 9% of non-opt-in cases.
- 77% of all opt-in cases were still resolved at a hearing, although opt-in cases had a lower rate of adjournment (9%) than non-opt in cases.
- Opt-in cases resulted in a slightly higher cost to the Tribunals Service (£222 per case for all opt-in cases and £202 for non-opt-in cases), although it also generated more savings in avoiding hearings or avoiding adjournments.
- ENE did not achieve swifter resolution of cases (an average of 46 working days for opt-in cases and 42 working days for non-opt-in cases).
- The pilot helped to build an effective working relationship between the Tribunals Service and the different stakeholder organisations.

- The overall conclusion was that there should be a limited roll-out into a wider and geographically diverse set of areas and further monitoring should take place before the scheme was rolled out nationally.

JUDICIAL ENE

In 2008, the Association of Her Majesty's District Judges put forward proposals to the Civil Justice Council for a judicial ENE scheme. It is anticipated that this will be the subject of a pilot in Cardiff, and, if successful, it may be rolled out into a national programme. **17.28**

KEY POINTS SUMMARY

- ENE is useful if the parties would benefit from an independent assessment of the merits of the case or an issue in the case. **17.29**
- It can be undertaken at any stage of the case, even during mediation.
- ENE is not binding on the parties.
- It is a confidential process.
- If the ENE is carried out by a judge, they will have no further involvement in the case.
- ENE assists the parties to negotiate a settlement by direct negotiations or in mediation.
- Judicial evaluation may be an area for growth in ADR in the future.

18

CONCILIATION

WHAT IS CONCILIATION? 18.01

AN OUTLINE OF THE PROCESS. 18.04

ADVISORY, CONCILIATION AND ARBITRATION
SERVICE CONCILIATION 18.06

CONCILIATION IN FAMILY CASES 18.14

KEY POINTS SUMMARY. 18.21

WHAT IS CONCILIATION?

18.01 Conciliation is a voluntary process whereby a neutral third party facilitates negotiations between the parties to a dispute and assists them to reach a settlement. The process is virtually identical to mediation. There is no international or national consistency over the terminology, so the terms 'conciliation' and 'mediation' can be used to describe the same process. Mediation is the term that is more commonly used now in the United Kingdom to describe ADR by third-party facilitation in civil and commercial disputes.

18.02 In conciliation, the conciliator may express an opinion on the merits of the dispute and may, and usually will, suggest a solution if the parties cannot put forward proposals themselves to resolve the matter. Therefore conciliation could be described as evaluative mediation.

18.03 Conciliation is most commonly encountered in family and employment disputes. The role of conciliation in such disputes is therefore the primary focus of this chapter.

AN OUTLINE OF THE PROCESS

18.04 Conciliation is a confidential and 'without prejudice' voluntary process. Either party can withdraw from it at any time before settlement is reached. The conciliator has no power to impose a solution on the parties. Whether a settlement is reached and, if so, the terms of that settlement, lies within the control of the parties themselves. Factors influencing the choice of conciliation as an ADR process are set out in Chapter 3, and the advantages and disadvantages of ADR are set out in Chapter 1.

The process is very similar to mediation (see Chapter 11–13). The only difference is that the parties usually do not select the conciliator. **18.05**

- The parties will not usually select and appoint the conciliator themselves. If they are able to do so, the factors that are described in 11.63–11.75 will be relevant.
- The conciliator will hold private and joint meetings with the parties in much the same way as a mediator (see Chapter 13), although some conciliators will prefer to use joint meetings.
- The conciliator will perform the same function as a mediator in moving the parties towards settlement, although he may be more active in putting forward proposals for the consideration of the parties. In that sense he will perform a role similar to that of an evaluative mediator rather than a facilitative mediator (see Chapter 11 and 13).
- Like mediation, the parties do not have to agree to any solution that is recommended by the conciliator, although they can agree (usually in writing in advance of the conciliation) that any solution put forward is binding on them.
- An agreement reached in conciliation can be recorded and enforced in the same way as agreements reached in other ADR processes (see Chapters 20 and 29).

ADVISORY, CONCILIATION AND ARBITRATION SERVICE CONCILIATION

The Advisory, Conciliation and Arbitration Service (ACAS) deals with all types of employment issues in the United Kingdom. It was founded in 1974 and is one of the most established ADR bodies in the United Kingdom. Full details of all services it provides can be found on its website: www.acas.org.uk. ACAS offer conciliation and mediation services. The only difference between the two ACAS processes is that conciliation is the term used to describe the ADR process if an employee has made or may make a claim to an employment tribunal. Mediation is used to resolve workplace disputes with the aim of restoring and maintaining the employment relationship between the parties. **18.06**

Post-claim conciliation

ACAS has a statutory duty to offer conciliation to the parties after a claim has been made to the employment tribunal in respect of employment rights. The aim is to help the parties to find a solution to the dispute without the need for a tribunal hearing. The conciliation service is voluntary and free of charge to the parties. ACAS conciliators are impartial and independent and they are not part of the Employment Tribunal Service. The conciliator will not impose a solution on the parties but will facilitate negotiations between the parties and assist them to reach their own solution. The parties can reach a settlement that a tribunal has no power to order (for example the provision of a reference, perhaps in agreed terms). ACAS conciliation is confidential and the tribunal will not be given details of what took place during the conciliation if settlement is not reached (Employment Tribunals Act 1996 s 18(7)). ACAS report on their website that about 75% of all claims made in employment tribunals are resolved by ACAS conciliation. **18.07**

The process

18.08 • When a complaint is lodged by a party in the employment tribunal, a copy will be forwarded by the tribunal to ACAS, who will then contact the parties to the dispute and offer conciliation to them.

• If all parties to the dispute agree to use the conciliation service, then ACAS will set up a conciliation meeting with the parties and the conciliator to explore settlement of the dispute. The parties will have no choice over the selection of a conciliator.

• At the meeting, the conciliator will explain the process, his role, and explore each party's case and discuss proposals for settlement with each party.

• If settlement is reached, it will be recorded on an ACAS settlement form and be signed by both parties. It will be legally binding on the parties.

• ACAS will inform the tribunal that settlement has been reached.

• If settlement is not reached at the conciliation, then the case will proceed to a hearing in the tribunal.

18.09 It is not the function of an ACAS conciliator to ensure that the terms of settlement are fair to the parties, and nor should he advise the parties about the merits or likely outcome of the case (*Clarke v Redcar & Cleveland Borough Council* [2006] IRLR 324).

Pre-claim conciliation

18.10 Since 9 April 2009, ACAS has a statutory discretion or power (not a statutory duty) to provide conciliation to parties who are *considering* making a claim to a tribunal in any type of workplace dispute (Employment Tribunals Act 1996 s 18(2)–(3) as substituted by Employment Act 2005 s 5). This is free of charge to the parties. ACAS will only exercise their discretion to offer conciliation in such cases if:

• the parties have already tried to resolve the dispute (perhaps through a grievance or complaints procedure);

• there are grounds to believe that a valid claim is likely to be made by a party eligible to make the claim;

• providing a conciliation service will not interfere with good employment relations in the employer's organisation, such as collective agreements and procedures.

18.11 Sometimes conciliation cannot be offered in a particular case due to high demand for ACAS services at that time. If that occurs, ACAS will select cases for conciliation on the basis of criteria that give priority to disputes in which conciliation is most likely to be of benefit (see the *Guidance Note: Conciliation in cases that could be the subject of employment tribunal proceedings after 6 April 2009* on www.acas.org.uk).

18.12 If conciliation is attempted before a claim is issued in the tribunal, it is the employee's responsibility to ensure that he complies with any time limits that may apply for making such a claim.

Collective conciliation

18.13 This is a term used to describe talks between representative groups such as trade unions and employers, which are facilitated by ACAS.

CONCILIATION IN FAMILY CASES

Conciliation is commonly employed in family disputes where the choice of process is driven **18.14**
by the court rather than the parties. In-court conciliation is offered in disputes by parents
over children on the breakdown of a marriage.

The process

In-court conciliation consists of a meeting at court, usually lasting around 30 minutes, **18.15**
between the parents with the assistance of a neutral independent party from the Children
and Family Court Advisory and Support Service (Cafcass) to help them to negotiate disputes
relating to contact and residence arrangements for children following separation or divorce.
The aim is to help them to resolve their dispute without the need for court intervention.
In-court conciliation is delivered by Cafcass in every county court in England and Wales
and in some magistrates' courts that handle family cases.

In family law cases, conciliation occurs in the following ways: **18.16**

- Conciliation appointments will be arranged before the district judge or registrar. The
  Principal Registry of the Family Division operates several conciliation lists each week.
- The parties will outline the nature of the application and the matters in dispute to the
  district judge and the Cafcass officer.
- The conciliation appointment will then be conducted with a view to the parties reaching
  an agreement about the arrangements concerning the children.
- All discussions at the conciliation appointment are privileged and will not be disclosed in
  any subsequent hearing other than a further conciliation appointment.
- If agreement is reached, the district judge will make the relevant orders by consent.
- If agreement is not reached, then the district judge will give directions for the hearing of the application. The Cafcass officer and the district judge will not be involved
  in any further applications between the parties other than further conciliation
  appointments.

Other conciliation schemes

Healthcare providers

The Independent Doctor's Forum (IDF) was formed to represent doctors in general practice **18.17**
and consultants carrying out private work in addition to their NHS work. The organisation
has implemented a code for complaints, which provides for complaints to be determined in
three stages. The first stage involves the doctor meeting with the patient to reach a resolution of the matter. If that does not resolve the complaint, it will be referred to conciliation. A
conciliator will be provided by IDF who will meet with the parties, and then make a written
report rejecting or upholding the complaint. If it is upheld the conciliator will put forward
proposals for resolving it. If the complaint cannot be resolved after conciliation, it will be
referred to mediation.

Many NHS trusts also operate conciliation schemes to resolve complaints. **18.18**

The Disability Conciliation Service

18.19 The Disability Conciliation Service (now known as The Equalities Mediation Service) offers individuals with a disability the opportunity to resolve disputes under the Disability Discrimination Act 1995 in relation to discrimination in the provision of goods, services, education and employment instead of pursuing court or tribunal proceedings (see www. dcs-gb.com). A conciliator will assist the parties to help them resolve the dispute. The service is free to the parties as it is funded by the Equality and Human Rights Commission (EHRC). Referrals to the Scheme must be made by the EHRC. For more details on the scheme see www.adrnow.org.uk.

The Furniture Ombudsmen Conciliation Scheme

18.20 The Furniture Ombudsmen (TFO) is an independent organisation offering ADR services for consumers of the furniture, home improvements and floor coverings industry. It is overseen by Trading Standards and by representatives of retailers and manufacturers. The service is available to consumers who purchase goods or services from members of TFO. A list of organisations who are members is available at www.thefurnitureombudsman.org/services). The TFO conciliator will look at the matters in dispute, at no cost to the consumer, and put forward proposals to enable the matter to be resolved. Consumers must try to resolve the complaint with the member using any internal complaints procedure before using the Scheme.

KEY POINTS SUMMARY

18.21
- Conciliation is very similar to mediation. The terms 'conciliation' and 'mediation' can be used interchangeably to describe the same process in some countries and by some commentators.
- In England and Wales, conciliation tends to be court-driven and it is most often used in family and employment cases.
- It is useful when the parties would benefit from the assistance of a neutral party to help them to settle their dispute.
- In employment cases, a free conciliation scheme is offered by ACAS where a claim has been, or is likely to be, made in the employment tribunal.
- In-court conciliation also takes place in family cases in disputes over contact and residence arrangements over children on the breakdown of the relationship between the parties.
- A number of independent conciliation schemes exist to help consumers solve disputes in relation to goods or services.

19

COMPLAINTS, GRIEVANCES AND OMBUDSMEN

INTRODUCTION. 19.01

COMPLAINTS AND GRIEVANCE PROCEDURES. 19.02

OMBUDSMEN 19.17

KEY POINTS SUMMARY. 19.29

INTRODUCTION

Grievance, complaints and ombudsman schemes are designed to provide effective and **19.01** speedy relief where problems arise between a customer and an organisation. It is recognised that the customer often wants no more than an explanation or an apology (such as in relation to medical care). These schemes seek to provide a local or in-house solution when a problem arises. However, complaints procedures have themselves grown in sophistication, and increasingly they provide for 'appeals' to national bodies where a matter cannot be resolved by the local organisation.

COMPLAINTS AND GRIEVANCE PROCEDURES

It has become increasingly common for companies and organisations that offer goods **19.02** or services to the general public to have internal complaints and grievance procedures to look into and respond to any problems raised by their customers of a formal nature. It is seen to be good for customer relations for problems to be investigated by someone within the organisation and for the problem to be resolved with the customer quickly and before it escalates into a contentious dispute. Efficient and effective complaints and grievance procedures also form part of an organisation's quality control or quality assurance procedures, which are aimed at ensuring that high levels of service are maintained, with any weaknesses being addressed swiftly before other customers are affected by similar problems.

19.03 In many areas of activity, having a formal complaints or grievance policy is simply a matter of good practice. In others, having these procedures may be:

- a requirement of a relevant code of professional conduct, such as the need to have a client complaints procedure for solicitors (Solicitors' Code of Conduct 2007, para. 2.05) and barristers (Bar Code of Conduct, para. 403.2(d));
- a statutory requirement, as in the case of grievance and disciplinary procedures in employment law (Employment Act 2002).

Definitions

19.04 'Complaints' and 'grievances' are obviously related concepts. According to ACAS (the Advisory, Conciliation and Advisory Service in relation to employment matters), a grievance is a concern, problem or complaint that an employee might raise with their employer, which would mean that complaints are subsumed within the general umbrella of 'grievances'. This is an area where there is a lack of generally agreed definitions, but for clarity:

- a 'complaint' may be regarded as a problem raised in the context of a one-off transaction or incident. Examples may include a defective item that has been purchased, or misleading advice, or a bad service given on a particular occasion; and
- a 'grievance' arises in the context of a continuing relationship, particularly that between employees and employers.

19.05 'Complaints' are often divided into formal and informal complaints. Usually the difference is that a formal complaint has to be made in writing, or on a complaints form prescribed by the relevant policy of the organisation. Most complaints procedures and policies only apply to formal, written, complaints. Informal complaints (those made orally, or not on the relevant form etc) may well be responded to, but not under the relevant complaints procedure, and probably without the investigation involved in a formal complaint.

Complaints, including legal profession complaints

19.06 Complaints are usually the first stage of resolution for many disagreements that members of the public have with companies or government departments. Some complaints procedures are handled at a local level, often informally. For example, the Bar Standards Board and the Solicitors Regulatory Authority both say that initially complaints should be made to the barrister's chambers or the solicitor's firm. It is if the complainant is unhappy with the response from chambers or the firm that a further complaint may be made to the professional regulator (Bar Standards Board or Solicitors' Regulatory Authority, Legal Complaints Service). The legal professional regulators have their own, highly developed, procedures for dealing with complaints that are not resolved by chambers or the firm. These procedures are likely to be replaced when the Office for Legal Complaints, which is being established as part of the changes made by the Legal Services Act 2007, begins operations in late 2010. A detailed complaint form needs to be completed and sent to the regulator. How the complaint will be dealt with depends on the circumstances. Some are dismissed after initial fact finding. Others are dealt with by conciliation between the client and firm (see Chapter 18). Others are investigated and end with a formal decision together with, if appropriate, a remedy for the complainant.

Employment grievances

A wide range of matters may be raised in employment grievances. These include: **19.07**

- an employee's contractual terms and conditions;
- new working practices and organisational changes;
- health and safety issues;
- bullying and harassment;
- equal opportunities.

Most employment grievances should be capable of being resolved amicably and quickly **19.08**
through discussions between the employee and their line manager. Others are best resolved
with the assistance of mediation (see Chapters 11–13). When a grievance affects several
employees in a similar way it may be necessary to have the interests of the employees represented by the relevant trade union. Where an employment-related grievance cannot be
resolved between the employee and employer, it may be necessary to refer the matter to
ACAS, which has a range of conciliation (see Chapter 18), mediation and other procedures
available to it together with considerable experience in resolving employment disputes.

Raising a complaint or grievance

Different organisations will have their own complaints and grievance policies, which vary **19.09**
quite widely in terms of detail and the different procedures that must be followed. Most
will start with the complainant lodging a formal complaint in writing. Many complaints
schemes have official complaints forms that must be used. There is often a fairly short time
limit for lodging the complaint.

An example of an employment grievance is shown in Figure 19.1. This example is worded **19.10**
in a fairly formal way, typical of the drafting to be expected from a lawyer. Many formal
complaints and grievances are written by the person affected, who will not be a lawyer and
who cannot be expected to set the matter out in the structured way shown in Figure 19.1. It
will be seen that in this case the written grievance makes specific reference to the company's
relevant policy document, sets out the incidents complained about, and indicates that what
has happened breaches the policy. It ends by setting out what the complainant wants to
achieve if the grievance is upheld. A large number of complaints and grievances are based
on anonymous information, and an example can be seen in para (c) of Figure 19.1. Most
organisations rightly refuse to investigate anonymous complaints, particularly when they
relate to the conduct of staff. This is because it is grossly unfair to the person identified in
such a complaint, who cannot reasonably be expected to respond to an incident involving
an unidentified person. Allegation (c) in this case would almost certainly be dismissed for
this reason.

Investigation and determination of complaints and grievances

The organisation will acknowledge receipt of the complaint in writing, and indicate a period **19.11**
over which it is intended that the matter will be investigated and a decision reached. A person (the 'investigator'), or sometimes a panel, typically of three people, will be designated by
the organisation to investigate the matter. Some procedures give the investigation and decision-making responsibilities to a single person. Others designate one person to investigate,

Figure 19.1 Employment grievance

Grievance

This Grievance is being made because I feel that bullying, intimidation and drunkenness by [*name of manager*] have not been dealt with seriously enough by the company. The company's Harassment and Dignity at Work policy document states:

'The company takes the issue of harassment and bullying very seriously and is committed to a working environment that is free from discrimination and intimidation, and in which the dignity of the individual is paramount.'

The policy also states:

• Individuals should have confidence to complain about harassment and bullying should it arise (clause 2)
• Staff are required to make it clear they find such behaviour unacceptable (clause 4)
• The company will foster a climate that discourages the occurrence of harassment and bullying (clause 10)
• The company will act upon potential breaches of this policy and unacceptable behaviour despite the absence of a formal complaint (clause 11)

There are three related matters:

a) On 15 July 2010 [*name of manager*] had been to the pub and was drunk. He exploded in anger over a batch of invoices which were a day late in being sent out. My supervisor wrote an email to him on 16 July saying: 'You cannot continue being so aggressive with members of staff. We all have to work together, and staff cannot cope with being bullied and belittled when due to pressures of work some things have to be slightly delayed.'
b) [*Name of manager*] swore at me repeatedly in a meeting I had with him on 26 July 2010 about 3.30pm. He repeatedly used the word 'f…ing' to describe me and a report I had sent to him. He was shouting at me, and refused to listen and talked over me when I tried to give an explanation to him. His breath smelt of alcohol on this occasion too.
c) These were not isolated incidents. I know of two occasions when [*name of manager*] was swearing and shouting at a female member of staff in the main office. This member of staff wants to remain anonymous, and has told me she will not make a formal complaint because, she says, it is far too dangerous to complain against [*name of manager*]. This shows that staff believe they will not be supported by the company if they make complaints about bullying.

The above falls within the definition of bullying set out in the company's policy, which includes:

• Using abusive language
• Shouting at or humiliating an individual in front of colleagues or in private

I raised these matters informally with [*name of senior manager*] on 27 July 2010.

What I would like is an assurance that the company's Harassment and Dignity at Work policy will be honoured. This should include taking these matters very seriously, and not tolerating conduct which creates an intimidating, hostile, degrading or humiliating environment. I would also like to know what if any disciplinary action is being taken against [*name of manager*].

Signed

Date   9 August 2010

who reports to a more senior person who makes the decision on the basis of the report. Some matters will be dealt with entirely on the basis of written materials. In others the complainant, and then any employees involved, will be interviewed, followed by a decision. In others there will be a meeting where the facts relating to the complaint will be raised and considered. Most complaints and grievance policies say very little about the investigation process, leaving a great deal to the discretion and good sense of the investigator or panel. Where the policy sets out a specific procedure, that of course should be followed.

When acting for either a complainant or the person against whom a complaint is raised, **19.12** it is first necessary to get the full story, both from the person involved and from the relevant documents. This may involve some investigation of what documents are or should be available. It may also become clear that other people may need to be contacted to find out what they know. It is vital to obtain a copy of the relevant complaints procedure or policy, together with any of the company's written procedures or guidance notes that may be relevant. It may be that a meeting or hearing will have been already convened by the company or organisation but, if not, consideration should be given to whether this would be helpful in conveying the case of the person who is being represented. Sometimes they will be best advised to have a matter considered on the papers, but in many cases, particularly serious matters, they will only have their side of events fully considered at a meeting or hearing.

Most investigators or panels will tailor the amount of time spent in investigating a matter **19.13** and the degree of formality to the nature of the complaint and its seriousness. The guiding principles are the rules of natural justice. These mean that anyone who may have an adverse finding against them must be notified of the nature of the allegations being made, and be given a reasonable opportunity to respond to them. Most investigators will also want to ensure that the real complaint is looked into, so will often meet with the complainant to ensure they have fully understood what lies behind the complaint.

Meetings and hearings take a variety of different forms. They usually start with the person **19.14** chairing the meeting getting each person to introduce themselves, and then explaining the nature of the investigation. The complainant is often asked to say what they are seeking from the investigation. The meeting can then take a number of different courses, from a general discussion to something more resembling a court hearing with questions being put to the different people in turn. Whatever form it takes, each person directly involved must be given a fair chance to state their case.

Decisions in complaints and grievance investigations

The primary decision that needs to be made is whether to uphold or dismiss the complaint **19.15** or grievance. This may be done at the meeting, or by letter shortly afterwards. It is best practice to give reasons for the decision, although these are usually short. Organisations should keep records of successful and unsuccessful complaints, and good practice is to take appropriate action to rectify problems identified by the process for the benefit of future customers and employees. Typical outcomes that may be available in an individual matter under different complaints and grievance processes include:

- an explanation;
- an apology;
- compensation;

- reduction of a bill or a refund;
- disciplinary action.

Effectiveness of complaints and grievance procedures

19.16 Grievance and complaints procedures can be quick, may cost nothing to the complainant, and can produce helpful solutions. However, many complaints procedures are inefficient and may take a long time to complete. Objections are sometimes raised that complaints procedures are not independent, because they are operated by the organisation against which the complaint is raised. If a complaints procedure does not produce the desired result, it may be necessary to take the matter further, such as through litigation, or with an ombudsman.

OMBUDSMEN

19.17 Ombudsmen act rather like umpires in complaints brought by individuals and public or private organisations. There are ombudsmen schemes for a range of different consumer services, including many professions, public utility companies such as energy, water, and telephones, and financial services such as banks and insurance companies. If an organisation is a member of an ombudsman scheme, it should make this clear in a brochure or on its letterhead. Most ombudsmen belong to the British and Irish Ombudsman Association (BIOA), which can provide information about the available public and private sector ombudsman schemes. Its website is www.bioa.org.uk.

19.18 Important ombudsmen include the Local Government Ombudsman (England) and the Parliamentary Ombudsman. The Local Government Ombudsman deals with complaints about services provided by local authorities in England: see www.lgo.org.uk.

19.19 The Parliamentary and Health Service Ombudsman deals with complaints about services provided by government departments and the NHS in England, the relevant website being www.ombudsman.org.uk.

Complaints handling by ombudsmen

19.20 Ombudsmen are independent from the organisations they investigate. Ombudsmen schemes usually provide that reference to the ombudsman is only permitted after attempting to resolve the complaint through an organisation's internal complaints procedure. Ombudsmen therefore frequently deal with the more difficult complaints that cannot be resolved by an organisation's internal complaints system. How complaints are investigated under ombudsman schemes varies considerably, but good practice has been formulated in the BOIA's *Guide to Principles of Good Complaints Handling*. Two key goals are that:

- complaints must be considered impartially and on their merits; and
- independent judgment must be brought to bear.

19.21 In order to achieve these aims, the *Guide to Principles of Good Complaints Handling* says that ombudsman schemes should be designed to comply with the following seven principles:

- *clarity of purpose*, with a clear statement of the role of the ombudsman and the aims of the scheme;

- *accessibility*, so that the scheme is free and open to anyone who needs to use it;
- *flexible procedures*, which can be adjusted to meet the requirements of each case. The *Guide* makes the point that it is important that each complainant is made to feel they are being treated as an individual with their complaint being dealt with on its own merits;
- *transparency*, so that information is readily available;
- *proportionality*, so that the process used is appropriate to the complaint;
- *efficiency*; and
- *quality outcomes*, with the process leading to positive change.

Procedure on references to ombudsmen

Many schemes provide that there will be a governing body with a chair and members who oversee the scheme. Most schemes use a 'documents-only' process. They may be started by a letter or the completion of a complaints form. The depth of any particular investigation will depend on the nature and complexity of the complaint. In some cases the primary function of the ombudsman is to explain the decision-making process or to provide other information to the complainant because the complaint is essentially one where the complainant does not understand what has been done because it has not previously been clearly explained. In most other cases the ombudsman has to enter into detailed correspondence with the complainant and the organisation in an attempt to identify exactly what lies behind the complaint, and to get the organisation's explanation for what it has done. In seeking to do this the ombudsman has to abide by the rules of natural justice, and an obvious danger here is that it is possible for the correspondence to become unbalanced, with either the complainant or the organisation appearing to be consulted more frequently than the other. There is no rule that there should be an equal number of letters to each party, but the ombudsman must be careful to ensure there is no appearance of favouring one side over the other. **19.22**

Ombudsmen are required to reach evidence-based decisions, having investigated the matter and after careful analysis of the evidence. It is therefore important the parties provide the ombudsman with the available contemporaneous documentation and any other relevant evidence, rather than basing what they say solely on assertions in their letters. **19.23**

Grounds on which ombudsmen make their decisions

Public sector ombudsmen normally only review how a decision was made, not whether it was right, and uphold a complaint if there was 'maladministration' that resulted in an injustice. Maladministration can include: **19.24**

- a public body not following its own policies or procedures;
- rudeness;
- taking too long;
- failing to act;
- treating the complainant less fairly than other people; and
- giving wrong or misleading information.

Private sector ombudsmen may come to a decision against the organisation on any of the above grounds, and also if it is felt that the organisation's conduct was unfair or unreasonable when compared with industry standards of good practice. **19.25**

Effect of ombudsman's decision

19.26 Decisions made by ombudsmen may or may not be binding, depending on the terms of the particular scheme. An example of a scheme that produces binding decisions is the Pensions Ombudsman, but this should be regarded as rather exceptional. While a government department is not bound by the findings of the Parliamentary Ombudsman, it may only reject the Ombudsman's findings if doing so is not irrational (*R (Bradley) v Secretary of State for Work & Pensions* [2009] QB 114).

19.27 Compensation is usually only available in private sector schemes. The primary relief in public sector schemes is the review of a decision or act of a government department or local authority, with a changed decision being the ultimate goal of the complainant. There are a number of cases where an apology will be the primary relief given.

19.28 In non-binding schemes complainants are able to bring court proceedings if they are not satisfied with the result. For the most part organisations will abide by ombudsmen's decisions, even though they are non-binding. A particular value of such schemes is that an impartial decision is obtained without the expense of litigation, which will be lost if the organisation does not honour the decision. In some schemes the decision is published, which may act as an additional incentive to put right anything identified by the ombudsman's decision.

KEY POINTS SUMMARY

19.29
- There is a large range of complaints, grievance and ombudsman schemes.
- Each one has its own procedure, which should be brought to the attention of customers and made available to them when asked for.
- These schemes usually seek an amicable resolution of the matter.
- If the procedure includes reaching a decision, in the absence of a contract to be bound it will only be binding on the professional person (through their professional code of conduct).
- These schemes can be quick and inexpensive. They can be time consuming, particularly if there is an appeal mechanism, and they can be ineffective.

PART 5

RECORDING SETTLEMENT

20

RECORDING SETTLEMENT

REACHING A CLEAR OUTCOME 20.01

FORMS OF RECORDED OUTCOME 20.07

RECORDS MADE DURING THE ADR PROCESS. 20.11

WHO SHOULD PRODUCE A FORMAL RECORD 20.14

ENFORCEABLE FORMS FOR RECORDING SETTLEMENT 20.16

DRAFTING TERMS OF SETTLEMENT. 20.23

METHODS OF RECORDING SETTLEMENT AGREEMENTS. 20.24

TERMS AS REGARDS COSTS. 20.55

INFORMING THE COURT OF SETTLEMENT 20.60

KEY POINTS SUMMARY. 20.61

REACHING A CLEAR OUTCOME

20.01 The purpose of an ADR process is to resolve a dispute. For the dispute to be effectively resolved there needs to be sufficient clarity about the outcome. If the basis for resolution is not sufficiently clear, detailed and comprehensive, there is a risk that the dispute will continue on some matters, or that a further dispute will arise over the outcome. In non-adjudicative processes there is a wide range of possible outcomes (see 10.122–10.127 for negotiated settlements and 13.46–13.49 in relation to mediation). In adjudicative processes, while the main focus will be on settling the dispute or difference, a settlement can still include terms going outside that dispute. Once a settlement has been agreed it needs to be recorded.

20.02 The relative informality of some ADR processes compared to litigation can lead to difficulties as regards outcome. A focus on key issues can lead to less central issues being overlooked. Particularly where the agreement is essentially oral, as in negotiation or mediation, something may be left a little vague to achieve an agreement, or each party may have a slightly different understanding of what has been agreed. As a party's representative, you should address rather than ignore such problems as they may lead to a breakdown in the agreement.

20.03   Recording a settlement is the final part of the ADR process, and the lawyer has several responsibilities in ensuring that the process is completed properly. They should ensure:

- the terms are comprehensive. They should cover everything at issue;
- each term is clear and sufficiently detailed;
- the client understands the agreement. The lawyer should explain to client what each side must do and not do under the agreement;
- the client accepts the agreement. Where the agreement is subject to client consent, the lawyer must provide the client with sufficient information and advice to ensure that the client takes an informed decision as to whether to accept the agreement;
- the terms are appropriately recorded. The options for this are given in this chapter;
- the terms are appropriately enforceable. The lawyer should explain to the client what steps may be taken if either side does not comply with the agreement: see Chapter 29.

20.04   It may not be easy to persuade your client to approve the terms of a compromise, especially following a difficult negotiation or mediation. The client may feel that the provisional agreement falls too far short of their objectives, especially if the client does not take a realistic view of the weaknesses of their case or the difficulties of obtaining certain concessions from the other side. It is important to prepare your client for the potential outcome in advance, and to do all you can to ensure your client is fully informed of the risks and benefits of the provisional settlement. Ultimately, it is the client's decision whether to accept a compromise, and the lawyer's role is to advise the client rather than imposing their own views on the client. You will also have to review whether there are other options such as ongoing litigation, and perhaps whether you can continue to represent the client if the client refuses a provisional settlement. In such a case the other side must be informed of the client's decision.

20.05   There can be a particular problem where the lawyer is acting under a conditional fee agreement, because the refusal of the client to accept a proposed settlement has implications for what the lawyer may recover in the case, and whether further costs should be incurred in pursuing the case when the lawyer feels it should be settled. Solicitors (under the Solicitor's Code of Conduct 2007) and barristers (under the Bar Council Conditional Fee Guidance) are under professional obligations to promote the client's best interests when advising on a settlement, without regard to the lawyer's own interests or any consequences for the lawyer. If there is a disagreement, careful consideration must be given to the lay client's interests, and whether the client might be left without legal representation. The lawyer should consider very carefully whether they are entitled to withdraw from the case if the client will not approve the settlement. This may be appropriate if, for example, the client had mislead the lawyer about the strength of the case.

20.06   Also note that if you are acting for a publicly funded client who does not accept an offer of settlement the client should be warned that there should be a report to the Community Legal Service, which may lead to funding being withdrawn.

FORMS OF RECORDED OUTCOME

20.07   The wide variety of ADR processes leads to a wide variety of outcomes.

Litigation leads to a judgment, which will be final and binding as regards all matters in dis-   **20.08**
pute, unless there is a successful appeal. An adjudicative form of ADR can lead to a similarly
binding outcome. Non-adjudicative ADR leads to a compromise, which is normally worded
to be in 'full and final settlement' of those matters that are resolved in the compromise.

The range of options is broadly as follows: **20.09**

- An adjudicative process such as arbitration will lead to a written decision such as an
  agreed arbitration award (see Chapter 27). This decision should cover all relevant matters,
  such as interest and costs. An expert determination will also produce a written decision
  (see Chapter 21).
- A non-adjudicative process can also lead to a written report from a third party, as for
  example happens with early neutral evaluation (see Chapter 17). This report will not provide a final outcome, but will inform further discussion between the parties.
- Some processes lead to relatively simple or limited outcomes. For example an ombudsman
  will often produce a letter (see Chapter 19).
- The outcome of some processes is not always clear or set. For example a grievance resolution scheme or conciliation will not necessarily reach any definite outcome, so long as the
  concern raised is addressed (see Chapters 18 and 19).
- The major processes of mediation and negotiation normally result in an oral agreement. It is here that most potential issues arise with regard to ensuring that what is
  agreed is properly recorded, and this chapter deals largely with the outcomes of these
  processes.

Note that the form of outcome is often at least partly governed by the original agreement   **20.10**
to enter ADR, for example a mediation agreement can include a statement of what form of
outcome is anticipated.

RECORDS MADE DURING THE ADR PROCESS

It is vital to keep a clear record of what is being agreed or provisionally agreed during a   **20.11**
negotiation or mediation. Make sure the record is sufficiently detailed and accurate—
you may think you will remember points but it is easy to forget, and quickly written
notes can be difficult to interpret later. You must check what is agreed—it is all too
common for the lawyers to have a slightly different understanding of what is agreed.
One lawyer can make a record and check the wording with the other. In a mediation,
the mediator will normally assist with the recording process as proposals are raised and
discussed.

At the end of a mediation or negotiation it is crucial to take time to agree a written version   **20.12**
of the terms agreed, see 10.122–10.127 and 13.46–13.49. It is advisable to write this note of
terms clearly on a fresh sheet of paper, to avoid any possible confusion from crossing out or
amendment, and that the lawyers on both sides check the wording. Normally one lawyer
will make a full note of the terms agreed, and check the words written down with the opponent. A copy of the note might be made and handed over straight away.

An accurate record may be needed for various purposes—as a basis for reporting to a judge   **20.13**
in court if you have negotiated outside court, or to provide a basis from which to write a

letter or contract. You may need a copy for the judge if your terms need court approval in an interim or consent order.

WHO SHOULD PRODUCE A FORMAL RECORD

20.14   You must agree who will draft the letter, contract or order that will formally record the outcome. The lawyers for one side will produce a draft in the form agreed, and send it to the lawyers on the other side for agreement. There may be an advantage to the side that agrees to do the draft as they will have some control over the written detail, though note that the side drawing up the document will also bear the costs of doing so unless it has been agreed that the costs be shared.

20.15   In addition to agreeing who should produce the draft it should be agreed when the draft will be sent to the other parties and who should pay the costs. Note that the wording of a draft order is subject to the discretion of the judge, even if it is an agreed consent order.

ENFORCEABLE FORMS FOR RECORDING SETTLEMENT

20.16   Any form of written or oral statement can set out the terms of a settlement. If the dispute is settled by an explanation, a clarification or an apology then nothing further may be needed. However when a dispute relating to legal rights is settled it will normally be in the interests of both parties to record the outcome in a form that is legally enforceable. It is important to understand what the options are, and to appreciate that some forms of ADR lead to more than one option, so that the most appropriate option needs to be chosen.

An oral contract

20.17   Non-adjudicative ADR processes often lead to an oral contract. Once both parties say they have reached agreement and the basic requirements of a contract exist (that is the terms are sufficiently certain, there is some form of consideration etc) there will be an enforceable contract: see *Chanel v FW Woolworth* [1981] 1 All ER 745 and *Soulsbury v Soulsbury* (2007) Times, 14 November. Once a contract is made it may be difficult or impossible to vary it or to challenge it in court. If that agreement is conditional, for example on the approval of the client, that condition must be stated at the time, and will need to be fulfilled.

A written contract

20.18   Non-adjudicative ADR processes also commonly lead to a written contract, either because the process was wholly or partly conducted in writing, or because the oral agreement is reduced to a written contract. If an oral agreement is to be recorded as a written contract it is important to be clear whether the oral terms are final, or will only become final once the written terms are agreed. Normal contractual principles will apply.

An award with statutory authority

Some awards carry statutory or other regulatory authority, because the ADR process is governed by statute or regulation (see Chapter 29). **20.19**

A court order

An ADR process can be wholly or partly incorporated into a court judgment, but only where proceedings have been issued. There are some restrictions in the CPR, Part 2, over which judges have jurisdiction to make certain orders, and the judge may not be prepared to make an order in the terms sought. Settlements restricted to common law relief (money, delivery of goods), the stay or dismissal of the case, and costs, can be made as consent orders without involving a judge (CPR 40.6). Where no proceedings have been issued there will be no basis for a judge to make an order. If the terms of an interim order are agreed by negotiation a judge can be asked to make an interim order in the terms agreed. **20.20**

Other legal documents

The terms of an agreement can be wholly or partly incorporated into some other appropriate form, such as a deed or conveyance. It may be agreed to vary or amend an existing contract, if for example the parties agree to vary an existing commercial relationship. **20.21**

The main difference between these options is that where a court is involved the terms can normally be enforced by returning to court within the existing proceedings. If the court is not involved it may be necessary to issue new proceedings for breach of contract to enforce the settlement (see Chapter 29). The above options are not mutually exclusive—an agreed interim order might deal with some terms with others being put into a separate contract. **20.22**

DRAFTING TERMS OF SETTLEMENT

Some points will apply to all forms of written settlement document. **20.23**

- The terms must be comprehensive and accurate—once the terms have been reduced to writing and agreed it will be difficult or impossible to argue that any additional oral term is part of the final agreement.
- All practical details should be included such as dates by which actions such as payment should be carried out.
- Court powers to award interest and make orders as to costs will only apply to a court order. Both matters should be dealt with specifically in an order or contract: *President of India v La Pintada Cia Navegacion* [1984] 2 All ER 773. If there is no mention of costs, each side will have to bear their own.
- Some enforcement options can be built in—for example that a payment will carry interest if it is not made on time. In doing so, be careful to avoid the term amounting to a penalty clause (under contract law). Alternatively, one term can be made a precondition to another.
- As a general matter, ensure the terms are enforceable—for example they do not seek to affect third party rights, unless the third party agrees to be bound.

- Double check the draft to avoid any vagueness or ambiguity that may have been left at the end of the ADR process.
- The terms may usefully bear in mind any foreseeable future events that may affect them, so that the agreement covers and is not undermined by foreseeable change, if for example there will be a continuing relationship,

METHODS OF RECORDING SETTLEMENT AGREEMENTS

Exchange of letters

20.24   It is common for the solicitor for one side to write a letter setting out terms of settlement, with the solicitors for the other side replying to indicate agreement. This is appropriate for a wide range of settlements in non-adjudicative ADR where there is no particular need for any more formal document. It is commonly used where proceedings have not been issued so a court order is not an option. It can also be used after proceedings have been issued if there is no particular need for a court order. An exchange of letters will normally be relatively cost effective. A typical exchange of letters settling a dispute can be seen in Figures 20.1 and 20.2.

20.25   It will need to be agreed which solicitor writes the first letter, and that solicitor will need to work from a full and accurate note of what was agreed. If the solicitor was involved in the negotiation or mediation this may be the solicitor's note; otherwise the solicitor will need a full note from the barrister.

20.26   An exchange of letters can form a contract in itself without any face-to-face ADR process where there is an appropriate offer and acceptance. A chain of letters on a single issue does not necessarily amount to a settlement: *Jackson v Tharker* [2007] EWHC 271 (TCC). If there has been a face-to-face process then the letters will evidence the oral agreement that was reached.

Contract or deed

Whether a contract is required or appropriate

20.27   Although there is no essential legal difference between a contract formed or evidenced in letters and a contract recorded in a separate document, there are circumstances where it may be preferable to have a separate signed contract or deed. Sometimes a specific form of contract may be needed to implement an agreement, for example matters which by law have to be evidenced or made in writing. Examples where writing is required include consumer credit agreements (Consumer Credit Act 1974 ss 60, 61 and 65), legal assignments (Law of Property Act 1925 s 136), guarantees (Statute of Frauds 1677 s 4), and contracts for the sale or disposition of land (Law of Property (Miscellaneous Provisions) Act 1989 s 2).

20.28   A contract or deed may be appropriate where the terms are complex, or where the outcome is particularly important and the parties want a formal separate legal document for later reference. A contract may be particularly appropriate where there will be an ongoing commercial relationship. If there is already a contract between the parties it is necessary to decide

Figure 20.1 Letter setting out terms of a negotiated settlement

16 September 2010

Dear Sir,

Groovy Music Ltd v Tracey Green

I am writing to you to record the terms of negotiated settlement of this case reached by counsel for the parties on 10 September 2010. These terms were subject to client approval, and we are pleased to inform you that our client, the claimant in these proceedings, has approved the terms. Please can you confirm in your reply that your client has also accepted the terms.

I am informed by counsel that the terms agreed are as follows:

1. There should be a new contract between the parties to commence on 1 November 2010. From that date this will replace the existing contract between the parties, which has been the subject of this dispute. The new contract will run for three years and be renewable. It will provide that the copyright of all songs written by the defendant within that period will vest in the claimant, and that the claimant will bear all costs of recording and publicising an album of twelve songs by the defendant, the album to be released within the contract period. All profit from merchandising will be shared equally by the parties. The defendant and a representative of the claimant will meet before 14 November 2010 to agree full detailed terms for this contract.

2. On the basis that the existing contract does not provide clearly for merchandising rights, but that income from existing merchandising sales is broadly equal to costs incurred by the claimant in producing merchandise, no payment will be made with regard to income from merchandising prior to the start of the new contract referred to above.

3. The defendant will pay to the claimant the sum of £16,759 in relation to income from her songs 'Climate Change' and 'Obama Rocks', which she released in contravention of her agreement with the claimant. This sum is to be paid within fourteen days of the date of this letter.

4. The position as regards the claimant's claim regarding income from the defendant's stall in Camden Market will be settled on the basis of a report from an agreed accountant. The accountant will be agreed by 1 November 2010, and the sum found due will be paid within 14 days of that accountant producing his or her report.

5. There will be no payment with regard to the defendant's alleged loss of profit from web-based downloads. However, the claimant and the defendant will discuss the possibility of developing a 'Green Gauge' blog, and the marketing options it may provide.

6. Each party will pay their own costs, save that the claimant will bear the costs of drawing up this agreement.

I look forward to hearing from you to confirm these terms, and your client's acceptance of them.

Yours sincerely
(Solicitor for the claimant)

Figure 20.2 Letter accepting the terms in Figure 20.1

21 September 2010

Dear Sir,

Groovy Music Ltd v Tracey Green

I am writing in reply to your letter of 16 September 2010 recording proposed terms of agreement for this case.

My client is prepared to accept these terms in full and final settlement of this case. She is sorry that the relationship between our clients deteriorated to this extent, and hopes that the new contract will prove beneficial to both parties.

I understand that it was also a term that your client would withdraw its claim on the basis of these terms. My client's acceptance is on the basis that your client will do this.

We are happy to nominate Ms Sophie Bennett to act as the accountant pursuant to term 4. Please can you let us know if this is acceptable to your client—I believe she is known to your client.

Yours sincerely,
(Solicitor for the defendant)

whether that contract will be varied or replaced, and to make that clear. It may sometimes be appropriate for some of the terms agreed to be put into a contract and others separately recorded, for example in covering letters.

20.29 A contract or deed may be appropriate where proceedings have not been issued, or where they have been issued but there is no need for court involvement in the settlement. A deed may be more appropriate than a contract in relatively limited circumstances where formality is important (for example as regards rights over land), or where it is not clear that one party is providing consideration, so there might otherwise be doubts over validity.

Drafting the contract or deed

20.30 The contract or deed will be a separately legally enforceable document, and all the normal rules for drafting such documents need to be followed. Normally the contract will be drawn up by the solicitor for one side and sent to the solicitor for the other for agreement as to terms. As with letters, the solicitor will need to work with a clear note of what was agreed. This option may well take more lawyer time than a simpler exchange of letters. Dependant on how much time is taken in drafting and negotiating the wording of the terms, potentially this is the most expensive method of recording a settlement.

20.31 It is common to include a preamble setting out that the contract is to resolve a dispute, summarising the matters that were in dispute and are covered by the agreement. This is for clarity as regards what issues have been resolved, but it is not essential if it is not appropriate for the contract envisaged. This is followed by the agreed terms. An example can be seen in Figure 20.3.

Figure 20.3 Example of a contract settling a dispute

THIS AGREEMENT is made on 1 October 2010 between Jon Collins of the one part and Phabulous Phasions Ltd of the other part.

WHEREAS the aforesaid Jon Collins and Phabulous Phasions Ltd have been in dispute regarding alleged breaches of a contract for the supply of garments by the claimant to the defendant in a contract dated 14 January 2009.

NOW IT IS HEREBY AGREED by way of compromise of the said dispute as follows:

1. For the three years following the date of this agreement Jon Collins will produce for by Phabulous Phasions 10 spring designs (to be produced by 10 January in each year) and 10 autumn designs (to be produced by 10 June each year). Each design will be for a dress, a suit or a coat, with a mix of designs in each category.
2. Phabulous Phasions will pay to Jon Collins the sum of £23,333 in respect of designs delivered up to the date of this agreement, and interest of £2,317. This sum is to be paid within twenty eight days of the date of this agreement, with interest at 5% pa if it is not paid when due.
3. Each party will pay their own costs, save that Phabulous Phasions will pay Jon Collins the costs he incurred with regard to an application for an interim injunction on a standard basis, such costs to be assessed if not agreed.

IN FURTHERANCE OF THIS AGREEMENT:

1. Jon Collins and a representative of Phabulous Phasions will meet within one month of the date of this agreement to vary the terms of their existing contract to reflect the terms of this agreement.
2. Phabulous Phasions will return to Jon Collins the five unique outfits that he created for the Brighton Bizarre show within 14 days of the date of this agreement.

Dated:

Signed   Signed

In the presence of   In the presence of

Settlements where there are existing court proceedings

Where there are existing court proceedings there are several different ways of recording **20.32** a settlement, which are set out in Table 20.1. In addition to dealing with the terms of settlement, where there are court proceedings important issue to be agreed include how to dispose of the proceedings and the costs of the proceedings.

Endorsement on briefs

When a barrister completes any task for which she or he is briefed, the brief is returned to **20.33** instructing solicitors with a written endorsement on the back sheet. The endorsement is primarily to confirm the nature of the work that has been done, but it is also commonly

Table 20.1 Different methods of recording settlements after proceedings have started

Method of recording settlement	Circumstances where it is appropriate
Judgment may be entered for immediate payment of the sum agreed together with costs.	Where settlement is for a sum of money (usually because the claim is for a debt or for damages). Often this form is used where a settlement is reached at the door of the court, with the judgment being pronounced when the case is called on before the judge. Immediate payment means within 14 days (CPR 40.11), so is not suitable if the defendant needs time to pay. Nor is this appropriate if the defendant wants to avoid an adverse judgment for credit-scoring purposes (because it will go onto the register of judgments if it is not paid immediately).
Judgment may be entered for the agreed sum (and costs), subject to a stay of execution pending payment by stated instalments.	Similar to the above, but provision is made for the principal sum to be paid by instalments, usually because the defendant cannot afford to pay the whole amount immediately. It has the disadvantage of having an adverse credit-scoring effect on the defendant.
The court may be informed that the case has been settled upon terms endorsed on counsel's briefs. This is the most informal compromise of a claim.	This is a long-established way of recording compromises at the door of the court. It can be used in a wide range of cases, from simple debt to family law to commercial claims. It is essential that counsel for both sides endorse their briefs in identical terms.
The court may be informed that the case has been settled, the terms being recorded in a contract.	Appropriate where the terms are detailed, or where signed writing is required. The outcome of the proceedings must still be dealt with.
Entry of a consent order setting out the agreement in the form of undertakings by both parties in a series of numbered paragraphs. There will also usually be a costs provision.	This is more suitable where the dispute is about non-monetary matters, such as a claim for injunctive relief, or specific performance. The undertakings will regulate the future relationship between the parties. For consent orders see 20.39.
Consent order staying all further proceedings upon the agreed terms. If the agreement is reached immediately before a hearing the terms will usually be endorsed on counsel's briefs and the court will be asked to make a consent order in those terms.	This is similar to the above, but goes further in that the court is asked to make a consent order as well. The consent order ensures all the parties leave court being confident everyone else has the same terms in mind. The stay of the court proceedings is intended to ensure that no further steps (which will mean incurring more costs) are needed (at least while the terms are being complied with).
Consent order providing for 'no order' save as to costs, but setting out the agreed terms in recitals.	This is more appropriate for non-money claims, and brings the proceedings to a conclusion other than quantifying costs. The terms of the compromise are recorded in the recitals, which means the parties can be confident each party will have the same terms in mind.
Recording the agreement in a Tomlin order.	Tomlin orders are dealt with at 20.48–20.54. They are particularly useful where either: • the agreed terms go outside the scope of the litigation; • the parties want to keep the agreed terms confidential.

used to record the outcome of the case. When the barrister appears in court the endorsement will include the outcome, and a summary of what order has been made. If the barrister is briefed to appear in an ADR process and an agreement is reached, that is often endorsed on the backsheet.

Making the endorsement

If barristers negotiate and reach a relatively simple agreement the terms may be written onto **20.34** the backsheet of the brief. If the settlement is very straightforward, for example an agreement for payment of a single figure, no additional written record of the agreement may be needed. If there will be no other document, make sure you set out what was agreed fully and accurately, including costs etc. It would be normal for the lawyer for each party to sign the other's endorsement signifying agreement. The parties may also sign to signify their agreement—useful if the client has been reluctant to agree. Make sure the same wording is used on both briefs. An example of an endorsement on counsel's brief in a case where the terms are relatively simple, and where the settlement is reached outside court, is shown in Figure 20.4.

Effect of endorsements on briefs

The endorsement is evidence of an oral agreement. It is relatively quick and inexpensive, **20.35** but it is only appropriate where the agreement is simple. It should only be used where the clients have confirmed the terms, for example where agreement is reached outside court. Endorsement is not appropriate where the terms are still subject to client approval as that means there is not yet a final outcome. A solicitor may write a letter to confirm the terms in the endorsement, but such a letter should not seek to add anything as the agreement is complete. The endorsement has no special form of enforcement, save that if the agreement relates to an interim matter it may be possible to go back to court if there is a change of circumstances, or it may be possible to ask that an undertaking be given to the judge as regards carrying out appropriate terms. In *Green v Rozen* [1955] 1 WLR 741 terms were endorsed on counsels' briefs with the words 'By consent all proceedings stayed on terms endorsed on briefs. Liberty to apply', but it was held that these words did not reserve a right to return to court and new proceedings would be required to enforce the terms.

Figure 20.4 Example of an endorsement on a brief

JANE TURBOT

v

QUENTIN SMITH

It is hereby agreed that:

(1) The Claimant shall have ownership of the cocker spaniel dog known as 'Rufus'.
(2) The Defendant shall have ownership of the statue known as 'Life goes on'.
(3) The collection of twenty drawings accumulated by the parties shall be sold and the proceeds divided equally between the Claimant and the Defendant.
(4) The claim herein is dismissed.
(5) Each side to bear their own costs.

Signed (client)   Signed (client)

Signed (barrister)   Signed (barrister)

Dated

Interim order

20.36 An interim order will only be a possibility once proceedings have been issued, and if there has been an application for an interim order. Where an agreement is reached outside court on the terms of the application, these may be recorded as undertakings or in a consent order 20.39–20.47. A typical scenario would be where there is an application for an interim injunction and the terms of the injunction, or undertakings to be given by the respective parties, are negotiated outside court.

20.37 However, it is not uncommon for negotiations prior to interim applications to result in the settlement of the whole case rather than just the interim application. When the application is called on before the judge, an order may be made staying, adjourning or dismissing the claim on the basis of the terms agreed by the parties. The terms may be recorded in the court's order, or as a schedule, or by a separate agreement such as a contract. An example of an interim order recording a settlement is shown in Figure 20.5.

20.38 This option is only relevant in very limited circumstances—primarily where there has been an application to court for a specific order and one party is prepared to give an undertaking to the court as regards their conduct rather than having an order made. For example, if there is an application for an interim injunction a negotiation outside court might result in a compromise under which one party gives an undertaking to the court and the application is not pursued (any failure to abide by the undertaking being contempt of court). This is most likely to happen if the party who has made the application for the interim order is sufficiently concerned about events and future compliance to want some form of protection, but is prepared to concede that a full order is not necessary. The undertaking must be very clearly worded so that it is very clear what conduct will or will not breach the undertaking.

Figure 20.5 Example of interim order

IN THE LANCASTER COUNTY COURT   Claim No. 10LA3595

Before Her Honour Judge Jenkins

BETWEEN

Mr. MOHAMAD AZIZ

Claimant

and

Mrs. CLARISSA VANE

Defendant

ORDER

BY CONSENT it is ordered that the claim and counterclaim in these proceedings be adjourned generally upon the terms set out below:

1. That the Defendant pays to the Claimant the sum of £11,750 within 14 days of the date of this order.

(Continued)

Figure 20.5 Example of interim order *(Continued)*

....

2. That the Claimant returns to the Defendant her laptop computer within 28 days of the date of this order.

AND IT IS FURTHER ORDERED that in the event of the terms being carried out by the parties the claim and counterclaim be and are hereby dismissed with no order as to costs.

AND IT IS FURTHER ORDERED that in the event of any of the terms not being carried out, either party shall be at liberty to restore the claim for trial.

DATED: 11 October 2010

....

Consent order

A consent order can only be made where proceedings have been issued so that a court has **20.39** jurisdiction over the case. There is no procedure in England and Wales to go to court simply to get a consent order where litigation has not been commenced. Exceptions where the courts consider settlements reached before proceedings are issued include cases where the approval of the court is required for a settlement involving a child or a person suffering from mental incapacity, representative claims, costs only proceedings under CPR, r 44.12A, and claims under the Road Traffic Accident Pre-action Protocol. The main benefit of having a consent order relates to enforcement, because a court order can be enforced with the full range of court enforcement powers without the need to start a new action to enforce a separate contract made to compromise a dispute (see Chapter 29).

The fact that a settlement is reached after proceedings have been issued does not mean that **20.40** the terms have to be recorded in a consent order. The terms can be recorded in an exchange of letters or a contract if appropriate. If the settlement is reached at the door of the court there may be no additional expense in going in to court to ask the judge to make an order. However if the settlement is reached away from court then going to court to have the consent order made could be an additional cost.

However once proceedings have been commenced, those proceedings must be dealt with **20.41** appropriately if a settlement is reached. The options, some of which are referred to in *Green v Rozen* [1955] 1 WLR 741, are as follows.

- The judge may make an order in terms agreed through a consent order or a Tomlin order, in which case the order will bring the case to an end.
- The judge can make an order discontinuing the claim at the request of the claimant. This will bring the claim to an end with no formal court decision. If a claim is discontinued, the claimant is required to pay the defendant's costs unless specific provision is made to the contrary (CPR, r 38.6). Also, the claimant is not necessarily barred from commencing fresh proceedings in respect of the same claim (see CPR, r 38.7, which says that court permission is required for subsequent proceedings).
- The judge can make an order dismissing the claim at the request of the claimant. If the claim is dismissed, that will involve a formal court decision that the case should not proceed.
- The judge may stay proceedings. A stay is normally made for a set period, though it can be indefinite. This means that no further steps can be taken, but does not end the case. It may

be appropriate where there is some concern that there may be problems in implementing the agreement.

• The judge can adjourn a hearing indefinitely.

Administrative consent orders

20.42 In limited circumstances a consent order can be entered by a purely administrative process, and sealed by a court officer without the need for the approval of a judge (CPR, r 40.6). This can be done to order the payment of money, the delivery up of goods, the dismissal of all or part of the proceedings, an order to stay on agreed terms, and some other cases. The order should be drawn up and sent to the court together with letters expressing the consent of the parties (PD 23A para 10). If there are any doubts or concerns, the draft consent order may be referred to a judge for consideration, which may be dealt with without a hearing. The judge has a discretion and does not have to accept the terms drafted by the parties if, for example, the terms are thought to be inappropriate or poorly drafted.

Drafting of consent orders

20.43 A consent order is normally drafted by a barrister, using the wording agreed in the settlement.

• It is important to note that the court can only make an order that is within its jurisdiction, that is an order that the court can normally make, such as an order for damages or costs, or a declaration: see *Hinde v Hinde* [1953] 1 All ER 171.

• The court cannot make an order it does not have the power to make, even if the terms are agreed by the parties.

• The court can only make an order based on the issues in the case, depending on the causes of action and claims for relief pleaded in the statements of case. If this is a problem you may ask for permission to amend the statements of case to provide a basis for the order you would like the court to make, though the judge may not allow a radical amendment.

• If the compromise includes matters outside the powers of the court and the issues in the case, the options are to use a Tomlin order or to record all or some of the terms in an alternative way.

• Consent judgments and orders must be expressed as being 'by consent' (CPR, r 40.6(7)(b)) and must be signed by the legal representatives for each party.

• Care should be taken to ensure that the wording used reflects the parties' intentions, especially where the order is enshrining an existing oral contract.

• The terms should cover all costs, including for example any previous interim costs orders. If the order does not contain a provision as to costs then each side will bear their own.

• The order should state whether the claim is being stayed, discontinued etc (see above).

20.44 An example of a consent order is shown in Figure 20.6.

True consent orders and submission to agreed terms

20.45 A true consent order is based on a contract between the parties. As such, the court order is evidence of the contract arrived at by bargaining between the parties: *Wentworth v Bullen* (1840) 9 B & C 840. To be a true consent order there must be consideration passing from each side. Unlike other orders, a true consent order can only be set aside on grounds such as fraud, misrepresentation or mistake, which would justify the setting aside of a contract:

Figure 20.6 Consent order

··

IN THE HIGH COURT OF JUSTICE   Claim No. HQ10 7564

QUEEN'S BENCH DIVISION

Before Mr Justice Maynard

BETWEEN

WEB WONDERS (a firm)   <u>Claimant</u>

and

GREAT GRAPHICS PLC   <u>Defendant</u>

DRAFT MINUTES OF ORDER

Upon hearing counsel for the Claimant and for the Defendant.

And upon the Defendant undertaking:

1. To continue to promote the services of the Claimant as agreed in the contract dated 3 March 2009.
2. Not to block or otherwise interfere with the access of the Defendant's customers to the Claimant's website.

By consent it is ordered:

1. The Defendant to pay to the Claimant damages of £33,700 within 14 days of the date of this order.
2. The Defendant to pay the Claimant's standard basis costs of this claim.

Dated

··

Purcell v F C Trigell Ltd [1971] 1 QB 358 and *Roult v North West Strategic Health Authority* [2010] 1 WLR 487 at [19].

There is a distinction between a consent order based on a real contract and a simple submis-   **20.46**
sion to an order. In *Siebe Gorman and Co Ltd v Pneupac Ltd* [1982] 1 WLR 185, Lord Denning
MR said at 189:

> 'It should be clearly understood by the profession that, when an order is expressed to be made
> "by consent", it is ambiguous...One meaning is this: the words 'by consent' may evidence
> a real contract between the parties. In such a case the court will only interfere with such an
> order on the same grounds as it would with any other contract. The other meaning is this: the
> words "by consent" may mean "the parties hereto not objecting". In such a case there is no real
> contract between the parties. The order can be altered or varied by the court in the same cir-
> cumstances as any other order that is made by the court without the consent of the parties.'

Family consent orders

In family proceedings the legal effect of a consent order derives from the order, not the   **20.47**
agreement of the parties. Consequently, there is no jurisdiction to vary a matrimonial consent order: *Thwaite v Thwaite* [1982] Fam 1. Where such an order has been obtained by fraud,
misrepresentation, or mistake, the remedy is to appeal or bring fresh proceedings: *de Lasala*

v de Lasala [1980] AC 546 per Lord Diplock. It may also be possible to appeal out of time where there has been an unforeseeable event that invalidates a fundamental assumption on which the order was made, provided only a relatively short period of time has passed since the order (*Barder v Caluori* [1988] AC 20, at 43, although there is some controversy over the procedural mechanism to be used to bring the matter back to the court: see *Harris v Manahan* [1996] 4 All ER 454).

Tomlin order

20.48 The Tomlin order is a form of consent order that offers particular advantages. The order is named after Tomlin J who created them (see *Practice Note* [1927] WN 290).

Drafting Tomlin orders

20.49 The court orders that further proceedings in the claim be stayed, except for the purpose of carrying out the terms of the compromise, those terms being set out in a schedule to the order. The order will also provide for each party to have liberty to apply to the court if necessary to compel compliance with the terms.

20.50 An example of a Tomlin order is shown in Figure 20.7. Note when you are drafting one that three things must be dealt with on the face of the order, with the other terms agreed normally being in the schedule:

- further proceedings in the claim be stayed, except for the purpose of carrying out the terms of the compromise, those terms being set out in a schedule to the order;
- each party to have liberty to apply to the court if necessary to compel compliance with the terms;
- the payment of costs. By PD 40B, para 3.5, where a consent order is in the form of a Tomlin order any direction for the payment of money out of court or for the payment and assessment of costs must be contained in the body of the order and not the schedule. The reason is that these two forms of direction require the involvement of the court, and must therefore be included in the public part of the order and not concealed in the schedule. If the amount of costs has been agreed, this can be included in the schedule.

Figure 20.7 Tomlin order

IN THE HIGH COURT OF JUSTICE   Claim No 10HC9876
CHANCERY DIVISION

Before Mr Justice Allbright

BETWEEN

TAKOA LIGHT ENGINEERING CO LIMITED

<u>Claimant</u>

and

(1) Mr. DAVID WALLACE
(2) NUCOMPONENTS LIMITED

(Continued)

Figure 20.7 Tomlin order *(Continued)*

<u>Defendants</u>

ORDER

An application was made on 20 September 2010 by counsel for the Claimant and was attended by solicitors for the Defendants.

Mr. Justice Allbright approved the following terms of settlement and made them an Order of the Court.

BY CONSENT IT IS ORDERED that:—

1. The Claimant and the Defendants having agreed to the terms set forth in the schedule hereto, it is ordered that all further proceedings in this claim be stayed, except for the purpose of carrying such terms into effect.

2. Liberty to apply as to carrying the terms in the schedule to this Order into effect.

3. The Defendants do pay the Claimant's standard basis costs to be agreed and if not agreed to be assessed by a detailed assessment by the court.

Dated

SCHEDULE

The parties have agreed to compromise their dispute in these proceedings on the following terms:—

(a) The First Defendant shall sign and deliver to the Claimant's solicitors the annual accounts and directors report for the Claimant for the years ended 5 April 2009 and 5 April 2010 in the form prepared by Boswell Field & Co on 10 June 2010 by 4pm on 24 September 2010;

(b) The First Defendant shall co-operate with Mr. Brian Gunn, the other director of the Claimant, in holding a meeting of the directors of the Claimant by 4pm on 1 October 2010 and shall co-operate with Mr. Brian Gunn in taking all steps necessary to ensure the transfer of 10 ordinary shares in the share capital of the Claimant from Mr. Brian Gunn to Mrs. Jane Gunn at that meeting;

(c) The First Defendant shall sign and deliver to the Claimant's solicitors a duly completed form of resignation as a director of the Claimant by 4pm on 1 December 2010;

(d) The First and Second Defendants or either of them shall pay the sum of £150,000 to the Claimant by 4pm 1 December 2010;

(e) Until 31 December 2011, the Second Defendant will not accept any business from any person who placed an order with the Claimant in the period between 1 January 2007 and 5 April 2010; and

(f) The Claimant accepts these terms in full and final settlement of its claim in these proceedings.

Advantages and disadvantages of Tomlin orders

20.51 The first advantage of a Tomlin order is privacy. A court order is a public matter, because the order will normally be announced in court, and then becomes part of the court record, unless there is some specific justification for the matter not to be dealt with in open court. However a schedule does not have to be made public in court, and the court can direct that the schedule should not be released to anyone other than the parties or their advisers. This can be useful where, for example, the compromise includes the payment of money, and the defendant does not want it recorded in a court judgment that will become available for credit-scoring purposes, which may have adverse effects on its future ability to borrow money, or where the actual amount that may be agreed between the parties is of a sensitive nature (which is why in high profile cases it is often reported in the news media only that a case has been settled for 'substantial damages').

20.52   The second advantage of a Tomlin order for an ADR process is that the schedule, unlike the order itself, is not limited to those orders that a judge has jurisdiction to make in the case. A schedule can therefore set out the terms agreed by the parties more fully, including matters that the judge could not order directly: see for example *E F Phillips and Sons Ltd v Clarke* [1970] Ch 322.

20.53   A third advantage is that a Tomlin order is better suited to record long or complex terms, as the schedule can be worded in a more flexible way than the order itself.

20.54   A possible drawback of a Tomlin order is that enforcement powers for the terms of the schedule are more limited than for the court order itself. If there is a difficulty with regard to the implementation of the terms of the schedule then the party seeking to enforce the terms must apply to court to have the matter brought back before the court, and seek an order requiring the other party to comply with the terms in the schedule. Any failure to comply with that order will be a contempt of court.

TERMS AS REGARDS COSTS

20.55   It is very important to include a provision relating to costs in any settlement, whether a court order or a contract. If the case is a substantial one, or has gone on for some time, then the costs may be substantial, quite possibly exceeding the amount in the substantive claim. If there is no provision then each side will bear their own costs.

20.56   However there can be significant difficulties in reaching a clear agreement about costs.

- The amount of costs incurred by each side will often not be known precisely when a claim is settled.
- If the agreement reached on costs is too vague it may not constitute an enforceable contractual term, which may in turn threaten the validity of the whole settlement.
- If agreement as to costs is simply deferred, the agreement reached could be undermined when costs are discussed.
- In litigation costs usually follow the event (CPR, r 44.3(2)(a)), so that the unsuccessful party is ordered to pay the costs of the successful party. The default position in ADR is that each party will pay their own costs. If the claimant's costs are high this can be a difficult point to agree.
- If litigation has been commenced there may already be some interim orders as to costs to be picked up as part of the settlement.
- If there are no existing court proceedings and the parties cannot agree the amount of costs payable, special proceedings under CPR, r 44.12A, using the Part 8 procedure will have to be used to obtain an order for the court to assess the amount of costs that should be paid.

It is important to have the clearest and most up-to-date information about the costs in the **20.57** case when you are involved in an ADR process so that a full and clear oral agreement can be reached. Terms as to costs should comply with the requirements of the CPR in order to ensure they are effective. This typically means the relevant term should provide for payment of costs on either the standard or indemnity basis, to be agreed (ie that the sum payable should be agreed between the parties if at all possible), but, if the parties cannot agree, with the amount of costs to be determined through a detailed assessment by the court. Possible agreements are therefore

- each side to bear their own costs;
- one side to contribute a stated sum towards the costs of the other side;
- one side to pay a percentage of the other side's costs, or costs on specific issues, the precise sum to be agreed or subject to detailed assessment;
- one side to pay the costs of the other side, the precise sum to be agreed or subject to detailed assessment.

It is important to draft the term as to costs with care, as poor drafting can result in the **20.58** whole compromise being void for uncertainty. The most common danger is in the use of the words 'reasonable costs', which are regularly used in settlements. To most litigators this term means standard basis costs (CPR, r 44.4(2)), to be agreed, or failing agreement, to be assessed by the court in a detailed assessment (CPR, Part 47). It is better to spell this out saying 'standard basis' rather than relying on a vague term. Note that technically the standard basis only applies to contentious costs, which applies where litigation has commenced. Where ADR procedures have been used without the issue of a claim form the costs incurred by the parties are technically non-contentious costs.

To illustrate the problems that can arise, in *Booker Belmont Wholesale Ltd v Ashford* **20.59** *Developments Ltd* (2000) LTL 18/7/2000 a Tomlin order provided that 'the fourth party do pay such proportion of the claimant's costs of the action as the court shall determine...'. The Court of Appeal commented that the order was not in a satisfactory form, but was plainly an order for costs as between the claimant and the fourth parties in a proportion to be fixed by the court. It required the court to consider, in light of the amount claimed by the claimant, the proportion of costs that it was right for the claimant to be awarded. As this was a case where there was pending (already issued) litigation, it only gave rise to the first problem. Cases where there is no existing litigation cause far more difficulty because the costs are non-contentious in nature.

INFORMING THE COURT OF SETTLEMENT

Once proceedings have been issued, there is a duty to inform the court if settlement is **20.60** reached, even if the court is not being asked to make a consent order. The solicitor will normally do this, unless the settlement is reached at the door of the court, in which case the advocate will inform the judge. Where a case is settled in advance of a hearing, each party has a responsibility to inform the court so that the time set aside for the hearing can be reallocated to other litigants. Any order giving effect to the settlement should be filed with the listing officer (PD 39, para 4.2). If the court is informed of a settlement at least seven days before the trial, all or part of the hearing fee is refunded (Civil Proceedings Fees Order 2008

(SI 2008/1053), fee 2.3: there is a 100% refund if more than 28 days' notice is given, 75% if 15–28 days, and 50% if 7–14 days).

KEY POINTS SUMMARY

20.61
- It is essential that all the issues between the parties are covered in a settlement agreement.
- If particular issues are deliberately left out of the agreement, or are left for further agreement, this should be made clear.
- The normal rules of contract law must be adhered to, or the settlement will not be binding.
- While oral agreements are usually binding, the risk of misunderstandings means that it is invariably best practice to record the agreement in writing.
- Choosing the method of recording a settlement depends on:
  - whether there are existing proceedings;
  - whether the matter has been referred to arbitration or adjudication;
  - the costs of different methods of recording the agreement;
  - whether the terms are to be kept confidential;
  - the ease with which different forms of agreement can be enforced. This is dealt with in Chapter 29.
- When drawing up the agreement it is important not to overlook how any existing proceedings are to be dealt with and on how the costs are to be paid.
- A Tomlin order can be used to keep terms confidential in a schedule.

PART 6

ADJUDICATIVE ADR

21

EXPERT OR NEUTRAL DETERMINATION

INTRODUCTION. 21.01

WHEN SHOULD NEUTRAL OR EXPERT DETERMINATION BE USED . . .21.07

AGREEMENT TO USE EXPERT (OR NEUTRAL) DETERMINATION . . .21.10

APPROACH OF THE COURTS TO EXPERT DETERMINATION. 21.11

ADVANTAGES OF EXPERT DETERMINATION 21.15

DIFFERENCES BETWEEN EXPERT DETERMINATION AND
NEGOTIATION, MEDIATION AND NEUTRAL EVALUATION 21.16

SIMILARITIES WITH OTHER FORMS OF ADR. 21.17

SELECTION OF THE NEUTRAL OR EXPERT DETERMINER. 21.18

THE PROCESS 21.21

CONFIDENTIAL INFORMATION 21.28

THE NATURE OF THE DECISION 21.29

REASONS FOR THE DECISION 21.32

CHALLENGING A FINAL DECISION BY COURT PROCEEDINGS. 21.35

PROCEDURE FOR MAKING A CHALLENGE 21.44

ENFORCING A DECISION 21.45

SUING THE EXPERT 21.47

HOW NEUTRAL OR EXPERT DETERMINATION DIFFERS FROM
ARBITRATION 21.50

DISPUTES REVIEW PANELS 21.51

KEY POINTS SUMMARY. 21.53

INTRODUCTION

21.01   With most of the forms of ADR discussed so far, the parties themselves devise their own solution to the dispute, rather than the court imposing a solution at the conclusion of litigation and arbitration.

21.02   Expert determination differs from early neutral or expert evaluation discussed in Chapter 17, because the parties will appoint an expert to make a decision or formal determination on the issues referred to the expert. The expert can only make a decision within the boundaries laid down by the parties. In this sense, expert determination is a determinative process, rather than a facilitative process (mediation) or an advisory evaluative process (neutral evaluation). Expert determination differs from evaluation because the expert is asked to do more than produce a non-binding evaluation, opinion or recommendation in relation to the issues in dispute, but rather to determine those issues.

21.03   Although, the parties usually agree that the determination should be carried out by an appropriate expert such as a judge, lawyer, accountant, surveyor or engineer, it is not always the case that an expert should be used. In appropriate cases, the parties can agree that the determination is carried out by an independent third party, or even by a panel consisting of a number of neutral third parties and a lawyer.

21.04   Depending on the nature of the agreement made between the parties as to the terms on which the determiner is instructed, the determiner's decision can be:

- finally binding on the parties, although they must agree in advance that this is to be so. If they do agree that it is binding, there is no right of appeal, although the decision can be challenged in court on a limited number of grounds;
- binding on them, but only for a temporary or interim period.

21.05   Expert determination should not be confused with the rules relating to expert evidence that can be adduced under the CPR, Part 35. In an expert determination, the expert is acting as the decision maker, not as a witness. In court proceedings, an expert acts as a witness, and the ultimate decision maker is the judge.

21.06   For further detail on all aspects of expert determination, see Kendall, Freedman and Farrell *Expert Determination* (4th edn, Thompson Sweet & Maxwell])

WHEN SHOULD NEUTRAL OR EXPERT DETERMINATION BE USED

Stage at which the parties may agree to expert determination

21.07   Expert or neutral determination tends to be used in three main situations:

- where the parties contractually bind themselves, in advance of any dispute arising, to use this method of ADR in order to resolve disputes arising out the contract between them; or

- where a case raises issues of a very technical nature, and the parties decide, after the dispute has arisen, to use expert (or neutral) determination as the preferred method of ADR; or
- during the course of mediation, with the parties settling the remainder of the issues between them when that determination has been obtained.

In these cases, the parties will enter into a contract with the determiner to determine the dispute. The relationship between the parties and the determiner is primarily governed by the law of contract. **21.08**

Cases where expert determination is particularly suitable

Expert determination is a very useful and cost-effective way of determining disputes of a highly technical nature. Examples of cases that are suitable for resolution using this form of ADR are: **21.09**

- rent reviews where the determination will usually be by a surveyor acting as an expert;
- disputes as to causation, for example the cause of subsidence or a medical condition;
- valuation of a company or share valuations;
- construction disputes;
- real property disputes such as boundary disputes or land valuations;
- energy disputes.

AGREEMENT TO USE EXPERT (OR NEUTRAL) DETERMINATION

If the parties agree to use expert or neutral determination to determine any disputes arising out of or in connection with the contract, care needs to be taken to ensure that these clauses are unambiguously drafted. They should make it clear which issues are to be referred to the determiner for determination and, where applicable, the type and qualifications of the expert that should be appointed to resolve the dispute. Some clauses will also spell out the procedure that must be followed to appoint the determiner, and even the procedure that should be followed by the determiner during the determination. An example of a standard clause is shown in Figure 21.1. **21.10**

Figure 21.1 Example of an expert determination clause

Any dispute arising out of this contract shall be referred to an independent chartered accountant or firm of chartered accountants ('the Expert') to be agreed between the Parties or, failing agreement, to be nominated by the president for the time being of the Instituted of Chartered Accountants in England and Wales. The Expert shall act as an expert and not as an arbitrator. The Parties agree to provide the Expert with such information as may reasonably be required by him to enable him to determine the dispute. The Expert's determination shall be conclusive and binding on the Parties.

APPROACH OF THE COURTS TO EXPERT DETERMINATION

Contractual effect of expert determination clauses

21.11   Expert determination clauses, if clearly and unambiguously drafted, will be upheld by the courts, and such clauses will generally prevent the parties having recourse to the courts to resolve their dispute (*Harper v Interchange Group Ltd* [2007] EWHC 1834 (Comm)).

21.12   If one party refuses to comply with an expert determination clause in the contract, the other party will be entitled to damages for breach of contract if it has to issue proceedings to have the dispute determined (*Sunrock Aircraft Corporation v Scandinavian Airlines System* [2007] EWCA Civ 882. See also *Union Discount v Zoller* [2002] 1 WLR 1517).

Applications to stay court proceedings pending expert determination

21.13   The court also has discretion to stay court proceedings that have been issued by a party who failed to use the contractually agreed machinery in the contract to determine the dispute (*Channel Tunnel Group Ltd v Balfour Beatty Construction Ltd* [1993] AC 334). The burden will on the party seeking to litigate the dispute to show grounds why the claim should not be stayed so that the parties can invoke the contractually agreed method of ADR (*Cott UK Ltd v FE Barber Ltd* [1997] 3 All ER 540). In exercising its discretion to enforce such clauses by staying proceedings commenced in breach of the clause, the court has considered the following factors:

- the extent to which the parties have complied with the requirements in any pre-action protocol;
- whether the dispute is suitable for determination by the ADR process the parties have contractually agreed to use (*Cott UK Ltd v FR Barber Ltd* [1997] 3 All ER 540);
- the costs of that ADR process compared to the costs of litigation;
- whether the dispute could be resolved more quickly by court proceedings than by requiring the parties to use the contractually agreed ADR machinery (*Thames Valley Power Ltd v Total Gas & Power Ltd* [2006] 1 Lloyd's Rep 441);
- whether a stay would accord with the overriding objective (*DGT Steel and Cladding Ltd v Cubitt Building & Interiors Ltd* [2007] BLR 371).

21.14   In *DGT Steel and Cladding Ltd v Cubitt Building & Interiors Ltd,* the court rejected an argument by the claimant that granting a stay would have the effect of debarring the claimant from pursuing its claim in court. The court held that a temporary stay of the proceedings, for a stated period, simply halts proceedings for a few weeks, until after the adjudication. If, following the adjudication, there is still a residual dispute, the court proceedings can be easily reactivated.

ADVANTAGES OF EXPERT DETERMINATION

21.15   Expert determination has many advantages:

- It is cost-effective.
- It provides for a speedy resolution of the dispute compared to litigation or arbitration.

- It removes the decision-making from the parties themselves into the hands of an independent third party.
- It is relatively informal, as the strict rules of evidence and procedure will not apply.
- The parties can agree the procedure that the determiner will have to follow.
- It can be kept confidential and private to the parties.
- It gives the parties a final determination of their dispute where the parties agree that the process is binding on them, with no right of appeal.

DIFFERENCES BETWEEN EXPERT DETERMINATION AND NEGOTIATION, MEDIATION AND NEUTRAL EVALUATION

The main differences between expert determination and negotiation, mediation and neutral evaluation are as follows: **21.16**

- Expert determination has less flexibility than the other processes.
- The outcome is not within parties control in expert determination.
- In expert determination, the determination will be decided on a correct application of the law and the facts whereas negotiation and mediation enable the parties to move away from their strict legal position to obtain a more creative outcome.
- The decision of the determiner in expert determination will usually be binding on the parties, whereas in evaluation, the decision is not binding on them.

SIMILARITIES WITH OTHER FORMS OF ADR

Expert determination also has a number of similarities with other forms of ADR: **21.17**

- Selection of the process is within the parties' control.
- The selection of the expert is within the parties' control.
- It is a more timely and cost-effective way to resolve a dispute than litigation.
- Parties generally control the amount of information to put before the determiner (although, if required, the expert determiner can carry out an investigative role independently of the parties).
- It remains a confidential process. Unlike litigation, any hearing will take place in private and the determination will usually be private unless the parties agree otherwise.

SELECTION OF THE NEUTRAL OR EXPERT DETERMINER

The parties may agree themselves on the identity of the expert they will appoint and **21.18** may approach him directly. Alternatively, they may enlist the help of bodies such as the Academy of Experts, the Royal Institute of Chartered Surveyors, the Institute of Chartered Accountants in England and Wales and the Law Society (see Appendix 1 for details of these bodies).

21.19   Some ADR providers also offer an expert determination service (see for example CEDR at www.cedr.co.uk). An ADR provider will advise on the most appropriate type of expert to resolve the dispute and will offer a selection of experts for the consideration of the parties. The provider will also administer the process. See Appendix 1 for a selection of ADR providers. Most ADR providers have their own standard rules for expert determination and a standard form of agreement that applies to the expert determination. For an example of this, see CEDR's Model Expert Determination Agreement and Rules of Conduct, which are reproduced in Appendix 3. These documents are updated from time to time, so check www.cedr.com for the most recent versions.

21.20   When appointing the expert, the parties should give consideration to the following matters:

- the nature of the expertise required;
- the procedure for appointing the expert;
- the issues to be referred to the expert;
- the procedure that the expert should employ to determine the dispute. In particular whether the expert should resolve the dispute from information supplied by the parties, conduct his own investigations and whether an oral hearing should take place. The parties may simply want to provide that, in the absence of agreement between them about the procedure, the relevant procedure should be determined by the expert;
- the information that should be provided to the expert;
- whether the determination is to be confidential;
- whether the determination is to be final and binding on the parties;
- whether the expert is to give reasons for the determination;
- the circumstances in which the parties can challenge the decision, for example for manifest error, fraud, or partiality;
- the time scale for the determination: this could include agreement on the date by which the determination should be provided;
- the dates for payment of the expert's fees and any monetary sum that the expert determines should be paid by one side to the other.

THE PROCESS

21.21   If the parties have spelt out the procedure that should be followed in advance in the substantive contract, or in the contract appointing the determiner, then this procedure should be followed. However, it is more usual for the parties simply to agree in advance to refer disputes to an expert for determination, leaving the parties and the expert to agree on the appropriate procedure once the dispute has arisen and the referral to the expert has been made.

21.22   The parties can retain a degree of control over the process and most experts will seek to agree any procedural directions with the parties. The parties can also tailor the process to suit their individual needs and requirements. There can be statements of case, disclosure, and a formal hearing with oral submissions and cross-examination of witnesses if the parties require this. If proceedings have not been issued, the determination can be done in a relatively informal way, with both parties simply making submissions on paper, and the expert providing his decision in writing.

The parties are under an implied duty to co-operate with each other and with the expert in relation to the determination.   **21.23**

If the parties agree on the procedure or machinery by which the determination is to be carried out, the court can intervene and provide its own machinery if the procedure agreed has broken down (*Sudbrook Trading Estate Ltd v Eggleton* [1983] 1 AC 444 and *Ursa Major Management Ltd v United Utilities Electricity plc* [2002] EWHC 3041 (Ch)).   **21.24**

In the absence of any agreement between the parties and the expert about the procedure that should be followed, an expert determination cannot be set aside on the basis that the expert failed to follow a fair procedure in accordance with the notions of natural justice (*Bernard Schulte GmbH v Nile Holdings Ltd* [2004] 2 Lloyd's Rep 352).   **21.25**

The procedure that is typically agreed will provide for each party to send to the expert: **21.26**

- written submissions setting out their case on each of the issues; and
- copies of all relevant documents (the parties should co-operate to produce an agreed bundle of documents if possible). If one party refuses to disclose relevant documents to the expert, having agreed to do so, the court may order him to do so (*Bruce v Carpenter* [2006] EWHC 3301 (Ch)).

In some cases, the parties may agree that the parties or their lawyers should make submissions at a meeting or hearing, or that live evidence should be called at a hearing before the expert, although this is usually not required. In some cases also, the parties may agree that the expert may conduct his own lines of inquiry.   **21.27**

CONFIDENTIAL INFORMATION

The parties may agree that they can each provide information to the expert on a confidential basis. If they do so, and the expert is obliged to give reasons for his determination, he should summarise any information that has been provided to him but that is not known to the other party, so that both parties can ascertain what the expert took into account in reaching the determination (per Cresswell J in *Halifax Life Ltd v Equitable Life Assurance Society* [2007] 1 Lloyd's Rep 528 at [48]). This is particularly important if the parties have agreed that the determination can be challenged on the grounds of manifest error. To avoid suggestions of bias in favour of one party, it is preferable if the parties openly exchange any information that is placed before the determiner, and that any hearings are held in the presence of all parties.   **21.28**

THE NATURE OF THE DECISION

In expert determination the parties will usually agree that the decision will be binding on them and, where this is so, the court will uphold the decision unless there are grounds for   **21.29** setting it aside (see 21.35–21.43 and *Thames Valley Power Ltd v Total Gas & Power Ltd* [2006] 1 Lloyd's Rep 441).

21.30   The decision does not take the form of an award or an order, unlike arbitration.

21.31   The agreement may also specify a time limit within which the determination may be challenged by court proceedings. Alternatively, the parties may agree to be bound by the determination with no right to challenge it in court or elsewhere.

REASONS FOR THE DECISION

21.32   The parties can agree whether written reasons should be provided for the determination. If the contract by which the expert is appointed does not require reasons for the determination, then the expert is not obliged to provide them. However if the parties agree that the expert should give reasons for the decision, and the expert fails to do so, he will be ordered to do so by the court (*Halifax Life Ltd v Equitable Life Assurance Society* [2007] 1 Lloyd's Rep 528). Although in an expert determination (unlike arbitration) there is no statutory provision directing the expert to give reasons, where the contract provided for him to do so, the court can require him to give reasons by enforcing the contractual provisions, or under its inherent jurisdiction.

21.33   Where reasons are to be given, they should be intelligible and adequate in all the circumstances. The reasons can be stated briefly, but they should explain the basis for the expert's conclusions on the issues he was asked to determine.

21.34   If the parties have agreed that the decision will not be binding on them in the event of a 'manifest error' by the expert, it will be very difficult for them to show that a manifest error has been made if the written reasons contracted for have not been provided, or indeed to show that he departed from his instructions.

CHALLENGING A FINAL DECISION BY COURT PROCEEDINGS

21.35   If the parties agree that their dispute should be resolved by expert determination and that the expert's decision is to be conclusive and binding for all purposes, then provided the expert has done exactly what he was instructed to do, the report, whether or not it contained reasons for the decision, can generally not be challenged by seeking to set it aside in court proceedings (*Jones v Sherwood Computer Services plc* [1992] 1 WLR 277). If the parties agree that the expert determination should be final, they will be bound by any decision made honestly and in good faith, and even if the expert has made a mistake. The decision will also be binding on the parties if the expert has erred in law on a question of construction, and answered the right question but in the wrong way (*Nikko Hotels (UK) Ltd v MEPC plc* [1991] 2 EGLR 103).

21.36   However it can be challenged on the following grounds.

Material departure from instructions

The decision can be challenged if the expert has departed from his instructions in a mate- **21.37**
rial way. This could be established if, for example, the expert was mistaken about the terms
of his instructions, or did not do what he was appointed to do; for example, if he valued the
wrong number of shares, or shares in the wrong company, or failed to carry out a test by a
contractually stipulated method (*Veba Oil Supply and Trading GmbH v Petrotrade Inc* [2002] 1
Lloyd's Rep 295). In *Kollerich & Cie SA v The State Trading Corporation of India* [1980] 2 Lloyd's
Rep 32 certificates of quality were set aside because they did not comply with the terms of
the expert determination clause in the contract. Any decision reached on an issue that was
not within the expert's terms of reference is also liable to be set aside. Any departure will be
material unless it can be said to be trivial or de minimis. Once any departure is material, it
is not necessary to show that it affected the result (*British Shipbuilders v VSEL Consortium plc*
[1997] 1 Lloyd's Rep 105).

Manifest error

The parties may agree in their contract that the expert's decision will only be binding on **21.38**
them in the absence of manifest error. If there is such an error the decision may be set aside
(*Veba Oil Supply and Trading GmbH v Petrotrade Inc* [2002] 1 Lloyd's Rep 295). However, even if
a determiner has clearly erred in law or in fact, in the absence of any contractual term enabling the parties to challenge the decision on the grounds of a manifest error, the decision
will be binding on the parties (*Jones v Sherwood Computer Services plc* [1992] 1 WLR 277).

The meaning of 'manifest error' was considered in *Conoco (UK) Ltd v Phillips Petroleum Co UK* **21.39**
Ltd (unreported, 19 August 1996) to be '...oversights and blunders so obvious as to admit of
no difference of opinion'. If the expert's reasoning is not apparent from the determination
itself, the court can look at other material that was available to the expert to determine if
a manifest error has been made and any subsequent reasons the expert may have given by
way of clarification (*Homepace Ltd v Sita South East Ltd* [2008] EWCA Civ 1).

Fraud or collusion

If the expert is guilty of fraud or has colluded with one party in reaching his decision, then **21.40**
it can be set aside (*Campbell v Edwards* [1976] 1 WLR 403). In the case of partiality, it must be
shown that the expert actually was biased. A mere possibility of bias will not suffice (*Marco*
v Thompson (No 3) [1997] 2 BCLC 36).

Failure to act lawfully or fairly

If the expert fails to act lawfully or fairly, his decision may be set aside (*John Barker* **21.41**
Construction Ltd v London Portman Hotel Ltd [1996] 83 BLR 31).

The decision not intended to be final on matters of construction

If it can be said that, by the terms under which the expert was appointed, the expert's deter- **21.42**
mination was not intended to oust the jurisdiction of the court in matters of interpretation

of the terms of the underlying contract between the parties, then the court can intervene if the expert issues a determination based on an incorrect interpretation. See *Mercury Communications Ltd v Director General of Telecommunications* [1996] 1 WLR 48, and *Homepace Ltd v Sita South East Ltd* [2008] EWCA Civ 1.

No reasons for decision

21.43 If the expert fails to provide reasons for his decision (a decision for which reasons have to be given is sometimes known as a 'speaking decision'), despite having agreed to do so, then the decision can be challenged. However the court is likely to order the expert to provide reasons, rather than set the decision aside (see above).

PROCEDURE FOR MAKING A CHALLENGE

21.44 A challenge to the decision in an expert determination will usually be made by issuing Part 8 proceedings. Part 8 proceedings may also be issued in advance of an expert determination to decide any disputes about the interpretation of the expert determination clause, or to resolve disagreement about matters that should be referred to the expert pursuant to the clause. If the decision is set aside, the court may, in some circumstances, make the determination itself, if necessary after considering expert evidence adduced by the parties, or it may direct a new expert to be instructed to determine the matter.

ENFORCING A DECISION

21.45 A decision reached by expert or neutral determination cannot be enforced in the same way as if it were a court decision.

21.46 However a failure by one side to honour the decision amounts to a breach of contract, and proceedings can be issued in relation to the breach. In those proceedings, the court can make an order giving effect to the decision of the expert. The court's decision can then be enforced in the same way as any other judgment. See Chapter 29 for more detail on enforcement proceedings. Winding-up or bankruptcy proceedings could also be brought against an individual or company or partnership that refused to pay a monetary sum awarded by an expert determination.

SUING THE EXPERT

21.47 An expert or neutral person carrying out a determination is not immune from suit in the same way as a member of the judiciary. An expert can be liable in negligence or breach of contract if he is negligent in the determination that he reaches or fails to act in accordance with the contract (*Sutcliffe v Thackrah* [1974] AC 727 and *Arenson v Casson Beckman Rutley and Co* [1977] AC 405).

Table 21.1 A comparison of early neutral evaluation (ENE), expert determination (ED), adjudication and arbitration

Characteristic	ENE	ED	Adjudication	Arbitration
Neutral third party involved	Yes	Yes	Yes	Yes
Parties have control over selection of the neutral third party	Yes	Yes	Yes	Yes—to an extent
It is a *facilitative* dispute resolution process	No—unless evaluation is being done in the context of mediation (evaluative mediation)	No	No	No
Neutral third party's determination is legally binding on the parties	No	Yes	Yes—provided no challenge is made to it within a specified time limit	Yes—subject to any right of appeal
Parties have some control over the procedure and the evidence to be placed before the neutral third party	Yes	Yes	Yes—usually	Yes
The outcome is negotiated by the parties	Yes	No	No	No
The decision is made by the neutral third party	No	Yes	Yes	Yes
Private and confidential process	Yes	Yes	Yes	Yes
Process can be abandoned by the party at any time	Yes	No	No	No
The determiner is subject to control by the court	No	No	No	Yes
Right of appeal from the decision	No	No	No	Yes—in some circumstances
Determiner can be liable for negligence/breach of contract	Yes	Yes	No	No
Decision can be enforced as a court order without the need for fresh proceedings	No	No	No	Yes

Many experts seek to secure immunity by inserting clauses in the agreement by which the parties agree that they will not hold the expert liable in respect of the determination or call the expert as a witness in any proceedings (see, for example, cll 13 and 15 in CEDR Model Expert Determination Agreement in Appendix 3).

21.48

21.49 These clauses may be unenforceable if they are unreasonable under the terms of the Unfair Contract Terms Act 1977.

HOW NEUTRAL OR EXPERT DETERMINATION DIFFERS FROM ARBITRATION

21.50 Expert determination differs from arbitration in the following ways:

- Unlike arbitration, the determiner has no power to make an order or an award.
- The determination does not take place within the formal scheme laid down in the Arbitration Act 1996, and that Act and the extensive body of common law that applies to arbitrations does not apply to neutral or expert determination.
- The parties retain a great deal of control over the timing and the procedure that applies to the determination.
- The parties retain a reasonable degree of control over the evidence that they place before the determiner.
- If it is an international dispute, it is not enforceable under the New York Convention 1958 (for which, see Chapter 29).

DISPUTES REVIEW PANELS

21.51 This can be a hybrid form of determination, which may or may not involve an expert. They can take a number of different forms, but typically they will allow for each party to appoint an independent party to the panel, and the independent parties will then choose a chairman. The chairman or the independent parties may or may not be experts, depending on the nature of the dispute that is being referred to the panel. Decisions made by the panel will be binding on the parties unless they agree that they will refer the decision to arbitration within a specified time limit.

21.52 A disputes review panel was used in the channel tunnel litigation (*Channel Tunnel Group Ltd v Balfour Beatty Ltd* [1993] 1 All ER 664).

KEY POINTS SUMMARY

21.53
- Expert determination is a speedy, cost-effective way of obtaining a determination on a case or an issue.
- It is useful in cases raising technical issues that would require expert evidence to resolve in court proceedings.
- The parties can choose the determiner.
- The decision is usually final and binding on the parties.
- The parties may agree on a speaking decision, or one without reasons.
- The decision can only be challenged in court proceedings in very limited circumstances.

22

CONSTRUCTION INDUSTRY ADJUDICATION

INTRODUCTION. 22.01

NATURE OF ADJUDICATION. 22.04

REQUIREMENTS. 22.05

EXPRESS CONTRACTUAL RIGHT TO ADJUDICATION 22.13

DEFAULT PROVISIONS IN THE SCHEME FOR CONSTRUCTION
CONTRACTS 22.16

COMMENCEMENT OF THE ADJUDICATION 22.17

PROCEDURE BEFORE THE HEARING. 22.27

ADJUDICATOR'S DECISION 22.36

BINDING, BUT INTERIM EFFECT, OF DECISIONS. 22.43

OVERALL COST 22.46

ADJUDICATION IN RESIDENTIAL BUILDING CONTRACTS. 22.47

COURT ENFORCEMENT OF SUM FOUND DUE ON ADJUDICATION . .22.48

KEY POINTS SUMMARY. 22.49

INTRODUCTION

22.01 ADR has tended to develop through initiatives in particular organisations and industries, usually aimed at finding cost-effective and swift means of resolving disputes as alternatives to bringing proceedings in court. Different solutions, which have developed into the different ADR processes described in this book, have been adopted in different industries. One particular process is adjudication in construction industry disputes. Adjudication resembles arbitration (see Chapters 23–28), in that it produces a decision on the dispute, but one that is only of a temporary nature. The process involves an adjudicator reaching a decision very swiftly (only 28 days after appointment), with the idea being to get a decision on how much a contractor should be paid, followed by a full-blown investigation through the courts or in a formal arbitration if either party does not agree with the adjudicator's decision. The underlying policy is 'pay now, argue later' (*RJT Consulting Engineers Ltd v DM Engineering (Northern Ireland) Ltd* [2002] 1 WLR 2344). An adjudication award is binding, but is not registrable as a judgment unlike an award in arbitration. Instead, enforcement is through suing on the adjudicator's decision, often followed by the entry of judgment in default or an application for summary judgment.

22.02 Adjudication procedures were laid down by the Housing Grants, Construction and Regeneration Act 1996, Part II. Before this was enacted there was a serious problem in the late payment of sums due in construction industry contracts. Large construction projects will be ongoing for many months or even years. If contracting parties are not paid until the completion of the project they will often fall into financial difficulties, which then has an impact on the other parties and may jeopardise the successful completion of the project. In large projects there are also usually several contractors, each dealing with a particular aspect of the overall scheme (such as architects, main contractors, ground works, scaffolding, cement, brickwork, structural work, glazing, roofing, electrical and other fitting out). If one of these stops work due to some dispute, it will have an adverse effect on all the other parties.

22.03 The Housing Grants, Construction and Regeneration Act 1996, Part II, deals with these problems by laying down a scheme aimed at ensuring fair dealing in construction contracts. Adjudication of construction industry disputes, which is dealt with in s 108, is the key provision for the purposes of this chapter. Related provisions deal with things like stage payments (s 109), a right to suspend performance for non-payment, but only after giving notice of the grounds (s 112), and a general prohibition on making payment to a contractor conditional on the paying party itself being paid by someone else (s 113). The common theme of these provisions is that they provide mechanisms for ensuring contractors are paid the sums they are contractually entitled to at the time they are contractually due, or as soon as the law can practically achieve this.

NATURE OF ADJUDICATION

22.04 Adjudication is an interim dispute resolution process, under which an impartial adjudicator gives a decision on a dispute arising during the course of a construction contract (*Macob Civil Engineering Ltd v Morrison Construction Ltd* (1999) 64 Con LR 1). While a dispute seeking any type of relief may be referred to adjudication, an adjudicator simply makes a decision, and does not have any of the coercive powers available to a court. Adjudication is therefore not likely to be effective if relief in the form of specific performance or an injunction is sought. In practical terms, the vast majority of disputes referred to adjudication are about how much money is payable under the contract. An adjudicator makes an interim decision, which is binding in the sense that the losing party has to pay the sum decided upon, but the unsuccessful party can reopen the matter in the courts or through arbitration, which will decide the dispute afresh without reference to the adjudicator's decision.

REQUIREMENTS

A party to a construction contract can refer a matter to adjudication if the following condi-   **22.05**
tions are satisfied:

(1)   the underlying contract is a construction contract (Housing Grants, Construction and
      Regeneration Act 1996 ss 104 and 105);
(2)   the underlying contract is a 'commercial' construction contract as opposed to a con-
      tract with a residential occupier (s 106). It is only contracts with the residential occupier
      that are excluded, so that contractor/sub-contractor and contractor/consultant con-
      tracts are covered if the other conditions are satisfied;
(3)   the underlying contract is made in writing (s 107);
(4)   the underlying commercial construction contract is required by s 108(2) to include
      terms providing a contractual right to refer disputes to adjudication. If it fails to do so,
      there is a default statutory right to refer disputes to adjudication;
(5)   there is a dispute between the parties;
(6)   the dispute is one relating to the underlying construction contract.

There are particular technical issues relating to requirements (1), (3) and (5) that are dis-   **22.06**
cussed next. They are followed by a discussion on express terms providing for adjudication,
and the default statutory scheme (requirement (4)).

Construction contract

A 'construction contract' is an agreement for the carrying out of construction operations,   **22.07**
either directly or through others such as by sub-contracting, or by the provision of labour
(Housing Grants, Construction and Regeneration Act 1996 s 104(1)). It includes architec-
tural, design and surveying work relating to construction operations (s 104(2)), but excludes
contracts of employment (s 104(3)) and construction operations outside England, Wales
and Scotland (s 104(6)(b)). 'Construction operations' is widely defined in s 105(1) to cover
the construction, alteration, repair, maintenance, extension, demolition or dismantling of
buildings or structures forming, or to form, part of land, and also various other activities,
including:

- similar activities relating to walls, roads, power-lines, aircraft runways, harbours, pipe-
  lines, sewers and reservoirs etc;
- installation of fittings for heating, lighting, air-conditioning, drainage, water supply etc;
- ground clearance, foundations, scaffolding, landscaping etc operations that are an inte-
  gral part of construction operations;
- cleaning in the course of construction, restoration etc, and painting and decorating inside
  and outside of any building or structure.

Extraction of oil and gas, mining for minerals, and building of nuclear power plants are   **22.08**
excluded, as are artistic works (s 105(2)). Also excluded is the manufacture of building components, materials etc, unless the contract also provides for these items to be installed in a
construction operation (s 105(2)(d)).

Agreement in writing

22.09 The provisions in the Housing Grants, Construction and Regeneration Act 1996, Part II, only apply to construction contracts that are in writing (s 107(1)). This is satisfied (s 107(2)) if the agreement is:

- made in writing, whether or not it is signed by the parties. This includes an agreement by reference to terms that are in writing (s 107(3)); or
- made by the exchange of communications in writing; or
- evidenced in writing. This applies where the agreement is recorded by one of the parties, or by a third party, with the authority of the parties to the agreement (s 107(4)). A signed credit reference application was regarded in *Estor Ltd v Multifit (UK) Ltd* [2009] EWHC 2108 (TCC) as sufficient evidence in writing for the purposes of s 107 to show the defendant was a party to a construction contract based on other contractual documentation that did not name the defendant.

22.10 References to writing include recording by any means (s 107(6)). An issue as to whether a term should be implied into the contract does not impact on the question of whether the contract is in writing for the purposes of s 107 (*Connex South Eastern Ltd v MJ Building Services Group plc* [2004] BLR 333). There will be no written contract where all that can be pointed to is a draft contract which says an official order will be issued, but where no order is in fact issued (*Adonis Construction v O'Keefe Soil Remediation* [2009] EWHC 2047 (TCC)).

Dispute

22.11 The Housing Grants, Construction and Regeneration Act 1996 s 108(1) gives the parties a right to refer any 'dispute' to adjudication. This is defined to include any difference, and so has the same meaning as 'dispute' in relation to arbitration (Arbitration Act 1996 s 82; and see 23.21). Making a claim is therefore not enough. There will be a dispute if there is an express disagreement by the responding party or if it can be inferred that a claim is not admitted. Not much is needed for this purpose. It is far from unknown for a party to make a reference to adjudication just hours after lodging a claim. This may be enough provided it is considered that a reasonable time to consider and respond to the claim has been given. This will depend on the nature of the claim: only a short time for consideration is required for a simple claim for money contracted for, whereas claims for extensions of time, or additional costs due to site constraints, are likely to require more time before they can be considered to be disputed.

22.12 It is only the disputed claim that can be referred to adjudication. The basic guidance is that only a single dispute should be referred to adjudication in one reference. Where the parties try to wrap several disputes into a single reference, costs tend to escalate, and keeping to the 28-day timetable becomes increasingly difficult. Once a reference is made, the referring party is not permitted to add further disputes at a later stage. An appearance of seeking to do just this is sometimes given where the referring party produces new documentation in the adjudication process that has not been seen by the responding party before the reference to adjudication. Experts' reports are particularly dangerous in this regard, because they often describe the dispute in more sophisticated ways than the terms used by the referring party. Practical advice is to ensure that all the evidence that will be used in the adjudication is sent to the responding party before making the formal reference to adjudication.

EXPRESS CONTRACTUAL RIGHT TO ADJUDICATION

Under the Housing Grants, Construction and Regeneration Act 1996 s 108(2), a construction contract must include terms that:　　**22.13**

- enable a party to give notice at any time of its intention to refer a dispute to adjudication;
- provide a timetable with the object of securing the appointment of the adjudicator and referral of the dispute to him within seven days of such notice;
- require the adjudicator to reach a decision within 28 days of referral or such longer period as is agreed by the parties after the dispute has been referred;
- allow the adjudicator to extend the period of 28 days by up to 14 days, with the consent of the party by whom the dispute was referred;
- impose a duty on the adjudicator to act impartially; and
- enable the adjudicator to take the initiative in ascertaining the facts and the law.

Further, by s 108(3) the contract must provide that the decision of the adjudicator is binding until the dispute is finally determined by legal proceedings, by arbitration (if the contract provides for arbitration or the parties otherwise agree to arbitration) or by agreement. However, the parties may agree to accept the decision of the adjudicator as finally determining the dispute.　　**22.14**

It is important that all these matters are addressed in the clause, otherwise whatever provision is made will be void. A clause that provided that the adjudicator's decision was valid even if issued out of time has been held in *Aveat Heating Ltd v Jerram Falkus Construction Ltd* [2007] EWHC 131 (TCC) to fail to comply with s 108(2)(c),(d), and the clause was void. Typical, fairly basic, express terms dealing with references to adjudication are shown in Table 22.1. Standard form contracts in the construction industry are often far more　　**22.15**

Table 22.1 Contract clauses referring construction disputes to adjudication

Type of clause	Wording
Reference to construction adjudication	A party to this contract ('the referring party') may at any time give notice ('the notice') in writing to the other party of its intention to refer a dispute arising under the contract to adjudication.
Clauses dealing with procedure on the adjudication	The parties may agree the identity of the adjudicator. Where an adjudicator is not agreed within two days of the notice being given, the referring party shall immediately apply to [*name of adjudication provider*] for the nomination of an adjudicator, which nomination shall be communicated to the parties within five days of receipt of the application.
	Within seven days of the notice the referring party shall refer the dispute to the adjudicator
	The adjudicator must act impartially and shall reach a decision within 28 days of referral or such longer period as is agreed by the parties after the dispute has been referred.
	The adjudicator may extend the period of 28 days by up to 14 days, with the consent of the party by whom the dispute was referred.
Clause to avoid conflict between enforcement of decision and any arbitration clause	The enforcement of any decision of an adjudicator is not a matter which may be referred to arbitration.

sophisticated. The adjudication clause in the JCT standard form contract, local authority without quantities, for example, has 32 paragraphs laying down detailed procedures for adjudications.

DEFAULT PROVISIONS IN THE SCHEME FOR CONSTRUCTION CONTRACTS

22.16 To the extent that a construction contract does not make express provision for adjudication in accordance with the above requirements, the Housing Grants, Construction and Regeneration Act 1996 s 108(5), and the Scheme for Construction Contracts (England and Wales) Regulations 1998 (SI 1998/649) provide for disputes to be referred to adjudication under 'the Scheme for Construction Contracts'. This covers cases where the contract fails to say anything about adjudication, and also cases where a purported adjudication clause is void through failing to comply with s 108 (*Aveat Heating Ltd v Jerram Falkus Construction Ltd* [2007] EWHC 131 (TCC)). The Scheme for Construction Contracts makes the same provision on all the main features of adjudication as an express clause complying with s 108(2), (3).

COMMENCEMENT OF THE ADJUDICATION

22.17 In the case of express adjudication clauses, the contract may lay down a detailed set of procedures to be followed, but it is more likely to adopt the standard rules of a commercial dispute resolution service provider. In a similar way to arbitration, such providers publish rules for conducting adjudications that can be adopted by agreement between the parties. Examples are the CEDR Rules for Adjudication and the TeCSA Adjudication Rules. Institutional rules tend to follow the basic scheme in the default provisions in the Scheme for Construction Contracts. Figure 22.1 is a flow diagram showing how an adjudication develops from making a claim to notification of the decision.

Notice of adjudication: the commencement of adjudication

22.18 Under the Scheme for Construction Contracts, para 1 an adjudication is commenced by the referring party giving a notice of adjudication to all the other parties to the contract. This is a notice in writing stating the referring party's intention to refer a stated dispute arising out of the construction contract to adjudication. The notice needs to contain:

- the names and addresses of the parties;
- details to identify the contract (technically this is not one of the requirements in the Scheme for Construction Contracts, but in practical terms this is needed to show the dispute comes within the scheme and to provide a basis for explaining the nature of the dispute);
- brief details of the dispute to be referred to adjudication;
- details of where and when the dispute arose; and
- details of the remedy sought.

22.19 A notice of adjudication may be in a letter or a formal notice. An example is shown in Figure 22.2. It relates to a dispute between a property development company and the main

Figure 22.1 Stages in adjudication

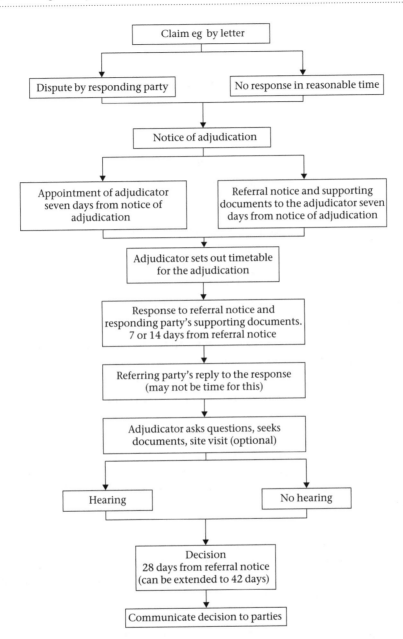

contractor over whether the property development company is entitled to liquidated damages for delay in completion of a building project, or whether the main contractor is entitled
to an extension of time. The notice of adjudication is often drafted at the same time as the
referral notice (see below), which has to be served within seven days of the notice of adjudication. In many ways a notice of adjudication is a summary of the key points from the details
that have to be included in the referral notice, and drafting them at the same time ensures
they are consistent with each other.

Figure 22.2 Notice of adjudication

....

IN THE MATTER OF THE HOUSING GRANTS, CONSTRUCTION
AND REGENERATION ACT 1996

AND

IN THE MATTER OF AN INTENDED ADJUDICATION

BETWEEN

PROPERTY DEVELOPERS LIMITED

<u>Referring party</u>

and

MAIN CONTRACTORS PLC

<u>Responding party</u>

NOTICE OF ADJUDICATION

This notice of adjudication is served on behalf of: Property Developers Ltd, whose registered office is 47 Bank Street, London EC2 5SL.

It is served on Main Contractors plc ('MCP'), whose registered office is at Greyfriars House, Munton Place, London WC3J 7ZP.

We refer to Property Developers Ltd's agreement with MCP for the carrying out of refurbishment and remodelling work to Hardy Mansions, Wellington Road, Stafford ('the Project').

The Agreement between Property Developers Ltd and MCP incorporates the Construction Industry Standard Form of Contract 2007 Edition incorporating Amendments 1 and 2 ('CIS/1-2 2007').

A dispute has arisen between Property Developers Ltd and MCP as a result of MCPs failure to complete the Project by the contractual Completion Date pursuant to Clause 16 of the CIS/1-2 2007 contract. As a result of late completion of the Project Property Developers Ltd is entitled to liquidated damages amounting to £467,125.00 based on practical completion of the Project taking place 185 days after the contractual completion date of 6 February 2010.

MCP has disputed its liability to pay the liquidated damages on the basis that Property Developers Ltd did not grant MCP a proper extension of time. Property Developers Ltd dispute that MCP is entitled to the alleged extension of time, and its case is that the liquidated damages are properly payable by MCP.

We hereby give MCP notice, on behalf of Property Developers Ltd, of its intention to refer the above dispute to Adjudication under Clause 35 of the CIS/1-2 2007, which forms part of the contract between Property Developers Ltd and MCP.

The relief claimed comprises:

(a) An order that MCP should pay to Property Developers Ltd the sum of £467,125.00 (or such other sum as the Adjudicator may consider appropriate) in respect of the late completion of the Project, plus interest pursuant to Clause 24 of the CIS/1-2 2007 contract (or such other Clause as may be relevant) within 7 days of the date of the Adjudicator's Decision.

(Continued)

Figure 22.2 Notice of adjudication *(Continued)*

(b) A declaration that, on the true construction of Clause 16 of the CIS/1-2 2007 contract and in the events that have happened in the execution of the works on the Project, MCP is not entitled to any extension of time to the Contractual Completion Date for the works of 6 February 2010 or, alternatively, that the Adjudicator declares that MCP is entitled to such extension as the Adjudicator considers appropriate.

DATED 21 September 2010

Signed: Wilkinson & Bradshaw, solicitors for Property Developers Ltd
Dunedin House, Victoria Road, London EC1H 5LD

Ambit of the reference

It is for the party making the reference to adjudication to define the issues to be adjudi- **22.20**
cated, and it is the notice of adjudication that achieves this. As the TeCSA Rules r 13 says, it is the notice of adjudication that identifies the scope of the adjudication. This means the adjudicator has no jurisdiction to decide matters outside these issues in the absence of agreement to vary by the parties (*McAlpine PPS Pipeline Systems Ltd v Transco plc* [2004] BLR 352 at [145]). The reason for including as relief in Figure 22.2 provision for substituting an extension period of such length as the adjudicator may consider appropriate (para. (b) at the end of Figure 22.2) is to avoid an argument that the adjudicator can either decide there should be no extension or the full 185 days claimed by the main contractor, but nothing in between. Any dispute about the ambit of the reference is decided by the adjudicator (TeCSA Rules r 14).

Nomination of adjudicator

An adjudicator needs to be appointed within seven days of the notice of adjudication. The **22.21**
adjudicator may be named in the construction contract, or else will have to be appointed in accordance with the machinery in the contract (which may adopt the institutional rules of a dispute resolution service provider) or the Scheme for Construction Contracts. These may provide for an adjudicator to be selected by a nominating body, such as the AICA, RIBA, RICS or TeCSA. Most appointing bodies have a five-day turn-around time for making appointments and aim to make the appointment within the seven-day deadline (eg TeCSA Rules r 5(ii)). The Scheme for Construction Contracts has default provisions dealing with situations where the named adjudicator or nominating body is unable or unwilling to act. The adjudicator has two days to confirm whether they are available to act.

A small fee is usually payable to the nominating body for making the nomination (it is £100 **22.22**
under the TeCSA Rules). The adjudicator will provide the parties with a copy of the terms on which they are prepared to act, including information regarding fees and expenses.

An appointment fee (typically in four figures) is often charged by the adjudicator on accept- **22.23**
ing an appointment, and further work and any hearings will be charged on an hourly or daily fee basis.

Referral notice

22.24   A written referral notice needs to be sent by the referring party to the adjudicator not later than seven days from the date of the notice of adjudication (see Scheme for Construction Contracts para 7). These seven days run in parallel with the seven days for appointing the adjudicator. Referral notices are in effect formal statements of case, and are often set out in points of dispute format (rather like the points of claim in arbitration shown in Figure 25.3, but usually more discursive). For an example of this style, see Figure 22.3. As it is addressed

Figure 22.3 Referral notice

IN THE MATTER OF THE HOUSING GRANTS, CONSTRUCTION AND REGENERATION ACT 1996

AND

IN THE MATTER OF AN INTENDED ADJUDICATION

BETWEEN

PROPERTY DEVELOPERS LIMITED

Referring party

and

MAIN CONTRACTORS PLC

Responding party

————————————

REFERRAL NOTICE

————————————

1. At all material times Property Developers Ltd has been the freehold owner of Hardy Tower, Wellington Road, Stafford, which is a 5-storey building divided into residential flats ('Hardy Mansions').
2. At all material times Main Contractors Plc ('MCP') were the main contractors on a project for the refurbishment and remodelling of Hardy Mansions ('the Project').
3. By a contract in writing dated 6 December 2009, MCP agreed with Property Developers Ltd to carry out of the refurbishment and remodelling works on the Project ('the Contract').
4. The Contract incorporates the Construction Industry Standard Form of Contract 2007 Edition incorporating Amendments 1 and 2 ('CIS/1-2 2007').
5. The full contractual documentation between Property Developers Ltd and MCP relating to the Project can be found in File B.
6. It was an express term of the Contract that the parties must refer any dispute to Adjudication under Clause 35 of the CIS/1-2 2007.
7. A dispute has arisen between Property Developers Ltd and MCP as a result of MCP's refusal to pay liquidated damages in the sum of £467,125.00 to Property Developers Ltd. Property Developers Ltd's right to liquidated damages arises from MCP's failure to complete the Project by 6 February 2010, the contractual date for practical completion of the Project.

(Continued)

Figure 22.3 Referral notice *(Continued)*

8. MCP has disputed its liability to pay the liquidated damages on the basis that Property Developers Ltd did not grant MCP a proper extension of time.

9. Notice of Adjudication was sent to MCP on 21 September 2010.

10. Property Developers Ltd do not believe there is any dispute that the contractual date for practical completion was 6 February 2010, or that there was a term in the Contract providing for liquidated damages at the daily rate of £2,525, or that practical completion was 185 days after 6 February 2010, or that no sum has been paid by MCP to Property Developers Ltd in respect of liquidated damages.

11. The dispute between the parties is as to whether MCP is entitled to an extension to the date for practical completion, and if so, for how long, with the result that the sum payable to Property Developers Ltd in respect of liquidated damages may be reduced or reduced to zero.

12. It was a further express term of the Contract that MCP should: 'Record progress on a copy of the programme kept on site. If any circumstances arise which may affect the progress of the works, put forward proposals or take other action as appropriate to minimize any delay and to recover any lost time' (clause 30.4).

13. In breach of the express term in paragraph 12 above MCP failed to record progress on any programme, on site or otherwise, and/or in breach of contract MCP failed to put forward proposals to minimize delay and/or to recover lost time. Property Developers Ltd submit that in consequence of the failure of MCP to comply with its contractual obligations it is now impossible with any degree of certainty to determine the date or duration that the various activities were undertaken by the various contractors on site, and also impossible to determine the impact or effect on other linked or non-linked activities. Property Developers Ltd submits that this being the case it is impossible to assess properly the true causes of the delay to the completion of the works, and the dates and durations of the delays claimed by MCP are therefore no more than speculation.

14. MCP has submitted the following as-built programmes (see file C, pages 1 to 231):

    FABP1: Critical Trade Activities
    FABP2: Stripping Out and Demolition Works
    FABP3: Brick and Block Works
    FABP4: Asphalt and Pitched Roofing Works
    FABP5: Carpentry Works
    FABP6: Window Installation Works
    FABP7: Decorating Works
    FABP8: Common Areas Works

15. Property Developers Ltd submits that the inadequate record keeping by MCP means that it can only report progress on a 'floor-by-floor' basis. Property Developers Ltd submits that such general records are hopelessly vague and inadequate. By way of example, a variation in one flat on one floor (file C, page 147, for example) may have a delaying effect on that flat but it is submitted would have no impact or effect on the non-affected flats even on the same floor. The manner in which MCP has recorded progress makes it simply impossible to isolate any individual event. Thus an event in one trade in one flat on one floor is depicted by MCP as a delay to all flats on the entire floor (see file C,

(Continued)

Figure 22.3 Referral notice *(Continued)*

pages 232 to 278). This is simply not credible and calls into question the entire reliability of all the programmes.

16. MCP programmed the works on a flat type basis, without identifying the critical path. A critical path would have made it possible to compare the planned progress with the actual progress in a meaningful way. Instead, MCP's method (see file C, pages 232 to 278) produces an aggregate of all planned time, and compares that with all the actual time on a trade by trade basis. No attempt has been made by MCP to demonstrate any link between the trades.

17. It is Property Developers Ltd's case that the programme of MCP does not conform or comply with any of the recognized and accepted delays analysis methods used in the industry. It is observed that MCP has provided no explanation as to why it has not used any of the accepted delay analysis techniques. Property Developers Ltd submits that this is because none of the accepted methods would substantiate the delays claimed by MCP.

18. In the circumstances Property Developers Ltd submits that it is entitled to liquidated damages at the rate of £2,525 per day for 185 days amounting to £467,125.00.

Property Developers Ltd therefore claims:—

(a) An order that MCP should pay to Property Developers Ltd the sum of £467,125.00 (or such other sum as the Adjudicator may consider appropriate) in respect of the late completion of the Project, plus interest pursuant to Clause 24 of the CIS/1-2 2007 contract (or such other Clause as may be relevant) within 7 days of the date of the Adjudicator's Decision.

(b) A declaration that, on the true construction of Clause 16 of the CIS/1-2 2007 contract and in the events that have happened in the execution of the works on the Project, MCP is not entitled to any extension of time to the Contractual Completion Date for the works of 6 February 2010 or, alternatively, that the Adjudicator declares that MCP is entitled to such extension as the Adjudicator considers appropriate.

DATED   28 September 2010

Signed: Wilkinson & Bradshaw, solicitors for Property Developers Ltd

Dunedin House, Victoria Road, London EC1H 5LD

to a particular adjudicator it takes a more personalised tone than court pleadings. Also, because there may be limited scope for oral argument, it seeks to explain and argue the referring party's case, unlike the more formal practice with court statements of case. Rule 4 of the CEDR Rules requires a referral notice to set out:

- the circumstances giving rise to the dispute;
- the reasons for entitlement to the remedy sought; and
- the evidence, including relevant documentation, in support of its case.

22.25 The referral notice should be consistent with the notice of adjudication, but will set out the full circumstances on each of these areas in some detail, and is the 'full version' of events rather than the summary as set out in the notice of adjudication. They can be very long.

The referral notice should include the notice of adjudication and copies of, or extracts from, **22.26** the construction contract and such other documents as the referring party intends to rely upon. Most adjudicators prefer to have documents in chronological order. There may or may not be a hearing, so the referring party has to ensure that everything the adjudicator will need to understand with regard to the dispute is included. As there may be little other opportunity to explain the significance of the documents, the referral notice may have to talk the adjudicator through the material. It is very unwise to think the documents will speak for themselves. Copies of the files containing the referral notice and supporting documents must be sent at the same time to the other parties.

PROCEDURE BEFORE THE HEARING

The adjudicator is required to decide the procedure to be followed in the adjudication **22.27** (Scheme for Construction Contracts, para 13; CEDR Rules r 7). This is often done through a telephone conference between the adjudicator and all the parties, shortly after the adjudicator is appointed.

Response to referral notice

The adjudicator will consider whether the responding party should be allowed to put in a **22.28** response to the referral notice, and when. Treating the parties fairly will mean that almost invariably a direction is given providing for the response within either 7 or 14 days of the referral notice. As the referring party will have had as long as they wanted to prepare before service of the notice of adjudication, it will often be fair to give as much as 14 days of the 28-day adjudication period for the response to the referral notice. The response often takes the form of points of response, and responds to the referral notice and sets out the responding party's case.

Like a referral notice, the response should be supported by the relevant documentary evi- **22.29** dence. The best practice is to include only such documentation as was not included with the referral notice, but is not uncommon for a completely new set of documents, including duplicated documents, to be sent with the response.

Subsequent statements of case

The short time before a decision has to be made may mean it is impractical to permit the **22.30** referring party time to serve a reply, but the financial consequences of not doing so frequently compel the referring party to do so despite the lack of time. Likewise, particularly in large cases, further statements of case may be provided in response to the one before, in the sequence: rejoinder, rebutter, surrebutter. Provided each party has been given a fair opportunity to present its case and to respond to the allegations made by the other side, the adjudicator is entitled to decide (on giving fair notice to both sides) that no further submissions will be accepted after a set date.

Timetable for procedural steps

The adjudicator is required to establish the timetable and procedure for the adjudication, which may include the consideration of any documentary or oral submission of the parties, site visits or inspections, and meeting the parties (CEDR Rules r 8). The adjudicator may seek expert advice (r 13). There is a general duty to avoid incurring unnecessary expense (Scheme for Construction Contracts, para 12(b)), and the need to make a decision within 28 days of referral means that the adjudication has to be conducted expeditiously. If a party fails to comply with a direction imposed by the adjudicator, the adjudicator may make a peremptory order, and ultimately the adjudicator (or a party with the consent of the adjudicator), can apply to the High Court for an order requiring compliance by the defaulting party (Arbitration Act 1996 s 42, as applied by the Scheme for Construction Contracts, para 24).

Documents, questions and impartiality

22.31 Powers given to the adjudicator include the right to request any party to supply such documents as may be reasonably required, including any written statement from any party, and answers to questions. Questions are sometimes put to a party or witness in a separate meeting with the adjudicator as part of the fact-gathering process.

22.32 All documents and information provided to the adjudicator must be made available to all the parties (Scheme for Construction Contracts, para 17), which is part of a wider duty of impartiality (Housing Grants, Construction and Regeneration Act 1996, s 108(2)(e)). This means that the adjudicator must inform the other parties of any information or evidence provided by the other parties so they have a fair opportunity to comment on it. Failure to do so may invalidate the ultimate decision on the ground of a breach of the rules of natural justice.

Site visits

22.33 Subject to obtaining any necessary consent from third parties, the adjudicator may make such site visits and inspections as seem appropriate, and may do so whether accompanied by the parties or not (Scheme for Construction Contracts, para 13(d)). The adjudicator may also carry out tests or experiments (para 13(e)), and particular rules may also make provision for opening up of work on site for the purpose of inspections or tests (an example is the JCT standard form contract adjudication clauses).

Related disputes

22.34 With the consent of all the parties, the adjudicator may adjudicate at the same time on more than one dispute, either under the same contract, or on related disputes under different contracts (Scheme for Construction Contracts, para 8).

Confidentiality

22.35 All materials disclosed in an adjudication must be kept confidential except to the extent necessary for purposes in connection with the adjudication (Scheme for Construction Contracts, para 18).

ADJUDICATOR'S DECISION

Inquisitorial approach

The adjudicator may take the initiative in ascertaining the facts and the law necessary to **22.36** decide the dispute (Housing Grants, Construction and Regeneration Act 1996 s 108(2)(f); Scheme for Construction Contracts, para 13). This form of words, which can also be found in relation to arbitration in the Arbitration Act 1996, s 34(2)(g), means the adjudicator can (but is not obliged to) adopt an inquisitorial as opposed to an adversarial approach in the adjudication.

Hearing

There is no obligation to have a hearing, although the adjudicator may decide to hear oral **22.37** evidence or representations (Scheme for Construction Contracts, para 16(2)). A hearing will be more necessary or helpful where the case involves complex law or where there is conflicting evidence in any witness statements included in the parties' referral notice and subsequent statements of case on matters material to the decision. If there is a hearing the parties may be assisted or represented by legally qualified or other advisers. If there is no hearing, something similar is frequently achieved through communications by telephone, conference calls, email etc, which often come in quick succession as the deadline for the decision draws near.

The decision-making process

Adjudicators are required to act impartially in carrying out their duties, and must decide **22.38** the dispute in accordance with the relevant terms of the contract and in accordance with the law applicable to the contract (Scheme for Construction Contracts, para 12(a)). The adjudicator will consider any relevant information provided by the parties, but must not take into consideration any document or statement that has not been made available to the other parties for comment (CEDR Rules r 10). The adjudicator has the power to review any certificates etc made under the contract, unless precluded by the terms of the contract (Scheme for Construction Contracts, para 20(a)).

The adjudicator is required to reach a decision within 28 days of the referral notice (*Aveat* **22.39** *Heating Ltd v Jerram Falkus Construction Ltd* [2007] EWHC 131 (TCC)), although this period may be extended by 14 days with the consent of the referring party or longer if agreed by all the parties (Housing Grants, Construction and Regeneration Act 1996. 108(2)(c), (d)). This is recognised as being a very tight timetable, which might result in injustice, but one which Parliament must be taken to have been aware of (*Macob Civil Engineering Ltd v Morrison Construction Ltd* (1999) 64 Con LR 1). While the priority is to give effect to the rough and ready adjudication process, in an exceptional case the court can intervene by way of declaratory relief to prevent a breach of natural justice (*Dorchester Hotel Ltd v Vivid Interiors Ltd* [2009] Bus LR 1026).

Communicating decision to the parties

Technically, it is the decision that has to be made within 28 days (or an agreed extended **22.40** period) from the referral notice. This means actually communicating the decision to the parties may happen after this 28-day period without a breach of the Act. However, given immediate communications provided by email, there may be no excuse for any delay in sending the decision to the parties.

Reasons, interest and costs

22.41 Reasons must be given at the same time as delivering the decision unless the parties agree to the contrary under the CEDR Rules r 17, but under the Scheme for Construction Contracts reasons are only required if one of the parties makes a request (para 22). Giving reasons gives scope to arguments that the adjudication may have been flawed, which would undermine the quick and decisive purpose of the process. However, where parties have presented detailed cases to the adjudicator, they may feel they deserve to know the reasons for the decision.

22.42 Interest may be awarded in addition to the principal sum if payable under the contract (para 20(c)). Under the CEDR Rules each party bears its own costs (r 22).

BINDING, BUT INTERIM EFFECT, OF DECISIONS

22.43 By the Housing Grants, Construction and Regeneration Act 1996 s 108(3), the construction contract must provide that the adjudicator's decision is binding until the dispute is finally determined by legal proceedings, by arbitration or agreement. Any sum found to be payable by the adjudicator must be paid in full without any deduction by way of set-off, counterclaim or abatement (CEDR Rules r 21). If there are multiple adjudications arising out of a single project, it is fundamental to the adjudication process that each decision must be complied with separately without set-offs (*Hart v Smith* [2009] EWHC (TCC) 2223).

22.44 As mentioned at the beginning of this chapter, the principle is 'pay now, argue later', so the losing party can reopen everything after the adjudication by litigating through the courts or referring the matter to arbitration. To protect the adjudicator, institutional rules often make provision to the effect that the adjudicator shall not be joined as a party to any subsequent litigation or arbitration, or be required to give evidence or provide any of his notes (eg TeCSA Rules r 36).

22.45 To avoid the expense of subsequent litigation, the parties may agree to accept the decision of the adjudicator as finally determining the dispute.

OVERALL COST

22.46 Adjudication is not necessarily a cheap alternative. In *Amec Projects Ltd v Whitefriars City Estates Ltd* [2004] EWHC 393 (TCC) the costs of adjudication and enforcement were estimated at £277,000. In *AWG Construction Services Ltd v Rockingham Speedway Ltd* [2004] EWHC 888 (TCC) the costs came to over £1 million. In *McAlpine PPS Pipeline Systems Ltd v Transco plc* [2004] BLR 352 the adjudication costs were about £100,000 in relation to a claim for £45,000.

ADJUDICATION IN RESIDENTIAL BUILDING CONTRACTS

While construction contracts with residential occupiers are excluded from the scheme in **22.47**
the Housing Grants, Construction and Regeneration Act 1996, Part II, by s 106 (see 22.05
above), this does not prevent the parties to such a contract including clauses in their contract making similar provision. There are even rules promulgated by the building industry
specifically providing for the adjudication of disputes in building contracts with owner/
occupiers. For example, the Joint Contracts Tribunal Limited ('JCT') Rules for Adjudication
are designed for use with the JCT building contract and the JCT consultancy agreement for
home owner/occupiers.

COURT ENFORCEMENT OF SUM FOUND DUE ON ADJUDICATION

A party with the benefit of an adjudicator's decision may bring enforcement proceedings **22.48**
in the courts by issuing a Part 8 claim form, and then applying for summary judgment.
In most cases summary judgment will be entered in accordance with the policy of the
Housing Grants, Construction and Regeneration Act 1996. This is discussed in more detail
in Chapter 29.

KEY POINTS SUMMARY

- The basic principle of adjudication is pay now, argue later. **22.49**
- Adjudication applies to written commercial construction contracts.
- An adjudicator must be appointed within seven days of a notice referring a dispute to
  adjudication.
- The adjudicator must act impartially.
- The adjudicator's decision must be made within 28 days of referral (although this can be
  extended).
- The adjudication is binding until the dispute is decided by litigation, arbitration or
  agreement.
- Normally the parties are required to comply with the adjudicator's decision immediately
  on delivery of the decision.
- Otherwise enforcement is normally through summary judgment of the adjudicator's
  decision.

23

ARBITRATION

INTRODUCTION 23.01

ARBITRATION AND LITIGATION 23.05

FUNDAMENTAL CONCEPTS IN ARBITRATION 23.06

HISTORY OF ARBITRATION 23.07

INTERPRETATION OF THE ARBITRATION ACT 1996 . . . . .23.09

CONTRACTUAL FOUNDATION TO ARBITRATION 23.11

REQUIREMENTS 23.20

OVERVIEW OF ARBITRATION PROCEDURE 23.52

GENERAL PRINCIPLES AND DUTIES .23.53

FAIR RESOLUTION OF DISPUTES 23.54

PARTY AUTONOMY 23.59

COURT APPLICATIONS 23.63

DIFFERENT TYPES OF ARBITRATIONS 23.65

STATUTORY ARBITRATION 23.70

CONSUMER ARBITRATION 23.71

MULTI-TIERED DISPUTE RESOLUTION 23.74

ONE-STOP ADJUDICATION 23.76

EUROPEAN CONVENTION ON HUMAN RIGHTS
AND ARBITRATION 23.77

MAIN FEATURES OF ARBITRATION .23.79

KEY POINTS SUMMARY 23.81

INTRODUCTION

Arbitration is an adjudicative dispute resolution process. It is based on an agreement **23.01** between the parties to refer a dispute or difference between them to impartial arbitrators for a decision. There is no statutory definition of the term 'arbitration', probably because it can take a wide variety of forms and can arise in a wide variety of legal contexts. It is not uncommon to distinguish arbitration from other forms of ADR on the grounds that it is adjudicative, in the sense that the arbitrators actually make a decision on which party succeeds on the dispute, whereas in non-adjudicative ADR processes the dispute resolution agency acts as a facilitator in order to seek to enable the parties to reach an agreement on resolving their dispute.

As a consequence of the contractual basis of arbitration, it is not every dispute that can go to **23.02** arbitration. This chapter considers the requirements for an effective reference to arbitration, but it should be noted that the agreement to arbitrate may be made before or after the relevant dispute has arisen. This means that there may be a pre-existing arbitration agreement which, when a dispute arises, one of the parties wishes to evade. There is a strong public policy in favour of upholding arbitration agreements, which is supported by the idea that an arbitration clause in a contract is separable from the rest of the substantive contract (and so continues to apply even if the substantive contract is avoided), and by the jurisdiction to stay court proceedings that are commenced in breach of an arbitration agreement (see Chapter 28).

Arbitrations in England and Wales are governed by the Arbitration Act 1996 (which is set **23.03** out in Appendix 4). A key philosophical question in arbitration law is the extent to which domestic law should prescribe how arbitrations should be conducted, and the extent to which the parties should be allowed to devise their own procedures. This is reflected in the distinction in the Arbitration Act 1996 between mandatory and non-mandatory provisions (discussed in this chapter). The intention is that the mandatory provisions cover only the matters that are essential to the effective resolution of matters referred to arbitration, with everything else covered by non-mandatory fall-back provisions, which the parties can change if they wish.

The Arbitration Act 1996 is also intended to lay down a highly developed set of proce- **23.04** dures for arbitrations, in keeping with this country's status as a leading venue for international arbitrations. These include rules for how to start an arbitration, and how a panel of arbitrators is appointed, matters discussed in Chapter 24. A detailed consideration of how commercial arbitrations are conducted can be found in Chapter 25, which includes a number of precedents and also considers a number of sets of rules used by arbitral institutions dealing with the procedures that should be followed. Chapter 26 looks at a number of particular issues that arise in international arbitrations. These include jurisdictional issues, questions of the proper law to be applied, as well as the institutional rules for arbitrations published by the International Chamber of Commerce and the United Nations Commission on International Trade Law. Arbitral awards are considered in Chapter 27, and Chapter 28 deals with applications that can be made to the courts in support of arbitrations, and to review arbitral decisions that might be wrong. Enforcement of arbitral awards is considered in Chapter 29.

ARBITRATION AND LITIGATION

23.05 Arbitration can be seen as a private version of litigation. It involves an independent arbitrator or tribunal considering both sides of the dispute and making a decision on the issues raised by the parties. Many commercial contracts include arbitration clauses under which the parties agree to refer any dispute to arbitration rather than going to court. The object is to obtain a fair resolution of the dispute by an impartial tribunal without unnecessary delay or expense (Arbitration Act 1996 s 1). Arbitration differs from litigation in two main respects:

- a dispute will only be referred to arbitration if that is the course agreed between the parties; and
- arbitrators are appointed by the parties (or through a mechanism agreed by the parties), whereas in litigation the judge will be appointed by the state.

FUNDAMENTAL CONCEPTS IN ARBITRATION

23.06 Where the parties have agreed to refer their disputes to arbitration, Lord Hoffmann said in *Fili Shipping Co Ltd v Premium Nafta Products Ltd* [2007] Bus LR 1719 that this implies they want their disputes decided:

- by a tribunal they have chosen (see Chapter 24);
- in a neutral location (this is of particular importance in international arbitration: see Chapter 26) and with neutral arbitrators;
- in privacy (see 25.06);
- by the arbitrators speedily and efficiently; and
- with light but efficient supervision by the courts (see Chapter 28).

HISTORY OF ARBITRATION

23.07 Despite the modern feel to most of the procedures described in this book, arbitration in fact has an impressive history. It can be traced back to Ancient Greece, and in England at least as far back as 1468 (see *Anon* [1468] YB 8 Edw IV, fo1, p1, at which time it was called arbitrament, a word still in use). For many years the Arbitration Act 1950 was the principal statute governing this area. It had a number of limitations, including giving excessive powers of review to the courts, and giving inadequate coverage of matters relating to procedure. It was amended by the Arbitration Act 1979 following a report by Lord Donaldson, and was replaced by the Arbitration Act 1996, which rectified these defects and provides a modern statement of the law that meets the needs of the international commercial community.

23.08 The Arbitration Act 1996 draws heavily on reports by the Departmental Advisory Committee ('DAC') on Arbitration set up by the Department of Trade and Industry. It also borrows from concepts to be found in the United Nations Commission on International Trade Law ('UNCITRAL') Model Law on arbitration. It has been very successful in ensuring that English law on arbitration is consistent with international practice.

INTERPRETATION OF THE ARBITRATION ACT 1996

The Arbitration Act 1996 restates and improves the law relating to arbitration. It was con- **23.09** sciously drafted in accessible English, with the intention that it would be read and understood by non-lawyers who may be engaged in arbitrations either as parties or arbitrators. In a passage endorsed by Lord Steyn in *Lesotho Highlands Development Authority v Impregilo SpA* [2006] 1 AC 221 at [19], Thomas J in *Seabridge Shipping AB v AC Orssleff's Eft's A/S* [1999] 2 Lloyd's Rep 685, said:

> '...it would in my view be a retrograde step if when a point arose reference had to be made to pre-Act cases. Reference to such cases should only generally be necessary in cases where the Act does not cover some point - as, for example, in relation to confidentiality or where for some other reason it is necessary to refer to the earlier cases. A court should, in general, comply with the guidance given [in *Patel v Patel* [2000] QB 551] and rely on the language of the Act. International users of London arbitration should, in my view, be able to rely on the clear "user-friendly language" of the Act and should not have to be put to the trouble or expense of having regard to the pre-1996 Act law on issues where the provisions of the Act set out the law. If international users of London arbitration are not able to act in that knowledge, then one of the main objectives of the reform will have been defeated.'

A large number of provisions in the Arbitration Act 1996 use the word 'shall' to describe **23.10** matters to be done by the parties, arbitrators or the courts. In 1996 'shall' was regarded by lawyers as connoting a mandatory requirement and as being synonymous with 'must'. That is the intention of the Arbitration Act 1996, and in this book the word 'shall' is used in a mandatory sense. In 2004 and 2006 two cases (*Metcalfe v Clipston* [2004] EWHC 9005 (Costs) and *Choudury v Kingston Hospital NHS Trust* [2006] EWHC 90057 (Costs)) decided that 'shall' is not mandatory. As a result, post-2006 legislation uses the word 'must' instead of shall, but this is not to be regarded as changing the legislative intent of the Arbitration Act 1996.

CONTRACTUAL FOUNDATION TO ARBITRATION

Almost any type of dispute can be referred to arbitration, regardless of the legal classification **23.11** of the underlying cause of action. That said, arbitration is most commonly used for resolving disputes arising out of a contract between the parties, frequently with the agreement to arbitrate being found in a clause in the substantive contract. Where such a dispute is referred to arbitration, from a technical legal point of view there will often be four contracts.

- the underlying substantive contract on which the dispute is based ('the substantive contract');
- the agreement to arbitrate. Even where the agreement to arbitrate is in point of form just one of many contractual clauses in the substantive contract, as a matter of arbitration law the clause is a separable contract, distinct from the substantive contract. See 23.12 below;
- the agreement between the parties and an arbitral institution referring the dispute to arbitration under the aegis of that institution. Often the institution's arbitration rules will apply to the arbitral proceedings;
- the agreement between the parties and/or the arbitral institution and the individuals who will act as arbitrators appointing those individuals to preside over the arbitration and make a decision on the dispute.

Separability of arbitration clause

23.12   The Arbitration Act, 1996 s 7, provides:

> 'Unless otherwise agreed by the parties, an arbitration agreement which forms or was intended to form part of another agreement (whether or not in writing) shall not be regarded as invalid, non-existent or ineffective because that other agreement is invalid, or did not come into existence or has become ineffective, and it shall for that purpose be treated as a distinct agreement.'

23.13   This is an important principle, and prevents arbitral proceedings becoming frustrated in cases where the arbitrators make a finding to the effect that the substantive agreement is invalid or discharged. Without s 7 such a finding would result in the arbitration clause also being ineffective, which would mean there is no decision on the substantive contract. If that was the position, a party who did not want a dispute referred to arbitration would always be tempted to argue for some invalidity in the substantive contract in order to undermine the jurisdiction of the arbitrators.

23.14   That this will not work was confirmed by *Fili Shipping Co Ltd v Premium Nafta Products Ltd* [2007] Bus LR 1719 (this case is also known as *Fiona Trust & Holding Corporation v Privalov*). Ship owners in this case had entered into charterparties (leases of ships) with the charterers. Each charterparty included a clause giving both parties the right to refer any dispute under the charter to arbitration. The owners alleged that the charterparties had been induced by bribery, and brought court proceedings in England seeking declarations that they were entitled to rescind the charterparties on the basis they had been procured by bribery, conspiracy and breach of fiduciary duty. The charterers wanted the disputes to be referred to arbitration, and applied to have the court litigation stayed under the Arbitration Act 1996 s 9 (see 28.07). The owners sought an injunction to restrain the charterers referring the disputes to arbitration pursuant to s 72 (see Table 26.1). It was held by the House of Lords that an argument that the substantive contract (the charterparties) had been procured by bribery did not prevent the arbitrators ruling on whether the substantive contract was invalid. It is only if the alleged invalidity affects the arbitration clause itself that the arbitrators will be deprived of jurisdiction on this ground. As there were no grounds for challenging the validity of the separable arbitration clauses, the court proceedings were stayed under s 9.

Mandate of the arbitral tribunal

23.15   The jurisdiction given to an arbitral tribunal depends on the mandate given to it by the parties. An arbitral tribunal will not have jurisdiction unless the dispute comes within the terms of the particular reference to arbitration. This will be limited by the terms of the arbitration agreement (which may be a standard clause in the substantive contract, or an agreement after the dispute has arisen to refer that dispute to arbitration), and the separate agreement between the tribunal and the parties appointing the tribunal. It means, for example, that the arbitrators cannot make a decision against a person who is not a party to the arbitration agreement, or on matters not covered by the arbitration agreement, or on matters not covered by the parties' agreement with the arbitrators. Restrictions based on the terms of the arbitration agreement are discussed at 23.41.

Further, the tribunal is only authorised to determine the dispute actually referred to it and **23.16**
on the terms of the agreement between the arbitrators and the parties. Once a dispute is
referred to arbitration, the courts tend to give a wide interpretation to what is included in
the tribunal's mandate. Partly this is in support of the 'one-stop' policy (see 23.76), that the
parties usually intend that all their current disputes should be resolved at the same time by
a single decision-making body. Partly this is a recognition that the precise scope of a dispute
inevitably tends to evolve as it is investigated.

Restrictions imposed by a tribunal's mandate mean that the arbitrators have to comply with **23.17**
the agreement between the parties on the procedure to be followed. This is the agreement
as at the time the tribunal is appointed, which may include a framework for further agreements between the parties on matters of procedure. This may include adhering to a set of
arbitral institutional rules and, if so, the tribunal does not have the power to go behind what
the parties have agreed.

By accepting their appointments, the arbitrators agree to consider the evidence and make **23.18**
decisions on the matters referred to them. They are obliged to make decisions on all the
central issues of the dispute(s). In this connection, a purposive construction is placed on
the 'issues' that are to be decided (*Checkpoint Ltd v Strathclyde Pension Fund* [2003] 1 EGLR
1). This means that decisions must be made on all the matters that are critical to the overall
decision, and also such subsidiary issues that have to be decided en route to those central
issues. It means that other matters, which may have appeared to be important at earlier
stages of the arbitration, may fall away once certain decisions are made. Where a tribunal
fails to reach a decision on a central issue in the dispute there is a serious irregularity for
the purposes of the Arbitration Act 1996 s 68, which means the award may be challenged
in court (*Ascot Commodities v Olam* [2002] CLC 277; and see 28.45).

These constraints do not necessarily prevent arbitrators making decisions on matters **23.19**
arising after their appointment. For example, in *Rederij Lalemant v Transportes Generales
Navigacion SA* [1986] 1 Lloyd's Rep 45 it was held that the arbitrators were entitled to decide
both the demurrage payable at the port of loading (arising from events before they were
appointed) and demurrage payable at the port of discharge (which arose after they were
appointed). What is covered depends on the terms of the appointment of the arbitrators.

REQUIREMENTS

In order for there to be an effective reference to arbitration the following requirements **23.20**
must be met:

- there must be a dispute or difference (see 23.21);
- the dispute must be 'arbitrable' (see 23.25);
- there must be an agreement to arbitrate (see 23.28);
- for the Arbitration Act 1996 to apply, the agreement to arbitrate must be in writing (see
  23.38);
- the nature of the dispute must come within the terms of the arbitration agreement (see
  23.41);

- the parties must have had the capacity to enter into the arbitration agreement (see 23.47);
- any condition precedent to arbitration must be complied with (see 23.49);
- the parties must find an arbitral tribunal willing to act and decide the dispute (see Chapter 24); and
- the dispute must come within the terms of the particular reference to arbitration (the tribunal's mandate: see 23.15 above).

Dispute or difference

23.21 Arbitration is a dispute resolution process, and if there is no dispute there is nothing for the arbitrators to decide. The Arbitration Act 1996 s 6(1) defines an arbitration agreement as one to submit present or future disputes (whether they are contractual or not) to arbitration. What frequently happens in practice is that one of the parties will make a 'claim' against the other, such as for payment of the price due under a contract, or damages for non-performance. Such situations do not develop into disputes if the claim is admitted (or paid). Any other type of response, for example a denial of liability, or an assertion that the money is not yet payable, converts the claim into a dispute that may be referred to arbitration.

23.22 'Dispute' is defined by s 82 to include any difference. A 'difference' was technically regarded as applying to a failure to agree, but the distinction between 'disputes' and 'differences' ceased being important when the Arbitration Act 1996 assimilated the two concepts. Both words must be given their natural meanings (*Cruden Construction Ltd v Commission for the New Towns* [1995] 2 Lloyd's Rep 387). They cover disputes of law or fact, and are intended to have a wide effect. They are even wide enough to cover a dispute whether there has been an effective compromise of a dispute arising out of the substantive contract (*Joseph Finney plc v Vickers* [2001] All ER (D) 235).

23.23 Before the enactment of the Arbitration Act 1996 the courts were allowed to take over and grant summary judgment despite an arbitration clause where the grounds of defence to a claim were regarded as 'not disputable'. This is now regarded as too great an invasion by the courts, and the present position is that the courts cannot intervene to stop an arbitration even if the court thinks the defendant does not have an arguable defence (*Halki Shipping Corp v Sopex Oils Ltd* [1998] 1 WLR 726).

23.24 Even under the modern law there will be no dispute if:

- the defendant does not dispute liability; or
- the contention now being relied upon by the defendant was never put to the claimant (*Edmund Nuttall Ltd v RG Carter Ltd* [2002] BLR 312);
- the right to dispute the matter has been lost under the contract or by law (*Watkins Jones and Sons Ltd v Lidl UK GmbH* (2002) 86 Con LR 155).

Arbitrable dispute

23.25 While most arbitrations relate to contractual disputes, any private dispute or difference is amenable to arbitration, regardless of the nature of the underlying cause of action. The only restriction is that arbitration is only available to resolve issues of a private law nature. This flows from the contractual basis of arbitration, which means that public law matters, and matters relating to legal status, cannot be determined by arbitration.

This means that the following are all examples of disputes that are *not* arbitrable: **23.26**

- marital status;
- care of children;
- validity of patents;
- status of a public right of way;
- bankruptcy;
- criminal liability; and
- judicial review of administrative decisions.

This does not mean that disputes that have a public element are entirely off-limits for **23.27** arbitration. For example, arbitrators are obliged to respect EU competition law (*Nordsee Deutsche Hochseefischerei GmbH v Reederei Mond Hochseefischerei Nordstern AG & Co KG* Case 102/81 [1982] ECR 1095). Likewise, the provisions of the European Convention on Human Rights have to be given effect to in arbitrations, because these are directed at determining the civil rights and obligations of the parties (Art 6(1); but see 23.77).

Agreement to arbitrate

Arbitration stems from an agreement to refer a dispute to arbitration. Such an agreement **23.28** can be made before or after the dispute has arisen. Where an arbitration clause is an express written term of the underlying contract there should be no problems other than construing what it requires. It is more difficult where the arbitration clause is in a connected contract, or a contract with someone else, or where a dispute covers a number of contracts each with different arbitration clauses (see 23.31–23.37).

Breach of an agreement to arbitrate

A party will be bound by its pre-dispute agreement to arbitrate if it subsequently changes **23.29** its mind. If a party insists on ignoring an arbitration clause any litigation may be stayed under the Arbitration Act 1996 s 9 (see 28.07). Starting court proceedings to determine the dispute in breach of an arbitration clause may also be a repudiatory breach of the arbitration agreement (*Delta Reclamantion Ltd v Premier Waste Management Ltd* [2008] EWHC 2579 (QB)). Correspondence denying the existence of the arbitration agreement may also be a repudiation (*Downing v Al Tameer Establishment* [2002] 2 All ER (Comm) 545). A party in breach of an arbitration agreement may be liable in damages (*Donohue v Armco* [2001] 1 Lloyd's Rep 425 (a jurisdiction clause case, and see *Russell on Arbitration* (23rd edn, Sweet & Maxwell, 2007), para 7–019).

Arbitration clauses

A selection of typical arbitration clauses, together with a post-dispute agreement to refer the **23.30** dispute to arbitration, are shown in Table 23.1. The level of detail found in different arbitration clauses varies very considerably. Such a clause can be very short and fully effective. Given the range of non-mandatory matters covered by the Arbitration Act 1996 (all or any of which may be addressed in an arbitration clause), and the range of solutions to just about every one of those elements, there is an almost infinite number of potential clauses that may be encountered. However, the clauses shown in Table 23.1 are fairly representative of clauses frequently found in standard form contracts.

Table 23.1 Arbitration contract clauses

Type of clause	Wording
Ad hoc arbitration, single arbitrator	Any dispute or difference arising out of or in connection with this contract shall be determined by the appointment of a single arbitrator to be agreed between the parties, or failing agreement within 14 days after either party has given to the other a written request to concur in the appointment of an arbitrator, by an arbitrator to be appointed by the President [*of a named arbitral institution or profession*]. The seat of the arbitration shall be England and Wales.
Ad hoc arbitration, clause referring dispute to two arbitrators	All disputes arising out of this contract shall be arbitrated at London and, unless the parties agree forthwith to a single arbitrator, be referred to the final arbitrament of two arbitrators, both to be commercial men, one to be appointed by each of the parties.
Rules for the arbitration	The arbitration shall be governed by both the Arbitration Act 1996 and the [*named Rules of an arbitral institution*] ('the Rules'), or any amendments to those provisions. The Rules are deemed to be incorporated by reference into this clause.
Facilitation of settlement in arbitration	The arbitral tribunal appointed under this agreement shall apply the [*name of arbitral institution*] Rules on the facilitation of settlement in arbitration.
Institutional arbitration, three arbitrators	Any dispute or difference arising out of or in connection with the present contract shall be administered by [*named arbitral institution*] and finally determined under the rules of the [*named Rules of the arbitral institution*] by three arbitrators appointed in accordance with those Rules.
Agreement to refer dispute to arbitration after dispute has arisen	A dispute having arisen between [*Party 1*] and [*Party 2*] concerning [*state the nature of the dispute*], the parties hereby refer that dispute to arbitration under the rules of the [*named Rules of an arbitral institution*]. Signed: Signed: Dated:

Two-contract cases

23.31 It is not unusual, particularly in shipping, reinsurance and construction cases, for there to be an arbitration clause in the main agreement, and a clause in a subsidiary contract to adopt all or some of the terms of the main agreement, including the arbitration clause. Whether this is effective to make the subsidiary contract subject to the arbitration clause is a matter of construction.

23.32 There will often be good reasons for not being too quick to assume that an arbitration clause from the main contract is intended to apply to the subsidiary contract. These include the common occurrence that the main contract is quite different in its nature from the subsidiary contract (particularly if the subsidiary contract is a sub-sub-contract or even further removed from the main contract), or if the subsidiary contract is a transferable document of title (such as a bill of lading, the document evidencing a contract of carriage of goods by sea) issued under a charterparty (a lease of a ship)). These considerations have resulted in a rule in construction and shipping cases that an arbitration clause in the main contract will only be imported into the subsidiary contract if there is a specific reference to the arbitration clause in the subsidiary contract. See *Aughton Ltd v MF Kent Services Ltd* [1991] 57 BLR 1 (construction contracts) and *Thomas and Co Ltd v Portsea SS Co Ltd* [1912] AC 1 (charterparty and bill of lading cases).

Contracts (Rights of Third Parties) Act 1999

Third parties may be subject to arbitration agreements in contracts between other parties in   **23.33** relation to contractual disputes over terms made for their benefit by virtue of the Contracts (Rights of Third Parties) Act 1999. Section 8(1) provides:

> 'Where—
>
> (a)   a right under section 1 to enforce a term ('the substantive term') is subject to a term providing for the submission of disputes to arbitration ('the arbitration agreement'), and
>
> (b)   the arbitration agreement is an agreement in writing for the purposes of Part I of the Arbitration Act 1996,
>
> the third party shall be treated for the purposes of that Act as a party to the arbitration agreement as regards disputes between himself and the promisor relating to the enforcement of the substantive term by the third party.'

Under s 1(1), a third party may in his own right enforce a term of a contract if: **23.34**

- the contract expressly provides that he may; or
- the term purports to confer a benefit on him. This is subject to s 1(2), which says this does not apply if on a proper construction of the contract it appears that the parties did not intend the term to be enforceable by the third party.

Where s 8(1) applies, not only is the third party able to rely on the arbitration clause,   **23.35** but the third party is also bound by it and can be required to refer any dispute covered by the clause to arbitration (*Nisshin Shipping Co Ltd v Cleaves and Co Ltd* [2004] 1 Lloyd's Rep 38).

It is only disputes over contractual terms that are covered by s 8(1). Arbitration over other   **23.36** causes of action, such as in tort, may be resorted to by third parties under s 8(2), which provides that where:

> '(a)   a third party has a right under section 1 to enforce a term providing for one or more descriptions of dispute between the third party and the promisor to be submitted to arbitration ("the arbitration agreement"),
>
> (b)   the arbitration agreement is an agreement in writing for the purposes of Part I of the Arbitration Act 1996, and
>
> (c)   the third party does not fall to be treated under subsection (1) as a party to the arbitration agreement,
>
> the third party shall, if he exercises the right, be treated for the purposes of that Act as a party to the arbitration agreement in relation to the matter with respect to which the right is exercised, and be treated as having been so immediately before the exercise of the right.'

Disputes covering several contracts

Where a single dispute raises issues based on a number of contracts each with different arbi-   **23.37** tration clauses, it is necessary to determine which clause takes precedence. It is best if this can be done by agreement between the parties. If this is not possible, the rule is that the arbitration clause in the contract at the commercial centre of the transaction is the one that applies (*UBS AG v HSH Nordbank AG* [2009] 2 Lloyd's Rep 272, a case on jurisdiction clauses).

The agreement to arbitrate

Written agreement

23.38   The provisions in the Arbitration Act 1996 only apply to arbitration agreements that are in writing (Arbitration Act 1996 s 5(1)). This is satisfied (s 5(2)) if the agreement is:

- made in writing, whether or not it is signed by the parties. This includes an agreement by reference to terms which are in writing (s 5(3)); or
- made by the exchange of communications in writing; or
- evidenced in writing. This applies where the agreement is recorded by one of the parties, or by a third party, with the authority of the parties to the agreement (s 5(4)).

23.39   References to writing include recording by any means (s 5(6)). An issue as to whether a term should be implied into the contract does not impact on the question of whether the contract is in writing for the purposes of s 5 (*Connex South Eastern Ltd v MJ Building Services Group plc* [2004] BLR 333, a case on construction industry adjudication). There will be no written contract where all that can be pointed to is a draft contract where the court finds that executing a formal signed agreement was a precondition to the parties being bound (*Sun Life Assurance Company of Canada v CX Reinsurance Co Ltd* [2004] Lloyd's Rep IR 58). On the other hand, where a charterparty with an arbitration clause had been signed by one party, both parties were held bound by the clause where the other party had on the evidence waived its entitlement to insist on a signature before being bound (*Oceanografia SA de CV v DSND Subsea AS* [2007] 1 Lloyd's Rep 37).

Oral agreements to refer disputes to arbitration

23.40   Without a written agreement, even with the extended meaning given to writing by the Arbitration Act 1996 s 5, an agreement to refer a dispute to arbitration will not be governed by the Arbitration Act 1996. Despite this, an oral agreement to refer a matter to arbitration is effective (s 81(1)(b)), but the reference will be governed by the common law. Essentially this means that the matter should be arbitrated in accordance with the agreement between the parties. There are obvious problems in establishing such an oral agreement and in deciding what has been agreed, particularly where the parties are in acrimonious dispute.

Dispute must come within the arbitration agreement

23.41   The range of disputes that will be covered by an arbitration agreement is a matter of contractual construction to determine what the parties intended. The underlying principle is that an arbitral tribunal can only have jurisdiction to determine matters that the parties have agreed should be referred to arbitration. The parties may agree to refer all disputes arising out of the substantive contract to arbitration, whether they are based on the law of contract, tort, unjust enrichment or any other type of cause of action. Alternatively, the parties may agree that only certain types of dispute will go to arbitration.

23.42   At one time a large number of technical distinctions were drawn by the courts over what disputes were and were not covered by different forms of words in arbitration clauses. The technicality of the rules left the law in some disrepute, and the modern approach is to give a broad and inclusive interpretation to most arbitration clauses.

In *Fili Shipping Co Ltd v Premium Nafta Products Ltd* [2007] Bus LR 1719, the arbitration clause **23.43** provided: 'Any dispute arising under this charter [lease of a ship] shall be decided...' by arbitration. Lord Hoffmann pointed out that in construing such a clause regard must be had to the commercial background, and that businessmen are assumed to make agreements that achieve some rational commercial purpose. Agreeing with Longmore LJ in the Court of Appeal, Lord Hoffmann said that a new start was needed (see [12]). Rather than undertaking a semantic analysis of the clause and how similar clauses have been construed in the past, the court must start from the assumption that the parties, as rational businessmen, are likely to have intended that any dispute arising out of their relationship should be decided by the same tribunal. As a result, the clause in the case itself was wide enough to cover both:

- disputes regarding the rights and obligations created by the charter of the ship itself; and
- disputes over matters said to invalidate the charter (on the facts these were allegations that the charter was vitiated through bribery).

It should follow that the same should apply on the question whether an arbitration clause in **23.44** a contract extends both to disputes:

- in contract; and
- in tort and other non-contract causes of action.

Support for this can be derived from *Et Plus SA v Welter* [2006] 1 Lloyd's Rep 251 and *Asghar* **23.45** *v Legal Services Commission* [2004] EWHC 1803 (Ch).

Of course, ultimately the parties may agree to whatever restrictions on the nature of the **23.46** disputes they intend to refer to arbitration, and the question remains one of contractual construction. Thus, in *Food Corp of India v Achilles Halcoussis* [1988] 2 Lloyd's Rep 56, the arbitration clause said that disputes relating to demurrage and freight could be referred to arbitration. A dispute arose over a claim to elevator overtime, and Steyn J said that as it could not be inferred from the clause that it included elevator overtime, that was simply not a matter that had been entrusted to the arbitrators.

Capacity

There will be no valid reference to arbitration if either of the parties lacked the legal capacity **23.47** to enter into the arbitration agreement. This is a matter of contract law, and means that in general children (those aged under 18) and persons suffering from mental incapacity within the meaning of the Mental Capacity Act 2005 cannot be parties to arbitrations. There may also be restrictions on the capacities of corporations that prevent them from entering into arbitration agreements, but the modern position is that registered companies under the Companies Acts have unlimited objects and therefore no restrictions on being parties to arbitrations (see Companies Act 2006 s 31).

Lack of capacity is a reason for not recognising an arbitration agreement when a party **23.48** seeks to enforce it through the court system (see Arbitration Act 1996 s 103(2)(a), and the New York Convention 1958, discussed in Chapter 29).

Conditions precedent to arbitration

Compliance with conditions precedent

23.49 Any condition precedent in the arbitration clause will need to be complied with. For example, it is not unusual for a clause to say that a dispute may be referred to arbitration 'at the request' of a party. In such as case a request must be made before arbitration becomes compulsory (*Secretary of State of the Environment, Transport and the Regions, ex p The Channel Group Ltd* [2001] EWCA Civ 1185). It has been known for other arbitration clauses to provide for arbitration 'after completion of the work' or 'after mediation', which have the effect that arbitration cannot be started until after these steps have been completed.

Scott v Avery clauses

23.50 A *Scott v Avery* clause (from *Scott v Avery* (1856) 25 LJ Ex 308) provides that court proceedings shall not be brought until after an arbitration award has been made. Its purpose is to ensure the parties arbitrate before they litigate. Such a clause is a condition precedent to litigation (as opposed to a condition precedent to arbitration). If the other side commence court proceedings without arbitrating, the *Scott v Avery* clause can be pleaded as a defence to the claim.

23.51 As the purpose of a *Scott v Avery* clause is to protect the right to arbitrate, it does not prevent a party applying for a court injunction for the purpose of enforcing the arbitration agreement (*Toepfer International GmbH v Societe Cargill France* [1998] 1 Lloyd's Rep 379).

OVERVIEW OF ARBITRATION PROCEDURE

23.52 Figure 23.1 is an overall flow diagram showing the stages that many arbitrations go through from the initial formation of a dispute through the appointment of a tribunal to the hearing and enforcement. On the right-hand side of the flow diagram are indications of the types of applications to the court that may be made at various stages of the process. As the actual procedures followed depends on the agreement of the parties, any arbitral institution rules that apply, and the approach of individual arbitrators, the steps taken in particular arbitrations may vary considerably from this basic model.

GENERAL PRINCIPLES AND DUTIES

23.53 Arbitrations governed by the Arbitration Act 1996 are subject to three general principles that are set out in s 1, as follows:

'(a) the object of arbitration is to obtain the fair resolution of disputes by an impartial tribunal without unnecessary delay or expense;

(b) the parties should be free to agree how their disputes are resolved, subject only to such safeguards as are necessary in the public interest; and

(c) the court should not intervene except as provided by the Arbitration Act 1996.'

Figure 23.1 Stages in arbitration flow diagram, with possible applications to court

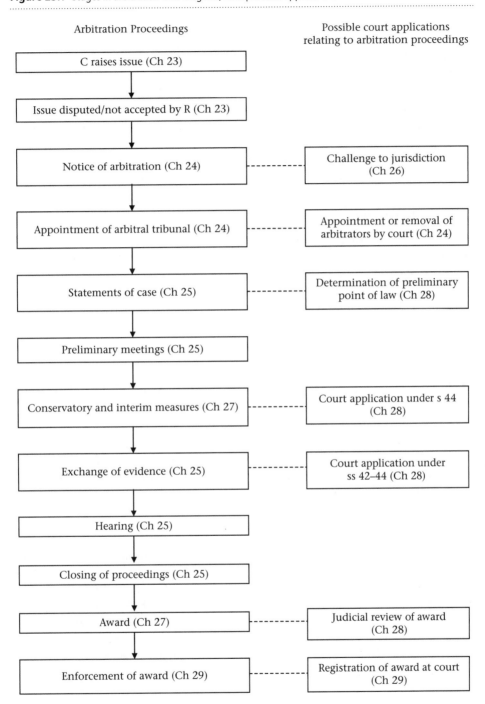

FAIR RESOLUTION OF DISPUTES

23.54   The first of the general principles is in many respects similar to the overriding objective in normal litigation to be found in CPR, r 1.1. There is a close affinity between obtaining the fair resolution of disputes in arbitration and dealing with litigation justly, and ensuring there is a fair trial pursuant to the European Convention on Human Rights ('ECHR') Art 6. In most arbitrations the tribunal will seek to resolve the dispute by applying the appropriate law, but this is not always the case, as the parties are able to agree that the tribunal should apply some other system of rules or principles in deciding their dispute. It will be noticed that the Arbitration Act 1996 s 1(a) says that the dispute must be resolved by an 'impartial' tribunal, as opposed to an independent tribunal. This will be explored further in Chapter 24.

Saving costs and expedition

23.55   In a similar way to litigation, the arbitral object of resolving the dispute fairly includes doing so without unnecessary delay or expense. To assist the tribunal in achieving this objective the parties are required to do all things necessary for the proper and expeditious conduct of the arbitral proceedings (s 40(1)). This includes complying without delay with any orders made by the tribunal on procedural or evidential matters and with any other orders and directions of the tribunal (s 40(2)).

General duty of the tribunal

23.56   The first general principle in the Arbitration Act 1996 s 1(a) is supported by s 33(1), which imposes the following general duties on the arbitral tribunal:

> '(a)   to act fairly and impartially as between the parties, giving each party a reasonable opportunity of putting its case and dealing with that of it's opponent; and
>
> (b)   to adopt procedures suitable to the circumstances of the particular case, avoiding unnecessary delay or expense, with a view to providing a fair means for the resolution of the matters falling to be determined.'

Duty to follow the rules of natural justice

23.57   It follows from the Arbitration Act 1996 s 33(1) that the arbitral tribunal is required to follow the rules of natural justice. They will be breached if the arbitrators fail to give the parties an opportunity to deal with factors that the arbitrators intend to take into account in making a decision (*Gbangola v Smith & Sherriff Ltd* [1998] 3 All ER 730). Giving the parties a fair opportunity to present their case does not mean that the arbitrators are obliged to follow the strict procedures to be found in court procedure. An example is *Margulead Ltd v Exide Technologies* [2005] 1 Lloyd's Rep 324, where the arbitrator allowed both sides a closing speech, but refused to allow the claimant the last word, which is the usual position in litigation.

Arbitration need not be adversarial

23.58   In fact arbitrators can go even further, and completely depart from the usual adversarial system found in the English courts. This follows from s 34(2)(e), which provides that, subject to the agreement of the parties, the arbitral tribunal can decide whether any and if so what questions should be put to and answered by the respective parties and when and in what form this should be done. This provision of course allows for minor variations on the adversarial system, for example the use of written questions. When s 34(2)(e) is read together with s 34(2)(g), which provides that the arbitral tribunal can decide whether and to what extent the tribunal should itself take the initiative in ascertaining the facts and the law, it is clear that arbitrators are able to adopt an inquisitorial rather than an adversarial system if that is preferred.

PARTY AUTONOMY

The second general principle in arbitration is that the parties should be free to decide how **23.59** their dispute should be resolved. This flows from the entire concept of arbitration, in that it is a consensual process based on an agreement between the parties to refer their dispute to an impartial arbitral tribunal. This principle is reflected throughout the Arbitration Act 1996, where it can be seen that the majority of its provisions are subject to any other agreement between the parties (the 'non-mandatory' provisions).

Mandatory and non-mandatory provisions

Mandatory provisions

Table 23.2 sets out the mandatory provisions of the Arbitration Act 1996, which apply to **23.60** all arbitrations under written arbitration agreements. They are listed in Sch 1 of the Act, and represent the essential minimum requirements that informed opinion would say are needed for an effective reference to arbitration. The mandatory provisions are aimed at supporting an arbitration and ensuring it is effective, and provide machinery for limited court intervention to prevent substantial errors or arbitrators acting without jurisdiction.

Non-mandatory provisions

Anything not covered by the mandatory provisions listed in Table 23.2 can be agreed **23.61** between the parties. One of the main things the Arbitration Act 1996 does is to lay down a detailed set of default provisions for just about everything else relating to an arbitration, which are subject to whatever other agreement may be reached between the parties. The areas covered by the non-mandatory provisions are set out in Table 23.3. The default provisions have been carefully crafted to provide a balanced and sensible set of rules for nearly all the non-mandatory issues that might arise, which will be adopted simply by not saying anything about the matter. However, if the parties do agree to a procedure that departs from the Arbitration Act 1996 scheme, the principle of party autonomy means that the parties' wishes will be respected.

Sources of party agreement

Party agreement departing from the non-mandatory provisions of the Arbitration Act 1996 **23.62** may be reached in four distinct ways:

- before the dispute arises, where the contrary provisions will be found in the detailed wording of the arbitration agreement;

Table 23.2 Mandatory provisions of the Arbitration Act 1996

Provision	Subject matter
ss 9–11	Stay of legal proceedings
s 12	Power of court to extend time limits for beginning arbitral proceedings
s 13	Application of the Limitation Acts to arbitration
s 24	Power of the court to remove an arbitrator if not impartial, or incapable etc
s 26(1)	Effect of death of an arbitrator
s 28	Liability of parties for the fees and expenses of arbitrators
s 29	Immunity of arbitrators
s 31	Objections to the substantive jurisdiction of arbitrators
s 32	Determination of preliminary point on jurisdiction
s 33	General duty of arbitral tribunals
s 37(2)	Items to be regarded as expenses of arbitrators
s 40	General duties of parties in arbitrations
s 43	Securing the attendance of witnesses
s 56	Power to withhold award on non-payment of arbitrators' fees
s 60	Agreements between the parties to pay costs in any event
s 66	Enforcement of the award
ss 67, 68, 70, 71	Challenging the award on the ground of lack of substantive jurisdiction or for serious irregularity
s 72	Parties not taking part in an arbitration
s 73	Loss of right to object
s 74	Immunity of arbitral institutions
s 75	Charge to secure payment of solicitors' costs

- as a variation on this method, where the arbitration clause in the underlying contract adopts the rules of an arbitral institution (s 4(3)). This is discussed further in Chapter 25;
- after the dispute has arisen in a case where there is no pre-existing arbitration agreement, by a subsequent written agreement between the parties to refer the matter to arbitration. This may include provisions dealing with non-mandatory matters; or
- during the course of the arbitration. The principal example is the Arbitration Act 1996 s 34, which says that all procedural and evidential matters are for the tribunal to decide, but subject to the right of the parties to agree any matter. This in effect allows the parties to override the wishes of the arbitral tribunal on the procedure they wish to follow in resolving their dispute.

COURT APPLICATIONS

23.63   The third principle is that the court should not intervene in an arbitration except as provided by the Arbitration Act 1996. The philosophy is that where parties have agreed that

Table 23.3 Non-mandatory matters that may be agreed between the parties

Provision	Subject matter
s 3	Seat of the arbitration
s 4	Whether to adopt institution rules
s 7	Whether to agree the arbitration agreement is not a separable agreement
s 8	Effect of death of a party
s 14	When arbitral proceedings are to be regarded to commence
ss 15–22	Constitution etc of the arbitral tribunal
s 23	Circumstances in which the arbitrator's authority may be revoked
s 30	Whether the arbitral tribunal can rule on its own jurisdiction
s 35	Conferring power to consolidate
s 36	Rights to be represented in the arbitration
s 37	Tribunal's power to appoint experts
ss 38–41	Powers available to the tribunal
s 44	Exclusion of court's powers in support of arbitration
s 45	Exclusion of court's power to determine points of law
s 46	Which substantive law should apply
ss 47–49	Powers available to the tribunal when making its award
ss 52–58	Form, date etc of the final award
s 69	Excluding appeals to the court on a point of law
ss 76–79	Time limits and service of notices

their dispute should be resolved by arbitration the court should not intervene except and to the extent that this is necessary. The two main reasons for court intervention are:

- in order to give support to the arbitral proceedings; or
- in order to put right any serious injustice.

23.64 The principle of non-intervention is to support the implementation of the parties' decision to refer their dispute to arbitration. If the courts were too ready to intervene much of the value in arbitrating as opposed to litigating would be lost. This topic is discussed further in Chapter 28.

DIFFERENT TYPES OF ARBITRATIONS

Institutional arbitration

23.65 An institutional arbitration is where the arbitration itself is administered by an arbitral institution. This should be distinguished from an ad hoc arbitration (see below). Very frequently an institutional arbitration will be conducted in accordance with the institution's own arbitration rules, although some institutions, such as CEDR, will apply the rules of another organisation (CEDR uses the UNCITRAL Model Law).

23.66 In an institutional arbitration the institution may well provide a range of support services. These may include machinery for appointing the arbitrators, arranging facilities for hearings, and support in ensuring that the arbitration proceeds expeditiously and smoothly, and that awards are drawn up in a manner that makes them readily enforceable through the courts if they are not complied with (see Chapters 27 and 29). Some institutions even include an internal appeal process against the arbitrators' award. The additional services that will be provided by the institution depends on what is on offer from the institution, whether any of these are required by the institution's arbitration rules, and what the parties are prepared to pay for.

23.67 Almost inevitably there will be additional costs involved in making use of an institution's services, but doing so may be less expensive than trying to agree an equivalent with the other side, and the parties may well find that the benefits of using effective systems that are already established far outweigh the costs.

Ad hoc arbitration

23.68 Particularly in maritime disputes, the parties may enter into what is known as an ad hoc arbitration agreement. This simply means that the parties have agreed to arbitrate and not to use one of the arbitral institutions for the administration of the arbitration. This does not prevent the parties using such an institution as an appointing authority, but often the parties to an ad hoc arbitration will appoint the arbitrators themselves. It also does not stop the parties adopting the arbitration rules from an arbitral institution (this can be an effective short-hand way to agree the detailed procedures that will be adopted), but they may leave the details of the procedures to be followed to the arbitrators to decide (if these have not been prescribed by the arbitration agreement).

23.69 The net result is that in an ad hoc arbitration the parties save the fees that would be charged by an arbitral institution, and free themselves to choose arbitrators in any manner that may be agreed between them, and to agree to any procedures for the arbitration that they may choose. This level of freedom has many attractions while parties are on amicable terms, but can be a major source of difficulties if their relationship becomes less harmonious. Delays and additional expense can easily result if one party or the other decides to become obstructive. These problems can become particularly acute in arbitrations, because arbitrators have limited powers to force the parties into making progress in preparing the case. Ultimately, arbitrators may need to resort to the courts if one of the parties becomes deliberately obstructive (see Chapter 28).

STATUTORY ARBITRATION

23.70 As an exception to the almost universal rule that arbitrations are based on agreement, the Arbitration Act 1996 ss 94–98 deal with statutory arbitrations. These occur where legislation requires certain types of dispute to be referred to arbitration. They are quite rare, but arise in some contexts in landlord and tenant and company law. The relevant legislation is treated for the purposes of the Arbitration Act 1996 as if it were an arbitration agreement between the parties.

CONSUMER ARBITRATION

There are restrictions, which can be found in the Arbitration Act 1996, ss 89–91, on the use **23.71** of arbitration in consumer disputes. These give effect to Council Directive 93/13, and are aimed at ensuring that arbitration clauses are not used against consumers as a means of preventing them from seeking redress from the courts.

Med-arb

Mediation-arbitration ('Med-arb') is a hybrid between mediation and arbitration. There **23.72** are various different forms this can take. One version is for a single person to be nominated as a mediator, who will then become the arbitrator if the matter cannot be resolved in the mediation. A different version is for one individual to act as the mediator, and for a different person to be appointed as the arbitrator if the matter is not resolved in the mediation.

While this combined approach may appear to give business people the best of both worlds, **23.73** there are problems:

- If the parties proceed first by referring the matter to mediation, and this is successful, the settlement will not be enforceable under the New York Convention 1958 or the Arbitration Act 1996 s 66 (see Chapter 29), because there is no 'dispute' as required by s 6. It is possible to ensure enforceability by starting with a formal reference to arbitration, then immediately referring the matter to mediation, and, if the matter is settled, recording the agreement in a consent award (see Chapter 28).
- There are obvious ethical problems in a person who has acted as a mediator changing roles and becoming an arbitrator (see Chapter 16).
- It is possible that important information may be disclosed in confidence in a mediation, which may influence the decision on the arbitration, and that private discussions with the mediator in the absence of the other party may turn out to be entirely improper when the process converts over to arbitration. These considerations may also mean that the parties are more reticent in the mediation part of the process than would otherwise be the case, which may make settling the matter more difficult.

MULTI-TIERED DISPUTE RESOLUTION

Some dispute resolution clauses are more complicated still, and provide for more than two **23.74** levels or tiers of ADR. For example, a clause may provide that where there is a dispute the parties must:

- submit the dispute to designated officers of the respective parties to attempt to negotiate a settlement;
- followed by mediation if the matter remains unresolved;
- followed by arbitration.

It is a matter of construction as to whether each of the tiers is a condition precedent to **23.75** proceeding to the next tier. If they are not, a party can proceed directly to arbitration.

ONE-STOP ADJUDICATION

23.76   Where the parties have made a clear agreement for Med-arb or multi-tiered dispute resolution, that will be upheld by the courts. However, there is a strong presumption that the parties will have intended that their dispute would be resolved through a single dispute resolution process (*Fili Shipping Co Ltd v Premium Nafta Products Ltd* [2007] Bus LR 1719). Reasonable businessmen are unlikely to have intended that their disputes should be looked into both by arbitrators and the courts. Consequently, the underlying purpose of the Arbitration Act 1996 is for one-stop adjudication (*Lesotho Highlands v Impreglio SpA* [2006] 1 AC 221 at [34]).

EUROPEAN CONVENTION ON HUMAN RIGHTS AND ARBITRATION

23.77   While arbitrators cannot ignore the requirements of the ECHR, the courts have upheld the main features of arbitration in the face of a number of attacks based on ECHR arguments. In *Stretford v Football Association* [2007] Bus LR 1052 it was argued that an arbitration clause in the Football Association Rules infringed the ECHR Art 6. The appellant was a football players' agent who had to submit to the Rules in order to be licensed. It was held that arbitrations comply with much of Art 6 in that the Arbitration Act 1996 provides for a fair hearing by an impartial tribunal, and gives the High Court jurisdiction to review issues such as apparent bias and procedural unfairness. Two remaining issues, namely the right to a hearing in public and a hearing before a tribunal established by law, were waived by the appellant through the incorporation of the arbitration clause into the appellant's licence agreement.

23.78   In *Sumukan Ltd v Commonwealth Secretariat* [2007] Bus LR 1075 it was argued that Art 6 was infringed by the exclusion of the right to appeal to the courts against the decision of the arbitrators on a point of law under the Arbitration Act 1996 s 69. The exclusion was made by a clause in the contract, that referred to a statute, which set out the relevant rules for the arbitration, that excluded the right to appeal. It was held that the exclusion did not infringe Art 6, being a common provision in arbitration rules, and it did not matter that the exclusion was in a document referred to in the substantive agreement, rather than being an express clause of that agreement.

MAIN FEATURES OF ARBITRATION

23.79   Given the range of matters that can be agreed between the parties, and the range of options available on almost every matter of principle and procedure, it is perhaps not surprising that the Arbitration Act 1996 avoids seeking to define arbitration as a concept. The closest thing in the Act is the definition of an arbitration agreement given by s 6(1); and see 23.21. Nevertheless, a number of common features to most arbitrations can be identified;

- Arbitrations are based on an agreement between the parties to have their dispute decided by impartial arbitrators.

- Arbitrators are frequently appointed by the parties, or through a mechanism agreed by the parties, rather than by the state (as happens in court proceedings). This should result in arbitrators being acceptable to the respective parties and who may have trade knowledge that will assist in coming to a decision. A disadvantage is that there is scope for a party who decides to be obstructive to delay the appointment of the arbitral tribunal, which can lead to the undesirable result of needing to go to court for the purpose of securing the appointment of the arbitrators (see Chapters 24 and 28). Another disadvantage is that it is difficult to find individuals better qualified than High Court judges, who are provided free as part of the service in High Court litigation, whereas arbitrators will charge fees at commercial rates, which can be expensive, particularly in tribunals of three arbitrators.
- Parties retain a measure of control over the procedures adopted by the tribunal (subject to their original agreement to arbitrate), whereas court procedures are controlled by the judge.
- Formality is often given to arbitrations by adopting institutional rules, but the parties can choose extremely informal procedures if they prefer.
- The level of formality adopted in an arbitration varies greatly between different arbitrators and different institutional arbitral rules, but are often less formal than court procedures.
- By choosing which set of institutional rules to adopt, or by entering into an ad hoc arbitration, the parties can decide between themselves the level of formality and the complexity of the procedures to be used in their arbitration. In court cases the procedures are largely laid down by the CPR and have to be followed.
- Most arbitrations are conducted in private, whereas court hearings have to be in public unless there are pressing counterveiling considerations (ECHR Art 6(1)). Many business people do not want their disputes becoming widely known, so this is a major factor in deciding whether to arbitrate or litigate.
- Following on from its consensual nature, arbitration usually works best when there are only two parties. While it is possible to arbitrate where there are three or more parties, there are problems. These include agreeing on the arbitral rules, particularly where the substantive contracts between the different parties have inconsistent arbitration clauses. Further, unless express provision is made for this, arbitrators have no power to join additional parties, or to consolidate two or more arbitrations. This can be useful to avoid irreconcilable decisions in related disputes, and is one of the advantages of litigation.
- LIkewise, arbitrators have no powers against third parties. This is a drawback where documentation, or property that needs to be inspected by an expert, is in the control of a third party.
- Arbitrators have relatively weak powers in relation to imposing sanctions on parties who do not comply with timetables and procedural orders. There is therefore more scope for parties to cause delays in arbitrations than in litigation, where judges impose a system of active case management.
- Unless the parties agree to confer such a power, arbitrators have no power to grant interim injunctions. They do have power to make final awards for injunctive relief (Arbitration Act 1996 s 48(5)), and there may be a limited power to grant interim injunctive relief under ss 38 and 39, but in any event arbitrators cannot enforce their orders by committal. Outside these provisions an application for an interim injunction has to be made to the court (Chapter 28).

- Similarly, arbitrators cannot grant orders equivalent to search orders and freezing injunctions.
- Generally, the decision of the arbitrators is final. There are exceptions, because some arbitral rules include an appeals process, and the courts have a limited power to review arbitral awards (Chapter 28). For business people finality is a great benefit. The CPR, however, have brought the English court system into a position that is fairly close to that in arbitration (almost all civil appeals require permission to appeal, and the grounds of appeal are quite limited), but it is generally regarded to be true that it is more difficult to overturn an arbitral award than a judgment of a court.
- In international arbitration there is a simple enforcement procedure through the New York Convention 1958 (see Chapter 29), which provides a huge advantage to arbitration compared with the more difficult overseas enforcement procedures that apply to court judgments. In cases where both parties are within the jurisdiction, enforcement will be more direct in litigation, because there is no need to go through the stage of registering the award as a judgment.

23.80 Whether it is cheaper to arbitrate than to go to court is an open question. It depends largely on the nature of the dispute and the approach taken by the parties. Often the balance is between the ability to save costs on simpler procedures in arbitration against the fees payable to the arbitrators (on a daily fee basis, and which may include international travel) and to the arbitral institution.

KEY POINTS SUMMARY

23.81
- The foundation of arbitration is the agreement to arbitrate, which is commonly found in an arbitration clause in the substantive contract between the parties.
- The arbitration agreement is separable from the substantive contract, which means that arbitrators can rule on the validity of the substantive contract without destroying their own jurisdiction.
- The three principles of arbitration law are:
  - the fair resolution of disputes by an impartial tribunal without unnecessary delay or expense;
  - party autonomy;
  - limited court interference.
- The Arbitration Act 1996 seeks to achieve a balance between these principles by setting out a relatively small number of mandatory provisions, which are those regarded as essential to support effective arbitrations, and a wider range of non-mandatory provisions that the parties can choose whether to adopt.
- Party autonomy has resulted in a wide range of procedures that are adopted in arbitrations. Despite this, by agreeing to arbitration through an arbitral institution under the institution's rules a degree of certainty can be achieved.
- While the Arbitration Act 1996 contains quite a large number of provisions that allow applications to be made to the court, these are operated in accordance with the principle that the courts will honour the agreement between the parties that they want their disputes decided privately by an arbitral tribunal.

- By agreeing to arbitrate, the parties effectively waive their right to trial in the courts for the purposes of the ECHR Art 6.
- The main features of arbitration discussed in the final section of this chapter set out many of the pros and cons of arbitrating compared with litigating. Often the advantage enjoyed by one party will be balanced by a corresponding disadvantage for the other side.
- Often the balance boils down to having the dispute decided in private by a tribunal chosen by the parties, against having the dispute decided by a professional judge in public and with the coercive powers granted to the courts.

24

ARBITRAL TRIBUNALS

INTRODUCTION...24.01

COMMENCEMENT OF ARBITRATION 24.02

NOTICE OF ARBITRATION 24.08

APPOINTMENT OF ARBITRAL TRIBUNAL 24.10

CONTRACTUAL BASIS OF THE ARBITRATORS' MANDATE 24.18

TERMS OF REFERENCE.................................24.23

REMOVAL, RESIGNATION AND VACANCIES.................24.24

IMMUNITIES 24.33

LIABILITY FOR ARBITRATORS' FEES.......................24.35

KEY POINTS SUMMARY 24.36

INTRODUCTION

24.01 This chapter describes how arbitrations are commenced with a notice of arbitration, and the appointment of arbitral tribunals. Typically arbitral tribunals will have either a sole arbitrator, or a panel of three arbitrators. There are a number of variations on this theme. Examples are tribunals with a chairman or an umpire, and the use of judge-arbitrators. The chapter also describes the contractual basis of the appointment of arbitrators, and the procedures dealing with the removal, resignation or death of an arbitrator.

COMMENCEMENT OF ARBITRATION

Importance of the date of commencement of an arbitration

24.02 There are potentially two sets of time-limits that may result in an arbitration being unsuccessful:

- any contractual restriction on bringing claims; and
- any limitation period.

Contractual time-limits

The arbitration agreement, some other contractual provision, or the arbitral institution **24.03** rules that apply to an arbitration, may include a requirement that any arbitration has to be commenced within a stated time-limit. The wording of the clause will determine the effect of such a time-limit. Unless the wording makes clear that compliance with the time-limit is a condition of any claim, but does not limit the right to arbitrate, expiry of a contractual time-limit will bar the commencement of the arbitration (*Metalfer Corp v Pan Ocean Shipping Co Ltd* [1998] 2 Lloyd's Rep 632).

Limitation periods

The normal limitation periods under the Limitation Act 1980 apply to arbitration: Arbitration **24.04** Act s 13(1). In contract and most claims in tort the limitation period is six years (Limitation Act 1980 ss 2 and 5). Detailed consideration of limitation can be found in Sime, *A Practical Approach to Civil Procedure* (13th edn, OUP, 2010), ch 7. Limitation runs from the day after the cause of action accrues until the date a claim is brought.

Date of commencement of arbitration

In arbitration proceedings the parties are entitled to agree when the arbitration is to be **24.05** regarded as having commenced for limitation purposes (Arbitration Act 1996 s 14(1)). If there is no such agreement s 14(3)–(5) sets out three rules for when the arbitration is to be regarded as having commenced, depending on how the arbitral tribunal is to be appointed. These are:

- where the arbitrator is named or designated in the arbitration agreement, arbitral pro-ceedings are commenced when one party serves on the other party or parties a notice in writing requiring him or them to submit the dispute to the person so named or designated (s 14(3));
- where the arbitrator or arbitrators are to be appointed by the parties, arbitral proceedings are commenced when one party serves on the other party or parties notice in writing requiring him or them to appoint an arbitrator or to agree to the appointment of an arbi-trator in respect of the dispute (s 14(4)); and
- where the arbitrator or arbitrators are to be appointed by a person other than a party to the proceedings, arbitral proceedings are commenced when one party gives notice in writing to that person requesting him to make the appointment in respect of the dispute (s 14(5)).

Avoiding the consequences of failing to comply with a time-limit

In the case of a contractual time-limit, there may be a provision in the arbitral institution's **24.06** rules giving a discretion to the tribunal or institution to grant more time. Alternatively, the claimant may apply to the High Court under the Arbitration Act 1996 s 12 for an exten-sion of time. Any arbitral process for extending time must be used before applying to court (s 12(2)). Successful applications to extend time are comparatively rare. In the further alter-native, the respondent may simply decide not to raise the time bar by way of defence.

Other than the provisions in the Limitation Act 1980 (such as ss 14A and 14B on latent dam- **24.07** age) that give the court some flexibility over certain limitation periods, there is no power to forgive a claimant who fails to comply with a Limitation Act time-limit. However, as limitation is a procedural defence and is only effective if raised by the respondent, a time-barred arbitration will continue if limitation is not pleaded.

NOTICE OF ARBITRATION

24.08 Under the Arbitration Act 1996 s 14(3)–(5) (see 24.05), a notice of arbitration (also known as a notice to arbitrate) has to be in writing and must comply with the requirements of the relevant subsection of s 14 on appointing the arbitral tribunal. These requirements can be met by a reasonably simple letter. In practice the letter tends to include various other details in order to comply with further requirements set out in any relevant institutional arbitral rules. Under the London Metal Exchange Ltd ('LME') rules, for example, a notice to arbitrate must contain at least the following information:

- the address for service of the claimant;
- a brief statement of the nature and circumstances of the dispute including a brief description of any contract, sufficient to enable the respondent to identify it, to which the dispute relates;
- a brief statement of the relief claimed;
- the claimant's proposal with regard to the number of arbitrators to form the tribunal;
- the claimant's nomination of one arbitrator from the LME panel; and
- the name and address of the respondent to which the notice to arbitrate has been sent.

24.09 Often, the notice of arbitration is sent to the respondent. Where the arbitrators are appointed by an appointing institution, or where institutional rules so require, the notice needs to be sent to the institution as well. For example, under the LME rules a claimant commences an arbitration by serving the notice to arbitrate on the respondent, and by sending a copy of the notice to the secretary of the LME accompanied by the registration fee and deposit (reg 2.1). An example of a notice of arbitration in a carriage of goods by sea case can be seen in Figure 24.1.

APPOINTMENT OF ARBITRAL TRIBUNAL

Number of arbitrators

24.10 In accordance with the principle of party autonomy, the parties are given considerable scope on how their arbitral tribunal will be constituted. The Arbitration Act 1996 s 15(1), says the parties are free to agree on the number of arbitrators to form the tribunal and whether there is to be a chairman or umpire. If there is no agreement as to the number of arbitrators, the tribunal shall consist of a sole arbitrator (s 15(3)). Having an even number of arbitrators risks deadlock. It will be recalled that the second arbitration clause in Figure 23.1 provided for the appointment of two arbitrators. Unless otherwise agreed by the parties s 15(2) says that an agreement that the number of arbitrators shall be two or any other even number shall be understood as requiring the appointment of an additional arbitrator as chairman of the tribunal.

Figure 24.1 Notice of arbitration under the Arbitration Act 1996 s 14(4)

....

Taylor, Andrews & Co.,
Solicitors
Tel 0121 847 4746 Fax 0121 857 8822

36 High Street,
Birmingham,
B4 8YD
Ref INA/863
Date: 28 April 2010

Dear Sirs,

M.V. ASIAN SUMMER

Bill of Lading KAY-3 of 6 January 2010

We are instructed on behalf of the subrogated underwriters, Seaborne Insurance plc, of a consignment of grapefruit carried from Seattle to Liverpool on board the M.V. 'Asian Summer', arriving at Liverpool on 1 February 2010. On arrival it was discovered that the consignment was subject to considerable physical damage. Our clients have suffered losses in the sum of US$210,563. We understand that the vessel is owned by Summer Navigation SA and is chartered by Ocean Shipping and Carriage plc. We further understand that the vessel is entered with the Bristol & Liverpool P & I Club.

We hereby notify you that we have appointed Mr James Morrison as arbitrator on behalf of our clients Seaborne Insurance plc and Midlands Fruit Importers plc in connection with all disputes and differences arising under the above mentioned bill of lading. We hereby require you to appoint a second arbitrator in accordance with clause 24 of the above mentioned bill of lading.

We look forward to receiving your acknowledgement of safe receipt of this letter within the next 14 days.

Yours faithfully,
Taylor, Andrews & Co

....

Appointing the arbitrators

24.11 The parties are free to agree on the procedure for appointing the arbitrator or arbitrators, including the procedure for appointing any chairman or umpire (Arbitration Act 1996 s 16(1)). Arbitrators may be chosen because they are known professionally by, or recommended to, the appointing parties. Alternatively, an approach may be made to a professional body, with an arbitrator being nominated by (say) the President of that organisation. Perhaps more frequently the parties will use an arbitral institution as a nominating authority. This usually involves completing a form applying for the necessary arbitral services, which will ask for details such as the nature of the dispute, whether there is an arbitration agreement, which institutional rules (if any) apply, and the seat, law and language of the arbitration (see Chapter 26 for these concepts).

24.12 In the absence of contrary agreement s 16 provides default for provisions for the main varieties of arbitral tribunal, as set out in Table 24.1.

Table 24.1 Default procedures for the appointment of arbitrators

Tribunal	Appointment procedure
Sole arbitrator	The parties jointly appoint the arbitrator not later than 28 days after service of a request in writing by either party to do so (s 16(3)). To prevent an appearance of unfairness, institutional arbitral rules often provide that where the parties are from different countries, a sole arbitrator should not be of the same nationality as any of the parties.
Two arbitrators (where this really is the intention of the parties)	Each party is required to appoint one arbitrator not later than 14 days after service of a request in writing by either party to do so (s 16(4)).
Three arbitrators	Each party is required to appoint one arbitrator not later than 14 days after service of a request in writing by either party to do so, and these arbitrators then forthwith appoint a third arbitrator as the chairman of the tribunal (s 16(5)). Again, to prevent an appearance of unfairness, institutional arbitral rules often provide that where the parties are from different countries, the chairman should not be of the same nationality as any of the parties.
Two arbitrators and an umpire	Each party is required to appoint one arbitrator not later than 14 days after service of a request in writing by either party to do so, and these arbitrators may appoint an umpire at any time after they themselves are appointed and must do so before any substantive hearing or forthwith if they cannot agree on a matter relating to the arbitration (s 16(6)).

Chairman

24.13 Where the arbitral tribunal has a chairman, the parties are free to decide on the chairman's functions and powers. In the absence of such an agreement, decisions, orders and awards of the tribunal are made by all or a majority of the arbitrators (including the chairman) (Arbitration Act 1996 s 20(3)). The view of the chairman prevails in relation to a decision, order or award where there is an evenly split decision (s 20(4)).

Umpire

24.14 Arbitral tribunals with umpires are a peculiarly English idea. In the absence of contrary agreement, the umpire shall attend the proceedings and be supplied with the same documents and other materials as are supplied to the other arbitrators (Arbitration Act 1996 s 21(3)). Decisions, orders and awards are made by the other arbitrators unless and until they cannot agree on a matter relating to the arbitration. In that event they must give notice in writing to the parties and the umpire, and the umpire then replaces them as the tribunal with power to make decisions, orders and awards as if he were sole arbitrator (s 21(4)). Paying an umpire to wait in the wings until the party-appointed arbitrators fail to agree is not usually regarded as an efficient way of proceeding, so this arrangement is not all that common.

Judges as arbitrators

24.15 A judge of the Commercial Court or of the Technology and Construction Court may, if in all the circumstances he thinks fit, accept appointment as a sole arbitrator or as umpire under an arbitration agreement (Arbitration Act 1996 s 93(1)). Such an appointment requires the permission of the Lord Chief Justice having regard to the state of business in the relevant courts.

There is a £1,800 appointment fee for a judge arbitrator and daily fees, also of £1,800 (Civil   **24.16**
Proceedings (Fees) Order 2008 (SI 2008/1053)), which are payable to the High Court. A judge arbitrator can exercise the jurisdiction of the High Court under various provisions of the Arbitration Act 1996 (s 93(6) and Sch 2), which may be attractive to the parties. However, pressure on court time makes such appointments very unusual.

Failure of appointment procedure

Where the above procedures break down, possibly because the other side does not make an   **24.17**
appointment, there are default powers in the Arbitration Act 1996 ss 17–19. These may result in the claimant's nominee becoming the sole arbitrator, or may require an application to the High Court to resolve the problem (see Chapter 28).

CONTRACTUAL BASIS OF THE ARBITRATORS' MANDATE

Where a person accepts an appointment as an arbitrator they enter into a contract with the   **24.18**
parties in the terms that are agreed. These will usually include:

* the identification of the dispute or difference that has to be adjudicated upon;
* the terms on which the adjudicator is prepared to act, which will include the fees payable to the arbitrator;
* the basis on which the arbitration is to be conducted, which will usually be in accordance with the terms of the arbitration agreement between the parties and any institutional rules that have been incorporated or otherwise agreed between the parties;
* an agreement by the arbitrator to conduct the arbitration and to issue an award without undue delay (Arbitration Act 1996 s 33(1)(b)) or within any time frame agreed with the parties or in accordance with the relevant institutional rules.

Once appointed, the arbitrators are contractually bound to complete their mandate, which   **24.19**
also has the effect of limiting the extent of their jurisdiction to the matters that have been referred to them in their mandate.

Qualifications of arbitrators

While there are no requirements in the general law imposing minimum qualifications on   **24.20**
arbitrators, it is not uncommon for arbitration agreements to specify such qualifications. These may specify minimum professional qualifications, or membership of an organisation (such as membership of the Baltic Exchange), or status (such as being in business in the City of London). Arbitrators appointed under the rules of arbitral institutions are invariably only on the relevant panel if they are suitably qualified.

Impartiality and independence

Arbitrators, even those appointed by a particular party, must be impartial (Arbitration Act   **24.21**
1996 ss 1, 24 and 33). The word used in the Act is 'impartial' rather than 'independent',

because, as the DAC report (Departmental Advisory Committee on Arbitration, set up by the Department of Trade and Industry, whose reports formed the basis for the Arbitration Act 1996) says, it is possible to be impartial even if the arbitrator is not independent. An arbitrator is liable to be removed if their impartiality is compromised (s 24). This may happen if there is actual bias or a real possibility of bias. This is approached on the basis of whether a fair-minded and informed observer would conclude there is a real possibility of bias (*Porter v Magill* [2002] 2 AC 357).

24.22 Some arbitral institution rules, such as the UNCITRAL Model Law Art 12, require arbitrators to be 'independent'. This has caused some controversy, but probably does not impose any substantially different standard than impartiality.

TERMS OF REFERENCE

24.23 Formal terms of reference are somewhat unusual, but do form part of the standard procedure in ICC arbitrations (ICC Rules Art 18). These are drawn up by the arbitral tribunal on the basis of the documents filed at the start of the arbitration or after an initial hearing with the parties. In addition to details of those involved, the place of the arbitration etc, this document summarises the respective claims and counterclaims and the relief sought. Importantly, it also sets out a list of the issues to be determined. It therefore provides a clear definition of the limits of the arbitrators' mandate.

REMOVAL, RESIGNATION AND VACANCIES

Removal

24.24 The parties are free to agree in what circumstances the authority of an arbitrator may be revoked (Arbitration Act 1996 s 23(1)). In the absence of such prior agreement, the authority of an arbitrator may not be revoked except by the parties acting jointly, or by an arbitral institution vested by the parties with such a power (s 23(3)). Revocation of the authority of an arbitrator by the parties acting jointly must be agreed in writing unless the parties also agree (whether or not in writing) to terminate the arbitration agreement (s 23(4)).

24.25 An early termination of an arbitrator's appointment is potentially a breach of contract that may lead to a claim of damages. It will not be a breach if the appointment contract has been discharged or if the termination of the appointment is for a reason permitted in the appointment contract. It may be discharged if the arbitrator is in fundamental breach of the agreement (which is accepted by the parties) or if it has become impossible for the arbitrator to continue.

24.26 In similar situations a party to arbitral proceedings may, provided avenues for the removal of the arbitrator under the arbitration agreement and any institutional rules have been exhausted, apply to the court for an order removing the arbitrator (s 24). Such an order can be made if:

- circumstances exist that give rise to justifiable doubts as to the arbitrator's impartiality;
- the arbitrator does not possess the qualifications required by the arbitration agreement;
- the arbitrator is physically or mentally incapable of conducting the proceedings or there are justifiable doubts as to his capacity to do so; or
- the arbitrator has refused or failed properly to conduct the proceedings, or to use all reasonable despatch in conducting the proceedings or making an award, and substantial injustice has been or will be caused to the applicant.

Where the court removes an arbitrator, it may make such order as it thinks fit with respect to his entitlement (if any) to fees or expenses, or the repayment of any fees or expenses already paid (s 24(4)). **24.27**

Resignation

Resignation by an arbitrator is also a potential breach of contract, so the Arbitration Act 1996 s 25(1) provides that the parties are free to agree with an arbitrator on: **24.28**

- the consequences of his resignation;
- in particular, on the arbitrator's entitlement (if any) to fees or expenses; and
- any liability incurred by the arbitrator as a result of having resigned.

If agreement cannot be reached, the arbitrator can apply to the court for relief on the ground that resigning was reasonable in the circumstances (s 25(3), (4)). **24.29**

Death

The authority of an arbitrator is personal and ceases on his death (Arbitration Act 1996 s 26(1)). This can have serious consequences for the parties, who may have to start all or part of the arbitration proceedings again. It is not uncommon for parties to insure against this eventuality. **24.30**

Vacancies

Where an arbitrator ceases to hold office, the Arbitration Act 1996 s 27(1), says that the parties are free to agree: **24.31**

- whether and if so how the vacancy is to be filled;
- whether and if so to what extent the previous proceedings should stand; and
- what effect (if any) his ceasing to hold office has on any appointment made by him (alone or jointly).

In the absence of agreement the same procedures apply as where there is a failure to make an initial appointment (s 27(2)–(3)). One possibility is that the vacancy will not be filled, which in a multi-member tribunal is called a truncated arbitral tribunal. The tribunal (when reconstituted) is required to determine whether and if so to what extent the previous proceedings should stand (s 27(4)). **24.32**

IMMUNITIES

Immunity of arbitrators

24.33 An arbitrator is not liable for anything done or omitted in the discharge or purported discharge of his functions as arbitrator unless the act or omission is shown to have been in bad faith (Arbitration Act 1996 s 29(1)). This immunity does not apply to any liability the arbitrator may have on account of resigning (s 29(3)).

Immunity of arbitral institutions

24.34 An arbitral institution which appoints or nominates an arbitrator at the request of the parties is not liable for anything done or omitted in the discharge or purported discharge of that function unless the act or omission is shown to have been in bad faith (Arbitration Act 1996 s 74(1)). Nor is such an arbitral institution liable, by reason of having appointed or nominated an arbitrator, for anything done or omitted by the arbitrator in the discharge or purported discharge of his functions as arbitrator (s 74(2)). These immunities do not cover every situation, and will not cover, for example, negligence in the way the institution administers an arbitration.

LIABILITY FOR ARBITRATORS' FEES

24.35 The parties are jointly and severally liable to pay to the arbitrators such reasonable fees and expenses (if any) as are appropriate in the circumstances (Arbitration Act 1996 s 28(1)). This does not affect any liability of a party to any other party to pay all or any of the costs of the arbitration (see 27.28) or any contractual right of an arbitrator to payment of his fees and expenses (s 28(5)). The tribunal may refuse to deliver an award to the parties except upon full payment of the fees and expenses of the arbitrators (s 56(1)). Applications may be made to the court under these sections in the event of an impasse.

KEY POINTS SUMMARY

24.36
- It is most usual to have either one- or three-person arbitral tribunals.
  - The procedure for having two party-appointed arbitrators, who then appoint a chairman, is designed to ensure the parties have an equal involvement in choosing the tribunal.
  - The appointment of an arbitrator creates a contract between him and the parties.
  - The contract(s) between the parties and the members of the tribunal creates the tribunal's mandate to make an award on the dispute or difference.
  - The Arbitration Act 1996 seeks to give effect to the parties' agreements (between themselves or with the arbitrators) if it becomes necessary for an arbitrator to resign or be removed, but there are fall-back provisions allowing applications to the court because it is recognised that agreement may not be possible given the possibly contentious nature of these situations.

25

THE COMMERCIAL ARBITRATION PROCESS

INTRODUCTION. 25.01

DEFINITION OF 'COMMERCIAL'. 25.03

PRIVACY AND CONFIDENTIALITY 25.05

RANGE OF PROCEDURAL APPROACHES IN ARBITRATION 25.10

PROCEDURAL RULES GOVERNING THE ARBITRATION 25.12

ROLE OF LEGAL REPRESENTATIVES IN ARBITRATION. 25.16

COMMENCEMENT 25.25

'LOOK–SNIFF' ARBITRATIONS 25.26

SHORT-FORM ARBITRATIONS 25.28

GENERAL PROCEDURE IN COMMERCIAL ARBITRATION. 25.31

EXAMPLE OF ARBITRAL RULES THAT CLOSELY FOLLOW COURT
PROCEDURES. 25.83

KEY POINTS SUMMARY 25.101

INTRODUCTION

This chapter will describe the procedures followed in commercial arbitrations involving **25.01**
parties who are all located within England and Wales. The seat of the arbitration, its law,
objections to the tribunal's jurisdiction and the language to be used could, in theory, arise
as issues in domestic commercial arbitration, but are far more frequently issues in international arbitration. These issues will therefore be considered in the next chapter on international arbitration. In most domestic arbitrations it will be obvious that the seat of the
arbitration is England, that the dispute should be determined applying English law and that
the language of the arbitration should be English.

25.02 'Commercial' disputes and commercial law potentially cover a wide range of legal areas. For most purposes English law does not draw distinctions between different types of arbitrations, with the two main areas where it does make a difference being:

- there are restrictions in the use of arbitration in consumer disputes (Arbitration Act 1996 ss 89–91); and
- enforcement of international arbitration agreements under the New York Convention 1958 (see Chapter 29) is limited to commercial disputes where a country has entered into a commercial reservation. About a third of the states that are parties to the Convention have entered such a reservation.

DEFINITION OF 'COMMERCIAL'

25.03 In English law, the distinction between commercial and consumer arbitration is that there will be a consumer arbitration agreement where one of the parties is a legal or natural person (Arbitration Act 1996 s 90) who is acting for purposes outside those of a trade, business or profession (Unfair Terms in Consumer Contracts Regulations 1999 (SI 1999/2083) reg 3(1)). This covers an individual acting in their private capacity, and also a company (which is a legal person) provided it was acting for a purpose outside its business.

25.04 The most important definition of commercial arbitration is that set out in the UNCITRAL Model Law Art 1(1). This provides:

> 'The term "commercial" should be given a wide interpretation so as to cover matters arising from all relationships of a commercial nature, whether contractual or not. Relationships of a commercial nature include, but are not limited to, the following transactions: any trade transaction for the supply or exchange of goods or services; distribution agreements; commercial representation or agency; factoring; leasing; construction of works; consulting, engineering; licensing; investment; financing; banking; insurance; exploitation agreements or concessions; joint venture; carriage of goods or passengers by air, sea, rail or road.'

PRIVACY AND CONFIDENTIALITY

25.05 It is a long-established principle of arbitration law that arbitral proceedings are private and confidential. Interestingly, there are no express provisions enshrining these principles in the Arbitration Act 1996. This is because both principles have a large number of exceptions and were too unsettled to formulate suitable provisions for the Act (DAC report, paras 11–17).

Privacy

25.06 Privacy relates to holding hearings in places where the public have no access. Privacy in arbitration is based on the fact that the parties have agreed to submit their dispute to arbitration between themselves, and only between themselves (*Oxford Shipping Co Ltd v Nippon Yusen Kaisha* [1984] 3 All ER 835 at 842).

Confidentiality

Confidentiality relates to an obligation on those participating in an arbitration not to dis-   **25.07**
close details, documents or information about the arbitration to anyone outside the arbitration. The duty of confidentiality arises as a corollary to the privacy of arbitration (*Ali
Shipping Corp v Shipyard Trogir* [1999] 1 WLR 314).

In *Michael Wilson & Partners Ltd v Emmott* [2008] Bus LR 1361 Lawrence Collins LJ pointed   **25.08**
out that the limits of the duty of confidentiality in arbitration proceedings are still being
developed, and will depend on the context and the nature of the documents or information
at issue. As the law now stands the principal cases where disclosure may be permitted are:

- where there is consent; and
- where a court grants permission, which it has a discretion to grant, where:
  - disclosure is reasonably necessary for the protection of the legitimate interests of an
    arbitrating party;
  - the interests of justice require disclosure; or
  - possibly, the public interest requires disclosure.

It may be in the interests of justice to permit the use of documents disclosed in an arbitration   **25.09**
where the party giving disclosure has advanced inconsistent cases in the arbitration and
in related litigation, to avoid the tribunal dealing with the related litigation being mislead
(*Michael Wilson & Partners Ltd v Emmott*).

RANGE OF PROCEDURAL APPROACHES IN ARBITRATION

A wide range of procedures are possible in arbitrations. These include: **25.10**

- very simple procedures, which do not even include a hearing. An example is the 'look-
  sniff' arbitration (see 25.26);
- short-form arbitrations (see 25.28 for an example);
- arbitrations that adopt the default procedures in the Arbitration Act 1996;
- arbitrations that adopt the rules of an arbitral institution. Institutional rules vary in
  length and detail, but will be typically 6–30 pages long. There will often be gaps in institutional rules, which will be filled by the default provisions of the Arbitration Act 1996.
  Arbitrations broadly following the Arbitration Act 1996 and the format of most domestic
  commercial arbitration rules are considered at 25.31;
- arbitrations where the parties, often in consultation with the arbitrators, agree on a
  bespoke procedure;
- arbitrations where the procedure draws heavily on the procedures in the CPR (or even
  the pre-CPR rules of court). An example is discussed at 25.83. This may happen because
  the particular institutional rules adopt CPR procedures, or because these are specifically
  adopted by the arbitrators. The CPR are vastly more detailed than even the most highly
  developed of the institutional rules on arbitration. One of the reasons for choosing arbitration is to enable the dispute to be resolved with a simpler set of procedures than those
  laid down in the CPR, so for many people wholesale adoption of the CPR in an arbitration
  would be a retrograde step.

25.11 Arbitration proceedings are usually less formal than court proceedings, although what actually happens depends on the parties, their lawyers, the arbitrators, and the institutional rules (if any) that govern the arbitration. It is a common fall-back in domestic commercial arbitrations to adopt the standard court procedures laid down in the CPR to fill in gaps in the relevant arbitral institution rules or as the basis for formulating the procedure in an ad hoc arbitration.

PROCEDURAL RULES GOVERNING THE ARBITRATION

Bespoke arbitration clause

25.12 As parties are allowed to agree anything not covered by the mandatory provisions (see Table 23.3 for the non-mandatory issues that may be included), the parties and their lawyers may decide to make detailed provision for the procedure to be followed in the event of any dispute being referred to arbitration. This is most likely to arise where a party contracts on terms drafted with this in mind by its lawyers. As a practical matter, it is when a contract is being negotiated that it is easiest to secure agreement to such matters.

Arbitral institution rules

25.13 There are many commercial and international organisations, trade associations and professions, as well specialist dispute resolution organisations that publish their own rules for arbitrations in their areas of interest. Examples of arbitral institutions are given in Table 25.1. Most institutional rules of arbitral institutions located in England and Wales have been written or redrafted in order to be consistent with the scheme of the Arbitration Act 1996. Obviously, the same cannot be said of international organisations, whose rules are intended for use in a wide range of jurisdictions, including non-common law countries.

25.14 The arbitral institutions listed in Table 25.1 are just examples, and with a very large number of different sets of rules there are inevitably differences in style, coverage and detail. Most rules cover:

- appointment of the arbitrators;
- pleadings;
- procedure and exchange of information and evidence;
- decision-making by the arbitrators;
- awards; and
- payment of fees and costs.

Silence in institutional rules

25.15 Where the rules of an arbitral institution apply to an arbitration, but are silent on a non-mandatory matter covered by the Arbitration Act 1996, the relevant provision of the Arbitration Act 1996 applies. This follows from s 4(3), which allows the parties to make use of institutional rules, read together with s 4(2). This provides that while the parties can make their own arrangements by agreement, the non-mandatory provisions lay down rules '...which apply in the absence of such agreement'.

Table 25.1 Arbitral institutions

Institution	Full name	Area covered by rules
AAA	American Arbitration Association	Wide range of domestic and international arbitrations
CEDR	Centre for Effective Dispute Resolution	Commercial. It acts as an appointing and administering institution, applying the UNICTRAL rules
CIA	Chartered Institute of Arbitrators	Arbitration schemes for trade associations and professional bodies
CIETAC	China International Economic and Trade Arbitration Commission	International commercial arbitration
FOSFA	Federation of Oils, Seeds and Fats Association	Commodity disputes
GAFTA	Grain and Feed Trade Association	Commodity disputes
HKIAC	Hong Kong International Arbitration Centre	International commercial arbitration
ICC	International Chamber of Commerce	International commercial, financial and technical disputes
ICE	Institute of Civil Engineers	Civil engineering disputes
ICSID	International Centre for Settlement of Investment Disputes	Investment disputes between states and nationals of other states
JCT	Joint Contracts Tribunal Ltd	Building disputes
LCIA	London Court of International Arbitration	International commercial arbitration
LMAA	London Maritime Arbitrators Association	Shipping arbitration
LME	London Metal Exchange Ltd	Metals trade etc disputes
PCA	Permanent Court of Arbitration	Differences between states
SIAC	Singapore International Arbitration Centre	Shipping, banking, insurance, construction
UNCITRAL	United Nations Commission on International Trade Law	International commercial contracts

ROLE OF LEGAL REPRESENTATIVES IN ARBITRATION

Being an adjudicative process, solicitors and barristers representing clients in arbitrations need to be adept at all the traditional lawyering skills, from legal analysis to drafting, advising and advocacy.   **25.16**

Advice on the arbitration clause

A lawyer's input starts from the time a client is being advised on the drafting of the terms and conditions to be included in its standard terms of trading. Decisions have to be made on whether to include an arbitration clause (or indeed, some other dispute resolution clause) in those terms and conditions, and on the nature of the clause to be included. Key questions include: **25.17**

- the composition of the arbitral panel;
- whether to include use of a named set of rules from an arbitral institution;

- whether the arbitration should be administered by a named arbitral institution;
- the seat of the arbitration (see 26.11);
- the governing law (see 26.21);
- whether, and how, any non-mandatory provisions in the Arbitration Act 1996 should be adjusted;
- whether to require or dispense with reasons for the arbitrators' decision;
- the extent to which appeals to the courts should be allowed.

25.18 Often this involves a consideration of the client's priorities and business needs, as well as a good understanding of the relative merits and drawbacks of the various different sets of institutional rules governing arbitrations.

Reference of a dispute to arbitration

25.19 When a dispute arises, the lawyer needs to come to a view on which documents constitute the substantive contract, and assess whether there is any arbitration clause and its effect. A clause may require reference of disputes to arbitration, or may permit such reference. Consideration is also needed on whether the actual dispute comes within the arbitration clause. Consideration is then required of the options available to the client, and tactically what is in the best interests of the client. This often depends on the nature of the dispute and what is needed in order to succeed. It may be that the strength of the case is primarily legal, which would make litigation attractive. On the other hand, privacy or obtaining a fair result may point towards arbitration. If there is a binding arbitration clause there will be no choice.

25.20 Proper case analysis is required in formulating the nature of the dispute and the remedies that should be sought, or in formulating a response to a claim brought by the other side. This requires obtaining as full a picture as possible of the background facts and evidence as early as possible, because it is important to ensure that the dispute identified in the early correspondence accurately reflects the real problem so that the correct matter can be referred to arbitration, and that costs are not wasted in investigating a mistaken version of events.

Defining the issues

25.21 A clear statement of the client's case is required in the early stages of an arbitration, both in the initial reference to arbitration and in the statements of case that are usually required shortly after the tribunal is appointed. Lawyers play a key role in identifying the right issues, ensuring the correct causes of action are relied upon, and sustainable relief is sought. When acting for the respondent, each allegation made in the points of claim has to be responded to, so detailed instructions are required from the client both on whether these allegations are disputed, and on the nature of any affirmative case that should be advanced by the respondent. For both sides, this involves having conferences and meetings with the clients and their witnesses, and ensuring that all the relevant documentation is identified and provided for use in the arbitration.

Putting together the case

25.22 In most arbitrations a great deal of time has to be taken in collating the relevant documentation and in taking evidence from potential witnesses for the purpose of drafting their witness statements. Likewise, identifying expert witnesses on matters requiring expertise, putting together the necessary documents for the experts, instructing them, and finalising their reports, requires a high level of expertise on the part of solicitors acting in arbitrations. Perhaps of even greater importance is deciding how to deal with the expert and other evidence provided by the other parties. Matters to consider include whether written questions should be put to the other side's experts, and whether a without prejudice meeting of the experts from both sides would be an advantage.

Considerable care is required over the disclosure of documents and the compilation of bun- **25.23** dles of documents for any hearings before the tribunal. This may involve considering the scope of disclosure and privilege in a number of jurisdictions, particularly in international arbitrations. An accurate appreciation of the issues is needed to ensure that the documentation used, whether in the disclosure process or included in the bundles for the tribunal, covers the issues that are relevant to the dispute. Translations may also be required, with care needing to be taken that these are accurate.

Hearings

While it is possible to have decisions in arbitrations on the papers, it is more usual to have **25.24** one or a number of hearings both for the tribunal to hear from the witnesses and for the parties to make submissions. Usually, English arbitrations follow an adversarial approach, but this is not an absolute requirement, and less formal approaches are encountered. Typically, counsel will be briefed, and counsel will produce written skeleton arguments or written submissions on how the facts and evidence should be analysed within the framework of the relevant legal principles. If witnesses are to be heard, the usual approach is to take their witness statements as their testimony on behalf of the party calling them (their evidence-in-chief), but they will be cross-examined by counsel for the other party, as well as being questioned by the tribunal. Legal representatives therefore need the full range of forensic skills in preparing for and appearing at arbitral hearings, which are often conducted with a similar level of formality as court hearings.

COMMENCEMENT

Arbitrations are commenced by sending a notice of arbitration (see 24.08) and then appoint- **25.25** ing the members of the arbitral tribunal (see 24.10–24.17). It is relatively unusual for terms of reference to be drawn up, but see 24.23.

'LOOK–SNIFF' ARBITRATIONS

'Look–sniff' arbitrations are most commonly met in disputes over the quality of goods in **25.26** import–export transactions. If the dispute boils down to whether the goods match the contract specification or description, it may be that all that is needed is for an expert in the field to go to the warehouse or storage tank, have a look at the goods, do other tests (such as sniffing them, but nowadays also more scientific tests), and to express a view on the quality of the goods (such as the appropriate grade of fruit, or the fineness of textiles or flour etc).

In these cases delay is to be avoided, because of possible market fluctuations and the risk of deterioration. The procedure is largely aimed at agreeing on a suitably qualified arbitrator, with a minimum of documents, and a minimum of argument (even on paper) from the parties, because all that is needed is a decision on the quality of the goods as seen by the arbitrator.

25.27 There is not a great deal of distinction between this type of arbitration and the process of expert evaluation (see Chapter 17).

SHORT-FORM ARBITRATIONS

25.28 It is recognised that the full-blown procedure under the Arbitration Act 1996 and the full arbitration rules of many arbitral institutions are too expensive and unnecessary for disputes of a simple nature or where the monetary value of the dispute is relatively low. A number of arbitral institutions have therefore promulgated short-form procedures to deal with these cases on a cost-efficient basis. An example is the ICE Short Procedure.

25.29 Under the ICE Short Procedure, r 14.2, within two working days after the appointment of the arbitrator the claimant is required to deliver a file setting out its case to the arbitrator and the respondent, which must contain:

- a statement of the orders or awards sought;
- a statement of the reasons for being entitled to those orders or awards; and
- copies of all the documents relied upon, including any witness statements relied upon.

25.30 The respondent must deliver its defence in the same format within 14 days of receiving the claimant's file. No counterclaim is permitted. If the respondent has a cross-claim it has to be brought as a separate reference (r 14.4). Following delivery of the respondent's file there is a 14-day period during which the parties may comment on the other side's case, and in which they may add to or remove documents from their file. Normally there is no formal hearing (r 14.9) and the arbitrator makes an award on considering the papers within 14 days of the close of the parties' files (r 14.6). There is a power to extend this period, and the arbitrator may hold a site visit, require either or both parties to submit further documents or information, or to attend a meeting for the purpose of answering questions (r 14.8). The arbitrator also has a discretion to hold a hearing with cross-examination of witnesses (r 14.9), although doing so rather detracts from the procedure being 'short'. The normal rule under the ICE Short Procedure rules is that each side bears its own costs (r 14.7).

GENERAL PROCEDURE IN COMMERCIAL ARBITRATION

25.31 Figure 25.1 is a flow diagram showing the main stages followed in an arbitration, which broadly adopts the procedures in the Arbitration Act 1996 and most domestic commercial arbitration rules. These are aimed at ensuring the fair resolution of the dispute without unnecessary delay or expense (Arbitration Act 1996 s 1(a)). This is achieved by adopting procedures suitable for the circumstances of the particular case (s 33(1)(b)). Different stages in the process may be heavily prescribed by the rules of an arbitral institution as chosen by

Figure 25.1 Typical steps in arbitration proceedings

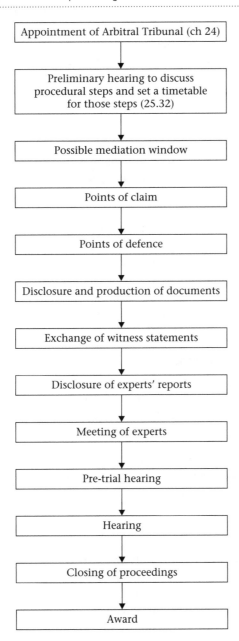

the parties. In the absence of agreement the default provisions of the Arbitration Act 1996 will apply.

Preliminary meeting

A preliminary meeting will often be convened shortly after the tribunal is appointed. Its **25.32** actual timing is a matter for the arbitrators, and there is no absolute requirement to hold such a meeting. It is an opportunity for the parties and arbitrators to see each other, but its main purpose is as a forum for the tribunal to discuss jurisdictional matters and to make procedural directions for the preparation of the evidence needed for deciding the reference. There is no set agenda for preliminary meetings. It may well be possible for directions to be agreed between the parties, which will make a preliminary meeting less necessary. It is becoming increasingly common to hold preliminary meetings by conference telephone calls or through video-conferencing.

Procedural orders

25.33 In accordance with the principle that the parties are free to agree how their dispute should be resolved (Arbitration Act 1996 s 1(b)), the following discussion on the powers of arbitrators to make provisional orders is subject to any contrary agreement between the parties.

Interim payments, security for costs, etc

25.34 The Arbitration Act 1996 s 39, gives an arbitral tribunal the power to make orders on a provisional basis on any relief which it had the power to grant in a final award. This includes, for example, making a provisional order for an interim payment, or for the disposition of property between the parties (s 39(2)), and to provide security for costs (s 38(3)). These subjects are considered in Sime, *A Practical Approach to Civil Procedure* (13th edn, OUP, 2010), chs 23 and 24. A provisional award for an interim payment, of course, has to be taken into account in the arbitral tribunal's final award (s 39(3)).

Directions on procedure and evidence

25.35 More generally, it is for the arbitration tribunal to decide all procedural and evidential matters that have been referred to it, subject to the right of the parties to agree such matters between themselves (Arbitration Act 1996 s 34(1)). By s 34(2), procedural and evidential matters include:

- when and where any part of the proceedings is to be held;
- the language or languages to be used in the proceedings and whether translations of any relevant documents are to be supplied;
- whether any and if so what form of written statements of claim and defence are to be used, when these should be supplied and the extent to which such statements can be later amended;
- whether any and if so which documents or classes of documents should be disclosed between and produced by the parties and at what stage;
- whether any and if so what questions should be put to and answered by the respective parties and when and in what form this should be done;
- whether to apply strict rules of evidence (or any other rules) as to the admissibility, relevance or weight of any material (oral, written or other) sought to be tendered on any matters of fact or opinion, and the time, manner and form in which such material should be exchanged and presented;
- whether and to what extent the tribunal should itself take the initiative in ascertaining the facts and the law; and
- whether and to what extent there should be oral or written evidence or submissions.

25.36 The tribunal may fix the time within which any directions given by it are to be complied with, and may if it thinks fit extend the time so fixed (whether or not it has expired) (s 34(3)).

Conservatory measures

There will be some cases where it is important to preserve the subject-matter of a dispute, **25.37** or to allow an expert retained by the other side to have access to land, goods or vehicles relevant to the dispute. In these cases the Arbitration Act 1996 s 38(4), provides:

'The tribunal may give directions in relation to any property which is the subject of the proceedings or as to which any question arises in the proceedings, and which is owned by or is in the possession of a party to the proceedings—

(a) for the inspection, photographing, preservation, custody or detention of the property by the tribunal, an expert or a party, or

(b) ordering that samples be taken from, or any observation be made of or experiment conducted upon, the property.'

It is to be noted that these powers may be exercised for the benefit of the arbitrators, an **25.38** expert or another party. This power only extends to property in the possession of another party to the proceedings. If the property belongs to a non-party, it may be possible to get a court order permitting inspection etc under s 44(2)(c) (see Chapter 28).

Procedural matters typically considered

The matters that need to be decided once the tribunal has been appointed, either at the **25.39** preliminary meeting, or in correspondence, depends on the nature of the dispute, the terms of the agreement to arbitrate, any institutional rules, and the preferences of the parties and arbitrators. Typical matters that might be considered are included in the directions that are set out in Figure 25.2, a set of interim directions in an arbitration to resolve a dispute relating to a contract alleged to have been tainted by bribery.

Figure 25.2 Interim directions in an arbitration

....

IN THE MATTER OF THE ARBITRATION ACT 1996

AND

IN THE MATTER OF AN ARBITRATION

BETWEEN

CHIPOKA AIRWAYS LIMITED

<u>Claimant</u>

and

RUNWAY AIRCRAFT MAINTENANCE LIMITED

<u>Respondent</u>

————————————

INTERIM DIRECTIONS

————————————

Upon hearing the solicitors for the parties the following directions are given:

1.   That there be statements of case in this arbitration as follows:

1.1 Points of Claim to be delivered within 21 days from this date.

1.2 Points of Defence (and Counterclaim if any) to be delivered within 21 days from delivery of the Points of Claim.

1.3 Points of Reply (and Defence to Counterclaim if any) to be delivered within 21 days from delivery of the Points of Defence (and Counterclaim).

(Continued)

Figure 25.2 Interim directions in an arbitration *(Continued)*

2. That the Claimant and the Respondent do each deliver to the other a list of the documents on which it relies within 14 days of delivery of the Points of Reply (and Defence to Counterclaim if any) together with copies of all the listed documents.

3. That the Claimant and Respondent mutually exchange written witness statements for each factual witness they intend to call at the hearing within 28 days after disclosure of documents.

4. That expert witnesses be limited to one forensic accountant for each party, and limited to an expert whose written report has been delivered to the other party within 56 days after the exchange of witness statements.

5. Within 14 days after the delivery of experts' reports the parties shall deliver to the Arbitrators their estimates for the length of the hearing and their and their witnesses' dates of availability.

6. There be a without prejudice discussion between the experts not less than 28 days before the hearing, and a statement of the areas of agreement and disagreement must be signed by both experts not less than 14 days before the hearing.

7. Any communication with the Arbitrators shall also be copied to the other party by the party writing to the Arbitrators.

8. The parties are to agree any financial loss and other financial figures if possible.

9. Not less than 14 days before the hearing each party shall deliver a written summary of their submissions on each of the matters to be decided.

10. Not less than 14 days before the hearing the Claimant shall deliver to the Arbitrators all the documents relevant to the hearing in ring binders with all the pages copied legibly and page numbered. Identical files shall be provided by the Claimant for both parties and a further copy must be available at the hearing for the use of witnesses.

11. The Claimant shall be responsible for hiring of suitable rooms for the hearing. The hire costs shall be costs in the arbitration.

12. The costs of the preliminary hearing shall be costs in the arbitration.

13. The dates for the hearing shall be notified to the parties after the Arbitrators have had the opportunity to consider the respective parties' and witnesses' availability.

14. Permission to apply for further or other directions.

DATED 1 March 2010

Signed: (1)
        (2)
        (3)
        Arbitrators

Other matters that may need to be considered include:

(a) any requirements that have to be followed in accordance with the terms of the arbitration agreement;

(b) any issues relating to the tribunal's jurisdiction (see 26.45);

(c) whether any interim measures are needed to preserve the position pending a decision;

(d) whether there will be an oral hearing, and if so, the form that it will take;

(e) the law that will be applied in deciding the dispute (see 26.21);

(f) the language that will be used in any hearings (see 26.59);

(g) any procedural complications, such as any related disputes, whether they should be consolidated etc; and

(h) the arbitrator's fees.

Peremptory orders

While the parties are free to agree on the powers of the arbitral tribunal to deal with proce- **25.40** dural default (Arbitration Act 1996 s 41(1)), unless otherwise agreed the powers in s 41(5)–(7) will apply. They apply where an order requires a step to be taken within a prescribed time, and one or other of the parties fails to comply within the time limit. These subsections give the tribunal a range of powers so that any default can be dealt with in a proportionate manner.

By s 41(5), the tribunal may make a peremptory order requiring the same steps to be taken as **25.41** an existing order where a party fails to comply with the previous order or direction without showing sufficient cause. These peremptory orders operate in much the same way as 'unless' orders in normal litigation (see Sime, *A Practical Approach to Civil Procedure* (13th edn, OUP, 2010), ch 28). The wording of s 41(5) means that a peremptory order may only be made if an ordinary order has been made first (*Wicketts v Brine Builders* [2001] CILL 1805).

If a party fails to comply with a peremptory order, by s 41(7) the arbitral tribunal may do **25.42** any of the following:

- direct that the defaulting party shall not be entitled to rely on any allegation or material that was the subject-matter of the order;
- draw such adverse inferences from the act of non-compliance as the circumstances justify;
- proceed to an award on the basis of such materials as have been properly provided to it; or
- make such order as it thinks fit as to the payment of costs of the arbitration incurred in consequence of the non-compliance.

What the arbitrators cannot do is to impose penal sanctions for default (committal to prison **25.43** or a fine), these being powers only exercisable by a court. Where the innocent party has exhausted all the available arbitral processes to seek compliance with an arbitral tribunal order, unless otherwise agreed by the parties the innocent party may apply to the High Court for an order requiring the defaulting party to comply with the peremptory order (s 42), which may include committal for non-compliance. Section 42 confers a discretion on the court, which does not act as a rubber stamp on orders made by the tribunal. However, it will be inconsistent with the general principle in s 1(c) (see 23.53) for the court to be too ready to review the decision made by the tribunal, the primary question for the court being whether a court order is required in the interests of justice to assist with the proper functioning of the arbitral process (*Emmott v Michael Wilson & Partners Ltd* [2009] 1 Lloyd's Rep 233).

Dismissal for inordinate and inexcusable delay

Where the claimant in an arbitration is guilty of inordinate and inexcusable delay that: **25.44**

- gives rise, or is likely to give rise, to a substantial risk that it is not possible to have a fair resolution of the issues in the arbitration; or
- has caused or is likely to cause, serious prejudice to the respondent,

the tribunal may make an award dismissing the claim (Arbitration Act 1996 s 41(3)).

Dismissal for inordinate and inexcusable delay is the equivalent of a former procedure by **25.45** the same name under the pre-CPR High Court procedural rules. There was a great deal of reported case law on this concept in relation to ordinary litigation, all of which is now redundant. The leading case was *Birkett v James* [1978] AC 297, but it is these principles that are enshrined in s 41(3). It is a restrictive concept, and there are not many cases where there is both the protracted delay contemplated by the subsection and the substantial risk that it is no longer possible to deal fairly with the arbitration or where there is serious prejudice to the respondent. An example where dismissal was upheld is *TAG Wealth Management v West* [2008] 2 Lloyd's Rep 699 where the claimant was responsible for five years of delay in dealing with disclosure of documents in the arbitration. Dismissal under s 41(3) is only possible if the limitation period has expired (*Lazenby (James) & Co v McNicholas Construction Co Ltd* [1999] 3 All ER 820).

Statements of case

25.46 Statements of case are intended to set out the respective contentions on the dispute by the parties. The Arbitration Act 1996 s 34(1) says it is for the tribunal to decide all procedural and evidential matters, subject to the right of the parties to agree any matter. Procedural matters by s 34(2)(d) include whether any and if so what form of written statements of claim and defence are to be used, when these should be supplied and the extent to which such statements can be later amended. It follows that the tribunal may decide against the use of formal pleadings, and this may be sensible where the dispute is reasonably straightforward. In some cases the tribunal may decide that the issues can best be defined by requiring the parties to provide lists of issues. In most other cases statements of case will be used. Like pleadings in court proceedings, these are intended:

- to set out what happened;
- to set out each side's case;
- to define the issues (through the responses to each allegation in subsequent statements of case); and
- to set out the relief sought and the respondent's response on whether that relief is available.

25.47 There are no set rules on what the statements of case should be called, or indeed on whether they should be called statements of case, pleadings or case summaries. Typically the claimant will start with its points of claim, with the respondent's case being set out in its points of defence. If the respondent has a cross-claim, the response is called the points of defence and counterclaim. The tribunal may allow further statements of case, which would continue with a claimant's points of reply (and defence to counterclaim). Examples of points of claim and points of defence in the same bribery case as the interim directions in Figure 25.2 can be seen in Figures 25.3 and 25.4.

25.48 Figures 25.3 and 25.4 broadly follow the approach in English court proceedings, but in a slightly less formal way. The technical rules of pleading in CPR, Part 16, do not apply in arbitrations. It is good practice to set out the facts and legal consequences in a statement of case, while avoiding setting out evidence and legal arguments. However, a wide range of practice is encountered, particularly in international arbitrations where the lawyers may practice in jurisdictions with very different traditions on setting out a client's statement of case.

Figure 25.3 Points of claim

IN THE MATTER OF THE ARBITRATION ACT 1996

AND

IN THE MATTER OF AN ARBITRATION

BETWEEN

CHIPOKA AIRWAYS LIMITED

<u>Claimant</u>

and

RUNWAY AIRCRAFT MAINTENANCE LIMITED

<u>Respondent</u>

POINTS OF CLAIM

1. The Claimant is a limited company incorporated and registered under the Companies Act 1985 and at all material times ran an international airline service operating from Chipoka Airport in Malawi, Africa.
2. The Respondent was at all material times a company providing aircraft maintenance and repair services.
3. In about October 2005 Aircraft Service Agencies plc approached the Claimant with a proposal that the Respondent was a suitable company to service the Claimant's fleet of four Boeing 737-800 jet airliners ('the four aircraft').
4. By a contract in writing dated 12 March 2006 ('the Contract') the Respondent agreed to provide aircraft maintenance services for the Claimant in respect of the four aircraft for a period of five years from 6 April 2006 to 5 April 2011.
5. The Claimant will rely on the Contract for its full terms, meaning and effect.
6. There were express terms of the Contract that:
   (a) the Claimant would pay sums to the Respondent on a power-by-the-hour basis under which specified sums would be paid in respect of each of the four aircraft for every hour it was in flight;
   (b) any work done on the four aircraft not covered by the power-by-the-hour clause would be charged by the Respondent to the Claimant at US $40.00 per hour;
   (c) the Respondent would undertake all maintenance and inspection work required on the four aircraft for the duration of the Contract; and
   (d) any dispute or difference arising out of or in connection with the Contract shall be administered by the London Court of International Arbitration and finally determined under the Rules of the London Court of International Arbitration by three arbitrators appointed in accordance with those Rules.
7. Unknown to the Claimant the Respondent paid certain sums to Aircraft Service Agencies plc which were used by Aircraft Service Agencies plc to pay bribes to the directors of the Claimant for the purpose of obtaining the Claimant's agreement to enter into the Contract.
8. The Claimant discovered the matters set out in paragraph 7 above on hearing of proceedings between Aircraft Service Agencies plc and the Respondent in which Aircraft Service Agencies plc sought to recover its commission from the Respondent, in which the Respondent set up the illegality of the commission payments on the basis of the bribes which the Respondent alleged were paid to the Claimant's directors.

(Continued)

Figure 25.3 Points of claim *(Continued)*

9. As a result of the matters set out in paragraph 7 above the Claimant is entitled to and does treat the Contract as vitiated for fraud and/or corruption.

10. By a letter from the Claimant's solicitors to the Respondent dated 26 October 2009 the Claimant sought to recover the sums it had paid to the Respondent under the Contract. By a letter dated 23 November 2009 the Respondent accepted that the Contract was vitiated for fraud and/or corruption, but disputed the amount that is payable to the Claimant.

11. It is common ground between the Claimant and the Respondent that the total amount paid by the Claimant to the Respondent pursuant to the Contract was the sum of US $55,553,886.03.

12. Of the sum of US $55,553,886.03 paid by the Claimant to the Respondent the amount paid by the Claimant to the Respondent as represented the provision for commissions payable to Aircraft Service Agencies plc in excess of the Respondent's selling price was the sum of US $9,887,480.38.

13. In the circumstances, the Claimant is entitled to repayment of the sum of US $55,553,886.03. Alternatively the Claimant, in the bona fide and reasonable, but mistaken, belief that the amounts were payable to the Respondent, effected payments totalling US $55,553,886.03 to the Respondent and the Respondent was unjustly enriched at the Claimant's expense in that amount.

14. Alternatively to paragraph 13, the Claimant is entitled to repayment of the sum of US $9,887,430,38, alternatively the Claimant, in the bona fide and reasonable, but mistaken, belief that the amounts were payable to the Respondent, effected payments totalling US $9,887,430,38 to the Respondent and the Respondent was unjustly enriched at the Claimant's expense in that amount.

15. The Claimant has demanded payment of the above sums and the Respondent has refused to make payment of all or any part of the sums so demanded.

AND the Claimant therefore seeks an award against the Respondent as follows:

(a)   Payment of the sum of US $55,553,886.03, alternatively

(b)   Payment of the sum of US $9,887,480.38;

(c)   Interest pursuant to the Arbitration Act 1996, section 49, on the amount found to be due to the Claimant at such rate and for such period as the arbitral tribunal considers appropriate.

(d)   Costs.

I believe that the facts stated in these Points of Claim are true.

SERVED this 22 day of March 2010 by Taylor, Andrews & Co., Solicitors, of 36 High Street, Birmingham, B4 8YD

Signed:

Dated: 22 March 2010

Evidence

25.49 An arbitral tribunal has a wide discretion on whether to apply the strict rules of evidence (or any other rules) as to the admissibility, relevance or weight of any material (oral, written or other) sought to be tendered on any matters of fact or opinion (Arbitration Act 1996 s 34(2)(f)). The discretion has to be exercised in ways that are consistent with the fair resolution of the dispute (s 1(a)).

Figure 25.4 Points of defence and counterclaim

IN THE MATTER OF THE ARBITRATION ACT 1996

AND

IN THE MATTER OF AN ARBITRATION

BETWEEN

CHIPOKA AIRWAYS LIMITED

<u>Claimant</u>

and

RUNWAY AIRCRAFT MAINTENANCE LIMITED

<u>Respondent</u>

POINTS OF DEFENCE
AND COUNTERCLAIM

1. The Respondent adopts the definitions used in the Points of Claim.
2. The allegations in paragraphs 1 to 6 of the Points of Claim are admitted.
3. Except that the Respondent is unable to admit or deny and requires the Claimant to prove that the payment of the bribes was unknown to the Claimant or when the Claimant discovered the matters set out in paragraph 7 of the Points of Claim, paragraphs 7 and 8 of the Points of Claim are admitted.
4. The allegations in paragraphs 9 to 11 of the Points of Claim are admitted.
5. The Respondent denies each and every allegation contained in paragraphs 12 and 13 of the Points of Claim as if specifically traversed and puts the Claimant to the proof of those allegations.
6. The Respondent denies each and every allegation contained in paragraph 14 of the Points of Claim as if specifically traversed and the Claimant is put to the proof of those allegations.
7. Without derogating from the generality of the denials in paragraphs 5 and 6, Respondent pleads that:
   7.1. it performed all its obligations under the Contract and gave good and proper value by way of its services and inspections provided under the Contract to the Claimant;
   7.2. it has not been unjustly enriched nor has the Claimant been prejudiced;
   7.3. the Claimant has received the services and inspections it required and for which it had contracted at a fair cost.
8. The Respondent:
   8.1. avers that if the Claimant were to succeed in these proceedings, it would receive the full value in respect of the services rendered by the Respondent without giving credit for the value of those services, and taking such benefit without giving credit would, in all the circumstances, be inequitable and not in accordance with the law;
   8.2 relies upon the Counterclaim set out below.
9. The allegations in paragraph 15 of the Points of Claim are admitted.
10. In the event of it being found that the Contract entered into by the Claimant and the Respondent was tainted by bribery and/or corruption and that, as a result, the Claimant

(Continued)

Figure 25.4 Points of defence and counterclaim *(Continued)*

is entitled to the relief sought in this arbitration, then and in that event the Respondent proceeds with the Counterclaim set out below.

POINTS OF COUNTERCLAIM

11. The Respondent repeats its Points of Defence.
12. The Respondent performed all its obligations under the Contract and gave good and proper value by way of its services under the Contract, in accordance with the provisions of the Claimant's approved maintenance schedule, and further, in accordance with such instructions as were given to the Respondent by the Claimant from time to time, the Respondent rendered technical services, in the form of, among other things, special inspections and/or replacement of parts on the four aircraft.
13. At the time it entered into the Contract, the Respondent was not aware of the possible illegality of the Contract and/or the possible illegality of the performance of the Contract.
14. The Respondent has performed under the Contract and has, in terms of the Contract, received payment in respect of the maintenance and inspection services rendered and the parts replaced on the four aircraft. In the circumstances an award to the effect that the Respondent should repay to the Claimant the amount of US $55,553,866.03 or any part of that sum would have the effect of enriching the Claimant at the expense of the Respondent in that sum of money, the Claimant having received the benefit of the servicing, parts and inspections in respect of the four aircraft under the alleged illegal Contract.
15. The retention by the Respondent of the amount of US $55,553,866.03 or any part of that sum would not be contrary to public policy, and/or would not be unjust and inequitable, in the circumstances.

AND the Respondent Counterclaims:

That the Respondent is entitled to a declaration to the effect that it is entitled to the retention of the amount of US $55,553,866.03 or such other sum as the arbitral tribunal shall decide.

I believe that the facts stated in these Points of Defence and Counterclaim are true.

SERVED this 13th day of April 2010 by Scott & Avery LLP., Solicitors, of 16-24 Archway Road, London WC2H 6SP

Signed:

Dated: 13th April 2010

Disclosure of documents

25.50 By the Arbitration Act 1996 s 34(2)(d), the tribunal must consider whether any, and if so which, documents or classes of documents should be disclosed between and produced by the parties and at what stage. From the use of the word 'any' it is clear the tribunal may decide against any form of disclosure of documents. Far more frequently, the tribunal will make a

direction requiring the parties to disclose to the tribunal and to each other the documents
that will assist the arbitrator in deciding the dispute. There is no requirement to import the
concept of 'standard disclosure' from the CPR, r 31.6. Disclosure may be limited to specified categories of documents, or to the documents on which each side relies. There are cases
where disclosure of adverse documents in the possession of each side, or documents that
support the other side's case, may also be required by the arbitrators' directions.

Method of disclosure

The form in which disclosure is given also does not have to follow court procedures. This **25.51**
may be done simply by providing copies to the other side and the tribunal. Sometimes a
list is specified in the arbitrators' directions, but it need not have the formalities laid down
in CPR, Part 31, unless that is specified too. A particular form used in arbitration is what is
called a 'Redfern Schedule' (after one of the authors of the *Law and Practice of International
Commercial Arbitration* by Redfern, Hunter and Blackaby (4th edn, Sweet & Maxwell)). An
example is shown in Figure 25.5.

Figure 25.5 Redfern schedule

IN THE MATTER OF THE ARBITRATION ACT 1996

AND

IN THE MATTER OF AN ARBITRATION

BETWEEN

CHIPOKA AIRWAYS LIMITED

<u>Claimant</u>

and

RUNWAY AIRCRAFT MAINTENANCE LIMITED

<u>Respondent</u>

REDFERN SCHEDULE

Description of document	Respondent's objection	Claimant's response	Arbitrators' ruling
Draft statement of James Morris	Protected by legal professional privilege	Agreed	Not required
Invoice 54546	Not relevant to the issues in this reference	Relevant to issue of how much the Respondent paid to Aircraft Service Agencies plc	Relevant and disclosable
Respondent's list of aircraft maintenance service parts and labour costs 2006	This document is a trade secret as it sets out cost prices for the Respondent's services which would undermine its business if disclosed to competitors or customers	Highly relevant to the issues in this reference. The confidentiality of the list can be maintained by the privacy of these proceedings and a suitable undertaking on behalf of the Claimant	To be disclosed on an undertaking on behalf of the Claimant and its lawyers

Implied obligation of confidentiality

25.52   Parties to an arbitration are under an implied obligation not to use or disclose any documents provided to them by the other parties for any purpose outside the scope of the reference (*Dolling-Baker v Merrett* [1991] 2 All ER 891). This is very similar to the implied undertaking relating to disclosed documents in litigation (CPR, r 31.22). A significant difference is that in litigation the undertaking is lifted once documents are used in open court, whereas the obligation in arbitration continues after a hearing because of the privacy of arbitration proceedings.

Witness statements

25.53   It is common for arbitrators to make directions for the exchange of witness statements from factual witnesses intended to be relied upon at the hearing.

Experts

Party-appointed experts

25.54   As with court proceedings, there are concerns in arbitrations over the cost of expert evidence. Directions frequently impose limits on the expert evidence that each party may rely upon, typically restricting the parties to one expert in each relevant field of expertise. Usually the directions will require the parties to deliver copies of their experts' written reports to each other and the tribunal by a specified date. It is also common for further directions to cover things like putting written questions to the other side's experts, which must be answered in writing, and for the experts in a particular field to have a without prejudice discussion for the purpose of seeking agreement and identifying where they disagree.

Tribunal-appointed experts

25.55   Under the Arbitration Act 1996 s 37(1), unless otherwise agreed by the parties the tribunal may appoint experts or legal advisers to report to it and the parties, or appoint assessors to assist it on technical matters. The parties must be given a reasonable opportunity to comment on any information, opinion or advice offered by an expert appointed by the tribunal, and the tribunal may allow the expert, legal adviser or assessor to attend the proceedings. The fees of a tribunal-appointed expert need to be provided for. Usually they are paid by the parties.

Pre-trial hearing/conference

25.56   If the arbitration is of some complexity it may be sensible to hold a pre-trial hearing or conference. This will usually take place a number of weeks before the expected start of the hearing. Frequently the tribunal will want the advocates who will be representing the parties at the final hearing to attend so that matters relating to the management of the hearing can be discussed with the lawyers who will be there. The main purpose is to review what has been done in preparation for the hearing, to assess whether the parties are going to be ready for the hearing (so there is no need to adjourn), to make any directions that will assist in ensuring both parties are ready for the hearing, and to agree how the hearing can be conducted in the most efficient manner. For example, it may be that costs will be saved by having the experts for both sides dealt with on specified days of the hearing, to avoid having to pay retainers when they are not needed. A procedural hearing at this stage can also be a catalyst for either settling the dispute or narrowing the issues.

No right to an oral hearing

Before the Arbitration Act 1996 the parties to an arbitration had the right to demand an oral **25.57** hearing. Under the Arbitration Act 1996 s 34(2)(h), subject to contrary agreement between the parties, the tribunal can decide whether and to what extent there should be oral or written evidence or submissions. In deciding whether to deal with the dispute on the documents or after an oral hearing the tribunal must bear in mind the need to act fairly, giving every party a reasonable opportunity of putting its case and dealing with that of the other side, and the need to avoid unnecessary expense and delay (s 33(1)). In *Boulos Gad Tourism and Hotels Ltd v Uniground Shipping Co Ltd* (2001) LTL 21/2/2002 Tomlinson J said it was unwise of the tribunal to have proceeded without a hearing on an arbitration where a substantial amount of money was at stake, although the arbitrators were acting within their powers in doing so.

While the Arbitration Act 1996 therefore allows a tribunal to make an award without an oral **25.58** hearing, a number of institutional rules reverse this and give the parties the right to insist on an oral hearing.

Bundles

Directions are usually made for the compilation of bundles for the hearing. This task is usu- **25.59** ally given to the claimant. Bundles will be needed for all members of the tribunal, each of the parties, and for the use of witnesses. Bundles should be paginated and identical.

Bundles are usually compiled in consultation between the parties. They will usually con- **25.60** tain the documents dealing with the reference to the arbitration and the appointment of the tribunal. They will then usually have the statements of case, in order (points of claim, then defence, then reply), with any amendments standing in place of the original, and any answers to requests for clarification of a statement of case coming immediately after the relevant statement of case. Procedural orders and directions usually come next.

It may well be that separate bundles will be required for the evidence. These files should be **25.61** divided into the contemporaneous documentation, the witness statements of the factual witnesses, and the expert evidence. Care is needed in organising the files of evidence where this is voluminous. It is usual to group similar documents together, and to maintain chronological order within sections of these files. There may also be a need for a correspondence file dealing with correspondence since the dispute arose.

A further file is likely to be needed to contain the written opening submissions or skeleton **25.62** arguments (and in due course the closing submissions or skeleton arguments), together with the legal authorities relevant to the dispute. Unless there is something unusual, all the authorities that the legal representatives wish to refer to will feature in the written submissions or skeleton arguments.

Arrangements for the hearing

25.63 Fixing dates for a hearing can be difficult, particularly where a number of witnesses and experts will need to attend, and where there is a multi-member tribunal. Directions are often made that the claimant must book the necessary rooms for the hearing (in addition to the main room for the hearing, other rooms are usually necessary for each of the parties and the tribunal). Hearings often take place in hotels or rooms provided by the arbitral institution. Arrangements may also be needed for the appointment of a secretary to the tribunal, and for the recording or transcription of the evidence and submissions given at the hearing. It is increasingly common for the evidence of some of the witnesses to be given through video-conferencing or similar means and, if so, arrangements will need to be in place for the hearing.

The hearing

Adversarial or inquisitorial

25.64 It is clear from the Arbitration Act 1996 s 34(2)(e) and (g), which provide that the arbitral tribunal can decide whether and to what extent it should take the initiative in ascertaining the facts and the law, that arbitrators can choose to adopt either an adversarial (the traditional English court method of conducting hearings) or inquisitorial (civil law system) approach to the hearing. In English arbitrations the adversarial system remains dominant.

Written submissions and skeleton arguments

25.65 The modern approach is for the opening and closing submissions by the advocates for the parties in an arbitration to be by or supported by written submissions or skeleton arguments. Written submissions tend to be reasonably full, and at their extreme completely replace oral submissions. They can be very long (it is not unknown for them to exceed 100 pages in complex cases). They perhaps merge with 'written briefs' that originated in other jurisdictions, which often contain a large amount of documentary evidence as well as written submissions on the law and how the party would like it applied to the facts.

25.66 Skeleton arguments are intended to summarise the main submissions that will be made, and include some of the detailed information or law that would otherwise have to be delivered at dictation pace at the hearing. In *Raja v Van Hoogstraten (No 9)* [2009] 1 WLR 1143 Mummery LJ said that skeleton arguments should not be prepared as verbatim scripts to be read out in public or as footnoted theses to be read in private. Good skeleton arguments are tools with practical uses: an agenda for the hearing, a summary of the main points, propositions and arguments to be developed orally, a useful way of noting citations and references, a convenient place for making cross-references, a time-saving means of avoiding unnecessary dictation to the court and laborious and pointless note-taking by the court. They are aids to oral advocacy, not substitutes for oral argument.

25.67 It is usually necessary to prepare these documents (or at least prepare the substance of them) well in advance of the hearing. There will usually be a direction for the exchange and delivery to the tribunal of opening written submissions or opening skeleton arguments a stated period in advance of the hearing.

Witnesses

Witnesses in arbitrations usually attend voluntarily, because the tribunal has no power to **25.68** issue witness summonses (which compel attendance). If a witness summons is needed for an unwilling witness, it is possible to obtain one by making an application to the High Court (Arbitration Act 1996 s 43).

Witnesses are rarely sworn in arbitrations. Their witness statements are usually taken as **25.69** their evidence-in-chief, so the party relying on their evidence will usually ask only a few questions to establish the witness' identity, involvement in the dispute, and to deal with any relevant documents or corrections to their statements. Unless the expected answer is not controversial, the usual rule is that questions during examination-in-chief should be non-leading (see below for leading questions). It is intended that everything that the witness knows that is relevant to establishing the case of the party calling them should be in the exchanged witness statement. By verifying their statement the witness adopts it, which is why there should be no need to ask further questions in-chief.

Witnesses are then tendered for cross-examination, which often follows the same format as **25.70** in court proceedings. In cross-examination the advocate is allowed to use leading questions (broadly, these are questions that suggest the intended answer, or that give the witness a choice of answering 'yes' or 'no'). The purpose of cross-examination is to advance the case of the cross-examining party. It may be that some witnesses who are cross-examined can help the cross-examining party on certain issues and, if so, the opportunity should not be lost in obtaining this helpful evidence. Otherwise, the cross-examining party may seek to undermine or limit the potential effect of the witness by asking questions designed to show the witness may be mistaken, or not to have understood what they think they saw, or that their memory may have faded, or to point out inconsistencies between their witness statement and other evidence in the case.

After being cross-examined each witness may be re-examined by the party who called **25.71** them. Strictly, questions in re-examination should be put in non-leading form, and should be restricted to points raised in cross-examination.

The tribunal is able to ask its own questions of witnesses at any point while they are giving **25.72** evidence.

Witness conferencing

An alternative to having witnesses called in sequence is to have a number of witnesses give **25.73** evidence simultaneously. This process is sometimes called witness conferencing, or colloquially as 'hot tubbing'. Precise mechanics vary, but fairly typically the tribunal will consult with the parties over which witnesses will be dealt with in this way, and to formulate a list of questions for the witnesses. Each witness will then be asked the same questions from the list. The process is not that popular in England and Wales because it severely inhibits the effectiveness of cross-examination.

Expert evidence at the hearing

The experts who should attend the hearing will be stated in the directions previously given **25.74** by the tribunal. Often the arbitrators will be minded to have the expert evidence presented in the form of the experts' reports, supplemented by any written answers to questions and any note produced following a without prejudice meeting of the experts. In other cases experts will appear at the hearing, either as witnesses for the parties or on behalf of the tribunal. Their reports are usually taken as their evidence-in-chief (perhaps with some supplementary questions), and they will be cross-examined and re-examined in a similar way to factual witnesses.

Views and site visits

25.75 In a number of arbitrations, such as rent review and construction disputes, the tribunal may well decide to include a view or site visit as part of the evidence it takes into account in making its decision.

Closing submissions

25.76 When the evidence is complete, the advocates for both sides make their closing submissions. These may be oral, but are increasingly given by written submissions, or in conjunction with a skeleton argument. Usually the respondent makes the first closing submission, followed by the claimant.

Closing of proceedings

25.77 The arbitrators will include a mechanism for closing the proceedings. This may be a date designated in the tribunal's directions, or a set period after a stage in the process, or after the last closing submission at the hearing. After the closure of proceedings the usual rule is that no further evidence or submissions can be given to the tribunal (although sometimes tribunals give permission for further material to be advanced even after the close of proceedings).

The decision

25.78 The arbitrators will need to confer to discuss the evidence and the submissions made by the parties, and make a decision. Arbitrators must act judicially, even if they are appointed on the basis of qualifications or experience that they possess (this follows from the duty to decide the reference fairly as stated by the Arbitration Act 1996 s 33). Appointing arbitrators with relevant experience means the parties must be taken to have agreed that such arbitrators will bring their own knowledge to bear in making their decisions (*Hawk Shipping Ltd v Cron Navigation* [2003 EWHC 1828 (Comm)). From *Checkpoint Ltd v Strathclyde Pension Fund* [2003] 1 EGLR 1, the dividing line is that:

- it is permissible for the arbitrator to use his technical knowledge and experience in evaluating the evidence presented by the parties, provided it is knowledge that the parties could reasonably expect the arbitrator to have; but
- it is impermissible for the arbitrator to supply evidence from his own knowledge without disclosing that knowledge to the parties so they can put in an answer either through submissions or with additional evidence.

25.79 *Checkpoint Ltd v Strathclyde Pension Fund* was a rent review arbitration that provided for the appointment of an arbitrator experienced in the letting and/or valuation of similar properties. The landlord's expert surveyor gave evidence of six similar properties. The tenant's surveyor's evidence was to the effect that only one of the landlord's comparables was in fact relevant. The Court of Appeal held that the arbitrator had not strayed over the line mentioned above in using his knowledge and experience in evaluating the evidence of the two experts. For example, he had not introduced any comparables of his own into the equation. There was therefore no need for the arbitrator to disclose anything to the parties, as all he did was to do what the parties should have expected given he was appointed on account of his experience.

Usually decisions are valid if made by a majority, although arbitrators usually seek to reach **25.80** a unanimous decision. They also need to consider their reasons for their decision, which should be included in the award (unless there has been an agreement that no reasons will be stated for the award).

Ex aequo et bono/amiable compositeur (equity clauses)

Normally, arbitrators in England and Wales will be expected to reach a decision in accord- **25.81** ance with English substantive law. Obviously judges in the courts are best placed to apply substantive law to a dispute. By choosing arbitration the parties may also intend that their dispute should be decided on principles other than the strict application of law. This is perfectly permissible given the provision in the Arbitration Act 1996 s 46(1), which says the arbitral tribunal shall decide the dispute either in accordance with the law chosen by the parties as applicable to the substance of the dispute, or, if the parties so agree, in accordance with such other considerations as are agreed by them or determined by the tribunal. One possibility is that the substantive dispute will be decided *ex aequo et bono*, or with the tribunal acting as an *amiable compositeur*. These concepts, together with deciding on the proper law of an arbitration, are considered in Chapter 26.

The award and appeals

Chapter 28 deals with the practice relating to the delivery of the tribunal's award. Appeals **25.82** to the High Court are dealt with in Chapter 29.

EXAMPLE OF ARBITRAL RULES THAT CLOSELY FOLLOW COURT PROCEDURES

This section will describe a system of commercial arbitration run by the London Metal **25.83** Exchange Ltd ('LME'). The LME's arbitration service is in fact used by a large number of enterprises who have no direct involvement in the metals trade. The parties will have agreed to refer their dispute to LME arbitration under the LME arbitration rules ('the LME rules'). Arbitrations under the LME rules are conducted in accordance with the provisions of the Arbitration Act 1996 as amended from time to time (reg 16).

Commencement of arbitration

Under the LME rules a claimant commences an arbitration by serving a notice to arbitrate **25.84** on the respondent, and by sending a copy of the notice to the secretary of the LME accompanied by the registration fee and deposit (reg 2.1). The date of receipt by the respondent of a valid notice to arbitrate is deemed to be the date on which the arbitration commenced (reg 2.4). The notice to arbitrate must contain at least the following information:

- the address for service of the claimant;
- a brief statement of the nature and circumstances of the dispute including a brief description of any contract, sufficient to enable the respondent to identify it, to which the dispute relates;
- a brief statement of the relief claimed;
- the claimant's proposal with regard to the number of arbitrators to form the tribunal;
- the claimant's nomination of one arbitrator from the LME panel; and
- the person and address of the respondent to which the notice to arbitrate has been sent.

Counter-notice

25.85 Within 21 days of receipt of the notice to arbitrate, the respondent is required to send to the claimant, with a copy to the secretary, a counter-notice (reg 2.5). A counter-notice must contain:

- the address for service of the respondent;
- confirmation that the respondent agrees to the number of arbitrators proposed by the claimant, or the respondent's counter-proposal; and
- if relevant, the respondent's nomination of one arbitrator from the LME panel.

25.86 If the respondent fails to serve a counter-notice the secretary of the LME will appoint the tribunal on receipt of a written application from the claimant.

Appointment of tribunal

25.87 LME tribunals consist of one, two, or three arbitrators. Arbitrators are only admitted to the LME panel if they have a broad experience of trading in metals. They are also required to have a legal or arbitration background.

25.88 Usually the tribunal has two arbitrators unless the parties agree to a tribunal of either one or three arbitrators (reg 3.1). If the tribunal is to consist of three arbitrators, the two arbitrators appointed by the parties nominate the third or inform the secretary that they are unable to agree. In this event the secretary appoints the third arbitrator (reg 3.3). The third arbitrator is the chairman of the tribunal (reg 3.6, and see 24.13). A challenge to the appointment of an arbitrator must be made within 28 days of the appointment of that arbitrator or within 28 days of the party becoming aware of the facts and circumstances on which the challenge is based. It is made by sending a written statement of the reasons for the challenge to the secretary (reg 3.12). Challenges can be made on grounds of non-independence, partiality, unfitness, or inability to act. Unless the other party agrees to the challenge or the arbitrator withdraws within seven days, the secretary refers the matter to the LME panel committee for a decision on whether the challenge should be sustained.

Procedure

25.89 The tribunal is by reg 4 given the widest discretion permitted by law to determine the procedure to be adopted, and to ensure the just, expeditious, economical, and final determination of the dispute.

Statements of case

Within 21 days of the appointment of the tribunal, the claimant is required to send to the **25.90** tribunal and to the respondent written points of claim that set out any facts or contentions of law on which it relies, and the relief claimed (reg 6.2). The claimant may serve the points of claim at the same time as the notice to arbitrate. If so, the information required by reg 2.2(b) and (c) need not be contained in the notice to arbitrate, and no further copies of the points of claim need be served.

Within 21 days of receipt of the points of claim, or of the appointment of the tribunal **25.91** if later, the respondent must send to the tribunal and to the claimant written points of defence (reg 6.4). Points of defence must state in sufficient detail which of the facts and contentions of law in the points of claim the respondent admits or not, or denies, on what grounds, and on what other facts and contentions of law it relies. Any counterclaims must be included in the points of defence in the same manner as claims are set out in the points of claim.

Within 21 days of receipt of the points of defence, the claimant may send to the tribunal **25.92** and to the respondent written points of reply which, where there are counterclaims, should include points of defence to counterclaims (reg 6.5). If the points of reply contain points of defence to counterclaims, the respondent may, within 21 days of receipt, send to the tribunal and to the claimant written points of reply regarding counterclaims (reg 6.6).

Documents and samples

All statements of case must be accompanied by legible copies, or if they are especially volu- **25.93** minous, lists of all essential documents on which the party concerned relies and, where appropriate, by any relevant samples (reg 6.8). Any document not in English must be accompanied by a translation into English and a note explaining who prepared the translation and the translator's qualifications, if any, to do so. The authority to be accorded to any translation is a matter for the tribunal (reg 6.9).

Directions

Within seven days of close of pleadings the tribunal is required to give directions for the **25.94** subsequent procedure of the arbitration and may convene a hearing for this purpose (reg 6.10). The tribunal fixes the date, time, and place of any meetings and hearings in the arbitration, and must give the parties reasonable notice (reg 7.2.1). Before any hearing, the tribunal may require either party to give notice of the identity and qualification of witnesses it wishes to call and may require the parties to exchange statements of evidence to be given by the witnesses a specified time in advance of the hearing (reg 9.1). The tribunal has the power either on its own motion or on the application of either party to order either party to take specified steps within a specified time (reg 10.1(a)). Among the powers given to the tribunal are those:

- to order either party to produce and to supply copies of, any documents in that party's possession, custody, or power, which, in the event of dispute, the tribunal determines to be relevant;
- to order either party to answer interrogatories (these are rather like requests for further information under CPR, Part 18);

- to require the parties to provide a written statement of their respective cases in relation to particular issues, to provide a written answer and to give reasons for any disagreement;
- to order the inspection, preservation, storage, interim custody, sale, or other disposal of any property or thing relevant to the arbitration under the control of either party;
- to make orders authorising any samples to be taken, or any observation to be made, or experiment to be tried which may, in the tribunal's discretion, be necessary or expedient for the purposes of obtaining full information or evidence; and
- to appoint one or more investigators or experts to report to the tribunal on specified issues.

25.95 The tribunal can also make orders for interim payments and security for costs. In other words, by agreeing to arbitration under the LME rules the parties confer on the tribunal almost all the powers of a court of law.

Hearings

25.96 Either party has the right to be heard before the tribunal, unless the parties have agreed to a documents-only arbitration (reg 7.1). The tribunal has a discretion to direct hearings to be conducted without the physical presence of every participant in the same room, but with participants linked through an audio or audio-visual telecommunication system (reg 7.2.2). The tribunal may submit to the parties a list of questions in advance of a hearing that it wishes them to treat with special attention (reg 7.3). Neither party may be represented at any hearing by a legal practitioner without the consent of the tribunal, such consent to be requested not later than close of pleadings (reg 8.1). Any consent has to be given on a reciprocal basis. Regulation 8.1 does not preclude either party from otherwise seeking legal advice.

25.97 The tribunal may allow, refuse, or limit the appearance of witnesses, whether witnesses of fact or expert witnesses (reg 9.2). Any witness who gives oral evidence may be questioned by each of the parties or their representative, under the control of the tribunal. The tribunal may put questions at any stage of the examination of the witnesses (reg 9.3). The tribunal may allow the evidence of a witness to be presented in written form either as a signed statement or by a duly sworn affidavit (reg 9.4). Either party may request that such a witness should attend for oral examination at a hearing. If the witness fails to attend, the tribunal may place such weight on the written evidence as it thinks fit, or exclude it altogether.

25.98 Everything that occurs in the arbitration is confidential save to the extent that disclosure may be required by a legal duty or to protect a legal right (reg 6.11).

Awards

25.99 The tribunal is required to make its award in writing and give reasons for the award (reg 12.1). If the tribunal consists of two arbitrators and they fail to agree on any issue, they shall request the secretary to appoint a third arbitrator (reg 12.2.1). If the tribunal consists of three arbitrators and they fail to agree on any issue, they shall decide by a majority. If an arbitrator refuses or fails to sign the award, the signatures of the majority are sufficient, provided that the reason for the omitted signature is stated (reg 12.2.2). In addition to the statutory power to award interest, the tribunal has the power to award interest on any monetary award at such rate and for such period as it considers fit on any sum after its due date but before commencement of the arbitration (reg 12.5). The award can also apportion costs between the parties (reg 13.2). Awards are final and binding on the parties as from the date they are made (reg 12.8). The award of the arbitrators is deposited with the secretary who notifies each party (reg 12.10). Either party may then take up the award upon payment by that party of the costs and expenses of the arbitration as specified in the award (including the remuneration of the arbitrators). Until the award is taken up by one of the parties it confers no rights upon either party.

Appeals

While there is the possibility of appeals on points of law to the High Court, the parties in LME arbitrations may exclude this possibility by agreement after the arbitration has commenced. **25.100**

KEY POINTS SUMMARY

- Arbitration is intended to be private and confidential, concepts that flow from the private agreement of the parties to refer the matter to arbitration rather than the courts. **25.101**
- Privacy and confidentiality are not absolute, and there are exceptions.
- There are many arbitral institutions, which may have their own institutional rules for arbitration, and they may also administer arbitrations.
- There are speedy, streamlined, arbitration procedures for the simpler types of dispute. These often dispense with hearings, and often have tight timetables for the delivery of written documentation to the tribunal.
- The procedural rules in the Arbitration Act 1996 are subject to contrary agreement by the parties.
- If institutional rules are silent on a procedural matter, the default provisions in the Arbitration Act 1996 apply.
- It is common in commercial arbitration for the process to follow the stages set out in Figure 25.1.
- The LME rules described towards the end of this chapter are an example of institutional rules that follow a system similar to the CPR. They adopt court procedures in a more overt way than the Arbitration Act 1996, but their general scheme is in fact very similar to that laid down by the Act.

26

INTERNATIONAL ARBITRATION

INTRODUCTION. 26.01

MEANING OF 'INTERNATIONAL' IN ARBITRATION. 26.06

ADVISING THE CLIENT. 26.08

SEAT 26.11

PROBLEMS CAUSED BY DIFFERENT SYSTEMS OF LAW 26.18

APPLICABLE LAW 26.21

OBJECTIONS TO JURISDICTION 26.45

PROCEDURAL MATTERS RELEVANT TO INTERNATIONAL
ARBITRATION 26.59

ICC RULES OF ARBITRATION 26.68

UNCITRAL MODEL LAW ON INTERNATIONAL COMMERCIAL
ARBITRATION 26.79

KEY POINTS SUMMARY 26.92

INTRODUCTION

26.01 International arbitration broadly covers any reference to arbitration involving parties in different states. A fuller definition is provided in the United Nations Commission on International Trade Law ('UNCITRAL') Model Law (see 26.06). So far as English law is concerned there is no fundamental difference between domestic commercial arbitration and international arbitration. There are provisions in the Arbitration Act 1996 (ss 85–88) that were intended to make special provision on a number of aspects of arbitration law for domestic arbitrations. These sections have not been brought into force (Arbitration Act 1996 (Commencement No 1) Order 1996 (SI 1996/3146)), and never will be (Department of Trade and Industry press release 30 January 1997).

26.02 International arbitration is most frequently met in the shipping, construction and engineering, oil and gas industries, and also in disputes involving insurance, banking and financial services.

A significant factor encouraging parties to use arbitration as their dispute resolution proc- **26.03** ess in international disputes is that the New York Convention 1958 (see Chapter 29) makes it easy to enforce the award made in an arbitration almost anywhere in the world. Another factor particularly of importance in international cases where the parties are in different states is that neither party may want the matter dealt with in the other side's country. By choosing arbitration the parties are able to find a neutral jurisdiction that is satisfactory to both sides. The parties may also agree to the tribunal applying a neutral system of law when making a decision on the dispute. In other cases the parties achieve a balance between themselves by agreeing on the arbitration being located in one jurisdiction but applying the law of another jurisdiction.

This chapter will consider a number of issues, such as the seat of the arbitration, the law **26.04** governing the arbitration, and disputes over jurisdiction, which often arise as important issues in international arbitrations. These issues apply to domestic arbitrations as much as to those of an international character, but in domestic arbitrations the answers are often uncontentious.

There are a number of arbitral institutions that deal with international arbitration. **26.05** Examples can be seen in Table 25.1. There are two well-known sets of institutional rules specifically aimed at international arbitration, namely the ICC rules of arbitration ('ICC rules') and the UNCITRAL Model Law. These will be considered towards the end of this chapter, as well as being referred to where appropriate in other parts of this chapter. It will be recalled from Chapter 23 that the Arbitration Act 1996 drew quite extensively from the UNCITRAL Model Law, so there is a large degree of affinity between these instruments. The ICC rules take a significantly different approach on a number of matters, as explained at the end of this chapter.

MEANING OF 'INTERNATIONAL' IN ARBITRATION

The ICC rules simply say they apply to business disputes 'of an international character' (Art **26.06** 1.1). A far more detailed definition is given in the UNCITRAL Model Law Art 1(3). This provides that an arbitration is international if:

'(a) the parties to an arbitration agreement have, at the time of the conclusion of that agreement, their places of business in different states; or

(b) one of the following places is situated outside the state in which the parties have their places of business:

(i)   the place of arbitration if determined in, or pursuant to, the arbitration agreement;

(ii) any place where a substantial part of the obligations of the commercial relationship is to be performed or the place with which the subject-matter of the dispute is most closely connected; or

(c) the parties have expressly agreed that the subject matter of the arbitration relates to more than one country.'

For the purposes of the UNCITRAL definition, if a party has more than one place of busi- **26.07** ness, the relevant place of business is the one with the closest relationship to the arbitration agreement (Art 1(4)(a)). Also, if a party does not have a place of business, the relevant place is his place of residence rather than his place of business (Art 1(4)(b)).

ADVISING THE CLIENT

26.08 Advising the client on the best venue for an arbitration, and on how to approach questions of the proper system of law or other rules to be applied in determining the dispute, is one of the most important responsibilities of solicitors retained in international arbitrations. There are obvious advantages in having the arbitration conducted in the client's home jurisdiction, but balanced against that are the costs and litigation risks in a full-blown dispute over jurisdiction, or over the proper law of the contract, with the other party. Assessing those risks, which will depend largely on how clearly the arbitration agreement is worded, is central in giving this advice.

26.09 Where an arbitration is to be conducted in England and Wales, but with a foreign system of law applying to the substantive contract, consideration has to be given to how that system differs from English law, whether to take a point on any such differences, and how to prove those differences. As discussed at 26.35, there is a presumption that foreign law is the same as English law, so if neither party takes a point, the tribunal simply applies English law. Advice invariably has to be taken from a law firm in the overseas jurisdiction, and if a point is to be taken, a lawyer from that jurisdiction has to give factual evidence of the relevant provisions of the foreign law.

26.10 Where the seat of the arbitration (see 26.11) is overseas, particularly where this is combined with hearings taking place in an overseas country, it is often best to advise the client to instruct local lawyers, sometimes instead of the English firm, sometimes in addition. The actual decision is usually based on questions of cost, expertise and convenience.

SEAT

26.11 The 'seat' and the 'place' of an arbitration are interchangeable terms. The Arbitration Act 1996 s 3, provides:

> ' "the seat of the arbitration" means the juridical seat of the arbitration designated—
> (a) by the parties to the arbitration agreement, or
> (b) by any arbitral or other institution or person vested by the parties with powers in that regard, or
> (c) by the arbitral tribunal if so authorised by the parties,
>
> or determined, in the absence of any such designation, having regard to the parties' agreement and all the relevant circumstances.'

26.12 Being the juridical seat means this is about the system of law that governs the arbitration. This implies there must be a country whose duty it is to administer, control or decide what control there should be over an arbitration (*Braes of Doune Wind Farm (Scotland) Ltd v Alfred McAlpine Business Services Ltd* [2008] 2 All ER (Comm) 493). If England is the seat of an arbitration, this means it is the Arbitration Act 1996 and English law that provide the framework for the procedural steps to be followed in the arbitration. It also means that the level of judicial intervention prescribed by the Arbitration Act 1996 applies.

The seat need not be the place where the arbitration hearings take place. In the mod- **26.13** ern world with digital communications and easy air travel, this produces very sensible results. If the seat of an arbitration was fixed by some other rule, such as where the tribunal conducted its hearings, or where the award is signed, bizarre results would be produced. For example, an arbitration conducted entirely in London would have its seat in France if the chairman of the tribunal took the draft award on holiday to France and signed it in Paris.

Designation of seat

The seat of an arbitration is decided on the basis of the intentions of the parties, either **26.14** directly or through a body they have chosen for the purpose (Arbitration Act 1996 s 3). An arbitration clause that provided for arbitration to be conducted in accordance with the rules of the ICC in Paris, and that included a provision that the venue of the arbitration was to be London, was held in *Shashoua v Sharma* [2009] 2 Lloyd's Rep 376 to be a designation of London as the juridical seat for the purposes of the Arbitration Act 1996 s 3. A surprising case is *Braes of Doune Wind Farm (Scotland) Ltd v Alfred McAlpine Business Services Ltd* [2008] 2 All ER (Comm) 493. In this case the arbitration clause provided that the seat of the arbitration was to be Glasgow, Scotland, but the High Court decided that England was the designated seat of the arbitration. Another clause of the contract provided that the courts of England and Wales had exclusive jurisdiction to settle disputes under the contract. It was held that the English jurisdiction clause had the effect that English law was the curial law of the arbitration, so England was the seat of the arbitration, whereas the Scottish 'seat' clause just meant that the arbitration hearings would take place in Scotland.

Where there is no express designation of the seat, important factors among the relevant **26.15** circumstances include whether the parties have agreed to arbitration administered by an institution located in a particular country (*Whitworth Street Estates (Manchester) Ltd v James Miller and Partners Ltd* [1970] AC 583) or whether a particular system of law has been agreed as the proper law of the substantive contract or as being the procedural law of the arbitration (*Egon Oldendorff v Liberia Corporation (No 2)* [1996] 1 Lloyd's Rep 380).

Supervisory jurisdiction

The courts of the seat of an arbitration have supervisory jurisdiction over the arbitration **26.16** (*C v D* [2008] Bus LR 843). This means that any challenge to an interim or final award made by the arbitrators may be made only in the courts of the place designated as the seat of the arbitration. Most applications to the courts in support of an arbitration (such as applications dealing with the appointment of arbitrators where there are problems in appointing a tribunal) are also brought in the country of the seat of the arbitration. It is recognised that the courts of the seat of an arbitration will not always have an effective jurisdiction over some matters, so that certain applications in a practical sense have to be brought in the courts of the country where an order will be effective. Examples are applications to secure the attendance of witnesses to attend the arbitration hearing and applications for injunctions in support of an arbitration (Arbitration Act 1996 s 2(3)). The need to give effect to the parties' agreement to arbitrate a dispute means that an English court will grant a stay of English litigation under s 9 whether or not the seat of the arbitration is in England and Wales (s 2(2)(a)). For similar practical reasons, applications relating to the enforcement of arbitral awards are made in the country where enforcement is to take place, rather than the seat of the arbitration (s 2(2)(b)).

Place of award

26.17 The seat of the arbitration is also, unless otherwise agreed by the parties, the place where any award is treated as having been made (Arbitration Act 1996 s 53). This is important because certain of the grounds for refusing to recognise arbitral awards in the New York Convention 1958 Art 5 apply to matters arising in the place of the award. Examples include if any of the parties was under an incapacity under the law of the place of the award, or if the award has been set aside by a court in the country in which the award was made.

PROBLEMS CAUSED BY DIFFERENT SYSTEMS OF LAW

26.18 Where the parties to a dispute are based in different countries they may well be totally unfamiliar with the system of law and the methods of resolving disputes that apply in the country of the other side to the dispute. International commerce covers every country on the globe, and the differences in the legal systems that may be met are far wider than those between different common law systems or that between common and civil law.

26.19 Prior to 1985, there were numerous recurrent problems faced by parties involved in international arbitrations. Most countries had developed laws that focussed on domestic arbitrations, which meant they were ill-suited to international disputes. Different countries dealt with the procedures to be followed in different levels of detail. It was most common for local laws to deal with procedure on a fragmentary basis, so there were a great many gaps that could lead to expensive litigation in resolving how to fill them. The range of mandatory and non-mandatory provisions in local laws varied widely (for the position in England and Wales, see 23.60), and was a source of considerable difficulty, with parties regularly falling victim of technical local laws that they were not expecting. While most systems provide for some form of supervision of arbitration by their courts, the degree of intervention, when it may be resorted to, and the grounds on which the courts may act have the potential for wide variations. Avoiding these problems invariably meant parties had to spend considerable sums in obtaining appropriate legal advice.

26.20 That said, there is a measure of consensus between different legal systems on the general nature of arbitration law and the procedures to be followed in arbitrations. It has also been recognised that it is desirable that states should work towards the harmonisation of their domestic arbitration laws, so that the business community can resort to arbitration in the reasonable expectation that the laws and procedures that will be followed will comply with internationally recognised principles that are acceptable to parties from a wide range of legal traditions. The most important development in achieving this goal was the promulgation of the UNCITRAL Model Law on International Commercial Arbitration of 1985 (as subsequently amended) (the 'UNCITRAL Model Law'). This is intended to provide a framework to be adopted by states when they codify or revise their local arbitration laws, with the consequence that as more countries do this, local arbitration laws will have a large measure of consistency around the world.

APPLICABLE LAW

The substantive contract, the arbitration clause, the contracts with the arbitrators, and each **26.21** part of the arbitration process, potentially has its own applicable system of law. There may therefore be systems of law from different countries dealing with:

- the substantive contract ('the proper law of the contract');
- the arbitration agreement (the law governing the obligation to refer the dispute to arbitration);
- the curial law (also known as the *lex arbitri*), which is the procedural law governing how the arbitration should be conducted;
- the law relating to the contracts with any arbitral institution and the individual arbitrators;
- the law of any place where actual hearings take place;
- the law relating to any agreement to compromise the dispute; and
- the law of the place or places where it is sought to register and enforce any arbitral award.

This can create unseemly complexities. There are many cases, however, where all these **26.22** matters (except possibly the law of the place of enforcement) are governed by the same system of law.

Proper law of the contract

The Arbitration Act 1996 s 46(1) provides that the arbitral tribunal shall decide the dispute: **26.23**

- in accordance with the law chosen by the parties as applicable to the substance of the dispute; or
- if the parties so agree, in accordance with such other considerations as are agreed by them or determined by the tribunal.

For this purpose the choice of the laws of a country by the parties shall be understood to **26.24** refer to the substantive laws of that country and not its conflict of laws rules (s 46(2)). If or to the extent that there is no such choice or agreement, the tribunal must apply the law determined by the conflict of laws rules that it considers applicable (s 46(3)). It is usually the conflict of laws rules from the country where the arbitration has its seat that are applied (*CGU International Insurance plc v Astrazeneca Insurance Co Ltd* [2006] CLC 162).

Law, or other rules

Usually, the proper law of the substantive dispute will be the system of law of a state. It can **26.25** be seen from the Arbitration Act 1996 s 46(1)(b) that it is open to the parties to agree that the substantive dispute is be decided in accordance with 'such other considerations' as they might agree or that may be determined by the arbitrators. One of the options available is that the tribunal could be authorised to decide the dispute as *amiable compositeur* or *ex aequo et bono* (see below). Another possibility is that the dispute may be determined by a system of rules that have not have been incorporated into the law of any particular state, for example, the United Nations Convention on Contracts for the International Sale of Goods.

Use of a system of rules that are not the laws of a named state is possible where the parties **26.26** so agree, or where the parties agree that the tribunal has this level of choice. If there is no such agreement, the default position is that the tribunal must apply a system of national law (s 46(3)) as determined by the conflict of laws rules that the tribunal considers applicable.

Amiable compositeur or ex aequo et bono (equity clauses)

26.27 The terms *amiable compositeur* and *ex aequo et bono* ('equity clauses') probably mean the same thing, although there may be a slight though ill-defined difference between them. Different legal systems recognise or do not recognise these concepts, and some provide definitions (which are not the same in every jurisdiction). Acting as an *amiable compositeur* allows the tribunal to decide the arbitration in according with the principles the arbitrators believe to be just rather than those that the law would technically apply. Deciding a matter *ex aequo et bono* means in justice and good faith. Equity clauses are not intended to give the tribunal complete scope to do whatever it wants, but they are intended to give the tribunal the flexibility to decide the dispute in accordance with notions of justice and equity.

26.28 Broadly, the idea is that by appointing arbitrators who are sensible and practical commercial people, the parties trust them to decide the dispute fairly and in accordance with the expectations and business ethics of reasonable people in the relevant trade. The risk is that by adopting such an ill-defined basis for deciding the matter, what may seem reasonable to one person may be wholly unacceptable to another, but there are limited means for saying one is to be preferred over the other.

26.29 Anticipating this problem, the UNCITRAL Model Law says at Art 28(4) that even in these cases the tribunal must decide the dispute in accordance with the terms of the contract, and must take into account the usages of the trade applicable to the transaction. This provision is not included in the Arbitration Act 1996, the view taken by the DAC report being that if the applicable law allows account to be taken of trade usages etc, the provision is unnecessary, whereas if it does not, the provision overrides the law. This misses the point that the clause ·is most aimed at providing minimum requirements when the tribunal is acting under an equity clause.

26.30 One particular effect of having a dispute decided under an equity clause is that doing so excludes the possibility of an appeal to the courts as there is no possibility of a 'question of law'.

Determination of the proper law

26.31 Where England is the seat of the arbitration (see 26.11), the proper law is determined:

- for contracts entered into before 17 December 2009 by applying the rules in the Contracts (Applicable Law) Act 1990, which gives effect to the Rome Convention 1980;
- for contracts entered into after 17 December 2009 by applying the rules in Regulation (EC) No 593/2008 ('Rome I'); and
- for non-contractual obligations from 11 January 2009 by applying the rules in Council Regulation (EC) No 864/2007 ('Rome II').

26.32 Under Rome I, the guiding principle is one of party autonomy on the choice of law. By Art 3(1), a contract shall be governed by the law chosen by the parties. The choice has to be made expressly or clearly demonstrated by the terms of the contract or the circumstances of the case. By their choice the parties can select the law applicable to the whole or to part only of the contract. The parties can subsequently agree to change their initial choice (Art 3(2)). Articles 4–8 deal with cases where there is no agreement, and provide special rules for consumer, employment and insurance contracts. Among the particular situations provided for, the following are important in the context of international arbitration:

- contracts for the sale of goods are governed by the law of the country where the seller is habitually resident (Art 4(1)(a));
- contracts for the provision of services are governed by the law of the country where the service provider is habitually resident (Art 4(1)(b));
- contracts for the carriage of goods are governed by the law of the country where the carrier is habitually resident, provided that the place of receipt or the place of delivery or the habitual residence of the consignor is also situated in that country. If those requirements are not met, the contract is governed by the law of the country where the place of delivery as agreed by the parties is situated (Art 5(1)).

Where it is clear from all the circumstances of the case that the contract is manifestly more **26.33** closely connected with a country other than that indicated in these provisions, the law of that other country applies instead (Arts 4(3) and 5(3)).

Under the Contracts (Applicable Law) Act 1990 it was held that a choice of seat in an arbitra- **26.34** tion agreement meant that the applicable law was that of the seat. Choosing a seat demonstrated a choice for that system of law with reasonable certainty (*Egon Oldendorff v Liberia Corporation (No 2)* [1996] 1 Lloyd's Rep 380). Although other circumstances may point in another direction, a choice of seat is also likely to be a sufficiently clear demonstration of the parties' choice for the purposes of Rome I Art 3(1)).

Presumption that the applicable law is the same as English law

In arbitrations, as much as in litigation, there is a presumption that any system of law that is **26.35** the proper law of a dispute is the same as the law of England and Wales (*Hussman (Europe) Ltd v Al Almeen Development and Trade Co* [2000] 2 Lloyd's Rep 83). As Thomas J said in this case, '...to hold otherwise would mean that international arbitrations held in London would be encumbered with the considerable extra expense of obtaining general evidence of foreign law relevant to the matters in issue in every case where the proper law of the contract was not the law of England and Wales'. What tends to happen is that the presumption is the starting point, but it is open to any of the parties to suggest that the applicable law is different on any specific issues. Where they do so, expert evidence from suitably qualified lawyers in the relevant jurisdiction will be required.

Law of the arbitration agreement

The law of the arbitration agreement governs matters such as the meaning and effect of **26.36** the agreement to arbitrate, the validity of any unusual provisions in the arbitration agreement (*Weissfisch v Julius* [2006] 1 Lloyd's Rep 716), and whether the dispute in question falls within the terms of the arbitration agreement (*Nova (Jersey) Knit Ltd v Kammgarn Spinnerei* [1977] 1 WLR 713).

Often the law of the arbitration agreement will be the same as the proper law of the con- **26.37** tract, particularly where the reference to arbitration is based on an arbitration clause in the substantive contract. There are cases where even in this situation the parties agree to different systems of law to govern the substantive contract and the arbitration agreement. It will be recalled that the agreement to arbitrate is separable from the substantive contract (see 23.12), so there is no objection in principle to having different systems of law for the two purposes. The possibility of having different systems of law for the two purposes is increased where the arbitration agreement is in a separate contract from the substantive contract.

26.38   Arbitration agreements are expressly excluded from the choice of law rules in Rome I (Art1(2)(e)), so different conflicts of laws rules apply in determining the applicable law of the arbitration agreement than apply in relation to the substantive contract. In English law, the law of an arbitration is that which is chosen by the parties (*Naviera Amazonica Peruana SA v Compania Internactional du Seguros del Peru* [1988] 1 Lloyd's Rep 116). Where there is no express statement of the applicable law, the court must consider all the circumstances, including the proper law of the substantive contract, the place of performance of the contract, and whether the parties agreed to a neutral forum for the arbitration (*Deutsche Schachtbau-und Tiefbohrgesellschaft mbH v Ras Al Khaimah National Oil Co* [1987] 2 All ER 769). Powerful indicators are the applicable law of the substantive contract and the location of the seat of the arbitration (*Sonatrach Petroleum Corp v Ferrell International Ltd* [2002] 1 All ER (Comm) 627).

Jurisdiction Regulation (Brussels Convention)

26.39   Regarding court proceedings, jurisdiction between member states of the EU is governed by Council Regulation (EC) No 44/2001 ('the Jurisdiction Regulation'), which replaced the Brussels Convention on Jurisdiction and Enforcement of Judgments in Civil and Commercial Matters 1968. The Jurisdiction Regulation covers litigation involving civil and commercial matters, but does not apply to arbitration (Art 1(2)(d)).

26.40   Proceedings relating to the incorporation or validity of an arbitration clause come within Art 1(2)(d), with the result that they are outside the scope of the Jurisdiction Regulation (*National Navigation Co v Endesa Generación SA* [2009] 1 Lloyd's Rep 666). The mere fact that a contract includes an arbitration clause does not mean the proceedings are outside the Jurisdiction Regulation (*Youell v La Réunion Aérienne* [2009] Bus LR 1504). It is the nature of the claim that is crucial. If any arbitration point is merely incidental to the proceedings, the claim is not excluded on this ground.

Procedural law of the arbitration (curial law)

26.41   The procedural law of an arbitration covers matters such as the appointment of the tribunal, the tribunal's powers and duties, defining the issues and preparation of the evidence, making of interim and final awards, and the degree to which the courts can intervene to support the arbitral process or to review decisions made by the arbitrators. The detailed framework of procedural law set out in the Arbitration Act 1996 ss 1–84 applies to any arbitration whose seat is in England or Wales (s 2(1)). Institutional arbitral rules only apply to the extent that the procedural law permits agreement between the parties on matters of procedure. Under the Arbitration Act 1996 in fact a great deal of scope is given to the parties in this regard, but the parties cannot override the mandatory provisions of the Act (for which, see Table 23.2).

An agreement between the parties that a particular country will be the seat of an arbitra- **26.42** tion operates as an agreement that the law of that country is the procedural law of the arbitration (*Shashoua v Sharma* [2009] 2 Lloyd's Rep 376).

Law of the place of enforcement

Enforcement of arbitral awards is considered in Chapter 29. As a practical matter, the par- **26.43** ties to an arbitration ought to have in mind in the early stages of the process the likely countries where they might wish to enforce an award, to make sure they comply with any local requirements as to procedure or the form of the award if it is to be enforceable in the countries where the other side are likely to have assets.

Stateless arbitrations

Academic lawyers, particularly from civil law jurisdictions, have argued for the recognition **26.44** of 'stateless' arbitrations, free from the law of any particular state. The appearance that this may have some validity comes from the contractual basis of arbitration (rather than state provided litigation) conducted in accordance with arbitration rules chosen by the parties. It is perfectly possible for such an arbitration to be conducted with the arbitrators deciding the dispute *ex aequo et bono* rather than under the laws of any particular country and without any involvement of any court. Like many aspects of business life, the appearance that there is no need for any system of law only survives as long as no-one needs to seek the assistance of a court. Stateless arbitration, 'delocalised' from any national system of law, is simply not recognised in English law (*Bank Mellat v Helliniki Techniki SA* [1984] 1 QB 291). Ultimately, every arbitration (other than arbitration under the ICSID rules) is required to have a seat (Arbitration Act 1996 s 3), which means that the law of the state of the seat is the procedural law of the arbitration.

OBJECTIONS TO JURISDICTION

The jurisdiction of an arbitral tribunal depends on it being appointed in accordance with **26.45** the terms of an agreement between the parties to refer the relevant dispute to arbitration. This means that the tribunal may not have jurisdiction for a number of reasons, which include:

- there was no effective arbitration agreement;
- the arbitration agreement was between parties that are different to the parties to the dispute;
- the dispute does not come within the terms of the arbitration agreement;
- the arbitrators have not been appointed in accordance with the terms of the arbitration agreement;
- the arbitrators are purporting to decide matters that have not been referred to them.

Objections to the jurisdiction of arbitrators can be used to cause delays and can be very **26.46** expensive. They are an obvious means of making life difficult for a claimant at the hands of a respondent who has no real grounds of defence. On the other hand, if the arbitrators have no jurisdiction they have no right to pronounce on a dispute.

Procedures available for raising an objection to jurisdiction

26.47   A person who is named in existing arbitration proceedings, or who may be named in a future arbitration, has a number of procedural routes for registering any jurisdictional objection they may have. The main options are set out in Table 26.1.

Table 26.1 Jurisdictional objections

Procedure	Description	Advantages/disadvantages
Ignore the arbitration, and challenge the award by seeking either: (a) an injunction; or (b) a declaration	A person who takes no part in an arbitration is allowed by the Arbitration Act 1996 s 72(1), to question: (a) whether there was a valid arbitration agreement; (b) whether the tribunal was properly constituted; or (c) whether the submission to arbitration was in accordance with the arbitration agreement	Taking no part in the arbitration avoids the costs involved in participation. It however runs the risk that the tribunal will make an adverse finding which, unless challenged successfully, will be enforceable. An application under s 72 made after an award therefore involves the loss of the right to defend the arbitration. There is no need to await the tribunal's decision, and it may be better to make an application early in the arbitration to see whether the challenge is successful. The applicant, however, can take no part in the arbitration while the challenge is being resolved.
Ignore the arbitration, and challenge enforcement of the award	Permission to enforce an award under s 66 will be refused where it is shown that the tribunal lacked substantive jurisdiction to make the award (s 66(2)).	As with the previous method, this is a high-risk strategy. Section 66 deals with domestic enforcement. There are different grounds for refusing to recognise an international award under the New York Convention 1958 (see s 103(2)).
Oppose the appointment of the arbitrators	By not agreeing to the appointment of a tribunal, the effect may be that the claimant is forced into applying to the court for the appointment of the necessary arbitrators under s 18.	This may not work at all because the arbitration agreement may contain sufficient machinery for the appointment of the tribunal. Even if the matter comes before the court under s 18, the objection may not be regarded as sufficient to warrant not appointing any tribunal at all.
Make an objection to the substantive jurisdiction of the arbitrators to the tribunal under s 31	The objection must be made no later than the time the party making the objection takes the first step to contest the merits (s 31(1)).	While the tribunal may well have jurisdiction to determine its own jurisdiction (s 30), its decision may be just the first step in the process, with a review by the courts.
Apply to the court to determine a question as to the substantive jurisdiction of the arbitrators under s 32	Requires the written agreement of the other parties or the permission of the tribunal (and other conditions set out in s 32(2)).	There are restrictions on the right to apply to the court (ss 32(2) and 73). The arbitration may continue (and costs continue being incurred) while the application to the court is pending (s 32(4)). These costs may be wasted if the court decides the tribunal does not have jurisdiction.

(Continued)

Table 26.1 Jurisdictional objections *(Continued)*

Procedure	Description	Advantages/disadvantages
Apply for an anti-suit injunction to restrain the arbitration	Interim application to the High Court supported by written evidence under CPR Parts 23 and 25.	While there technically may be jurisdiction to grant such an injunction under the Senior Courts Act 1981 s 37, the principle that the court has no supervisory jurisdiction over arbitrations beyond those set out in the Arbitration Act 1996 (see s 1(c)) means the court should rarely if ever exercise this power.
Start normal court proceedings relating to the substantive dispute	Normal Part 7 claim form followed by the CPR procedures for litigation.	The other side may apply for a stay of the court proceedings under s 9. The dispute over the jurisdiction to arbitrate may be argued on the s 9 application.
Challenge the tribunal's award as to its substantive jurisdiction under s 67	This is only available if the applicant has exhausted any available arbitral process of appeal or review (s 70(2)). The challenge is brought as an arbitration claim under CPR, Part 62. There are detailed procedures in PD 62 that have to be followed.	There are restrictions on the right to apply to the court (ss 70(2), (3) and 73). The arbitration may continue (and costs continue being incurred) while the application to the court is pending (s 67(2)). These costs may be wasted if the court decides the tribunal does not have jurisdiction.

Substantive jurisdiction

Objections to a tribunal's substantive jurisdiction cover: **26.48**

- whether there is a valid arbitration agreement;
- whether the tribunal is properly constituted; and
- what matters have been submitted to arbitration in accordance with the arbitration agreement.

See the Arbitration Act 1996 s 82, which adopts the above wording from s 30(1)). **26.49**

Time when an objection to jurisdiction should be taken

Although there are numerous different procedures that can be used in raising a jurisdic- **26.50** tional objection, unless the party making the objection takes no part in the arbitration, the objection must be made at the time it arises or when it was first discovered. Further, a party is not allowed to contest an arbitration on its merits, and then raise a jurisdictional objection for the first time if the award is unfavourable. As was stated by Thomas J in *Hussmann (Europe) Ltd v Al Ameen Development and Trade Co* [2000] 2 Lloyd's Rep 83, a party is not allowed to '... keep a point "up his sleeve" and wait and see what happens while considerable expense is incurred. A party cannot be allowed to take part in proceedings and then challenge the award if he is dissatisfied with it on the basis of a point about which he knows or ought with reasonable diligence to have discovered'.

Reserving client's position

26.51 Solicitors not infrequently seek to avoid the problems mentioned in the previous paragraph by raising an objection at an early stage in correspondence, stating that they are reserving their client's rights in relation to the objection, and then proceeding with contesting the arbitration on the merits. Such an attempt to reserve the right to raise the objection later in the process was held to be ineffective in *ASM Shipping Ltd of India v TTMI Ltd of England* [2006] 1 Lloyd's Rep 375 (a case under the Arbitration Act 1996 s 68). Instead, the arbitral tribunal should be invited to rule that it will deal with the matter in its final award under s 31(4)(b), if a party wants to take part in the arbitration, but leave the determination of the jurisdictional issue to the end. Where all the parties agree this is the best course, the tribunal has to comply with the parties' wishes (s 31(4)).

Taking a step in the arbitration

26.52 The right to challenge the arbitral tribunal's jurisdiction under the Arbitration Act 1996 s 72 (the first entry in Table 26.1) will be lost if the applicant takes any part in the arbitration (s 72(1)).

26.53 By s 31(1), any objection to the substantive jurisdiction of the tribunal must be raised no later than the time the applicant takes the first step in the arbitration proceedings to contest the merits of the matter relating to the jurisdictional challenge. Further, by s 73(1) any objection that:

- the tribunal lacks substantive jurisdiction;
- the proceedings have been improperly conducted;
- there has been a failure to comply with the arbitration agreement or with any provision of the Arbitration Act 1996 ss 1–84; or
- there has been any other irregularity affecting the tribunal or the proceedings,

can only be raised if the applicant shows that, at the time he took part or continued to take part in the arbitral proceedings, he did not know and could not with reasonable diligence have discovered the grounds for the objection.

26.54 Appointing, or participating in the appointment, of the arbitrators by a party does not preclude a challenge to the substantive jurisdiction of the tribunal (s 31(1)). This is because it is legitimate to appoint a tribunal to decide a dispute over its own jurisdiction (see *Kompetenz-Kompetenz* below). Almost any other action in the arbitration, and sometimes doing nothing, will operate as a bar to later objecting to the tribunal's jurisdiction by virtue of ss 31 and 73. Contesting the merits will amount to taking a step, as will taking up an award (*Thyssen Canada Ltd v Mariana Maritime SA* [2005] 1 Lloyd's Rep 640). It is clear from *Rustal Trading Ltd v Gill and Duffas SA* [2000] 1 Lloyd's Rep 14 that simple inaction may amount to taking a step. Moore-Bick J said: '. . . there might well be periods in the arbitration during which no formal step is required of one or other party but, during these periods, the parties will be taking part in the proceedings'.

Kompetenz-Kompetenz

26.55 Purists will say that it is impossible to allow a tribunal to decide a dispute over its own jurisdiction. If it decides it has no jurisdiction, what is the status of that decision? Intellectual difficulties of this kind find no home in the modern law of arbitration, which is firmly rooted in providing practical justice. However, this can be pushed too far, particularly when married to the idea that there should be limited or no court review of decisions made by arbitrators. At its extreme is the German concept of *Kompetenz-Kompetenz*. This meant that not only was an arbitral tribunal empowered to decide on its own jurisdiction, but also that its decision was not amenable to review by the courts. Such an extreme position no longer applies in Germany, and does not apply in England either. However, the expression *Kompetenz-Kompetenz* is still commonly used to describe any system that provides for a tribunal ruling on its own jurisdiction (even if that decision is reviewable by the courts).

The Arbitration Act 1996 s 30(1) provides that unless otherwise agreed by the parties, the **26.56** arbitral tribunal may rule on its own substantive jurisdiction. In construing any arbitration agreement, the presumption is that the parties will have intended that any dispute arising out of their relationship is to be decided by the same tribunal rather than having some matters decided by the courts, and others by the arbitrators (*Fili Shipping Co Ltd v Premium Nafta Products Ltd* [2007] Bus LR 1719). This, together with s 30, means that where the parties have included an arbitration clause, the arbitrator can decide any objection to his jurisdiction, even if there is a dispute over the validity of the substantive contract.

It is not uncommon for arbitrators to be called upon to consider submissions that they are **26.57** not competent to act by reason of bias. An arbitrator's decision on jurisdiction is not final, provided the seat of the arbitration was in a country, such as England, where the courts exercise a supervisory jurisdiction over arbitration (*Weissfisch v Julius* [2006] 1 Lloyd's Rep 716; and see Chapter 28).

Anti-suit injunctions

It is incompatible with the Jurisdiction Regulation (see 26.39) for an English court to grant **26.58** an anti-suit injunction to restrain proceedings in another member state on the ground that those proceedings are inconsistent with an arbitration agreement (*West Tankers Inc v Riunione Adriatica di Sicurtà SpA* (Case C-185/07) [2009] 1 AC 1138). It is exclusively for the courts of the member state seised of the original proceedings to determine any objection to its jurisdiction.

PROCEDURAL MATTERS RELEVANT TO INTERNATIONAL ARBITRATION

Language of the arbitration

Having an arbitration conducted in a party's first language is a significant advantage both at **26.59** a practical level and in ensuring that the party's case is conveyed as effectively as is possible. While there are translation services available, even the best translations are never as effective as being able to address a tribunal directly in a shared language.

The parties will not infrequently make express provision for the language to be used in any **26.60** arbitration in the substantive contract. If they do the tribunal is obliged to adopt what the parties have agreed.

26.61 If there is no express agreement on the language of the arbitration, the Arbitration Act 1996 s 34(2)(b) provides that it is for the tribunal to decide the language or languages to be used in the proceedings and whether translations of any relevant documents are to be supplied. Institutional rules often deal with these matters, and will often deal with translations of the statements of case and documentary evidence. Directions will, as a practical matter, also have to cover the translation services required for the final hearing (both for the parties and witnesses).

26.62 Under the ICC rules, in the absence of an agreement by the parties, the tribunal is required to determine the language or languages of the arbitration (Art 16). In making this decision the tribunal is to have due regard to all relevant circumstances, including the language of the substantive contract. The UNCITRAL Model Law is similar (Art 22(1)), but this also says that the language of the arbitration shall apply, unless otherwise provided, to any written statement by a party, as well as to the hearing, the award and any other communication by the tribunal. Article 22(2) gives the tribunal the power to order that any documentary evidence must be accompanied by a translation into the language or languages of the arbitration.

Meetings and hearings

26.63 Considerations of cost and distance mean that greater thought is required of how and where meetings and hearings should take place in international arbitrations. In addition to the parties and their witnesses, who are likely to be based in different countries, there may also be a panel of (say) three arbitrators all based in different countries. Telephone conferences and video-conferences may be effective ways of conducting at least certain meetings at reasonable cost. Where actual hearings and meetings take place, consideration has to be given to where these can take place with the least inconvenience to those who need to attend, which is why on occasions hearings take place in countries otherwise unconnected with the dispute but which are the most easily accessible to those who need to attend.

Privilege

26.64 A particular issue in international arbitration is that there is a distinct possibility that the scope of the rules relating to privilege and the right not to disclose documents to other parties often differ between different countries. It is obviously unfair if one side gives the other side wider access to its documents than it receives in return. Further, there can be difficulties in requiring a party to an arbitration to disclose documents that would be protected from production under the law where it conducts its business. If it had known that certain categories of documents that would be protected under its domestic law might be disclosable in a dispute with a party from another jurisdiction, those documents may never have been written or compiled in the first place.

26.65 It ought to be that the procedural law of the arbitration (the curial law) should govern the scope of disclosure to be given by all the parties in an arbitration. Disclosure is traditionally regarded as a procedural issue, so the procedural law should prevail. The contrary argument is that privilege has become established as a substantive right (see *McE v Prison Service of Northern Ireland* [2009] 1 AC 908), and that therefore the scope of privilege should be decided in accordance with the law of the state where the documents were created.

Security for costs

One of the powers given to arbitral tribunals (unless the parties agree otherwise) is a power **26.66** to order the claimant to provide security for costs (Arbitration Act 1996 s 38). Unlike CPR, r 25.13, which specifies the grounds on which security for costs may be ordered in court proceedings, an arbitral tribunal is given a general discretion untrammeled by any conditions. However s 38(3) prohibits an arbitral tribunal from ordering security for costs on the ground that the claimant is incorporated or ordinarily resident outside the United Kingdom. This is to avoid the power to order security for costs acting as a disincentive to overseas parties using England and Wales as the seat for their arbitrations.

This means that security for costs will typically be ordered where the claimant is a corpor- **26.67** ation (whether or not it is a registered company) and there is reason to believe it will be unable to pay the respondent's costs, or if the claimant fails to give an address, or changes its address to avoid having to pay costs, or if the claimant is acting in a nominal capacity, or if it has taken steps to make it difficult to enforce a costs award (compare CPR, r 25.13, which English arbitrators normally apply by analogy).

ICC RULES OF ARBITRATION

The International Chamber of Commerce ('ICC') is based in Paris, and has published an **26.68** internationally recognised set of rules of arbitration (1998, as amended). The ICC has established the International Court of Arbitration ('ICA'), which oversees arbitrations conducted under the ICC rules and scrutinises ICC awards. The ICA is not a court of law, and its members are not permitted to act as arbitrators or counsel in cases submitted to ICC arbitration (Internal Rules of the ICA Art 2(1)). The ICA secretariat has various delegated functions, and may issue notes and guidance for parties and arbitrators involved in ICC arbitrations. All documents in ICC arbitrations are provided to the secretariat as well as the parties and arbitrators (Art 3(1)).

Request for arbitration

An ICC arbitration is commenced by the submission of a request for arbitration to the secre- **26.69** tariat (ICC rules Art 4(1)). This must include:

- the names, description and address for each party;
- a description of the nature and circumstances of the dispute;
- a statement of the relief sought;
- copies of all relevant contracts, including the arbitration agreement;
- the number of arbitrators required by the arbitration agreement, and details of any nominations; and
- any comments on the place of arbitration, applicable law and the language of the arbitration.

By submitting their dispute to arbitration under the ICC rules, the parties undertake to carry **26.70** out any award without delay (Art 28(6)). After receipt of the request the ICC can request the claimant to pay a provisional advance to cover the costs of the arbitration until the terms of reference have been drawn up (Art 30(1)).

Answer to the request

26.71 The request for arbitration is sent to the respondent by the secretariat (Art 4(5)). Within 30 days of receipt of the request the respondent is required to file an answer, which sets out the respondent's comments on the dispute, the relief claimed, and matters relating to the arbitration (Art 5(1)). At the same time the respondent may file a counterclaim (Art 5(5)). A copy of the answer and any counterclaim is sent to the claimant by the secretariat (Art 5(4)). The claimant is required to respond to any counterclaim within 30 days of receipt (Art 5(6)).

ICC arbitral tribunals

26.72 ICC arbitral tribunals have either one or three arbitrators (Art 8(1)). Where there are to be three arbitrators, each party nominates one arbitrator, subject to confirmation by the ICA, with the third arbitrator being appointed by the ICA (Art 8(4)). There are default provisions to deal with cases where a party fails to make a nomination, where the ICA refuses to confirm a nomination, and where there are challenges to arbitrators (for example, for alleged lack of independence). Each arbitrator has to sign a statement of independence before they are appointed (Art 7(2)).

Seat of the arbitration

26.73 The seat of the arbitration is fixed by the ICA (Art 14(1)).

Terms of reference

26.74 Once the tribunal is constituted the secretariat will provide it with a copy of the secretariat's file. The tribunal then draws up, on the basis of the documents or in the presence of the parties and on considering their representations, a document defining the tribunal's terms of reference (Art 18). This will include the following particulars:

- the names and descriptions of the parties;
- their addresses;
- a summary of the respective claims and relief sought by the parties;
- a list of issues (which may be dispensed with);
- names and addresses of the arbitrators;
- the place (seat) of the arbitration; and
- details of the applicable law, and whether the tribunal is to act as *amiable compositeur* or to decide *ex aequo et bono*.

26.75 The terms of reference have to be signed by the parties and the arbitral tribunal, and filed with the ICA within two months of transmission of the file to the tribunal (Art 18(2)).

Procedure prior to the hearing

26.76 At the same time as considering its terms of reference, the tribunal will consult the parties on a timetable for the procedural steps needed to prepare the matter for the final disposal of the matter. A provisional timetable for these steps is recorded in a separate document that is sent to the ICA and the parties with the terms of reference or as soon as practicable thereafter (Art 18(2)).

Hearings and the decision

ICC tribunals are required to establish the facts within as short a time as possible, and **26.77** by using all appropriate means (Art 20(1)). These are likely to include contemporaneous documents provided by the parties, written submissions, and may include hearings with witnesses being called to give evidence (Art 20(2), (3)). Decisions may be made without a hearing, but a hearing must be held if requested by any of the parties (Art 20(6)). Expert evidence may be necessary, and the tribunal may appoint its own experts (with their own terms of reference (Art 20(4)). Actual meetings and hearings can be held anywhere as decided by the tribunal in consultation with the parties (Art 14(2)). Hearings are held in private (Art 21(3)), and parties may be legally represented (Art 21(4)).

When the tribunal is satisfied that the parties have had a reasonable opportunity to present **26.78** their cases, the tribunal will declare the proceedings closed (Art 22). Once the proceedings are closed, no further submissions or evidence will be admitted without the authorisation of the tribunal. The tribunal indicates to the secretariat when the draft award will be submitted. There is a time limit of six months from the signing of the terms of reference until the final award (Art 24(1)). This time limit may be extended by the ICA (Art 24(2)). ICC awards give reasons as well as the decision (Art 25(2)). A final award will fix the costs of the arbitration, and will include a decision on which of the parties will bear the costs (Art 31(3)). Before the award is signed, a draft is provided to the ICA for scrutiny. The ICA may lay down modifications, and no ICC award can be finalised until it has been approved by the ICA (Art 27).

UNCITRAL MODEL LAW ON INTERNATIONAL COMMERCIAL ARBITRATION

The UNCITRAL Model Law is published by United Nations Commission on International **26.79** Trade Law, whose secretariat is based in Vienna. UNCITRAL is a subsidiary body of the General Assembly of the United Nations. A particular function of UNCITRAL is in promoting the harmonisation and modernisation of international trade law. The Model Law is just one of many publications dealing with different aspects of international trade published by UNCITRAL. Unlike the ICC, UNCITRAL is not an arbitral institution, and neither is it an appointing institution. Its Model Law has, however, been used as the basis of arbitration law reform in many countries, including England and Wales. While the primary purpose of the Model Law was to provide a framework for law reform, it contains a detailed set of rules which (with one or two minor exceptions) provide a comprehensive set of rules that can be adopted by parties as the rules for ad hoc arbitrations. Some arbitral institutions, such as CEDR in England, adopt the Model Law as their standard rules for international arbitrations.

Interpretation of the Model Law

When interpreting the Model Law regard is to be had to its international origin, and the **26.80** need to promote uniformity in its application and the observance of good faith (Art 2A(1)). To assist in the interpretation of the Model Law the secretariat of UNCITRAL has published an explanatory note, which is technically for information purposes only. UNCITRAL also publishes a series of decisions from around the world on the Model Law and other UNCITRAL texts (Case Law on UNCITRAL Texts).

Commencement of Model Law arbitration

26.81 Unless the parties otherwise agree, an arbitration under the Model Law commences on the date a request for a particular dispute to be referred to arbitration is received by the respondent (Art 21).

Model Law arbitral tribunals

26.82 The Model Law allows the parties to determine the number of arbitrators on their tribunal (Art 10(1)). In the absence of agreement, there are three arbitrators in Model Law arbitrations (Art 10(2)). In these cases, each party appoints one arbitrator, and the two party-appointed arbitrators appoint the third arbitrator (Art 11(3)(a)). One of the abuses the Model Law seeks to address is that of a party delaying matters by not co-operating in the appointment of the tribunal. It therefore lays down strict 30-day time-limits for the appointment of arbitrators, and provides for a right to apply to the courts of the seat of the arbitration to make the necessary orders to ensure the tribunal is properly constituted in the case of default (Art 11(4)). There are express provisions in Art 16 stating that the arbitration agreement is separable from the substantive contract and that the arbitrators have power to rule on their own jurisdiction (matching the position in English law: see 23.12 and 26.56).

Interim measures

26.83 There are detailed provision in the Model Law, in Arts 17–17J, dealing with preliminary orders and interim measures. A preliminary order resembles a without notice application in English civil litigation (for which, see Sime, *A Practical Approach to Civil Procedure* (13th edn, OUP, 2010), ch 20). Preliminary orders are available unless otherwise agreed by the parties (Art 17B(1)). They are made without notice to the respondent, and usually last for up to 20 days, when there should be a decision by the tribunal on whether to adopt or modify the preliminary order as an interim measure (Art 17C(4)). They are available where there is a risk that giving advance notice to the respondent will frustrate the purpose of the measure (Art 17B(2)).

26.84 Interim measures under the Model Law are broadly equivalent to conservatory measures and procedural orders in English law (see 25.37 and 27.04). They are any temporary measure, whether or not in the form of an award, which orders a party to maintain the status quo pending determination of the dispute, or to take action to prevent imminent harm, or to preserve assets (a freezing order) or evidence (Art 17(2)). Under the Model Law a tribunal has the power to grant interim measures unless otherwise agreed by the parties (Art 17(1)).

26.85 Article 17A says that an interim measure in the form of an interim injunction is only available if the arbitral tribunal is satisfied that:

- it is likely there will be harm that is not adequately reparable in damages without the measure;
- such harm substantially outweighs the harm that the respondent is likely to suffer if the measure is granted; and

- there is a reasonable possibility that the requesting party will succeed on the merits of the arbitration.

The arbitral tribunal can require the party seeking an interim measure to provide security, **26.86** and will usually do so if it grants a preliminary order (Art 17E). There is a continuing duty on the requesting party to disclose any material change in the circumstances (Art 17F). The requesting party is under an obligation to pay any costs and damages caused by the measure if it later transpires it should not have been granted (Art 17G). One of the drawbacks in arbitration is that arbitrators themselves have no coercive powers, and the parties have to resort to the courts for enforcement if arbitrators' decisions are not complied with. To make this as easy as possible, Arts 17H and 17I say that interim measures are enforceable in the courts on the same basis as final awards (ie with limited grounds for objecting to recognition or enforcement by the courts). Preliminary orders, however, are not recognised or enforceable in the courts.

Statements of case under the Model Law

Either the parties may agree, or the tribunal may direct, the times when the parties must pro- **26.87** vide their statements of case (Art 23). The claimant's statement of claim must state the facts supporting the claim, the points at issue, and the relief or remedies sought. The respondent responds in a statement of defence, which must answer the particulars set out in the statement of claim. Article 23(1) says that the parties may provide supporting documents with their statements of case, or they may choose to make references to the relevant documents or other evidence that they say support their version of events.

Subsequent procedure

In accordance with the principle of party autonomy, the parties are free to agree on the pro- **26.88** cedure to be followed in the conduct of proceedings under the Model Law (Art 19(1)). In the absence of agreement, the tribunal may conduct the arbitration in such manner as it considers appropriate (Art 19(2)). It will usually make directions for the steps to be taken by the parties to prepare for the final determination of the reference. All statements, documents or other information supplied to the arbitral tribunal must be communicated to all the parties (Art 24(3)). Procedural matters can be decided by a presiding arbitrator (Art 29).

The tribunal has the power (unless otherwise agreed by the parties) to appoint one or more **26.89** experts to report on specific issues (Art 26(1)(a)), and may direct any of the parties to provide access to any relevant documents, goods or other property for inspection (Art 26(1)(b)). All experts' reports must be communicated to all the parties (Art 24(3)). A tribunal-appointed expert should attend any hearing for the purpose of answering questions from the parties (Art 26(2)). The parties must be given sufficient notice of any hearing (Art 24(2)).

Hearings

Where the tribunal feels it appropriate, and provided there is no objection from the parties, **26.90** the tribunal can decide to determine the reference without a hearing. In such a case the tribunal decides the dispute on the basis of the documents and any other materials available to it (Art 24(1)). However, unless the parties have previously agreed there will be no hearings, any party may request a hearing, in which event a hearing will take place at an appropriate stage of the proceedings (Art 24(1)). There is nothing in this provision laying down any minimum requirements on the length, number or timings of any hearings. However, art 18 says the parties must be treated with equality, and each party must be given a full opportunity of presenting its case.

26.91   Article 19(2) gives the tribunal an express power to determine the admissibility, relevance, materiality and weight of any evidence submitted to it. Decisions are made in accordance with the proper law of the dispute (Art 28). Where there is a tribunal with more than one member, any decision may be made by a majority of its members (Art 29). Reasons must be stated, unless the parties have agreed that no reasons be given (Art 31(2)). The proceedings, and the tribunal's mandate, terminate with the signing of the final award (Art 32).

KEY POINTS SUMMARY

26.92   • In English law, there are no differences in the Arbitration Act 1996 between domestic and international commercial arbitrations.
- Other jurisdictions often draw a distinction between domestic and international arbitrations.
- The seat of an arbitration is its juridical location.
- Different systems of law may govern the substantive contract, the agreement to arbitrate, and the procedural law of an arbitration.
- Ideally the parties will have reached express agreement on the system(s) of law governing each of these areas.
- If there is no express agreement on the system of law, it will be determined from all the circumstances. There are particular rules, for example Rome I, that provide a framework for determining the proper law of contracts etc.
- There is a range of possible challenges to the jurisdiction of a tribunal.
- There are also several different ways in which a challenge to the tribunal's jurisdiction can be brought.
- These include the tribunal deciding its own jurisdiction (*Kompetenz-Kompetenz*) and challenges being made to the court.
- International arbitrations give rise to issues such as the language to be used in the process, and possibly different concepts on things like the scope of the law of privilege, which present difficulties in ensuring the process is fair to all sides.
- The UNCITRAL Model Law and ICC arbitration rules are widely used across the globe in international arbitration.

27

ARBITRATION AWARDS AND ORDERS

INTRODUCTION. 27.01

PROCEDURAL ORDERS 27.04

INTERIM AWARDS AND AWARDS ON DIFFERENT ISSUES. 27.06

SETTLEMENT. 27.09

MAIN AWARDS 27.10

AWARD OF COSTS. 27.28

KEY POINTS SUMMARY. 27.31

INTRODUCTION

Making awards, which are binding decisions, is what distinguishes arbitration from the **27.01** non-adjudicatory methods of ADR. These other ADR processes are aimed at facilitating the parties in coming to a consensual arrangement between themselves. Arbitration, on the other hand, is designed to ensure the final disposal of a dispute by an impartial arbitral tribunal agreed upon by the parties.

There are four different types of awards and orders that are available to arbitrators, **27.02** namely:

- *procedural orders*, which provide procedural directions and measures designed to preserve evidence or the subject-matter of the dispute ('conservatory measures') while an arbitration is proceeding;
- *interim awards and awards on different issues*, which finally dispose of one or more of the substantive issues in the arbitration, leaving the other issues to be decided later;
- *main awards*, finally disposing of the arbitration; and
- *costs awards*, which provide for the payment of the costs incurred in the arbitration between the parties.

Usually, once an order or award is made it is binding on the parties. Most sets of institu- **27.03** tional arbitral rules include provision for parties making suggestions for the correction of clerical mistakes in orders and awards. In addition to making such checks, lawyers need to advise their clients on the meaning and effect of the tribunal's decision, and where there is further work to be done, to take the client's instructions on the next steps. If it is a procedural order these will be the further steps needed in preparing the matter for the final decision. If it is a final award, and if the decision is adverse to the client, consideration needs to be given to whether there are grounds for challenging the award, for which see Chapter 28.

PROCEDURAL ORDERS

27.04   Arbitrators have the power to make a range of orders and to give directions in the period between the time they are appointed and when they make their final award. The various types of order available are considered in Chapter 25, and fall into the following categories:

- *procedural directions*, which will set out a timetable for the parties to follow in preparing for the hearing (see 25.33);
- *interim remedies*, such as security for costs and interim payments on account of the sum that may eventually be awarded (see 25.34);
- *conservatory measures*, which are designed to preserve the subject-matter of the dispute, or give one side access to property in the control of the other party (see 25.37);
- *peremptory orders*, which are usually backed by sanctions in default, which are used where a party fails to comply with earlier orders of the tribunal (see 25.40); and
- *orders dismissing the arbitration*, which is the ultimate sanction for non-compliance with the timetable laid down by the arbitrators (see 25.44).

27.05   An example of a tribunal's order for directions can be seen at Figure 25.2.

INTERIM AWARDS AND AWARDS ON DIFFERENT ISSUES

27.06   Unless otherwise agreed by the parties, arbitrators have powers to make interim awards and awards on different issues under the Arbitration Act 1996 s 47. Interim awards are to be distinguished from provisional orders in that they are final awards, but only on part of the dispute, whereas provisional orders regulate the position of the parties during the interim stages of an arbitration, but do not finally dispose of any of the issues in the arbitration.

27.07   Particular powers given by s 47(2) include:

- making an award relating to an issue affecting the whole claim; and
- making an award relating to a part only of the claims or cross-claims remitted to the arbitrators.

27.08   These powers may be useful, for example, where it is possible to identify a single issue that may be capable of being disposed of swiftly, and once there is a final decision on that issue the parties may be enabled to settle the rest of their dispute. Alternatively, it may be that resolution of part of a claim, for example liability, may avoid the need to investigate and determine other issues, such as those relating to remedies, thereby saving costs.

SETTLEMENT

If the parties settle their dispute before the arbitrators make their final decision, unless **27.09** otherwise agreed by the parties, the arbitral tribunal will terminate the substantive proceedings and will record the settlement in the form of an agreed award (Arbitration Act 1996 s 51(1), (2)). An agreed award must state that it is an award of the arbitration tribunal, and has the same status and effect as any other award on the merits of the case (s 51(3)). A duly authenticated original award of a settlement makes it possible to effect enforcement overseas under the New York Convention 1958 (see Chapter 29).

MAIN AWARDS

Again in accordance with the principle that the parties are free to agree on the way in which **27.10** their dispute is determined (Arbitration Act 1996 s 1(b)), the parties can agree on the form of their award in an arbitration (s 52(1)). However, the default provisions in the Arbitration Act 1996 are usually adopted because they provide a sensible and practical regime for ensuring that awards are properly recorded and enforceable. Section 52(3) provides that the award shall be in writing signed by all the arbitrators or all those assenting to the award. The award must also contain the reasons for the decision (see 27.15) unless it is an agreed award or the parties have agreed to dispense with reasons (s 52(4)). Dispensing with reasons will mean that it is impossible to appeal the decision to the High Court on a point of law under s 69 (see Chapter 28), and also excludes the jurisdiction of the court to determine preliminary points of law (s 45(1)).

The award must state the seat of the arbitration (see 27.16), and the date when the award is **27.11** made (see 27.17) (s 52(5)).

An example of a final award based on the bribery case in Chapter 25 is shown in Figure 27.1. **27.12** After the heading the award has a number of recitals (under the word 'whereas'). There then follow three procedural issues dealing with the seat of the arbitration and the applicable law. The substantive provisions of the award then follow. The short para 1 means that the claimant won on liability, with the other paragraphs dealing with costs (which are to be decided later in a separate award on costs).

Majority decisions

An obvious reason for having an odd number of arbitrators is to avoid the risk of stale- **27.13** mate. If the arbitral tribunal has more than one member, the usual rule is that decisions are made by a majority. In accordance with the principle of party autonomy, the parties may agree some other method of decision making (such as unanimous decisions), but the risks of having to start again with a new tribunal are such that such arrangements are rare.

Where the arbitral tribunal includes a chairman (see 24.13), decisions, orders and awards **27.14** are made by all or a majority of the arbitrators, including the chairman (Arbitration Act 1996 s 20(3)). The view of the chairman prevails where there is neither unanimity nor a

Figure 27.1 Final award in an arbitration

IN THE MATTER OF THE ARBITRATION ACT 1996
AND
IN THE MATTER OF AN ARBITRATION
BETWEEN

CHIPOKA AIRWAYS LIMITED

<u>Claimant</u>

and

RUNWAY AIRCRAFT MAINTENANCE LIMITED

<u>Respondent</u>

—————————
FINAL AWARD
—————————

WHEREAS:

(1) By a contract in writing dated 12 March 2006 ('the Contract') the Respondent agreed to provide aircraft maintenance services for the Claimant in respect of four aircraft for a period of five years from 6 April 2006 to 5 April 2011.

(2) The Contract provided that any dispute or difference arising out of or in connection with the Contract shall be administered by the London Court of International Arbitration and finally determined under the Rules of the London Court of International Arbitration ('the Rules') by three arbitrators appointed in accordance with the Rules.

(3) By a letter dated 18 January 2010 the Claimant appointed James Benson to act as an arbitrator for the determination of such disputes and differences who accepted his appointment by a letter dated 29 January 2010.

(4) By a letter dated 28 January 2010 the Respondent appointed Margaret Swaledale to act as an arbitrator for the determination of such disputes and differences who accepted her appointment by a letter dated 2 February 2010.

(5) By an instrument in writing dated 10 February 2010 the arbitrators appointed Philip Wilson to be the third arbitrator and chairman in the matter of this arbitration.

(6) Formal statements of case having been exchanged, an oral hearing took place opening on 22 November 2010 and closing on 25 November 2010.

(7) The oral hearing was attended by the parties and their legal representatives, and oral evidence was heard from witnesses called by both parties.

PROCEDURAL ISSUES

1. In accordance with article 16.1 of the Rules the parties agreed that the place of the arbitration should be London.
2. The seat of the arbitration is accordingly London, England.
3. By clause 26 of the Contract the parties agreed that the proper law of the Contract was the law of England and Wales.

THE AWARD

Having considered the oral and written evidence, and the oral and written submissions by the legal representatives of both parties, and for the reasons set out in the annex to this

(Continued)

Figure 27.1 Final award in an arbitration *(Continued)*

award, we hereby award and direct as follows:

1. The Respondent shall pay to the Claimant the sum of US$ 8,421,765 being the sum we award in respect of the matters arising for decision on the disputes in this reference.
2. This award is final on all matters except costs.
3. The arbitrators' award as to costs and the fees of the arbitrators is reserved.
4. If either party wishes to make oral submissions regarding costs they must give notice in writing to the arbitrators at the address set out in the covering letter to this award within 14 days of the date of this award.
5. If no such written notice is received within the time limited in paragraph 4 above, the parties are at liberty to deliver to the arbitrators at the same address written submissions on costs no later than 28 days after the date of this award.

DATED 14 January 2011

Signed: (1)
          (2)
          (3)
          Arbitrators

Witnessed by:

ANNEX

[The reasons for the award will be set out in an annex, unless the parties have agreed that no reasons should be given.]

majority (s 20(4)). Where the arbitral tribunal has an umpire (see 24.14), decisions, orders and awards shall be made by the other arbitrators unless and until they cannot agree on a matter relating to the arbitration (s 21(4)). Where there is stalemate between the other arbitrators, they are required give notice in writing to the parties and the umpire, whereupon the umpire replaces them as the tribunal with power to make decisions, orders and awards as if he were the sole arbitrator. Where the parties agree that there shall be two or more arbitrators with no chairman or umpire, in the absence of contrary agreement between the parties, decisions, orders and awards are made by all or a majority of the arbitrators (s 22).

Reasons

Reasons, where they are to be given for an award, need to be adequate, and capable of being understood by the parties. There is no requirement for the tribunal to deal with every possible argument in the case, nor is there any duty to explain why greater weight was given to some items of evidence rather than others (*World Trade Corporation v Czarnikow Sugar Ltd* [2005] 1 Lloyd's Rep 422). The arbitral tribunal does however need to deal with each of the essential issues to be decided in the case. What these are depends in part on the statements of case of the parties and in part on the nature of the decision that has to be made (*Hussmann (Europe) Ltd v Al Ameen Development and Trade Co* [2000] 2 Lloyd's Rep 83; *Checkpoint Ltd v Strathclyde Pension Fund* [2003] 1 EGLR 1).

27.15

Seat of the arbitration

27.16 The need to include the seat of the arbitration in an award is important for enforcement in other jurisdictions. Establishing the seat of an arbitration is considered at 26.14. Failing to state the seat of the arbitration in an award will not prevent enforcement of the award within England and Wales (see for example *Ranko Group v Antarctic Maritime SA* (1998) LMLN 492). Ultimately, where a failure to state the seat of the arbitration does cause a problem, it may be cured by an application to the High Court under the Arbitration Act 1996 s 68, as an irregularity causing substantial injustice (see Chapter 28).

Date of award

27.17 Unless otherwise agreed by the parties, the arbitration tribunal may decide what is to be taken to be the date on which the award is made (Arbitration Act 1996 s 54(1)). In the absence of such a decision the award shall be taken to be dated when it is signed by the arbitrator, or where there is more than one arbitrator, when it is signed by the last of them (s 54(2)).

27.18 Institution rules may provide machinery for dealing with difficulties, such as the death or lack of co-operation of one of the arbitrators after a decision has been reached. The LME rules provide that if an arbitrator refuses or fails to sign the award, the signatures of the majority are sufficient, provided that the reason for the omitted signature is stated (reg 12.2.2).

27.19 The date of the award is important for the purposes of any challenge or appeal. By s 70(3) any application or appeal must be brought within 28 days of the date of the award (see Chapter 28). The date of the award is also important for the purposes of calculating interest (see below).

Place where award is made

27.20 Unless otherwise agreed by the parties, where the seat of the arbitration is in England and Wales, the award is treated as being made here (Arbitration Act 1996 s 53). This is regardless of where the award was signed, dispatched or delivered. This section reverses the decision in *Hiscox v Outhwaite* [1992] 1 AC 562, where an English arbitration happened to have been signed in Paris. Section 53 makes clear that the accident of where an arbitration award happens to have been signed does not affect where it is treated as a matter of law to have been made. Section 53 is consistent with the rule relating to enforcement under the New York Convention 1958 (see s 100(2)(b), and see Chapter 29).

Remedies

27.21 The parties are free to agree on the remedies available to the arbitral tribunal (Arbitration Act 1996 s 48(1)). Unless otherwise agreed by the parties, the arbitrators have the following powers:

- to make declarations (s 48(3));
- to order payment of a sum of money in any currency (s 48(4));
- the same powers as a court to order a party to do or be refrained from doing anything (s 48(5));
- to order specific performance of a contract other than a contract relating to land, if and so far as it relates to land (s 48(5)(b) and *Tilia Sonera Ab v Hilcourt (Docklands) Ltd* [2003]

EWHC 3540 (Ch), where it was held that specific performance could be ordered in respect of remedial works on land); and

- to order the rectification, setting aside or cancellation of a deed or other document (s 48(5)(c)).

Injunctions

While the Arbitration Act 1996 s 48(5)(a) gives arbitrators a power equivalent to granting mandatory and prohibitory injunctions, this is restricted to final awards and does not give arbitrators the power to make the equivalent of interim injunctions (*Kastner v Jason* [2004] 2 Lloyd's Rep 233 and see the further discussion at 28.25). **27.22**

Interest

Unless otherwise agreed by the parties, arbitrators may award simple or compound interest from such dates and at such rates and with such rests as are considered to meet the justice of the case (Arbitration Act 1996 s 49). Interest may be awarded both up to the date of the award and also for the period after the award until the date of payment (s 49(3), (4)). Interest is usually awarded at a rate equivalent to the rate that the successful party would have had to pay on money borrowed from its bank. **27.23**

Notification of award

Subject to the agreement of the parties, the award shall be notified to them by service of copies of the award, which must be done without delay (Arbitration Act 1996 s 55(2)). This provision does not affect the power of the arbitrators to withhold their award in the case of non-payment of their fees (ss 55(3) and 56). **27.24**

Binding effect

Unless otherwise agreed by the parties a final award is both final and binding upon the parties and any persons claiming through or under them (Arbitration Act 1996 s 58(1)). This does not affect the right of a party to challenge the award either by an internal appeal under the arbitration provider's institutional rules, or through an appeal to the High Court (for which see Chapter 28). **27.25**

Different arbitration institutions either do or do not provide for an appeal mechanism within their institutional rules. A challenge to the arbitrators' award is not permitted to the High Court before the appellant has first exhausted any available arbitral process of appeal or review (s 70(2)), but the 28-day period for making the application to the High Court does not run until the internal appeal or review process has been completed (s 70(3)). **27.26**

Different institutional rules make various different provisions for the mechanics for finalising an award. Awards of the arbitrators in commercial arbitration under the LME rules are deposited with the secretary to the LME, who notifies each party (reg 12.10). Either party may then take up the award upon payment by that party of the costs and expenses of the arbitration as specified in the award (including the remuneration of the arbitrators). Until the award is taken up by one of the parties it confers no rights upon either party. **27.27**

AWARD OF COSTS

27.28　An arbitral tribunal may make an award allocating costs of the arbitration between the parties, this power being subject to any agreement between parties (Arbitration Act 1996 s 61(1)). It will be seen from paragraphs 2–5 in the final award shown in Figure 27.1 that the tribunal reserved the question of costs when making its award on liability and quantum. The outstanding matters cover whether the losing party (in this instance the respondent) should pay the successful party's costs, how much should be payable under the award of costs, and also payment of the arbitrators' fees.

27.29　Arbitration costs awards are made on similar principles to those applicable in court litigation (see Sime, *A Practical Approach to Civil Procedure* (13th ed, OUP), ch 43). The main principle is that the arbitrators shall award costs in favour of the successful party (s 61(2)), except where this appears to be inappropriate. Similar factors to those affecting the usual principle in court litigation apply also to arbitrations. Arbitrators will therefore take into account factors such as the conduct of the parties in the arbitration, whether the claim has been exaggerated, and the degree, if any, to which the successful party was only partially successful.

27.30　In the example shown in Figure 27.1 it would be very difficult for the respondent to mount a successful argument avoiding paying all the claimant's costs. From the statements of case, the respondent did not dispute liability, but argued on how much should be paid to the claimant. While the claimant made a claim for US $55 million odd, and recovered only US $8.5 million odd, the claim was put forward in alternative ways. The US $55 million claim was based on the whole amount the claimant had paid to the respondent under the contract, and while this is considerably more than the sum recovered, the alternative claim based on what the claimant thought was either the total amount of the bribes or the amount by which the respondent was unjustly enriched by the transaction, namely US $9.9 million odd, was clearly set out in the points of claim. It is not therefore an exaggeration case. All the respondent can reasonably point to is that the claimant sought US $9.9 million on the alternative case, and recovered 'only' US $8.5 million. Therefore, to some extent, the claimant was not totally successful in the reference, both because the respondent defeated the total amount paid (US $55 million) basis of the claim, and by paring off US $1.4 million on the alternative way of quantifying the claim. Whether these points have any effect on the costs award depends on the view taken by the arbitrators of how important these two areas of partial success by the respondent were in the overall picture of the reference. If, for example, the main issue was whether the sum awarded should be based on the total outlay (US $55 million) or the amount by which the respondent was unjustly enriched (US $8.5 million), a substantial deduction from the claimant's award of costs would be likely. If the US $55 million basis of quantification was not a major issue (because the claimant recognised early that it was unlikely to be awarded), suffering a US $1.4 million reduction on the sum set out in the points of claim is unlikely to be regarded as a sufficiently clear partial success on the part of the respondent to justify any departure from the usual rule that the losing party pays the whole costs of the successful party. If the tribunal does decide there was partial success, this is likely to be reflected by ordering the respondent to pay only a percentage of the claimant's costs.

KEY POINTS SUMMARY

- The provisions in the Arbitration Act 1996 on awards are all subject to the agreement of   **27.31**
  the parties.
- Arbitrators have wide powers to make procedural orders enabling them to lay down time-
  tables for the steps to be taken by the parties to prepare for the arbitration hearing and to
  preserve property pending the final award.
- Interim awards are final decisions on aspects of the whole dispute, but are not all that
  common. They can be a useful method of saving expense.
- Final awards finally determine the dispute between the parties.
- Final award must be in writing and comply with certain formalities.
- The normal position is that the final award should also state reasons, but the parties may
  agree to dispense with reasons, in which case it will not be possible to mount an appeal on
  a point of law
- Although there are some restrictions, arbitrators have wide-ranging powers on remedies
  and interest.
- The purpose of the formalities on awards is to ensure that they are enforceable, for example under the New York Convention 1958.

28

HIGH COURT JURISDICTION IN ARBITRATION CLAIMS

INTRODUCTION. 28.01

ORDERS TO PREVENT PARTIES BREACHING AGREEMENTS TO
ARBITRATE 28.05

APPOINTMENT, REMOVAL AND REPLACEMENT OF ARBITRATORS . .28.15

PROCEDURAL ORDERS TO ASSIST IN THE DETERMINATION OF
ARBITRAL PROCEEDINGS 28.23

JUDICIAL REVIEW OF ARBITRAL PROCEEDINGS. 28.40

PRELIMINARY POINTS OF LAW 28.41

SERIOUS IRREGULARITY 28.45

APPEAL ON A POINT OF LAW 28.61

PROCEDURE IN ARBITRATION CLAIMS .28.82

APPEALS TO THE COURT OF APPEAL. 28.91

KEY POINTS SUMMARY. 28.95

INTRODUCTION

28.01 Achieving a balance between the autonomy of arbitration proceedings and judicial intervention to ensure arbitral proceedings are conducted fairly and in accordance with the rights of the parties is a difficult issue. Different solutions have been advanced in different jurisdictions and at different times. In England they are largely summarised by two of the general principles in the Arbitration Act 1996 s 1, namely:

- the parties are free to agree how their disputes are resolved, subject only to such safeguards as are necessary in the public interest (s 1(b)); and
- the court should not intervene except as provided by the Arbitration Act 1996 (s 1(c)).

There is a significant public interest in preserving the binding effect of decisions made by **28.02** arbitrators. If these are readily overturned by the courts, arbitration would be little more than a precursor to the 'real' litigation in the courts, which would be expensive for the parties and would drive arbitration business away from this country. Balanced against this is the need to ensure the parties in arbitration proceedings are treated fairly, have a proper chance to present their version of events, and are able to put right any burning injustices that may occur in an arbitration. Despite being founded on an agreement to arbitrate between the parties, with the passing of time there are cases where one side loses its enthusiasm for arbitration. Witnesses of course were not parties to the agreement to arbitrate, so are not under a contractual obligation to assist the parties to an arbitration.

To deal with these situations, the Arbitration Act 1996 gives the civil courts a number of **28.03** powers to support or intervene in arbitrations. These powers fall into five broad categories:

- court orders to prevent parties breaching agreements to arbitrate;
- court assistance in the appointment of arbitrators where there has been a problem in making the necessary appointments;
- court orders over procedural steps that the arbitral tribunal either cannot make or cannot enforce;
- interim remedies granted by the court to preserve the status quo; and
- judicial review and enforcement of arbitral awards to ensure arbitral decisions have the effect intended when the arbitral agreement was entered into.

In this context, arbitration lawyers use the expression 'judicial review' (see above) to describe **28.04** going to court to challenge an award for want of jurisdiction or for serious irregularity, or to appeal to the court on a point of law. This is not to be confused with the High Court's jurisdiction of judicial review of administrative decisions of local and central government decisions under the Senior Courts Act 1981 s 31.

ORDERS TO PREVENT PARTIES BREACHING AGREEMENTS TO ARBITRATE

A party may bring court proceedings in breach of an existing arbitration agreement for **28.05** a number of reasons. It may be that the existence of the arbitration clause is simply overlooked, or it may be that the party bringing the court proceedings hopes that the other side will not object to the matter being dealt with by the courts rather than through arbitration. In some cases the question of arbitrating or litigating has already been canvassed in correspondence, and the claimant may take the view that the other side have also stated a preference for going to court rather than arbitration. Rather more difficult issues may be raised where there is a disagreement between the parties over whether an arbitration clause applies to the current dispute, or whether there is a valid arbitration clause at all. See Chapter 25 for a number of the issues that might arise.

Where court proceedings have already been started, the appropriate application to make **28.06** is for a stay of those proceedings. If successful, such an application prevents the court proceedings being taken any further. Where it is feared that proceedings are about to be commenced, it may be possible to apply for an anti-suit injunction. Anti-suit injunctions are also sometimes sought from the courts in England and Wales to prevent proceedings being either started or continued in another state contrary to an arbitration agreement. There is a great reluctance in granting anti-suit injunctions.

Stay of legal proceedings

28.07 To prevent a party from breaching an agreement to arbitrate by bringing court proceedings, the Arbitration Act 1996 s 9(1) allows the other side to apply for a stay of those court proceedings. A stay can be sought whether the legal proceedings said to breach the arbitration agreement are brought by way of claim or counterclaim (s 9(1)). A stay imposes a halt on the legal proceedings, apart from taking any steps allowed by the terms of the stay. While in technical terms the proceedings can be continued if the stay is lifted (see the glossary to the CPR), in practical terms stays under s 9 are usually permanent, because the usual consequence is that the dispute will be referred for final determination by arbitration.

Procedure for seeking a stay

28.08 Applications for stays under the Arbitration Act 1996 s 9 are made in the court in which the claim is proceeding (s 9(1)). The party seeking the stay is required to file an acknowledgment of service (form N9) in the court proceedings before making the application (s 9(3)), and will tick the box on the form stating an intention to contest the court's jurisdiction. The application for the stay needs to be made before taking any other steps in the litigation. It is made by issuing an application notice in form N244 (CPR, r 62.3(3)). A witness statement in support will need to set out all the relevant circumstances, including the arbitration agreement as an exhibit, and explain why the dispute comes within that agreement. The application has to be served on all the other parties to the litigation (CPR, r 62.8(1), (2)).

Determination of the application for a stay

28.09 The main question under the Arbitration Act 1996 s 9 is whether the dispute raised in the litigation is a matter '... which under the [arbitration] agreement is to be referred to arbitration ...' (s 9(1)). If it is s 9(4) says the court 'shall' grant a stay (so this is mandatory rather than discretionary), unless the court is satisfied that the arbitration agreement is null and void, inoperative, or incapable of being performed.

Whether the dispute comes within arbitration agreement

28.10 It sometimes happens that the claimant in the court proceedings raises a question as to:

- whether there was a concluded arbitration agreement; or
- whether the dispute in the court proceedings falls within the terms of the arbitration agreement.

28.11 The court cannot grant a stay under the Arbitration Act 1996 s 9 if the parties to the court proceedings are not the parties, or persons claiming through or under a party, to the arbitration agreement (*City of London v Sancheti* [2009] Bus LR 996). For a stay to be granted, both parties in the litigation have to be parties to the arbitration agreement. It is not enough if one or other of the parties to the litigation has a mere commercial connection with one of the parties to the arbitration agreement.

28.12 In cases where there is a dispute over whether the dispute comes within the arbitration agreement, the court may by CPR, r 62.8(3), either:

- decide that question on the hearing of the application for the stay; or

- give directions as how that question is to be decided and, if so, consider granting a stay of the proceedings pending that decision.

Anti-suit injunctions

It is in theory possible to obtain an injunction to restrain another party to an arbitration **28.13** agreement from bringing court proceedings in breach of that agreement. This was considered in Chapter 26 in the context of disputes over the jurisdiction of arbitrators. These injunctions are regarded as being available only in exceptional circumstances (*Industrie Italia Centrale v Alexander Tsaviris and Sons Maritime Co, The Choko Star* [1987] 1 Lloyd's Rep 508), and are only available where it is necessary to restrain the breach of the arbitration agreement (*Compagnie Europeenne de Cereals SA v Tradax Export SA* [1986] 2 Lloyd's Rep 301).

Applications for interim injunctions are governed by CPR, Part 25. They will typically be **28.14** brought in the Commercial Court of the High Court, by an application notice supported by evidence in witness statements. The application will need to be served on the other party to the arbitration agreement, and will have to comply with the additional requirements in CPR, Part 58, PD 58, and the *Commercial Court Guide*. These impose time-limits for the filing of witness statements by the applicant and respondents (PD 58, paras 13.1–13.4), and various requirements for the compilation and filing of bundles of papers for the hearing (*Commercial Court Guide*, paras F5.4 and F11), skeleton arguments (paras F5.5 and F6.5) and authorities (para F13).

APPOINTMENT, REMOVAL AND REPLACEMENT OF ARBITRATORS

The usual position is that arbitrators are appointed by the parties or through mechanisms **28.15** agreed by the parties without any involvement of the courts (see Chapter 24). Where there are problems in securing the appointment of the tribunal, or in the continuation of an arbitration caused by problems with members of the panel, there are a number of provisions in the Arbitration Act 1996 that give the courts power to make orders that may be exercised to provide solutions to the problems.

Extending time for beginning arbitral proceedings

Arbitration clauses sometimes provide that claims will be barred, or the claimant's rights will **28.16** be extinguished, unless specified steps to begin the arbitration are taken within some fixed time-limit. The Arbitration Act 1996 s 12(1) provides that in these cases the court has power to extend the time for beginning the arbitration. An extension can be granted either before or after the time-limit has elapsed (s 12(4)) on the grounds either that there has been a change of circumstances that was not contemplated by the parties, or the conduct of the other side makes it unjust to hold the applicant to the strict terms of the time-limit (s 12(3)).

Setting aside appointment of sole arbitrator

Where an arbitration agreement provides for both sides to appoint one arbitrator each, and **28.17** one side refuses to do so, the party not in default can give notice under the Arbitration Act

1996 s 17(1) appointing its arbitrator as a sole arbitrator. Where this happens, the defaulting party is given a right to apply to the court to set aside the appointment of the sole arbitrator (s 17(3)).

Failure of the appointment procedure

28.18   Where there is a failure in the procedure agreed by the parties for the appointment of the tribunal, either party may apply to the court for directions or other orders under the Arbitration Act 1996 s 18(3), which are aimed at ensuring that there is a properly constituted tribunal. Powers in s 18(3) include the court making any necessary appointments itself. The courts have similar powers where a vacancy arises during the course of an arbitration (s 27(3)).

Removal of arbitrators

28.19   A party to an arbitration is permitted to apply to the court under the Arbitration Act 1996 s 24 for the removal of an arbitrator. Grounds for removal set out in s 24(1) are:

- justifiable doubts over the arbitrator's impartiality;
- the arbitrator does not have the qualifications required by the arbitration agreement;
- mental or physical incapacity; and
- refusal or failure to conduct the arbitration properly or with all reasonable despatch.

28.20   Bias, or a lack of impartiality, is a recurrent issue in arbitrations. This is often caused by there being a limited pool of qualified people in the relevant field, so that it becomes difficult to find someone who has not had dealings (whether these be business dealings, or previous arbitrations) with one or other of the parties. To reduce the risks of such dealings only becoming known to both sides after substantial progress has been made in the arbitration, it is good practice for arbitrators both to conduct a 'conflicts of interest' check and to communicate the results to both sides before their appointment is confirmed. Institutional arbitration rules on occasions make express provision for this. The UNCITRAL Model Law Art 12(1), provides that when approached in connection with possibly being appointed as an arbitrator, a person is under an obligation to disclose any circumstances likely to give rise to justifiable doubts as to his impartiality or independence. This duty continues after an appointment is made.

28.21   A doubt about partiality is only justifiable if a fair-minded and informed observer would conclude there was a real possibility that the arbitrator was biased, or if there was a reasonable appearance of bias (*Porter v Magill* [2002] 2 AC 357). The guidance given in *Locabail (UK) Ltd v Bayfield Properties Ltd* [2000] QB 451 (see Sime, *A Practical Approach to Civil Procedure* (13th edn, OUP, 2010), ch 39) is of general application and is just as relevant in arbitration as in litigation. It is not any appearance of bias that will justify the removal of an arbitrator. In *Andrews v Bradshaw* [2000] BLR 6 both parties were supposed to contribute to the arbitrator's fees, but only one had done so, and the arbitrator wrote a number of angry letters about the non-payment of his fees. While accepting the appointment with this one-sided payment arrangement and the tone of the letters was clearly unwise, neither was regarded by the Court of Appeal as sufficient to call into question the arbitrator's impartiality.

Relief from liability after resignation of an arbitrator

After resigning from his appointment, an arbitrator may apply to the court for relief from   **28.22**
any liability for breaking his contract to conduct the arbitration, and for an order relating to his entitlement to any fees or expenses (Arbitration Act 1996 s 25(3)). Whether any
relief is granted depends on whether in all the circumstances it was reasonable to resign
(s 25(4)).

PROCEDURAL ORDERS TO ASSIST IN THE DETERMINATION
OF ARBITRAL PROCEEDINGS

Powers to secure evidence etc available to tribunals

The powers available to an arbitral tribunal depend primarily on what the parties have   **28.23**
chosen to confer on their tribunal. These may be set out in the arbitration agreement, or
in any institutional rules adopted by the parties. In the absence of contrary agreement by
the parties, arbitral tribunals have various powers by virtue of the Arbitration Act 1996
for:

- appointing experts (s 37);
- inspecting, preserving and ordering samples and experiments of the subject-matter of the
  arbitration if it is in the possession of a party (s 38(4));
- preserving evidence in the custody or control of a party (s 38(6)); and
- giving permission to a party to apply to the court for a witness summons to secure the
  attendance of a witness at the tribunal's hearings if the witness is in the United Kingdom
  (s 43).

There are limitations on these powers, which stem from the contractual basis of arbitra-   **28.24**
tion. Tribunals can only make orders about inspection of property or the preservation of
evidence between the parties, so these orders are only available where the property is in
the control of a party to the arbitration. While in many cases the tribunal will give permission to apply for a witness summons (s 43 also applies where all the parties agree), there
will be cases where one party wants a witness summons, but the tribunal and other parties
disagree.

There is an unresolved issue over whether the Arbitration Act 1996 permits an arbitral tri-   **28.25**
bunal to make an order for an interim injunction. There is no express provision giving
such a power. It is often thought that such a power can be seen in s 48. This provides in s
48(5)(a) that the tribunal has the same powers as the court to order a party to do or refrain
from doing anything. The problem is that s 48 is located within ss 46–58, which deal with
the final award. Cases like *Econet Wireless Ltd v Vee Networks Ltd* [2006] 2 Lloyd's Rep 428
assume that tribunals do have such a power. The doubt over this may be dispelled by the
institutional rules that may be adopted by the parties. The clearest rules are those in the
UNCITRAL Model Law Arts 17–17J (see Chapter 26), which contain detailed provisions for
interim injunctions granted by arbitral tribunals.

Court jurisdiction on procedural matters

28.26 Given the gaps and limitations on the powers available to arbitrators, the Arbitration Act 1996 s 44, makes the following provision in support of arbitral proceedings:

> '(1) Unless otherwise agreed by the parties, the court has for the purposes of and in relation to arbitral proceedings the same power of making orders about the matters listed below as it has for the purposes of and in relation to legal proceedings.
>
> (2) These matters are—
>> (a) the taking of the evidence of witnesses;
>> (b) the preservation of evidence;
>> (c) making orders relating to property which is the subject of the proceedings or as to which any question arises in the proceedings [...];
>> (d) the sale of any goods the subject of the proceedings;
>> (e) the granting of an interim injunction or the appointment of a receiver.'

28.27 Under these provisions the courts may make orders for recording the evidence of witnesses in depositions, orders for the preservation of evidence or for the inspection, sampling etc of property that is the subject-matter of the arbitration, which may be in the possession of someone who is not a party to the arbitration.

28.28 The purpose of s 44 is to give the court powers to be used when the arbitral tribunal is unable to act effectively. In *Belair LLC v Basel LLC* [2009] EWHC 725 (Comm) this was satisfied because the tribunal had not been constituted. An order was made to enable a party to deal with certain property, which was the only asset in the case, in the period until the tribunal could be constituted. Once this had happened it was for the tribunal to decide whether steps were required to preserve the property.

Disclosure in aid of arbitration

Norwich Pharmacal orders

28.29 Where a dispute is referred to arbitration, the Arbitration Act 1996 s 43 provides that court procedures to procure documents or other material evidence may only be used with the permission of the arbitral tribunal or the agreement of the other parties. This provision does not prevent a court making a *Norwich Pharmacal* order (see see Sime, *A Practical Approach to Civil Procedure* (13th edn, OUP, 2010), ch 30) in the period before a dispute has been referred to arbitration, where the power is used for preserving assets or remedies (*Glidepath Holding BV v Thompson* [2005] 1 All ER (Comm) 434).

Pre-action disclosure

28.30 It has been held that the Senior Courts Act 1981 s 33(2) is limited to likely court proceedings, and does not confer jurisdiction to order pre-action disclosure in aid of arbitration (*EDO Corporation v Ultra Electronics Ltd* [2009] Bus LR 1306).

Non-party disclosure

28.31 The five powers specified under the Arbitration Act 1996 s 44(2) do not include orders for non-party disclosure under the Senior Courts Act 1981 s 34(3) and CPR, r 31.17. Where there is a risk that documents may cease to exist or become unavailable, it may be possible to obtain an order for their preservation, such as by copying, under s 44(2)(b): see *Assimina Maritime Ltd v Pakistan National Shipping Corporation* [2005] 1 All ER (Comm) 460.

Interim injunctions

Courts are given jurisdiction to grant interim injunctions to preserve the status quo in **28.32** support of arbitral proceedings by the Arbitration Act 1996 s 44(2)(e). The purpose of this power is to provide protection for the period before an arbitrator can be appointed (*Econet Wireless Ltd v Vee Networks Ltd* [2006] 2 Lloyd's Rep 428). In *Econet Wireless Ltd v Vee Networks Ltd* it was held to be inappropriate to seek an interim injunction in England under s 44 when the arbitration is to take place in another jurisdiction. Such an application should be made in the courts for the seat of the arbitration.

In *Cetelem SA v Roust Holdings Ltd* [2005] 1 WLR 3555 a dispute arose between parties to a **28.33** share sale contract containing a London arbitration clause. A condition precedent under the contract was that approval had to be given by the Russian Central Bank. Five weeks before the expiry of the time for obtaining approval, no action had been taken by the defendant, so the claimant applied for an urgent mandatory interim injunction requiring the defendant to lodge the necessary papers in Russia. It was held that such an order could only be made if it was necessary for the preservation of evidence or assets, and there was no jurisdiction to make the order on any wider basis. Nevertheless the injunction satisfied the test. 'Assets' to be preserved under s 44(3) could include things in action. In this case the injunction was necessary to preserve the claimant's contractual right to purchase the shares, because the right to purchase them would be lost if no application was made for Russian Central Bank approval.

An application to the court for a freezing injunction in support of arbitration proceedings **28.34** under the Arbitration Act 1996 s 44 has the advantages that the court's order will bind third parties and is buttressed by sanctions (*Pacific Maritime (Asia) Ltd v Holystone Overseas Ltd* [2008] 1 Lloyd's Rep 371).

Apart from the Arbitration Act 1996 s 44, the High Court also has an inherent jurisdiction **28.35** to grant interim injunctions. This jurisdiction can be invoked even if there is an arbitration clause in the contract underlying the dispute that might be invoked at a later stage and lead to a stay of the court proceedings (*Glidepath Holding BV v Thompson* [2005] 1 All ER (Comm) 434).

Applications for procedural orders

On-notice applications

Applications for interim remedies under the Arbitration Act 1996 s 44 are usually made **28.36** on notice to the other parties to the arbitration, using the arbitration claim form (form N8: see PD 62, para 8.1, and discussed at 28.82 below). A Part 8 claim form is used because the dispute is being dealt with by arbitration, which means there will be no existing court proceedings.

Urgent applications

If an application for a procedural order is urgent, the Arbitration Act 1996 s 44(3) provides **28.37** that the court may, on the application of a party or proposed party to the arbitral proceedings, make such orders as it thinks necessary for the purpose of preserving evidence or assets. These are usually made without notice to the other party, which in technical terms means without giving the usual three clear days' notice of the hearing to the other side

(CPR, r 23.7(1)). Even in urgent cases, such notice as can be given must be attempted (such as by telephone or email informing the other party of the nature of the application and when it will be considered by the court). It is only if secrecy is essential (such as in applications for freezing injunctions), or where the urgency makes it impossible to give even informal notice, that giving no notice at all can be justified (*National Bank of Jamaica Ltd v Olint* [2009] 1 WLR 1405).

Procedure for seeking interim injunctions

28.38 As with other procedural orders in support of arbitration, applications for interim injunctions under the Arbitration Act 1996 s 44(2)(e), are brought using the arbitration claim form. As the power under s 44(2)(e) is to preserve the position pending the appointment of the tribunal, it is necessary to set out the steps being taken to appoint an arbitrator in the evidence in support, and there must be an undertaking to appoint an arbitrator without delay.

Exclusion of section 44

28.39 In accordance with the principle of party autonomy (see Chapter 23), the opening words of the Arbitration Act 1996 s 44 say it applies unless otherwise agreed by the parties. The powers given by s 44 are designed to support the effectiveness of arbitral proceedings, and are regarded as being highly beneficial. Accordingly, any purported exclusion of the section requires clear words, and the courts are not prone to finding the section has been excluded by reference to allegedly inconsistent provisions in the arbitration agreement (*SAB Miller Africa v East African Breweries* [2010] EWCA Civ 1564). Clauses that make equivalent provision to s 44 will not be taken to have excluded the section. It was held in *SAB Miller Africa v East African Breweries* that if the parties want to agree that interim relief is to be granted under the Senior Courts Act 1981 s 37 (for which, see Sime, *A Practical Approach to Civil Procedure* (13th edn, OUP, 2010), ch 35) free from the provisions of the Arbitration Act 1996 s 44, very clear provision would have to be made to that effect.

JUDICIAL REVIEW OF ARBITRAL PROCEEDINGS

28.40 Judicial review of arbitral proceedings takes four forms:

- challenges to the jurisdiction of arbitrators (see 26.45);
- preliminary points of law (see 28.41);
- challenges to decisions for serious irregularity (see 28.45); and
- appeals on a point of law (see 28.61).

PRELIMINARY POINTS OF LAW

28.41 Unless otherwise agreed by the parties, a party to arbitral proceedings may apply to the court for the determination of any question of law arising in the course of the arbitral proceedings (Arbitration Act 1996 s 45(1)). If such an application is made the tribunal may continue with the arbitration while the application to the court is pending (s 45(4)).

Conditions to be satisfied

An application to the court for the determination of a preliminary question of law may   **28.42** only be brought if:

- the application is made with the agreement of all the other parties to the arbitration or with the permission of the tribunal (Arbitration Act 1996 s 45(2)). The agreement should ideally be in writing. Where reliance is placed on the permission of the tribunal rather than the consent of the parties, the court must be satisfied that:
  - the determination of the question is likely to produce substantial savings in costs; and
  - the application has been made without delay;
- there is no agreement to dispense with reasons for the tribunal's award (s 45(1)). Dispensing with reasons means the tribunal cannot make an error of law; and
- the court is satisfied that the point substantially affects the rights of one or more of the parties (s 45(1)). This is primarily directed at how important the point is in determining the rights of the parties. There is some authority that the value of the claim may be a factor in deciding whether a party's rights are substantially affected (*Retla Steamship Co v Gryphon Shipping Co SA* [1982] 1 Lloyd's Rep 55).

Procedure on applications on preliminary points of law

The application is an arbitration claim, and follows the procedure in CPR, Part 62 (see below).   **28.43** The arbitration claim form must identify the question of law to be determined (Arbitration Act 1996 s 45(3)). The witness statement in support should state whether the application is made with the consent of the parties or with the tribunal's permission, exhibiting the relevant documents. If the application is brought with the tribunal's permission, the witness statement must state the grounds on which it is alleged the question should be determined by the court (s 45(3) and PD 62, para 9.2).

In an application is made with the tribunal's permission, as soon as practical after the writ-   **28.44** ten evidence of all the parties has been filed, the court will decide whether or not it should consider the application. Unless the court otherwise directs, the court will make its decision under s 45(2)(b) on whether to allow the application to proceed without a hearing (PD 62, paras 9.3 and 10.1).

SERIOUS IRREGULARITY

Challenges to an arbitral award may be made under the Arbitration Act 1996 s 68 on the   **28.45** ground of serious irregularity. A challenge on this ground will only be successful if the claimant establishes both that:

- there was a serious irregularity affecting the tribunal, the proceedings or the award; and
- it caused or will cause substantial injustice (s 68(1) and *Commercial Court Guide*, para O8.6(a)).

Meaning of 'serious irregularity'

28.46   The meaning of 'serious irregularity' is set out in the Arbitration Act 1996 s 68(2). This provides that a serious irregularity is one involving either:

- a failure by the tribunal to comply with the general duty to act fairly and impartially between the parties, giving each party a reasonable opportunity to put its case, as set out in s 33 (see Chapter 23);
- the tribunal exceeding its powers;
- a failure by the tribunal to conduct the arbitration in accordance with the procedure agreed by the parties;
- a failure by the tribunal to deal with the issues put before it;
- an arbitral institution exceeding its powers;
- uncertainty or ambiguity as to the effect of the award;
- obtaining the award by fraud or by means contrary to public policy;
- a failure to comply with the requirements as to the form of the award (see Chapter 27); or
- any irregularity in the conduct of the proceedings or in the award that is admitted by the tribunal or arbitral institution.

28.47   In considering these grounds, the court must be astute not to impose the standards that would be expected of judges and the courts in civil litigation. Having chosen to refer their dispute to arbitration, the parties must be taken to have accepted that the process adopted by the arbitrators may well lack the formality found in court proceedings. It is only if the complaint discloses a defect that cannot on any view be justified as an acceptable consequence of having chosen to arbitrate that s 68 may be engaged (*Petroships Pte Ltd v Petec Trading and Investment Corporation* [2001] 2 Lloyd's Rep 348).

General duty to act fairly and impartially

28.48   Matters that have been held to come within the Arbitration Act 1996 s 68(2)(a) include an arbitrator failing to recuse himself where there was a real possibility of bias (*ASM Shipping Ltd v TTMI Ltd* [2006] 1 Lloyd's Rep 375) and delegating decision-making to an expert witness (*Brandeis Brokers Ltd v Black* [2001] 2 Lloyd's Rep 359). Deciding the case by overriding common ground between the parties without giving the parties the opportunity to address the contrary view on that matter taken by the arbitrator comes within s 68(2)(a) (*Omnibridge Consulting Ltd v Clearsprings (Management) Ltd* [2004] EWHC 2276 (Comm)). Failing to follow court practice, such as not giving the claimant's representative the final speech at the hearing, would not of itself come within s 68(2)(a) (*Margulead Ltd v Exide Technologies* [2005] 1 Lloyd's Rep 324).

Exceeding powers

28.49   A tribunal will exceed its powers within the meaning of the Arbitration Act 1996 s 68(2)(b) where it exercises a power it does not have. Section 68(2)(b) is not engaged by merely wrongly exercising a power it does have (*Lesotho Highlands Development Authority v Impregilo SpA* [2006] 1 AC 221). One of the complaints in this case was that the arbitrators had exceeded their powers by expressing their award in favour of the contractors for payments due under a contract for the construction of a dam in European currencies rather than in Lesotho malotis. The significance was that in the period between the date the payments should have been made under the contract and the award the maloti had fallen dramatically against the European currencies. The majority view in the House of Lords was that the arbitrators had made an error of law in either misinterpreting the substantive contract or in misinterpreting s 48(4) (on making awards in any currency) by making the award in the European currencies.

Lord Steyn at [32] said that in deciding whether s 68(2)(b) is engaged it is necessary to focus **28.50** intensely on the particular power under the arbitration agreement, the terms of reference, or the Arbitration Act 1996, in the context of all the circumstances of the case. The mere '...erroneous exercise of an available power cannot by itself amount to an excess of power. A mere error of law will not amount to an excess of power under s 68(2)(b))'. Accordingly, the court could not intervene under s 68 despite the error of the tribunal. Being an error of law it would have been possible to mount a challenge under s 69, but that was not available on the facts because the parties had excluded rights of appeal on points of law under s 69.

Failing to deal with all the issues

The Arbitration Act 1996 s 68(2)(d) provides for situations where there has been a 'fail- **28.51** ure by the tribunal to deal with all the issues that were put to it'. Morison J in *Fidelity Management SA v Myriad International Holdings BV* [2005] EWHC 1193 (Comm) at [9] said that s 68(2)(d):

- is designed to cover the essential issues in the arbitration. These are the issues that it is essential for the tribunal to determine in coming to a decision on the claims or defences raised in the course of the arbitration;
- is concerned with cases where the arbitral tribunal has not dealt at all with the case of a party. Examples are where a claim has been overlooked or where the decision cannot be justified as a particular key issue that is crucial to the result has not been decided;
- does not require arbitrators to deal with every argument on every point that is raised;
- is not to be used as a means of launching a detailed enquiry into the manner in which the tribunal considered the various issues, or with whether there has been a failure to come to the right answer on an issue; and
- is not concerned with the reasons given by the arbitrators on the issues. Deficiency of reasons is dealt with separately in s 70(4).

Fraud and public policy

In order to amount to fraud within the Arbitration Act 1996 s 68(2)(g) the alleged con- **28.52** duct must amount to serious impropriety, and requires cogent evidence (*Cuflet Chartering v Carousel Shipping Ltd* [2001] 1 Lloyd's Rep 707).

Substantial injustice

It is clear from the second requirement under the Arbitration Act 1996 s 68(2), that any **28.53** irregularity either must have caused, or will cause, substantial injustice to the applicant, and that the section imposes a high hurdle. The DAC report (Departmental Advisory Committee on Arbitration, set up by the Department of Trade and Industry, whose reports formed the basis for the Arbitration Act 1996) at para 280 commented that s 68 '...is really designed as a long stop only available in extreme cases where the tribunal has gone so wrong in its conduct of the arbitration that justice calls out for it to be corrected'. This passage has been cited with approval in a number of cases, including *Lesotho Highlands Development Authority v Impreglio SpA* [2006] 1 AC 221 (Lord Steyn).

28.54   Where the decision would clearly have been different if the irregularity had not occurred, there will almost certainly have been a substantial injustice (*Newfield Construction Ltd v Tomlinson* (2004) 97 Con LR 148); likewise where the irregularity results in the denial of a fair hearing (*Checkpoint Ltd v Strathclyde Pension Fund* [2003] 1 EGLR 1). An arbitrator's failure to recuse himself in circumstances where the court found there was a real possibility of bias was regarded as of itself a substantial injustice in *ASM Shipping Ltd v TTMI Ltd* [2006] 1 Lloyd's Rep 375.

28.55   In deciding whether an injustice is substantial, all the circumstances must be taken into account. The monetary value of the claim may be a factor in this assessment (*Groundshire v VHE Construction* [2001] 1 Lloyd's Rep 395).

28.56   It is to be noted that substantial injustice is not the sole test, but the second limb of the test. The mere fact something has or has not occurred in an arbitration that may have caused a substantial injustice is not sufficient to satisfy the test in s 68. In addition, one of the specific irregularities set out in s 68(2) must be established.

28.57   Where an irregularity has been remedied, no relief should be given under s 68. For example, where reasons have not been given, the availability of applying for reasons or further reasons under s 70(4) would make it impossible to contend there was any substantial injustice (*Fidelity Management SA v Myriad International Holdings BV* [2005] EWHC 1193 (Comm)).

Loss of right to object

28.58   The right to object under the Arbitration Act 1996 s 68, that the proceedings have been improperly conducted or that there has been a failure to comply with the arbitration agreement or with the provisions of the Arbitration Act 1996, or that there has been any other irregularity affecting the tribunal or the proceedings, is lost if it is not taken at the time (s 73). This arises if the party making the complaint takes part, or continues to take part, in the arbitral proceedings without making the objection either forthwith or within such time as is allowed by the arbitration agreement or the tribunal or by any provision of the Arbitration Act 1996 (s 73(1)).

Powers available to deal with a serious irregularity

28.59   Where the court finds there has been a serious irregularity that causes a substantial injustice, the Arbitration Act 1996 s 68(3), says the court may:

- remit the award to the tribunal, in whole or in part, for reconsideration;
- set aside the award in whole or in part; or
- declare the award to be of no effect, in whole or in part.

28.60   The choice between these powers will depend on the nature of the problem. Most problems within s 68 will be dealt with by setting aside, although remitting to the tribunal may be appropriate if the tribunal failed to deal with the issues, if the award is ambiguous, or if there is a formal defect in the award. The proviso to the subsection says that setting aside and declarations under sub-paras (b) and (c) cannot be made unless the court is satisfied that it would be inappropriate to remit the matters in question to the tribunal for reconsideration.

APPEAL ON A POINT OF LAW

Unless otherwise agreed by the parties, a party to arbitral proceedings may appeal to the **28.61** court on a question of law arising out of an award (Arbitration Act 1996 s 69(1)). This is a controversial provision, because many arbitration lawyers believe it goes too far in allowing a court to interfere with decisions made by arbitrators. It is a commonly held view that as the parties have agreed to have their dispute decided by arbitration, it is inconsistent to have that decision reviewed by a court. The contrary view, which s 69 seeks to promote, is that where the parties have agreed to have their dispute decided in accordance with a system of law, it is right that the courts should be able to review decisions if they were not in the event decided in a way consistent with that law.

There are a large number of restrictions on appeals under s 69, which are discussed below, **28.62** which mean that successful appeals under s 69 are comparatively rare.

Question of law

The Arbitration Act 1996 s 69 only applies to questions of law. The courts are vigilant in **28.63** preventing the parties from seeking to dress up questions of fact as questions of law (*Demco Investments and Commercial SA v SE Banken Forsakring Holding Aktiebolag* [2005] EWHC 1398 (Comm)). On an appeal under s 69 the parties must take the arbitrator's findings of fact as the starting point. The appellant must then identify the question of law arising from those facts, and explain why the arbitrator's decision on that question was in error. Questions of law include disputes over the legal principles to be applied, the meaning of statutory provisions, and questions of construction of contracts.

For this purpose, 'law' means the law of England and Wales (s 82(1)). Questions of foreign **28.64** law, where this is the proper law of the dispute, are questions of fact. As such, errors of foreign law do not come within s 69. They are still questions of fact if the foreign law is presumed to be, or if it is in fact, the same as English law. In *Reliance Industries Ltd v Enron Oil and Gas India Ltd* [2002] 1 All ER (Comm) 59, the parties had agreed that the proper law of the substantive contract was Indian law, which applies the same rules of contractual construction as English law. An appeal against the arbitrators' decision on the construction of the contract was not possible under s 69 because this was a matter of Indian law and therefore a question of fact.

No contrary agreement

The opening words of the Arbitration Act 1996 s 69(1) expressly say that its provisions apply **28.65** unless otherwise agreed by the parties. It is therefore open to the parties to oust judicial review on points of law by agreement. Such agreement may be included in the arbitration clause in the substantive contract, or subsequently. Clear wording is required for a clause to have the effect of excluding the court's jurisdiction (*Essex CC v Premier Recycling Ltd* [2007] BLR 233). In *Shell Egypt West Manzala Gmbh v Dana Gas Egypt Ltd* [2010] 1 Lloyd's Rep 109 the phrase 'final, conclusive and binding' in the parties' arbitration agreement was not construed as an exclusion agreement. It was no more than a fairly standard governing law and arbitration clause. 'Final and binding' traditionally means simply that the arbitrators' award creates a res judicata between the parties.

28.66 Adoption of institutional arbitral rules may have the result of ousting the court's jurisdiction under s 69 if those rules prohibit appeals on points of law. For example, by adopting the ICC rules (see Chapter 26) the parties waive their right to any form of recourse in so far as such waiver can validly be made (ICC rules Art 28(6)). This amounts to a contrary agreement, ousting s 69 (see *Lesotho Highlands Development Authority v Impregilo SpA* [2006] 1 AC 221 at [3]).

No agreement to dispense with reasons

28.67 A written agreement to dispense with reasons for the tribunal's decision excludes the court's jurisdiction over points of law (the proviso to the Arbitration Act 1996 s 69(1), and s 5). Without reasons for the award, it is impossible to identify any error of law.

Tribunal asked to determine the point

28.68 Permission to appeal under the Arbitration Act 1996 s 69 cannot be granted unless the arbitral tribunal was asked to determine the question (s 69(3)(b)).

Exhaustion of arbitral appeals and reviews

28.69 An appeal under the Arbitration Act 1996 s 69, can only be made once all arbitral appeal and review opportunities have been exhausted (ss 57 and 70(2)).

Point must arise from an award

28.70 Appeals under the Arbitration Act 1996 s 69 can only be made on points arising from awards. They are not available from procedural orders that do not amount to awards. See Chapter 27 for the distinction between awards and orders.

Appeal must be made within 28 days

28.71 By virtue of the Arbitration Act 1996 s 70(3), an appeal on a point of law must be made within 28 days of the award (see 28.84).

Agreement or permission to appeal

28.72 An appeal under the Arbitration Act 1996 s 69 can only be made with the agreement of the other parties to the arbitration or with the permission of the court (s 69(2)).

28.73 Agreements to enable appeals on points of law are the reverse of agreements to exclude such appeals. Their effect is to remove the need to obtain the court's permission for an appeal under s 69. Such agreements can be made in the arbitration agreement (they are sometimes found in construction contracts, such as the JCT standard terms) or after the dispute has arisen.

Permission of the court

28.74 In the absence of the consent of the other parties, a party seeking to appeal on a point of law has to obtain the court's permission for the appeal (Arbitration Act 1996 s 69(2)(b)). When seeking permission, the party bringing the appeal must issue an arbitration claim form supported by a witness statement, which must address the requirement for seeking permission as set out in s 69(3) (see PD 62, para 12.2). Permission will not be granted (see s 69(3)) unless the court is satisfied that:

(a) the determination of the question will substantially affect the rights of one or more parties;
(b) the question was raised with the tribunal (see 28.68 above);
(c) on the basis of the findings of fact in the award either:
  (i) the decision of the tribunal on the question is obviously wrong; or
  (ii) the question is one of general public importance and the decision of the tribunal is at least open to serious doubt; and
(d) despite the agreement of the parties to resolve the matter by arbitration, it is just and proper in all the circumstances for the court to determine the question.

As these are statutory criteria for granting permission, there is no scope for the courts to **28.75** amplify or adapt them to changing circumstances (*CMA CGM SA v Beteiligungs-KG MS 'Northern Pioneer' Schiffahrtgesellschaft mbH and Co* [2003] 1 WLR 1015). They are based on the criteria laid down by Lord Diplock in *The Nema* [1982] AC 724, but sub-para. (b) is new and sub-para (c)(ii) is a little wider than the guidance given in *The Nema*.

Substantially affect the rights of the parties

In criterion (a), 'substantially' means of major importance (*International Sea Tankers Inc v* **28.76** *Hemisphere Shipping Co Ltd* [1982] 1 Lloyd's Rep 128). 'Rights' means the issues in dispute in the arbitration (*CMA CGM SA v Beteiligungs-Kg MS 'Northern Pioneer' Schiffahrtgesellschaft mbH and Co* [2003] 1 WLR 1015). Permission therefore will not be granted on technical points. In the *Northern Pioneer* case the claimant raised an issue over whether its right to withdraw from a charterparty within a reasonable time under a war clause arose from an implied term or through the principles of waiver, election or estoppel. While this was an arguable point of law, it had no substantial impact on either party's rights because whatever the juridical basis of the right to withdraw, it had to be exercised within a reasonable time, and the arbitrators' decision that the claimant was too late to raise it was not open to serious doubt.

Obviously wrong

If the point of law is not of general public importance, it is necessary to show that the arbitra- **28.77** tors' decision is obviously wrong. In *The Kelaniya* [1989] 1 Lloyd's Rep 30, Lord Donaldson MR said that permission will only be given if the decision is 'plainly wrong', which is the same test as is used in overturning first instance court decisions on appeals under the CPR Part 52. It means 'unsustainable' (*Abrahams v Lenton* [2003] EWHC 1104 (QB)).

General public importance

If the point of law is of general public importance, rather than having to show the arbitra- **28.78** tors' decision was obviously wrong, it is only necessary to show that the decision is open to serious doubt (Arbitration Act 1996 s 69(3(c)(ii)). The distinction is often between points of law arising from one-off clauses (which do not raise questions of general public impor- tance), and those arising from standard form contracts in common use (which do): see *The Nema* [1982] AC 724. Additional factors suggested by *Geogas Ltd v Trammo Gas Ltd* [1991] 1 Lloyd's Rep 349 are whether the point raises a matter of general legal principle, and whether it is likely to arise often in other cases. Events operating outside standard form contracts, such as whether the closure of a sea lane or shipping canal is a frustrating event, or whether the conflict in Kosovo amounted to a war for the purpose of shipping and insurance con- tracts (*The Northern Pioneer*), can therefore be of general public importance.

28.79 Showing a decision is open to serious doubt is plainly a lower test than showing it is obviously wrong. It may be satisfied, for example, where there is a split decision by the arbitrators (*The Northern Pioneer*) or where there are conflicting decisions in the courts or in previous arbitrations.

Overall discretion

28.80 Even if the three main conditions in sub-paras (a)–(c) of the Arbitration Act 1996 s 69(3), are satisfied, permission to bring an arbitration claim on a point of law will only be granted if it is just and proper for the court to determine the matter in all the circumstances of the case. The fact the parties have agreed to arbitrate rather than litigate is an important and powerful factor (DAC report, para 290).

Powers available to deal with points of law

28.81 On an appeal on a point of law, the Arbitration Act 1996 s 69(7), says the court may:

- confirm the award;
- vary the award;
- remit the award to the tribunal, in whole or in part, for reconsideration; or
- set aside the award in whole or in part.

PROCEDURE IN ARBITRATION CLAIMS

Application or Part 8 claim

28.82 Arbitration claims are commenced using the arbitration claim form (form N8), and follow the procedure for Part 8 as amended by Part 62 (CPR, r 62.3(1); and see Sime, *A Practical Approach to Civil Procedure* (13th edn, OUP, 2010), ch 19). An application to stay legal proceedings (which have already started) is made by making an interim application within those proceedings (CPR, r 62.3(2)).

28.83 An example of an arbitration claim form is shown in Figure 28.1. It is a claim seeking permission to appeal on a point of law under the Arbitration Act 1996 s 69. The question of law is one of the proper construction of a term in a standard form shipping contract, and is identified in para (a). As it arises in a standard form contract the claimant takes the view that the lower test in s 69(3)(c)(ii) applies on the merits of the application. The statutory criteria for granting permission to appeal are dealt with in paras 1–12, with paras 5–11 dealing with why it is said the arbitrator's decision is open to serious doubt. Paragraph 13 deals with the no alternative review requirement in s 70(2), and para 14 with the need to bring the claim within 28 days of the award (s 70(3)).

Time-limit

28.84 An application to challenge an award under the Arbitration Act 1996 s 67 or 68, or to appeal under s 69, must be brought within 28 days of the date of the award (s 70(3)). The 28-day time-limit in s 70(3) may be extended, either under s 79 (the view favoured by the DAC)

Figure 28.1 Arbitration claim form

Claim Form (arbitration)	**In the** HIGH COURT OF JUSTICE QUEEN'S BENCH DIVISION, COMMERCIAL COURT
	for court use only
	Claim No.
	Issue date

In an arbitration claim between

Claimant
ANTAIOS COMPANIA NAVIERA SA

SEAL

Defendant(s)
SALEN REDERIERNA AB

In the matter of an [intended] arbitration between

Claimant
ANTAIOS COMPANIA NAVIERA SA
30 AFENTOULI STR.
158 27, PIRAEUS
GREECE

Respondent(s) *Set out the names and addresses of persons to be served with the claim form stating their role in the arbitration and whether they are defendants.*

SALEN REDERIERNA AB (DEFENDANT)

MR. JONATHAN HODSON (ARBITRATOR)

Defendant's name and address	SALEN REDERIERNA AB (DEFENDANT) SYDATLANTEN 7 SKANDIAHAMMMEN, GOTHENBURG 411 72 SWEDEN	☐ This claim will be heard on: at am/pm ☐ This claim is made without notice.

The court office at

When corresponding with the court, please address forms or letters to the Court Manager and quote the case number.

N8 Claim form (arbitration)

Figure 28.1 Arbitration claim form *(Continued)*

	Claim No.	

Remedy claimed and grounds on which claim is made

The Claimant seeks orders pursuant to the Arbitration Act 1996, section 69:

(a) granting permission to appeal from the award of Mr Jonathan Hodson ('the Arbitrator') dated 13 September 2010 ('the Award') in an arbitration between the Claimant and the Defendant on the following question of law ('the question'), namely: Whether clause 5 of the New York Produce Exchange standard form time charterparty ('the New York charterparty') applies to any breach of the New York charterparty, or to any serious breach of the New York charterparty, or only to repudiatory breaches of the New York charterparty; and

(b) that if permission to appeal is granted by this Court that the Award be:

(i) varied;

(ii) remitted in whole or in part for reconsideration in the light of this Court's determination in this claim; or

(iii) set aside in whole or in part; and

(c) that the costs of the application for permission to appeal be costs in the appeal.

The grounds for the application for permission to appeal are that:

1. Determination of the question will substantially affect the rights of the Claimant and/or the Defendant.

2. The question is one that the Arbitrator was asked to determine.

3. On the basis of the findings of fact of the Arbitrator, the question is one of general public importance in that:

(a) the question is one as to the proper construction of the New York charterparty, which is a standard form contract in common use in the shipping industry;

(b) there have been numerous conflicting court and arbitral decisions on the question; and

(c) determination of the question by this Court is necessary to promote legal certainty.

4. On the basis of the findings of fact of the Arbitrator, the decision of the Arbitrator on the question is open to serious doubt for the reasons set out in paragraphs 5 to 11.

5. Clause 5 of the New York charterparty confers a right on the owner of the vessel to withdraw the vessel from the charterparty failing punctual and regular payment of the hire "or for any breach of this charterparty".

6. There is a dispute between the Claimant and the Defendant on the question whether clause 5 of the New York charterparty applies to any breach of the New York charterparty, or to any serious breach of the New York charterparty, or only to repudiatory breaches of the New York charterparty.

7. The Arbitrator found as facts that sub-charterers of a vessel chartered from the Claimant by the Defendant had procured false bills of lading, which were false in that they were antedated, issued in respect of cargo not yet shipped, or unclaused despite defects in the condition of the goods shipped. The Arbitrator also found that the Defendant was responsible for the bills of lading procured by the sub-charterers.

8. The Arbitrator found that clause 5 of the New York charterparty only applies to repudiatory breaches.

9. The Arbitrator also found that the breaches referred to in paragraph 7 above were not repudiatory breaches.

10. The Arbitrator's decision referred to in paragraph 8 above was wrong in that it is inconsistent with the decisions in The Tropwind [1977] 1 Lloyd's Rep 397, and The Athos [1981] 2 Lloyd's Rep 74 and [1983] 1 Lloyd's Rep 127.

11. The Arbitrator should have held that the words "any breach" in clause 5 of the New York charterparty include the breaches of the kind referred to in paragraph 7 above, which are breaches, alternatively serious breaches, of the New York charterparty.

12. In the circumstances it is just and proper for this Court to determine the question.

13. There is no arbitral process of appeal or review available to the Claimant.

14. This application is brought within 28 days of the date of the Award.

Figure 28.1 Arbitration claim form *(Continued)*

	Claim No.	

The claimant seeks an order for costs against

SALEN REDERIERNA AB

Statement of Truth
*(I believe)(The Claimant believes) that the facts stated in these particulars of claim are true.
* I am duly authorised by the claimant to sign this statement

Full name _____

Name of claimant's solicitor's firm _____

signed_____ position or office held _____
        *(Claimant)(Claimant's solicitor)   (if signing on behalf of firm or company)

*delete as appropriate

Scott and Avery LLP, solicitors,
16-24 Archway Road,
London
WC2H 6SP

Claimant's or claimant's solicitor's address to which documents should be sent if different from overleaf. If you are prepared to accept service by DX, fax or e-mail, please add details.

or s 80(5) (which seems more consistent with the scheme of the Arbitration Act 1996). An application to extend time is made by issuing an application notice if the time-limit has not expired, or in a separately identified part of the arbitration claim form if the 28 days have expired (CPR, r 62.9 and PD 62, para 11.1). Respondents are permitted to file witness statement evidence in opposition to an application to extend time (CPR, r 62.9(3)). On applications to extend time, according to *Nagusina Naviera v Allied Maritime Inc* [2003] 2 CLC 1 the three most important considerations are:

- the length of the delay;
- whether, in allowing the time-limit to expire and the subsequent delay to occur, the defaulting party nevertheless acted reasonably in the circumstances; and
- whether the respondent to the application or the arbitrator contributed to the delay.

28.85   A number of other factors were also identified in *AOOT Kalmneft v Glencore* [2001] 1 Lloyd's Rep 128, such as any irremediable prejudice that may be suffered by the respondent (which may in some circumstances outweigh all other factors), the strength of the application, and any unfairness to the applicant.

Defendants to the arbitration claim

28.86   Where a provision of the Arbitration Act 1996 requires notice to be given of a court application, that requirement is fulfilled by making the relevant person a defendant to the arbitration claim (CPR, r 62.6). Thus, the arbitrator must be made a defendant in the following cases:

- applications to remove an arbitrator (Arbitration Act 1996 s 24);
- applications to consider and adjust the arbitrator's fees and expenses (s 28); and
- applications to determine the arbitrator's fees and expenses where the award has been withheld pending payment (s 56).

Courts having jurisdiction over arbitration claims

28.87   The courts that can deal with arbitration claims are listed in PD 62, para 2.3(1), and include the Admiralty and Commercial Registry, the TCC, and the Mercantile Courts. Arbitration claims involving landlord and tenant matters are dealt with in the Chancery Division (para 2.3(2)).

Procedure on arbitration claims

28.88   An arbitration claim form must be served within one month of issue (CPR, r 62.4(2)). The court may grant permission for service outside the jurisdiction (CPR, r 62.5). A defendant must acknowledge service within 14 days of service by filing form N15 or form N210(CC) (CPR, r 10.3(1)(b)). All arbitration claims are allocated to the multi-track, and there is no requirement to file allocation questionnaires (CPR, r 62.7). Automatic directions apply, unless the court orders otherwise, as set out in Table 28.1 (PD 62, paras. 6.1 to 6.7). An application for alternative directions is made using the procedure in CPR, Part 23 (see Sime, *A Practical Approach to Civil Procedure* (13th edn, OUP, 2010), ch 20). The claimant should apply for a hearing date as soon as possible after issuing the claim (*Commercial Court Guide*, para O6.2).

Table 28.1 Automatic directions in arbitration claims

Step	Time-limit
Defendant files and serves witness statements	21 days after acknowledgment of service
Claimant files witness statements in reply	Seven days after service of defendant's evidence
Agreed, indexed, and paginated bundles (prepared by claimant)	Five days before the hearing
Time estimates and complete documentation to be filed	Five days before the hearing
Chronology, list of persons involved (if necessary), skeleton argument filed by claimant	Two days before the hearing
Skeleton argument filed by defendant	Day before the hearing

Hearings in arbitration claims under Part 62

Arbitration hearings are usually held in private, although preliminary determinations of **28.89** points of law under the Arbitration Act 1996 s 45, and appeals under s 69, are usually heard in public (CPR, r 62.10).

The following questions in applications in arbitration claims are usually made without **28.90** hearings:

- decisions in preliminary points of jurisdiction and preliminary points of law as to whether determining the question is likely to produce substantial savings in costs and whether the application is made without delay (ss 32(2)(b) and 45(2)(b); see PD 62, para 10.1);
- whether to grant permission to appeal on a point of law (s 69(5)); and
- whether to extend the 28-day time-limit prescribed by s 70(3) (PD 62, para 10.2).

APPEALS TO THE COURT OF APPEAL

As mentioned at the start of this chapter, any scope for making applications to court where **28.91** a matter has been referred to arbitration derogates from the principle of one-stop dispute resolution. The various situations discussed in this chapter where it is seen as appropriate to allow recourse to the courts are aimed at supporting the arbitral process, and to put right the most serious kinds of injustices that may occur from time to time. Allowing parties to go further, and to bring appeals against the decisions of the High Court judges dealing with matters dealt with in this chapter, is seen as being contrary to the ethos of the Arbitration Act 1996, as this risks the parties being tied up in the courts for years, with costs escalating out of control. Consequently, almost all the provisions in the Arbitration Act 1996 that allow applications to the courts also contain restrictions on appeals.

A fairly typical provision is s 68(4) (in the context of challenges for serious irregularity), **28.92** which says: 'The leave of the court is required for any appeal from a decision of the court under this section.' In this context, 'the court' is the High Court judge dealing with the arbitration claim (s 105(1)). This means that an appeal to the Court of Appeal can only be made if the High Court judge grants permission to appeal. If the judge refuses permission, the Court of Appeal has no jurisdiction to overrule that decision (*Athletic Union of Constantinople v National Basketball Association* [2002] 1 WLR 2863). The effect is that decisions of the judges in the High Court are usually final in arbitration claims.

28.93 A first instance judge should apply the same test for granting permission to appeal as the appeal court. A non-arbitration appeal can only be made if the court considers the appeal would have a real prospect of success or if there is some other compelling reason why the appeal should be heard (CPR, r 52.3(6)). In arbitration appeals there may be an additional element of whether the appeal warrants the consideration of the Court of Appeal (*Geogas SA v Trammo Gas Ltd* [1991] 1 Lloyd's Rep 349). There is some doubt whether there is such an additional requirement. Leggatt LJ, who was in the majority in that case, expressly said that, given the restrictions on appeals from arbitrators to the court at first instance, there was no apparent justification for making arbitration appeals more difficult to maintain than other appeals to the Court of Appeal.

28.94 While usually a refusal of permission to appeal by the judge at first instance means no appeal can be brought to the Court of Appeal, there are authorities that the Court of Appeal can review such a refusal if either:

- the first instance judge had no jurisdiction to make the order under appeal (*Cetelem SA v Roust Holdings Ltd* [2005] 1 WLR 3555). A very restricted approach is taken to finding matters over which the judge had no jurisdiction as opposed to merely cases where the judge made an error in exercising his jurisdiction (see 28.49); or
- the refusal of permission at first instance was unfair or arbitrary (*CGU International Insurance plc v Astrazenca Insurance Co Ltd* [2007] Bus LR 162). These will be exceptionally rare cases where there has been a failure of intellectual engagement with the arguments, or where there has been an absence of a decision on the issue.

KEY POINTS SUMMARY

28.95
- Intervention by the courts in arbitrations is restricted to those situations allowed by the Arbitration Act 1996 (s 1(c)).
- The situations where the courts have a role in arbitration are those where the judicial system can offer support to the arbitral process to make it effective, and to correct obvious injustices.
- Applications in support of the arbitral process include applications relating to the appointment of arbitrators and procedural orders to secure evidence for use in arbitrations.
- Judicial review of arbitral awards is strictly restricted. The main provisions deal with serious irregularities (s 68) and appeals on points of law (s 69).
- Rights to object are in general lost if the objection is not raised forthwith (s 73).
- Challenges and appeals under ss 67–69 must be brought within 28 days of the award (s 70(3)).
- Applications to stay court proceedings under s 9 are made within the existing litigation.
- All the other types of application are made by issuing an arbitration claim form under CPR, Part 62.
- Arbitration claims are brought by a special form of Part 8 claim form, and must be brought in designated specialist courts within the High Court.
- Arbitration claims are automatically allocated to the multi-track.
- Appeals to the Court of Appeal are (with minor exceptions) only available with the permission of the High Court judge.

29

ENFORCEMENT OF SETTLEMENTS AND AWARDS

INTRODUCTION. 29.01

BASIC METHODS OF ENFORCING COMPROMISE AGREEMENTS. . .29.04

MERGER, OR DISCHARGE OF ORIGINAL OBLIGATION,
BY COMPROMISE. 29.05

MAKING A CHOICE ON ENFORCEMENT OPTIONS 29.09

ENFORCEMENT OF COMPROMISES RECORDED AS A CONTRACT. .29.12

CHALLENGING A SETTLEMENT RECORDED AS A CONTRACT. 29.18

ENFORCEMENT OF COURT ORDERS. 29.19

COSTS ONLY PROCEEDINGS. 29.20

ENFORCEMENT OF CONSTRUCTION INDUSTRY ADJUDICATION
DECISIONS. 29.23

ARBITRATION SETTLEMENTS AND AWARDS 29.27

KEY POINTS SUMMARY. 29.36

INTRODUCTION

Entering into a compromise agreement as a result of negotiation or mediation, or obtaining **29.01**
an award through arbitration or adjudication, produces a solution to the underlying difference or dispute between the parties. In most cases, the fact that the parties have agreed
to use an ADR process, and that they will have agreed to the terms of the settlement in
a non-adjudicative process, will hopefully mean that there are no difficulties as regards
enforcement, and the parties will willingly honour the terms of settlement and what they
have agreed to do.

Unfortunately, there are many cases where there are difficulties with enforcement. This **29.02**
may happen where a party is not happy with the outcome of an adjudicative process, where

a party realises that the terms agreed are not as attractive as they seemed, or when practical problems arise. Obligations may not be honoured on time, or in the correct form, or at all. In these cases the party with the benefit of the compromise or award will need to consider how to enforce compliance by the other side.

29.03 Some methods are simpler and less expensive than others. The importance of choosing an appropriate form in which to record a settlement where there is a choice was dealt with in Chapter 20, and the point was made there that any concern about enforcement is a relevant criterion. The enforcement methods available to a large extent depend on the form taken by the compromise agreement. It is therefore important that the legal advisers for the parties take into account how the agreement can be enforced when formulating the compromise agreement, to minimise the risks and difficulties that may arise at a later stage.

BASIC METHODS OF ENFORCING COMPROMISE AGREEMENTS

29.04 The approach taken to enforcement of compromises in large measure depends on the nature of the process used to resolve the original dispute. Essentially:

- in adjudicative procedures, the tribunal will make an award. Enforcement will often be through registering the award with the courts of the state where enforcement is to take place, and then enforcing the award as a civil judgment (see 29.28–29.35);
- an exception is construction industry adjudications (Chapter 22), where the decision is not itself registrable. Instead it may be enforced through bringing court proceedings and entering judgment (see 29.23);
- in non-adjudicative procedures, if the parties have resolved their dispute, they will have entered into a contract of compromise. Enforcement is through suing on that contract;
- alternatively in a non-adjudicative procedure the parties may convert the compromise agreement into a court judgment or order, and then enforce that judgment or order.

MERGER, OR DISCHARGE OF ORIGINAL OBLIGATION, BY COMPROMISE

29.05 In each of the situations set out in the previous paragraph it will be seen that enforcement is of the compromise, decision or award, rather than the original dispute. In other words, by settling the original claim or having it adjudicated, the original cause of action is merged or converted into a contract of compromise or an adjudicative award. In fact, as a result it is no longer open to either party to sue on the original cause of action, and their rights and obligations are now defined by the compromise or adjudicative award.

There are three apparent exceptions to this rule, namely where:

- there is a an express term reviving old obligations in the event of non-performance;
- compromise is based on performance of the agreed terms;
- the compromise is ineffective.

Express term reviving old obligations in the event of non-performance

It is not uncommon for a compromise of a money claim to provide for payment by instal-   **29.06**
ments and also that in the event of default of an instalment the whole amount then outstanding shall become due and payable immediately. If there is a default, the old obligations
revive, subject to deduction of any instalments paid under the compromise. An express
term to this effect in the compromise agreement is required if this is to be the consequence
of non-performance (*Smith v Shirley and Bayliss* (1875) 32 LT 234).

Compromise based on performance of the agreed terms

Most compromises take effect from the time the parties reach agreement (sometimes   **29.07**
referred to as an accord). The old dispute then immediately merges into the new compromise (*Jameson v Central Electricity Generating Board* [1998] QB 323). However, as a matter of
construction it is possible for the parties to agree that their compromise will only become
effective when one of the parties performs its obligations under the compromise (*British
Russian Gazette and Trade Outlook Ltd v Associated Newspapers Ltd* [1933] 2 KB 616). In such a
case the party who has agreed to perform on the compromise agreement remains liable on
the old cause of action until performance is completed.

Compromise ineffective

It sometimes happens that an apparent compromise agreement does not comply with the   **29.08**
requirements for the formation of a valid contract. This ought not to happen, but there are
occasions where, for example, lax language in the compromise agreement leads to such
uncertainty of terms that the alleged compromise is held to be ineffective. In such a case,
as there is no valid compromise, the parties revert back to the original position with the
underlying cause of action (although with the passing of time there may be limitation or
other difficulties).

MAKING A CHOICE ON ENFORCEMENT OPTIONS

In giving professional advice to a client, you should not ignore enforcement until some   **29.09**
problem with enforcement arises. It should be a relevant consideration from the time you
first advise on the case. If there are likely to be enforcement problems, this should be built in
to earlier decisions so that enforcement can be as efficient as possible in terms of what can
be done, in what time frame, and at what cost.

If it is envisaged that enforcement may be a significant issue, because of what is at stake, the   **29.10**
complexity of the case, or the attitudes of the parties, then enforcement possibilities will be
an important issue from the time the lawyer is first consulted. The factors relevant to selecting an ADR option were dealt with in Chapters 2–3. The use of litigation or an adjudicative
option will bring with it specific recording and enforcement options. If arbitration is used
an arbitration award should be the outcome. The availability of the full enforcement powers
of the court may be a reason for selecting litigation.

Some ADR processes leave options on enforcement open to a later stage. The factors rele-   **29.11**
vant to recording a settlement are dealt with in Chapter 20, and the client may need to be

advised as to which form for recording the settlement will give the best enforcement options. The main distinction is between some form of contract, which will need to be enforced by starting new court proceedings, or a consent order, which can be enforced through appropriate court enforcement powers without the need for separate proceedings.

ENFORCEMENT OF COMPROMISES RECORDED AS A CONTRACT

Enforcement by civil proceedings

29.12 As mentioned above, where a compromise or full and final settlement is reached in a dispute at a time when no proceedings have been started, the old dispute is merged with the compromise agreement, and the parties can then sue on the compromise if it is breached. 'No proceedings' includes both litigation in the courts and references to arbitration. If a party fails to comply with the agreed terms, in most cases there will be an obvious breach of the compromise contract. A civil claim based on that breach should be reasonably straightforward. In most cases there will be no defence, and it would be expected that entering judgment should be a matter of either:

- entering judgment in default if the defendant does not respond to the particulars of claim within 14 days of the deemed date of service; or
- applying for summary judgment if there is a response, on the basis that the defendant has no real prospect of defending the claim.

29.13 Once judgment has been entered, the claimant can use the normal court enforcement processes. These include execution against goods, warrants of delivery and of possession, charging orders, third-party debt orders, attachment of earnings orders, and receivership orders.

29.14 If the contract is repudiated, is invalid, or a dispute arises outside the matters covered by the agreement, proceedings can be started on the original subject-matter of the dispute, so long as the limitation period has not expired.

Defences to claims for breach of compromise agreements

29.15 Exceptionally, a party who is sued for breach of a compromise agreement may be able to defend the claim by relying on one of the usual defences to claims in contract. The difficulty is in persuading the court that the defence is available on the facts. What cannot be done is to rely on an argument to the effect that there was no merit in the underlying dispute. Two exceptions to this rule are:

- where the original claim was not made in good faith; and
- where an undisputed claim for a liquidated amount is compromised by an agreement to pay a smaller sum (the rule in *Pinnel's Case* (1602) 5 Co Rep 117a, although there are restrictions on this principle: see *Chitty on Contracts* (30th edn, Sweet & Maxwell)).

29.16 General defences under contract law that may be available include:

- no offer or acceptance in relation to the alleged compromise agreement;
- the terms of the compromise being too uncertain;

- consideration being past or there being no consideration;
- incapacity of a party to the compromise (unless the compromise is approved by the court under CPR, r 21.10);
- lack of writing where that is required by contract law;
- mistake;
- misrepresentation;
- duress;
- undue influence;
- lack of authority if the compromise was apparently entered into by an agent;
- illegality;
- frustration;
- performance;
- renunciation;
- impossibility;
- fundamental breach which has been accepted; or
- discharge of the compromise by a further agreement.

Bankruptcy and winding up

Insolvency is often an alternative to enforcement by proceedings in the civil courts. Breach of **29.17** a compromise agreement may well be evidence that the other party is unable to pay its debts as they fall due (or any of the other grounds set out in the Insolvency Act 1986), which may make use of bankruptcy or winding-up procedures attractive. Bankruptcy is used in the case of individuals, and winding up for companies. They are not inexpensive alternatives to litigation, and operate as relief on behalf of all the creditors of the individual or company rather than specifically for the person bringing the proceedings. These insolvency procedures are swift, and can be very effective in obtaining payment from a reluctant payer. However, if the individual is made bankrupt or the company is wound up, the petitioning creditor is extremely unlikely to see any of their money, so these can be risky procedures to use.

CHALLENGING A SETTLEMENT RECORDED AS A CONTRACT

As regards challenging the terms of a settlement: **29.18**

- A settlement can only be set aside in limited circumstances, for example if it was obtained by fraud or misrepresentation (*Detz v Lennig* [1969] 1 AC 170), mutual mistake, unilateral mistake encouraged by the other side (*Huddersfield Banking Co Ltd v Henry Lister & Son Ltd* [1895] 2 Ch 273), mutual mistake of law (*Brennan v Bolt Burden (a firm)*) Times, 7 November 2003) or for economic duress or undue influence: *D & C Builders v Rees* [1966] 2 QB 107. It is unlikely that it can be argued that the agreement should be rectified if it was drawn up by lawyers.
- It is not normally possible to appeal against a consent order, or to apply to court to vary its terms: *Peacock v Peacock* [1991] Fam Law 139. It might be possible to get the agreement rectified, but this is unlikely where it has been drawn up by lawyers.
- The court may decline to enforce a compromise if there is equitable reason for not doing so, or if it can be argued that the terms of compromise have been frustrated. One side

may not be bound by the terms of a settlement if they can argue that the other side has breached or repudiated it.

- A court may refuse to enforce a consent order for someone who is not abiding by its terms: *Thwaite v Thwaite* [1981] FLR 280.

ENFORCEMENT OF COURT ORDERS

29.19 Where a compromise is reached in a case where there are existing court proceedings, it is likely that the compromise will be recorded in a court order or a Tomlin order as set out in Chapter 20. Normally the terms will be complied with but, if they are not, a key question is whether the party with the benefit of the compromise can immediately use the court's enforcement processes, or whether it is first necessary to take some other step. Table 29.1 sets

Table 29.1 Enforcement of the different methods of recording settlements

Method of recording settlement	Enforcement procedure
Judgment entered for immediate payment of the sum agreed together with costs.	Enforcement proceedings (by execution against goods, charging order etc) can be taken on such a judgment immediately (which means 14 days after judgment).
Judgment entered for the agreed sum (and costs), subject to a stay of execution pending payment by stated instalments.	If the instalments fall into arrears, the stay will be lifted, and the judgment creditor can immediately bring enforcement proceedings.
Consent order setting out the agreement in the form of undertakings by both parties in a series of numbered paragraphs.	If any of the terms are not complied with, enforcement may be possible immediately or on application to the court depending on the nature of the term in question.
Tomlin order.	• Substantive terms in a Tomlin order take effect and are enforceable as they stand without the need for any further court order. Figure 20.7 is a fairly typical Tomlin order. If there is no agreement on the amount of costs to be paid under para 3 of Figure 20.7, the claimant can proceed directly to a detailed assessment of its costs under CPR, Part 47. • In the event of the scheduled terms being breached, enforcement is a two-stage process. First, the claim must be restored under the 'liberty to apply' clause, and an order obtained to compel compliance with the term breached. Secondly, if that order is itself breached, enforcement can follow in the usual way.
Settlement upon terms endorsed on counsel's briefs.	The effect of this type of arrangement is to supersede the original claim with the compromise. Any breach can only be enforced by issuing fresh proceedings.
Consent order staying all further proceedings upon agreed terms.	The courts are very unwilling to remove the stay imposed by this type of order, so enforcement can usually be effected only by bringing fresh proceedings for breach of the contract embodied in the compromise (see *Rofa Sport Management AG v DHL International (UK) Ltd* [1989] 1 WLR 902).
Consent order providing for 'no order' save as to costs, but setting out the agreed terms in recitals.	*Atkinson v Castan* (1991) *Times*, 17 April, held that the recitals in the consent order could be enforced without the need to bring a fresh claim.

out for each of the processes, whether enforcement is either a one-stage or two-stage process, and the nature of the procedure to be followed.

If the claim has been adjourned or stayed on terms then it may be possible to revive it.

COSTS ONLY PROCEEDINGS

29.20 In cases where costs have to be assessed, but there are no existing substantive proceedings between the parties, the claimant may use the procedure in CPR, r 44.12A to obtain an order for a detailed assessment of its costs pursuant to the compromise agreement. This rule is intended to provide a solution to the problem that, as a technical matter, in the absence of court proceedings between the parties there was no mechanism for the court to conduct a detailed assessment of costs. CPR, r 44.12A sets out a procedure which may be followed where:

- the parties to a dispute have reached an agreement on all issues (including which party is to pay the costs), which is made or confirmed in writing; but
- they have failed to agree the amount of those costs; and
- no proceedings have been started.

29.21 In such a case either party may commence proceedings using the CPR Part 8 procedure (CPR, r 44.12A(2)) seeking an order that the compromised costs be determined by the court by a detailed assessment. The only orders the court can make under CPR, r 44.12A are an order for a detailed assessment (thus allowing the assessment of the costs to be dealt with by the court despite there being no substantive proceedings) or an order dismissing the claim (CPR, r 44.12A(4)). The claim will be dismissed if it is opposed (CPR, r 44.12A(4)(b)). The intention is that Part 8 proceedings under the rule should effectively be brought with the consent of both parties as a convenient way of resolving the dispute over the amount of the compromised costs.

29.22 What CPR, r 44.12A does not do is to provide a means of resolving what the parties meant by an unclear term as to costs in a compromise agreement (see 20.58). As soon as the defendant raises such a problem, the Part 8 claim under CPR, r 44.12A will be dismissed. A dispute over whether a compromise agreement is enforceable or over what it means can only be dealt with by normal litigation (using the usual CPR, Part 7, procedure). Guidance issued by the Senior Costs Judge in 2000 was to the effect that if a claimant is forced to commence proceedings under Part 7, rather than costs only proceedings under Part 8, defendants will find themselves having to pay not only the reasonable and proportionate costs of the claim, but also the costs of the Part 7 proceedings and any related assessment proceedings. If the defendant has acted unreasonably in compelling the commencement of Part 7 proceedings, consideration should be given to making an order for costs on the indemnity basis.

ENFORCEMENT OF CONSTRUCTION INDUSTRY ADJUDICATION DECISIONS

29.23 A party with the benefit of an adjudicator's decision under the Housing Grants, Construction and Regeneration Act 1996 s 108 (Chapter 22) may bring enforcement proceedings in the courts by issuing a Part 8 claim form, and then entering default judgment (*Coventry Scaffolding Co (London) Ltd v Lancsville Construction Ltd* [2009] EWHC 2995 (TCC)) if there is no acknowledgment of service, or otherwise applying for summary judgment. In most cases summary judgment will be entered in accordance with the policy of the Act (see Chapter 22).

29.24 Summary judgment will be refused, however, if the defendant advances a properly arguable jurisdictional objection. A dispute as to whether there was a written construction contract between the parties (*Pegram Shopfitters Ltd v Tally Weijl (UK) Ltd* [2004] 1 WLR 2082), or a dispute that the defendant was a party to the relevant contract (*Estor Ltd v Multifit (UK) Ltd* (2009) 126 Con LR 40), or whether the agreement has been replaced (*Lead Technical Services Ltd v CMS Medical Ltd* [2007] BLR 251), may be effective objections.

29.25 A number of other situations where a valid objection to the adjudicator's decision may be mounted include cases where:

- the adjudicator was not the person nominated by the contract, or was not appointed in accordance with the agreed procedure (*Amec Projects Ltd v Whitefriars City Estates Ltd* [2004] EWHC (TCC) 393);
- there is a real risk the adjudicator was biased (*Glencott Development v Barrett* [2001] BLR 207);
- the decision was not responsive to the issues referred to adjudication (*Ballast plc v The Burrell Company* [2001] BLR 529);
- there is no dispute, because the matter was not previously brought to the attention of the other party (*Fastrack v Morrison* [2000] BLR 168); and
- the adjudicator acted unfairly, resulting in significant prejudice, such as where the adjudicator allowed new claims to be added without giving the defendant an opportunity to respond (*Project Services v Opek Prime Development Ltd* [2000] BLR 402).

29.26 If the defendant has agreed that the adjudicator can rule on the issue of jurisdiction and that they will be bound by the adjudicator's decision, summary judgment will be entered even if the adjudicator is wrong (*Thomas-Fredric's (Construction) Ltd v Wilson* [2004] BLR 23 at [20]). Summary judgment may also be entered if the defendant has not submitted to the adjudicator's jurisdiction, provided the adjudicator's decision is plainly right (*Thomas-Fredric's (Construction) Ltd v Wilson*). Summary judgment will also be entered where the defendant has not paid the amount due under an architect's certificate, unless the defendant has given an effective notice of intention to withhold payment under s 111. This is so even if the certificate might be wrong (*Rupert Morgan Building Services (LLC) Ltd v Jervis* [2004] 1 WLR 1867).

ARBITRATION SETTLEMENTS AND AWARDS

Negotiated settlements in arbitration proceedings

29.27 Where the parties settle their dispute after referring the matter to arbitration, it will be necessary to bring the arbitration to an end, and also to deal with the costs of the arbitration and the arbitrator's fees. As with litigation, the form of the settlement may have itself effected an end of the dispute, or the settlement may be conditional on performance by one of the parties, or it may require the entry of an award in the agreed terms. One great advantage in recording the agreed terms in an arbitrator's award is that it will then be enforceable, such as under the New York Convention 1958, in the same way as other arbitral awards (see 29.29).

Enforcement of domestic arbitral awards

Under the Arbitration Act 1996 s 66(1) the court may grant permission to enforce an award **29.28** of an arbitral tribunal in the same manner as a judgment or order of the court. Permission is sought by issued an arbitration claim form in the High Court, which is considered without notice (CPR 62.18). Permission to enforce an award will not be given where, or to the extent that, the person against whom it is sought to be enforced shows that the tribunal lacked substantive jurisdiction to make the award (s 66(3), which is considered at 26.48). There are very strong policy reasons in favour of granting permission, and unless there are grounds for impeaching the award, permission is usually granted (*Tongyuan (USA) International Trading Group v Uni-Clan Ltd* (unreported, 19 January 2001).

Recognition and enforcement of New York Convention arbitration awards

The New York Convention 1958 on the recognition and enforcement of arbitral awards is **29.29** one of the most successful international treaties of its kind, having been ratified by no less than 144 countries (at the last count only 51 countries, mostly quite small countries, had not ratified it). In practical terms it means that arbitral awards are enforceable almost all over the world, and this alone is one of the major advantages of using arbitration over most other ways of resolving disputes. Enforcement of an arbitration award under the New York Convention is in addition to seeking permission to enforce under the Arbitration Act 1996 s 66 (see ss 66(4) and 104).

The New York Convention applies to arbitral awards made in the territory of a state other **29.30** than the state where the recognition and enforcement of such awards are sought, and arising out of differences between persons, whether physical or legal (Art I). It also applies to arbitral awards not considered as domestic awards in the state where their recognition and enforcement are sought. In deciding whether the Convention applies, an award shall be treated as made at the seat of the arbitration, regardless of where it was signed, despatched or delivered to any of the parties (Arbitration Act 1996 s 100(2)).

A New York Convention award may be relied on by way of defence or set-off in any legal **29.31** proceedings, or, with the permission of the court, be enforced in the same manner as a judgment or order of the court (s 101). Where permission is given, judgment may be entered in terms of the award (s 101(3)). Technically, there are two procedures that may be used:

- to apply for permission to enforce the award as if it were a High Court judgment, but without entering the award as a judgment in the court; or
- to apply for permission to enter the award as a High Court judgment. It then has the status of a High Court judgment, and can be enforced as such.

A party seeking the recognition or enforcement of a New York Convention award must by **29.32** s 102(1) produce:

- the duly authenticated original award or a duly certified copy; and
- the original arbitration agreement or a duly certified copy.

29.33 If the award or agreement is in a foreign language, the party seeking recognition must also produce a translation certified by an official or sworn translator or by a diplomatic or consular agent (s 102(2)).

Grounds for refusing recognition or enforcement of a New York Convention award

29.34 Recognition or enforcement of a New York Convention award may be refused (see the Arbitration Act 1996 s 103) only if the person against whom it was made proves that:

- a party to the arbitration agreement was under some incapacity;
- the arbitration agreement was not valid under the law to which the parties subjected it or, failing any indication on the award itself, under the law of the country where the award was made;
- he was not given proper notice of the appointment of the arbitrator or of the arbitration proceedings or was otherwise unable to present his case;
- the award deals with a difference not contemplated by or not falling within the terms of the submission to arbitration or contains decisions on matters beyond the scope of the submission to arbitration;
- the composition of the arbitral tribunal or the arbitral procedure was not in accordance with the agreement of the parties or, failing such agreement, with the law of the country in which the arbitration took place;
- the award has not yet become binding on the parties, or has been set aside or suspended by a competent authority of the country in which, or under the law of which, it was made;
- the award is in respect of a matter that is not capable of settlement by arbitration; or
- it would be contrary to public policy to recognise or enforce the award.

Enforcement of Geneva Convention awards

29.35 The Arbitration Act 1996 s 99 provides for the continuing effect of the UK's obligations under the Geneva Convention on the execution of foreign arbitral awards that are not also New York Convention awards. While there are 49 countries that are signatories to the Geneva Convention (Arbitration (Foreign Awards) Order 1984 (SI 1984/1168)), there is a great deal of overlap with countries that are parties to the New York Convention. As the latter takes precedence over the Geneva Convention, the Geneva Convention has relatively limited practical application.

KEY POINTS SUMMARY

29.36
- Most compromises operate as contracts, and can be enforced by suing on the compromise agreement.
- There are some exceptions, such as where a compromise agreement is conditional on the performance by one side of the compromise terms (in which case the original cause of action revives).
- Construction adjudication awards can be enforced by suing on the award and entering default or summary judgment. Judgment is usually entered in accordance with the policy of 'pay now, argue later'.

- Where there are existing court proceedings, a compromise is often incorporated into a consent order or Tomlin order.
- Compromises recorded in court orders and judgments can usually be enforced directly using the court's enforcement procedures.
- Sometimes, for example terms included in the schedule to a Tomlin order, enforcement follows a two-stage process.
- Where there is a compromise of a dispute on terms that one side will pay the other's costs, but there are no existing proceedings, CPR, r 44.12A, provides a special procedure commenced by a Part 8 claim form to get a court order for the assessment of those costs.
- Domestic arbitration awards can be enforced as a court judgment with the leave of the court under the Arbitration Act 1996 s 66.
- International arbitration awards can be enforced and recognised cheaply and easily under the New York Convention.

APPENDICES

ADR providers

The Academy of Experts
3 Gray's Inn Square
Gray's Inn
London
WC1R 5AH
Tel: 0207 430 0333
www.academy-experts.org

ACAS (Advisory, Conciliation and Arbitration Service)
Euston Tower
286 Euston Road
London
NW1 3JJ
Tel: 020 7396 0022
National Helpline: 08457 47 47 47
www.acas.org.uk

ADR Chambers (UK) Limited
City Point
1 Ropemaker Street
London
EC2Y 9HT
Tel: 0845 072 0111
www.adrchambers.co.uk

ADR Group
Grove House
Grove Road
Redland
Bristol
BS6 6UN
Tel: 0117 946 7180
www.adrgroup.co.uk

ADR NOW
Advice Services Alliance
The Administrative Team
12th floor, New London Bridge House
25 London Bridge Street
London
SE1 9SG
www.adrnow.org.uk

Association of Midlands Mediators
PO Box 14188
Birmingham
B2 2HJ
Tel: 0800 633 5460
www.ammediators.co.uk

Association of Northern Mediators
Icon Business Centre
4100 Park Approach
Thorpe Park
Leeds
LS15 8GB
Tel: 0113 399 3435
www.northernmediators.co.uk

Centre for Effective Dispute Resolution (CEDR)
International Dispute Resolution Centre
70 Fleet Street
London
EC4Y 1EU
Tel: 020 7536 6000
www.cedr.co.uk
info@cedr-solve.com

The City Disputes Panel (specialists in ADR in financial services industry
24 Angel Gate
City Road
London EC1V 2PT
Tel: 020 7520 3817
www.citydisputespanel.org

Civil Mediation Council
The Secretary
Civil Mediation Council
Fourth Floor 218 Strand
London
WC2R 1AT
www.civilmediation.org

**Conflict Management Plus Ltd
(specialists in workplace mediation)**
Low Farm
Bassingbourn
Royston
Herts
SG8 5NT
Tel: 0844 504 8874
www.conflictmanagementplus.com

**Construction Contracts Mediators'
Group (CCMG) (specialists in
construction mediation)**
70 Fleet Street
London
EC4Y 1EU
Tel: 020 7353 8000
www.ccmg.co.uk

**Council of the Bar of England and Wales
(barristers who are accredited mediators)**
289–293 High Holborn
London
WC1V 7HZ
Tel: 020 7242 0082
www.barcouncil.org.uk

**Hardwicke Building (barristers
providing Commercial Dispute
Resolution Service)**
Hardwicke Building
New Square
Lincoln's Inn
London
WC2A 3SB
Tel: 020 7242 2523
www.hardwicke.co.uk.

**IDRS Ltd Dispute Resolution Services (a
subsidiary of the Chartered Institute of
Arbitrators undertaking ADR processes
for the construction and property sector)**
24 Angel Gate
City Road
London
EC1V 2PT
Tel: 020 7520 3800
www.idrs.ltd.uk

In Place of Strife
The International Dispute Resolution
Centre
70 Fleet Street
London EC4Y 1EU
Tel: 020 7917 9449
www.mediate.co.uk

**InterMediation (part of the Intersolve
Group)**
International House
1 St Katherine's Way
London
E1W 1UN
Tel: 0207 977 0600

Littleton Dispute Resolution Services Ltd
Littleton Chambers
3 Kings Bench Walk North
Temple
London
EC4Y 7HR
Tel: 0207 797 8600
www.littletonchambers.com

**Maritime Solicitors Mediation Service
(MSMS) (specialists in mediation in
maritime disputes and all matters
relating to carriage of goods by sea and
marine insurance)**
www.msmsg.com

Midlands Mediation
8 Green Lane
Belper
Derbyshire
DE56 1BY
Tel: 0845 200 8232
www.ukmediation.net

National Mediation Helpline
Clerksroom
Equity House
Blackbrook Park Avenue
Taunton
TA1 2PX
Tel: 0845 60 30 809
www.nationalmediationhelpline.com

Resolution (healthcare industry specialists)
Central Office
PO Box 302
Orpington
Kent BR6 8QX
Tel: 01689 820272
www.resolution.org.uk

UK College of Family Mediators (sets professional standards for family mediation)
3rd Floor, Alexander House
Telephone Avenue
Bristol BS1 4BS
Tel: 01179 047 223
www.ukcfm.co.uk

EXPERT DETERMINATION PROVIDERS

The Academy of Experts
Details set out above.

CEDR
Details set out above.

The Chartered Institute of Arbitrators (CIArb) International Arbitration and Mediation Centre
12 Bloomsbury Square
London
WC1A 2LP
Tel: 0207 421 7444
www.arbitrators.org.uk

The City Disputes Panel
24 Angel Gate
City Road
London
EC1V 2PT
Tel: 020 7520 3800/ 020 7520 3817
www.idrs.ltd.uk/www.citydisputespanel.org

Institute of Civil Engineers
1 Great George Street
Westminster
London
SW1P 3AA
Tel: 020 7222 7722
www.ice.org.uk

The Law Society of England and Wales
113 Chancery Lane
London
WC2A 1PL
Tel: 020 7242 1222
www.lawsociety.org.uk

Royal Institute of British Architects
66 Portland Place
London
W1B 1AD
Tel: 020 7580 5533
www.architecture.com

Royal Institute of Chartered Surveyors
Dispute Resolution Service
Surveyor Court
Westwood Way
Coventry
CV4 8JE
Tel: 0207 334 3608
www.rics.org

INTERNATIONAL ADR SERVICE PROVIDERS

International Mediation Institute (IMI)
Laan van Meerdervoort 70
2517 AN The Hague
The Netherlands
www.imimediation.org
Includes a directory of IMI certified
mediators throughout the world.

**World Intellectual Property Organisation
Arbitration and Mediation Centre
(WIPO)**
34, chemin des Colombettes
CH-1211 Geneva 20
Switzerland
Tel: +41 22 338 9111
www.wipo.int.

This is based in Geneva, Switzerland.

Useful for international commercial disputes between private parties in technology and intellectual property and entertainment disputes.

APPENDIX 2

Agreement to Mediate

Ref No.	If applicable

We the undersigned, namely:

_____

       (*Print name*)

and:_____

    (*Print name*)

and:_____

    (*Print name*)

and:_____

    (*Print name*)

agree to the mediation of the dispute between us on the following terms and conditions.

1. The Mediation

Mediation is a non-adversarial procedure in which a neutral, specially trained professional assists the parties in reaching a settlement of a dispute or difference. The mediator avoids being judgmental, but rather employs techniques, which facilitate constructive and productive negotiations. Throughout, the parties remain in complete control and ultimately decide whether and how a dispute will be settled. In the event that the parties agree to settle, that settlement will be documented in a form called a Mediation Settlement.

The mediation session normally begins with a brief joint meeting at which the all the parties come together to understand the background to the dispute and any underlying issues, to identify the party's true interests and to explore possible ways in which the dispute might be resolved. Thereafter the mediator conducts a series of private sessions with each party during which settlement positions are discussed.

The parties may wish to consult with their legal and/or other advisers before and during the mediation as the mediator at no time acts as legal adviser to any of the parties.

The parties must agree to have present at the mediation such persons as are authorised to agree settlement terms. Most mediators will request the attendance of the individuals involved in the dispute at the mediation in addition to any representatives they may wish to attend.

Note: This Agreement may be amended from time to time. Check www.nationalmediation helpline.com for the most up to date edition of this agreement.

The Mediator may ask the parties' consent to a co-mediator or observer being present at the mediation.

2. The Mediator

The parties (all sides to the dispute) agree to an appointment of an Accredited Mediator by [**Name of organisation**] to assist in the resolution of their dispute. The parties understand that:—

- the mediator is independent, neutral and is not employed by or acting as a representative of the Ministry of Justice (MoJ)
- the role of the mediator is to facilitate settlement of the dispute by negotiation and agreement where possible
- the mediator does not give legal advice and will not adjudicate the dispute
- the mediator will not and cannot compel the parties to settle, nor even to continue negotiating should they not wish to do so
- the parties agree to participate in negotiations in good faith with the aim of achieving a settlement

Save in the case of gross error or misconduct the parties agree that they will respect the neutrality of the mediator, any professional body to which the mediator may belong and HMCS and not bring any claim, demands or proceedings against any or all of theses, arising out of the appointment of the mediator or the conduct of the mediation.

3. Private Sessions

During the mediation, the mediator will speak to the parties separately in order to improve the mediator's understanding of each party's views. Information given to the mediator during such private talks will be confidential unless the party involved confirms that they are happy for the mediator to give such information to the other party.

4. Confidentiality

Other than what is contained within a Mediation Settlement, any information—whether written in a document prepared for the mediation or written or spoken during the mediation—can only be used for the purpose of the mediation and cannot be referred to in any subsequent action unless all parties agree.

The parties agree that no recording or transcript will be made at the time of the mediation and that they will not call the mediator, or the mediation provider [or MoJ] to give evidence in any subsequent action.

5. Costs

Unless the parties otherwise agree, the fees and expenses of the mediator will be borne by the parties in equal share. Each party will also pay its own expenses of individual representation in the mediation. The fees of the mediator are payable in advance. In the event that the mediation does not result in a settlement, this clause does not prevent a court or other tribunal with appropriate power from treating both the mediator's fee and each party's legal costs as costs of, or incidental to, the proceedings.

If prior to the mediation or during the mediation itself it becomes apparent that the amount in dispute is higher than that originally discussed with either the NMH adviser or the Mediation Provider and / or Mediator allocated, and upon which the mediation fee invoiced by the Mediation Provider and / or Mediator was based; then the Mediation Provider and / or Mediator reserves the right to invoice the Parties for any additional amount that would have been due, in accordance with the published NMH fee scales.

6. Ending the mediation

The mediator, or any party to the mediation, may end the mediation at any time without giving a reason. If one of the parties wishes to end the mediation the mediator may request that they give him/her a few minutes notice.

In this event if the dispute is subject to court proceeding the trial judge will only be made aware that a mediation had taken place and a settlement had not been reached.

7. Ongoing evaluation

Both the NMH and the accredited mediator providers supporting this scheme are continually looking at ways to improve the service we provide our customers.

Please indicate below if you are willing to be contacted by the NMH for feedback in relation to the mediation process from first contact to actual mediation. Any information given will remain confidential.

<u>Acceptance</u>

Name	
Address	
Signed	
Date	
☐	Yes, I agree to being contacted by the NMH for feedback of the service provided after the mediation.

Name	
Address	
Signed	
Date	
☐	Yes, I agree to being contacted by the NMH for feedback of the service provided after the mediation.

Name	
Address	
Signed	
Date	
☐	Yes, I agree to being contacted by the NMH for feedback of the service provided after the mediation.

Name	
Address	
Signed	
Date	
☐	Yes, I agree to being contacted by the NMH for feedback of the service provided after the mediation.

Mediators Signature: _____

Mediators Name:
_____
              (*Print name*)

Date: _____

Once completed, please return to: [**Provider's name and address**]

CEDR MODEL MEDIATION AGREEMENT

CEDR Centre for Effective Dispute Resolution

Model Mediation Agreement

Eleventh Edition
January 2010

Note: This Agreement may be amended from time to time. Check www.cedr.com for the latest version of this agreement.

CEDR Centre for Effective Dispute Resolution

www.cedr.co.uk

CEDR Model Mediation Agreement

THIS AGREEMENT   dated   **IS MADE BETWEEN**

Party A

....*of* ....

Party B

.... *of* ....
(together referred to as "**the Parties**")

The Mediator
.... *of* ....

(a term which includes any agreed **Assistant Mediator**)

and

CEDR Solve of IDRC, 70 Fleet Street, London EC4Y 1EU

in relation to a mediation to be held

on ....
at ....
("**the Mediation**")

concerning a dispute between the Parties in relation to

....
....
....
....

("**the Dispute**")

IT IS AGREED by those signing this Agreement THAT:

The Mediation

1   The Parties agree to attempt in good faith to settle the Dispute at the Mediation. All signing this Agreement agree that the Mediation will be conducted in accordance with its terms and consistent with the CEDR Solve Model Mediation Procedure and the CEDR Code of Conduct for Mediators current at the date of this Agreement.

Centre for Effective Dispute Resolution International Dispute Resolution Centre 70 Fleet Street London EC4Y 1EU
Tel +44 (0)20 7536 6000 Fax +44 (0)20 7536 6001 E-mail info@cedr.co.uk www.cedr.com
Registered in England as Centre for Effective Dispute Resolution Limited number 2422813 Registered Charity number 1060369

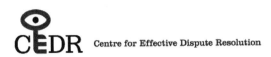

CEDR Centre for Effective Dispute Resolution

Authority and status

2 The person signing this Agreement on behalf of each Party warrants having authority to bind that Party and all other persons present on that Party's behalf at the Mediation to observe the terms of this Agreement, and also having authority to bind that Party to the terms of any settlement.

3 The Mediator is operating as an independent contractor (unless an employee of CEDR Solve), and neither the Mediator nor CEDR Solve is an agent for any of the Parties in relation to the Dispute or this Agreement.

4 Neither the Mediator nor CEDR Solve shall be liable to the Parties for any act or omission in relation to the Mediation unless the act or omission is proved to have been fraudulent or involved wilful misconduct.

Confidentiality and without prejudice status

5 Every person involved in the Mediation:

5.1 will keep confidential all information arising out of or in connection with the Mediation, including the fact and terms of any settlement, but not including the fact that the Mediation is to take place or has taken place or where disclosure is required by law to implement or to enforce terms of settlement; and

5.2 acknowledges that all such information passing between the Parties, the Mediator and/or CEDR Solve, however communicated, is agreed to be without prejudice to any Party's legal position and may not be produced as evidence or disclosed to any judge, arbitrator or other decision-maker in any legal or other formal process, except where otherwise disclosable in law.

6 Where a Party privately discloses to the Mediator any information in confidence before, during or after the Mediation, the Mediator will not disclose that information to any other Party or person without the consent of the Party disclosing it, unless required by law to make disclosure.

7 The Parties will not call the Mediator or any employee or consultant of CEDR Solve as a witness, nor require them to produce in evidence any records or notes relating to the Mediation, in any litigation, arbitration or other formal process arising from or in connection with the Dispute and the Mediation; nor will the Mediator nor any CEDR Solve employee or consultant act or agree to act as a witness, expert, arbitrator or consultant in any such process. If any Party does make such an application, that Party will fully indemnify the Mediator or the employee or consultant of CEDR Solve in respect of any costs any of them incur in resisting and/or responding to such an application, including reimbursement at the Mediator's standard hourly rate for the Mediator's time spent in resisting and/or responding to such application.

Centre for Effective Dispute Resolution International Dispute Resolution Centre 70 Fleet Street London EC4Y 1EU
Tel +44 (0)20 7536 6000 Fax +44 (0)20 7536 6001 E-mail info@cedr.co.uk www.cedr.com
Registered in England as Centre for Effective Dispute Resolution Limited number 2422813 Registered Charity number 1060369

www.cedr.co.uk

8   No verbatim recording or transcript of the Mediation will be made in any form.

Settlement formalities

9   No terms of settlement reached at the Mediation will be legally binding until set out in writing and signed by or on behalf of each of the Parties.

Fees and costs of the Mediation

10   The Parties will be responsible for the fees and expenses of CEDR Solve and the Mediator (**"the Mediation Fees"**) in accordance with CEDR Solve's Terms and Conditions of Business current at the date of this Agreement.

11   Unless otherwise agreed by the Parties and CEDR Solve in writing, each Party agrees to share the Mediation Fees equally and also to bear its own legal and other costs and expenses of preparing for and attending the Mediation (**"each Party's Legal Costs"**) prior to the Mediation. However, each Party further agrees that any court or tribunal may treat both the Mediation Fees and each Party's Legal Costs as costs in the case in relation to any litigation or arbitration where that court or tribunal has power to assess or make orders as to costs, whether or not the Mediation results in settlement of the Dispute.

Legal status and effect of the Mediation

12   Any contemplated or existing litigation or arbitration in relation to the Dispute may be started or continued despite the Mediation, unless the Parties agree or a Court orders otherwise.

13   This Agreement is governed by the law of [England and Wales] and the courts of [England and Wales] shall have exclusive jurisdiction to decide any matters arising out of or in connection with this Agreement and the Mediation.

14   The referral of the dispute to the Mediation does not affect any rights that exist under Article 6 of the European Convention of Human Rights, and if the Dispute does not settle through the Mediation, the Parties' right to a fair trial remains unaffected.

Changes to this Agreement

15   All agreed changes to this Agreement and/or the Model Procedure are set out as follows:

Centre for Effective Dispute Resolution International Dispute Resolution Centre 70 Fleet Street London EC4Y 1EU
Tel +44 (0)20 7536 6000 Fax +44 (0)20 7536 6001 E-mail info@cedr.co.uk www.cedr.com
Registered in England as Centre for Effective Dispute Resolution Limited number 2422813 Registered Charity number 1060369

CEDR Centre for Effective Dispute Resolution

www.cedr.co.uk

Signed

Party A _____

Party B _____

Mediator _____

CEDR Solve _____

Centre for Effective Dispute Resolution International Dispute Resolution Centre 70 Fleet Street London EC4Y 1EU
Tel +44 (0)20 7536 6000 Fax +44 (0)20 7536 6001 E-mail info@cedr.co.uk www.cedr.com
Registered in England as Centre for Effective Dispute Resolution Limited number 2422813 Registered Charity number 1060369

CEDR NOTES TO MODEL MEDIATION AGREEMENT

| Centre for Effective Dispute Resolution | **www.cedr.com**

Notes for CEDR Solve's Model Mediation Agreement and Model Procedure and Code of Conduct

CEDR Solve keeps its Model Mediation Agreement and Procedure under constant review in the light of developments in law and practice and to keep it as useful and effective as possible.

The CEDR Model Mediation Agreement is intended for use with the CEDR Model Mediation Procedure (**Model Procedure**). The Model Procedure explains what mediation is and explains the roles of the mediator, each party and their adviser, and explains how complaints can be made.

In the UK, the whole legal framework of any mediation is largely dependent on the contract formed between the parties to the mediation, which makes its terms absolutely crucial. The following notes highlight some particularly topical or recently changed provisions but parties should carefully review each term of the Mediation Agreement and Model Procedure to ensure that it accurately reflects their requirements:

- In **Clause 1** of the Agreement, all parties agree that the mediation is to be conducted in accordance with the Model Procedure. This ensures for the purposes of ADR contract clauses in commercial contracts that, as required by *Cable & Wireless v IBM*, there is a clearly defined procedure to the parties to follow, preventing any suggestion that such a clause is a mere "agreement to agree". Also, the mediator contracts to abide by the CEDR Code of Conduct.
- In **Clause 2**, each party warrants that someone has authority to bind them to the mediation agreement and to any settlement terms. In public cases, this may need amendment where a party only has authority to recommend settlement to a departmental Minister, local authority or board.
- **Clause 4** limits liability for a mediator to cases of fraudulent acts or omissions, or those involving wilful misconduct.
- **Clause 7** confirms that the mediator shall not act as a witness and includes provision for indemnification of the mediator's costs in resisting and/or responding to any such application by a party.
- **Clause 11** provides that where a court or tribunal has power to assess or order costs against a party, it may treat the mediation fees and any party's legal costs of preparing for and attending the mediation as costs in the case, and therefore awardable on the merits of the litigation. It does **not** enable the court to enquire about what happened at the mediation to inform that decision: what happened at the mediation remains confidential by virtue of Clauses 5 to 8.

Centre for Effective Dispute Resolution

CEDR Solve code of conduct for third party neutrals

April 2008

1 Introduction

This Code of Conduct ("the Code") applies to any person who acts as a Mediator or other neutral third party ("the Neutral") in any dispute resolution procedure ("the Process") conducted under the auspices of the Centre for Effective Dispute Resolution ("CEDR Solve") in relation to an attempt to resolve a dispute or difference ("the Dispute") between all the parties ("the Parties") to the Dispute under the terms of a written agreement signed by the Parties the Neutral and CEDR Solve ("the Process Agreement") to seek resolution of the Dispute.

2 Competence and availability

The Neutral assures the Parties that he or she:

2.1 possesses the necessary competence and knowledge about the Process to deal with the Dispute, based on proper training and updating of education and practice in the necessary skills; and

2.2 has sufficient time to prepare properly for and conduct the Process expeditiously and efficiently.

3 Fees and expenses

The Neutral undertakes:

3.1 to make clear either directly to the Parties or through CEDR Solve the basis for charging fees and expenses as between CEDR Solve and the Parties for the conduct of the Process before the Process starts; and

3.2 not to prolong the Process unnecessarily where there is, in the Neutral's opinion, no reasonable likelihood of progress being made towards settlement of the Dispute through the Process.

4 Independence and neutrality

The Neutral:

4.1 will at all times act, and endeavour to be seen to act fairly, independently and with complete impartiality towards the Parties in the Process, without any bias in favour of, or discrimination against, any of the Parties;

4.2 will ensure that the Parties and their representatives all have adequate opportunities to be involved in the Process;

CEDR 2008

Centre for Effective Dispute Resolution International Dispute Resolution Centre 70 Fleet Street London EC4Y 1EU
Tel +44 (0) 20 7536 6000 Fax +44 (0)20 7536 6001 E-mail info@cedr.co.uk www.cedr.com
Registered in England as Centre for Effective Dispute Resolution Limited number 2422813 Registered Charity number 1060369

4.3 will disclose to the Parties any matter of which the Neutral is or at any time becomes aware which could be regarded as being or creating a conflict of interest (whether apparent, potential or real) in relation to the Dispute or any of the Parties involved in the Process, and, having done so, will not act or continue to act as Neutral in relation to the Dispute unless the Parties specifically acknowledge such disclosure and agree to the Neutral's continuing to act in the Process: such matters include but are not limited to:

- any personal or business relationship with any of the Parties;
- any financial or other interest in the outcome of the Mediation;
- having acted (either personally or through the Neutral's own firm or business) in any capacity other than as a Neutral in another Process for any of the Parties;
- being in prior possession of any confidential information about any of the Parties or about the subject-matter of the Dispute (but excluding any confidential information given to the Neutral by one of the Parties while acting as Neutral in relation to the Dispute)
- any such matters involving a close member of the Neutral's family.

4.4 will not (nor will any member of the Neutral's own firm or business or close family) act for any of the Parties individually in relation to the Dispute either while acting as Neutral or at any time thereafter, without the written consent of all the Parties.

5   Conduct of the Process

The Neutral will observe all the terms of the Process Agreement (especially as regards confidentiality) and will conduct the Process consistent with any relevant CEDR Model Procedure.

6   Professional Indemnity Insurance

The Neutral will take out professional indemnity insurance in an adequate amount with a responsible insurer against such risks as may arise in the performance of the Neutral's duties in relation to the Dispute before acting as a Neutral.

7   Withdrawing from any Process

7.1 The Neutral **will** withdraw from the Process and cease to act as such in relation to the Dispute if the Neutral:

- is requested to do so by one of the Parties, except where the Parties have agreed to a procedure involving a binding decision by the Neutral to conclude the Mediation;

Centre for Effective Dispute Resolution International Dispute Resolution Centre 70 Fleet Street London EC4Y 1EU
Tel +44 (0) 20 7536 6000 Fax +44 (0)20 7536 6001 E-mail info@cedr.co.uk www.cedr.com
Registered in England as Centre for Effective Dispute Resolution Limited number 2422813 Registered Charity number 1060369

- would be in breach of the Code if continuing to act as the Neutral; or
- is required by one or more of the Parties to act or refrain from acting in a way which would be in material breach of the Code or in breach of the law.

7.2   The Neutral **may** withdraw from the Process at the Neutral's own discretion and after such consultation with the Parties as the Neutral deems necessary and appropriate (and always subject to the Neutral's obligations as to confidentiality) if:

- any of the Parties is acting in material breach of the Process Agreement;
- any of the Parties is acting in an unconscionable or criminal manner;
- the Neutral decides that continuing the Process is unlikely to result in a settlement;
- any of the Parties alleges that the Neutral is in material breach of the Code.

8   Complaints

The Neutral will respond to, and co-operate with, any complaints procedure initiated by a party through CEDR Solve in relation to the Process in which the Neutral acted, including attending (without charging a fee or claiming any expenses for attending) any meeting convened by CEDR Solve as part of that complaints procedure.

Centre for Effective Dispute Resolution International Dispute Resolution Centre 70 Fleet Street London EC4Y 1EU
Tel +44 (0) 20 7536 6000 Fax +44 (0)20 7536 6001 E-mail info@cedr.co.uk www.cedr.com
Registered in England as Centre for Effective Dispute Resolution Limited number 2422813 Registered Charity number 1060369

CEDR MODEL EXPERT DETERMINATION AGREEMENT

CEDR Centre for Effective Dispute Resolution

Model Expert Determination Agreement

Including guidance notes

Note: This Agreement may be amended from time to time. Check www.cedr.com for the latest version of this agreement.

CEDR Centre for Effective Dispute Resolution

www.cedr.co.uk

Model Expert Determination Agreement

Text in italics indicates where information has to be added.
Text in square brackets indicates where a choice has to be made.

Please refer to the guidance notes for commentary on and help with the completion of this Agreement.

Date

Parties

_____ ("Party A")

_____ ("Party B")

_____ ("Party C") etc.
(jointly "the Parties")   *Add full names and addresses*

_____ ("the Expert")

Centre for Effective Dispute Resolution Limited ("CEDR Solve") of IDRC, 70 Fleet Street, London EC4Y1EU

Dispute
("the Dispute")

Here set out the scope of the dispute to be determined.

_____

_____

_____

_____

_____

Centre for Effective Dispute Resolution, International Dispute Resolution Centre, 70 Fleet Street London EC4Y 1EU
Tel +44 (0)20 7536 6000 Fax +44 (0)20 7536 6001 E-mail info@cedr.co.uk www.cedr.co.uk
Registered in England as Centre for Dispute Resolution Limited number 2422813 Registered Charity number 1060369

CEDR Centre for Effective Dispute Resolution

www.cedr.co.uk

Appointment of Expert

1   CEDR Solve will appoint an Expert to resolve the Dispute and has exclusive rights to do so under this Procedure. The Parties agree that the Expert will resolve the Dispute by Expert Determination. The Expert will act as an expert and not as an arbitrator or legal adviser.

Purpose of Expert Determination

2   Unless the Parties subsequently agree otherwise, this Expert Determination leads to a decision ("the Decision") being issued by the Expert via CEDR Solve. The Decision will be final and binding on the Parties.

Confidentiality

3   The Expert Determination process is private and confidential. The Parties, the Expert and CEDR Solve will keep confidential all information arising out of or in connection with the Expert Determination except where disclosure is required by law.

Independence

4   The Expert and CEDR Solve are independent of the Parties. They are neutral and impartial, and do not act as advisers to the Parties.

Conduct of Expert Determination

5   The Expert will conduct the Expert Determination in accordance with procedural directions which the Expert will seek to agree with the Parties. If they cannot be agreed, the Expert's directions will prevail.

Challenge to the procedure

6   The Parties agree that they are not permitted to challenge the Expert's directions on issues arising during the procedure including those on the Expert's own jurisdiction.

Mediation option

7   At any time before the issue of the Expert's decision the Parties may agree to refer the Dispute to mediation, in accordance with CEDR's Model Mediation Procedure. In that case each of the Parties notifies the Expert and CEDR Solve, and the Expert Determination is suspended. If the dispute is settled by mediation, the Expert Determination comes to an end and the Parties settle the fees and expenses of the Expert and of CEDR Solve. If the dispute is not settled by mediation, the Expert Determination resumes, and if the Expert has been acting as mediator, the Expert may take up his / her previous role.

Reasons in the Decision

8   The Expert's Decision [shall/shall not] include reasons.

Centre for Effective Dispute Resolution, International Dispute Resolution Centre, 70 Fleet Street London EC4Y 1EU
Tel +44 (0)20 7536 6000 Fax +44 (0)20 7536 6001 E-mail info@cedr.co.uk www.cedr.co.uk
Registered in England as Centre for Effective Dispute Resolution Limited number 2422813 Registered Charity number 1060369

Interest

9 The Expert is empowered to award interest as part of the Decision.

Fees and expenses

10 Unless the Parties agree otherwise, the parties are jointly and severally liable for the fees and expenses of the Expert Determination. The fees and expenses will be estimated by CEDR Solve upon receipt of the Agreement and paid to CEDR Solve, to be held on account before the Expert Determination starts. The Expert will be paid fees and expenses from the account and interim bills may be raised by CEDR Solve to cover these fees should the account run out of funds. A final account of the fees and expenses will be sent to the Parties by CEDR Solve when the Decision is ready for issue to the Parties and the Decision will be released on payment by the Parties of any further amounts due, if any. CEDR Solve will reimburse the Expert. If the Parties agree not to proceed with Expert Determination, CEDR Solve will refund a proportionate amount of the fees and expenses advanced, depending on the amount of work done by the Expert and CEDR Solve.

Implementation of the Decision

11 The Parties agree to implement the Decision within [e.g. - seven] days of the Decision being published to them.

Challenge to the Decision

12 The Parties agree that the decision of the Expert is final and binding and that the dispute cannot be referred to a subsequent tribunal.

No liability

13 The Parties expressly acknowledge that neither the Expert nor CEDR Solve shall be liable to the Parties for any act or omission whatsoever in connection with this Expert Determination.

Role of CEDR Solve

14 CEDR Solve appoints the Expert. The Expert is responsible for the procedure from then on. CEDR Solve may be consulted by any of the Parties to this Agreement in case of difficulty. Should the Expert be unable to complete the task, CEDR Solve will appoint a substitute Expert within a reasonable time. The same costs will apply in respect of CEDR Solve's fee for the appointment of any substitute Expert.

Centre for Effective Dispute Resolution, International Dispute Resolution Centre, 70 Fleet Street London EC4Y 1EU
Tel +44 (0)20 7536 6000 Fax +44 (0)20 7536 6001 E-mail info@cedr.co.uk www.cedr.co.uk
Registered in England as Centre for Effective Dispute Resolution Limited number 2422813 Registered Charity number 1060369

After the Decision

15 None of the Parties will call the Expert or CEDR Solve (or any employee, consultant, officer or representative of CEDR Solve) as a witness, consultant, arbitrator or expert in any litigation or arbitration in relation to the Dispute and the Expert and CEDR Solve will not act voluntarily in any such capacity.

Law and jurisdiction

16 This Agreement shall be governed by English law and under the jurisdiction of the English courts. All the Parties to this Agreement agree to refer any dispute arising in connection with it to mediation first.

Signed

On behalf of Party A _____

On behalf of Party B _____

[Signed on behalf of Party C_____]

Signed by the Expert _____

Signed on behalf of CEDR Solve _____

Schedule

CEDR Solve professional support fee	£	
Expert's fees	£	per hour
Payment to be made on account by each Party	£	by [date]

© CEDR 2008

Centre for Effective Dispute Resolution, International Dispute Resolution Centre, 70 Fleet Street London EC4Y 1EU
Tel +44 (0)20 7536 6000 Fax +44 (0)20 7536 6001 E-mail info@cedr.co.uk www.cedr.co.uk
Registered in England as Centre for Effective Dispute Resolution Limited number 2422813 Registered Charity number 1060369

Guidance Notes

Essential Information

The CEDR Model Expert Determination Agreement refers to the Parties to the Dispute, CEDR Solve and, of course, the Expert. The role of CEDR Solve is defined in paragraph 14 of the Agreement.

The section "Dispute", when completed, sets out how the dispute arose with a brief description of the issue(s).

Paragraphs 1 and 2 establish the appointment of the Expert, that the process is Expert Determination, and that the result is a Decision, which will be final and binding on the Parties. Paragraphs 3 and 4 establish the confidentiality of the process and the independence of the Expert and CEDR Solve.

The Procedure

Once appointed, the Expert will wish to establish the procedure. Paragraph 5 states that the Expert will seek to agree the procedure with the Parties, and that if agreement cannot be reached, the Expert's directions will prevail.

Procedural directions may deal with any or all of the following:
* a timetable for the submission of case summaries and supporting documents to the Expert with copies to each other;
* whether submissions are to be simultaneous or sequential;
* whether there should be one round or two rounds of submissions;
* whether the Expert has the power to call for documents; or
* whether the Expert has the power to award costs.

Challenge to the procedure

Paragraph 6 provides that the Parties have no right to challenge the Expert Determination procedure before the Decision is issued. This enhances the use of Expert Determination, is in the spirit of ADR and allows the Expert to do the work for the Parties as agreed without the time and expense of court applications.

Mediation option

Paragraph 7 provides that the Parties may agree to refer the dispute to mediation at any time before the Decision is made, provided the fees and expenses to date are paid, and that CEDR Solve will organise the mediation.

© CEDR 2008

Centre for Effective Dispute Resolution, International Dispute Resolution Centre, 70 Fleet Street London EC4Y 1EU
Tel +44 (0)20 7536 6000 Fax +44 (0)20 7536 6001 E-mail info@cedr.co.uk www.cedr.co.uk
Registered in England as Centre for Effective Dispute Resolution Limited number 2422813 Registered Charity number 1060369

Reasons in the Decision

Paragraph 8 gives the Parties a choice as to whether to include reasons in the Decision. The inclusion of reasons increases the cost, but may make the resolution of the Dispute by this means more attractive and therefore worth the extra cost.

Interest

The Expert does not have the power to award interest unless the Parties agree, so paragraph 9 gives the Expert that power.

Fees and expenses

Paragraph 10 deals with fees and expenses, some of which are payable in advance.

Consequences of the Decision

Paragraphs 11 and 12 deal with the consequences of the Decision. The Parties agree to implement it within an agreed period and agree that the Decision cannot be challenged.

No Liability

Paragraph 13 gives immunity from liability to the Expert and CEDR Solve.

Role of CEDR Solve

Paragraph 14 explains CEDR Solve's role, in making the appointment and other arrangements, and collecting the fees and expenses.

After the Decision

Paragraph 15 ensures that those involved in the Expert Determination do not get involved in future proceedings without the consent of all the Parties.

Law and Jurisdiction

Paragraph 16 establishes English law as the governing law of the Agreement, with disputes referred first to mediation and then to the English court. It may be necessary in international cases to provide that the language of the Expert Determination is to be English.

Centre for Effective Dispute Resolution, International Dispute Resolution Centre, 70 Fleet Street London EC4Y 1EU
Tel +44 (0)20 7536 6000 Fax +44 (0)20 7536 6001 E-mail info@cedr.co.uk www.cedr.co.uk
Registered in England as Centre for Effective Dispute Resolution Limited number 2422813 Registered Charity number 1060369

CEDR EARLY NEUTRAL EVALUATION AGREEMENT

CEDR Centre for Effective Dispute Resolution

Model Early Neutral Evaluation Agreement

Including guidance notes

Note: This Agreement may be amended from time to time. Check www.cedr.com for the latest version of this agreement.

CEDR Centre for Effective Dispute Resolution

Model Early Neutral Evaluation Agreement

Introduction

Early Neutral Evaluation:

- is quick, inexpensive and confidential;
- is informal; and
- produces a non-binding result that aims to provide an objective and independent assessment of the merits of a case.

Early Neutral Evaluation differs from arbitration in that it is non-binding and has greater informality. Unless the Parties agree that it should be, it is not subject to "due process" and can therefore be more flexible. In particular there is no need for a trial-type hearing. Unless the Parties agree otherwise, the Evaluator may conduct investigations independently of the Parties, and make the Recommendation based on those investigations without reference to the Parties. Parties should obtain legal advice when embarking on an Early Neutral Evaluation, but do not strictly need to be legally represented during the procedure.

Centre for Effective Dispute Resolution International Dispute Resolution Centre 70 Fleet Street London EC4Y 1EU
Tel +44 (0)20 7536 6000 Fax +44 (0)20 7536 6001 E-mail info@cedr.co.uk www.cedr.co.uk
Registered in England as Centre for Effective Dispute Resolution Limited number 2422813 Registered Charity number 1060369

CEDR   Centre for Effective Dispute Resolution

www.cedr.co.uk

Model Early Neutral Evaluation Agreement

Text in Italics indicates where information has to be added.
Text in square brackets indicates where a choice has to be made.

Please refer to the guidance notes for commentary on and help with the completion of this Agreement.

Date:

Parties

_____ ("Party A")

_____ ("Party B")

[_____ ("Party C")
etc.]

(jointly "the Parties")

Add full names and addresses

_____ ("the Evaluator")

Centre for Effective Dispute Resolution Limited ("CEDR Solve") of 70 Fleet Street, London, EC4Y 1EU

Dispute
("the Dispute")

Here set out details of the contract(s) or other legal relationship(s) and brief details of the dispute(s) to be resolved by Early Neutral Evaluation.

_____
_____
_____
_____
_____
_____
_____
_____
_____

Centre for Effective Dispute Resolution International Dispute Resolution Centre 70 Fleet Street London EC4Y 1EU
Tel +44 (0)20 7536 6000 Fax +44 (0)20 7536 6001 E-mail info@cedr.co.uk www.cedr.co.uk
Registered in England as Centre for Effective Dispute Resolution Limited number 2422813 Registered Charity number 1060369

CEDR Centre for Effective Dispute Resolution

Appointment of Evaluator

1   CEDR Solve has appointed the Evaluator to provide a non-binding recommendation on the Dispute.

Purpose of Early Neutral Evaluation

2   Unless the Parties subsequently agree otherwise, this Early Neutral Evaluation leads to a non-binding Recommendation ("the Recommendation") being issued by the Evaluator.

Confidentiality

3   The Early Neutral Evaluation process is private and confidential. The Parties, the Evaluator and CEDR Solve will keep the matter entirely confidential except as is required by law.

Independence

4   The Evaluator and CEDR Solve are independent of the Parties, neutral and impartial, and do not act as advisers to the Parties.

Conduct of Early Neutral Evaluation

5   The Evaluator will conduct the Early Neutral Evaluation in accordance with procedural directions which the Evaluator will seek to agree with the Parties. If they cannot be agreed, the Evaluator's directions will prevail.

Mediation Option

6   At any time before the issue of the Evaluator's Recommendation the Parties may agree to refer the Dispute to mediation, in accordance with CEDR's Model Mediation Procedure. In that case each of the Parties notifies the Evaluator and CEDR Solve, and the Early Neutral Evaluation is suspended. If the Dispute is settled by mediation, the Early Neutral Evaluation comes to an end and the Parties settle the fees and expenses of the Evaluator and of CEDR Solve. If the Dispute is not settled by mediation, the Early Neutral Evaluation resumes.

Reasons in the Recommendation

7   The Recommendation of the Evaluator [shall/shall not] include reasons.

Fees and Expenses

8   Unless the Parties agree otherwise, the fees and expenses of the Early Neutral Evaluation will be borne by the parties in equal shares. The fees and expenses will be estimated by CEDR Solve and paid to CEDR Solve as a condition precedent for the Early Neutral Evaluation to start. The Evaluator will be paid fees and expenses. Interim bills may be raised by CEDR Solve to cover the Evaluator's fees at the Evaluator's option. A final account of the fees and expenses will be sent to the parties by CEDR Solve when the Recommendation is ready for issue to the Parties and the Recommendation will be released on payment by the Parties of any further amounts due. CEDR Solve will reimburse the Evaluator. If the Parties agree not to proceed with Early Neutral Evaluation, CEDR Solve will refund a proportionate

Centre for Effective Dispute Resolution International Dispute Resolution Centre 70 Fleet Street London EC4Y 1EU
Tel +44 (0)20 7536 6000 Fax +44 (0)20 7536 6001 E-mail info@cedr.co.uk www.cedr.co.uk
Registered in England as Centre for Effective Dispute Resolution Limited number 2422813 Registered Charity number 1060369

amount of the fees and expenses advanced, depending on the amount of work done by the Evaluator and CEDR Solve.

No Liability

9   The Parties expressly acknowledge that neither the Evaluator nor CEDR Solve shall be liable to the Parties for any act or omission whatsoever in connection with this Early Neutral Evaluation.

Role of CEDR Solve

10   CEDR Solve appoints the Evaluator. The Evaluator is responsible for the procedure from then on. CEDR Solve may be consulted by any of the Parties to this Agreement in case of difficulty. Should the Evaluator be unable to complete the task, CEDR Solve will appoint a substitute Evaluator within a reasonable time.

After the Recommendation

11   None of the Parties will call the Evaluator or CEDR Solve (or any employee, consultant, officer or representative of CEDR Solve) as a witness, consultant or arbitrator in any litigation or arbitration in relation to the Dispute and the Evaluator and CEDR Solve will not act voluntarily in any such capacity without the written agreement of all the Parties.

Law and Jurisdiction

12   This Agreement shall be governed by English law and under the jurisdiction of the English courts. All the Parties to this Agreement agree to refer any dispute arising in connection with it to mediation first.

_____

Signed on behalf of Party A

_____

Signed on behalf of Party B

_____

Signed by the Evaluator

_____

Signed on behalf of CEDR Solve

© CEDR 2001

Centre for Effective Dispute Resolution International Dispute Resolution Centre 70 Fleet Street London EC4Y 1EU
Tel +44 (0)20 7536 6000 Fax +44 (0)20 7536 6001 E-mail info@cedr.co.uk www.cedr.co.uk
Registered in England as Centre for Effective Dispute Resolution Limited number 2422813 Registered Charity number 1060369

Centre for Effective Dispute Resolution

Guidance Notes

Essential Information

The CEDR Model Early Neutral Evaluation Agreement includes CEDR Solve as well as the Parties to the Dispute and, of course, the Evaluator. The role of CEDR Solve is defined in paragraph 10 of the Agreement.

The section "Dispute", when completed, sets out how the dispute arose with a brief description of the issue(s).

Paragraphs 1 and 2 establish the appointment of the Evaluator, that the process is Early Neutral Evaluation, and that the result is a Recommendation which will be non-binding on the Parties.

Paragraphs 3 and 4 establish the confidentiality of the process and the independence of the Evaluator and CEDR Solve.

The Procedure

Once appointed, the Evaluator will wish to establish the procedure. Paragraph 5 states that the Evaluator will seek to agree the procedure with the Parties, and that if agreement cannot be reached, the Evaluator's directions will prevail.

Procedural directions may deal with any or all of the following:
- a timetable for the submission of case summaries and supporting documents to the Evaluator with copies to each other;
- whether submissions are to be simultaneous or sequential;
- whether there should be one round or two rounds of submissions;
- whether the Evaluator has the power to call for documents; or
- whether the Evaluator has the power to award costs.

Mediation Option

Paragraph 6 provides that the Parties may agree to refer the dispute to mediation at any time before the Recommendation is made, provided the fees and expenses to date are paid, and that CEDR Solve will organise the mediation.

Reasons in the Recommendation

Paragraph 7 gives the Parties a choice as to whether to include reasons in the Recommendation. The inclusion of reasons increases the cost, but may make the resolution of the Dispute by this means more attractive and therefore worth the extra cost.

Fees and Expenses

Paragraph 8 deals with fees and expenses, some of which are payable in advance.

Centre for Effective Dispute Resolution International Dispute Resolution Centre 70 Fleet Street London EC4Y 1EU
Tel +44 (0)20 7536 6000 Fax +44 (0)20 7536 6001 E-mail info@cedr.co.uk www.cedr.co.uk
Registered in England as Centre for Effective Dispute Resolution Limited number 2422813 Registered Charity number 1060369

CEDR Centre for Effective Dispute Resolution

No Liability

Paragraph 9 gives immunity from liability to the Evaluator and CEDR Solve.

Role of CEDR Solve

Paragraph 10 explains CEDR Solve's role, in making the appointment and other arrangements, and collecting the fees and expenses.

After the Recommendation

Paragraph 11 ensures that those involved in the Early Neutral Evaluation do not get involved in future proceedings without the consent of all the Parties.

Law and Jurisdiction

Paragraph 12 establishes English law as the governing law of the Agreement, with disputes referred first to mediation and then to the English court. It may be necessary in international cases to provide that the language of the Early Neutral Evaluation is to be English.

Centre for Effective Dispute Resolution International Dispute Resolution Centre 70 Fleet Street London EC4Y 1EU
Tel +44 (0)20 7536 6000 Fax +44 (0)20 7536 6001 E-mail info@cedr.co.uk www.cedr.co.uk
Registered in England as Centre for Effective Dispute Resolution Limited number 2422813 Registered Charity number 1060369

APPENDIX 4

Arbitration Act 1996

PART I   ARBITRATION PURSUANT TO AN ARBITRATION AGREEMENT 534

INTRODUCTORY 534
  1. General principles. 534
  2. Scope of application of provisions 534
  3. The seat of the arbitration. 535
  4. Mandatory and non-mandatory provisions. 535
  5. Agreements to be in writing 535

THE ARBITRATION AGREEMENT 536
  6. Definition of arbitration agreement. 536
  7. Separability of arbitration agreement. 536
  8. Whether agreement discharged by death of a party 536

STAY OF LEGAL PROCEEDINGS 536
  9. Stay of legal proceedings. 536
  10. Reference of interpleader issue to arbitration. 537
  11. Retention of security where Admiralty proceedings stayed. 537

COMMENCEMENT OF ARBITRAL PROCEEDINGS 537
  12. Power of court to extend time for beginning arbitral
      proceedings, &c. 537
  13. Application of Limitation Acts 538
  14. Commencement of arbitral proceedings 538

THE ARBITRAL TRIBUNAL 538
  15. The arbitral tribunal 538
  16. Procedure for appointment of arbitrators. 539
  17. Power in case of default to appoint sole arbitrator 539
  18. Failure of appointment procedure 539
  19. Court to have regard to agreed qualifications. 540
  20. Chairman 540
  21. Umpire. 540
  22. Decision-making where no chairman or umpire. 540
  23. Revocation of arbitrator's authority 541
  24. Power of court to remove arbitrator 541
  25. Resignation of arbitrator. 541
  26. Death of arbitrator or person appointing him 542
  27. Filling of vacancy, &c 542
  28. Joint and several liability of parties to arbitrators for
      fees and expenses 542
  29. Immunity of arbitrator 542

JURISDICTION OF THE ARBITRAL TRIBUNAL 543
  30. Competence of tribunal to rule on its own jurisdiction 543
  31. Objection to substantive jurisdiction of tribunal. 543
  32. Determination of preliminary point of jurisdiction 543

THE ARBITRAL PROCEEDINGS 544

33. General duty of the tribunal. 544
34. Procedural and evidential matters 544
35. Consolidation of proceedings and concurrent hearings 544
36. Legal or other representation 545
37. Power to appoint experts, legal advisers or assessors 545
38. General powers exercisable by the tribunal 545
39. Power to make provisional awards 545
40. General duty of parties 546
41. Powers of tribunal in case of party's default. 546

POWERS OF COURT IN RELATION TO ARBITRAL PROCEEDINGS 546

42. Enforcement of peremptory orders of tribunal 546
43. Securing the attendance of witnesses. 547
44. Court powers exercisable in support of arbitral proceedings. 547
45. Determination of preliminary point of law 548

THE AWARD 548

46. Rules applicable to substance of dispute. .548
47. Awards on different issues, &c. 548
48. Remedies 549
49. Interest. 549
50. Extension of time for making award. 549
51. Settlement 549
52. Form of award 550
53. Place where award treated as made. 550
54. Date of award. 550
55. Notification of award 550
56. Power to withhold award in case of non-payment. 550
57. Correction of award or additional award .551
58. Effect of award. 551

COSTS OF THE ARBITRATION 551

59. Costs of the arbitration 551
60. Agreement to pay costs in any event 551
61. Award of costs 552
62. Effect of agreement or award about costs .552
63. The recoverable costs of the arbitration 552
64. Recoverable fees and expenses of arbitrators 552
65. Power to limit recoverable costs 552

POWERS OF THE COURT IN RELATION TO AWARD 553

66. Enforcement of the award. 553
67. Challenging the award: substantive jurisdiction 553
68. Challenging the award: serious irregularity 553
69. Appeal on point of law 554
70. Challenge or appeal: supplementary provisions 555
71. Challenge or appeal: effect of order of court 555

MISCELLANEOUS 556

72. Saving for rights of person who takes no part in proceedings 556
73. Loss of right to object 556
74. Immunity of arbitral institutions, &c. 556
75. Charge to secure payment of solicitors' costs 557

SUPPLEMENTARY 557
   76. Service of notices, &c. 557
   77. Powers of court in relation to service of documents. 557
   78. Reckoning periods of time 557
   79. Power of court to extend time limits relating to
      arbitral proceedings 558
   80. Notice and other requirements in connection with
      legal proceedings 558
   81. Saving for certain matters governed by common law 559
   82. Minor definitions 559
   83. Index of defined expressions: Part I 559
   84. Transitional provisions. 560

PART II   OTHER PROVISIONS RELATING TO ARBITRATION 560

DOMESTIC ARBITRATION AGREEMENTS 560
   85. Modification of Part I in relation to domestic
      arbitration agreement. 560
   86. Staying of legal proceedings 560
   87. Effectiveness of agreement to exclude court's jurisdiction 561
   88. Power to repeal or amend sections 85 to 87 561

CONSUMER ARBITRATION AGREEMENTS. 561
   89. Application of unfair terms regulations to consumer
      arbitration agreements 561
   90. Regulations apply where consumer is a legal person 561
   91. Arbitration agreement unfair where modest amount sought 562

SMALL CLAIMS ARBITRATION IN THE COUNTY COURT 562
   92. Exclusion of Part I in relation to small claims
      arbitration in the county court. 562
   93. Appointment of judges as arbitrators 562

STATUTORY ARBITRATIONS 562
   94. Application of Part I to statutory arbitrations 562
   95. General adaptation of provisions in relation to
      statutory arbitrations 563
   96. Specific adaptations of provisions in relation to
      statutory arbitrations 563
   97. Provisions excluded from applying to statutory arbitrations. 563
   98. Power to make further provision by regulations 563

PART III   RECOGNITION AND ENFORCEMENT OF
CERTAIN FOREIGN AWARDS. 564

ENFORCEMENT OF GENEVA CONVENTION AWARDS 564
   99. Continuation of Part II of the Arbitration Act 1950 564

RECOGNITION AND ENFORCEMENT OF NEW YORK CONVENTION AWARDS. . 564
   100. New York Convention awards. 564
   101. Recognition and enforcement of awards .564
   102. Evidence to be produced by party seeking recognition or
       enforcement 564
   103. Refusal of recognition or enforcement. 564
   104. Saving for other bases of recognition or enforcement 565

PART IV   GENERAL PROVISIONS 565
    105. Meaning of 'the court': jurisdiction of High Court and
          county court 565
    106. Crown application 566
    107. Consequential amendments and repeals .566
    108. Extent 566
    109. Commencement 566
    110. Short title. 566

SCHEDULE 1
    Mandatory provisions of Part I 567

SCHEDULE 2
    Modifications of Part I in relation to judge-arbitrators 567

SCHEDULE 3
    Consequential amendments [*not reproduced here*]

SCHEDULE 4
    Repeals [*not reproduced here*]

An Act to restate and improve the law relating to arbitration pursuant to an arbitration agreement; to make other provision relating to arbitration and arbitration awards; and for connected purposes.

[17th June 1996]

BE IT ENACTED BY THE QUEEN'S MOST EXCELLENT MAJESTY, BY AND WITH THE ADVICE AND CONSENT OF THE LORDS SPIRITUAL AND TEMPORAL, AND COMMONS, IN THIS PRESENT PARLIAMENT ASSEMBLED, AND BY THE AUTHORITY OF THE SAME, AS FOLLOWS:—

PART I   ARBITRATION PURSUANT TO AN ARBITRATION AGREEMENT

INTRODUCTORY

1 General principles

The provisions of this Part are founded on the following principles, and shall be construed accordingly—

    (a) the object of arbitration is to obtain the fair resolution of disputes by an impartial tribunal without unnecessary delay or expense;

    (b) the parties should be free to agree how their disputes are resolved, subject only to such safeguards as are necessary in the public interest;

    (c) in matters governed by this Part the court should not intervene except as provided by this Part.

2 Scope of application of provisions

(1) The provisions of this Part apply where the seat of the arbitration is in England and Wales or Northern Ireland.

(2) The following sections apply even if the seat of the arbitration is outside England and Wales or Northern Ireland or no seat has been designated or determined—

    (a) sections 9 to 11 (stay of legal proceedings, &c.), and

    (b) section 66 (enforcement of arbitral awards).

(3) The powers conferred by the following sections apply even if the seat of the arbitration is outside England and Wales or Northern Ireland or no seat has been designated or determined—

    (a) section 43 (securing the attendance of witnesses), and

    (b) section 44 (court powers exercisable in support of arbitral proceedings);

but the court may refuse to exercise any such power if, in the opinion of the court, the fact that the seat of the arbitration is outside England and Wales or Northern Ireland, or that when designated or determined the seat is likely to be outside England and Wales or Northern Ireland, makes it inappropriate to do so.

(4) The court may exercise a power conferred by any provision of this Part not mentioned in subsection (2) or (3) for the purpose of supporting the arbitral process where—

    (a) no seat of the arbitration has been designated or determined, and

    (b) by reason of a connection with England and Wales or Northern Ireland the court is satisfied that it is appropriate to do so.

(5) Section 7 (separability of arbitration agreement) and section 8 (death of a party) apply where the law applicable to the arbitration agreement is the law of England and Wales or Northern Ireland even if the seat of the arbitration is outside England and Wales or Northern Ireland or has not been designated or determined.

3 The seat of the arbitration

In this Part 'the seat of the arbitration' means the juridical seat of the arbitration designated—

    (a) by the parties to the arbitration agreement, or

    (b) by any arbitral or other institution or person vested by the parties with powers in that regard, or

    (c) by the arbitral tribunal if so authorised by the parties,

or determined, in the absence of any such designation, having regard to the parties' agreement and all the relevant circumstances.

4 Mandatory and non-mandatory provisions

(1) The mandatory provisions of this Part are listed in Schedule 1 and have effect notwithstanding any agreement to the contrary.

(2) The other provisions of this Part (the 'non-mandatory provisions') allow the parties to make their own arrangements by agreement but provide rules which apply in the absence of such agreement.

(3) The parties may make such arrangements by agreeing to the application of institutional rules or providing any other means by which a matter may be decided.

(4) It is immaterial whether or not the law applicable to the parties' agreement is the law of England and Wales or, as the case may be, Northern Ireland.

(5) The choice of a law other than the law of England and Wales or Northern Ireland as the applicable law in respect of a matter provided for by a non-mandatory provision of this Part is equivalent to an agreement making provision about that matter.

For this purpose an applicable law determined in accordance with the parties' agreement, or which is objectively determined in the absence of any express or implied choice, shall be treated as chosen by the parties.

5 Agreements to be in writing

(1) The provisions of this Part apply only where the arbitration agreement is in writing, and any other agreement between the parties as to any matter is effective for the purposes of this Part only if in writing.

The expressions 'agreement', 'agree' and 'agreed' shall be construed accordingly.

(2) There is an agreement in writing—

    (a) if the agreement is made in writing (whether or not it is signed by the parties),

    (b) if the agreement is made by exchange of communications in writing, or

    (c) if the agreement is evidenced in writing.

(3) Where parties agree otherwise than in writing by reference to terms which are in writing, they make an agreement in writing.

(4) An agreement is evidenced in writing if an agreement made otherwise than in writing is recorded by one of the parties, or by a third party, with the authority of the parties to the agreement.

(5) An exchange of written submissions in arbitral or legal proceedings in which the existence of an agreement otherwise than in writing is alleged by one party against another party and not denied by the other party in his response constitutes as between those parties an agreement in writing to the effect alleged.

(6) References in this Part to anything being written or in writing include its being recorded by any means.

THE ARBITRATION AGREEMENT

6 Definition of arbitration agreement

(1) In this Part an 'arbitration agreement' means an agreement to submit to arbitration present or future disputes (whether they are contractual or not).

(2) The reference in an agreement to a written form of arbitration clause or to a document containing an arbitration clause constitutes an arbitration agreement if the reference is such as to make that clause part of the agreement.

7 Separability of arbitration agreement

Unless otherwise agreed by the parties, an arbitration agreement which forms or was intended to form part of another agreement (whether or not in writing) shall not be regarded as invalid, non-existent or ineffective because that other agreement is invalid, or did not come into existence or has become ineffective, and it shall for that purpose be treated as a distinct agreement.

8 Whether agreement discharged by death of a party

(1) Unless otherwise agreed by the parties, an arbitration agreement is not discharged by the death of a party and may be enforced by or against the personal representatives of that party.

(2) Subsection (1) does not affect the operation of any enactment or rule of law by virtue of which a substantive right or obligation is extinguished by death.

STAY OF LEGAL PROCEEDINGS

9 Stay of legal proceedings

(1) A party to an arbitration agreement against whom legal proceedings are brought (whether by way of claim or counterclaim) in respect of a matter which under the agreement is to be referred to arbitration may (upon notice to the other parties to the proceedings) apply to the court in which the proceedings have been brought to stay the proceedings so far as they concern that matter.

(2) An application may be made notwithstanding that the matter is to be referred to arbitration only after the exhaustion of other dispute resolution procedures.

(3) An application may not be made by a person before taking the appropriate procedural step (if any) to acknowledge the legal proceedings against him or after he has taken any step in those proceedings to answer the substantive claim.

(4) On an application under this section the court shall grant a stay unless satisfied that the arbitration agreement is null and void, inoperative, or incapable of being performed.

(5) If the court refuses to stay the legal proceedings, any provision that an award is a condition precedent to the bringing of legal proceedings in respect of any matter is of no effect in relation to those proceedings.

10 Reference of interpleader issue to arbitration

(1) Where in legal proceedings relief by way of interpleader is granted and any issue between the claimants is one in respect of which there is an arbitration agreement between them, the court granting the relief shall direct that the issue be determined in accordance with the agreement unless the circumstances are such that proceedings brought by a claimant in respect of the matter would not be stayed.

(2) Where subsection (1) applies but the court does not direct that the issue be determined in accordance with the arbitration agreement, any provision that an award is a condition precedent to the bringing of legal proceedings in respect of any matter shall not affect the determination of that issue by the court.

11 Retention of security where Admiralty proceedings stayed

(1) Where Admiralty proceedings are stayed on the ground that the dispute in question should be submitted to arbitration, the court granting the stay may, if in those proceedings property has been arrested or bail or other security has been given to prevent or obtain release from arrest—
   (a) order that the property arrested be retained as security for the satisfaction of any award given in the arbitration in respect of that dispute, or
   (b) order that the stay of those proceedings be conditional on the provision of equivalent security for the satisfaction of any such award.

(2) Subject to any provision made by rules of court and to any necessary modifications, the same law and practice shall apply in relation to property retained in pursuance of an order as would apply if it were held for the purposes of proceedings in the court making the order.

COMMENCEMENT OF ARBITRAL PROCEEDINGS

12 Power of court to extend time for beginning arbitral proceedings, &c

(1) Where an arbitration agreement to refer future disputes to arbitration provides that a claim shall be barred, or the claimant's right extinguished, unless the claimant takes within a time fixed by the agreement some step—
   (a) to begin arbitral proceedings, or
   (b) to begin other dispute resolution procedures which must be exhausted before arbitral proceedings can be begun,
   the court may by order extend the time for taking that step.

(2) Any party to the arbitration agreement may apply for such an order (upon notice to the other parties), but only after a claim has arisen and after exhausting any available arbitral process for obtaining an extension of time.

(3) The court shall make an order only if satisfied—
   (a) that the circumstances are such as were outside the reasonable contemplation of the parties when they agreed the provision in question, and that it would be just to extend the time, or
   (b) that the conduct of one party makes it unjust to hold the other party to the strict terms of the provision in question.

(4) The court may extend the time for such period and on such terms as it thinks fit, and may do so whether or not the time previously fixed (by agreement or by a previous order) has expired.

(5) An order under this section does not affect the operation of the Limitation Acts (see section 13).

(6) The leave of the court is required for any appeal from a decision of the court under this section.

13 Application of Limitation Acts

(1) The Limitation Acts apply to arbitral proceedings as they apply to legal proceedings.

(2) The court may order that in computing the time prescribed by the Limitation Acts for the commencement of proceedings (including arbitral proceedings) in respect of a dispute which was the subject matter—

    (a) of an award which the court orders to be set aside or declares to be of no effect, or

    (b) of the affected part of an award which the court orders to be set aside in part, or declares to be in part of no effect,

the period between the commencement of the arbitration and the date of the order referred to in paragraph (a) or (b) shall be excluded.

(3) In determining for the purposes of the Limitation Acts when a cause of action accrued, any provision that an award is a condition precedent to the bringing of legal proceedings in respect of a matter to which an arbitration agreement applies shall be disregarded.

(4) In this Part 'the Limitation Acts' means—

    (a) in England and Wales, the Limitation Act 1980, the Foreign Limitation Periods Act 1984 and any other enactment (whenever passed) relating to the limitation of actions;

    (b) in Northern Ireland, the Limitation (Northern Ireland) Order 1989, the Foreign Limitation Periods (Northern Ireland) Order 1985 and any other enactment (whenever passed) relating to the limitation of actions.

14 Commencement of arbitral proceedings

(1) The parties are free to agree when arbitral proceedings are to be regarded as commenced for the purposes of this Part and for the purposes of the Limitation Acts.

(2) If there is no such agreement the following provisions apply.

(3) Where the arbitrator is named or designated in the arbitration agreement, arbitral proceedings are commenced in respect of a matter when one party serves on the other party or parties a notice in writing requiring him or them to submit that matter to the person so named or designated.

(4) Where the arbitrator or arbitrators are to be appointed by the parties, arbitral proceedings are commenced in respect of a matter when one party serves on the other party or parties notice in writing requiring him or them to appoint an arbitrator or to agree to the appointment of an arbitrator in respect of that matter.

(5) Where the arbitrator or arbitrators are to be appointed by a person other than a party to the proceedings, arbitral proceedings are commenced in respect of a matter when one party gives notice in writing to that person requesting him to make the appointment in respect of that matter.

THE ARBITRAL TRIBUNAL

15 The arbitral tribunal

(1) The parties are free to agree on the number of arbitrators to form the tribunal and whether there is to be a chairman or umpire.

(2) Unless otherwise agreed by the parties, an agreement that the number of arbitrators shall be two or any other even number shall be understood as requiring the appointment of an additional arbitrator as chairman of the tribunal.

(3) If there is no agreement as to the number of arbitrators, the tribunal shall consist of a sole arbitrator.

16 Procedure for appointment of arbitrators

(1) The parties are free to agree on the procedure for appointing the arbitrator or arbitrators, including the procedure for appointing any chairman or umpire.

(2) If or to the extent that there is no such agreement, the following provisions apply.

(3) If the tribunal is to consist of a sole arbitrator, the parties shall jointly appoint the arbitrator not later than 28 days after service of a request in writing by either party to do so.

(4) If the tribunal is to consist of two arbitrators, each party shall appoint one arbitrator not later than 14 days after service of a request in writing by either party to do so.

(5) If the tribunal is to consist of three arbitrators—
  (a) each party shall appoint one arbitrator not later than 14 days after service of a request in writing by either party to do so, and
  (b) the two so appointed shall forthwith appoint a third arbitrator as the chairman of the tribunal.

(6) If the tribunal is to consist of two arbitrators and an umpire—
  (a) each party shall appoint one arbitrator not later than 14 days after service of a request in writing by either party to do so, and
  (b) the two so appointed may appoint an umpire at any time after they themselves are appointed and shall do so before any substantive hearing or forthwith if they cannot agree on a matter relating to the arbitration.

(7) In any other case (in particular, if there are more than two parties) section 18 applies as in the case of a failure of the agreed appointment procedure.

17 Power in case of default to appoint sole arbitrator

(1) Unless the parties otherwise agree, where each of two parties to an arbitration agreement is to appoint an arbitrator and one party ('the party in default') refuses to do so, or fails to do so within the time specified, the other party, having duly appointed his arbitrator, may give notice in writing to the party in default that he proposes to appoint his arbitrator to act as sole arbitrator.

(2) If the party in default does not within 7 clear days of that notice being given—
  (a) make the required appointment, and
  (b) notify the other party that he has done so,
  the other party may appoint his arbitrator as sole arbitrator whose award shall be binding on both parties as if he had been so appointed by agreement.

(3) Where a sole arbitrator has been appointed under subsection (2), the party in default may (upon notice to the appointing party) apply to the court which may set aside the appointment.

(4) The leave of the court is required for any appeal from a decision of the court under this section.

18 Failure of appointment procedure

(1) The parties are free to agree what is to happen in the event of a failure of the procedure for the appointment of the arbitral tribunal.
  There is no failure if an appointment is duly made under section 17 (power in case of default to appoint sole arbitrator), unless that appointment is set aside.

(2) If or to the extent that there is no such agreement any party to the arbitration agreement may (upon notice to the other parties) apply to the court to exercise its powers under this section.

(3) Those powers are—
    (a) to give directions as to the making of any necessary appointments;
    (b) to direct that the tribunal shall be constituted by such appointments (or any one or more of them) as have been made;
    (c) to revoke any appointments already made;
    (d) to make any necessary appointments itself.
(4) An appointment made by the court under this section has effect as if made with the agreement of the parties.
(5) The leave of the court is required for any appeal from a decision of the court under this section.

19 Court to have regard to agreed qualifications

In deciding whether to exercise, and in considering how to exercise, any of its powers under section 16 (procedure for appointment of arbitrators) or section 18 (failure of appointment procedure), the court shall have due regard to any agreement of the parties as to the qualifications required of the arbitrators.

20 Chairman

(1) Where the parties have agreed that there is to be a chairman, they are free to agree what the functions of the chairman are to be in relation to the making of decisions, orders and awards.
(2) If or to the extent that there is no such agreement, the following provisions apply.
(3) Decisions, orders and awards shall be made by all or a majority of the arbitrators (including the chairman).
(4) The view of the chairman shall prevail in relation to a decision, order or award in respect of which there is neither unanimity nor a majority under subsection (3).

21 Umpire

(1) Where the parties have agreed that there is to be an umpire, they are free to agree what the functions of the umpire are to be, and in particular—
    (a) whether he is to attend the proceedings, and
    (b) when he is to replace the other arbitrators as the tribunal with power to make decisions, orders and awards.
(2) If or to the extent that there is no such agreement, the following provisions apply.
(3) The umpire shall attend the proceedings and be supplied with the same documents and other materials as are supplied to the other arbitrators.
(4) Decisions, orders and awards shall be made by the other arbitrators unless and until they cannot agree on a matter relating to the arbitration.
In that event they shall forthwith give notice in writing to the parties and the umpire, whereupon the umpire shall replace them as the tribunal with power to make decisions, orders and awards as if he were sole arbitrator.
(5) If the arbitrators cannot agree but fail to give notice of that fact, or if any of them fails to join in the giving of notice, any party to the arbitral proceedings may (upon notice to the other parties and to the tribunal) apply to the court which may order that the umpire shall replace the other arbitrators as the tribunal with power to make decisions, orders and awards as if he were sole arbitrator.
(6) The leave of the court is required for any appeal from a decision of the court under this section.

22 Decision-making where no chairman or umpire

(1) Where the parties agree that there shall be two or more arbitrators with no chairman or umpire, the parties are free to agree how the tribunal is to make decisions, orders and awards.

(2) If there is no such agreement, decisions, orders and awards shall be made by all or a majority of the arbitrators.

23 Revocation of arbitrator's authority

(1) The parties are free to agree in what circumstances the authority of an arbitrator may be revoked.

(2) If or to the extent that there is no such agreement the following provisions apply.

(3) The authority of an arbitrator may not be revoked except—
   (a) by the parties acting jointly, or
   (b) by an arbitral or other institution or person vested by the parties with powers in that regard.

(4) Revocation of the authority of an arbitrator by the parties acting jointly must be agreed in writing unless the parties also agree (whether or not in writing) to terminate the arbitration agreement.

(5) Nothing in this section affects the power of the court—
   (a) to revoke an appointment under section 18 (powers exercisable in case of failure of appointment procedure), or
   (b) to remove an arbitrator on the grounds specified in section 24.

24 Power of court to remove arbitrator

(1) A party to arbitral proceedings may (upon notice to the other parties, to the arbitrator concerned and to any other arbitrator) apply to the court to remove an arbitrator on any of the following grounds—
   (a) that circumstances exist that give rise to justifiable doubts as to his impartiality;
   (b) that he does not possess the qualifications required by the arbitration agreement;
   (c) that he is physically or mentally incapable of conducting the proceedings or there are justifiable doubts as to his capacity to do so;
   (d) that he has refused or failed—
      (i) properly to conduct the proceedings, or
      (ii) to use all reasonable despatch in conducting the proceedings or making an award,
   and that substantial injustice has been or will be caused to the applicant.

(2) If there is an arbitral or other institution or person vested by the parties with power to remove an arbitrator, the court shall not exercise its power of removal unless satisfied that the applicant has first exhausted any available recourse to that institution or person.

(3) The arbitral tribunal may continue the arbitral proceedings and make an award while an application to the court under this section is pending.

(4) Where the court removes an arbitrator, it may make such order as it thinks fit with respect to his entitlement (if any) to fees or expenses, or the repayment of any fees or expenses already paid.

(5) The arbitrator concerned is entitled to appear and be heard by the court before it makes any order under this section.

(6) The leave of the court is required for any appeal from a decision of the court under this section.

25 Resignation of arbitrator

(1) The parties are free to agree with an arbitrator as to the consequences of his resignation as regards—
   (a) his entitlement (if any) to fees or expenses, and
   (b) any liability thereby incurred by him.

(2) If or to the extent that there is no such agreement the following provisions apply.

(3) An arbitrator who resigns his appointment may (upon notice to the parties) apply to the court—

    (a) to grant him relief from any liability thereby incurred by him, and

    (b) to make such order as it thinks fit with respect to his entitlement (if any) to fees or expenses or the repayment of any fees or expenses already paid.

(4) If the court is satisfied that in all the circumstances it was reasonable for the arbitrator to resign, it may grant such relief as is mentioned in subsection (3)(a) on such terms as it thinks fit.

(5) The leave of the court is required for any appeal from a decision of the court under this section.

26 Death of arbitrator or person appointing him

(1) The authority of an arbitrator is personal and ceases on his death.

(2) Unless otherwise agreed by the parties, the death of the person by whom an arbitrator was appointed does not revoke the arbitrator's authority.

27 Filling of vacancy, &c

(1) Where an arbitrator ceases to hold office, the parties are free to agree—

    (a) whether and if so how the vacancy is to be filled,

    (b) whether and if so to what extent the previous proceedings should stand, and

    (c) what effect (if any) his ceasing to hold office has on any appointment made by him (alone or jointly).

(2) If or to the extent that there is no such agreement, the following provisions apply.

(3) The provisions of sections 16 (procedure for appointment of arbitrators) and 18 (failure of appointment procedure) apply in relation to the filling of the vacancy as in relation to an original appointment.

(4) The tribunal (when reconstituted) shall determine whether and if so to what extent the previous proceedings should stand.

This does not affect any right of a party to challenge those proceedings on any ground which had arisen before the arbitrator ceased to hold office.

(5) His ceasing to hold office does not affect any appointment by him (alone or jointly) of another arbitrator, in particular any appointment of a chairman or umpire.

28 Joint and several liability of parties to arbitrators for fees and expenses

(1) The parties are jointly and severally liable to pay to the arbitrators such reasonable fees and expenses (if any) as are appropriate in the circumstances.

(2) Any party may apply to the court (upon notice to the other parties and to the arbitrators) which may order that the amount of the arbitrators' fees and expenses shall be considered and adjusted by such means and upon such terms as it may direct.

(3) If the application is made after any amount has been paid to the arbitrators by way of fees or expenses, the court may order the repayment of such amount (if any) as is shown to be excessive, but shall not do so unless it is shown that it is reasonable in the circumstances to order repayment.

(4) The above provisions have effect subject to any order of the court under section 24(4) or 25(3)(b) (order as to entitlement to fees or expenses in case of removal or resignation of arbitrator).

(5) Nothing in this section affects any liability of a party to any other party to pay all or any of the costs of the arbitration (see sections 59 to 65) or any contractual right of an arbitrator to payment of his fees and expenses.

(6) In this section references to arbitrators include an arbitrator who has ceased to act and an umpire who has not replaced the other arbitrators.

29 Immunity of arbitrator

(1) An arbitrator is not liable for anything done or omitted in the discharge or purported discharge of his functions as arbitrator unless the act or omission is shown to have been in bad faith.

(2) Subsection (1) applies to an employee or agent of an arbitrator as it applies to the arbitrator himself.

(3) This section does not affect any liability incurred by an arbitrator by reason of his resigning (but see section 25).

JURISDICTION OF THE ARBITRAL TRIBUNAL

30 Competence of tribunal to rule on its own jurisdiction

(1) Unless otherwise agreed by the parties, the arbitral tribunal may rule on its own substantive jurisdiction, that is, as to—
   (a) whether there is a valid arbitration agreement,
   (b) whether the tribunal is properly constituted, and
   (c) what matters have been submitted to arbitration in accordance with the arbitration agreement.

(2) Any such ruling may be challenged by any available arbitral process of appeal or review or in accordance with the provisions of this Part.

31 Objection to substantive jurisdiction of tribunal

(1) An objection that the arbitral tribunal lacks substantive jurisdiction at the outset of the proceedings must be raised by a party not later than the time he takes the first step in the proceedings to contest the merits of any matter in relation to which he challenges the tribunal's jurisdiction.

A party is not precluded from raising such an objection by the fact that he has appointed or participated in the appointment of an arbitrator.

(2) Any objection during the course of the arbitral proceedings that the arbitral tribunal is exceeding its substantive jurisdiction must be made as soon as possible after the matter alleged to be beyond its jurisdiction is raised.

(3) The arbitral tribunal may admit an objection later than the time specified in subsection (1) or (2) if it considers the delay justified.

(4) Where an objection is duly taken to the tribunal's substantive jurisdiction and the tribunal has power to rule on its own jurisdiction, it may—
   (a) rule on the matter in an award as to jurisdiction, or
   (b) deal with the objection in its award on the merits.

If the parties agree which of these courses the tribunal should take, the tribunal shall proceed accordingly.

(5) The tribunal may in any case, and shall if the parties so agree, stay proceedings whilst an application is made to the court under section 32 (determination of preliminary point of jurisdiction).

32 Determination of preliminary point of jurisdiction

(1) The court may, on the application of a party to arbitral proceedings (upon notice to the other parties), determine any question as to the substantive jurisdiction of the tribunal.

A party may lose the right to object (see section 73).

(2) An application under this section shall not be considered unless—
   (a) it is made with the agreement in writing of all the other parties to the proceedings, or
   (b) it is made with the permission of the tribunal and the court is satisfied—
      (i) that the determination of the question is likely to produce substantial savings in costs,
      (ii) that the application was made without delay, and
      (iii) that there is good reason why the matter should be decided by the court.

(3) An application under this section, unless made with the agreement of all the other parties to the proceedings, shall state the grounds on which it is said that the matter should be decided by the court.

(4) Unless otherwise agreed by the parties, the arbitral tribunal may continue the arbitral proceedings and make an award while an application to the court under this section is pending.

(5) Unless the court gives leave, no appeal lies from a decision of the court whether the conditions specified in subsection (2) are met.

(6) The decision of the court on the question of jurisdiction shall be treated as a judgment of the court for the purposes of an appeal.

But no appeal lies without the leave of the court which shall not be given unless the court considers that the question involves a point of law which is one of general importance or is one which for some other special reason should be considered by the Court of Appeal.

THE ARBITRAL PROCEEDINGS

33 General duty of the tribunal

(1) The tribunal shall—
   (a) act fairly and impartially as between the parties, giving each party a reasonable opportunity of putting his case and dealing with that of his opponent, and
   (b) adopt procedures suitable to the circumstances of the particular case, avoiding unnecessary delay or expense, so as to provide a fair means for the resolution of the matters falling to be determined.

(2) The tribunal shall comply with that general duty in conducting the arbitral proceedings, in its decisions on matters of procedure and evidence and in the exercise of all other powers conferred on it.

34 Procedural and evidential matters

(1) It shall be for the tribunal to decide all procedural and evidential matters, subject to the right of the parties to agree any matter.

(2) Procedural and evidential matters include—
   (a) when and where any part of the proceedings is to be held;
   (b) the language or languages to be used in the proceedings and whether translations of any relevant documents are to be supplied;
   (c) whether any and if so what form of written statements of claim and defence are to be used, when these should be supplied and the extent to which such statements can be later amended;
   (d) whether any and if so which documents or classes of documents should be disclosed between and produced by the parties and at what stage;
   (e) whether any and if so what questions should be put to and answered by the respective parties and when and in what form this should be done;
   (f) whether to apply strict rules of evidence (or any other rules) as to the admissibility, relevance or weight of any material (oral, written or other) sought to be tendered on any matters of fact or opinion, and the time, manner and form in which such material should be exchanged and presented;
   (g) whether and to what extent the tribunal should itself take the initiative in ascertaining the facts and the law;
   (h) whether and to what extent there should be oral or written evidence or submissions.

(3) The tribunal may fix the time within which any directions given by it are to be complied with, and may if it thinks fit extend the time so fixed (whether or not it has expired).

35 Consolidation of proceedings and concurrent hearings

(1) The parties are free to agree—
   (a) that the arbitral proceedings shall be consolidated with other arbitral proceedings, or
   (b) that concurrent hearings shall be held,
   on such terms as may be agreed.

(2) Unless the parties agree to confer such power on the tribunal, the tribunal has no power to order consolidation of proceedings or concurrent hearings.

36 Legal or other representation

Unless otherwise agreed by the parties, a party to arbitral proceedings may be represented in the proceedings by a lawyer or other person chosen by him.

37 Power to appoint experts, legal advisers or assessors

(1) Unless otherwise agreed by the parties—
  (a) the tribunal may—
    (i) appoint experts or legal advisers to report to it and the parties, or
    (ii) appoint assessors to assist it on technical matters,
  and may allow any such expert, legal adviser or assessor to attend the proceedings; and
  (b) the parties shall be given a reasonable opportunity to comment on any information, opinion or advice offered by any such person.
(2) The fees and expenses of an expert, legal adviser or assessor appointed by the tribunal for which the arbitrators are liable are expenses of the arbitrators for the purposes of this Part.

38 General powers exercisable by the tribunal

(1) The parties are free to agree on the powers exercisable by the arbitral tribunal for the purposes of and in relation to the proceedings.
(2) Unless otherwise agreed by the parties the tribunal has the following powers.
(3) The tribunal may order a claimant to provide security for the costs of the arbitration.
  This power shall not be exercised on the ground that the claimant is—
  (a) an individual ordinarily resident outside the United Kingdom, or
  (b) a corporation or association incorporated or formed under the law of a country outside the United Kingdom, or whose central management and control is exercised outside the United Kingdom.
(4) The tribunal may give directions in relation to any property which is the subject of the proceedings or as to which any question arises in the proceedings, and which is owned by or is in the possession of a party to the proceedings—
  (a) for the inspection, photographing, preservation, custody or detention of the property by the tribunal, an expert or a party, or
  (b) ordering that samples be taken from, or any observation be made of or experiment conducted upon, the property.
(5) The tribunal may direct that a party or witness shall be examined on oath or affirmation, and may for that purpose administer any necessary oath or take any necessary affirmation.
(6) The tribunal may give directions to a party for the preservation for the purposes of the proceedings of any evidence in his custody or control.

39 Power to make provisional awards

(1) The parties are free to agree that the tribunal shall have power to order on a provisional basis any relief which it would have power to grant in a final award.
(2) This includes, for instance, making—
  (a) a provisional order for the payment of money or the disposition of property as between the parties, or
  (b) an order to make an interim payment on account of the costs of the arbitration.
(3) Any such order shall be subject to the tribunal's final adjudication; and the tribunal's final award, on the merits or as to costs, shall take account of any such order.
(4) Unless the parties agree to confer such power on the tribunal, the tribunal has no such power.

This does not affect its powers under section 47 (awards on different issues, &c.).

40 General duty of parties

(1) The parties shall do all things necessary for the proper and expeditious conduct of the arbitral proceedings.

(2) This includes—

  (a) complying without delay with any determination of the tribunal as to procedural or evidential matters, or with any order or directions of the tribunal, and

  (b) where appropriate, taking without delay any necessary steps to obtain a decision of the court on a preliminary question of jurisdiction or law (see sections 32 and 45).

41 Powers of tribunal in case of party's default

(1) The parties are free to agree on the powers of the tribunal in case of a party's failure to do something necessary for the proper and expeditious conduct of the arbitration.

(2) Unless otherwise agreed by the parties, the following provisions apply.

(3) If the tribunal is satisfied that there has been inordinate and inexcusable delay on the part of the claimant in pursuing his claim and that the delay—

  (a) gives rise, or is likely to give rise, to a substantial risk that it is not possible to have a fair resolution of the issues in that claim, or

  (b) has caused, or is likely to cause, serious prejudice to the respondent,

  the tribunal may make an award dismissing the claim.

(4) If without showing sufficient cause a party—

  (a) fails to attend or be represented at an oral hearing of which due notice was given, or

  (b) where matters are to be dealt with in writing, fails after due notice to submit written evidence or make written submissions,

  the tribunal may continue the proceedings in the absence of that party or, as the case may be, without any written evidence or submissions on his behalf, and may make an award on the basis of the evidence before it.

(5) If without showing sufficient cause a party fails to comply with any order or directions of the tribunal, the tribunal may make a peremptory order to the same effect, prescribing such time for compliance with it as the tribunal considers appropriate.

(6) If a claimant fails to comply with a peremptory order of the tribunal to provide security for costs, the tribunal may make an award dismissing his claim.

(7) If a party fails to comply with any other kind of peremptory order, then, without prejudice to section 42 (enforcement by court of tribunal's peremptory orders), the tribunal may do any of the following—

  (a) direct that the party in default shall not be entitled to rely upon any allegation or material which was the subject matter of the order;

  (b) draw such adverse inferences from the act of non-compliance as the circumstances justify;

  (c) proceed to an award on the basis of such materials as have been properly provided to it;

  (d) make such order as it thinks fit as to the payment of costs of the arbitration incurred in consequence of the non-compliance.

POWERS OF COURT IN RELATION TO ARBITRAL PROCEEDINGS

42 Enforcement of peremptory orders of tribunal

(1) Unless otherwise agreed by the parties, the court may make an order requiring a party to comply with a peremptory order made by the tribunal.

(2) An application for an order under this section may be made—

  (a) by the tribunal (upon notice to the parties),

(b) by a party to the arbitral proceedings with the permission of the tribunal (and upon notice to the other parties), or

(c) where the parties have agreed that the powers of the court under this section shall be available.

(3) The court shall not act unless it is satisfied that the applicant has exhausted any available arbitral process in respect of failure to comply with the tribunal's order.

(4) No order shall be made under this section unless the court is satisfied that the person to whom the tribunal's order was directed has failed to comply with it within the time prescribed in the order or, if no time was prescribed, within a reasonable time.

(5) The leave of the court is required for any appeal from a decision of the court under this section.

43 Securing the attendance of witnesses

(1) A party to arbitral proceedings may use the same court procedures as are available in relation to legal proceedings to secure the attendance before the tribunal of a witness in order to give oral testimony or to produce documents or other material evidence.

(2) This may only be done with the permission of the tribunal or the agreement of the other parties.

(3) The court procedures may only be used if—

(a) the witness is in the United Kingdom, and

(b) the arbitral proceedings are being conducted in England and Wales or, as the case may be, Northern Ireland.

(4) A person shall not be compelled by virtue of this section to produce any document or other material evidence which he could not be compelled to produce in legal proceedings.

44 Court powers exercisable in support of arbitral proceedings

(1) Unless otherwise agreed by the parties, the court has for the purposes of and in relation to arbitral proceedings the same power of making orders about the matters listed below as it has for the purposes of and in relation to legal proceedings.

(2) Those matters are—

(a) the taking of the evidence of witnesses;

(b) the preservation of evidence;

(c) making orders relating to property which is the subject of the proceedings or as to which any question arises in the proceedings—

(i) for the inspection, photographing, preservation, custody or detention of the property, or

(ii) ordering that samples be taken from, or any observation be made of or experiment conducted upon, the property;

and for that purpose authorising any person to enter any premises in the possession or control of a party to the arbitration;

(d) the sale of any goods the subject of the proceedings;

(e) the granting of an interim injunction or the appointment of a receiver.

(3) If the case is one of urgency, the court may, on the application of a party or proposed party to the arbitral proceedings, make such orders as it thinks necessary for the purpose of preserving evidence or assets.

(4) If the case is not one of urgency, the court shall act only on the application of a party to the arbitral proceedings (upon notice to the other parties and to the tribunal) made with the permission of the tribunal or the agreement in writing of the other parties.

(5) In any case the court shall act only if or to the extent that the arbitral tribunal, and any arbitral or other institution or person vested by the parties with power in that regard, has no power or is unable for the time being to act effectively.

(6) If the court so orders, an order made by it under this section shall cease to have effect in whole or in part on the order of the tribunal or of any such arbitral or other institution or person having power to act in relation to the subject-matter of the order.

(7) The leave of the court is required for any appeal from a decision of the court under this section.

45 Determination of preliminary point of law

(1) Unless otherwise agreed by the parties, the court may on the application of a party to arbitral proceedings (upon notice to the other parties) determine any question of law arising in the course of the proceedings which the court is satisfied substantially affects the rights of one or more of the parties.

An agreement to dispense with reasons for the tribunal's award shall be considered an agreement to exclude the court's jurisdiction under this section.

(2) An application under this section shall not be considered unless—
    (a) it is made with the agreement of all the other parties to the proceedings, or
    (b) it is made with the permission of the tribunal and the court is satisfied—
        (i) that the determination of the question is likely to produce substantial savings in costs, and
        (ii) that the application was made without delay.

(3) The application shall identify the question of law to be determined and, unless made with the agreement of all the other parties to the proceedings, shall state the grounds on which it is said that the question should be decided by the court.

(4) Unless otherwise agreed by the parties, the arbitral tribunal may continue the arbitral proceedings and make an award while an application to the court under this section is pending.

(5) Unless the court gives leave, no appeal lies from a decision of the court whether the conditions specified in subsection (2) are met.

(6) The decision of the court on the question of law shall be treated as a judgment of the court for the purposes of an appeal.

But no appeal lies without the leave of the court which shall not be given unless the court considers that the question is one of general importance, or is one which for some other special reason should be considered by the Court of Appeal.

THE AWARD

46 Rules applicable to substance of dispute

(1) The arbitral tribunal shall decide the dispute—
    (a) in accordance with the law chosen by the parties as applicable to the substance of the dispute, or
    (b) if the parties so agree, in accordance with such other considerations as are agreed by them or determined by the tribunal.

(2) For this purpose the choice of the laws of a country shall be understood to refer to the substantive laws of that country and not its conflict of laws rules.

(3) If or to the extent that there is no such choice or agreement, the tribunal shall apply the law determined by the conflict of laws rules which it considers applicable.

47 Awards on different issues, &c

(1) Unless otherwise agreed by the parties, the tribunal may make more than one award at different times on different aspects of the matters to be determined.

(2) The tribunal may, in particular, make an award relating—
    (a) to an issue affecting the whole claim, or
    (b) to a part only of the claims or cross-claims submitted to it for decision.

(3) If the tribunal does so, it shall specify in its award the issue, or the claim or part of a claim, which is the subject matter of the award.

48 Remedies

(1) The parties are free to agree on the powers exercisable by the arbitral tribunal as regards remedies.
(2) Unless otherwise agreed by the parties, the tribunal has the following powers.
(3) The tribunal may make a declaration as to any matter to be determined in the proceedings.
(4) The tribunal may order the payment of a sum of money, in any currency.
(5) The tribunal has the same powers as the court—
    (a) to order a party to do or refrain from doing anything;
    (b) to order specific performance of a contract (other than a contract relating to land);
    (c) to order the rectification, setting aside or cancellation of a deed or other document.

49 Interest

(1) The parties are free to agree on the powers of the tribunal as regards the award of interest.
(2) Unless otherwise agreed by the parties the following provisions apply.
(3) The tribunal may award simple or compound interest from such dates, at such rates and with such rests as it considers meets the justice of the case—
    (a) on the whole or part of any amount awarded by the tribunal, in respect of any period up to the date of the award;
    (b) on the whole or part of any amount claimed in the arbitration and outstanding at the commencement of the arbitral proceedings but paid before the award was made, in respect of any period up to the date of payment.
(4) The tribunal may award simple or compound interest from the date of the award (or any later date) until payment, at such rates and with such rests as it considers meets the justice of the case, on the outstanding amount of any award (including any award of interest under subsection (3) and any award as to costs).
(5) References in this section to an amount awarded by the tribunal include an amount payable in consequence of a declaratory award by the tribunal.
(6) The above provisions do not affect any other power of the tribunal to award interest.

50 Extension of time for making award

(1) Where the time for making an award is limited by or in pursuance of the arbitration agreement, then, unless otherwise agreed by the parties, the court may in accordance with the following provisions by order extend that time.
(2) An application for an order under this section may be made—
    (a) by the tribunal (upon notice to the parties), or
    (b) by any party to the proceedings (upon notice to the tribunal and the other parties),
    but only after exhausting any available arbitral process for obtaining an extension of time.
(3) The court shall only make an order if satisfied that a substantial injustice would otherwise be done.
(4) The court may extend the time for such period and on such terms as it thinks fit, and may do so whether or not the time previously fixed (by or under the agreement or by a previous order) has expired.
(5) The leave of the court is required for any appeal from a decision of the court under this section.

51 Settlement

(1) If during arbitral proceedings the parties settle the dispute, the following provisions apply unless otherwise agreed by the parties.

(2) The tribunal shall terminate the substantive proceedings and, if so requested by the parties and not objected to by the tribunal, shall record the settlement in the form of an agreed award.

(3) An agreed award shall state that it is an award of the tribunal and shall have the same status and effect as any other award on the merits of the case.

(4) The following provisions of this Part relating to awards (sections 52 to 58) apply to an agreed award.

(5) Unless the parties have also settled the matter of the payment of the costs of the arbitration, the provisions of this Part relating to costs (sections 59 to 65) continue to apply.

52 Form of award

(1) The parties are free to agree on the form of an award.

(2) If or to the extent that there is no such agreement, the following provisions apply.

(3) The award shall be in writing signed by all the arbitrators or all those assenting to the award.

(4) The award shall contain the reasons for the award unless it is an agreed award or the parties have agreed to dispense with reasons.

(5) The award shall state the seat of the arbitration and the date when the award is made.

53 Place where award treated as made

Unless otherwise agreed by the parties, where the seat of the arbitration is in England and Wales or Northern Ireland, any award in the proceedings shall be treated as made there, regardless of where it was signed, despatched or delivered to any of the parties.

54 Date of award

(1) Unless otherwise agreed by the parties, the tribunal may decide what is to be taken to be the date on which the award was made.

(2) In the absence of any such decision, the date of the award shall be taken to be the date on which it is signed by the arbitrator or, where more than one arbitrator signs the award, by the last of them.

55 Notification of award

(1) The parties are free to agree on the requirements as to notification of the award to the parties.

(2) If there is no such agreement, the award shall be notified to the parties by service on them of copies of the award, which shall be done without delay after the award is made.

(3) Nothing in this section affects section 56 (power to withhold award in case of non-payment).

56 Power to withhold award in case of non-payment

(1) The tribunal may refuse to deliver an award to the parties except upon full payment of the fees and expenses of the arbitrators.

(2) If the tribunal refuses on that ground to deliver an award, a party to the arbitral proceedings may (upon notice to the other parties and the tribunal) apply to the court, which may order that—

(a) the tribunal shall deliver the award on the payment into court by the applicant of the fees and expenses demanded, or such lesser amount as the court may specify,

(b) the amount of the fees and expenses properly payable shall be determined by such means and upon such terms as the court may direct, and

(c) out of the money paid into court there shall be paid out such fees and expenses as may be found to be properly payable and the balance of the money (if any) shall be paid out to the applicant.

(3) For this purpose the amount of fees and expenses properly payable is the amount the applicant is liable to pay under section 28 or any agreement relating to the payment of the arbitrators.

(4) No application to the court may be made where there is any available arbitral process for appeal or review of the amount of the fees or expenses demanded.

(5) References in this section to arbitrators include an arbitrator who has ceased to act and an umpire who has not replaced the other arbitrators.

(6) The above provisions of this section also apply in relation to any arbitral or other institution or person vested by the parties with powers in relation to the delivery of the tribunal's award.
As they so apply, the references to the fees and expenses of the arbitrators shall be construed as including the fees and expenses of that institution or person.

(7) The leave of the court is required for any appeal from a decision of the court under this section.

(8) Nothing in this section shall be construed as excluding an application under section 28 where payment has been made to the arbitrators in order to obtain the award.

57 Correction of award or additional award

(1) The parties are free to agree on the powers of the tribunal to correct an award or make an additional award.

(2) If or to the extent there is no such agreement, the following provisions apply.

(3) The tribunal may on its own initiative or on the application of a party—
  (a) correct an award so as to remove any clerical mistake or error arising from an accidental slip or omission or clarify or remove any ambiguity in the award, or
  (b) make an additional award in respect of any claim (including a claim for interest or costs) which was presented to the tribunal but was not dealt with in the award.
These powers shall not be exercised without first affording the other parties a reasonable opportunity to make representations to the tribunal.

(4) Any application for the exercise of those powers must be made within 28 days of the date of the award or such longer period as the parties may agree.

(5) Any correction of an award shall be made within 28 days of the date the application was received by the tribunal or, where the correction is made by the tribunal on its own initiative, within 28 days of the date of the award or, in either case, such longer period as the parties may agree.

(6) Any additional award shall be made within 56 days of the date of the original award or such longer period as the parties may agree.

(7) Any correction of an award shall form part of the award.

58 Effect of award

(1) Unless otherwise agreed by the parties, an award made by the tribunal pursuant to an arbitration agreement is final and binding both on the parties and on any persons claiming through or under them.

(2) This does not affect the right of a person to challenge the award by any available arbitral process of appeal or review or in accordance with the provisions of this Part.

COSTS OF THE ARBITRATION

59 Costs of the arbitration

(1) References in this Part to the costs of the arbitration are to—
  (a) the arbitrators' fees and expenses,
  (b) the fees and expenses of any arbitral institution concerned, and
  (c) the legal or other costs of the parties.

(2) Any such reference includes the costs of or incidental to any proceedings to determine the amount of the recoverable costs of the arbitration (see section 63).

60 Agreement to pay costs in any event

An agreement which has the effect that a party is to pay the whole or part of the costs of the arbitration in any event is only valid if made after the dispute in question has arisen.

61 Award of costs

(1) The tribunal may make an award allocating the costs of the arbitration as between the parties, subject to any agreement of the parties.

(2) Unless the parties otherwise agree, the tribunal shall award costs on the general principle that costs should follow the event except where it appears to the tribunal that in the circumstances this is not appropriate in relation to the whole or part of the costs.

62 Effect of agreement or award about costs

Unless the parties otherwise agree, any obligation under an agreement between them as to how the costs of the arbitration are to be borne, or under an award allocating the costs of the arbitration, extends only to such costs as are recoverable.

63 The recoverable costs of the arbitration

(1) The parties are free to agree what costs of the arbitration are recoverable.

(2) If or to the extent there is no such agreement, the following provisions apply.

(3) The tribunal may determine by award the recoverable costs of the arbitration on such basis as it thinks fit.

If it does so, it shall specify—

(a) the basis on which it has acted, and

(b) the items of recoverable costs and the amount referable to each.

(4) If the tribunal does not determine the recoverable costs of the arbitration, any party to the arbitral proceedings may apply to the court (upon notice to the other parties) which may—

(a) determine the recoverable costs of the arbitration on such basis as it thinks fit, or

(b) order that they shall be determined by such means and upon such terms as it may specify.

(5) Unless the tribunal or the court determines otherwise—

(a) the recoverable costs of the arbitration shall be determined on the basis that there shall be allowed a reasonable amount in respect of all costs reasonably incurred, and

(b) any doubt as to whether costs were reasonably incurred or were reasonable in amount shall be resolved in favour of the paying party.

(6) The above provisions have effect subject to section 64 (recoverable fees and expenses of arbitrators).

(7) Nothing in this section affects any right of the arbitrators, any expert, legal adviser or assessor appointed by the tribunal, or any arbitral institution, to payment of their fees and expenses.

64 Recoverable fees and expenses of arbitrators

(1) Unless otherwise agreed by the parties, the recoverable costs of the arbitration shall include in respect of the fees and expenses of the arbitrators only such reasonable fees and expenses as are appropriate in the circumstances.

(2) If there is any question as to what reasonable fees and expenses are appropriate in the circumstances, and the matter is not already before the court on an application under section 63(4), the court may on the application of any party (upon notice to the other parties)—

(a) determine the matter, or

(b) order that it be determined by such means and upon such terms as the court may specify.

(3) Subsection (1) has effect subject to any order of the court under section 24(4) or 25(3)(b) (order as to entitlement to fees or expenses in case of removal or resignation of arbitrator).

(4) Nothing in this section affects any right of the arbitrator to payment of his fees and expenses.

65 Power to limit recoverable costs

(1) Unless otherwise agreed by the parties, the tribunal may direct that the recoverable costs of the arbitration, or of any part of the arbitral proceedings, shall be limited to a specified amount.

(2) Any direction may be made or varied at any stage, but this must be done sufficiently in advance of the incurring of costs to which it relates, or the taking of any steps in the proceedings which may be affected by it, for the limit to be taken into account.

POWERS OF THE COURT IN RELATION TO AWARD

66 Enforcement of the award

(1) An award made by the tribunal pursuant to an arbitration agreement may, by leave of the court, be enforced in the same manner as a judgment or order of the court to the same effect.

(2) Where leave is so given, judgment may be entered in terms of the award.

(3) Leave to enforce an award shall not be given where, or to the extent that, the person against whom it is sought to be enforced shows that the tribunal lacked substantive jurisdiction to make the award.

     The right to raise such an objection may have been lost (see section 73).

(4) Nothing in this section affects the recognition or enforcement of an award under any other enactment or rule of law, in particular under Part II of the Arbitration Act 1950 (enforcement of awards under Geneva Convention) or the provisions of Part III of this Act relating to the recognition and enforcement of awards under the New York Convention or by an action on the award.

67 Challenging the award: substantive jurisdiction

(1) A party to arbitral proceedings may (upon notice to the other parties and to the tribunal) apply to the court—
    (a) challenging any award of the arbitral tribunal as to its substantive jurisdiction; or
    (b) for an order declaring an award made by the tribunal on the merits to be of no effect, in whole or in part, because the tribunal did not have substantive jurisdiction.

     A party may lose the right to object (see section 73) and the right to apply is subject to the restrictions in section 70(2) and (3).

(2) The arbitral tribunal may continue the arbitral proceedings and make a further award while an application to the court under this section is pending in relation to an award as to jurisdiction.

(3) On an application under this section challenging an award of the arbitral tribunal as to its substantive jurisdiction, the court may by order—
    (a) confirm the award,
    (b) vary the award, or
    (c) set aside the award in whole or in part.

(4) The leave of the court is required for any appeal from a decision of the court under this section.

68 Challenging the award: serious irregularity

(1) A party to arbitral proceedings may (upon notice to the other parties and to the tribunal) apply to the court challenging an award in the proceedings on the ground of serious irregularity affecting the tribunal, the proceedings or the award.

     A party may lose the right to object (see section 73) and the right to apply is subject to the restrictions in section 70(2) and (3).

(2) Serious irregularity means an irregularity of one or more of the following kinds which the court considers has caused or will cause substantial injustice to the applicant—
    (a) failure by the tribunal to comply with section 33 (general duty of tribunal);

(b) the tribunal exceeding its powers (otherwise than by exceeding its substantive jurisdiction: see section 67);

(c) failure by the tribunal to conduct the proceedings in accordance with the procedure agreed by the parties;

(d) failure by the tribunal to deal with all the issues that were put to it;

(e) any arbitral or other institution or person vested by the parties with powers in relation to the proceedings or the award exceeding its powers;

(f) uncertainty or ambiguity as to the effect of the award;

(g) the award being obtained by fraud or the award or the way in which it was procured being contrary to public policy;

(h) failure to comply with the requirements as to the form of the award; or

(i) any irregularity in the conduct of the proceedings or in the award which is admitted by the tribunal or by any arbitral or other institution or person vested by the parties with powers in relation to the proceedings or the award.

(3) If there is shown to be serious irregularity affecting the tribunal, the proceedings or the award, the court may—

(a) remit the award to the tribunal, in whole or in part, for reconsideration,

(b) set the award aside in whole or in part, or

(c) declare the award to be of no effect, in whole or in part.

The court shall not exercise its power to set aside or to declare an award to be of no effect, in whole or in part, unless it is satisfied that it would be inappropriate to remit the matters in question to the tribunal for reconsideration.

(4) The leave of the court is required for any appeal from a decision of the court under this section.

69 Appeal on point of law

(1) Unless otherwise agreed by the parties, a party to arbitral proceedings may (upon notice to the other parties and to the tribunal) appeal to the court on a question of law arising out of an award made in the proceedings.

An agreement to dispense with reasons for the tribunal's award shall be considered an agreement to exclude the court's jurisdiction under this section.

(2) An appeal shall not be brought under this section except—

(a) with the agreement of all the other parties to the proceedings, or

(b) with the leave of the court.

The right to appeal is also subject to the restrictions in section 70(2) and (3).

(3) Leave to appeal shall be given only if the court is satisfied—

(a) that the determination of the question will substantially affect the rights of one or more of the parties,

(b) that the question is one which the tribunal was asked to determine,

(c) that, on the basis of the findings of fact in the award—

(i) the decision of the tribunal on the question is obviously wrong, or

(ii) the question is one of general public importance and the decision of the tribunal is at least open to serious doubt, and

(d) that, despite the agreement of the parties to resolve the matter by arbitration, it is just and proper in all the circumstances for the court to determine the question.

(4) An application for leave to appeal under this section shall identify the question of law to be determined and state the grounds on which it is alleged that leave to appeal should be granted.

(5) The court shall determine an application for leave to appeal under this section without a hearing unless it appears to the court that a hearing is required.

(6) The leave of the court is required for any appeal from a decision of the court under this section to grant or refuse leave to appeal.

(7) On an appeal under this section the court may by order—
    (a) confirm the award,
    (b) vary the award,
    (c) remit the award to the tribunal, in whole or in part, for reconsideration in the light of the court's determination, or
    (d) set aside the award in whole or in part.
    The court shall not exercise its power to set aside an award, in whole or in part, unless it is satisfied that it would be inappropriate to remit the matters in question to the tribunal for reconsideration.

(8) The decision of the court on an appeal under this section shall be treated as a judgment of the court for the purposes of a further appeal.
    But no such appeal lies without the leave of the court which shall not be given unless the court considers that the question is one of general importance or is one which for some other special reason should be considered by the Court of Appeal.

70 Challenge or appeal: supplementary provisions

(1) The following provisions apply to an application or appeal under section 67, 68 or 69.

(2) An application or appeal may not be brought if the applicant or appellant has not first exhausted—
    (a) any available arbitral process of appeal or review, and
    (b) any available recourse under section 57 (correction of award or additional award).

(3) Any application or appeal must be brought within 28 days of the date of the award or, if there has been any arbitral process of appeal or review, of the date when the applicant or appellant was notified of the result of that process.

(4) If on an application or appeal it appears to the court that the award—
    (a) does not contain the tribunal's reasons, or
    (b) does not set out the tribunal's reasons in sufficient detail to enable the court properly to consider the application or appeal,
    the court may order the tribunal to state the reasons for its award in sufficient detail for that purpose.

(5) Where the court makes an order under subsection (4), it may make such further order as it thinks fit with respect to any additional costs of the arbitration resulting from its order.

(6) The court may order the applicant or appellant to provide security for the costs of the application or appeal, and may direct that the application or appeal be dismissed if the order is not complied with.
    The power to order security for costs shall not be exercised on the ground that the applicant or appellant is—
    (a) an individual ordinarily resident outside the United Kingdom, or
    (b) a corporation or association incorporated or formed under the law of a country outside the United Kingdom, or whose central management and control is exercised outside the United Kingdom.

(7) The court may order that any money payable under the award shall be brought into court or otherwise secured pending the determination of the application or appeal, and may direct that the application or appeal be dismissed if the order is not complied with.

(8) The court may grant leave to appeal subject to conditions to the same or similar effect as an order under subsection (6) or (7).
    This does not affect the general discretion of the court to grant leave subject to conditions.

71 Challenge or appeal: effect of order of court

(1) The following provisions have effect where the court makes an order under section 67, 68 or 69 with respect to an award.

(2) Where the award is varied, the variation has effect as part of the tribunal's award.

(3) Where the award is remitted to the tribunal, in whole or in part, for reconsideration, the tribunal shall make a fresh award in respect of the matters remitted within three months of the date of the order for remission or such longer or shorter period as the court may direct.

(4) Where the award is set aside or declared to be of no effect, in whole or in part, the court may also order that any provision that an award is a condition precedent to the bringing of legal proceedings in respect of a matter to which the arbitration agreement applies, is of no effect as regards the subject matter of the award or, as the case may be, the relevant part of the award.

MISCELLANEOUS

72 Saving for rights of person who takes no part in proceedings

(1) A person alleged to be a party to arbitral proceedings but who takes no part in the proceedings may question—
   (a) whether there is a valid arbitration agreement,
   (b) whether the tribunal is properly constituted, or
   (c) what matters have been submitted to arbitration in accordance with the arbitration agreement,
   by proceedings in the court for a declaration or injunction or other appropriate relief.

(2) He also has the same right as a party to the arbitral proceedings to challenge an award—
   (a) by an application under section 67 on the ground of lack of substantive jurisdiction in relation to him, or
   (b) by an application under section 68 on the ground of serious irregularity (within the meaning of that section) affecting him;
   and section 70(2) (duty to exhaust arbitral procedures) does not apply in his case.

73 Loss of right to object

(1) If a party to arbitral proceedings takes part, or continues to take part, in the proceedings without making, either forthwith or within such time as is allowed by the arbitration agreement or the tribunal or by any provision of this Part, any objection—
   (a) that the tribunal lacks substantive jurisdiction,
   (b) that the proceedings have been improperly conducted,
   (c) that there has been a failure to comply with the arbitration agreement or with any provision of this Part, or
   (d) that there has been any other irregularity affecting the tribunal or the proceedings,
   he may not raise that objection later, before the tribunal or the court, unless he shows that, at the time he took part or continued to take part in the proceedings, he did not know and could not with reasonable diligence have discovered the grounds for the objection.

(2) Where the arbitral tribunal rules that it has substantive jurisdiction and a party to arbitral proceedings who could have questioned that ruling—
   (a) by any available arbitral process of appeal or review, or
   (b) by challenging the award,
   does not do so, or does not do so within the time allowed by the arbitration agreement or any provision of this Part, he may not object later to the tribunal's substantive jurisdiction on any ground which was the subject of that ruling.

74 Immunity of arbitral institutions, &c

(1) An arbitral or other institution or person designated or requested by the parties to appoint or nominate an arbitrator is not liable for anything done or omitted in the discharge or purported discharge of that function unless the act or omission is shown to have been in bad faith.

(2) An arbitral or other institution or person by whom an arbitrator is appointed or nominated is not liable, by reason of having appointed or nominated him, for anything done or omitted by the arbitrator (or his employees or agents) in the discharge or purported discharge of his functions as arbitrator.

(3) The above provisions apply to an employee or agent of an arbitral or other institution or person as they apply to the institution or person himself.

75 Charge to secure payment of solicitors' costs

The powers of the court to make declarations and orders under section 73 of the Solicitors Act 1974 or Article 71H of the Solicitors (Northern Ireland) Order 1976 (power to charge property recovered in the proceedings with the payment of solicitors' costs) may be exercised in relation to arbitral proceedings as if those proceedings were proceedings in the court.

SUPPLEMENTARY

76 Service of notices, &c

(1) The parties are free to agree on the manner of service of any notice or other document required or authorised to be given or served in pursuance of the arbitration agreement or for the purposes of the arbitral proceedings.

(2) If or to the extent that there is no such agreement the following provisions apply.

(3) A notice or other document may be served on a person by any effective means.

(4) If a notice or other document is addressed, pre-paid and delivered by post—
   (a) to the addressee's last known principal residence or, if he is or has been carrying on a trade, profession or business, his last known principal business address, or
   (b) where the addressee is a body corporate, to the body's registered or principal office,
   it shall be treated as effectively served.

(5) This section does not apply to the service of documents for the purposes of legal proceedings, for which provision is made by rules of court.

(6) References in this Part to a notice or other document include any form of communication in writing and references to giving or serving a notice or other document shall be construed accordingly.

77 Powers of court in relation to service of documents

(1) This section applies where service of a document on a person in the manner agreed by the parties, or in accordance with provisions of section 76 having effect in default of agreement, is not reasonably practicable.

(2) Unless otherwise agreed by the parties, the court may make such order as it thinks fit—
   (a) for service in such manner as the court may direct, or
   (b) dispensing with service of the document.

(3) Any party to the arbitration agreement may apply for an order, but only after exhausting any available arbitral process for resolving the matter.

(4) The leave of the court is required for any appeal from a decision of the court under this section.

78 Reckoning periods of time

(1) The parties are free to agree on the method of reckoning periods of time for the purposes of any provision agreed by them or any provision of this Part having effect in default of such agreement.

(2) If or to the extent there is no such agreement, periods of time shall be reckoned in accordance with the following provisions.

(3) Where the act is required to be done within a specified period after or from a specified date, the period begins immediately after that date.

(4) Where the act is required to be done a specified number of clear days after a specified date, at least that number of days must intervene between the day on which the act is done and that date.

(5) Where the period is a period of seven days or less which would include a Saturday, Sunday or a public holiday in the place where anything which has to be done within the period falls to be done, that day shall be excluded.

In relation to England and Wales or Northern Ireland, a 'public holiday' means Christmas Day, Good Friday or a day which under the Banking and Financial Dealings Act 1971 is a bank holiday.

79 Power of court to extend time limits relating to arbitral proceedings

(1) Unless the parties otherwise agree, the court may by order extend any time limit agreed by them in relation to any matter relating to the arbitral proceedings or specified in any provision of this Part having effect in default of such agreement.

This section does not apply to a time limit to which section 12 applies (power of court to extend time for beginning arbitral proceedings, &c.).

(2) An application for an order may be made—
    (a) by any party to the arbitral proceedings (upon notice to the other parties and to the tribunal), or
    (b) by the arbitral tribunal (upon notice to the parties).

(3) The court shall not exercise its power to extend a time limit unless it is satisfied—
    (a) that any available recourse to the tribunal, or to any arbitral or other institution or person vested by the parties with power in that regard, has first been exhausted, and
    (b) that a substantial injustice would otherwise be done.

(4) The court's power under this section may be exercised whether or not the time has already expired.

(5) An order under this section may be made on such terms as the court thinks fit.

(6) The leave of the court is required for any appeal from a decision of the court under this section.

80 Notice and other requirements in connection with legal proceedings

(1) References in this Part to an application, appeal or other step in relation to legal proceedings being taken 'upon notice' to the other parties to the arbitral proceedings, or to the tribunal, are to such notice of the originating process as is required by rules of court and do not impose any separate requirement.

(2) Rules of court shall be made—
    (a) requiring such notice to be given as indicated by any provision of this Part, and
    (b) as to the manner, form and content of any such notice.

(3) Subject to any provision made by rules of court, a requirement to give notice to the tribunal of legal proceedings shall be construed—
    (a) if there is more than one arbitrator, as a requirement to give notice to each of them; and
    (b) if the tribunal is not fully constituted, as a requirement to give notice to any arbitrator who has been appointed.

(4) References in this Part to making an application or appeal to the court within a specified period are to the issue within that period of the appropriate originating process in accordance with rules of court.

(5) Where any provision of this Part requires an application or appeal to be made to the court within a specified time, the rules of court relating to the reckoning of periods, the extending or abridging of periods, and the consequences of not taking a step within the period prescribed by the rules, apply in relation to that requirement.

(6) Provision may be made by rules of court amending the provisions of this Part—

    (a) with respect to the time within which any application or appeal to the court must be made,

    (b) so as to keep any provision made by this Part in relation to arbitral proceedings in step with the corresponding provision of rules of court applying in relation to proceedings in the court, or

    (c) so as to keep any provision made by this Part in relation to legal proceedings in step with the corresponding provision of rules of court applying generally in relation to proceedings in the court.

(7) Nothing in this section affects the generality of the power to make rules of court.

81 Saving for certain matters governed by common law

(1) Nothing in this Part shall be construed as excluding the operation of any rule of law consistent with the provisions of this Part, in particular, any rule of law as to—

    (a) matters which are not capable of settlement by arbitration;

    (b) the effect of an oral arbitration agreement; or

    (c) the refusal of recognition or enforcement of an arbitral award on grounds of public policy.

(2) Nothing in this Act shall be construed as reviving any jurisdiction of the court to set aside or remit an award on the ground of errors of fact or law on the face of the award.

82 Minor definitions

(1) In this Part—

    'arbitrator', unless the context otherwise requires, includes an umpire;

    'available arbitral process', in relation to any matter, includes any process of appeal to or review by an arbitral or other institution or person vested by the parties with powers in relation to that matter;

    'claimant', unless the context otherwise requires, includes a counterclaimant, and related expressions shall be construed accordingly;

    'dispute' includes any difference;

    'enactment' includes an enactment contained in Northern Ireland legislation;

    'legal proceedings' means civil proceedings in the High Court or a county court;

    'peremptory order' means an order made under section 41(5) or made in exercise of any corresponding power conferred by the parties;

    'premises' includes land, buildings, moveable structures, vehicles, vessels, aircraft and hovercraft;

    'question of law' means—

        (a) for a court in England and Wales, a question of the law of England and Wales, and

        (b) for a court in Northern Ireland, a question of the law of Northern Ireland;

    'substantive jurisdiction', in relation to an arbitral tribunal, refers to the matters specified in section 30(1)(a) to (c), and references to the tribunal exceeding its substantive jurisdiction shall be construed accordingly.

(2) References in this Part to a party to an arbitration agreement include any person claiming under or through a party to the agreement.

83 Index of defined expressions: Part I

In this Part the expressions listed below are defined or otherwise explained by the provisions indicated—

agreement, agree and agreed	section 5(1)
agreement in writing	section 5(2) to (5)
arbitration agreement	sections 6 and 5(1)
arbitrator	section 82(1)
available arbitral process	section 82(1)
claimant	section 82(1)

commencement (in relation to arbitral proceedings)	section 14
costs of the arbitration	section 59
the court	section 105
dispute	section 82(1)
enactment	section 82(1)
legal proceedings	section 82(1)
Limitation Acts	section 13(4)
notice (or other document)	section 76(6)
party—	
—in relation to an arbitration agreement	section 82(2)
—where section 106(2) or (3) applies	section 106(4)
peremptory order	section 82(1) (and see section 41(5))
premises	section 82(1)
question of law	section 82(1)
recoverable costs	sections 63 and 64
seat of the arbitration	section 3
serve and service (of notice or other document)	section 76(6)
substantive jurisdiction (in relation to an arbitral tribunal)	section 82(1) (and see section 30(1)(a) to (c))
upon notice (to the parties or the tribunal)	section 80
written and in writing	section 5(6)

84 Transitional provisions

(1) The provisions of this Part do not apply to arbitral proceedings commenced before the date on which this Part comes into force.

(2) They apply to arbitral proceedings commenced on or after that date under an arbitration agreement whenever made.

(3) The above provisions have effect subject to any transitional provision made by an order under section 109(2) (power to include transitional provisions in commencement order).

PART II   OTHER PROVISIONS RELATING TO ARBITRATION

DOMESTIC ARBITRATION AGREEMENTS

85 Modification of Part I in relation to domestic arbitration agreement

(1) In the case of a domestic arbitration agreement the provisions of Part I are modified in accordance with the following sections.

(2) For this purpose a 'domestic arbitration agreement' means an arbitration agreement to which none of the parties is—

(a) an individual who is a national of, or habitually resident in, a state other than the United Kingdom, or

(b) a body corporate which is incorporated in, or whose central control and management is exercised in, a state other than the United Kingdom,

and under which the seat of the arbitration (if the seat has been designated or determined) is in the United Kingdom.

(3) In subsection (2) 'arbitration agreement' and 'seat of the arbitration' have the same meaning as in Part I (see sections 3, 5(1) and 6).

86 Staying of legal proceedings

(1) In section 9 (stay of legal proceedings), subsection (4) (stay unless the arbitration agreement is null and void, inoperative, or incapable of being performed) does not apply to a domestic arbitration agreement.

(2) On an application under that section in relation to a domestic arbitration agreement the court shall grant a stay unless satisfied—

    (a) that the arbitration agreement is null and void, inoperative, or incapable of being performed, or

    (b) that there are other sufficient grounds for not requiring the parties to abide by the arbitration agreement.

(3) The court may treat as a sufficient ground under subsection (2)(b) the fact that the applicant is or was at any material time not ready and willing to do all things necessary for the proper conduct of the arbitration or of any other dispute resolution procedures required to be exhausted before resorting to arbitration.

(4) For the purposes of this section the question whether an arbitration agreement is a domestic arbitration agreement shall be determined by reference to the facts at the time the legal proceedings are commenced.

87 Effectiveness of agreement to exclude court's jurisdiction

(1) In the case of a domestic arbitration agreement any agreement to exclude the jurisdiction of the court under—

    (a) section 45 (determination of preliminary point of law), or

    (b) section 69 (challenging the award: appeal on point of law),

    is not effective unless entered into after the commencement of the arbitral proceedings in which the question arises or the award is made.

(2) For this purpose the commencement of the arbitral proceedings has the same meaning as in Part I (see section 14).

(3) For the purposes of this section the question whether an arbitration agreement is a domestic arbitration agreement shall be determined by reference to the facts at the time the agreement is entered into.

88 Power to repeal or amend sections 85 to 87

(1) The Secretary of State may by order repeal or amend the provisions of sections 85 to 87.

(2) An order under this section may contain such supplementary, incidental and transitional provisions as appear to the Secretary of State to be appropriate.

(3) An order under this section shall be made by statutory instrument and no such order shall be made unless a draft of it has been laid before and approved by a resolution of each House of Parliament.

CONSUMER ARBITRATION AGREEMENTS

89 Application of unfair terms regulations to consumer arbitration agreements

(1) The following sections extend the application of the Unfair Terms in Consumer Contracts Regulations 1994 in relation to a term which constitutes an arbitration agreement.

For this purpose 'arbitration agreement' means an agreement to submit to arbitration present or future disputes or differences (whether or not contractual).

(2) In those sections 'the Regulations' means those regulations and includes any regulations amending or replacing those regulations.

(3) Those sections apply whatever the law applicable to the arbitration agreement.

90 Regulations apply where consumer is a legal person

The Regulations apply where the consumer is a legal person as they apply where the consumer is a natural person.

91 Arbitration agreement unfair where modest amount sought

(1) A term which constitutes an arbitration agreement is unfair for the purposes of the Regulations so far as it relates to a claim for a pecuniary remedy which does not exceed the amount specified by order for the purposes of this section.

(2) Orders under this section may make different provision for different cases and for different purposes.

(3) The power to make orders under this section is exercisable—

(a) for England and Wales, by the Secretary of State with the concurrence of the Lord Chancellor,

(b) for Scotland, by the Secretary of State, and

(c) for Northern Ireland, by the Department of Economic Development for Northern Ireland with the concurrence of the Lord Chancellor.

(4) Any such order for England and Wales or Scotland shall be made by statutory instrument which shall be subject to annulment in pursuance of a resolution of either House of Parliament.

(5) Any such order for Northern Ireland shall be a statutory rule for the purposes of the Statutory Rules (Northern Ireland) Order 1979 and shall be subject to negative resolution, within the meaning of section 41(6) of the Interpretation Act (Northern Ireland) 1954.

SMALL CLAIMS ARBITRATION IN THE COUNTY COURT

92 Exclusion of Part I in relation to small claims arbitration in the county court

Nothing in Part I of this Act applies to arbitration under section 64 of the County Courts Act 1984.

93 Appointment of judges as arbitrators

(1) A judge of the Commercial Court or an official referee may, if in all the circumstances he thinks fit, accept appointment as a sole arbitrator or as umpire by or by virtue of an arbitration agreement.

(2) A judge of the Commercial Court shall not do so unless the Lord Chief Justice has informed him that, having regard to the state of business in the High Court and the Crown Court, he can be made available.

(3) An official referee shall not do so unless the Lord Chief Justice has informed him that, having regard to the state of official referees' business, he can be made available.

(4) The fees payable for the services of a judge of the Commercial Court or official referee as arbitrator or umpire shall be taken in the High Court.

(5) In this section—

'arbitration agreement' has the same meaning as in Part I; and

'official referee' means a person nominated under section 68(1)(a) of the Supreme Court Act 1981 to deal with official referees' business.

(6) The provisions of Part I of this Act apply to arbitration before a person appointed under this section with the modifications specified in Schedule 2.

STATUTORY ARBITRATIONS

94 Application of Part I to statutory arbitrations

(1) The provisions of Part I apply to every arbitration under an enactment (a 'statutory arbitration'), whether the enactment was passed or made before or after the commencement of this Act, subject to the adaptations and exclusions specified in sections 95 to 98.

(2)   The provisions of Part I do not apply to a statutory arbitration if or to the extent that their application—
   (a)   is inconsistent with the provisions of the enactment concerned, with any rules or procedure authorised or recognised by it, or
   (b)   is excluded by any other enactment.

(3)   In this section and the following provisions of this Part 'enactment'—
   (a)   in England and Wales, includes an enactment contained in subordinate legislation within the meaning of the Interpretation Act 1978;
   (b)   in Northern Ireland, means a statutory provision within the meaning of section 1(f) of the Interpretation Act (Northern Ireland) 1954.

95   General adaptation of provisions in relation to statutory arbitrations

(1)   The provisions of Part I apply to a statutory arbitration—
   (a)   as if the arbitration were pursuant to an arbitration agreement and as if the enactment were that agreement, and
   (b)   as if the persons by and against whom a claim subject to arbitration in pursuance of the enactment may be or has been made were parties to that agreement.

(2)   Every statutory arbitration shall be taken to have its seat in England and Wales or, as the case may be, in Northern Ireland.

96   Specific adaptations of provisions in relation to statutory arbitrations

(1)   The following provisions of Part I apply to a statutory arbitration with the following adaptations.

(2)   In section 30(1) (competence of tribunal to rule on its own jurisdiction), the reference in paragraph (a) to whether there is a valid arbitration agreement shall be construed as a reference to whether the enactment applies to the dispute or difference in question.

(3)   Section 35 (consolidation of proceedings and concurrent hearings) applies only so as to authorise the consolidation of proceedings, or concurrent hearings in proceedings, under the same enactment.

(4)   Section 46 (rules applicable to substance of dispute) applies with the omission of subsection (1)(b) (determination in accordance with considerations agreed by parties).

97   Provisions excluded from applying to statutory arbitrations

The following provisions of Part I do not apply in relation to a statutory arbitration—
   (a)   section 8 (whether agreement discharged by death of a party);
   (b)   section 12 (power of court to extend agreed time limits);
   (c)   sections 9(5), 10(2) and 71(4) (restrictions on effect of provision that award condition precedent to right to bring legal proceedings).

98   Power to make further provision by regulations

(1)   The Secretary of State may make provision by regulations for adapting or excluding any provision of Part I in relation to statutory arbitrations in general or statutory arbitrations of any particular description.

(2)   The power is exercisable whether the enactment concerned is passed or made before or after the commencement of this Act.

(3)   Regulations under this section shall be made by statutory instrument which shall be subject to annulment in pursuance of a resolution of either House of Parliament.

PART III RECOGNITION AND ENFORCEMENT OF CERTAIN FOREIGN AWARDS

ENFORCEMENT OF GENEVA CONVENTION AWARDS

99 Continuation of Part II of the Arbitration Act 1950

Part II of theArbitration Act 1950 (enforcement of certain foreign awards) continues to apply in relation to foreign awards within the meaning of that Part which are not also New York Convention awards.

RECOGNITION AND ENFORCEMENT OF NEW YORK CONVENTION AWARDS

100 New York Convention awards

(1) In this Part a 'New York Convention award' means an award made, in pursuance of an arbitration agreement, in the territory of a state (other than the United Kingdom) which is a party to the New York Convention.

(2) For the purposes of subsection (1) and of the provisions of this Part relating to such awards—

(a) 'arbitration agreement' means an arbitration agreement in writing, and

(b) an award shall be treated as made at the seat of the arbitration, regardless of where it was signed, despatched or delivered to any of the parties.

In this subsection 'agreement in writing' and 'seat of the arbitration' have the same meaning as in Part I.

(3) If Her Majesty by Order in Council declares that a state specified in the Order is a party to the New York Convention, or is a party in respect of any territory so specified, the Order shall, while in force, be conclusive evidence of that fact.

(4) In this section 'the New York Convention' means the Convention on the Recognition and Enforcement of Foreign Arbitral Awards adopted by the United Nations Conference on International Commercial Arbitration on 10th June 1958.

101 Recognition and enforcement of awards

(1) A New York Convention award shall be recognised as binding on the persons as between whom it was made, and may accordingly be relied on by those persons by way of defence, set-off or otherwise in any legal proceedings in England and Wales or Northern Ireland.

(2) A New York Convention award may, by leave of the court, be enforced in the same manner as a judgment or order of the court to the same effect.

As to the meaning of 'the court' see section 105.

(3) Where leave is so given, judgment may be entered in terms of the award.

102 Evidence to be produced by party seeking recognition or enforcement

(1) A party seeking the recognition or enforcement of a New York Convention award must produce—

(a) the duly authenticated original award or a duly certified copy of it, and

(b) the original arbitration agreement or a duly certified copy of it.

(2) If the award or agreement is in a foreign language, the party must also produce a translation of it certified by an official or sworn translator or by a diplomatic or consular agent.

103 Refusal of recognition or enforcement

(1) Recognition or enforcement of a New York Convention award shall not be refused except in the following cases.

(2) Recognition or enforcement of the award may be refused if the person against whom it is invoked proves—

  (a) that a party to the arbitration agreement was (under the law applicable to him) under some incapacity;

  (b) that the arbitration agreement was not valid under the law to which the parties subjected it or, failing any indication thereon, under the law of the country where the award was made;

  (c) that he was not given proper notice of the appointment of the arbitrator or of the arbitration proceedings or was otherwise unable to present his case;

  (d) that the award deals with a difference not contemplated by or not falling within the terms of the submission to arbitration or contains decisions on matters beyond the scope of the submission to arbitration (but see subsection (4));

  (e) that the composition of the arbitral tribunal or the arbitral procedure was not in accordance with the agreement of the parties or, failing such agreement, with the law of the country in which the arbitration took place;

  (f) that the award has not yet become binding on the parties, or has been set aside or suspended by a competent authority of the country in which, or under the law of which, it was made.

(3) Recognition or enforcement of the award may also be refused if the award is in respect of a matter which is not capable of settlement by arbitration, or if it would be contrary to public policy to recognise or enforce the award.

(4) An award which contains decisions on matters not submitted to arbitration may be recognised or enforced to the extent that it contains decisions on matters submitted to arbitration which can be separated from those on matters not so submitted.

(5) Where an application for the setting aside or suspension of the award has been made to such a competent authority as is mentioned in subsection (2)(f), the court before which the award is sought to be relied upon may, if it considers it proper, adjourn the decision on the recognition or enforcement of the award.

  It may also on the application of the party claiming recognition or enforcement of the award order the other party to give suitable security.

104 Saving for other bases of recognition or enforcement

Nothing in the preceding provisions of this Part affects any right to rely upon or enforce a New York Convention award at common law or under section 66.

PART IV   GENERAL PROVISIONS

105 Meaning of 'the court': jurisdiction of High Court and county court

(1) In this Act 'the court' means the High Court or a county court, subject to the following provisions.

(2) The Lord Chancellor may by order make provision—

  (a) allocating proceedings under this Act to the High Court or to county courts; or

  (b) specifying proceedings under this Act which may be commenced or taken only in the High Court or in a county court.

(3) The Lord Chancellor may by order make provision requiring proceedings of any specified description under this Act in relation to which a county court has jurisdiction to be commenced or taken in one or more specified county courts.

  Any jurisdiction so exercisable by a specified county court is exercisable throughout England and Wales or, as the case may be, Northern Ireland.

(4) An order under this section—

  (a) may differentiate between categories of proceedings by reference to such criteria as the Lord Chancellor sees fit to specify, and

  (b) may make such incidental or transitional provision as the Lord Chancellor considers necessary or expedient.

(5) An order under this section for England and Wales shall be made by statutory instrument which shall be subject to annulment in pursuance of a resolution of either House of Parliament.

(6) An order under this section for Northern Ireland shall be a statutory rule for the purposes of the Statutory Rules (Northern Ireland) Order 1979 which shall be subject to annulment in pursuance of a resolution of either House of Parliament in like manner as a statutory instrument and section 5 of the Statutory Instruments Act 1946 shall apply accordingly.

106 Crown application

(1) Part I of this Act applies to any arbitration agreement to which Her Majesty, either in right of the Crown or of the Duchy of Lancaster or otherwise, or the Duke of Cornwall, is a party.

(2) Where Her Majesty is party to an arbitration agreement otherwise than in right of the Crown, Her Majesty shall be represented for the purposes of any arbitral proceedings—
(a) where the agreement was entered into by Her Majesty in right of the Duchy of Lancaster, by the Chancellor of the Duchy or such person as he may appoint, and
(b) in any other case, by such person as Her Majesty may appoint in writing under the Royal Sign Manual.

(3) Where the Duke of Cornwall is party to an arbitration agreement, he shall be represented for the purposes of any arbitral proceedings by such person as he may appoint.

(4) References in Part I to a party or the parties to the arbitration agreement or to arbitral proceedings shall be construed, where subsection (2) or (3) applies, as references to the person representing Her Majesty or the Duke of Cornwall.

107 Consequential amendments and repeals

(1) The enactments specified in Schedule 3 are amended in accordance with that Schedule, the amendments being consequential on the provisions of this Act.

(2) The enactments specified in Schedule 4 are repealed to the extent specified.

108 Extent

(1) The provisions of this Act extend to England and Wales and, except as mentioned below, to Northern Ireland.

(2) The following provisions of Part II do not extend to Northern Ireland—
section 92 (exclusion of Part I in relation to small claims arbitration in the county court), and
section 93 and Schedule 2 (appointment of judges as arbitrators).

(3) Sections 89, 90 and 91 (consumer arbitration agreements) extend to Scotland and the provisions of Schedules 3 and 4 (consequential amendments and repeals) extend to Scotland so far as they relate to enactments which so extend, subject as follows.

(4) The repeal of the Arbitration Act 1975 extends only to England and Wales and Northern Ireland.

109 Commencement

(1) The provisions of this Act come into force on such day as the Secretary of State may appoint by order made by statutory instrument, and different days may be appointed for different purposes.

(2) An order under subsection (1) may contain such transitional provisions as appear to the Secretary of State to be appropriate.

110 Short title

This Act may be cited as the Arbitration Act 1996.

SCHEDULE

Section 4(1)

SCHEDULE 1
MANDATORY PROVISIONS OF PART I

sections 9 to 11 (stay of legal proceedings);

section 12 (power of court to extend agreed time limits);

section 13 (application of Limitation Acts);

section 24 (power of court to remove arbitrator);

section 26(1) (effect of death of arbitrator);

section 28 (liability of parties for fees and expenses of arbitrators);

section 29 (immunity of arbitrator);

section 31 (objection to substantive jurisdiction of tribunal);

section 32 (determination of preliminary point of jurisdiction);

section 33 (general duty of tribunal);

section 37(2) (items to be treated as expenses of arbitrators);

section 40 (general duty of parties);

section 43 (securing the attendance of witnesses);

section 56 (power to withhold award in case of non-payment);

section 60 (effectiveness of agreement for payment of costs in any event);

section 66 (enforcement of award);

sections 67 and 68 (challenging the award: substantive jurisdiction and serious irregularity), and sections 70 and 71 (supplementary provisions; effect of order of court) so far as relating to those sections;

section 72 (saving for rights of person who takes no part in proceedings);

section 73 (loss of right to object);

section 74 (immunity of arbitral institutions, &c.);

section 75 (charge to secure payment of solicitors' costs).

Section 93(6).

SCHEDULE 2
MODIFICATIONS OF PART I IN RELATION TO JUDGE-ARBITRATORS

Introductory

1   In this Schedule 'judge-arbitrator' means a judge of the Commercial Court or official referee appointed as arbitrator or umpire under section 93.

General

2(1)   Subject to the following provisions of this Schedule, references in Part I to the court shall be construed in relation to a judge-arbitrator, or in relation to the appointment of a judge-arbitrator, as references to the Court of Appeal.

(2)   The references in sections 32(6), 45(6) and 69(8) to the Court of Appeal shall in such a case be construed as references to the House of Lords.

Arbitrator's fees

3(1)   The power of the court in section 28(2) to order consideration and adjustment of the liability of a party for the fees of an arbitrator may be exercised by a judge-arbitrator.

(2)   Any such exercise of the power is subject to the powers of the Court of Appeal under sections 24(4) and 25(3)(b) (directions as to entitlement to fees or expenses in case of removal or resignation).

Exercise of court powers in support of arbitration

4(1)   Where the arbitral tribunal consists of or includes a judge-arbitrator the powers of the court under sections 42 to 44 (enforcement of peremptory orders, summoning witnesses, and other court powers) are exercisable by the High Court and also by the judge-arbitrator himself.

(2)   Anything done by a judge-arbitrator in the exercise of those powers shall be regarded as done by him in his capacity as judge of the High Court and have effect as if done by that court. Nothing in this sub-paragraph prejudices any power vested in him as arbitrator or umpire.

Extension of time for making award

5(1)   The power conferred by section 50 (extension of time for making award) is exercisable by the judge-arbitrator himself.

(2)   Any appeal from a decision of a judge-arbitrator under that section lies to the Court of Appeal with the leave of that court.

Withholding award in case of non-payment

6(1)   The provisions of paragraph 7 apply in place of the provisions of section 56 (power to withhold award in the case of non-payment) in relation to the withholding of an award for non-payment of the fees and expenses of a judge-arbitrator.

(2)   This does not affect the application of section 56 in relation to the delivery of such an award by an arbitral or other institution or person vested by the parties with powers in relation to the delivery of the award.

7(1)   A judge-arbitrator may refuse to deliver an award except upon payment of the fees and expenses mentioned in section 56(1).

(2)   The judge-arbitrator may, on an application by a party to the arbitral proceedings, order that if he pays into the High Court the fees and expenses demanded, or such lesser amount as the judge-arbitrator may specify—

(a) the award shall be delivered,

(b) the amount of the fees and expenses properly payable shall be determined by such means and upon such terms as he may direct, and

(c) out of the money paid into court there shall be paid out such fees and expenses as may be found to be properly payable and the balance of the money (if any) shall be paid out to the applicant.

(3)   For this purpose the amount of fees and expenses properly payable is the amount the applicant is liable to pay under section 28 or any agreement relating to the payment of the arbitrator.

(4)   No application to the judge-arbitrator under this paragraph may be made where there is any available arbitral process for appeal or review of the amount of the fees or expenses demanded.

(5)   Any appeal from a decision of a judge-arbitrator under this paragraph lies to the Court of Appeal with the leave of that court.

(6)   Where a party to arbitral proceedings appeals under sub-paragraph (5), an arbitrator is entitled to appear and be heard.

Correction of award or additional award

8   Subsections (4) to (6) of section 57 (correction of award or additional award: time limit for application or exercise of power) do not apply to a judge-arbitrator.

Costs

9 Where the arbitral tribunal consists of or includes a judge-arbitrator the powers of the court under section 63(4) (determination of recoverable costs) shall be exercised by the High Court.

10(1) The power of the court under section 64 to determine an arbitrator's reasonable fees and expenses may be exercised by a judge-arbitrator.

(2) Any such exercise of the power is subject to the powers of the Court of Appeal under sections 24(4) and 25(3)(b) (directions as to entitlement to fees or expenses in case of removal or resignation).

Enforcement of award

11 The leave of the court required by section 66 (enforcement of award) may in the case of an award of a judge-arbitrator be given by the judge-arbitrator himself.

Solicitors' costs

12 The powers of the court to make declarations and orders under the provisions applied by section 75 (power to charge property recovered in arbitral proceedings with the payment of solicitors' costs) may be exercised by the judge-arbitrator.

Powers of court in relation to service of documents

13(1) The power of the court under section 77(2) (powers of court in relation to service of documents) is exercisable by the judge-arbitrator.

(2) Any appeal from a decision of a judge-arbitrator under that section lies to the Court of Appeal with the leave of that court.

Powers of court to extend time limits relating to arbitral proceedings

14(1) The power conferred by section 79 (power of court to extend time limits relating to arbitral proceedings) is exercisable by the judge-arbitrator himself.

(2) Any appeal from a decision of a judge-arbitrator under that section lies to the Court of Appeal with the leave of that court.

CPR, Part 62 Arbitration Claims

62.1 Scope of this Part and interpretation

(1) This Part contains rules about arbitration claims.

(2) In this Part—

    (a) 'the 1950 Act' means the Arbitration Act 1950;

    (b) 'the 1975 Act' means the Arbitration Act 1975;

    (c) 'the 1979 Act' means the Arbitration Act 1979;

    (d) 'the 1996 Act' means the Arbitration Act 1996;

    (e) references to—

       (i) the 1996 Act; or

       (ii) any particular section of that Act

include references to that Act or to the particular section of that Act as applied with modifications by the ACAS Arbitration Scheme (England and Wales) Order 2001; and

    (f) 'arbitration claim form' means a claim form in the form set out in Practice Direction 62

(3) Part 58 (Commercial Court) applies to arbitration claims in the Commercial Court, Part 59 (Mercantile Court) applies to arbitration claims in the Mercantile Court and Part 60 (Technology and Construction Court claims) applies to arbitration claims in the Technology and Construction Court, except where this Part provides otherwise.

I CLAIMS UNDER THE 1996 ACT

62.2 Interpretation

(1) In this Section of this Part 'arbitration claim' means—
    (a) any application to the court under the 1996 Act;
    (b) a claim to determine—
        (i) whether there is a valid arbitration agreement;
        (ii) whether an arbitration tribunal is properly constituted; or
    what matters have been submitted to arbitration in accordance with an arbitration agreement;
    (c) a claim to declare that an award by an arbitral tribunal is not binding on a party; and
    (d) any other application affecting—
        (i) arbitration proceedings (whether started or not); or
        (ii) an arbitration agreement.
(2) This Section of this Part does not apply to an arbitration claim to which Sections II or III of this Part apply.

62.3 Starting the claim

(1) Except where paragraph (2) applies an arbitration claim must be started by the issue of an arbitration claim form in accordance with the Part 8 procedure.
(2) An application under section 9 of the 1996 Act to stay legal proceedings must be made by application notice to the court dealing with those proceedings.
(3) The courts in which an arbitration claim may be started are set out in Practice Direction 62.
(4) Rule 30.5 applies with the modification that a judge of the Technology and Construction Court may transfer the claim to any other court or specialist list.

62.4 Arbitration claim form

(1) An arbitration claim form must—
    (a) include a concise statement of—
        (i) the remedy claimed; and
        (ii) any questions on which the claimant seeks the decision of the court;
    (b) give details of any arbitration award challenged by the claimant, identifying which part or parts of the award are challenged and specifying the grounds for the challenge;
    (c) show that any statutory requirements have been met;
    (d) specify under which section of the 1996 Act the claim is made;
    (e) identify against which (if any) defendants a costs order is sought; and
    (f) specify either—
        (i) the persons on whom the arbitration claim form is to be served, stating their role in the arbitration and whether they are defendants; or
        (ii) that the claim is made without notice under section 44(3) of the 1996 Act and the grounds relied on.
(2) Unless the court orders otherwise an arbitration claim form must be served on the defendant within 1 month from the date of issue and rules 7.5 and 7.6 are modified accordingly.
(3) Where the claimant applies for an order under section 12 of the 1996 Act (extension of time for beginning arbitral proceedings or other dispute resolution procedures), he may include in his arbitration claim form an alternative application for a declaration that such an order is not needed.

62.5 Service out of the jurisdiction

(1) The court may give permission to serve an arbitration claim form out of the jurisdiction if—
    (a) the claimant seeks to—
        (i) challenge; or

        (ii) appeal on a question of law arising out of,

      an arbitration award made within the jurisdiction;

        (The place where an award is treated as made is determined by section 53 of the 1996 Act.)

  (b) the claim is for an order under section 44 of the 1996 Act; or

  (c) the claimant—

        (i) seeks some other remedy or requires a question to be decided by the court affecting an arbitration (whether started or not), an arbitration agreement or an arbitration award; and

        (ii) the seat of the arbitration is or will be within the jurisdiction or the conditions in section 2(4) of the 1996 Act are satisfied.

(2) An application for permission under paragraph (1) must be supported by written evidence—

  (a) stating the grounds on which the application is made; and

  (b) showing in what place or country the person to be served is, or probably may be found.

(3) Rules 6.40 to 6.46 apply to the service of an arbitration claim form under paragraph (1).

(4) An order giving permission to serve an arbitration claim form out of the jurisdiction must specify the period within which the defendant may file an acknowledgment of service.

62.6 Notice

(1) Where an arbitration claim is made under section 24, 28 or 56 of the 1996 Act, each arbitrator must be a defendant.

(2) Where notice must be given to an arbitrator or any other person it may be given by sending him a copy of—

  (a) the arbitration claim form; and

  (b) any written evidence in support.

(3) Where the 1996 Act requires an application to the court to be made on notice to any other party to the arbitration, that notice must be given by making that party a defendant.

62.7 Case management

(1) Part 26 and any other rule that requires a party to file an allocation questionnaire does not apply.

(2) Arbitration claims are allocated to the multi-track.

(3) Part 29 does not apply.

(4) The automatic directions set out in Practice Direction 62 apply unless the court orders otherwise.

62.8 Stay of legal proceedings

(1) An application notice seeking a stay of legal proceedings under section 9 of the 1996 Act must be served on all parties to those proceedings who have given an address for service.

(2) A copy of an application notice under paragraph (1) must be served on any other party to the legal proceedings (whether or not he is within the jurisdiction) who has not given an address for service, at–

  (a) his last known address; or

  (b) a place where it is likely to come to his attention.

(3) Where a question arises as to whether—

  (a) an arbitration agreement has been concluded; or

  (b) the dispute which is the subject-matter of the proceedings falls within the terms of such an agreement,

the court may decide that question or give directions to enable it to be decided and may order the proceedings to be stayed pending its decision.

62.9 Variation of time

(1) The court may vary the period of 28 days fixed by section 70(3) of the 1996 Act for—

    (a) challenging the award under section 67 or 68 of the Act; and

    (b) appealing against an award under section 69 of the Act.

(2) An application for an order under paragraph (1) may be made without notice being served on any other party before the period of 28 days expires.

(3) After the period of 28 days has expired—

    (a) an application for an order extending time under paragraph (1) must—

        (i) be made in the arbitration claim form; and

        (ii) state the grounds on which the application is made;

    (b) any defendant may file written evidence opposing the extension of time within 7 days after service of the arbitration claim form; and

    (c) if the court extends the period of 28 days, each defendant's time for acknowledging service and serving evidence shall start to run as if the arbitration claim form had been served on the date when the court's order is served on that defendant.

62.10 Hearings

(1) The court may order that an arbitration claim be heard either in public or in private.

(2) Rule 39.2 does not apply.

(3) Subject to any order made under paragraph (1)—

    (a) the determination of—

        (i) a preliminary point of law under section 45 of the 1996 Act; or

        (ii) an appeal under section 69 of the 1996 Act on a question of law arising out of an award,

    will be heard in public; and

    (b) all other arbitration claims will be heard in private.

(4) Paragraph (3)(a) does not apply to—

    (a) the preliminary question of whether the court is satisfied of the matters set out in section 45(2)(b); or

    (b) an application for permission to appeal under section 69(2)(b).

II OTHER ARBITRATION CLAIMS

[CPR 62.11–62.16 concern arbitration claims to which the old law applies.]

III ENFORCEMENT

62.17 Scope of this Section

This Section of this Part applies to all arbitration enforcement proceedings other than by a claim on the award.

62.18 Enforcement of awards

(1) An application for permission under—

    (a) section 66 of the 1996 Act;

    (b) section 101 of the 1996 Act;

    (c) section 26 of the 1950 Act; or

    (d) section 3(1)(a) of the 1975 Act,

to enforce an award in the same manner as a judgment or order may be made without notice in an arbitration claim form.

(2) The court may specify parties to the arbitration on whom the arbitration claim form must be served.

(3) The parties on whom the arbitration claim form is served must acknowledge service and the enforcement proceedings will continue as if they were an arbitration claim under Section I of this Part.

(4) With the permission of the court the arbitration claim form may be served out of the jurisdiction irrespective of where the award is, or is treated as, made.

(5) Where the applicant applies to enforce an agreed award within the meaning of section 51(2) of the 1996 Act—

    (a) the arbitration claim form must state that the award is an agreed award; and

    (b) any order made by the court must also contain such a statement.

(6) An application for permission must be supported by written evidence—

    (a) exhibiting—

        (i) where the application is made under section 66 of the 1996 Act or under section 26 of the 1950 Act, the arbitration agreement and the original award (or copies);

        (ii) where the application is under section 101 of the 1996 Act, the documents required to be produced by section 102 of that Act; or

        (iii) where the application is under section 3(1)(a) of the 1975 Act, the documents required to be produced by section 4 of that Act;

    (b) stating the name and the usual or last known place of residence or business of the claimant and of the person against whom it is sought to enforce the award; and

    (c) stating either—

        (i) that the award has not been complied with; or

        (ii) the extent to which it has not been complied with at the date of the application.

(7) An order giving permission must—

    (a) be drawn up by the claimant; and

    (b) be served on the defendant by—

        (i) delivering a copy to him personally; or

        (ii) sending a copy to him at his usual or last known place of residence or business.

(8) An order giving permission may be served out of the jurisdiction—

    (a) without permission; and

    (b) in accordance with rules 6.40 to 6.46 as if the order were an arbitration claim form.

(9) Within 14 days after service of the order or, if the order is to be served out of the jurisdiction, within such other period as the court may set—

    (a) the defendant may apply to set aside the order; and

    (b) the award must not be enforced until after—

        (i) the end of that period; or

        (ii) any application made by the defendant within that period has been finally disposed of.

(10) The order must contain a statement of—

    (a) the right to make an application to set the order aside; and

    (b) the restrictions on enforcement under rule 62.18(9)(b).

(11) Where a body corporate is a party any reference in this rule to place of residence or business shall have effect as if the reference were to the registered or principal address of the body corporate.

62.19 Interest on awards

(1) Where an applicant seeks to enforce an award of interest the whole or any part of which relates to a period after the date of the award, he must file a statement giving the following particulars—

    (a) whether simple or compound interest was awarded;

    (b) the date from which interest was awarded;

    (c) where rests were provided for, specifying them;

    (d) the rate of interest awarded; and

    (e) a calculation showing—

        (i) the total amount claimed up to the date of the statement; and

        (ii) any sum which will become due on a daily basis.

(2) A statement under paragraph (1) must be filed whenever the amount of interest has to be quantified for the purpose of—

    (a) obtaining a judgment or order under section 66 of the 1996 Act (enforcement of the award); or

    (b) enforcing such a judgment or order.

62.20 Registration in High Court of foreign awards

(1) Where—

    (a) an award is made in proceedings on an arbitration in any part of a British overseas territory or other territory to which Part I of the Foreign Judgments (Reciprocal Enforcement) Act 1933 ('the 1933 Act') extends;

    (b) Part II of the Administration of Justice Act 1920 extended to that part immediately before Part I of the 1933 Act was extended to that part; and

    (c) an award has, under the law in force in the place where it was made, become enforceable in the same manner as a judgment given by a court in that place,

rules 74.1 to 74.7 and 74.9 apply in relation to the award as they apply in relation to a judgment given by the court subject to the modifications in paragraph (2).

(2) The modifications referred to in paragraph (1) are as follows—

    (a) for references to the State of origin are substituted references to the place where the award was made; and

    (b) the written evidence required by rule 74.4 must state (in addition to the matters required by that rule) that to the best of the information or belief of the maker of the statement the award has, under the law in force in the place where it was made, become enforceable in the same manner as a judgment given by a court in that place.

62.21 Registration of awards under the Arbitration (International Investment Disputes) Act 1966

(1) In this rule—

    (a) 'the 1966 Act' means the Arbitration (International Investment Disputes) Act 1966;

    (b) 'award' means an award under the Convention;

    (c) 'the Convention' means the Convention on the settlement of investment disputes between States and nationals of other States which was opened for signature in Washington on 18th March 1965;

    (d) 'judgment creditor' means the person seeking recognition or enforcement of an award; and

    (e) 'judgment debtor' means the other party to the award.

(2) Subject to the provisions of this rule, the following provisions of Part 74 apply with such modifications as may be necessary in relation to an award as they apply in relation to a judgment to which Part I of the Foreign Judgments (Reciprocal Enforcement) Act 1933 applies—

    (a) rule 74.1;

    (b) rule 74.3;

    (c) rule 74.4(1), (2)(a) to (d), and (4);

    (d) rule 74.6 (except paragraph (3)(c) to (e)); and

    (e) rule 74.9(2).

(3) An application to have an award registered in the High Court under section 1 of the 1966 Act must be made in accordance with the Part 8 procedure.

(4) The written evidence required by rule 74.4 in support of an application for registration must—

    (a) exhibit the award certified under the Convention instead of the judgment (or a copy of it); and

    (b) in addition to stating the matters referred to in rule 74.4(2)(a) to (d) state whether—

        (i) at the date of the application the enforcement of the award has been stayed (provisionally or otherwise) under the Convention; and

(ii) any, and if so what, application has been made under the Convention, which, if granted, might result in a stay of the enforcement of the award.

(5) Where, on granting permission to register an award or an application made by the judgment debtor after an award has been registered, the court considers—

(a) that the enforcement of the award has been stayed (whether provisionally or otherwise) under the Convention; or

(b) that an application has been made under the Convention which, if granted, might result in a stay of the enforcement of the award,

the court may stay the enforcement of the award for such time as it considers appropriate.

Practice Direction 62: Arbitration

SECTION I

1.1 This Section of this Practice Direction applies to arbitration claims to which Section I of Part 62 applies.

1.2 In this Section 'the 1996 Act' means the Arbitration Act 1996.

1.3 Where a rule provides for a document to be sent, it may be sent—

(1) by first class post;

(2) through a document exchange; or

(3) by fax, electronic mail or other means of electronic communication.

Starting the claim: r. 62.3

2.1 An arbitration claim under the 1996 Act (other than under section 9) must be started in accordance with the High Court and County Courts (Allocation of Arbitration Proceedings) Order 1996 by the issue of an arbitration claim form.

2.2 An arbitration claim form must be substantially in the form set out in Appendix A to this practice direction.

2.3 Subject to paragraph 2.1, an arbitration claim form—

(1) may be issued at the courts set out in column 1 of the table below and will be entered in the list set out against that court in column 2;

(2) relating to a landlord and tenant or partnership dispute must be issued in the Chancery Division of the High Court.

Court	List
Admiralty and Commercial Registry at the Royal Courts of Justice, London	Commercial list
Technology and Construction Court Registry, St. Dunstan's House, London	TCC list
District Registry of the High Court (where mercantile court established)	Mercantile list
District Registry of the High Court (where arbitration claim form marked 'Technology and Construction Court' in top right hand corner)	TCC list

2.3A An arbitration claim form must, in the case of an appeal, or application for permission to appeal, from a judge-arbitrator, be issued in the Civil Division of the Court of Appeal. The judge hearing the application may adjourn the matter for oral argument before two judges of that court.

Arbitration claim form: service: r. 62.4

3.1 The court may exercise its powers under rule 6.15 to permit service of an arbitration claim form at the address of a party's solicitor or representative acting for that party in the arbitration.

3.2 Where the arbitration claim form is served by the claimant he must file a certificate of service within 7 days of service of the arbitration claim form.
(Rule 6.17 specifies what a certificate of service must show).

Acknowledgment of service or making representations by arbitrator or ACAS

4.1 Where—
 (1) an arbitrator; or
 (2) ACAS (in a claim under the 1996 Act as applied with modifications by the ACAS Arbitration Scheme (England and Wales) Order 2001)
is sent a copy of an arbitration claim form (including an arbitration claim form sent under rule 62.6(2)), that arbitrator or ACAS (as the case may be) may—
 (a) apply to be made a defendant; or
 (b) make representations to the court under paragraph 4.3.
4.2 An application under paragraph 4.1(2)(a) to be made a defendant—
 (1) must be served on the claimant; but
 (2) need not be served on any other party.
4.3 An arbitrator or ACAS may make representations by filing written evidence or in writing to the court.

Supply of documents from court records

5.1 An arbitration claim form may only be inspected with the permission of the court.

Case management: r. 62.7

6.1 The following directions apply unless the court orders otherwise.
6.2 A defendant who wishes to rely on evidence before the court must file and serve his written evidence—
 (1) within 21 days after the date by which he was required to acknowledge service; or,
 (2) where a defendant is not required to file an acknowledgement of service, within 21 days after service of the arbitration claim form.
6.3 A claimant who wishes to rely on evidence in reply to written evidence filed under paragraph 6.2 must file and serve his written evidence within 7 days after service of the defendant's evidence.
6.4 Agreed indexed and paginated bundles of all the evidence and other documents to be used at the hearing must be prepared by the claimant.
6.5 Not later than 5 days before the hearing date estimates for the length of the hearing must be filed together with a complete set of the documents to be used.
6.6 Not later than 2 days before the hearing date the claimant must file and serve—
 (1) a chronology of the relevant events cross-referenced to the bundle of documents;
 (2) (where necessary) a list of the persons involved; and
 (3) a skeleton argument which lists succinctly—
 (a) the issues which arise for decision;
 (b) the grounds of relief (or opposing relief) to be relied upon;
 (c) the submissions of fact to be made with the references to the evidence; and
 (d) the submissions of law with references to the relevant authorities.
6.7 Not later than the day before the hearing date the defendant must file and serve a skeleton argument which lists succinctly—
 (1) the issues which arise for decision;
 (2) the grounds of relief (or opposing relief) to be relied upon;
 (3) the submissions of fact to be made with the references to the evidence; and
 (4) the submissions of law with references to the relevant authorities.

Securing the attendance of witnesses

7.1 A party to arbitral proceedings being conducted in England or Wales who wishes to rely on section 43 of the 1996 Act to secure the attendance of a witness must apply for a witness summons in accordance with Part 34.

7.2 If the attendance of the witness is required within the district of a district registry, the application may be made at that registry.

7.3 A witness summons will not be issued until the applicant files written evidence showing that the application is made with—

(1) the permission of the tribunal; or

(2) the agreement of the other parties.

Interim remedies

8.1 An application for an interim remedy under section 44 of the 1996 Act must be made in an arbitration claim form.

Applications under sections 32 and 45 of the 1996 Act

9.1 This paragraph applies to arbitration claims for the determination of—

(1) a question as to the substantive jurisdiction of the arbitral tribunal under section 32 of the 1996 Act; and

(2) a preliminary point of law under section 45 of the 1996 Act.

9.2 Where an arbitration claim is made without the agreement in writing of all the other parties to the arbitral proceedings but with the permission of the arbitral tribunal, the written evidence or witness statements filed by the parties must set out any evidence relied on by the parties in support of their contention that the court should, or should not, consider the claim.

9.3 As soon as practicable after the written evidence is filed, the court will decide whether or not it should consider the claim and, unless the court otherwise directs, will so decide without a hearing.

Decisions without a hearing

10.1 Having regard to the overriding objective the court may decide particular issues without a hearing. For example, as set out in paragraph 9.3, the question whether the court is satisfied as to the matters set out in section 32(2)(b) or section 45(2)(b) of the 1996 Act.

10.2 The court will generally decide whether to extend the time limit under section 70(3) of the 1996 Act without a hearing. Where the court makes an order extending the time limit, the defendant must file his written evidence within 21 days from service of the order.

Variation of time: r. 62.9

11.1 An application for an order under rule 62.9(1)—

(1) before the period of 28 days has expired, must be made in a Part 23 application notice; and

(2) after the period of 28 days has expired, must be set out in a separately identified part in the arbitration claim form.

Applications for permission to appeal

12.1 Where a party seeks permission to appeal to the court on a question of law arising out of an arbitration award, the arbitration claim form must—

(1) identify the question of law; and

(2) state the grounds

on which the party alleges that permission should be given.

12.2 The written evidence in support of the application must set out any evidence relied on by the party for the purpose of satisfying the court—

    (1) of the matters referred to in section 69(3) of the 1996 Act; and

    (2) that permission should be given.

12.3 The written evidence filed by the respondent to the application must—

    (1) state the grounds on which the respondent opposes the grant of permission;

    (2) set out any evidence relied on by him relating to the matters mentioned in section 69(3) of the 1996 Act; and

    (3) specify whether the respondent wishes to contend that the award should be upheld for reasons not expressed (or not fully expressed) in the award and, if so, state those reasons.

12.4 The court will normally determine applications for permission to appeal without an oral hearing.

12.5 Where the court refuses an application for permission to appeal without an oral hearing, it must provide brief reasons.

12.6 Where the court considers that an oral hearing is required, it may give such further directions as are necessary.

SECTION II

[This section deals with arbitration claims under the old law.]

SECTION III

15.1 This Section of this Practice Direction applies to enforcement proceedings to which Section III of Part 62 applies.

Registration of awards under the Arbitration (International Investment Disputes) Act 1966: r 62.21

16.1 Awards ordered to be registered under the 1966 Act and particulars will be entered in the Register kept for that purpose at the Admiralty and Commercial Registry.

BIBLIOGRAPHY

Many books are available for further study, especially in the areas of mediation and negotiation. The following books may be of particular use to a lawyer working in England and Wales.

GENERAL ADR

The Law and Practice of Compromise: with precedents by David Foskett et al (7th edn, London: Sweet & Maxwell, 2005).

The ADR Practice Guide: commercial dispute resolution by Karl Mackie et al (3rd edn, Haywards Heath: Tottel, 2007).

ADR A Practical Guide by Charles Chatterjee (London: Routledge 2007).

Essentials of ADR by Susan Patterson (New Jersey: Prentice Hall, 2008).

ADR: A Conflict Diagnosis Approach by Laurie Coltri (New Jersey: Prentice Hall, 2009).

ADR Principles & Practice by Henry Brown (London: Sweet & Maxwell, 1999).

Dispute Processes: ADR and the Primary Forms of Decision Making by Michael Palmer (Cambridge: Cambridge University Press, 2005)

The Handbook of Dispute Resolution by Michael L Moffitt and Robert C Bordone (eds) (San Francisco: Jossey-Bass, 2005).

Alternative dispute resolution: an essential competency for lawyers by Mark Partridge (Oxford: Oxford University Press, 2009).

Dispute processes: ADR and the primary forms of decision-making by Simon Roberts and Michael Palmer (Cambridge: Cambridge University Press, 2005).

Restorative justice: ideas, values, debates by Gerry Johnstone (Cullompton: Willan, 2002).

COMPARISON WITH LITIGATION PRINCIPLES

A Practical Approach to Civil Procedure by Stuart Sime (13th edn, Oxford: Oxford University Press, 2010).

A Practical Approach to Effective Litigation by Susan Blake (7th edn, Oxford: Oxford University Press, 2010).

ARBITRATION

Russell on Arbitration by David St John, Judith Gill, Matthew Gearing (23rd edn, London: Sweet & Maxwell, 2007).

Gill: The law of arbitration by Enid A Marshall, William H Gill (4th edn, London: Sweet & Maxwell, 2001).

Arbitration Law by Robert Merkin (St Helier: Informa Business Publishing, 2004).

Arbitration Practice and Procedure by D Cato (London: LLP Professional Publishing, 1999).

Arbitration Awards: A Practical Approach by Ray Turner (Oxford: WileyBlackwell, 2005).

Arbitration Act 1996 by Robert Merkin (4th edn, London: Sweet & Maxwell, 2008).

The Arbitration Act 1996: a commentary by Bruce Harris, Rowan Planterose and Jonathan Tecks (Oxford: Blackwell, 2007).

Construction Arbitration by Peter Coulson (Oxford: Oxford University Press, 2007).

COMMERCIAL ADR

Arbitration of Commercial Disputes: International and English Law and Practice by Andrew Tweeddale and Karen Tweeddale (Oxford: Oxford University Press, 2007).

ADR in Commercial Disputes by Russell Caller (London: Sweet & Maxwell, 2001).

The ADR Practice Guide: commercial dispute resolution by Karl Mackie et al (3rd edn, Haywards Heath: Tottel, 2007).

The law and practice of commercial arbitration in England by Michael Mustill (London: Butterworths, 1989).

Butterworths Commercial Court and arbitration pleadings by Charles Macdonald and Chirag Karia Macdonald (Haywards Heath: Tottel, 2005).

Commercial dispute resolution by Michael Waring (Guildford: College of Law 2009).

MEDIATION

Mediation: Skills, Techniques and Strategies by Miryana Nesic and Laurence Boulle (Haywards Heath: Tottel, 2009).

Mediators Handbook by Ruth Charlton (Australia: Law Book Company, 2004).

Mediation Law and Practice by David Spenser and Michael Brogan (Cambridge: Cambridge University Press, 2007).

The Mediator's Handbook by Jennifer Beer (British Columbia: New Society Publishers, 2007).

The Mediation Process by Christopher Moore (San Francisco: Jossey Bas, 2003).

Mediation, conciliation and emotions: a practitioner's guide for understanding emotions in dispute resolution by Peter Ladd (Lanham (Maryland): University Press of America, 2005).

The EU Mediation Atlas: Practice and Regulation by CEDR (London: Butterworths Law, 2006).

Mediators on Mediation, Leading Mediator Perspectives on the Practice of Commercial Mediation by Chris Newmark and Anthony Monaghan (Haywards Heath: Tottel, 2005).

Mediation Advocacy by Andrew Goodman and Alastair Hammerton (2nd edn, St Albans: XPL Publishing, 2006)

NEGOTIATION

Getting to Yes: Negotiating an agreement without giving in by Roger Fisher, William Ury and Bruce Patton (London: Random House Business Books, 2003).

Getting Past No: Negotiating with difficult people by William Ury (London: Random House Business Books, 1992).

The Art and Science of Negotiation by Howard Raiffa (Cambridge Mass.: Harvard University Press, 1990).

Negotiation Analysis: The Science and Art of Collaborative Decision Making by Howard Raiffa (Cambridge Mass.: Harvard University Press, 2007).

Effective Negotiation by Ray Fells (Cambridge: Cambridge University Press, 2010).

Negotiation by Roy Lewicki, David Saunders and Bruce Barry (Ohio: McGraw-Hill Higher Education, 2009).

OTHER FORMS OF ADR

Expert Determination by John Kendall (London: Sweet & Maxwell, 2008).

Disciplinary and Grievance Procedures: ACAS Code of Practice by ACAS (London: Stationery Office, 2009).

Enhanced Dispute Resolution through the use of Information Technology by Arno Lodder and John Zeleznikov (Cambridge: Cambridge University Press, 2010).

INTERNATIONAL ADR

International Commercial Dispute Resolution by Jonathan Warne (Haywards Heath: Bloomsbury Professional, 2009).

ADR: A Developing World Perspective by Albert Fiadjoe (London: Routledge Cavendish, 2004).

Law and Practice of International Commercial Arbitration by Martin Hunter and Alan Redfern (5th edn, London: Sweet & Maxwell, 2009).

Principles and Practice of International Commercial Arbitration by Margaret Moses (Cambridge: Cambridge University Press, 2008).

International mediation: the art of business diplomacy by Eileen Carroll and Karl Mackie (2nd edn, Haywards Heath: Tottel, 2006).

International arbitration: a Handbook by Philip Capper (London: Informa, 2004).

International arbitration rules: a comparative guide by Bridget Wheeler (ed) (London: LLP 2000).

INDEX

Abruptness 129
ACAS (Advisory, Conciliation and Arbitration
        Service) 305–6
    codes 260
    collective conciliation 306
    Conciliation Scheme 260
    confidentiality 305
    criteria for selection of cases 306
    employment tribunals 305–6
    mediation 260, 305
    post-claim conciliation 305–6
    pre-claim conciliation 306
    process 306
    role 8, 31
    terminology 305
    time limits for employment tribunal claims 306
    trade unions 306
    website 8, 305
accreditation *see* training and accreditation
ad hoc arbitration 388
adjudication *see also* construction industry
        adjudication
    advantages 34
    agreements to adjudicate 34
    construction disputes 34
    definition 34
    disadvantages 34
    expert or neutral determination 351
    process, key elements of 34
    professional ethics 289
    specialist fields 34
    TeCSA Adjudication Rules 358, 361
    third parties 34
adjudicative options 32–5, 49, 321, 371 *see also*
        adjudication
administration 193, 250, 293
administrative consent orders 332
Admiralty and Commercial Courts Guide 77, 110
admissions 288
ADR Group 259
ADR Now research 10, 17–18
advantages and disadvantages of ADR 4, 6–7,
        13–15
    adjudication 34
    choice of forum 13
    clear and public finding, lack of 16
    client satisfaction 15
    confidentiality 14
    confusion of process 17
    control of process 13
    costs 13, 15, 16
    court orders required, where 43, 180

delay 15, 185
early neutral and/or expert evaluation 32
evidence
    disclosure 16–17
    flexibility 14
    pre-action protocols 16
    rules, loss of potential advantages of
        evidential 16–17
expense, increases in 15
flexibility of process 14
judgments 16, 321
litigation 7, 16, 43, 44–5, 180, 181
mediation 30–1, 177–8, 181–2, 185, 188–9
negotiation 27–8
outcome compared to judgments, possible
        reduction in 16
Part 36 offers 26
personal injury claims 261
potential outcomes, wider range of 14
precedent 7, 16, 43, 44–5, 180, 181
problem-solving approach, use of 14
professional ethics 270
risk reduction 15
specific benefits, suggesting 53
speed of settlement 13
strategic use of procedural steps, loss of potential
        use of 16
summary judgments 16
Tomlin orders 335–6
weighing up disadvantages and advantages 17
wider range of issues, consideration of 13–14
written offers 26
adversarial procedure 7, 14, 23, 46, 47, 384–5, 409,
        424
advice 39–41
    acceptance of settlements 24–5
    arbitration clauses 407–8
    best interests of client 40
    case management hearings 40
    conferences or meetings 40
    costs 61, 280–1
    evidence, disclosure of 41
    fees, concern over 39
    hearings, before 40, 41
    initial advice 40
    international arbitration 434
    issue of proceedings, prior to 40, 41
    litigation, familiarity with 39
    opinions 40
    Part 36 offers 41
    privilege 243
    problems with advice 38–9

advice (*cont.*)
    professional conduct 39–40, 280–3
    professional duty 39–40
    reviews prior to hearings 40
    selection of ADR options, factors influencing 38–41
    settlements 24–5, 282–3
    stage in case 48–9
    track allocation stage 41
    when to give advice 40–1
    witness statements, exchange of 41
advocates
    case analysis 236
    counsel, instructions to 236
    litigation and mediation, difference between 237
    mediation advocacy 236–40
    opening statements at opening joint meetings, delivery of 238
    persuasive arguments, identification of 141
    precedents 239
    preparation 236
    private closed meetings, role during 238
    role 236–40
    settlements 238–40
    skills 237–8
    Standing Council of Mediation Advocates 236–7
after the event insurance 66, 192–3
agendas, agreeing 156
agreement to ADR, securing 53–4
agreements/contracts *see also* arbitration agreements or clauses; settlement agreements/contracts
    adjudication 34
    ADR clauses 87, 89
    appeals on points of law 476
    arbitral tribunal, mandate of 399–400
    BATNA (best alternative to a negotiated agreement) 146–7, 201, 215
    breach 89, 350
    clarity 42
    compromise agreements 261
    conciliation 305
    confidentiality 54–5, 244–5
    construction industry adjudication 355–6, 356–7, 369
    costs 337
    courts 87–9
    damages 89, 400
    definition of contractual ADR clauses 89
    enforcement 42, 245
    example 87
    exchange of letters 324
    expert or neutral determination 342, 343–4, 350
    international context 11
    JCT standard form 258
    jurisdiction 43
    mediation 28–9, 65, 183, 203–5, 219, 230–1, App 2
    memorandum 29
    National Mediation Helpline App 2
    negotiation 42, 173–5
    options as part of contracts 22

    outcomes 321
    provisional agreements 320
    setting aside agreements 240
    settlements, recording 324, 326–7
    standard forms 204
    unfair contract terms 247, 352
    WATNA (worse alternative to a negotiated agreement) 147, 201, 215
    without prejudice communications 240–3
    writing 356
aggression 130
allocation stage
    advice 41
    fast track claims 83
    High Court jurisdiction in arbitration claims 483
    mediation 84–5
    multi-track claims 83
    questionnaires 83–5
    service 84
    small claims track 83
    stay of proceedings 85
    time limits 84
amiable compositeur 427, 437, 438, 441
ancillary relief 82, 258
animosity between parties 44
anonymous information 311
anti-suit injunctions
    breach of arbitration agreements 465
    bundles 465
    High Court jurisdiction in arbitration claims 465
    interim injunctions 465
    time limits 465
    witness statements 465
apologies 48, 316
appeals
    agreements to appeal 476
    arbitration
        Arbitration Act 1996 475–6, 478
        arbitration awards 475–6
        awards 431, 459
        commercial arbitration 427, 431
        High Court jurisdiction in arbitration claims 475–8, 483–4
        points of law 475–8
    avoidance of appeals 7
    contrary agreement, where there is no 475–6
    costs sanctions 103
    Court of Appeal mediation service 9, 90, 103, 249
    discretion 478
    exhaustion of appeals and reviews 476
    fair trials 390
    foreign law, questions of 475
    general public importance, points of law of 477–8
    Her Majesty's Courts Service (HMCS) Small Claims Mediation Scheme 256
    ICC Rules 476
    ousting the jurisdiction of the court 476
    permission to appeal 476–8, 483–4
    point must arise from an award 476
    points of law 475–8

question of law 475
reasons for decisions, no agreement to dispense
with 476
substantially affecting rights of parties 477
time limits 476
tribunal asked to determine points 476
wrong, where arbitrators' decision is
obviously 477
applicable law 437–41
appointments
arbitral tribunal 375, 391, 396–9, 428, 444, 450,
465–6
commercial arbitration 428
conciliators 305
construction industry adjudication 361
early neutral and/or expert evaluation 298, 300
experts 342, 345–6
fees 361
judges as arbitrators 398–9
mediation 193–7, 204
parties, by 391
arbitral tribunal 394–402
appeals on points of law 476
appointments 396–9
commercial arbitration 428
date of commencement 395
default procedure 398
failure of procedure 399, 466
High Court jurisdiction in arbitration
claims 465
international arbitration 444
judges as arbitrators 398–9
mandate 375
parties, by 391
setting aside 465–6
UNCITRAL Model Law 450
capacity 466
chair 396, 398
commercial arbitration 428
conflicts of interest 366
contractual basis of mandate 399–400
damages for breach of contract 400
date of commencement 395
death 401
Departmental Advisory Committee report 400
expenses 401
experts 422
fees 399, 401, 402, 467
general duty 384
High Court jurisdiction 465–7
ICC Rules of Arbitration 448–9
immunities 402
impartiality 399–400
independence 399–400
institutional rules 400–1
international arbitration 444
judges as arbitrators 398–9
jurisdiction 374–5, 465–6
mandate 374–5, 399–400
mental capacity 466

number of arbitrators 396, 398
parties
appointment 391
autonomy 396
physical capacity 466
procedure 375
qualifications 399, 466
removal 400–1, 466
resignation 401, 467
sole arbitrators 396, 398–9, 465–6
terms of agreement, dispute within 374–5
terms of reference 400
umpires 396, 398–9
UNCITRAL Model Law 400, 450–1
vacancies 401
arbitration 32–4, 370–92 *see also* **arbitral
tribunal; arbitration agreements or
clauses; arbitration awards; commercial
arbitration; international arbitration**
ACAS 8, 31, 305–6
ad hoc arbitration 388
adjudicative, as 371
advantages 33
adversarial procedure 384–5
anti-suit injunctions 465
appeals 388, 390, 392, 475–8, 483–4
arbitrable dispute, definition of 376–7
Arbitration Act 1697 8
Arbitration Act 1950 372
Arbitration Act 1996 32–3, 371–2, 374–6, 382–92
interpretation 373
text App 4
Arb-Med 234–5
Chartered Institute of Arbitrators 20
claims procedure 478–83
commencement of arbitration 394–6, 450, 465
competition law 377
confidentiality 389
construction industry adjudication 353–4
consumer arbitration 389
costs 65, 384, 388, 392
courts
applications 386–7
High Court jurisdiction in arbitration
claims 462–84
procedural orders 454, 467–70
date of commencement 394, 395
definition 32, 371
delay 384, 388
Departmental Advisory Committee report 372, 400
disadvantages 33–4
dispute or difference, definition of 376
EU competition law 377
EU law 377, 389
European Convention on Human Rights 377,
384, 390
evidence 375
expenses 467
expert or neutral determination 351, 352
failure, reasons for 34

arbitration (*cont.*)
fair resolution of disputes 384–5, 390
fees 466–7
flexibility 32
flowchart 382, 383
formality 391
fundamental concepts 372
hearings 483
High Court jurisdiction in arbitration
  claims 462–84
history 372
impartiality 466
independence 466
injunctions 391
institutional arbitration 373, 387–8, 391
interpretation 373, 375, 389
issues, interpretation of 375
judicial review 463, 470–4
jurisdiction 462–84
key elements 33
landlord and tenant 388
latent damage 395–6
legal representation 24, 65
limitation periods 395–6
litigation, as alternative to 32–3, 372
London Metal Exchange 396
main features 390–2
mandatory and non-mandatory provisions 385–6
maritime disputes 388
med-arb 35, 234, 389, 390
multi-tiered dispute resolution 389
natural justice 384
negotiations 493–4
New York Convention 1958 389
non-adjudicative, as 371
non-intervention principle 386–7
notice of arbitration 396, 397
one-stop adjudication 390
overriding objective 384
Part 8 claims 478
party autonomy 385–6
procedural orders 453–4, 467–70
procedure 371, 382–3, 388
professional ethics 289
providers' fees 65
public law disputes 376–7
public policy 371
remedies 391–2
requirement for effective references 375–82
rules of institutions 373, 391
serious irregularity 472–4
settlements, enforcement of 493–4
statutory arbitration 388
stay of proceedings 464–5
success, reasons for 34
third parties 32, 391
time limits 394–6, 465, 478, 482
types of arbitration 387–8
UNCITRAL Model Law 372, 466
venue 33, 65

arbitration agreements or clauses 371–81
advice 407–8
anti-suit injunctions 465
Arbitration Act 1996 380
breach 377, 400, 463–5
capacity 381–2
commercial arbitration 406, 407–8
conditions precedent 382
Contracts (Applicable Law) Act 1990 439
Contracts (Rights of Third Parties) Act 1999 379
corporations, capacity of 381
damages 400
dispute must come within agreement 374–5,
  380–1
enforcement by court system 381
High Court jurisdiction in arbitration
  claims 463–5
international arbitration 439–40
interpretation 380–1
key element of arbitration, as 33
law of arbitration agreements 439–40
med-arb 35
Mental Capacity Act 2005 381
oral agreements 380
party autonomy 385–6
Scott v Avery clauses 382
separability 374
several contracts, disputes covering 379–80
standard terms 407
stay of proceedings 464–5
substantive contracts 373
time limits 395
two-contract cases 378–9
typical clauses 377–8
writing or evidenced in writing 380
arbitration awards
appeals 431, 459, 475–6
Arbitration Act 1996 455, 460, 493–4
binding effect 354, 459
chair, view of the 455, 457
challenging awards 459
commercial arbitration 427, 430–1
construction industry adjudication 354
costs 453, 460
date of award 455, 458
declarations 458
enforcement 455, 458, 486, 493–4
fees 402
final award, example of 456–7
foreign awards, enforcement of 493–4
Geneva Convention awards, enforcement of 494
ICC Rules of Arbitration 477
injunctions 459
institutional rules 447, 458–9
interest 459
interim awards 453–4
international arbitration 436
London Metal Exchange 458, 459
main awards 453, 455–9
majority decisions 455, 457

merger 486
New York Convention 1958 493–4
notification 459
outcomes 321
place where award is made 436, 458
provisional orders 454
reasons 430, 457
recognition of awards 493–4
recording settlements 321
rectification 459
remedies 458–9
seat of arbitration 436, 455, 458
serious irregularity 471–4
settlements 321, 455, 493–4
signatures 430, 458
specific performance 458–9
stalemate 455, 457
types 453
Arb-Med 234–5
attendance
    experts 208
    insurers 207
    lawyers 206–7, 290
    mediation 29–30, 64–5, 205–8
    negotiation 27, 151–2
    professional ethics 290
awards *see* arbitration awards

bankruptcy 350, 489
bargaining tactics
    escalating demands 168
    extreme demands 168
    false issues 168
    mediation 219, 229–30, 233, 273
    multiple concessions 168
    negotiation 168–9
    preconditions 168
    splitting the difference 169
    stress, inducing 168
    take it or leave it 168
barristers *see also* lawyers; legal professional
    privilege
    advocacy 236
    attendance 290
    Bar Code of Conduct 281, 283–6
    Bar Council 195–6
    Bar Standards Board 20
    competence 285
    conditional fee agreements 283
    consent orders 332
    costs 61, 63–4
    drafting 285–6, 332
    endorsement on briefs 327–30
    fees 61, 63–4
    instructions 236
    mediation 284
    negotiations 63–4
    professional ethics 280, 281, 283–6
    records 290
    relationship with professional clients 290

service, lawyers providing an ADR 281
solicitors, relationship with 290
training and accreditation 195–6
BATNA (best alternative to a negotiated
    agreement) 146–7, 201, 215
bespoke arbitration procedure 405, 406
best endeavours 50
best interests of the client
    advice 40
    agreement to ADR, securing 53
    compliance with rules 40
    litigation 51
    professional ethics 280, 282–3
bibliography 577–9
binding effect
    arbitration awards 354, 459
    construction industry adjudication 354
    expert or neutral determination 342, 347–8
    ombudsmen 316
    settlements 231, 238–40
bluffing 130
body language 151–2
bogged down, getting 170–1
breaks 180
briefs, endorsement on 327–30
British and Irish Ombudsman Association
    (BIOA) 314
British Coal Miners Mediation Scheme for
    Respiratory and Vibration White
    Finger 262
Brussels I Regulation 278, 440
building contracts *see* construction disputes
bundles 208, 210–13, 423, 465

Cafcass (Children and Family Court Advisory and
    Support Service) 307
capacity
    arbitration agreements or clauses 381–2
    arbitrators 466
    corporations 381
    mental capacity 381, 466
    settlements 240
'cards on the table' approach 51, 185
case analysis 236
case management
    active case management 82–3
    Admiralty and Commercial Courts Guide 77
    advice 40
    Chancery Guide 77
    Civil Procedure Rules 82–3
    conferences 77–9, 83–4, 151, 219
    encouragement of ADR 83
    hearings 40
    list of duties 83
    negotiation 151
    overriding objective 83
    position statements 219
    powers 83
    Technology and Construction Court Guide 78–9
    Ungley Orders 83, 84

CEDR (Centre for Effective Dispute Resolution)
CEDR Commission 234
CEDR Solve code of conduct for third party
neutrals, copy of App 2
Clinical Negligence Mediation Scheme 267
construction industry adjudication 358, 368
costs 62
early neutral and/or expert evaluation 298, 301
expert or neutral determination 346
fees 62
med-arb 234
mediation 177, 182, 291, 293
Model Early Neutral Evaluation Agreement, copy
of App 3
Model Expert Determination Agreement, copy
of App 3
Model Mediation Agreement 113, 204, App 2
PIU (Personal Injury Unit) eValuate (CEDR) 300–1
PIU (Personal Injury Unit) Telephone
Mediation 262
professional ethics 291, 293
project mediation 264
role 8
Rules for Adjudication 358, 368
training and accreditation 20
website 8, 182
**Central London County Court Compulsory
Mediation pilot scheme** 254–5
**Central London County Court Voluntary
Mediation Scheme** 254, 255
Centre for Effective Dispute Resolution *see* **CEDR
(Centre for Effective Dispute Resolution)**
chair 396, 398, 455, 457
Chancery Division
ADR orders, example of 79
Chancery Guide 77
change of position 228
Chartered Institute of Arbitrators (CIA) 20
children
Cafcass (Children and Family Court Advisory and
Support Service) 307
contact arrangements 258
London SEN Mediation Service 264
views of the child 259
choice of forum 13
choice of law 437, 440
chronology 210
Civil Justice Council (CJC) 303
Civil Mediation Council (CMC) 183, 195–6, 250,
268, 276, 291, 293
Civil Procedure Rules
case management 82–3
commercial arbitration 405–6
costs 491
encouragement of ADR 4, 9–10, 76
historical background 75–6
overriding objective 9, 82
Part 8 procedure 350, 466, 478, 491–2
Part 36 offers 25–6, 41, 67, 97
Woolf reforms 76
civil proceedings *see* **litigation**

claim forms 479–81
clarity 16, 26, 147–8, 319–20
clauses *see* arbitration agreements or clauses
client satisfaction 15, 48
closing phases 173–5, 219, 230–3
closing submissions 426
codes of conduct
ACAS 260
Bar Code of Conduct 281, 283–6
CEDR Solve code of conduct for third party
neutrals, copy of App 2
Civil Mediation Council 293
complaints and grievance procedures 307, 310
early neutral and/or expert evaluation 298
EU Code of Conduct for Mediators 12, 18, 270–1,
277
Independent Doctor's Forum (IDF) 307
Independent Healthcare Forum code of
practice 267
mediation 12, 18, 272, 275–7, 291–3
professional ethics 281–7
solicitors 282, 283, 285–7
collaborative style 121–4, 152, 154, 160–3, 167–8
collusion 349
commencement of proceedings
arbitration 394–6 409, 427–8, 450
commercial arbitration 409, 427–8
construction industry adjudication 358–65
commercial arbitration 403–31
adversarial approach 409, 424
appeals 427, 431
appointment of tribunal 428
Arbitration Act 1996 406, 410–23, 427
arbitration clauses 406, 407–8
awards 427, 430–1
bespoke procedure 405, 406
bundles 423
Civil Procedure Rules 405–6
closing submissions 426
commencement 409, 427–8
confidentiality 404–5, 422
conservatory measures 413
consumer disputes 404
costs 412, 423, 430–1
counterclaims 410
counter-notices 428
court procedures, rules that follow 427–31
cross-examination, examination and
re-examination 425, 430
dates for hearings 424
decisions 426–7
defence 410, 428
definition of commercial 404
delay 415–16, 428
directions 412, 421–4, 429–30
disclosure 405, 420–2, 430
documents 429
enforcement of agreements 404
equity clauses (*ex aequo et bono/amiable
compositeur*) 427
evidence 408–9, 412, 418, 420, 423

experts 405, 409–10, 422, 425–6, 430
flowchart 411
formalities 406
general procedure 410–27
hearings 409, 422–6, 430
'hot tubbing' 425
ICE Short Procedure 410
inordinate and inexcusable delay, dismissal
    for 415–16
inquisitorial approach 424
institutions
    list 407
    rules 405, 406, 410–11, 427–31
interest 430–1
interim directions, example of 413–14
interim payments 412, 430
issues, defining the 408
legal representatives, role of 407–9
London Metal Exchange 427–31
look-sniff arbitration 405, 409–10
New York Convention 1958 404
notice 409, 427–8
oral hearings 423
peremptory orders 415
points of claim, example of 417–18, 419–20
preliminary meetings 411–12
pre-trial hearings/conferences 422–3
procedural orders 412–14
procedure 405–7, 412–18, 428
putting together the case 408–9
reasons for awards 430
Redfern Schedule, example of 421
reference of disputes 408
rules 405–7, 410–11, 427–31
samples 429
sanctions 415
scope 404
security for costs 412, 430
short-form arbitration 405, 410
signatures 430
silence in institutional rules 406
site visits 426
skeleton arguments 424, 426
standard terms 407
statements of case 416, 429
summonses 425
time limits 412, 428–9
UNCITRAL Model Law 404
venue 424
video-conferencing 424, 430
views 426
witnesses
    arrangements 525
    conferencing 425
    cross-examination, examination and
      re-examination 425, 430
    statements 422, 425
    summonses 425
written submissions 424
commercial cases
    Commercial Court, ADR orders in 78, 257

complexity 258
court mediation schemes and other schemes 258
early neutral and/or expert evaluation 32,
    299–300, 301
encouragement of ADR 9
mediation 257–8
Practice Note 9
statistics 257
communication
    body language 151–2
    collaborative approach 152, 154
    competitive approach 152
    concentration 154
    cooperative approach 152, 154
    decisions 367–8
    effectiveness 152–5
    gaps 155
    listening effectively 154
    mislead, duty not to 155
    negotiation 152–5
    non-verbal communication 151–2
    presentation, effective 152–3
    psychological factors 152
    questioning effectively 154
    reciprocal or mirroring behaviour 152
    responding effectively 153–4
community mediation 268–9
competence 277, 285, 291
competition 377
competitive/confrontational style
    communication 152
    concessions 164, 165, 167
    deals, making 167
    escalating demands 168
    negotiation 118–21, 127, 151, 161, 162, 171
    poorly prepared opponents, dealing with 171
    stress, inducing 168
    tactics 125
    take it or leave it 168
complaints and grievance procedures 309–14 *see*
    also **ombudsmen**
    anonymous information 311
    Civil Mediation Council 195
    codes of conduct 307, 310
    decisions 313–14
    definitions 35–6, 310
    determination of complaints and grievances 311,
      313
    effectiveness of procedures 314
    employment grievances 260–1, 311–13
    examples 35–6
    formal and informal complaints 310
    hearings 313
    Independent Doctor's Forum 307
    investigations 311–14
    lawyers 18–20, 310
    meetings 313
    natural justice 313
    outcomes 321
    raising a complaint or grievance 311
    records 313, 321

complaints and grievance procedures *(cont.)*
  regulation 18
  settlements, recording 321
  statutory requirements 310
complexity 6, 43–4, 189, 258
compromise agreements 261
compulsion
  access to courts 91
  Central London County Court Compulsory
    Mediation pilot scheme 254–5
  encouragement of ADR 90–1
  fair hearings 12, 90–1
  mediation 177, 275
  United States 11
concealing information 126
concentration 154
concessions
  admissions 288
  checklist 166
  collaborative style 167–8
  competitive style 164, 165, 167
  cooperative style 167
  demands, making 165
  false issues 169
  final offers 166
  gaining concessions 165
  implementing plans 164–5
  linking concessions 146, 166–7
  making concessions 166
  multiple concessions 168
  plans 143–6, 164–5
  preparation for negotiation 143–6
  professional ethics 288
  refusal to concede 166
  size of concessions 164
  strategies 167–8
  terminology 165
  timing 164
conciliation 304–8 *see also* **ACAS (Advisory,
    Conciliation and Arbitration Service)**
  agreements, records of 305
  conciliator
    role 305
    selection 305
  confidentiality 304
  court-based conciliation 307
  definition 31, 304
  Disability Conciliation Service (Equalities
    Mediation Service) 308
  family cases 259, 307
  Furniture Ombudsman Conciliation Scheme 308
  healthcare providers 307–8
  Independent Doctor's Forum 307
  mediation 199, 304–5
  meetings 305
  NHS trusts 307
  outcomes 321
  process 304–5
  recording settlements 321
  settlements 304–5, 321
  terminology 304

  third party, appointment of a neutral 304
  without prejudice communications 304
conclusions, drawing 215
conditional fee agreements (CFAs)
  after the event insurance 66, 192–3
  barristers 283
  costs 66
  disbursements 66
  mediation 192–3
  professional ethics 283
  recording settlements 320
  settlements 66, 320
  success fees 66, 193, 283
conduct *see also* **codes of conduct; costs sanctions
    for failure to consider ADR**
  advice 39–40
  costs sanctions 94–5, 96, 101–3, 105
  Practice Direction Pre-Action Conduct 80–1,
    101–3
  reasonableness of pre-action conduct 9
  wasted costs orders 19, 281
conferences *see also* **meetings**
  advice 40
  case management conferences 77–9, 83–4, 151,
    210
  negotiation 26, 151
  pre-trial conferences 422–3
  telephone calls 26
  video-conferencing 424, 430, 446
  witnesses 425
confidentiality
  ACAS 305
  advantages and disadvantages of ADR 14
  arbitration 389, 405, 422
  breach 244
  Cafcass (Children and Family Court Advisory and
    Support Service) 307
  commercial arbitration 404–5, 422
  conciliation 304
  construction industry adjudication 366
  contractual clauses 54–5, 244–5
  criminal activities, disclosure of 246
  damages 244
  early neutral and/or expert evaluation 298, 300
  enforcement 245
  EU Code of Conduct for Mediators 277
  evidence 49
  exceptions 246
  expert or neutral determination 347
  experts 287
  family mediation 246, 259
  Financial Services Authority Mediation Service 266
  harm, risk of significant 246
  information given to mediator 244–5
  interests of justice 245–6
  law, disclosure required by 246
  legal professional privilege 12, 54, 55
  litigation 6, 14
  Med-Arb 389
  mediation 181, 185, 212, 232, 244–6, 276–7, 292
  professional ethics 284, 286–8, 292

public statements 46
selection of ADR options, factors influencing 46, 54–7
solicitors 286–7
Tomlin orders 46, 335–6
waiver 245
without prejudice communications 54, 55–7, 241, 244–5
conflicts of interest 281, 283, 290, 466
confrontational style *see* competitive/confrontational style
consent orders
administrative consent orders 332
barristers, drafting by 332
consideration 332
court door, settlements at the 331
discontinuance 331
drafting 332
enforcement 331, 490
example of consent order 333
family consent orders 333–4
fraud, misrepresentation or mistake 333–4
litigation 331
mediation 278
negotiation 174
purpose 331
settlements
agreements 278
enforcement of 490
recording 331–6
stay of proceedings 331–2
submission to agreed terms 332–3
Tomlin orders 331, 334–6
true consent orders 332–3
conservatory measures 413, 454
construction disputes *see also* construction industry adjudication
complexity 258
court mediation schemes and other schemes 258
JCT standard form 258
pre-action meetings 81–2
pre-action protocol 81–2
specialisation 36
construction industry adjudication 34, 353–69
agreements in writing 356
ambit of the reference 361
appointment fees 361
arbitration 353–4
awards, binding nature of 354
before hearing, procedure 365–6
binding awards 354
CEDR Rules for Adjudication 358, 368
commencement of adjudication 358–65
communication of decisions 367–8
conditions for adjudication 355
confidentiality 366
construction operations, definition of 355
contracts 355, 356–7, 369
costs 368, 369
court enforcement 369
damages 359

decisions 367–8
binding 368
communication 367–8
enforcement 491–2
interim effect 368
process 367
reasons 368
time limits 354
default judgments 354
delay 366
dispute, definition of 356
documentation 365, 366
enforcement 354, 369, 491–2
evidence 365–6, 367
experiments 366
experts' reports 355
express contractual right to adjudication 357–8
fair dealing 354
fees 361
flowchart 359
hearings 367
impartiality 366, 367
inquisitorial approach 367
interest 368
interim effect of decisions 368
JCT standard form 358
jurisdiction 492
late payment of sums 354
manufacture of building components 355
mining 355
nature of adjudication 354
nomination of adjudicator 361
notice 358–65
nuclear power plants 355
oil and gas, extraction of 355
oral hearings 367
Part 8 procedure 491–2
procedure 354, 365–7
questions 366
reasons 368
referral notices 362–5
related disputes 366
requirements 355–6
residential building contracts 369
Scheme for Construction Contracts, default provisions in the 358, 361, 368
single disputes 356
site visits 366
stages in adjudication 359
statements of case 365
summary judgments 354, 492
TeCSA Adjudication Rules 358, 361
tests 366
time limits 361, 365–6, 367–8
timetable for procedural steps 366
writing or evidenced in writing 356
consumers
arbitration 389, 404
commercial arbitration 404
EU law 389
ombudsmen 314

contempt of court 336

continuing professional development (CPD) 196, 276, 291

contracts *see* agreements/contracts; arbitration agreements or clauses

control of process 13, 23–4, 46, 51

cooperative style 118–20, 152, 167

corporations

    capacity 381

    mini-trials or executive tribunals 264–5

costs 58–71 *see also* **costs sanctions for failure to consider ADR; Jackson Review**

    ADR processes 62–5

    Admiralty and Commercial Courts Guide 77, 110

    advance, agreement in 24

    advantages and disadvantages of ADR 13, 15, 16

    advice 61, 280–1

    agreements 337

    amount at stake 60

    arbitration 65, 384, 388, 392, 412, 423, 430–1, 447, 453, 460

    BATNA (best alternative to a negotiated agreement) 147

    barristers' fees 61, 63–4

    budget 24

    CEDR 62, 113

    checklist 68

    Civil Procedure Rules 491

    conditional fee agreements 66

    construction industry adjudication 368, 369

    costs only proceedings 491

    court fees 62

    court orders 336

    determination on all issues apart from costs, settlement or 113

    disbursements 62

    discretion 109

    drafting terms 337

    earliest opportunity, choosing ADR at 52

    elements of costs 61–2

    enforcement 491

    evidence 61

    example 70–1

    expenses 191–2

    extent to which costs have already been incurred 60

    failed ADR as part of costs of litigation, costs of 110

    fees 61–3, 108, 191

    financial analysis 68–71

    follow the event 336

    general considerations 59–61

    hearings 109

    ICC Rules of Arbitration 447

    incidental costs 110

    indemnity basis 337

    information 61

    insurance 66–7

    international arbitration 447

    investigations 61

    IT-based processes 63

Law Works organisation 62

legal funding 60, 66–7

Legal Services Commission funding 67

liability, agreement between parties determines 110–11

litigation 24, 61, 108–14, 181, 336

main elements of costs 60

Mayor's and City of London County Court Mediation Scheme 254

mediation 62–3, 64–5, 110–11, 190–2, 214, 271–2

National Mediation Helpline 63, 77, 112–13

negotiation 63–4, 134

NHS pilot scheme for medical negligence 8

non-adjudicative ADR 52

Part 8 procedure 491

parties 67–8

pre-action protocols 112

preparation for negotiation 134

process fees 62

professional ethics 280

proportionality 60, 491

provider's fees 62–3

reasonableness 60, 337

recording settlements 320, 322, 336–7

recovery of costs in litigation 108–14

retainers 61

review of ADR options 22, 24

risk assessment 68–9

savings, ADR not resulting in 51–2

security for costs 412, 430, 447

settlements 108, 110–11, 113, 320, 322–3, 336–7, 491

shifting costs 60–1

solicitors

    fees 61, 63–4

    negotiations 63–4

    professional ethics 280–1

standard basis 337

success, chances of 60

terms 323, 336–7

Tomlin orders 334, 337

unsuccessful ADR processes, recovery of 109–13

updated, duty to keep clients 68

venue 191

wasted costs orders 19, 281

withdrawal from process 111–12

without prejudice communications 57, 242

costs sanctions for failure to consider ADR 10, 93–114

    ADR orders have been made by court, whether 100

    advice 280–1

    appeals, rejection of ADR before 103

    both parties at fault 106

    cap on solicitor-client costs 105

    circumstances that court has regard to 94

    clarification of issues, obtaining 100–1

    conduct 94–5, 96, 101–3, 105

    consent to ADR, delay in 104

    Court of Appeal mediation service 103

    court's general powers 94–5

damages, interest on 105
delay
    consent 104
    prejudicial, where delay would be 98–9
discretion 94
expert evidence 101
extent to which other settlement methods have
        been attempted 97–8
failure to initiate ADR processes 102–3
fair hearings 12
follow the event 94
further information, obtaining 100–1
high, where costs would be disproportionately 98
indemnity costs 105–6
issue of proceedings, rejection before 101
judgment, rejection of ADR after 103
list of court orders 95
mediation 95–107, 185, 186
merits of case 96–7
nature of disputes 96
negotiations, failure to take part in 102
Part 36 offers 97
Practice Direction Pre-action Conduct 101–3
precedent 96
privileged material, how court treats 106–7
proportionality 98
pulling out of ADR 104
reasonable prospect of success 99–100
rejection of offers 97–8, 102
solicitor-client costs, cap on 105
unreasonableness 95–7, 100–1, 105
without prejudice communications 106–7
counsel *see* **barristers**
county courts
    Central London County Court 9
    Mayor's and City of London County Court
            Mediation Scheme 254
    mediation officers 10
    mediation pilot scheme 9
    National Mediation Helpline 10, 63
    small claims 90, 249
court door, settlements at 26, 135, 151, 331
Court Guides 76–9
    Admiralty and Commercial Courts
            Guide 77, 110
    Chancery Guide 77
    list 76–7
    professional ethics 280
    Queen's Bench Guide 77–8
    Technology and Construction Court Guide 78–9
court mediation schemes and other
        schemes 249–69 *see also* **National
        Mediation Helpline**
    Central London County Court Compulsory
            Mediation pilot scheme 254–5
    Central London County Court Voluntary
            Mediation Scheme 254, 255
    commercial disputes 258
    community mediation 268–9
    complex construction and commercial
            disputes 258
    consensus building in environmental disputes
            or disputes that involve public policy
            issues 265
    construction disputes 258
    Court of Appeal 9, 90, 103, 186, 249
    environment 265
    family disputes 258–9, 264
    Financial Services Authority Mediation
            Service 266
    healthcare sector 266–7
    Her Majesty's Court Service (HMCS) Small Claims
            Mediation Scheme 255–7
    intellectual property cases 258
    LawWorks 269
    London SEN Mediation Service 264
    Mayor's and City of London County Court
            Mediation Scheme 254
    Mediation in Civil and Commercial Matters
            Directive 275
    mini-trials or executive tribunals 264–5
    multi-party disputes 262–3
    Pensions Mediation Service 267
    Performing Arts Mediation Service 268
    personal injury 261–2
    pro bono mediation 269
    project mediation 264
    public policy 265
    research 182
    sector mediation 266–7
    Small Claims Scheme 249
    telephone mediations 256
    time-limited schemes 189
    workplace mediation 260–1
Court of Appeal Mediation Scheme 9, 90, 103,
        186, 249
court orders
    advantages of litigation 43, 180
    costs 100, 336
    costs sanctions 100
    enforcement 490–1
    evidence 49–50
    list of court orders 95
    settlements, recording 323
    Tomlin orders 46, 331, 334–6
    Ungley orders 83, 84
    wasted costs orders 19, 281
courts and ADR 75–92 *see also* **court mediation
        schemes and other schemes; court orders;
        litigation; particular courts**
    access to courts 91
    allocation stage questionnaires 83–5
    case management 82–3
    Civil Procedure Rules 75–6
    compelling use of ADR 90–1
    conciliation 307
    construction industry adjudication, enforcement
            and 369
    contractual clauses 87–9
    costs 62, 94–5
    Court Guides 76–9, 110, 280
    early neutral evaluation schemes 90, 298

courts and ADR (*cont.*)
  encouragement 85–7
  enforcement 369
  expert or neutral determination
    approach of courts 344
    challenging decisions of 348–50
  family cases 307
  fees, refund of 337–8
  flowchart 88
  High Court jurisdiction in arbitration
    claims 462–84
  mediation schemes 90
  National Mediation Helpline, referral to 250
  overriding objective 82
  pre-action protocols 79–82
  settlements, approval of 180
  stay of proceedings 85
criminal activities
  confidentiality 246
  fraud 180, 333–4, 349, 473
  quasi-criminal allegations 44
cultural differences 196, 272
curial law 440–1, 446

daily rates 191
damages 89, 105, 244, 344, 359
date of commencement 394–5
deadlock 129, 170–1, 227–9
deals, reaching 167–8
death of arbitrators 401
decisions
  binding decisions 342, 347–8, 368
  commercial arbitration 426–7
  communication 367–8
  complaints and grievance procedures 310, 313–14
  construction industry adjudication 354, 367–8, 491–2
  enforcement 350, 491–2
  expert or neutral determination 342, 347–50
  ICC Rules of Arbitration 449
  interim effect 368
  process 367
  reasons 348, 350, 368
  time limits 354
declarations 180, 458
deeds of settlement 174, 324, 326
default judgments 354, 488
definition of ADR 5–6
delay
  advantages and disadvantages of ADR 13, 15, 185
  arbitration 384, 388, 415–16, 428
  commercial arbitration 415–16, 428
  consent to ADR 104
  construction industry adjudication 354 366
  costs sanctions 98–9, 104
  ICC Rules of Arbitration 447
  inordinate and inexcusable delay, dismissal
    for 415–16
  international arbitration 441
  litigation 185
  mediation 180, 181, 185

  prejudicial, where delay is 98–9
  tactics 52
demands, planning and making 127–8, 143–6, 161–9
Departmental Advisory Committee (DAC) 372, 400
detail, points of 173
difficulties, dealing with 170–1
directions
  commercial arbitration 412, 421–4, 429–30
  High Court jurisdiction in arbitration
    claims 482–3
  interim directions, example of 413–14
  litigation 50
  mediation 179
  procedural arbitration orders 454
  stay of proceedings 50
Directory of UK Mediation 268
**Disability Conciliation Service (Equalities
  Mediation Service)** 308
disadvantages of ADR *see* **advantages and
  disadvantages of ADR**
disbursements 62, 66
disciplinary proceedings 247, 260
disclosure
  advice 41
  commercial arbitration 405, 420–2, 430
  criminal activities 246
  experts 288–9
  international arbitration 446
  law, required by 246
  litigation 7
  mediation 185, 189, 212
  non-adjudicative ADR 288–9
  pre-action disclosure 468
  procedural arbitration orders 468–9
  professional ethics 288–9
  selection of ADR options, factors
    influencing 49–50
discontinuance 331
discrimination 285
dispute management systems, definition of 36
Dispute Review Panel 352
disputes, definition of 354, 376
documents *see also* **forms and precedents**
  bundles 208, 210–13, 423, 465
  commercial arbitration 429
  construction industry adjudication 365, 366
  documents-only processes 315
  mediation, preparation for 210–13
  National Mediation Helpline 251
  position statements 210
drafting
  barristers 285–6, 332
  consent orders 332
  costs 337
  deeds of settlement 326
  position statements 208–9
  professional ethics 285–6
  recording settlements 322, 323–4
  settlements 231, 322, 323–4, 326–7

tactics 129
terms 231, 323–4
Tomlin orders 334–5
duress 243

earliest opportunity, choosing ADR at 52, 187
early neutral and/or expert evaluation 297–318
    Admiralty and Commercial Courts Guide 77
    advisory process, as 297
    advantages 32
    CEDR 298, 301, App 3
    Civil Justice Council 303
    code of conduct 298
    Commercial Court 32, 299–300, 301
    confidentiality 298, 300
    courts 90, 298
    definition 31, 297–8
    disadvantages 32
    elements of process 31–2
    evaluative process, as 297
    evaluator
        code of conduct 298
        impartiality 298
        selection 298
    evidence 299
    example of order providing for judicial
        evaluation 301
    expert, appointment of an 298, 300
    expert or neutral determination 345, 351, 352
    facilitative process, as 297
    fact finding 299
    fees 300–1
    flexibility 299
    hearings 299
    impartiality 298
    investigations 299
    judicial ENE scheme pilot 303
    judicial evaluation 299–300, 301
    lawyers 24–5, 32
    litigation 298
    mediation 199, 297, 298
    Mercantile Court 300
    Model Early Neutral Evaluation Agreement
        (CEDR), copy of App 3
    oral hearings 299
    personal injury 300–1
    PIU (Personal Injury Unit) eValuate (CEDR) 300–1
    procedure 299
    providers 298
    recommendations 299
    reports 32
    senior judges 32, 299–300
    Social Security and Child Support (SSCS) Tribunal
        pilots 301–3
    stage of process 298
    Technology and Construction Court 32, 300
    third parties, appointment of neutral 31, 297–8
    timing 32
    when it should be used 298
EC law *see* **EU law**
economic duress 243

emotion 171–2
employment *see also* **ACAS (Advisory, Conciliation
    and Arbitration Service)**
    complaints and grievance procedures 260,
        311–13
    compromise agreements 261
    determination of grievances 311, 313
    disciplinary procedures 260
    employment tribunals 260, 305–6
    determination of grievances 311, 313
    grievance procedures 260–1
    judicial mediation pilots 261
    mediation 260–1
    raising a complaint or grievance 311
    register of providers 260
encouragement of ADR
    Admiralty and Commercial Courts Guide 77
    case management conferences 83
    Chancery Guide 77
    Civil Procedure Rules 4, 9–10, 76
    commercial cases 9
    compulsion 90–1
    courts 85–7
    evidence of consideration of ADR 10
    examples of judicial encouragement 85–7
    Jackson Review 4
    litigation 10, 12
    mediation 177, 179, 183, 185–6
    National Mediation Helpline 90
    offers to settle 8–9
    pre-action protocols 9–10, 81
    robust encouragement 90–1
    stay of proceedings 10, 12
    Technology and Construction Court Guide 78–9
    Woolf reforms 9
endorsement on briefs
    barristers 327–9
    effect of endorsements 329–30
    example of endorsement 329–30
    negotiation 174
    recording settlements 327–30
    signatures 329
    solicitors 327–8
enforcement *see also* **enforcement of arbitration
    awards; enforcement of settlements**
    agreements 42, 381
    arbitration agreements or clauses 381, 404
    compromise agreements 485–6
    confidentiality 245
    consent orders 331, 490
    construction industry adjudication 354, 369,
        491–2
    costs only proceedings 491
    court orders 490–1
    expert or neutral determination 350
    judgments 50
    Mediation in Civil and Commercial Matters
        Directive 276
    negotiation 42
    New York Convention 1958 404
    selection of ADR options, factors influencing 50

enforcement (cont.)
  settlements
    recording 322–3
    terms 323
  Tomlin orders 336
  written offers 25
enforcement of arbitration awards
  Arbitration Act 1996 493–4
  domestic arbitral awards 493
  foreign awards 493–4
  Geneva Convention awards, enforcement of 494
  grounds for refusal of recognition or enforcement
      of New York Convention awards 494
  international arbitration 392, 441
  law of place of enforcement 441
  merger 486
  New York Convention 1958 493–4
  permission 486, 493
  recognition of awards 493–4
  seat of arbitration 458
  settlements 455, 493–4
enforcement of settlements 240, 485–90
  arbitration awards 455, 493–4
  bankruptcy 489
  basic methods 486
  breach of compromise agreements, defences to
      claims for 488–9
  challenging settlements recorded as
      contracts 489–90
  choice of options 487–8
  civil proceedings 488
  consent orders, refusal to enforce 490
  contracts, recorded as 488–90
  default judgments 488
  defences to claims for breach of compromise
      agreements 488–9
  discharge of original obligation 486
  express terms 487
  ineffective compromises 487
  merger 486
  mistake 489–90
  negotiated settlements in arbitration
      proceedings 493–4
  non-performance, express terms reviving old
      obligations in event of 487
  performance of agreed terms 487
  recording settlements, method of 488–90
  rectification 489
  summary judgments 488
  winding up 489
environmental disputes 265
Equality and Human Rights Commission
    (EHRC) 308
equity clauses (*ex aequo et bono/amiable
    compositeur*) 427, 437, 438, 441
escalating demands 168
ethics *see* professional ethics
EU Code of Conduct for Mediators 12, 18, 270–1,
    277, 291–3
EU law
  arbitration 377, 389

Brussels I Regulation 278, 440
  competition 377
  consumer arbitration 389
  Mediation in Civil and Commercial Matters
      Directive 270–1, 274–7, 291–3
  mediators, code of conduct for 12, 18, 270–1, 277
Europe, growth of mediation in 273
European Convention on Human Rights
  arbitration 377, 384, 390
  fair trials 12, 390
evaluative ADR
  conciliation 199
  early neutral and/or expert evaluation 199, 297
  mediation 197–9, 233–4
  mini-trials or executive tribunals 264–5
evasion 129
evidence
  adjudicative ADR 49
  advantages and disadvantages of ADR 14, 16–17
  advice 41
  arbitration 375, 408–9, 412, 418, 420, 423, 452,
      467–8
  commercial arbitration 408–9, 412, 418, 420, 423
  confidentiality 49
  consideration of ADR, evidence of 10
  construction industry adjudication 354, 365–6,
      367
  costs 61
  court orders, need for 49–50
  early neutral and/or expert evaluation 299
  flexibility 14
  litigation 6
  mediation, preparation for 214
  negotiation 137–9, 163
  non-adjudicative ADR 49
  ombudsmen 315
  pre-action protocols 16
  preparation for negotiation 137–9
  procedural arbitration orders 467–8
  rules, loss of potential advantages of
      evidential 16–17
  selection of ADR options, factors
      influencing 49–50
  UNCITRAL Model Law 452
ex aequo et bono/amiable compositeur 427, 437,
    438, 441
examples of documents *see* forms and precedents
exchange of letters
  accepting terms, example letter on 326
  example letters 325–6
  formation of contract 324
  negotiation 174
  non-adjudicative ADR 324
  notes, working from full and accurate 324
  offers 25–6
  recording settlements 324–6
  terms
    accepting terms, example letter on 326
    example letters 325–6
    setting out terms 325
exclusion clauses 247

expenses 15, 191–2, 401, 467
experience 172, 194–5
experiments 366
expert or neutral determination 341–52
  adjudication, distinguished from 351
  advantages 344–5
  agreements 342, 343–4
  appointment of experts 342, 345–6
  arbitration, distinguished from 351, 352
  bankruptcy 350
  binding decisions 342, 347–8
  breach of contract 350
  CEDR 346, App 3
  challenging decisions in court proceedings
    grounds 348–50
    time limit for 348
  collusion 349
  confidentiality 347
  construction, decisions not intended to be final
    on matters of 349–50
  contractual effect of clauses 344
  cooperate, duty to 347
  courts, approach of 344
  damages for refusal to comply in breach of
    clause 344
  decisions
    binding decisions 342, 347–8
    challenging 348–50
    construction, not intended to be final on
      matters of 349–50
    enforcement 350
    nature of 342, 347–8
    procedure for challenges 350
    reasons 348, 350
  definition 35, 342
  Dispute Review Panels 352
  early neutral evaluation, distinguished from 345,
    351, 352
  enforcement 350
  example clause 343
  expert evidence, rules on 342
  facilitative process, as 342
  fairly or lawfully, failure to act 349
  fraud 349
  immunity of experts 351–2
  instructions, material departure from 349
  lawyers 24–5
  litigation against experts 350–1
  manifest error 347, 348, 349
  mediation 343, 345
  Model Expert Determination Agreement (CEDR),
    copy of App 3
  natural justice 347
  negligence 350
  negotiations, distinguished from 345
  Part 8 proceedings 350
  process 346–7
  reasons for decisions 348, 350
  rules of providers 346
  selection of neutral or expert determiner 345–6
  similarities with other forms of ADR 345

  specialist knowledge 35
  stage at which parties may agree to expert
    determination 342–3
  stay of proceedings 344
  submissions 347
  suitable, cases where expert determination is
    particularly 343
  third parties, appointment of independent 342,
    345–6
  time limits 348
  unfair contract terms 352
  when expert or neutral determination should be
    used 342–3
  winding up 350
  witnesses as experts 351–2
experts *see also* **expert or neutral determination**
  agreement on experts 45
  attendance 208
  commercial arbitration 405, 409–10, 422, 425–6,
    430, 451
  confidentiality 287
  construction industry adjudication 355
  costs sanctions 101
  disclosure 288–9
  expert or neutral determination 342
  hearings 425–6, 430
  immunity 351–2
  joint experts 207
  litigation 7, 350–1
  look-sniff arbitration 405, 409–10
  mediation 193–5, 207–8, 224–5, 230, 233–4, 273
  meetings 230
  party-appointed 422
  professional ethics 287–9
  reports 45, 211, 355, 425–6
  selection of ADR options, factors influencing 45
  tribunal-appointed 422
  UNCITRAL Model Law 451
  without prejudice communications 207, 241
exploration or information phase 219, 226–9, 233
extreme demands 168

facilitative ADR
  early neutral and/or expert evaluation 297
  expert or neutral determination 342
  mediation 197–8, 199, 201, 233
  negotiation 151
factors influencing selection of ADR options
    see **selection of ADR options, factors**
    influencing
facts, arguments based on 141
failure to consider ADR *see* **costs sanctions for**
    failure to consider ADR
fair trials
  appeals 390
  arbitration 384–5, 390
  compulsion 12, 90–1
  costs sanctions 12
  European Convention on Human Rights 12
fairness *see also* **fair trials**
  construction industry adjudication 354

fairness (*cont.*)
  expert or neutral determination 349
  High Court jurisdiction in arbitration claims 463
  mediation 292
  preparation for negotiation 142
  professional ethics 285
  serious irregularity 472
false issues 168
family disputes *see also* **family mediation**
  ancillary relief 82, 258
  Cafcass (Children and Family Court Advisory and
    Support Service) 307
  conciliation 307
  confidentiality 307
  consent orders 333–4
  contact 307
  court-based conciliation 307
  court mediation schemes and other
    schemes 258–9, 264, 307
  pre-action protocols 82
  residence 307
Family Housing Group Mediation Scheme 264
family mediation
  accreditation 258
  ADR Group 259
  ancillary relief 258
  anti-social behaviour 264
  children
    contact arrangements 258
    views of the child 259
  conciliation 259
  confidentiality 246, 259
  contact arrangements 258
  duration of sessions 259
  Family Housing Group Mediation Scheme 264
  Family Mediation Association 258–9
  Family Mediation Council 195, 258
  Family Mediation Helpline 259
  harm, confidentiality and risk of significant 246
  Her Majesty's Courts Service (HMCS) Small
    Claims Mediation Scheme 256
  landlords 264
  Legal Services Commission funding 259
  mediator, role of 259
  meetings 233
  National Family Mediation 258–9
  negotiations 259
  process 259
  public funding 258, 259
  regulation 259
  social landlords 264
  Solicitors' Regulation Authority 259
  specialist providers 258–9
  views of the child 259
  West Midlands Family Mediation Scheme 257
fast track claims 63, 83
fees
  advance payments 191
  advice 39
  agreement to ADR, securing 54
  appointment fees 361

arbitration
  arbitral tribunal 399, 401, 402
  awards 402
  High Court jurisdiction in arbitration
    claims 466–7
  judges as arbitrators 399
  providers 65
  barristers 61, 63–4
  CEDR 62
  construction industry adjudication 361
  costs 61–3, 108, 181
  daily rates 191
  early neutral and/or expert evaluation 300–1
  fixed fees 251
  hourly rates 191
  LawWorks 62
  mediation 64–5, 191
  National Mediation Helpline 251–2
  negotiations 63–4
  non-payment 466
  PIU (Personal Injury Unit) eValuate (CEDR) 300–1
  reasonableness 54
  refund for informing court of settlement 337–8
  resignation of arbitrator, relief from liability
    after 467
  success fees 66, 193, 283
figures, dealing with 139–40, 148
final offers 166
**Financial Services Authority Mediation
  Service** 266
flexibility 7, 14, 32, 35, 299
flowcharts
  arbitration 382, 383, 411
  courts 88
  mediation 216, 220, 251, 252–3
  National Mediation Helpline 251, 252–3
foreign arbitration awards, enforcement of 493–4
foreign law 434, 475
forms and precedents
  accepting terms, letter 326
  CEDR Solve code of conduct for third party
    neutrals, copy of App 2
  Chancery Division ADR order 79
  claim forms 479–81
  Commercial Court ADR order 78
  contractual ADR clauses 87
  employment grievance 312
  exchange of letters 325–6
  expert or neutral determination, clause for 343
  interim directions 413–14
  interim orders 330
  Model Early Neutral Evaluation Agreement, copy
    of App 3
  Model Expert Determination Agreement, copy
    of App 3
  Model Mediation Agreement, copy of App 2
  points of claim 417–18, 419–20
  professional negligence actions 19
  Redfern Schedule 421
  referral notices 362–4
  settlement agreements/contracts 327

stay of proceedings 86
Tomlin orders 334–5
Ungley orders 84
fraud 180, 333–4, 349, 473
freezing injunctions 469
funding *see* legal funding
Furniture Ombudsman Conciliation Scheme (TFO) 308
further information, obtaining 100–1, 180, 213
future relationships 47, 133

gaps 138–9, 155, 170, 173, 228
Geneva Convention awards, enforcement of 494
good faith 50
government, use of mediation by 182–3
grievance processes *see* complaints and grievance procedures
growth of ADR processes 7–11
guides *see* Court Guides

Harvard Negotiation Project 17–18
healthcare sector
CEDR Clinical Negligence Mediation Scheme 267
complaints 307
conciliation 307–8
court mediation schemes and other schemes 266–7
Healthcare Commission Mediation Scheme 267
Independent Doctor's Forum 267, 307
Independent Healthcare Forum code of practice 267
mediation 266–7
NHS Litigation Authority 267
NHS trusts 267, 307
Parliamentary and Health Service Ombudsman 314
hearings *see also* fair trials
advice 40, 41
commercial arbitration 409, 413–6, 430, 451–2
complaints and grievance procedures 313
construction industry adjudication 367
costs 109
early neutral and/or expert evaluation 299
experts 425–6, 430
High Court jurisdiction in arbitration claims 483
ICC Rules of Arbitration 449
international arbitration 435, 446
preparation 135
pre-trial hearings 422–3
public hearings 483
UNCITRAL Model Law 451–2
Her Majesty's Courts Service (HMCS) Small Claims Mediation Scheme 90, 249, 255–7
annual reports 256
appeals 256
awards 256
Exeter model 255
family cases 256
key features of scheme 256–7
Manchester model 255
pilots 255
Reading pilot 255
success 256
telephone mediations 256
High Court jurisdiction in arbitration claims 462–84
allocation to track 483
anti-suit injunctions 465
appeals 475–8, 483–4
applications 386–7
appointment of arbitrators 465
Arbitration Act 1996 462–3, 466, 482–4
arbitrators, appointment of 465–6
breaching of agreements to arbitrate, orders to prevent parties 463–5
claim forms
example 479–81
Part 8 claims 478
service 482
commencement of arbitration, extension of time for 465
conflicts of interest 466
Court of Appeal 483–4
defendants 482
directions 482–3
expenses 467
fairness 463
fees
non-payment 466
resignation of arbitrator, relief from liability after 467
hearings 483
impartiality 466
independence 466
intervention 386–7
judicial review 463, 470–4
jurisdiction
courts, with 482
ousting the jurisdiction of the court 476
mental or physical incapacity of arbitrators 466
ousting the jurisdiction of the court 476
Part 8 claims 478
powers of court 463
procedural orders 454, 467–70
procedure 478–83
public hearings 483
qualifications of arbitrators 466
removal of arbitrators 466
resignation of arbitrator, relief from liability after 467
service of claim forms 482
sole arbitrators, setting aside appointments of 465–6
stay of proceedings 464–5
time limits 465, 478, 482
UNCITRAL Model Law 466
HMCS (Her Majesty's Courts Service) Small Claims Mediation Scheme *see* Her Majesty's Courts Service (HMCS) Small Claims Mediation Scheme
'hot tubbing' 425
hourly rates 191

human rights *see* European Convention on Human Rights
hybrid processes 35

ICC Rules of Arbitration 433, 447–9
  answers to requests 448
  appeals on points of law 476
  awards 447
  costs 447
  counterclaims 448
  decisions 449
  delay 447
  hearings 449
  International Court of Arbitration 447–8
  languages 446
  procedure 448
  regulation 18
  requests for arbitration 447–8
  seat 448
  secretariat 447–8
  terms of reference 448
  tribunals 448–9
ICE Short Arbitration Procedure arbitration 410
idle time, strategies for 263
immunity
  arbitral tribunal 402
  expert or neutral determination 351–2
  experts 351–2
  lawyers 19
impartiality
  arbitral tribunal 399–400
  construction industry adjudication 366, 367
  early neutral and/or expert evaluation 298
  High Court jurisdiction in arbitration claims 466
  mediation 198–9, 292
  ombudsmen 314
  professional ethics 292
  serious irregularity 472
independence
  arbitral tribunal 399–400
  EU Code of Conduct for Mediators 277
  High Court jurisdiction in arbitration claims 466
  mediation 277, 291
  ombudsmen 314
  professional ethics 283, 291
  solicitors 283
Independent Doctor's Forum (IDF) 267, 307
Independent Healthcare Forum code of practice 267
information *see also* confidentiality
  agreement to ADR, securing 53
  anonymous information 311
  concealing information 126
  costs 61
  exploration or information phase 219, 226–9, 233
  further information, obtaining 100–1, 180, 213
  IT-based options 36
  litigation 180
  negotiation 139, 160–1
  options, offering information on 53
  preparation for negotiation 139

revealing information as a tactic 126
  tactics 125–7
injunctions
  anti-suit injunctions 465–6
  arbitration 391, 450–1, 459, 467, 469–70
  freezing injunctions 469
  interim injunctions 330–1, 391, 465
  litigation 180
  UNCITRAL Model Law 450–1
inquisitorial approach
  commercial arbitration 424
  construction industry adjudication 367
inspections 6
Institute of Civil Engineers (ICE) Short Arbitration Procedure 410
institutional rules
  agreement on rules 391
  application 373
  appeals on points of law 476
  arbitral tribunal 400–1
  awards 458–9
  commercial arbitration 405–7, 410–11, 427–31
  ICC Rules of Arbitration 433, 446, 447–9
institutions *see also* institutional rules; particular institutions (eg Chartered Institute of Arbitrators)
  appeals 388
  arbitration 387–8
  commercial arbitration 405, 406, 407, 410–11, 427–31
  international arbitration 433
  list of arbitral institutions 407
  support services 388
instructions, acting within 282
insurance
  after the event insurance 66, 192–3
  attendance 207
  costs 66–7
  mediation, preparation for 207
integrity 283–4, 288
intellectual property disputes 258
inter-client discussions 25
interest 105, 323, 368, 430–1, 453
interest groups 207
interim arbitration awards
  Arbitration Act 1996 454
  powers 454
  provisional orders 454
  purpose 454
  UNCITRAL Model Law 450–1
interim orders
  anti-suit injunctions 465
  arbitration 454, 467, 469–70
  commercial arbitration 413–14
  conservatory measures 413, 454
  directions, example of 413–14
  example 330
  importance 49
  injunctions 330–1, 375, 465
  litigation 43
  negotiation 174

payments 412, 430
recording settlements 323, 330–1
selection of ADR options, factors influencing 49
undertakings 330
international arbitration 432–52
advising the client 434
anti-suit injunctions 445
appointment of arbitrators 444
applicable law 437–41
Arbitration Act 1996 432, 434, 437, 440, 445
arbitration agreements, law of 439–40
awards, place of 436
Brussels I Regulation 440
choice of law 437, 440
close connection 439
Contracts (Applicable Law) Act 1990 439
costs 447
curial law 440–1, 446
delay 441
different systems of law, problems caused by 436
disclosure 446
enforcement 392, 441
English law, presumption that applicable law is
    same as 439
equity clauses (*ex aequo et bono/amiable
    compositeur*) 437, 438, 441
foreign law 434
hearings 435, 446
ICC Rules 18, 433, 446, 447–9
institutions 433
International Court of Arbitration 447–8
international, definition in 433
jurisdiction 43, 444–5
    anti-suit injunctions 445
    appointment of arbitrators 444
    kompetenz-kompetenz 444–5
    objections 441–5
    reserving client's position 444
    step in arbitration, taking a 44
    substantive 443, 444–5
    supervisory jurisdiction 435–6
    time when objection should be taken 443
kompetenz-kompetenz 444–5
language 445–6
law, or other rules 437–8
mandatory and non-mandatory provisions 436
meetings 446
New York Convention 1958 392, 433
place of arbitration 434
place of award 436
place of business 433
privilege 446
procedure 440–1, 445–7
proper law 437–9
reserving client's position 444
Rome I Regulation 438–9
security for costs 447
seat of arbitration 434–6, 438–9, 441
stateless arbitrations 441
step in arbitration, taking a 44
supervisory jurisdiction 435–6

telephone conferences 446
treaties and conventions 18
UNCITRAL Model Law 18, 432–3, 436, 438, 446,
    449–52
video conferencing 446
International Court of Arbitration (ICA) 447–8
international mediation 43, 270–8
advantages 271–2
bargaining phase 273
Brussels I Regulation 278
codes of practice 272
consent orders 278
context 11
costs 271–2
cultural differences 272
EU Code of Conduct for Mediators 270–1, 277
EU law 270–1, 273–7
Europe, growth of mediation in 273
expert evidence 273
harmonisation 274
International Mediation Institute 272
International Mediation Services Alliance
    (MEDAL) 272
jurisdiction 43, 441–5
language 272
Mediation in Civil and Commercial Matters
    Directive 270–1, 274–7
meetings 272, 273
New York Convention 1958 277–8
position statements 272
preparation 272
process 273
rules 272
settlement agreements, enforceability of 277–8
shuttle diplomacy 273
time pressures 273
UNCITRAL Model Law 274
United States 270
websites 272
Internet 36, 235–6
interpretation
arbitration 373, 375, 380–1, 449–50
expert or neutral determination 349–50
issues 375
UNCITRAL Model Law 449–50
introductions 219–20
investigations 61, 299, 311–14
irregularity *see* **serious irregularity**
irritation 171–2
issue of proceedings 40, 41, 101, 135
issues
adding issues 173
commercial arbitration 408
definition 408
failure to deal with the issues 473
identification of issues 135–6, 209
law, issues of 180
making your case on the issues 161–3
negotiation 135–6, 161–3, 173
parking issues 128
position statements 209

issues (*cont.*)
   renegotiation 173
   serious irregularity 473
IT-based options 36, 63, 235–6

Jackson Review
   costs 4, 59
   encouragement of ADR 4
   mediation 177
   recommendations 11, 59
   review of ADR options 22
   under-use of costs 11
JCT standard form 358
judgments
   costs sanctions 103
   default judgments 354, 488
   enforcement 50
   litigation, advantages of 321
   outcomes, comparison of 16
   recording settlements 323
   rejection of ADR after judgment 103
   summary judgments 16, 43, 452, 488, 492
judicial precedent *see* **precedent**
judicial review
   arbitration 463, 470–4
   preliminary points of law, determination
     of 470–1
   serious irregularity 471–4
judiciary
   arbitrators, as 398–9
   attitude of judiciary 10
   costs penalties 10
   early neutral and/or expert evaluation 299–300,
     301, 303
   fees 399
   judicial ENE scheme pilot 303
   judicial mediation pilots 261
   mediation 179, 261
   role and power 7
jurisdiction
   agreements 43
   arbitration 43, 462–84
   construction industry adjudication 492
   High Court jurisdiction in arbitration
     claims 462–84
   international arbitration 43, 441–5
   international mediation 43
   ousting the jurisdiction of the court 476
   selection of ADR options, factors influencing 43

key questions, asking 157
kompetenz-kompetenz 444–5

landlord and tenant arbitration 388
languages 196, 272, 445–6
late payment of sums 354
latent damage 395–6
law
   arguments based on application of 141
   legal analysis 214
   legal context 136–7

   legal terminology and tests 131
   tactics 130–1
Law Society 195–6
LawWorks organisation 62, 269
lawyers *see also* **advice; barristers; legal
     professional privilege; professional ethics;
     solicitors**
   ADR services, providing 281
   advocates, role of 236–40
   arbitration 24, 65, 407–9
   attendance 206–7
   commercial arbitration 407–9
   complaints 19, 310
   control of process 24, 51
   early neutral evaluation 24–5, 32
   expert-assisted determinations 24–5
   expertise 194
   familiarity with litigation, lawyer's 30
   immunity 19
   inter-client discussions 25
   joint meetings 230
   legal analysis 214
   litigation 24, 39
   mediation 25, 29–30, 194, 205–7, 214, 236–40
   meetings 205
   negotiations 25–7
   Office for Legal Complaints 310
   professional negligence actions 19–20
   regulation 18–20
   research 214
   review of ADR options 24–5
   selection of ADR options, factors influencing 51
   training and accreditation 20, 24
   wasted costs orders 19
legal analysis 214
legal context 136–7
legal funding
   after the event insurance 66
   conditional fee agreements 66, 283, 320
   costs 60, 66–7
   family mediation 258, 259
   Funding Code 192
   Legal Services Commission funding 67, 192
   mediation 192–3
   withdrawal 192
   withdrawal from case for non-approval of
     settlement 320
legal professional privilege
   advice 243
   confidentiality 12, 54, 55
   costs sanctions 106–7
   economic duress 243
   definition 55
   international arbitration 446
   mediation 243
Legal Services Commission (LSC) funding
   costs 67
   family mediation 259
   mediation 67, 192
   negotiations 67
   Part 36 offers 67

settlements 67
statutory charge 67
letters *see* **exchange of letters**
limitation periods *see* **time limits**
listening effectively 154
litigation 3–7 *see also* **stay of proceedings**
  advantages and disadvantages 4, 6–7, 13–15
  adversarial process 7, 14, 23, 46, 47
  advice 39
  advocacy 237
  allocation stage questionnaires 83–5
  animosity between parties 44
  appeals, avoiding 7
  arbitration 32–3, 372
  best interests of the client 51
  'cards on the table' approach 51, 185
  choice of forum 13
  Civil Procedure Rules 4, 9–10, 75–6, 82–3, 405–6,
    491
  client satisfaction 15, 48
  complexity 6, 43–4
  confidentiality 6, 14
  consent orders 331
  control of process 13, 46
  costs 13, 24, 61, 106–14, 181, 336
  court orders required, where 43, 180
  declaratory relief required, where 180
  delay 13, 185
  directions 50
  disadvantages and advantages 4, 6–7, 13–15
  disclosure 7
  during litigation, encouragement of ADR 10
  early neutral and/or expert evaluation 298
  encouragement of ADR 10, 12
  enforcement 488
  evidence 6, 14
  experts 7, 350–1
  facts, complexity of 44
  familiarity with litigation, lawyer's 39
  fast track claims 83
  flexibility 7, 14
  fraud cases 180
  further information, need for 180
  historic process, as 47
  injunctions 180
  inspection 6
  intentional wrongdoing, cases involving 181
  interim orders 43
  judges, role and power of 7
  judgments 321
  law, issues of 180
  lawyers 24
  London 4
  mediation 180–1, 187–9, 237, 247
  mediators, litigation against 247
  multi-track claims 83
  need for court orders 45
  NHS Litigation Authority 267
  norm, as 5
  parties, where there are many 44
  potential outcomes, wider range of 14

precedent 7, 43, 44–5, 180, 181
pre-eminence 4
problem-solving approach, use of 14
public policy 44
publicity required 44, 180
quasi-criminal allegations 44
remedies 46–7
risk reduction 15
selection of ADR options, factors influencing 51
settlements
  court approval 180
  enforcement 488
  existing litigation, where there is 327
  termination of litigation 239–40
small track claims 83
stay of proceedings 12, 50
strong case, where client has 43, 180
success, relevance of chances of 47, 180
summary judgments 43
test cases 180
undermining litigation, ADR as 51
weak cases 52
weighing up disadvantages and advantages 17
wider range of issues, consideration of 13–14
without prejudice communications 55–6
Local Government Ombudsman 314
London, litigation in 4
London Metal Exchange (LME) 396, 427–31,
  458–9
London SEN Mediation Service 264
look-sniff arbitration 405, 409–10

majority decisions 455, 457
maladministration 315
mandatory and non-mandatory
  provisions 385–6, 436
maritime disputes 388
Mayor's and City of London County Court
  Mediation Scheme 254
med-arb
  agreements 35
  Arb-Med 234–5
  CEDR Commission 234
  confidentiality 389
  criticism 234
  New York Convention 1958 389
  one-stop adjudication 390
  settlements 234
  website 234
mediation 28–31, 176–202 *see also* **family**
  mediation; international mediation;
  mediation, preparation for
  ACAS 260, 305
  adjournments 228, 232
  administration 193
  advantages 30–1, 177–8, 181–2, 188
  advocates, role of 236–40
  after commencement of litigation 189
  after the event insurance 192–3
  agreements
    mediate, to 28–9, 183

mediation (*cont.*)
  memorandum 29
  settlements 230–1
  signatures 29, 219
  written 28–9, 65
allocation stage questionnaires 84–5
apologies 48
Arb–Med 234–5
attendance 29–30, 64–5
audits 182
bargaining phase 219, 229–30, 233
barristers 284
before commencement of litigation 187–9
CEDR 177, 182
  CEDR Clinical Negligence Mediation
    Scheme 267
  Model Mediation Agreement 113, App 2
  success rate 182
  website 182
change of position 228
Civil Mediation Council 183, 195–6, 250, 268,
  276, 291, 293
closing phase 219, 230–3
commercial cases 257–8
community mediation 268–9
complex disputes 189, 258
compulsion 177
conciliation 199, 304–5
conditional fee agreements 192–3
confidentiality 181, 185, 232, 244–6
construction disputes 258
costs 190–2
  after commencement of litigation 189
  expenses 191–2
  fees 191
  Jackson Review 177
  litigation 181
  mediation party costs 190–1
  recovery 110–11
  sanctions 95–107, 185, 186
county courts 10
court-based schemes 9, 90, 182, 186, 189, 249–69
Court of Appeal Mediation Scheme 9, 90, 103, 186
daily rates 191
deadlock, strategies to deal with 227–9
definition 28, 177
delay 180, 181, 185
directions 179
Directory of UK Mediation 268
disadvantages 31, 185, 188
disclosure 185, 189
duration 29, 64, 184, 189, 190
early neutral evaluation 199, 297, 298
early stages of dispute, success at 187
effectiveness, reasons for 184
encouragement from court 177, 179, 183, 185–6
environment 265
evaluative mediation 197–9, 233–4
expenses 191–2
expert or neutral determination 343, 345
experts 224–5, 230, 233–4

explanations 48
exploration or information phase 219, 226–9, 233
extension of plenary sessions 225
face to face meetings 29
facilitative mediation 197–8, 199, 233
facilities 190
failure, reasons for 31
fees 64–5, 191
files 29–30
final joint meetings 231
Financial Services Authority Mediation
  Service 266
flowchart of process 220
funding 192–3
Funding Code 192
future relationships, importance of 47
gap, closing the 228
government, use by the 182–3
healthcare sector 266–7
Her Majesty's Courts Service (HMCS) Small
  Claims Mediation Scheme 255–7
hourly rates 191
impartiality 198–9
Independent Doctor's Forum 267, 307
intellectual property cases 258
Internet mediations 235–6
introductions 219–20
Jackson Review 177
joint meetings 219–22, 225, 230–2
judicial endorsement 179
LawWorks 269
lawyers
  advocates, role of 236–40
  professional ethics 284, 287–8
  role 25, 29–30, 236–40
lay clients, joint meetings between 230
lay witnesses 224
layout of meeting rooms 190
legal funding 192–3
legal advice privilege 243
Legal Services Commission (LSC)
  funding 67, 192
litigation 180–1, 187–9, 237
  after commencement 189
  before commencement 187–9
London SEN Mediation Service 264
Med-Arb 35, 234, 389, 390
Mediation in Civil and Commercial Matters
  Directive 270–1, 274–7
meetings 29–30, 200–1
  closing joint meetings 225, 231–2
  experts 230
  family disputes 233
  final joint meetings 231
  joint meetings 219–22, 225, 230–2
  lay clients 230
  opening joint meetings 219–22, 230
  private meetings 225–7
  representatives 230
Ministry of Justice annual reports 182–3
mini-trials or executive tribunals 264–5

Model Mediation Agreement (CEDR), copy of App 2

multi-party disputes 262–3

National Mediation Helpline 177

negotiations 30, 177–8, 197, 219, 229–30, 233

NHS Litigation Authority 267

NHS trusts 267

no settlement reached, where 231

objectives of clients 47

offices of solicitors or parties, held at 190

opening phase 219–26, 230

opening statements 219–24

outcomes 321

Pensions Mediation Service 267

Performing Arts Mediation Service 268

personal injury 261–2

plenary sessions 219–20, 225

preparation 236

presentation of case 49

private meetings 225–7

pro bono mediation 269

procedure 29, 218–48

professional ethics 284, 287–8

project mediation 264

providers
    administration 193
    premises of 189–90

public funding 192

public policy 265

reality checks 227

reasons for use of mediation 183–4

recording settlements 321

regulation 12, 18

reluctant parties, persuading 185–6

representatives, joint meetings of 230

research 182

rooms
    required, number of 190
    visiting clients in 219

seating plan 219–20, 221

sector mediation 266–7

separate private meetings 225–6

settlements
    advocates 238–40
    after the mediation, helping settlement 182
    agreements 230–1
    binding 231
    closing phase 219, 230–1
    creativity 181, 228–9
    evaluative mediation 198–9
    final joint meetings 231
    no settlement reached, where 231
    recording 321
    success rate 182–3
    terms, drawing up 231

shuttle mediation 229–30

Small Claims Scheme 90, 249

stages 219–29

Standing Council of Mediation Advocates 236–7

statistics 182–3

stay of proceedings 186

strategies 227–9

stress, avoiding 181

styles of mediation 195, 197–9

success fees 193

success, reasons for 31, 187

suitability of disputes 179–81

tactics 184

telephone mediations 235

termination of mediation 232

terminology 304

terms of settlement, drawing up 231

third parties 28, 30, 177, 181

time frame 29, 200–1

timing 30, 186–9

training 29

transformative mediation 200

types 28–9

unrepresented parties 30

variations in process 233–6

venue 189–91

voluntary process, as 177

website 268

without prejudice communications 240–3

witnesses 246–7

workplace mediation 260–1

works, whether mediation 31, 182–3, 187

written agreements 28–9, 65

Mediation in Civil and Commercial Matters Directive 270–1, 274–7

application 275

Civil Mediation Council 276

codes of conduct 275–6

confidentiality 276–7

continuous professional development 276

court-ordered compulsory mediation 275

cross-border disputes, definition of 275

definition of mediation 274–5

enforceability of agreements 276

implementation timetable 274

key obligations of member states 275–6

limitation periods, effect of mediation of 277

objective 274–5

prescription periods, effect of mediation of 277

publicity 277

quality, ensuring 275–6

Registered Mediation Organisation Scheme 276

Registered Mediator Scheme 276

Registered Training Organisation Scheme 276

settlements 275

training 276

website 274

mediation, preparation for 203–17, 272

agreed bundles 211–12

agreement 203–5

analysis stage 213–15

attendees 205–8

BATNA (best alternative to a negotiated agreement) 215

bundles 210–13

conclusions, drawing 215

confidentiality 212

mediation, preparation for *(cont.)*
  cost analysis 214
  defences 214
  disclosure of position statements and
    documents 212
  documentation 210–13
  evidential analysis 214
  experts 207–8, 211
  factual analysis 214
  flowchart 216
  further information, seeking 213
  insurers, attendance of 207
  interest groups 207
  lawyers
    attendance 206–7
    legal analysis 214
    research 214
  legal analysis 214
  meetings 205
  position statements 208–10, 212
  pre-mediation meetings/contact 205
  preparation 213–15
  research 214
  settlements
    attendance of persons with authority to
      settle 206
    factors, analysis of 214–15
    insurers 207
    undue pressure 247
  signatures 204
  standard form agreements 204
  strategies, preparation of 213
  style, preparation of 215
  tactics, preparation of 213, 215
  telephone, contact by 213
  WATNA (worse alternative to a negotiated
    agreement) 215
  without prejudice communications 204, 207
  witnesses of fact 208
  writing, contact by 213
mediators
  accreditation 195–6
  administration 193, 293
  agreement 204
  appointment 193, 204
  at the meeting, role of mediator 200–1
  BATNA (best alternative to a negotiated
    agreement) 201
  before meeting, role of mediator 200
  CEDR 291, 293
  Civil Mediation Council 291, 293
  civil proceedings against mediators 247
  codes of conduct 291–3
  competence 277, 291
  conclusion of mediation, role following
    the 232–3
  confidentiality 277, 292
  contacting 186
  continuing professional development 291
  cultural considerations 196
  disciplinary proceedings against mediators 247

EU Code of Conduct for Mediators 12, 18, 277,
  291–3
  exclusion clauses 247
  experience 194–5
  expertise 193, 194–5
  facilitator, as 201
  factors influencing selection 194–7
  fairness 292
  family mediation 259
  fees 191
  impartiality 292
  independence 277, 291
  intermediatory, acting as 201
  interviews 196
  language considerations 196
  lawyers
    attendance 206
    expertise gained by mediator 194
    meetings with parties' lawyers 205
    professional ethics 290–3
  more than one mediator 193, 263
  multi-party disputes 263
  negligence 247
  organisation of process 200–1
  personal recommendation 194
  personality 194
  post-mediation role 201, 205
  practical experience 195
  procedure 292
  professional ethics 290–3
  professional in other fields, expertise gained as
    a 195
  providers 193
  qualities 193–4
  Registered Mediation Organisation Scheme 291
  Registered Mediation Scheme 291
  regulation 290–1
  repeat instructions 293
  representatives of parties, attendance of 206
  role 184, 200–1, 232–3, 259
  selection 193–7
  shortlist 193
  styles of mediation 195, 197–9
  sued, whether mediator can be 247
  team of mediators 196–7
  telephone, contact by 205
  termination of mediation 292–3
  training 290–1
  unfair contract terms, exclusion clauses and 247
  WATNA (worse alternative to a negotiated
    agreement) 201
  witness, mediator as 246–7
  without prejudice communications 243
meetings *see also* **conferences**
  advice 40
  closing joint meetings 225, 231–2
  complaints and grievance procedures 313
  conciliation 305
  construction disputes 81–2
  experts 230
  family disputes 233

final joint meetings 231
international arbitration 446
joint meetings 219–22, 225, 230–2
mediation 29–30, 200–1, 205, 219–22, 225–7,
    230–3
lawyers 205
lay clients 230
opening joint meetings 219–22, 230, 238
opening statements at opening joint meetings,
    delivery of 238
pre-action protocols 81–2
preliminary meetings 411–12
private meetings 225–7, 238
representatives 230
mental capacity 381, 466
Mercantile Court 300
merits of the case, presenting the 162
merger 476
mining 355
Ministry of Justice 17–18, 182–3
mini-trials or executive tribunals 264–5
mirroring behaviour 152
mislead, duty not to 155
misrepresentation 333–4
mistake 333–4, 489–90
mixed arguments 142
model documents *see* forms and precedents
Model Law *see* UNCITRAL Model Law
monitoring 196
moral arguments 142
moving on 128
multi-party disputes 44, 262–3
multi-tiered dispute resolution 389
multi-track claims 63, 83

National Health Service (NHS)
    NHS Litigation Authority 267
    NHS pilot scheme for medical negligence 8, 267
    NHS trusts, conciliation and 307
National Mediation Helpline (NMH) 249–54
    administration 250
    agreement to mediate, copy of App 2
    Central London County Court Voluntary
        Mediation Scheme 254
    Civil Mediation Council 250
    costs 63, 77, 112–13
    county courts 10, 63
    court, referral by 250
    criticism 250
    definition of mediation 177
    documentation 251
    encouragement of ADR 90
    family mediation 258–9
    fast track claims 63
    fees 251–2
    fixed fees 251
    flowcharts 251, 252–3
    Ministry of Justice 250
    multi track claims 63
    online enquiry form 250
    process 250–2

Queen's Bench Guide 77
    referrals 250–3
    small claims 250, 251
    telephone enquiries 250
    Telephone Helplines Association 250
    Thompson Report 250
    time-limited mediation 251, 254
    training and accreditation 196
    website 10, 63, 196, 250
natural justice
    arbitration 384
    complaints and grievance procedures 313
    expert or neutral determination 347
    ombudsmen 315
need for ADR, reasons for 6–7
negligence 8, 247, 281
negotiation 26–8 *see also* preparation for
        negotiation
    abruptness 129
    additional outcomes, proposing 128
    advantages 27–8
    agendas
        agreements 156
        setting 155–6
    aggression 130
    agreed easily, starting with items that can be 158
    agreements
        arbitration 493–4
        negotiate, to 42
        no agreement reached 174–5
        oral 173–4
        provisional 173
    attendance 27, 151–2
    bargaining tactics 168–9
    barristers' fees 63–4
    BATNA (best alternative to a negotiated
        agreement) 146–7, 201, 215
    bluffing 130
    body language 151
    bogged down, getting 170–1
    breaks 170
    case management conferences 151
    clients
        attendance 151
        satisfaction 48
    closing 173–5
    collaborative approach 121–3, 124, 160–3, 167
    communicating effectively 152–5
    competitive style 118–21, 125, 127, 129–30, 151,
        161, 162, 171
    complex or commercial negotiations 27
    concealing information 126
    concessions, planning and timing 163–9
    conference calls 26
    confusion 173–4
    cooperative strategies 118–20
    costs 63–4, 102
    court, door of the 26, 151
    deadlock, reaching 129, 170–1
    deals, reaching 167–8
    demands, planning and timing 127–8, 161–9

negotiation (*cont.*)
detail, points of 173
difficulties, dealing with 170–2
disadvantages 28
emotion 171–2
enforcement 42
escalating demands 168
evasion 129
evidence 163
expert or neutral determination 345
extreme demands 168
face to face 26, 27
facilitative start 151
failure, reasons for 28
failure to take part in negotiations, costs sanctions for 102
false issues 168
family mediation 259
figures 163
frustration 171–2
gaps 170, 173
Getting Past No. Ury, William 171–2
Harvard Negotiation Project 17–18
inexperience, concern about 172
information, seeking 125–7, 160–1, 170
interests rather than positions, focus on 122–3
irritation 171–2
issues
adding 173
making your case on the 161–3
key questions, asking 157
law, bringing out 130–1, 163
lawyer, role of the 25–7
Legal Services Commission funding 67
legal terminology and tests 131
mediation 30, 177–8, 197, 219, 229–30, 233
merits of case, presenting the 162
moving on 128
multiple concessions 168
objectives of clients 47
offers, planning and timing 127–9, 163–9
opening 156–60
agenda, agreeing an 156
agreed easily, starting with items that can be 158
key questions, asking 157
opponents to open, inviting 157–8
problems, dealing with 159–60
statements or proposals, with 157
strong, starting with items where your case is 158
opponents to open, inviting 157–8
option-creation 156
oral arguments, additions to 163
oral contracts 173–4
outcomes 163, 321
parameters, setting 127
parking issues 128
persuasive arguments 162
photos 163
plans 123–4, 163

poorly prepared opponents, dealing with 171
position statements 209
positional approach 120–1, 126, 172
power game, negotiation as a 172
pragmatic approach 123
preconditions 127, 168
presentation of case 49, 129–31
principled or problem solving 121–3
problems, dealing with 156, 159–60
procedure 26–7, 149–75
professional ethics 284–8
progress, making 169–70
proposals, opening with 157
questioning 126
recording the outcome 174, 321
reframing 127
renegotiation of issues 173
research 131
seating 151
separating people from the problem 122
settlements
enforcement 493–4
limits on authority 158–9
provisional settlements 159
recording 321
silence 128
splitting the difference 169
stages in case 27
stages of negotiation 149–50
statements, opening with a 157
strategies and style 118–24
stress, inducing 168
strong, starting with items where your case is 158
structure 128–9, 155–6
benefits of clarity 155
choices 155
implementation, problems in 155–6
summaries of progress 170
tables 151
tactics 125–31, 157–8
take it or leave it 168
telephone, by 26, 27, 151
terms of agreement, clarification of 26
threats 130
time to think 129
ultimatums 127
venue 26, 151
WATNA (worse alternative to a negotiated agreement) 147, 201, 215
weaknesses in case, addressing 162
weaknesses in opponent's case, bringing out 162–3
who needs to attend 151–2
without prejudice negotiations 55–7, 159
writing 26, 27
neutral determination *see* **expert or neutral determination**
neutrality 48
New York Convention 1958 277–8, 389, 392, 404, 433, 493–4
NHS Litigation Authority 267

NHS pilot scheme for medical negligence 8, 267
NHS trusts, conciliation and 307
non-adjudicative ADR 25–32
   arbitration 371
   costs 52
   definition 25
   disclosure 288–9
   evidence 49
   exchange of letters 324
   professional ethics 288–9
   recording settlements 321, 322
   settlements 49, 321, 322
non-verbal communication 151–2
Norwich Pharmacal orders 468
notice
   arbitration 396, 397, 409, 427–8, 459
   awards 459
   commercial arbitration 409, 427–8
   construction industry adjudication 358–61
   referral notices 362–5
nuclear power plants, construction of 355

objectives of clients
   identification 133–4
   mediation 47
   negotiations 47, 133–4
   personal objectives 133
   position statements 209
   remedies 46–7
   selection of ADR options, factors
      influencing 46–7
offers to settle
   costs sanctions 97–8, 102
   encouragement of ADR 8–9
   exchange of letters 25–6
   Legal Services Commission funding 67
   negotiation 143–6, 163–9
   Part 36 offers 25–6, 41, 67, 97
   planning and timing 143–6, 163–9
   rejection of offer 97–8, 102
   tactics 127–8
   writing 25–6
oil and gas extraction 355
ombudsmen 314–16
   apologies 316
   binding decisions 316
   British and Irish Ombudsman Association 314
   compensation 316
   consumer services 314
   definition 8
   documents-only process 315
   effect of decisions 316
   evidence-based decisions 315
   Furniture Ombudsman Conciliation Scheme 308
   grievance processes 35–6
   grounds for decisions 315
   Guide to Principles of Good Complaints
      Handling 314–15
   handling of complaints 314–15
   impartiality 314
   independence 314

   internal complaints 314
   Local Government Ombudsman 314
   maladministration 315
   natural justice 315
   Parliamentary and Health Service
      Ombudsman 314
   Pensions Ombudsman 316
   private sector ombudsman 315–16
   procedure 315
   public sector ombudsman 314–16
   publication of decisions 316
   recording settlements 321
   review of decisions 316
   use 8
   websites 314
one-stop adjudication 390
opening phases 156–60, 219–26, 230
opening statements 219–24, 238
opinions 40
oral agreements
   arbitration agreements or clauses 380
   negotiation 173–4
   outcomes 321
   recording settlements 321, 322
oral hearings 288, 367, 423
ousting the jurisdiction of the court 476
outcomes
   additional outcomes, proposing 128
   adjudicative ADR 321
   advantages and disadvantages of ADR 14, 16
   agreements 321
   arbitration awards 321
   clear outcomes, reaching 319–20
   conciliation 321
   forms of recorded outcome 320–1
   grievance procedure 321
   judgments, compared to 16
   litigation 14
   mediation 321
   negotiations 321
   non-adjudicative ADR 321
   ombudsmen 321
   oral agreements 321
   range of outcomes 14
   recording outcomes 174
   reports from third parties 321
overriding objective 9, 82–3, 280, 384

parameters, setting 127
parking issues 128
Parliamentary and Health Service
   Ombudsman 314
Parliamentary Commissioner for Administration
   (PCA) 8
Part 8 procedure 350, 466, 478, 491–2
Part 36 offers 25–6, 41, 67, 97
parties
   animosity between parties 44
   apologies 48
   arbitration 385–6, 391
   arbitrators

parties (*cont.*)
    agreements 385–6
    appointment 391
    autonomy 396, 451
  attitudes 44, 48
  autonomy 395–6, 470
  control 24
  costs 67–8
  experts 422
  multi-party disputes 44, 262–3
  terminology 6
  UNCITRAL Model Law 451
Pensions Mediation Service 267–8
Pensions Ombudsman 316
peremptory orders 415, 454
Performing Arts Mediation Service 268
personal injury claims
  advantages of ADR 261
  British Coal Miners Mediation Scheme for
    Respiratory and Vibration White Finger 262
  CEDR
    Personal Injury Unit (PIU) Telephone
      Mediation 262
    PIU Mediation 262
  court mediation schemes and other
    schemes 261–2
  early neutral and/or expert evaluation 300–1
  fees 300–1
  mediation 261–2
  PIU (Personal Injury Unit) eValuate (CEDR) 300–1
  Trust Meridian Ltd's Personal Injury Scheme 262
personality 194
persuasive arguments 140–2, 162
photographs 163
pilot schemes
  Central London County Court Compulsory
    Mediation pilot scheme 254–5
  Her Majesty's Courts Service (HMCS) Small
    Claims Mediation Scheme 255
  judicial mediation pilots 261
  NHS pilot scheme for medical negligence 8
  Social Security and Child Support (SSCS) Tribunal
    pilots 301–3
plenary sessions 219–20, 225
points of claim, example of 417–18, 419–20
points of law
  appeals 475–8
  preliminary points of law 470–1
poorly prepared opponents, dealing with 171
position statements
  bundles 208
  case management conferences 210
  case summaries 208, 209–10
  chronology 210
  contents 209–10
  definition 208
  documentation, accompanying 210
  drafting, aims on 208–9
  dramatis personae 210
  facts 209
  issues, identification of 209

joint statements 210
  mediation, preparation for 208–10, 212
  negotiations, explanation of 209
  objectives of parties 209
  outline of case 208
  time limits 208
positional approach 120–1, 126, 172
practical experience 195
Practice Direction Pre-Action Conduct 80–1,
  101–3
pragmatic approach 123
pre-action protocols 79–82
  ancillary relief 82
  Construction and Engineering Disputes 81–2
  costs 112
  encouragement of ADR 9–10, 81
  evidence 16
  family proceedings 82
  list of protocols 80
  Practice Direction Pre-Action Conduct 80–1, 101–3
  preparation for negotiation 134–5
precedent
  ADR as undermining development of law 44–5
  advantages and disadvantages of ADR 7, 16, 43,
    44–5, 180, 181
  advocacy 239
  costs sanctions 96
  test cases 180
precedents *see* **forms and precedents**
preliminary meetings 411–12
preliminary points of law
  conditions to be satisfied 471
  determination 470–1
  procedure 471
  witness statements 471
preparation *see* **mediation, preparation for;**
    preparation for negotiation
preparation for negotiation 132–48
  authority to settle, clarification of 147–8
  BATNA (best alternative to a negotiated
    agreement) 146–7
  concessions, planning potential 143–6
  costs 134
  court door, negotiation at the 135
  demands, planning potential 143–6
  early stage, case is at a very 134
  evidence, dealing with 137–9
  facts
    arguments based on 141
    client's views 137–8
    dealing with 137–9
    opponent's view 138
  fairness 142
  figures, preparing to deal with 139–40, 148
  foreseeability 137
  future relationships 133
  gaps and ambiguities, dealing with 138–9
  identification of issues 135–6
  importance of preparation 132–3
  information, dealing with 139
  instructions, clarification of 147–8

issue of proceedings, after the 135
law, arguments based on application of 141
legal context, relevance of 136–7
legal rights 133
linking concessions 146
merit based on moral argument 142
mixed arguments 142
money claims 133
objectives
    identification 133–4
    personal 133
offers, planning potential 143–6
personal objectives 133
persuasive arguments, identification of 140–2
    advocacy 141
    facts, arguments based on 141
    law, arguments based on application of 141
    merit based on moral argument 142
    mixed arguments 142
    practical or personal arguments 142
practical or personal arguments 142
pre-action protocol stage 134–5
priorities 143
procedural stage, importance of 134–5
settlements 134, 147–8
statements of case 134–6
trial, preparation for 135
WATNA (worse alternative to a negotiated
    agreement), identifying the 147
prescription 277
presentation 49, 129–31, 152–3
pre-trial hearings/conferences 422–3
principled or problem solving approach 121–3
priorities 143
privacy *see* **confidentiality**
private meetings 225–7, 238
privilege *see* **legal professional privilege**
pro bono mediation 264
problem-solving approach 14, 156, 159–60
procedural arbitration orders 453–4
    applications 469–70
    Arbitration Act 1996 467–9
    commercial arbitration 412–14
    conservatory measures 454
    determination of proceedings, assisting
        in 467–70
    directions 454
    disclosure 468–9
    dismissal of arbitration 454
    evidence 467–8
    freezing injunctions 469
    injunctions 467, 469–70
    interim remedies 454, 467, 469–70
    jurisdiction 468
    Norwich Pharmacal orders 468
    on-notice applications 469
    party autonomy 470
    peremptory orders 454
    pre-action disclosure 468
    UNCITRAL Model Law 467
    urgent applications 469–70

professional ethics 279–303
    adjudication 289
    administration 293
    admissions 288
    advancing client's case, duties when 285–6
    advantages over litigation 270
    advice 39–40, 280–3
    arbitration 289
    attendance 290
    authority to settle 289
    barristers 280, 281, 283–6
        attendance 290
        Bar Code of Conduct 281, 283–6
        competence 285
        conditional fee agreements 283
        drafting documents 285–6
        mediation 284
        records 290
        relationship with professional clients 290
        service, lawyers providing an ADR 281
        solicitors, relationship with 290
    best interests of clients 280, 282–3
    CEDR 291, 293
    Civil Mediation Council code 293
    codes of practice 281–7
    competence 285, 291
    concessions 288
    conditional fee agreements 283
    confidentiality 284, 286–8, 292
    conflicts of interest 281, 283, 290
    continuing professional development 291
    core duties 281–5
    costs, duty to consider 280
    court guides 280
    disclosure 288–9
    discrimination 285
    drafting documents 285–6
    experts
        confidentiality 287
        disclosure 288–9
    fairness 285
    impartiality 292
    independence 283, 291
    instructions, acting within 282
    integrity 283–4, 288
    mediation 284, 287–8
    mediators 290–3
    negotiation 284–8
    non-adjudicatory ADR, disclosure and 288–9
    overriding objective 280
    professional negligence 281
    records 290
    regulation 290–1
    repeat instructions 293
    service, lawyers providing an ADR 281
    settlements
        advice 282–3
        authority to settle 289
        instructions 289
        reasonableness 282–3
    solicitors 280–3, 285

professional ethics (*cont.*)
    barristers, relationship with 290
    Code of Practice 282, 283, 285–7
    competence 285
    confidentiality 286–7
    costs, advice on 280–1
    independence 283
    sanctions, advice on 280–1
  suitability for ADR, duty to consider 280
  termination of mediation 292–3
  wasted costs orders 281
  without prejudice communications 286–7
professional negligence actions 19–20, 281
progress, making 169–70
proper law 437–9
proportionality of costs 60, 98, 491
protocols *see* **pre-action protocols**
providers
  administration 193
  arbitration 65
  early neutral and/or expert evaluation 298
  employment 260
  expert or neutral determination 346
  fees 65
  increase in number of bodies offering ADR 8
  list 20, 196, App 1
  mediation 189–90, 193
  register 260
  review of ADR options 22
  venue 189–90
psychological factors 152
public funding *see* **legal funding**
public hearings 483
public law disputes 376–7
public policy 44, 265, 371, 473
publicity 44, 180, 277, 316 *see also* **confidentiality**

quasi-criminal allegations 44
Queen's Bench Guide 77–8
questioning effectively 126, 154
questionnaires at allocation stage 83–5

reality checks 227
reasons
  appeals on points of law 476
  arbitration awards 430, 457
  commercial arbitration 430
  construction industry adjudication 368
  decisions 348, 350, 368
  expert or neutral determination 348, 350
reciprocal or mirroring behaviour 152
recognition of arbitration awards 493–4
recording outcomes 174
recording settlements 319–38
  adjudicative ADR 321
  advocates 239
  arbitration awards 321
  checking agreement 321
  clear outcomes, reaching 319–20
  conciliation 321
  conditional fee agreements 320

  consent orders 331–6
  contracts 174, 324, 326–7, 488–90
  costs 320, 322, 336–7
  court of settlement, informing 337–8
  court orders 323
  deeds 174, 324, 326–7
  drafts 322, 323–4
  during process, records made 321–2
  endorsement on briefs 174, 327–30
  enforceable forms for recording
    settlements 322–3
  exchange of letters 174, 324–6
  formal records, who should produce 322
  forms of recorded outcome 320–1
  grievance procedure 321
  informing court of settlement 337–8
  interim court orders 174, 323, 330–1
  judgments 323
  legal documents 323
  litigation, settlements where there is existing 327
  mediation 321
  methods of recording settlement
    agreements 324–36, 488–90
  negotiations 321
  non-adjudicative ADR 321, 322
  ombudsmen 321
  oral agreements 321, 322
  outcomes
    forms 320–1
    reaching clear 319–20
  provisional agreements 320
  purpose of records 321–2
  reports from third parties 321
  statutory authority, awards with 323
  terms of settlement
    approval 320
    costs 323, 336–7
    drafting 323–4
    enforcement 323
    interest 323
    writing 321
  Tomlin orders 334–6
  withdrawal from case for non-approval of
    settlement 320
  writing 321–2
records
  barristers 290
  complaints and grievance procedures 313
  professional ethics 290
recovery of ADR costs in litigation 108–14
  Admiralty and Commercial Court Guide 110
  CEDR Model Mediation Agreement 113
  costs in the case, agreements between parties for
    costs of ADR process to be 112–13
  determination on all issues apart from costs,
    settlement or 113
  discretion 109
  failed ADR as part of costs of litigation, costs of 110
  fees 108
  hearings 109
  incidental costs 110

interim applications 109
lawyers 108
liability, agreement between parties
    determines 110–11
mediation 110–11
National Mediation Helpline 112–13
no agreement, where there is 111–12
pre-action protocols 112
refusal to engage in ADR process 109
settlements 108, 110–11, 113
unsuccessful ADR processes, recovery of 109–13
withdrawal from process 111–12
rectification 459, 489
Redfern Schedule, example of 421
referrals 257, 362–5
reframing 127
Registered Mediation Organisation Scheme
    (CMC) 276
Registered Mediator Scheme (CMC) 276
Registered Training Organisation Scheme
    (CMC) 276
regulation 18–20
    Arbitration Act 1996 18
    complaints 19
    family mediation 259
    international arbitration 18
    lawyers 18–20
    mediation 12, 18, 290–1
    professional ethics 290–1
    Solicitors' Regulation Authority 20, 259
    treaties and conventions 18
reluctant parties, persuading 185–6
remedies *see also* **injunctions**
    arbitration 391–2, 458–9
    awards 458–9
    damages 89, 105, 244, 344, 359
    declarations 180, 458
    interim remedies 454, 467, 469–70
    litigation 46–7
    objectives of clients 47
removal of arbitrators 400–1, 466
research 10, 17–18, 131, 182, 214
residential building contracts 369
resignation of arbitrators 401, 467
responding effectively 153–4
retainers 61
review of ADR options 22–37
    adjudicative options 32–5
    areas of practice 22–3
    contracts, options as part of 22
    costs 22, 24
    dispute management systems 36
    factors differentiating between objects 23–4
    grievance processes 35–6
    hybrids 35
    IT-based options 36
    Jackson Review 22
    key elements 23–4
    lawyers
        control 24
        role 24–5

non-adjudicative options 25–32
parties, control of 24
providers 22
specialist systems 36
terminology 23
third parties, control by 23
risk 15, 68–9
Rome I Regulation 438–9
rooms used for mediation
    required, number of 190
    visiting clients 219
rules *see* **institutional rules**

samples 429
sanctions *see* **costs sanctions**
Scheme for Construction Contracts, default
    provisions in the 358, 361, 368
Scott v Avery clauses 382
seat of arbitration
    awards 436, 455, 458
    choice of seat 438–9
    definition 434
    designation 435
    enforcement 458
    ICC Rules of Arbitration 448
    international arbitration 434–6, 441
seating 151, 219–20, 221
sector mediation 266–7
security for costs 412, 430, 447
selection of ADR options, factors
    influencing 38–57
    advance selection 41–2
    agreement to ADR, securing 53–4
    appropriateness 43–4
    attitudes of parties 44, 48
    confidentiality 46, 54–7
    control wanted by client, amount of 46
    costs 45, 51–2
    delaying tactic, ADR used as 52
    disclosure 49–50
    enforcement 50
    evidence, need for orders relating to 49–50
    expert knowledge, importance of 45
    future relationships, importance of 47
    interim orders 49
    jurisdiction 43
    lack of faith in case, proposing ADR means 51
    lawyer's control of case, ADR as undermining 51
    legal advice 38–41
    litigation, as undermining 51
    neutral assistance 48
    objectives of client 46–7
    potential concerns 50–3
    robust process, ADR as not being a 52–3
    settlement, pressures for 52
    stage case has reached 48–9
    success, relevance of chances of 43, 47
separability of clauses 374
serious irregularity
    Arbitration Act 1996 472–4
    arbitration awards 471–4

serious irregularity (*cont.*)
  definition 472
  exceeding powers 472–3
  failing to deal with the issues 473
  fairly and impartially, general duty to act 472
  fraud 473
  judicial review 471–4
  object, loss of right to 474
  powers available 474
  public policy 473
  substantial injustice 473–4
service 84
settlement agreements/contracts
  appropriateness 324, 326
  breach, defences to 488–9
  challenging settlements recorded as
      contracts 489–90
  consent orders 278
  costs 491
  drafting 326–7
  example 327
  mediation 277–8, 230–1
  necessity 324, 326
  reciprocal arrangements 278
  recorded as contracts, settlements 488–90
  writing or evidenced in writing 324
settlements *see also* **enforcement of settlements;**
      offers to settle; recording settlements
  advice 24–5, 282–3
  advocacy 238–40
  arbitration awards 455
  Arb-Med 234–5
  attendance 206
  authority
    limits 158–9
    preparation for negotiation 147–8
    professional ethics 289
    tactics 127
  binding settlements 238–40
  capacity 240
  conciliation 304–5
  conditional fee agreements 66
  costs 108, 110–11, 113
  court approval 180
  deeds 324, 326
  factors, analysis of 214–15
  fees, refund of 337–8
  instructions 289
  insurers 207
  litigation, termination of 239–40
  med-arb 234
  mediation 181–3, 206–7, 214–15, 219, 228–31,
      247, 275
  negotiation 134, 147–8, 158–9
  non-adjudicative ADR 49
  Part 36 offers 41
  preparation for negotiation 134, 147–8
  professional ethics 282–3, 289
  provisional settlements 159
  reasonableness 282–3
  selection of ADR options, factors influencing 52

  stay of proceedings 85
  terms 231, 239–40
  undue pressure 247
  withdrawal from case for non-approval of
      settlements 320
  without prejudice communications 242
  written offers 25–6
short-form arbitration 405, 410
shuttle mediation 229–30, 273
signatures
  arbitration awards 430, 458
  commercial arbitration 430
  endorsement on briefs 329
  mediation 29, 204, 219
silence as a tactic 129
site visits 366, 426
skeleton arguments 424, 426
small claims
  National Mediation Helpline 250, 251
  Her Majesty's Courts Service Small Claims
      Mediation Scheme 90, 249, 255–7
  small claims track 83
Social Security and Child Support (SSCS)
    Tribunal pilots 301–3
sole arbitrators 396, 398–9
solicitors *see also* **lawyers; legal professional**
      privilege
  barristers, relationship with 290
  cap on solicitor-client costs 105
  Code of Practice 282, 283, 285–7
  competence 285
  confidentiality 286–7
  costs
    advice 280–1
    sanctions 105
  endorsement on briefs 327–8
  fees 61, 63–4
  independence 283
  Law Society 195–6
  negotiations 63–4
  professional ethics 280–3, 285–7, 290
  sanctions, advice on 280–1
  Solicitors' Regulation Authority 20, 259
  TeCSA Adjudication Rules 358, 361
special educational needs 264
specialisation
  adjudication 34
  construction industry 36
  definition 36
  expert or neutral determination 35
  family mediation 258–9
  review of ADR options 36
  training and accreditation 20
specific performance 458–9
splitting the difference 169
standard terms 204, 358, 407
Standing Council of Mediation Advocates
    (SCMA) 236–7
stateless arbitration 441
statements of case 134–6, 365, 416, 429, 451
statutory arbitration 388

statutory charge 67
stay of proceedings
  agreement to ADR, securing 54
  allocation to track 85
  Arbitration Act 1996 464
  best endeavours 50
  breach of arbitration agreements 464–5
  consent orders 331–2
  determination of applications 464
  directions 50
  dispute coming within agreement 464–5
  encouragement of ADR 10, 12
  example of order 86
  expert or neutral determination 344
  good faith 50
  High Court jurisdiction in arbitration
      claims 464–5
  management powers of court 85
  mediation 186
  persuading judge to order a stay 54
  procedure 464
  settlements 85
  Technology and Construction Court Guide 78–9
  Tomlin orders 334
strategies and styles
  advantages and disadvantages of ADR 16
  bargaining tactics 168
  characteristic approach 119–23
  choice of strategy or style 118–19, 123–4
  collaborative strategies 121–3, 124, 152, 154,
      167–8
  comparison of strategies 126
  competitive/confrontational style 118, 119–21,
      127, 129, 130, 152, 164, 165, 167–8, 171
  concessions 167–8
  cooperative strategies 118–20, 152, 167
  definition of strategy 118
  definition of style 117
  idle time, strategies for 263
  importance 117–18
  interaction of strategies 124
  interests rather than positions, focus on 122–3
  listening effectively 154
  mediation 195, 197–9, 213, 215, 227–9, 263
  negotiations 118–24
  planning 123–4
  positional strategies 120–1
  pragmatic strategies 123
  principled or problem solving 121–3
  procedural steps, use of 16
  responding effectively 153
  separating people from the problem 122
stress 168, 181
strong case, where client has 43, 180
studies, list of 18
styles in negotiation *see* strategies and styles
substantial injustice 473–4
success fees 66, 193, 283
success of ADR
  ADR Now, research on website of 17–18
  assessment 17–18

CEDR 182
costs 60, 99–100
Harvard Negotiation Project 17
Her Majesty's Courts Service (HMCS) Small
    Claims Mediation Scheme 256
litigation 47, 180
mediation 31, 182–3, 187
Ministry of Justice 17–18
relevance of chances of success 47, 180
research 17–18
selection of ADR options, factors influencing 43, 47
settlements 182–3
studies, list of 18
suitability
  expert or neutral determination 343
  mediation 179–81
  professional ethics 280
summaries of progress 170
summary judgments 16, 43, 354, 488, 492
summonses 425

tables 151
tactics in negotiation 125–31, 157–8
  abruptness 129
  additional outcomes, proposing 128
  aggression 130
  authority to settle 127
  bargaining 168–9, 219, 229–30, 273
  bluffing 130
  concealing information 126
  confrontational approach 126
  deadlock, avoiding 129
  definition of tactics 118, 125
  delay 15
  draft, preparation of 129
  escalating demands 168
  evasion 129
  extreme demands 168
  false issues 168
  ignoring structure 128
  importance 117–18
  imposing structure 128
  information, relating to 126
  just one more thing 128–9
  law, relating to 130–1
  legal terminology and tests 131
  mediation 184, 213, 215, 219, 229–30, 233, 273
  moving on 128
  multiple concessions 268
  objective standards 127
  offers and demands 127–8
    additional outcomes, proposing 128
    authority to settle 127
    objective standards 127
    parameters, setting 127
    ultimatums 127
  parameters, setting 127
  parking issues 128
  positional approach 126
  pre-conditions 127, 168
  preparation 213, 215

tactics in negotiation *(cont.)*
  presentation, relating to 129–31
  questioning 126
  reframing 127
  research, using 131
  responding effectively 153
  silence 129
  splitting the difference 169
  stress, inducing 168
  structure for negotiation, relating to 128–9
  take it or leave it 168
  threats 130
  time to think 129
  ultimatums 127
take it or leave it 168
Technology and Construction Court (TCC)
  early neutral and/or expert evaluation 32, 300
  encouragement of ADR 78–9
  Guide 78–9
  stay of proceedings 78–9
  TeCSA Adjudication Rules 358, 361
TeCSA Adjudication Rules 358, 361
telephone, ADR by
  conference calls 26
  Her Majesty's Courts Service (HMCS) Small
    Claims Mediation Scheme 256
  international arbitration 446
  mediation 205, 213, 235
  National Mediation Helpline 250
  negotiation 26, 27, 151
  PIU (Personal Injury Unit) Telephone Mediation
    (CEDR) 262
  Telephone Helplines Association 250
terminology 5–6
  ACAS 305
  concessions 165
  conciliation 304
  legal terminology and tests 131
  mediation 304
  parties 6
  revealing information 126
  review of ADR options 23
  statements 126
terms
  accepting terms, example letter 326
  approval 320
  clarification 26
  consent orders 332–3
  costs 323, 336–7
  drafting 231, 323–4
  enforcement 323
  exchange of letters 325–6
  interest 323
  mediation 232
  negotiation 26
  settlements
    enforcement 487
    mediation 232
    performance of agreed terms 487
    recording 320–1, 323–4, 336–7
  standard terms 358, 407

  submission to agreed terms 332–3
  unfair contract terms 247, 352
  writing 321
test cases 180
textbooks 20–1
Thompson Report 250
threats 130
time limits
  ACAS 306
  allocation stage questionnaires 84
  anti-suit injunctions 465
  appeals on points of law 476
  arbitration 394–6, 412, 428–9, 465
  construction industry adjudication 361, 365–6,
    367–8
  decisions 354
  employment tribunals 306
  expert or neutral determination 348
  extension of time 465
  High Court jurisdiction in arbitration claims 465,
    478, 482
  Mediation in Civil and Commercial Matters
    Directive 277
  position statements 208
  prescription periods 277
time to think 129
timetable
  construction industry adjudication 366
  early neutral and/or expert evaluation 32
  mediation 29–30, 200–1
  offers 173–9
Tomlin orders 334–6
  advantages and disadvantages 335–6
  confidentiality 46
  consent orders 331, 334–6
  contempt of court 336
  costs 334, 337
  definition 334
  drafting 334–5
  enforcement 336
  example 334–5
  failure to comply 336
  privacy 335–6
  schedule 336
  stay of proceedings 334
trade unions 306
training and accreditation 20–1
  Bar Council 195–6
  Bar Standards Board 20
  CEDR 20
  Chartered Institute of Arbitrators 20
  Civil Mediation Council 195–6
  continuous professional development 196, 276
  disciplinary proceedings 247
  Family Mediation Council 195
  Law Society 195–6
  lawyers 20, 24
  list of providers 20, 196
  mediation 29, 290–1, 195–6, 276
  monitoring 196
  National Mediation Helpline 196

negotiation 20–1
Solicitors' Regulation Authority 20
specialisations 20
textbooks 20–1
websites 20, 196
treaties and conventions 18
tribunals *see also* **arbitral tribunal**
employment tribunals 260, 305–6
executive tribunals 264–5
Social Security and Child Support (SSCS) Tribunal
pilots 301–3
unified structure 8
use 8
Trust Meridian Ltd's Personal Injury Scheme 262

ultimatums 127
umpires 396, 398–9
**UNCITRAL Model Law on International
Commercial Arbitration** 449–52
appointment of arbitrators 450
Arbitration Act 1996 372, 433
commencement of arbitration 450
definition of commercial 404
equity clauses (*ex aequo et bono/amiable
compositeur*) 438
evidence 452
experts 451
harmonisation 449
hearings 451–2
High Court jurisdiction in arbitration claims 466
injunctions 450–1
interim measures 450–1
international arbitration, definition of 432
interpretation 449–50
language 446
legal systems, problems caused by different 436
mediation 274
party autonomy 451
preliminary orders 450–1
procedural orders 467
reform 449
regulation 18
statements of case 451
subsequent procedure 451
tribunals 400, 450–1
undertakings 330
unfair contract terms 247, 352
Ungley Orders 83, 84
United States 11, 270
urgent applications 469–70

venue
arbitration 33, 65, 424
commercial arbitration 424
costs 191
facilities 190
Mayor's and City of London County Court
Mediation Scheme 254
mediation 189–91
negotiation 26, 151
neutral venues 190

offices of solicitors or parties 190
providers, premises of 189–90
rooms required, number of 190
video-conferencing 424, 430, 446
views 426

wasted costs orders 19, 281
**WATNA (worse alternative to a negotiated
agreement)** 147, 201, 215
weaknesses in case, addressing 162
**weaknesses in opponent's case, bringing
out** 162–3
websites
ACAS 8, 305
ADR Now 10
British and Irish Ombudsman Association 314
CEDR 192
Chartered Institute of Arbitrators 20
community mediation 268
Disability Conciliation Service (Equalities
Mediation Service) 308
Financial Services Authority Mediation
Service 266
Furniture Ombudsman Conciliation
Scheme 308
Harvard Negotiation Project 17–18
international mediation 272
med-arb 234
Mediation in Civil and Commercial Matters
Directive 274
Ministry of Justice annual reports 182–3
National Mediation Helpline 10, 63, 196, 250
ombudsmen 314
Parliamentary and Health Service
Ombudsman 314
training and accreditation 20, 196
West Midlands Family Mediation Scheme 257
winding up 350, 489
without prejudice communications
abuse of rule 56–7
agreements 240–3
conciliation 304
confidentiality 54, 55–7, 241, 244–5
costs 57, 106–7, 242
costs sanctions 106–7
exceptions 56–7
experts 207, 241
litigation 55–6
mediation 204, 207, 240–3
negotiation 55–7, 159
professional ethics 286–7
protected communications, list of 241
reliance on rule by mediator 243
settlements 242
unprotected communications, list of 241–3
waiver 243
witnesses
advice 41
anti-suit injunctions 465
arrangements for witnesses 425
commercial arbitration 425, 430

witnesses (*cont.*)
    conferencing 425
    cross-examination, examination and
        re-examination 425, 430
    exchange of statements 41, 422, 425
    experts as witnesses 351–2
    fact, witnesses of 208
    mediation 208, 224, 246–7
    mediator as witness 246–7
    preliminary points of law 471
    statements 41, 465, 471
    summonses 425
    unfair contract terms 352

Woolf reforms 9, 76
workplace mediation *see* ACAS (Advisory,
        Conciliation and Arbitration Service);
        employment
writing or evidence in writing
    arbitration agreements or clauses 380
    construction industry adjudication 356
    mediation 28–9, 65, 213
    negotiation 26, 27
    offers 25–6
    recording settlements 322
    settlement agreements/contracts 324
    terms 321